THE FRIEDMAN-
LUCAS TRANSITION IN
MACROECONOMICS

THE FRIEDMAN-LUCAS TRANSITION IN MACROECONOMICS
A Structuralist Approach

PETER GALBÁCS

ACADEMIC PRESS
An imprint of Elsevier

Academic Press is an imprint of Elsevier
125 London Wall, London EC2Y 5AS, United Kingdom
525 B Street, Suite 1650, San Diego, CA 92101, United States
50 Hampshire Street, 5th Floor, Cambridge, MA 02139, United States
The Boulevard, Langford Lane, Kidlington, Oxford OX5 1GB, United Kingdom

Notices
Knowledge and best practice in this field are constantly changing. As new research and experience
broaden our understanding, changes in research methods, professional practices, or medical
treatment may become necessary.

Practitioners and researchers must always rely on their own experience and knowledge in
evaluating and using any information, methods, compounds, or experiments described herein. In
using such information or methods they should be mindful of their own safety and the safety of
others, including parties for whom they have a professional responsibility.

To the fullest extent of the law, neither the Publisher nor the authors, contributors, or editors,
assume any liability for any injury and/or damage to persons or property as a matter of products
liability, negligence or otherwise, or from any use or operation of any methods, products,
instructions, or ideas contained in the material herein.

Library of Congress Cataloging-in-Publication Data
A catalog record for this book is available from the Library of Congress

British Library Cataloguing-in-Publication Data
A catalogue record for this book is available from the British Library

ISBN 978-0-12-816565-2

For information on all Academic Press publications
visit our website at https://www.elsevier.com/books-and-journals

Publisher: Brian Romer
Editorial Project Manager: Emerald Li
Production Project Manager: Kiruthika Govindaraju
Cover Designer: Matthew Limbert

Typeset by SPi Global, India

To my granny, my most enthusiastic fan and critic.

Contents

4. Realism and instrumentalism along the Friedman–Lucas transition

5. The end of economics?

Foreword

In an age of scepticism about the relevance of neoclassical economics for today's economic policy, it is easy to argue that what went wrong lay primarily with the discipline's over-reliance on highly idealized theories such as rational choice and rational expectations in applied policy research. Fingers are pointed, most often, at the University of Chicago Nobel laureates, especially Milton Friedman and Robert Lucas. Of course, their opponents often have just as simplistic and highly idealized theories; they just come from a perspective that they consider more 'realistic', 'true', or laden with the 'right' ethical perspective. But what is really needed is an evaluation of the Chicago approach—especially the macroeconomic perspective that emerges from the work of Friedman and Lucas—that takes seriously, and hence, as its own starting point, the epistemic, methodological, economic, and institutional assumptions that Lucas actually held.

Such a starting point may produce an internalist account of a thinker that does not provide room for the historian as critic. On the other hand, these days hagiographic works are out-numbered by accounts written by those who already know before they begin what critical flaw they believe exists in the economist's work and how they will exploit it, without considering that a Nobel-worthy economist is likely to have thought about that potential flaw. Galbács avoids both extremes, providing instead a nicely balanced hermeneutics, simultaneously accepting the inevitability of some kind of hermeneutic circle—if the author's work is a seamless whole, where does one enter?—with recognition that the author's own understanding of their work is inevitably incomplete, and hence there are disjunctions that provide an opening.

Most interpreters of Friedman and Lucas assume they work from modern philosophies of science—instrumentalism, realism, etc. They then proceed to show how Lucas follows Friedman into whatever mistaken direction the methodologist or historian thinks they fell into. Usually, their story proceeds from Friedman's instrumentalism to Lucas' hyper-abstractionism, criticizing the lack of accuracy in describing individual rationality on the assumption that only a correctly described account of individual intentionality and reasonability can provide an accurate account of human decisions and their consequences.

But what if the purpose of Lucas's work, at least, is different? What if his purpose was to understand the interplay between the components of the overarching structure of an economy? Is a realistic account of individual motivation and action necessary for such a structuralist study? What if all one needs to test the interplay within the economy's structure is a variety of ideal types, to use a Weberian phrase, that act in predictable ways in order to examine outcomes from changes in the overarching structure? What if the structures emerging from human action are the object of study, rather than the process of their emergence? Friedman's toolkit of models took us always toward this approach, but not far enough. Lucas's context is not the same as the contemporary methodologist's, nor is it the same as Friedman's, Stigler's, and the other first-generation Chicago School economists'. Instead, Lucas starts from a Weberian methodology that does not require accurate descriptions of individual rationality and motivation as a starting point. The Weberian approach Lucas chooses is remarkably similar to that of Frank Knight. The goal is not predicting individual actions, but rather understanding the underlying causal forces at work within an institutional structure that account for systemic fluctuations. The rational agent is an ideal type, whose actions depend upon the institutional setting in which the agent can be found. Testing the institutional setting against the ideal type provides us with a way of understanding the consequences for the system that arise from individual action.

Galbács's approach to studying Lucas also merits recognition. He blends the philosophical interests of the methodologist with an historian's sensibility for diving deep into the context and history of an economist's work. Thus, this volume is as much a contribution to the history of economics as it is to economic methodology. His careful historical study of Lucas's life and work not only helps explicate the method Lucas adopted but also helps us appreciate its subtlety.

The blend of methodology and history raises my final point. Galbács's story of the transition from Friedman to Lucas tells us that the history may lie in the methodology, not the policy. So often we tell the history of economic thought as the history of theory and policy. But here, Galbács tells us that the most important part of that history may well lie in the history of methodology and the philosophical shifts behind that. Thus, Lucas's theory, which sounds like a return to something more classically liberal, may in fact be a movement forward in thinking about methodology. So while the methodologist is called to pay attention to the history of the theorist, the theorist is called to pay attention to the history of the methodology. Galbács does both sides of that duality well.

Ross B. Emmett
School of Civic and Economic Thought and Leadership,
Center for the Study of Economic Liberty, Arizona State University,
Tempe, AZ, United States

Preface

Beauty is truth, truth beauty,—that is all
Ye know on earth, and all ye need to know.
John Keats: Ode on a Grecian urn

To begin with I was laughed at, of course, always a sure promise of eventual
triumph. It took them quite a while to get the point, but when they did, my,
what a fuss.
John Banville: The infinities

I accomplished my studies in economics in a state of weird confusion. Following the prevalent pattern a student acquires the basic command of economics by being exposed to neoclassical orthodoxy only to be convinced later about the irrelevance of what she has learnt, be it the history of economic thought or applied economics. This is something I was also unable to shake off. As early as during my undergraduate years I nurtured familiarity with some most influential historical assessments of neoclassical economics, but it was all the same whether I read Mirowski, Blaug, or De Vroey, just to mention a few household names, all of these narratives proved to be deeply infused with scepticism and dissatisfaction with the theory in point. Whilst neoclassical high theory kept burgeoning in spite of all these critiques and challenges, it seemed to me that historians of economic thought have the common tendency of turning away from neoclassical economics and subscribing to the streams of malevolent flavour in order to turn back to the orthodox approach from a renegade and a critical point of view. One of the consequences of this negative and rejective attitude is an emphasis upon the alleged failures of neoclassical economics instead of seeking its adequate scope. Given this, it promised to be particularly exciting for me to remain faithful and to discuss the history and methodology of neoclassical theory as a neoclassical economist and with a supportive and positive attitude.

Economics in a slightly schizophrenic way is deeply disappointed in itself. I thought that such negative assessments had placed economics into a plight as it is its own historiography that calls the point of the achievements of economics into question. This could be still reasonable, acceptable, and even inspiring should the opinions not be voiced by utterly separate academic circles. The cutting edge of economics pays no attention to the critique, whilst the critics are outsiders to the cutting edge. This duality has rendered economics dissatisfied with the history of economic thought as a subdiscipline, which is a deplorable fact of life, whereas I was inclined to regard the way leading here not as a failure of economics but rather its histories. Harsh and unfruitful critique and rejection inevitably desensitize the target of the critique. If the history of our discipline supposes economics to be a failure in a large part, on what ground could we expect economics to consider the concerns of its historiography?

It was more and more difficult for me to live with this contrast. Where textbooks on the history of economic thought found increasing irrelevance, the absence of social responsibility, and empty instrumentalist formalism, when reading the original texts I found brilliance, focused attention, efficient and straightforward theorizing, genuine questions and genuine answers behind the powerful abstractions. The contradiction was especially shocking in the case of Robert Lucas, who is widely blamed for the degeneration of modern macroeconomics. Even before studying his unpublished papers and notes I started building strong reservations about the official sceptical views. It was unclear for me why Lucas had invested such serious intellectual efforts into a research project that had no promise of providing substantive answers. Instead of degeneration I found an ambitious programme through which Lucas, reopening some fundamental questions of economics, strove to renew the world view of economics and to get economics back on the usual causal realist track. Today's physics is rumoured to be still struggling to properly understand and assess what Albert Einstein taught and left behind as his academic heritage. The idea dawned on me that the misgivings about Lucas's theory may stem both from an incomprehension of this type and the overshot self-confidence of the history of economic thought. Painting something flawed may easily be a symptom of incomplete understanding. This idea was considerably enticing to me all the more because it promised to facilitate a comprehensive realist reading with the aim of opening an unconducted chapter of the debate between the neoclassical orthodoxy and its critique. This book is the outcome of my labours, which is intended to be definitely neoclassical by its viewpoint, so it is an endeavour to put forward a history that neoclassical theory writes on itself. My specific plan was to re-formulize the methodological and epistemological principles of the Lucas of the 1960–70s in the framework of a philosophy of science that suits the basic problems of the microfoundations project. I expected this way we could have a deeper understanding of Lucas's methodology. I was convinced that the scepticism around his economics stems from incomplete comprehension and the confusion he triggered by his radical methodological guidelines having proved to be too huge a leap forward.

During my disillusionment from contemporary history of economic thought I found shelter and inspiration in Uskali Mäki's philosophy. It is the realist methodological programme he initiated that first showed me the possibility of elaborating effective arguments for the relevance and causal adequacy of modern macroeconomics. Reading Mäki's enormous and intriguing oeuvre has rendered it clear to me that the realist rendition of economics is viable, plausible, and tenable. Of course, this realist interpretation is less evident and requires more preliminary considerations as compared to the easily accessible but suspiciously oversimplifying anti-realist reading, which implicitly permeates the whole history of postwar economics. I found Mäki's philosophy even more exciting as it treats Milton Friedman's methodology as a problem of central importance. Mäki's keen interest in Friedman's methodological principles, Friedman's formative role in the evolution of modern macroeconomics, and the tensions between Friedman and Lucas convinced me to believe that a comparative methodological assessment could aid in understanding how modern macroeconomics really works, which is also a question for historiography. A further factor was my own unrelenting interest in Lucas's lifework.

In this endeavour of mine Mäki's realist philosophy turned out to be an insufficient underpinning after a while. Mäki's permissive and supportive attitude towards modern economics and its success story inevitably glosses over some methodological discrepancies. Whilst at the textual level Friedman and Lucas seem to have provided dissimilar answers to some methodological questions, which suggests a serious divergence in spite of the theoretical parallelisms, I was lacking both in concepts and theories that could help me to highlight how Friedman and Lucas disagreed on the way and the necessity of connecting models to reality. Structuralist philosophies, especially Anjan Chakravartty's semirealism, have proved to be such a framework via which we can adequately emphasize these discrepancies. I agreed with the Mäkian philosophy of economics on the claim that the relationship of modern macro to reality is to be analyzed in the context of realism and instrumentalism, whilst I was unable to conciliate Mäki's realist reading on Friedman with the way Friedman in his methodology belittled the importance of the real properties of economic agents. By contrast, for Lucas the real entity properties served as the very fundament of all theorizing. Had I argued for Lucas's realism along such lines, their disagreements would have faded away under the all-covering realist banner. Thus in order to underline Lucas's realist efforts I needed to argue for Friedman's instrumentalism. In so doing, structuralist philosophies aided me by showing how intimately entity properties and the structures entities form are related. Along these lines a break between Friedman and Lucas showed up that, I believe, might raise the interest of the history of economic thought as well.

Thus the approach of the book stems from a twofold dissatisfaction. Historical narratives of modern macroeconomics, with some sporadic exceptions, disregard the results of the methodology and philosophy of economics. In spite of the revolutionary attitude of Mäki and his philosophy, historiography pays no attention to these considerations. At the same time, economic methodology rests upon a rather narrow textual base, so it falls closer to armchair philosophy than to historiography. Even though methodology obviously requires more complex arguments, somehow these considerations are cut adrift from the texts. Paragraphs appearing to be arbitrarily chosen for analysis cannot always convince the reader that the suggested interpretations adequately reflect the intentions of the authors or effectively underpin the posteriorly formed readings. I firmly believe that history and methodology can mutually benefit from each other's approaches and that the histories of modern macroeconomics in the 21st century can only be flawed and partial if the recent methodological considerations remain unnoticed. Likewise, letting in the methods of historiography promised to enhance the robustness of methodology. Apart from the attempts to provide a realist interpretation of Lucasian macro, I wanted to show what a methodologically underpinned neoclassical history of economic thought would look like.

Accordingly, Chapter 1 calls the attention of historiography to methodology. The purpose was to demonstrate why and how the results of cognition are dependent upon the methodology and the epistemological principles one follows when theorizing. If knowledge depends upon methodology, then analyzing knowledge as cut adrift from methodology can only lead to distorted results of limited relevance. It is particularly true of macroeconomics after Friedman, the revolutions of which were mainly of methodological nature.

Chapter 2 also serves as an introductory part. The present book identifies the most crucial aspect of the theoretical and methodological transition between Friedman and Lucas as a switch in the way models connect to reality, and as a consequence outlines a way from Friedmanian instrumentalism to Lucas's realism. This switch, however, was a highly complex and multidimensional process. From its facets Chapter 2 investigates three; thus it is the way Chicago economics evolved between Friedman's and Lucas's times, some subsequent episodes of the one and only Marshall–Walras divide, and an analysis of how the transition from Friedman's orthodox monetarism to Lucasian new classical macro altered some key theoretical claims and economic policy conclusions of monetary macroeconomics that stand in the focus. It is argued that along these aspects it is equally easy for us to characterize their theoretical and methodological relationship in terms of a special continuity as it is to describe it as a tense opposition.

Having completed the preparation, Chapter 3 launches the detailed methodological analysis that also takes up Chapter 4. In Chapter 3, starting from the basic problem of the microfoundations project, the problematic relationship of parts and wholes, some theories in modern philosophy of physics, and general philosophy of science are reviewed to understand how and to what extent the properties of objects, broadly conceived and taken as either atoms or economic agents, determine the properties of structures objects form. These philosophies, which sometimes front up in the scums as opponents, argue that features of the well-defined objects play a key role in structuring; thus Lucas's realist microfoundations project turns from an attempt doomed to failure into a product of a natural ontological and epistemological attitude. As long as societies are made up of individuals making decisions, social phenomena and institutions are to be conceived as the consequences of choices.

Chapter 4 is the stage for the comparative methodological analysis of the Friedman–Lucas transition. Even though the title of the book contains both names, Chapter 4 makes it clear that the roles Friedman and Lucas play in the investigation are dissimilar. Friedman serves rather as a contrasting background only; thus the book is more about Lucas, the realist Lucas, who is characterized as a mind having re-established economics after Friedman's instrumentalist misstep. In Friedman's case I did not aim to overwrite the well-known and widely accepted anti-realist reading. Accordingly, the analysis is pointed at his most prominent methodological works, from which some strong points in favour of the instrumentalist interpretation follow. It is mentioned only as a question of secondary importance whether in his theorizing practice Friedman really and consistently followed the instrumentalist methodological principles he suggested. After turning to Lucas, of course, the focus remains on methodology, even though the analysis is placed upon a broader textual basis. In order to study Lucas's fragments I had the privilege of spending some periods of time in 2016 and 2018 at the David M. Rubenstein Rare Book & Manuscript Library, Duke University (making the photocopies was only the first stage of the textual analysis), and those are the most cherished parts of this book that put forward the interpretive results and that let Lucas speak to underpin the arguments. The manuscripts are published in Chapter 4 at greatest length, though all the chapters contain some excerpts. While working, it was exciting to realize, on the one hand, how much attention Lucas paid to the clarification of his methodological principles and, on the other, that he really regarded these considerations as preparations, perhaps for methodology was not yet regarded as a high-ranked topic for research in those days; these papers thus remained unpublished. Analyzing such methodological studies he left in background, however, made it possible for me to provide a more comprehensive insight into Lucas's manuscripts as compared to the existing literature.

Chapter 5 takes aim at the existing Lucas interpretations with a view to stirring up a fruitful debate between the alternative readings. The arguments here are quite simple as the suggested interpretation is defended by underlining some shortcomings of the challenged understandings. The proposed and the prior readings are contrasted through the lens of some hermeneutic considerations that, on the one hand, suggest broadening the textual basis in order to avoid or minimize the implied distortions and that, on the other hand, draw attention to the dynamism of interpretive hypotheses. It is also this concluding chapter that highlights those aspects of the methodological transition from Friedman to Lucas that could have been analyzed only ineffectively without a structuralist framework and that points out why this structuralist analysis is to be regarded as an additional point in favour of a stricter reading of scientific realism in economics.

Acknowledgements

Thanks to the generous support of the Fulbright Scholar Program in academic year 2018–19, I had the honour of working under Ross B. Emmett's academic supervision as a visiting scholar at the Center for the Study of Economic Liberty, Arizona State University, with the possibility of carrying out extensive library research at the University of Chicago and Duke University, the most vibrant academic communities one can imagine. My warmest gratitude goes to Charles Jókay, Krisztina Kováts, and Csanád Nagypál as but for their supportive attitude this intellectual adventure could never have come true and culminated in the present publication.

The exchange of ideas with Robert Lucas started at the University of Chicago in the autumn of 2018, and the subsequent year exerted a fundamental influence on the manuscript. I am grateful to Virginia Bova for taking a huge and indispensable part in organizing the first appointment and the succeeding joint work. Her kindness, attentiveness, and helpfulness are among my most beloved memories from Chicago.

When I met Professor Lucas I could show him the first albeit ample drafts of a reading I had had in mind for a long time. I am particularly grateful to him for the suggestions he made as a reader and by which he called my attention to some underdeveloped parts; thus I am happy and proud to say that some sections of the book bear marks of his comments. As the preface and the acknowledgements are the only personal parts of a book, here I do not have to conceal that under the influence of this episode now I can no longer see his character as a simple role model but an idol.

During my scholarship Ross Emmett was my supervisor, and I still regard him as my master and the Center for the Study of Economic Liberty as my intellectual home. Even though I spent months at the libraries of Chicago and Duke, after my returning to the Tempe campus we had plenty of time to work together. A magnanimous professor with enormous knowledge—and a great friend. Never was he tired or busy for our long conversations. The stories about Friedman as a legendary teacher gained tangible reality for me by Ross's patronage. Thanks to him I could also experience what it means if a young researcher can learn from an outstanding mentor. Besides Ross, it is Kim Birchall, his wife, and Melissa Castle-Kirincic, his programme operations specialist (it is only a fancy name for being a part of the glue that holds everything together, as she would simply label herself), who did the most for me, so I was lucky to have the opportunity to spend the greatest time of my life with them, even if my heart broke into pieces when I had to leave. Although I am writing these rows from a distance, I am still far richer than I was before we met as they are my sweetest friends—though no Fulbright orientation could prepare me to lead a life far away from them. This book could never have been born without their support, encouragement, and love. I sincerely hope it is not all over to us.

Anjan Chakravartty provided an immeasurably great and valuable academic support in completing my research. When I started showing interest in structural realism, I found myself in hot water as I needed to give an account of a highly complex philosophy and the related scholarly debates to nonphilosophers as a nonphilosopher. Anjan was enthusiastic to keep supporting me throughout the project. I am particularly indebted to him as he immediately realized the point of the application of structuralism in the history and methodology of economics. As a leading figure of contemporary scientific realism he honoured me with his reading my first lame drafts that could hardly have contained anything new to him. However, instead of losing interest or discouraging me, he posed questions to inspire me to walk my way and offered me the opportunity of learning from him. His open mind and supportive attitude make him an exceptional scholar, and his friendship is perhaps the greatest gift of this research project.

Over and above these highly different albeit equally indispensable and unique key contributions, I am in hock to others as well for their help and assistance. Scott Bentley and Susan Ikeda are the first to mention. As an acquisition editor, it was Scott Bentley who picked up on the key idea of the book and invited me to make my point as an Elsevier author. Due to Scott's retirement, unfortunately, we could not complete this book together. With her editorial suggestions and instructions Susan helped me a lot to get through the pitfalls of the final phases of writing. Her cheerful personality emitted calmness even in the most stressful situations, and thanks to her the work with the publisher became a smooth creative process. Even though we started working together only in the final stages of the publication process, I would like to express my gratitude to Emerald Li, my editorial project manager, and to Kiruthika Govindaraju, my production project manager, for providing efficacious editorial support.

My special appreciation goes to László Muraközy. From the very first times he was intensely interested in the creative process leading to this publication, and kept encouraging me to go on even in the times of sudden difficulties. Even though we do not see eye to eye on the merits of the neoclassical orthodoxy, he being a follower of the historicist wing of institutional economics is one of the few who does not regard the touted outrage against neoclassical theory as a prerequisite of reaching his academic aims. His objective and unbiased attitude is an exception. I am proud of having him as a close friend.

Daniel Meyer, Barbara Gilbert, and Jessica Seet (Special Collections Research Center, the University of Chicago), Elizabeth Dunn, Kate Collins (David M. Rubenstein Rare Book & Manuscript Library, Duke University), and Diana Sykes (Hoover Institution Library & Archives, Stanford University) offered me effective assistance during the library stages of the research. Bruce Caldwell (Center for the History of Political Economy, Duke University) proved to be a cordial host for multiple times. Invited by Ross Emmett, on January 28, 2018 I had the privilege of giving a summarizing lecture on the project at the 'Philosophy, Politics and Economics Workshop' of the Center for the Study of Economic Liberty, where Edward C. Prescott and Scott Scheall offered me some impulses with their questions and remarks I could benefit from when finishing off the manuscript. Edit Koncz, my language supervisor, did an exceptionally great job about polishing the text. Her precision is accompanied by flexibility, which renders her an irreplaceable help. I am also grateful to Sára Csillag, who as the vice-rector of my home institution, Budapest Business School, did her best to support the project.

1

Methodology…?! Why?

> *Some people laughed to see the alteration in him, but he let them laugh, and little heeded them; for he was wise enough to know that nothing ever happened on this globe, for good, at which some people did not have their fill of laughter in the outset; and knowing that such as these would be blind anyway, he thought it quite as well that they should wrinkle up their eyes in grins, as have the malady in less attractive forms*
> **Charles Dickens: A Christmas carol**

> *Our responsibility is to create new knowledge by pushing research into new, and hence necessarily controversial, territory. Consensus can be reached on specific issues, but consensus for a research area as a whole is equivalent to stagnation, irrelevance and death.*
> **Robert E. Lucas**

The purpose of this chapter is to introduce economic methodology as a general analytical framework. From a brief review on the evolution of modern methodology our road leads to some intriguing methodological problems of contemporary macroeconomics. Here it is argued that the evolution of our discipline raises a number of issues that can only be understood, analyzed, and solved in a methodological approach; these questions thus lie beyond the boundaries of our common theoretical debates. Of these issues the treatment of complexity, the use of economics in economic policy, and its relation to other social sciences are highlighted.

In this overview the realist turn initiated by Uskali Mäki emerges as one of the most important developments in economic methodology. This turn fundamentally changed the image our discipline draws of itself. Thanks to him, realism could effectively challenge the dominant anti-realist interpretations of economics. Scientific realism in the general philosophy of science is an optimistic epistemological attitude or belief according to which it is possible to make grounded claims regarding even the unobservable realm of reality. Whilst anti-realism denies this possibility, various albeit conflicting methodological strategies of gaining knowledge

1

about socio-economic reality have emerged in the realist tradition. Tracing back the methodological disagreements to the underlying epistemological principles, it is argued that no analysis of economic theories can be complete without taking into account the epistemological, ontological, and methodological principles and strategies as well.

One of the most important accomplishments of the chapter is a simple definition of scientific realism easy to apply in the textual-based methodological analyses of the subsequent chapters. The absence of some incontrovertible evidences is perhaps the most cumbrous problem of scientific realism. Only such an evidence could by its undeniable verity convince sceptics to take a realist position. Accordingly, instead of making further troublesome attempts to by-pass or overcome the constraints that stem from the very nature of the connection between our senses and reality, the realist position is characterized below as a positive epistemological attitude or belief that is typical of theorists striving towards the causal understanding of reality. A crucial element of this attitude is the additional claim a realist attaches to her theories. Realists really believe that their theories are capable of unravelling the hidden levels of reality.

A case study on the neoclassical-institutionalist debate concludes the chapter to call attention to how and why methodological considerations ought to play a crucial role in theory assessment and interpretation.

1.1 Economic methodology as a juvenile subdiscipline suggesting some new aspects for theoretical analyses

1.1.1 Emergence and development

Economic methodology is one of the most novel subdisciplines of our science. In economics the term 'methodology' is applied in a twofold sense: there exist a 'small-m' and a 'big-M' methodology. Their approaches, scopes, and the researchers they involve are dissimilar. Small-m methodology is the playground of methodologically inclined economists, who seek answers to the practical questions of model building and forming assumptions. How to build 'good' economic models, what is meant by 'goodness' in this context, or how economists proceed in their research programmes, just to mention some of the typical questions. By contrast, big-M methodology is dominated by philosophers who as philosophers approach the questions raised by the ontological and cognitive status of economic models. These fields are of course overlapping to a certain extent. For the sake of a clear-cut distinction, Boland (2016) suggests the terms 'methodology of economics' (small-m methodology) and 'philosophy of economics' (big-M methodology). On the basis of the scientific background, quite a unanimous demarcation can be drawn in between as by profession economists are economists and philosophers are philosophers. Interestingly, Boland suggests that economists know more about philosophy (even if their knowledge does not stem from systematic studies) than philosophers know about economics. As a consequence, he argues, it would be unfortunate for economics if studies in its methodology were dominated by researchers alien to the field.

Methodological self-reflection became a constituent part of economic thinking relatively early as neoclassical founding fathers attached methodologies to their theories,[1] which as a matter of fact were inseparable from the theories themselves. However, an independent economic methodology only emerged as late as in the 1980s. The early days of systematic methodological studies date back to the 1960s. From the preceding decades economists and economically interested philosophers of science bequeathed some sporadic methodological works only (Hands, 2015, pp. 61–62). In the 1960s, by contrast, the attention paid to economic methodology quickly intensified and one of the focus points of this newly emerged interest was Friedman's (1953/2009) positivist methodology. Feelings evoked by the paper began to run so high that starting some systematic studies to clarify the methodological foundations of economics was no longer delayable.

The first occasion took place at the 1962 meeting of the American Economic Association, where apropos of Friedman's positivist suggestions an intense debate flared up over the nature of a proper economic methodology (a recurrent topic of Chapter 4 below). After 1962, however, papers, book chapters, and books on economic methodology were still published only occasionally. It is also 1962 that Mark Blaug's well-known textbook on the history of economics came out (Blaug, 1962). Blaug devoted its 17th chapter (A methodological postscript) to some methodological questions. Later Blaug developed this part into a complete volume (Blaug, 1980) the success and warm reception of which finally convinced the publishers to be open to methodology as an intriguing topic. This was thus the book that opened the avenue for the subsequent series of volumes in economic methodology (Boland, 2016, p. 20). From the period prior to the later breakthrough witnessed in the 1980s, Hands (2015) mentions only two books. One is a conference proceedings publication (Latsis, 1976). The 1974 conference was dedicated to the question what relevance Lakatos's methodology of scientific research programmes has had in economics. The other is Wong's tiny book on Samuelson's revealed preference theory (Wong, 1978). Amongst the pathbreaking intellectual efforts Wong's and Boland's analyses on Friedman's positivist methodology are also worth mentioning (Boland, 1979; Wong, 1973). As further positive examples, Rosenberg's (1976) and Hausman's (1981) studies are items to be labelled as philosophy of science with a specific interest in economics

---

[1] Here it is enough to mention Book I of Marshall's (1920/2013) 'Principles of economics' or Lesson 22 (especially Section 222) of Walras's (1926/1954) 'Elements of pure economics'.

(Hausman, 2009, p. 36). After the mid-1970s the literature in economic methodology started an intense expansion.

Even though economic methodology showed up as a topic claiming wide attention, circumstances in the 1980s were still unfavourable. In those years the opinion leaders in both the neoclassical orthodoxy and the heterodox camp had passionate interest in methodology. In such a situation a branch of methodologists lying outside the cutting edge camp could seem to be a horde of kibitzers at best. First and foremost, it followed from the fact that methodology has sharply distinguished itself from purely descriptive history of science, so it could not avoid getting accused of normativity (Mäki, 2009a, p. 93). Economic methodologists seemed to know better how to do science than the theorists actively doing research. Blaug (1980) provides the best example of mixing some normative suggestions into the history of economic methodology, considerably weakening the scientific merit of his narrative.

The early development of economic methodology was fundamentally influenced by a debate taken place between economic historian E. Roy Weintraub and Uskali Mäki, who established economic methodology as we know it today. In this controversy Weintraub (1989) was particularly hostile against methodology and by calling its practical relevance into question he regarded even the idea of an outsider subdiscipline of economics as utterly harmful. Weintraub's line of reasoning is problematic to say the least as the idea of a methodological subdiscipline torn apart from economics is difficult even to imagine. What is more, even practical economists engaging in methodological self-reflection cannot avoid taking such an outsider position, at least temporarily. Rather, methodology with its outsider point of view is likely to prove indispensable to rational self-control as disciplines cannot solve their methodological problems within their boundaries. In resolving our methodological debates, marginal utility theory is of no help.

Soon thereafter Mäki (1994a) responded to Weintraub's suggestions and digging as down as to the level of the ultimate concepts and definitions refuted his concerns one by one. The significance of the debate is clearly indicated by the fact that a number of economic historians applying the widely neglected methodological aspect joined it later. For instance, Bruce Caldwell (1990) set the doubts over a possible normative role of methodology at rest. Quite ironically, many of the parties in the controversy later became colleagues at Duke University.

Economic methodology today covers an exceptionally wide range of research topics. It is no longer uncommon for economists to embark upon topics conquered by philosophers. This is due to the fact that in order to do methodology better economists started acquiring more and more profound knowledge in philosophy. By today philosophy has become a key part of economic programmes at the universities all over the world. The most intriguing questions regard the fundamental problems of how

to do economics: causality and the role and possibilities of causal inference in theorizing and econometrics, the relationship between economic
models and socio-economic reality, the emergence of scientific realism and
anti-realism in economics, the distinction between positive and normative
forms of economics or the connection between theory and political ideol-
ogies. The purpose is thus to have a deeper understanding of the practice
of science and the interplay of theorizing, research methods, and applications. Today nobody remembers the initial self-identification problems—
clear questions and sensible research programmes dominate the field. The
evolution of our discipline instantaneously leaves a mark on methodology
as the moment a new method emerges, a critical reflection in methodology
immediately follows.

The philosophy of economics (or big-M methodology) regards an even
wider range of questions. Certain ethical questions, the philosophical implications of well-being and happiness, or the problems of fairness lie far
beyond the usual questions of model-building and theorizing to the discussion of which small-m methodology was given birth. Economics thus
still has such implications that are inaccessible to economists via their
usual theorizing methods and that still belong to the realm of philosophy.
In a narrow sense, they are not methodological problems.

The young discipline of economic methodology soon entered the subsequent stage of its evolution as, simultaneously with the debate mentioned above, a series of grandiose summarizing works by the leading
methodologists came out. It is the general philosophy of science that still
served as the analytical framework which means that a philosophy explicitly customized to the needs of economics was still missing. This was accomplished only in the early 2000s (Hands, 2015, pp. 66–72), and as a great
achievement, the emerging new economic methodology was capable of
reacting to the developments taking place at the frontiers of economics
(behavioural and experimental economics, neuroeconomics, etc.). In the
general philosophy of science stream, Boland (1992) sought the problems to which neoclassical economics could provide adequate answers.
His purpose was not to defend neoclassical orthodoxy but to get critics
back on a right track as without identifying the scope no critique can be
satisfactory. In the light of this profound recognition some of our controversies seem no more than pseudo-debates fuelled by ill-understanding.
Caldwell (1994) scrutinized the scientific status of economics on the basis
of aspects taken from the general philosophy of science. As his book is
rooted in the methodological era of the 1970s, Caldwell's purpose was
also to improve the philosophical background available to economists
for methodological discussions. Hausman's (1992) seminal work is still
regarded as a book of fundamental importance as treading in J.S. Mill's
footsteps, he effectively underlines the selectivity of economic theorizing.
As economic models can accentuate only some selected mechanisms of

the complex causal structure of social phenomena, due to the omission of influencing factors, even our best models are likely to have moderate empirical success at best. In the absence of predictive success, however, the validity of our principles rests upon our belief or conviction in the validity of our principles. Rosenberg (1992), who is widely cited even in the general philosophy of science, discusses the most intriguing questions of economic methodology by taking into account the interplay between economics and general philosophy of science. Today Rosenberg is a leading figure of a movement gaining popularity that intends to regard biology instead of physics as the model of economics.

Starting with the 1990s books devoted to the systematic study of some subtle methodological questions were published in a row (Mäki, 2001, 2002a; Mäki, Gustafsson, & Knudsen, 1993/2005). The millennium was the time of corpulent handbooks (Backhouse, Hausman, Mäki, & Salanti, 1997; Davis, Hands, & Mäki, 1998; Kincaid & Ross, 2009; Mäki, 2012a) that testify the emergence of an encyclopaedically describable corpus of knowledge. As another milestone, the philosophy of economics in 2003 received a lengthy and oft-augmented entry in the Stanford Encyclopaedia of Philosophy (Hausman, 2012), the key forum of contemporary philosophy and the history of philosophy. At the same time, economic methodology has become as mature as it made sense to interconnect recent and past methodological considerations to portray how the methodology of economics has developed (Boumans & Davis, 2016; Hands, 2001).

1.1.2 Academic centres and organizations

It is impossible to overestimate how profoundly Uskali Mäki, also a philosopher showing keen interest in economics, influenced the development of economic methodology. As a remarkable achievement, he contributed to the establishment of two research institutes. One of them (Erasmus Institute for Philosophy and Economics, EIPE) is run by Erasmus University, Rotterdam, and has internationally leading master and doctoral programmes in the philosophy of economics. By today it has grown into the number one centre of methodology. EIPE publishes its own methodological journal (Erasmus Journal for Philosophy and Economics) that is also open to the research outputs of scholars working at the frontiers of the philosophy of economics. EIPE as a research institute and an outstanding education centre shows a wide-spreading interest with a firm philosophical perspective. In this complex research interest reflecting all the recent developments on the edges of economics, all methodological questions (assumptions and ontology, causation, experiments, simulations, etc.) are studied in a broad philosophical context. EIPE's approach is so complex and pluralistic that its research agenda can hardly be confined to small-m methodology.

The research agenda of the slightly younger institution of the University of Helsinki (Centre for Philosophy of Social Science) is characterized by an explicit focus upon the philosophy of social sciences and the general philosophy of science. The topics the researchers follow treat economics in a comprehensive social scientific context as the differences between the theorizing practices of the disciplines rule out the plausibility of a methodologically unified social science. The problems of scientific realism and surrogative reasoning, the topics that hold Mäki spellbound, are of course accentuated as distinguished research streams.

Today these institutions are unanimously conceived as the leading centres of the methodologist profession. Researchers graduating and working there dominate the field whilst the institutions themselves are widely acknowledged as centres of gravity at the international level. Economic methodology is admittedly worth attention. Doubly so as the philosophy of economics is one of the few disciplines where Europe has played the leading role for a long time. Bearing in mind the oft-blamed Americanization of economics, this development in itself can enhance the respect of methodology. Over and above these centres, it is the Polish and French methodologists who are particularly active.

Methodologists have some international organizations (there exists a dedicated European association: the European Network for the Philosophy of the Social Sciences, ENPOSS) of which the International Network for Economic Method (INEM) is undoubtedly the most significant. The early days of the network date back to the 1980s when a few dozen of researchers decided upon the creation of an international organization with a view to catapulting the subdiscipline into a new stage of its history. In 1989 the newly established organization started its own journal, 'Methodus' that has still been in operation under the new title 'Journal of Economic Methodology' since the 1990s. Today INEM has even a book series (INEM advances in economic methodology). As parts of the system of international institutions, the periodical 'Research in the History of Economic Thought and Methodology', founded in 1983, and the journal 'Economics & Philosophy', founded in 1985, are also worth attention. Some journals in the general philosophy of science and the history of economic thought are further examples of forums interested in and open to economic methodology.

1.2 Major methodological problems in contemporary macroeconomics

1.2.1 Some preliminary remarks on the history of modern macroeconomics

Today Keynes is widely regarded as the initiator of modern macroeconomics. Even though it is not him who coined macroeconomics, in his

'General theory' he distinguished two subfields of economics. In general terms, the first branch was conceived to regard the problems and returns of economizing on scarce resources at the level of the individual firms or agents. This has become today's microeconomics. The other branch was supposed to study the issues of output and unemployment at the aggregate level: this is what we call macroeconomics today (Keynes, 1936, p. 293). Traditionally, the history of economic thought regards Ragnar Frisch as the inventor of the term macroeconomics. A few years before the 'General theory', Frisch (1933, pp. 2–3) used the terms micro-dynamic analysis and macro-dynamic analysis basically in the same meaning as we today use microeconomics and macroeconomics. As Hoover (2012, p. 22) points out, Frisch applied the Norwegian adjectives mikroøkonomiske and makroøkonomiske. However, these are only terminological questions. De Vroey (2016) distinguishing 'the economics of Keynes' and 'Keynesian economics' as characteristic periods begins telling the story of modern macroeconomics at Keynes's 'General theory' and ties the first, pre-Lucasian chapter of the history of modern macro to Keynes.

As Keynes's era faded away, macroeconomics underwent pivotal changes, and these changes were typically of methodological nature. Our discipline shifted towards a high level of formalism and generality. It is not an overstatement to say that the history of modern macro is the history of methodology. As early as in the 1940s, a methodological debate commonly regarded in the literature as the 'Marshal–Walras divide' started, which was about the desired level of abstractness and generality of economic models and the use of formalism. The transition from Friedman's Marshallian monetarism to Lucasian macro resulted in the victory of the Walrasian general equilibrium framework, and after the developments of the 1970s Marshallian partial equilibrium approach seemed to be only an unfruitful and perhaps extravagant attempt (Snowdon & Vane, 2005, p. 286). By the neo-Walrasian economics of the Arrow–Debreu–McKenzie model and Lucas and by today's DSGE models, economics was given a unified, stable, and mathematically well-formed theory, which the philosophy of science regards as its ideal. This development opened the avenue for the philosophy of science and the methodology of economics to scrutinize economics in the framework of general equilibrium theory. On the methodological problems raised by general equilibrium economics and on the suggested answers Ross and Kincaid (2009) provide a good summary. These are the questions and answers that dominated the first notable books written on the methodology of economics from the 1980s (Blaug, 1980; Hausman, 1992; Rosenberg, 1992). As the striving for the high level of formalism was accompanied by the desire to place macroeconomics on well-elaborated microfoundations, these books discussed the methodology of economics as a close interplay between micro and macro, so in this regard we had better talk about the methodology of neoclassical economics.

The ontological status of modern macroeconomics is amongst the most fundamental methodological problems of economics. What are these models at all? Do they represent anything from the underlying and hidden structure of our social reality, or are they nothing but useful instruments used for generating predictions? Can we understand the causes of social processes or do we need to make do with saving the phenomena? According to the positivist–instrumentalist–anti-realist interpretation endorsed by M. Friedman (1953/2009) as well, our theories are to be judged by their predictive performance only, and the truth of theories is not supposed to be a concern. For the anti-realist approaches it is dubious whether causal understanding is a feasible objective of science or the truth of theories is not problematized at all (Sugden, 2002). Starting at the end of the 1980s the initially domineering positivist–empiricist account, according to which prediction is to be cut away from causal explanations (Manicas, 2006, pp. 18–19), was gradually replaced by a realist approach (Caldwell, 1990, pp. 67–69), initiated by Uskali Mäki (1989, 1990a, 1992a). The drive for Mäki's realist philosophy is autobiographical (Mäki, 2009a, pp. 69–70). Even though in his realist mission he has gone to the extremes by providing some implausible realist interpretations (Mäki, 2009b), thanks to him economics today is not deprived of its connections with the deep structures of socio-economic reality. His efforts helped us understand that the unrealisticness of models is not a hindrance to economics' becoming or remaining a science of reality. It is Mäki who constructed a realist interpretation of economics and an economics-specific terminology on the basis of which economics could become superior to a superficial discipline that operates only at the level of social phenomena. It is difficult if not impossible to overestimate the importance of Mäki's contribution to the self-esteem of modern macroeconomics and economics as a whole.

The acute questions of scientific realism do not belong to economics only. For physics idolized by modern economics (Mirowski, 1984) these questions are also unresolved at the moment. Due to this idolization economics inherited these problems. An ultimate question of scientific realism regards the unobservables, the particles that are too little to be observed by unaided human senses (Psillos, 2011, p. 303). The underlying causal mechanisms, the mapping of which is one of the duties of a discipline having realist aspirations, also belong to this unobservable realm (Boyd, 1983). Whilst the majority of methodologists today see eye to eye on causal understanding having been the traditional objective of economics before (and perhaps even after) the positivist turn (Hoover, 2009a), until recently we have known only a little about the proper methodological strategies for sound causal understanding. It is the philosophy of physics where some pathbreaking studies have related causality to the underlying structures (Esfeld, 2009; Ladyman & Ross, 2007; Schmidt, 2010). At the same time, the plausibility and feasibility of the major selective realist strategies are also under scrutiny (Hacking, 1982a; Worrall, 1989). In these debates an approach relevant to economics as well seems to be standing out that derives causality from the (first-order) causal properties of relata in structures (Chakravartty, 1998, 2007). As causal connections can be understood there as working along the relations stretched by the properties of entities, this approach may be particularly fruitful for the methodological analysis of the microfoundations project. For economics the most important application of these studies may be an in-depth understanding of the way we ought to set up our descriptively inaccurate (in Mäki's terms: unrealistic) assumptions in order to bolster causal adequacy.

1.2.2 Complexity

If we problematize causal understanding, the first obstacle to overcome is the complexity of social phenomena. There exist complex causal structures underlying social (and natural) phenomena that render it impossible to reveal all the causes of events. Not only does mathematical tractability set limits on this endeavour as, plainly put, some facets or mechanisms of any causal structure are unknown to us. It is also true that one ought not to forget about the fact that some social phenomena are likely to resist the mechanical analogy of economics for their very nature. Perhaps societies, at least in part, are unopen to the mathematical–mechanical approach of modern macro. Complexity leads to confusions in understanding.

After some early attempts dated back even to Adam Smith (Colander, 2008), studying economies as complex organizations was initiated in the early 1990s (Lewin, 1992; Rosser, 1999; Waldrop, 1992). There are alleged to exist some spontaneous, self-organizing dynamics in economic processes that we cannot understand via our regular mechanical analogies. According to complexity economics, equilibrium is not the natural state of economic systems, since agents constantly alter their behavioural patterns and strategies. In this non-equilibrium framework agents continuously react to their continuously changing environment, and via this adaptation they also contribute to this continuous change. A recursive loop works here. An aggregate pattern emerges from the individual actions, and individuals also respond to the aggregate patterns. Thus an economy is not a pre-given and unchanging system that strives towards or fluctuates around a well-defined equilibrium. An economy is in motion and undergoes changes every moment as it is being created continuously. A manifestation of this creation process is the constant change in institutions, innovations, and arrangements, triggering off further changes in institutions, innovations, and arrangements (Arthur, 2015).

An emphasis upon complexity emerged early as an argument against the extensive use of the representative agent in economics. A suggested shift towards heterogeneity was expected to produce more sensible results as compared to the homogenous societies built from the multiplication of the one and only representative agent (Kirman, 1992). In the past few years or decades agent-based modelling (Berry, Kiel, & Elliott, 2002; Bonabeau, 2002), genetic–algorithm-based modelling (Tesfatsion, 2003) and evolutionary economics (Nelson & Winter, 2002) came up as some pathbreaking subdisciplines that aim to scrutinize, on the one hand, the continuous changes in economies and societies and, on the other hand, the macro-level outcomes of the interaction of heterogeneous and adaptable agents.

To sort out the problem of complexity, authors in mechanics–physics-based economics have put forward various suggestions. The simplest reaction is to carefully circumscribe the scope of economics. Citing Schumpeter (1911/1934), Knight (1935/1999) emphasized (at the time when the intellectual foundations for today's neoclassical orthodoxy were taking shape) that physical–mechanical analogies are not always proper for economics as a social science. Mechanics works with three ultimate dimensions: time, space, and mass. However, amongst them only time has hopes for direct applications in economics. Thus physics can provide economics with a useful framework only if we can endow the physical concepts of space and mass with sensible economic content. As a consequence, these concepts could really become applicable as analogies in economics. However, as long as this remains uncompleted, by idolizing physics we have no chance to elaborate dynamic economics. In other words, we cannot scientifically describe large-scale historical changes typical of human societies via our mechanical analogies capable of static analyses only. Mechanics has no place for evolutionary categories.

Even though in the same text Knight disapproves of the extensive use of ceteris paribus clauses as the other things to be assumed to remain unchanged cannot be equal in most of the cases, cutting the causal structure into parts whilst keeping other things equal is a widely used approach in economics as a further reaction to the complexity problem. The standards for this methodological strategy date back to as early as John Stuart Mill (Hausman, 1992, 2001). As one needs to hide behind ceteris paribus clauses all other factors that disturb the operation of the one causal mechanism under scrutiny, studying the causal factors of an event or process one by one amounts to a proper scientific strategy. Once we are cognizant of the effects of the causes in separation, we can turn to the effects of causes in combination. Weber (1968/1978) also argued that causal mechanisms are separable and that economics is only one approach to study the complex causal structures. Along this train of thought Weber made the case for a comprehensive social science. Here economics via its mechanical analogies scrutinizes pure instrumentally rational actions only and lets sociology, history, or social psychology study all other factors that disturb this rational core. Thus dealing with the problem of complexity is related to the connection between economics and other social sciences. As a consequence of crucial importance, economics only has probabilistic laws, which are not more than tendencies and not regarded as strict as the laws of physics (Manicas, 2006, p. 9).

1.2.3 Connections to politics

Remaining within the tradition of the mechanical analogies the idea known as the Lucas critique drew attention to the changeability and dynamic character of the macrostructures, previously conceived to be stable (Lucas, 1976/1981). One of the most important applications of macroeconomic models has been the evaluation of the effects of alternative economic policies. Taking a change in policy as an input we try to predict the effects of this change. Lucas identified as a major fault in the macroeconometric practice of his time the assumption that the parameters in the equations describing the behaviour of agents were supposed to be constant. In Lucas's views this is only an ungrounded presumption: any change in politics (or whatever) may alter the environment of the optimizing agents who try to adjust to this change. In other words, parameters in macroeconometric models depend on agents' expectations about future economic policies. Policy changes also modify the decision rules of agents, and consequently the parameters of equations as well, since the equations are estimated on the basis of these rules. A change in politics results in an altered macroeconomy and we have no reasons to expect the behavioural rules of the previous stage to persist. The Lucas critique was a strong point in favour of DSGE (dynamic stochastic general equilibrium) modelling and contributed to its subsequent triumph. Both De Vroey (2016, pp. 261–266) and Woodford (1999) assess Lucas's contribution as pathbreaking that set the stage for the later developments in dynamic stochastic general equilibrium modelling. Whilst the framework remained the same in that it contained forward-looking agents (dynamic), some shocks to the economic system (stochastic), an abstract-idealized form of the entire economy (general), and some (equilibrium) constraints and objectives for the agents (Kocherlakota, 2010, p. 10), post-Lucasian DSGE modelling rendered Lucas's theoretical considerations applied and quantitative.

The Lucas critique directed theoretical economics towards economic policy rules to find out how and why such rules aid agents in optimizing. Subsequent theoretical results played down discretionary economic policies for not maximizing the social objective function (Kydland & Prescott, 1977; Rudebusch, 2005). Needless to say, the introduction of rational expectations as an assumption failed to relieve the negative attitude of the approaches traditionally critical of the neoclassical orthodoxy.

Whilst the neoclassical paradigm responded actively and fruitfully, econometrics was reluctant to change (Ericsson & Irons, 1995), so the Lucas critique concerned theoretical economics and econometric practice in dissimilar ways. Macroeconometrics faced a twofold concern. Models built upon the erroneous theoretical basis were condemned, first, as useless for evaluating prospective or hypothetical changes in policy, and second, as unable to correctly represent the current structure of an economy (Hoover, 2008a). The reluctance of econometrics is clearly indicated by the fact that the most influential textbooks of the early 2000s either only mention the Lucas critique and its consequences for econometric practice (Maddala & Lahiri, 2009) or completely disregard it. In his widely used textbook, Ramanathan (2002) refuses to bring up Lucas and DSGE modelling even as a nuance. The use of DSGE models has become a scientific standard whilst some influential institutions (e.g. FED) still insist on their traditional models. It must be noted, however, that there exists a class of econometric models capable of good empirical performance (e.g. VAR models) where the representation of structures does not even arise as a problem. Even though his critique set strict limits on how to model macroeconomies, Lucas was ready to approve of the possibility of achieving good empirical results with models involving no economics at all (Snowdon & Vane, 2005, p. 287).

The future of DSGE modelling is blurred. One of the threads of the critique questions the plausibility of the idea. Microfounded models entailed by the DSGE approach are widely regarded as mistaken since the macro-structure oftentimes seems not to be supervenient on the micro-level (Epstein, 2009, 2014, 2015) or it is supervenient albeit irreducible to the micro (Hoover, 2001, 2008b, 2009b). This metaphysical–ontological debate regards the ultimate building blocks of our social reality and the plausibility of the idea that agents constitute a sufficient ground to carry the macro-level. If they do not, there must exist an irreducible macro-level over and above the agents, no matter how carefully they are represented. The calibration method applied in DSGE models also strengthens the scepticism (Hoover, 1995).

There is a practical thread as well. According to this line initiated by Blanchard (2017), the current hegemony of DSGE models is detrimental to the future developments of macroeconomics. Blanchard distinguishes theory models and policy models and argues that it is only by ad hoc (i.e. unsupported by any micro-theory and micro-evidence) assumptions that theory models can be made fit the data (Kuorikoski & Lehtinen, 2018). This technique spoils the theoretical consistency whilst fails to increase practicality. At the same time policy models having good fit with the data (i.e. good predictive-empirical performance) can also hardly be traced back to a solid choice-theoretic framework. A possible solution may be the separation of these two families, which, however, may result in hunting DSGE models away into the ivory tower of high-brow science. Bad news for the former revolutionists of theoretical and applied economics.

However, letting policy models get rid of solid microfoundations and making them have only loose theoretical underpinning amount to a justification for the instrumentalism of F53. On this showing the Lucas critique and DSGE models seem to have added a further requirement to the traditional standard of good empirical performance: the requirement of theoretical consistency which, however, was conceived to be detrimental to applied modelling (Wren-Lewis, 2018).

1.2.4 The broader scientific environment: Connections to heterodoxy

The negative attitude towards the Lucas critique and DSGE models draws attention to the connections between modern macroeconomics and the heterodox approaches. Since the 2007 global financial crisis modern macroeconomics has been hotly criticized for being deficient and wrongheaded. The arguments are not novel: modern macro is too reliant on mathematics; the assumption according to which asset markets are efficient in conveying information to the individuals is mistaken and misses the target; we have no reason to expect free competition to result in favourable outcomes; the idea of human beings formed in the rational expectations hypothesis is only a fiction and, therefore, modern macro is in need of a more intense dialogue with behavioural economics; and models disregard too many frictions of real-world markets. According to this critique it is exactly its very approach that deprives modern macro of the capability of paying attention to some peculiarities of crucial importance in the socio-economic universe. Thus letting heterodox approaches penetrate neoclassical orthodoxy is supposed to improve the overall performance of the latter (Colander, Holt, & Rosser, 2004).

But what does penetration mean in this context? As it is argued, the abstract-idealized and partial neoclassical approach does not meet the scientific standards, it is thus an inadequate framework for scrutinizing socio-economic problems. This is the reason why a fundamental revision of economics is supposed to be no longer postponed. The main objection of the heterodox critique against neoclassical economics is that it leaves a plethora of questions unanswered—questions related to factors clearly known as determinants of macroeconomic performance. Structural specialities, intersectoral relations, the problem of increasing returns to scale, our natural environment, the society itself with its norms and moral, specific patterns in the growth of world population: there is a wide range of problems uncovered by the neoclassical orthodoxy (Lawson, 2006). It is recognized on this ground that we have certain approaches able to provide answers to these questions—or, to be more specific, these are the questions we can answer by them.

Admittedly, the neoclassical orthodoxy as we know it today is really in need of a critical attitude, since its world view is highly fragmentary and incomplete. However, the next step to take is doubtful. Do we really need completeness in vision? Crying out for a complete makeover is almost the same thing as an argument for squeezing all the ignored facets of social reality into modern economics. By so doing, we cannot but put forward the notion of an economic science capable of providing answers to all our economic–social-demographic questions, including questions raised by the distorting effects of society or the natural environment. This would be the idea of totalist economics. However, if we take the complementarity or the division of labour of scientific approaches into account (Gilboa, Postlewaite, Samuelson, & Schmeidler, 2014; Grüne-Yanoff & Marchionni, 2018; Rodrik, 2015; Sugden, 2002), it is dubious whether such a totalist approach is still necessary or beneficial. Probably not, once we have model pluralism.

What would be the point of integrating all the successful heterodox approaches into neoclassical economics? Would there be any point in radically modifying the reigning orthodoxy only to have again the answers heterodox economics has already provided? Is it the only argument for these incredibly huge intellectual efforts that we are obstinate to require mainstream economics to be our 'Swiss army knife', to be the universal tool available to us for any scientific purposes? Is it really true that if a theory claims to be the current paradigm, it is not allowed to be partial in its vision and to ignore some alarming questions of modern societies? Yes, this train of thought seems to be the argument. Science ought to be regarded as a rational activity even if it resists being rationally reconstructed in some respects. The rock-solid rationality of cost–benefit analysis obviously prevails. It is worthwhile to initiate a scientific endeavour only if the expected returns and benefits are likely to offset the costs. However, there are no such returns and benefits in the case of total economics, since the possible answers are already available. Heterodox approaches are undisturbed in providing answers to problems modern macro does not address on purpose. We have to put up with the plain fact that neoclassical economics is not a 'Swiss army knife', rather a simple hammer that ought to be used for hammering nails, even if amongst the hammers we can find some masterpieces awarded the Nobel prize. It makes no sense to place a sign of equality between economics as a social science and the neoclassical orthodoxy, let alone modern macro. For looking into problems that lie outside the scope of neoclassical formalism we need specific tools, and no matter which approach one chooses, she will be justified to define herself as an economist.

Modern macroeconomics undergoes changes, even though this transformation process is slow, and it is the leading insiders who decide on its pace and directions. New results emerge time and again that grab the attention of the hard core of the camp and seem to be capable of lacing the highly esoteric world of neoclassical economics with reality. However, this is still a far cry from a radical departure from the beaten path. It is rather a series of subtle refinements to the time-tested framework (Rolnick, 2010). But this is everything the change amounts to. Neoclassical orthodoxy resists outsider reforms. Any efforts to modify from the outside will probably rebound from the neoclassicals' theoretical shield. Even if it may be difficult to accept, it is easier for the subdisciplines of economics to work in cooperation than to exhaust their intellectual ammunition in a battle against one another. In this one-sided war neoclassical economics and modern macro take refuge in the attitude of calm disinterest.

As Hands (2015) points out, today the connections of modern macro to its scientific environment cannot be properly described in the orthodox–heterodox relation and consequently this contrast seems to be rather outdated. Some of the most promising recent developments of economics occurred in experimental and behavioural economics, evolutionary economics (already mentioned above in the context of complexity) and neuroeconomics, whilst traditional heterodox approaches are still on stage. These fields are regarded as neither orthodox nor heterodox, not belonging to any of the camps traditionally labelled as heterodox. Neoclassical theory responds to these new developments in a way not typical of its prior reactions to the flow of heterodox critiques. Whilst the heterodox dissatisfaction has been mainly ignored, these new results raise the attention of neoclassical theorists, we thus had better talk about pluralistic mainstream economics and, consequently, pluralistic economic methodology today. However, at the moment it is difficult to predict how macroeconomics is going to change as a response to developments in new microeconomics, or whether there will be a change at all.

1.2.5 Looking ahead: What needs to be done?

We have come a long way by now. Today the relevance of economic methodology is out of question. However, it is not the end of the road. The methodology of economics works in a special twofold isolation. First, by voicing our normative results we are unable to exhort 'cutting-edge' economists to change their research strategies and methodological programmes. In these analyses the methodology of economics and the history of economic methodology characterize modern macroeconomics as a deficient endeavour doomed to failure. Such an attitude can induce nothing but ignorance. Second, for one reason or another our positive (i.e. descriptive) analyses cannot find their way to the related branches of knowledge. The only exception is the general philosophy of science. Here the leading economic methodologists have already been capable of making themselves heard, rendering the methodology of economics a mature and original subfield of the philosophy of science. However, the most important candidate for partnership is reluctant: the historiography of modern macroeconomics still walks its own path and refuses to utilize the results economic methodology provides. After decades of methodological research the history of economics still confines itself to taking descriptive performance as the only dimension of realism (De Vroey, 2016, p. 71). Based on the weakening of this performance, today modern macroeconomics is conceived by historiography as a long-drawn-out triumphal march of instrumentalism. Perhaps our task of the greatest urgency is to feed methodological aspects and results as inputs into the historiography of economics. It is difficult if not impossible to predict how hard-core methodological arguments could change the way we tell the story of modern macroeconomics.

Unfortunately, the current position of modern macro standing in the crossfire of various critiques is far from favourable. This widely held rejection is also fuelled by the narratives of both economic methodology and the history of economic thought. Formalism and the alleged lack of relevance to real-world economic and social problems have been the major arguments against modern macro and neoclassical economics as a whole. This attitude is highly detrimental or even destructive as this critique against mainstream economics has not led to a fruitful or constructive plan of rebuilding economics. Hands (2015, pp. 68–69) lists several examples for critiques that completely undermine the endeavour of modern economics without providing any ways out of the messy situation of high-level formalism and the alleged irrelevance. Both orthodox and heterodox approaches are understood as problematic in methodological terms. Consequently, economics has a unique status in the realm of sciences, since experts on its past and present are prone to reject it, hand in hand with the critics. In order to change this setting, to relieve the ignorance towards methodology and to avoid writing papers and books for ourselves inside our isolated intellectual circles perhaps we need to change our attitude. Quite ironically, critics regarding neoclassical orthodoxy as a 'closed shop' (Fullbrook, 2007, p. 18) and reluctant to let in any new insights are the same reluctant to consider the merits and to understand the motives of the neoclassical way of thinking. We ought to be more open-minded towards and perhaps more tolerant of the frontline of our discipline. We ought to make more efforts to have a more in-depth knowledge of both the practice and the objectives of the economics profession. Instead of placing the blame on others for an alleged failure, we may need to keep on digging deeper and deeper and to find the faults in our own thinking. This amounts to taking on a critical attitude towards ourselves: our judgements might have missed the target thus far by neglecting some crucial aspects. Perhaps economics has not reached the end of its story yet and there is room for improvements. However, if we are ready to pay attention to the objectives and intellectual efforts of the cutting-edge economists and to understand how serious and sophisticated these efforts have been, an economic science will emerge which is incomplete but capable of considerable progress.

1.3 On scientific realism in general

Before moving on, it is worthwhile to dwell upon the idea of scientific realism. The more so as Mäki's realist turn is characterized above as a radical breakthrough of economic methodology, and the ultimate purpose of this book is to argue for a plausible realist reading of Lucas. An overview of scientific realism also proves beneficial when it comes to understanding how science works. According to the key tenet of scientific realism, mind-independent reality is accessible to human knowledge, and the development of our theories is a convergence process towards this mind-independent truth in both the observable and unobservable realms. Confirmation is conceived as an evidence of this convergence, so the theoretical terms of such confirmed theories are genuinely referring expressions (Boyd, 1983, p. 45).

The controversy scientific realism conducts against anti-realism regards some fundamental questions of our discipline as for which an economist must have a definite stance even before making any narrowly conceived methodological considerations. The boundaries of scientific knowledge, the fundaments of ontological statements, the proper way of forming the underlying assumptions (which ought to be in consonance with what we think of the limits of scientific knowledge), the limitations of abstraction and idealization, the purpose of causal understanding: all the ultimate questions of modern, both predictivist and explanatory science (McMullin, 1984, p. 51), are the questions of scientific realism. Accordingly, every time an economist draws model-based inferences as for reality, she always takes a stand on the basic questions of scientific realism, even if she does so in an implicit way. It may seem an overstatement, but it is not: the basic problems of scientific realism as a philosophy precede any other scientific questions.

As a part of this introduction thus it is useful to provide a summary upon the rise of scientific realism and the main threads of its critique. On the basis of these sketchy notes a story emerges in which realism turns up as a natural and quite an ancient scientific attitude. With time, however, this scientific ideal turned out to be crying out for some refinements and, as a consequence, the realist notion of science came to be forced into the defensive. Current scientific realism is more sophisticated than its prior, naïve version, and its scope has also been narrowed down. Even though the realist philosophy of science is thus still alive and active, its main purpose today is to find a territory regarding which both realist philosophers of science and practicing scientists can form grounded realist commitments on. But what is scientific realism?

1.3.1 Scientific realism as an optimistic and ambitious philosophy

In McMullin's (1984) narrative, the earliest goal of science was simple prediction. Babylonian astronomers wanted to predict the movements of heavenly bodies, but they did not pose the question why celestial bodies moved in the observed way. The desire of causal understanding did not arise, not even in cases where causal knowledge would have aided in making forecasts. On McMullin's account, simple numerical prediction (or, in modern parlance, saving the phenomena) is an earlier and inferior form of curiosity than the ambition of causal understanding. In the era of the sole focus upon predictive performance the theoretical dimension as identified with causal understanding was completely absent. McMullin relates the latter to the antique Greek scientific ideal the purpose of which was to understand the world, even if the close association between 'understanding' and 'causal understanding' has been diluted by now, so today the modern use of the term 'understanding' does not imply causal knowledge (see Chapter 4 for more on this). Greek science was built upon premises and assumptions the truth of which was obvious. Right for the evidence and causal plausibility of the basis, the confirmation of theorems deduced from such evidently true presumptions did not require predictions and hence empirical confirmation (Hacking, 1982b). This tradition implies a realist science, i.e. striving towards the causal understanding of a chosen facet of nature via latching intellectually onto it, that does not rely upon empirics. This mix seems to be strange at a minimum as a causally relevant theory is obviously expected to save the phenomena to a certain extent. However, as it is argued in Chapter 3, the extensive use of abstraction and idealization gets along with scientific realism, even though these cognitive techniques are likely to deteriorate the empirical success of theories. As a consequence, plausible causal systems were meant to have no predictive capabilities. Mere prediction and causal understanding were thus two separate purposes in the early history of science.

It is a realist science also interested in empirical performance that interlinked these two distinct traditions. In the new ideal, predictions in line with experience became strong points in favour of the success of causal understanding. Mathematics played a significant role in this synthetizing transformation. The culmination was Newton's mechanics having completed the Copernicus–Galileo–Kepler–Newton evolution: it was successful in saving the phenomena, and Newton also intended it to be a sound causal explanation for the orbital movement of planets. Assumptions were getting less and less evident. By contrast, scientists were encouraged to apply assumptions that contradicted everyday experience (Galilei, 1632/1967, pp. 327–328), whilst the resulting theories proved to be good at predicting some well-known phenomena. Explanation and prediction in the new methodological standards thus came to form a close-knit unity (Manicas, 2006, p. 11). This detail effectively underlines that correct realist causal analyses need no theories, hypotheses, and assumptions in harmony with the common sense or our everyday experience. Judged by the scientific and everyday way of thinking of the era, assuming the Earth to be revolving around the Sun (and not to the contrary!) was an absurd idea. In a similar vein: 'In monetary matters, appearances are deceiving; the important relationships are often precisely the reverse of those that strike the eye' (Friedman & Schwartz, 1963, p. 676).

This methodological turn was a joint achievement by Descartes and Bacon. According to the new scientific method they suggested, theorists form causal hypotheses as to some observed phenomena conceived as effects (Marshall, 1920/2013, p. 36 and p. 638), then via observations they check whether the hypotheses are adequate. Good empirical performance is the evidence of their success in uncovering (a facet of) the causal structure (see Section 1.5.3). From satisfying predictions a theorist infers that her model provides at least an approximately true description of reality. In other words, empirical success makes it possible for a realist to argue for the causal truth of her theory. As Popper (1962, p. 97) argues, the natural and evident purpose of science is causal understanding (Manicas, 2006, p. 16), 'to uncover the secrets of our world—the reality hidden behind its appearance'. Mature science in the Newtonian tradition is thus evidently realist about the causal mechanisms working in the world, and that science seems to have abandoned this purpose during its history is only a compromise.

The relationship of causal understanding and predictive success, however, is contentious. A basic question regards what claims good empirical performance justifies. The assumed and approximate truth of theories is not a necessary part of the catalogue of the features of good or satisfying theories. Over and above truth there are further aspects that can render a theory acceptable. Anti-realist[2] instrumentalists are satisfied with mere predictive success—that is, with cases where there is a relevant set of phenomena on which a theory provides satisfactory predictions that save the phenomena. However, as a strength, realism distinguishes (more or less) *true and useful* (as realists also regard their theories as practical computing devices that can be true as well) and *nothing but useful* theories. For

---

[2] Under 'anti-realism' Fine (1984, p. 96) sorts all the antagonists of scientific realism including *idealism* (mind-independent reality is impossible to know), *instrumentalism* (empirical success is the only concern for science, thus truth or truth-likeness do not emerge as problems), *phenomenalism* (physical reality is reduced to perceptual phenomena), *empiricism* (the primary source of scientific knowledge is sensory experience), and *conventionalism* (scientific knowledge unable to latch onto mind-independent reality is a kind of social agreement), just to name a few.

economists the very question of the realism–anti-realism conflict regards whether empirically successful theories can provide causally adequate accounts on man and the socio-economic universe, and whether causal adequacy is a requisite at all. It is thus important to see that it is not the focus upon empirical success that renders one an anti-realist. Rather, it is her regarding the generation of predictions as the only justified purpose of science. If, however, striving towards sound causal understanding and truth was left out of the goals of science, we cannot but return to the minimalist purpose of mere predictions. At the same time, we would unavoidably abandon the option of predicting new kinds of events or new effects with the aid of theories. If theories are conceived as not more than useful devices, only known phenomena can be predicted: phenomena in the case of which the given theory has already been successfully applied (Popper, 1962, p. 117). On this basis, however, no later success of a theory is guaranteed, and, more importantly, even when predictive success holds, we have no answers to the causal questions.

The association between realism and empirical performance is particularly strong in Putnam's (1975a) interpretation. Putnam argues that the success of science would be a miracle (today this is known as the *no miracle argument*) or a chance (a given theory is known to be untrue, though things somehow happen to behave as if their behaviour was governed by the unobservable entities, their characteristics, and the causal relations the theory postulates) if our hypotheses were false and if the assumed unobservable entities were inexistent or if they fundamentally differed from their real counterparts. The success of science serving as an aid in manipulating the surrounding reality is also a strong point in favour of this argument. If our theories did not facilitate realist commitments, it would be impossible for us to explain why physical and social reality responds to our manipulating efforts in the expected ways. Shortly put, from the fact that reality works as if our theory successfully seized the causal structure, a realist infers that her theory successfully seizes the causal structure.

A related problem of scientific realism regards the realm of unobservables: entities inaccessible to our unaided senses. As causal relations in many contexts are regarded as unobservable (Manicas, 2006, pp. 16–17), the issue of causality is intimately related to the justification of knowledge about unobservable entities. Realists do believe in their theories providing true descriptions of reality even regarding the unobservables, whilst anti-realists excluding adherents of the extreme Cartesian form of scepticism dare to make statements only as for phenomena in the observable sphere (Boyd, 1983, p. 62). It means that anti-realists may probably confine their attention to simple co-occurrences and want 'theories' that are successful in predictive terms only, whilst the underlying assumptions regarding the observable realm are all the same. Fine (1991) labels this extreme stance as pragmatist instrumentalism (we shall return to this idea in Section 3.4

apropos of Friedman's methodology). As Fine argues, it is truth that realists strive towards even at the level of unobservables, and reliability in empirical terms is a bonus only. At the same time, anti-realists want to have highly reliable theories and truth is a concern at the level of observables at best. However, realists call into question whether a high degree of reliability is achievable at all in cases where truth is neglected (Hausman, 1992).

The stance on the importance of empirical performance, however, is crucial. If empirical reliability is only regarded as an additional bonus to truth, realism becomes an alternative to instrumentalism. This is how Fines conceives scientific realism. Neither realism nor instrumentalism can be more than a compromise. In this case, science would apply a two-fold language. We would have some models for predictive purposes, whilst these models would be abandoned when it comes to answering causal questions. Empirical performance in the realist tradition, however, is not simply a bonus but an evidence or a sign of truth-likeness. In this case, realism proves to be a higher order epistemic attitude as compared to anti-realism: as well as being empirically successful, realist theories are true. Now the question inevitably arises whether realists can line up some powerful arguments to convince sceptical anti-realists (Fig. 1.1).

Realists' commitment is thus problematic. Empirical performance is not an incontrovertible evidence of truth-likeness. Realism without some careful refinements[3] cannot but remain an insufficiently underpinned belief easy to refute. Suffice it to suggest some commonly known untrue theories as counterexamples. Empirical success of a theory does not necessarily underpin further conclusions beyond this success. Some caution is thus needed when establishing our theory-based ontological inferences.

Objectives	Scientific realism *á la* Putnam and Popper	Scientific realism *á la* Fine	Instrumentalism
Truth-likeness	Primary objective	Primary objective	Only a bonus as for observables; not problematized at the level of unobservables
Empirical performance	Primary objective	Only a bonus	Primary objective

FIG. 1.1   The relationship between truth-likeness and empirical performance as scientific objectives for realism and instrumentalism.

---

[3] Such refinements can be made along various strategies. One of them is selective optimism (surveyed in Chapter 3) resulting in entity realism and structural realism. Instead of solving all problems of scientific realism, these selective strategies have raised some further issues: first and foremost the fact that selectivity has multiple incompatible approaches. As another example for refinements, some authors confine approximate truth to the best theories only, or even to some parts of the best theories.

When a theory is successful, it excels at saving the phenomena, though as the causal structure underlying the phenomena is unobservable, and so are certain entities and entity properties, any consonance with observations cannot but serve only as an unjustified basis for inferences regarding the unobservables. It is possible to construct various theories leading to identical empirical consequences, so predictive success does not seem to be an efficient argument for the truth of theories. As Putnam argues, however, an emphasis upon the truth of theories and the reference of theoretical terms constitute a sufficient ground for scientists to choose between empirically equivalent theories. For realists, the problem of empirically equivalent theories in cases where accounts are in line with widely held theoretical beliefs or prejudices on how the world works (Manicas, 2006, pp. 101–102) boils down to a choice to be made on plausibility grounds.

Putnam's arguments draw attention to a key characteristic of scientific realism. A realist believes in the existence of the referents of her terms, in the (approximate) truth of her qualified (e.g. best) theories, and it is on this basis that she theorizes or prefers certain theories to others. Scientific realism can be characterized with an effort to tell the truth, so scientific goals may effectively point to the cases where realism as an aspiration works in the background. It is worthy of note, however, that realists would strongly disagree that empirical success is always a sign of truth. Only a subset of theories deserves realist commitments. At the same time, we have empirically useful albeit obviously untrue or false theories, and there is also an edge where the ontological status of theories is opaque for the time being.

This fact has some implications as for the history of economic thought as when judging the capabilities of any theory economists ought to pay attention to the goals of its elaborator, even if economics, like physics (Fine, 1984, pp. 91–92), also shows interest in evaluating the theories (in both methodological and ontological terms) irrespective of the underlying goals. Van Fraassen (1980) also characterizes scientific realism with realists' efforts towards truth, but it is not a naïve truth conceived at face value. Accordingly, the acceptance of a theory stems from a belief in its truth. Aspirations to truth and the resulting realist beliefs are the distinctive features of the realist attitude. It is not empirical success but realists' desire to build true theories and their success evaluated on plausibility grounds that is decisive. This is a commitment in a strict sense and the consonance between data and predictions may be a strong point in favour of the truth of theories, but only in the case of a qualified set of theories. At the same time, the truth of theories is not a concern for anti-realists, either for the question of truth is unanswerable in the unobservable realm (truth is not a meaningful term); or for truth is a low-ranked aspect as compared to other virtues of theories (a theory may even be true, but it is completely unimportant); or for, in a radical case, anti-realists do not believe in anything hidden behind the appearances as nature is only a 'world of mere phenomena' (Popper, 1962, p. 99). Anti-realists only 'use' their theories and regard them as efficient instruments, since 'explanatory efficacy can be achieved without the explanatory hypothesis being true' (Fine, 1984, p. 100). For anti-realists, empirical success has no implications beyond itself. If a theory performs well in empirical terms, an anti-realist only claims that reality works as if her theory was a successful representation, whilst she refuses to think it is a successful representation in causal terms in the unobservable region. The difference between realism and anti-realism stands in the amount of beliefs the acceptance of a theory involves. Do we believe in something beyond the simple fact of empirical adequacy and do we conceive this belief as sufficiently grounded?

A realist can thus hardly persuade an anti-realist. For those not sharing realists' beliefs empirical success is not an effective argument for the truth of theories. As long as such arguments are unavailable, realism only remains an unproven hypothesis. As Fine (1984) argues, realists only suppose that successful predictions (i.e. confirmation) ought to be regarded as signs of an approximately correct ontology.

However, Fine's portrayal is distorted as realists do not think that confirmation in itself is a sufficient basis for sound ontological inferences. For instance, no realist would think that Friedman's (1953/2009) leaves are rational utility maximizers just because a model built upon this assumption is empirically successful. Likewise, even if there is a statistical correlation between the size of stork populations and human birth rates (Matthews, 2000), this numerical result is not conceived to be a confirmation for a realist ontology. Causal plausibility and a commitment to the goals of realist science constitute a key element of the realist attitude. In this framework empirical performance only enhances a previously given realist commitment or surmise to say the least. Fine, however, underlines that such a supposition or belief cannot be proven in the strict sense, so realism lacks all kinds of ultimate rational support. For this reason, realists irrevocably rely upon their ungrounded conviction; thus the whole system of realist beliefs is said to rest upon an elusive presumption. Realists cannot portray their conviction as a logical necessity. As a consequence, the realist–anti-realist controversy has become a holy war in which the anti-realist camp demands evidence and logical necessity which realists are unable to present in a convincing way.

Realists try to substitute a belief for logical necessity: we do believe that there are well-identifiable causes working behind the phenomena and that our theories can latch onto the underlying causal structure. The belief cast in the truth of theories cannot of course reach full certainty as testing can be partial at best and as we cannot go farther than some falsifying tests (Popper, 1962, p. 103). Whilst admittedly truth cannot be known for certain, the lack of complete certainty does not imply the untruth of theories. Any theory currently supposed to be true can fail a falsifying test at any time. An anti-realist may thus be malevolent to suggest that even realists themselves have no definite answers to causal questions. So what is the supremacy of scientific realism over anti-realism? Its eminence exactly stems from the fact that a realist theory is wanted to be true and supposed to be able to be true, and we claim to have plausibility grounds for identifying the true theories (this is our purpose). Anti-realists abandon this system of beliefs and ambitions. And even though we have no conclusive answers to causal questions, we have some answers at least, whilst anti-realists have nothing to say in this respect. Commonsensibles, introspection, and the detection properties of unobservables (all surveyed in Chapter 3 below) can do a lot to underpin our realist beliefs. Commonsensibles as concepts and introspection as a theorizing strategy provide our theories with assumptions having even the power of evidence.

Realists, however, do not take truth at face value (Chakravartty, 2013, p. 114) for it was so strong a requirement that no theories would meet it. Putnam (1975b, p. 73) phrases very carefully: our mature (or best or non-ad-hoc or non-cooked-up) scientific theories are approximately true.[4] Not all our theories and not the whole truth: these are the simplest limitations to scientific realism. This is a highly liberal understanding of truth. Realists regard their terms as genuinely referring if theoretical entities bear approximate resemblance to their real counterparts, which is not too demanding a requirement. What is more, it is only the central terms the so-defined reference of which matters, which further dilutes the realist notion of truth (Laudan, 1981). It is easy to find certain elements in realist theories that, plainly put, cannot be regarded as true, and not only because of the extensive use of abstraction and idealization, but because even realists do not insist all parts of their theories be true (Mäki, 1994b). At the same time, any realist theory has an 'essential core' that can carry realist commitments.[5] Admittedly, a postulated entity may have no real counterpart if the theoretical description is taken at face value, but there is still something out there which our description approximately fits. So, as Putnam argues, we can subscribe to scientific realism along such terms and postulated mechanisms that provide only rough descriptions of reality.[6] This in itself is a strong point in favour of the realism of abstract-idealized economic models.

After these early impressions it is about time to draw up a brief albeit systematic overview of the arguments *for* and *against* scientific realism. Devitt (2007) and Chakravartty (2017) provide detailed and only partially overlapping summaries.

---

[4] Approximate truth is a loose term definable in both quantitative and qualitative terms.

[5] As it is argued in Chapters 3 and 4, such core parts in Lucas's economics are the abstract-idealized figures of the representative agent or the island models representing the scattered information structure of capitalist economies.

[6] The term 'approximately' is problematic. Anything can be approximately true, and anything can bear approximate resemblance to another thing if approximation is loosely defined. In such a case, a theory taken literally is false, whilst it is true if appropriately interpreted. Many find this claim too vague.

1.3.2 Arguments for scientific realism

The above-mentioned success or no-miracle argument is supposed to be the strongest pillar of scientific realism. As this argument underlines, the observational predictions of some theories come out true which would be impossible to explain if such theories were not approximately true even in unobservable terms. So, in other words, if reality so behaves that the underlying assumptions of a theory seem to be true (and they do if the theory is empirically successful), then they are (approximately) true. If they were not, by contrast, the success of science would be a miracle.

At this point, admittedly, realists are in hot water as there exist empirically successful albeit obviously false theories in the case of which empirical success does not imply truth claims. Realists thus need to provide further criteria of theory choice over and above empirical success. Such a criterion is causal plausibility or other explanatory considerations, even if they are hotly debated.[7] Views on causal connections are also influenced by the scientific community (Manicas, 2006, p. 7), so the reference to causal plausibility is an insufficient ground for realists to reach the desired level of certainty. Detectable and experienceable entity properties can serve as a proper footing for delineating the causal connections. As it is argued in Chapter 3, Hacking (1982a) has detectability and causal manipulability as the fundaments of his realism. His line of reasoning rests upon a version of the no-miracle argument: if we can experience or detect an entity and its properties, it is irrational to call their existence into question.

Popper lays a huge emphasis upon aspects beyond empirical success. He argues that even before empirical testing we do know whether a theory if empirically successful is an advancement as compared to its antecedents. In other words, the outlines of a good theory or a theory better than the preceding systems are known prior to the tests. For Popper (1962, p. 216), a preferable theory

> tells us more; that is to say, [a] theory which contains the greater amount of empirical information or *content*; which is logically stronger; which has the greater explanatory and predictive power; and which can therefore be *more severely tested* by comparing predicted facts with observations. In short, we prefer an interesting, daring, and highly informative theory to a trivial one.

Empirical performance on falsifying tests only strengthens our pregiven surmises on the basis of which a new theory is suggested. Such a theory is expected to be a step forward and hence to have a higher degree of verisimilitude or truth-likeness. It follows that realists apply some

---

[7] Explanatory considerations such as simplicity, consistency, or unity, just to name a few, also play a crucial role in rejecting the underdetermination argument against scientific realism, according to which data can never constitute the sole basis for theory choice.

criteria of theory choice irrespectively of empirical success. From the tests we cannot but infer what we already know, and Popper (1962, p. 218) also points out that theories with increased content are likely to perform worse in empirical terms. This consideration endows great power to empirics as the less probable a successful test is, the higher value an affirmative test has. Even though realists also pay attention to predictive success, for them it is not the only aspect of theory choice. What is more, it is some qualitative considerations of theorizing that foreshadow subsequent good empirical performance.

As Quine (1975) argues, by contrast, theory choice on qualitative grounds is neither feasible nor needed. If there are empirically equivalent albeit logically incompatible theories (i.e. that by no means can be reconciled), conducting decisive observations is not necessarily possible. As a further option, even though theories may be possible to re-specify in logically compatible ways, perhaps nobody finds such a specification. Quine underlines that it is possible to have some empirically equivalent theories which are the same simple: they all have the qualitative features on the basis of which realists try to choose. Given this, how and on what ground can a realist regard a theory as approximately true? According to Quine's answer, this decision does not need to be made. Conceiving a theory as true is neither necessary nor possible. Any attempt to do so would inevitably imply an irrational commitment, so explicit pluralism or, in fortunate cases, dualism is the only viable option. In such a case, of course, we have some rival and incompatible theories, but it is exactly this oscillation in between that best describes scientific practice. Refraining from decisions amongst rival theories amounts to thoroughly scrutinizing and evaluating some alternative hypotheses. This does not necessarily mean that theory choice is *ab ovo* infeasible, but cases may admittedly occur where it turns out impossible. What is more, gridlock situations may be long-lasting. Our best bet in such a case is thus to apply all our theories whilst highlighting our multi-theory or 'switching' approach. But even if theory choice is possible on some qualitative grounds, it infuses an objectionable inconsistency into theorizing. Paying attention to other aspects cuts science adrift from its empirical grounds (Boyd, 1983, p. 48) and science inevitably merges into metaphysics. If empirics is an insufficient basis for theory choice, then no decision is needed as decisions rest upon aprioristic considerations of contentious value.[8] We shall return to this problem in Section 1.3.3 apropos of the controversy between Jones and Musgrave.

---

[8] As a further option, some auxiliary hypotheses as additions can render theories empirically inequivalent. Such auxiliary hypotheses may be needed in order that we could derive testable predictions from the initial, unadjusted theories (Boyd, 1983, pp. 54–55). After introducing these adjustments it may be possible to decide on empirical grounds.

The success of methodology argument is related to our methodology of producing empirically or instrumentally successful theories. Even anti-realists would agree on the empirical success of empirically successful theories. As Boyd (1983, p. 64) argues, our methods are 'instrumentally reliable' and scientific realism is the only viable explanation. For Boyd, our methods are theory-laden, and he explains the fact that scientific methods work with a high degree of instrumental success by saying that it is only (approximate) truth that can underpin this success (Fine, 1991). In this framework, methodology progresses dialectically: our current methods underlying approximately true theories work as reliable guides, so with their help we can improve our theories and hence have new discoveries. Simultaneously, methodology also develops and aids in finding even better theories. Methodology helps to comprehend reality more and more accurately. Anti-realists only have dissatisfactory answers when it comes to understanding why scientific methods are instrumentally reliable.

Devitt (2007) mentions that both the success argument and the success of methodology argument are strongly reliant upon abduction when realists infer the existence of unobservables and their properties from empirical success. Anti-realists doubt the validity of abductive reasoning. However, as Devitt argues, such a critique is precarious as abduction may be needed for gaining new knowledge about the observable realm as well.

Last but not least, the basic abductive argument bears resemblance to the success arguments, though some subtle differences exist. Whilst the success arguments focus upon the success of theories that have certain ontological assumptions, the basic abductive argument highlights that by supposing some entities and characteristics in the unobservable realm science can provide good explanations of behaviour and properties in the observable realm. Here realism is thus used for explaining observed phenomena, but not for explaining success. However, these two arguments are closely interrelated for it is by empirical success that the explanation of observed phenomena is tested.

1.3.3 Arguments against scientific realism

Whilst the no-miracle argument is the strongest point in favour of scientific realism, the underdetermination argument (more technically, the underdetermination of theory by data) is the most effective case against it (Boyd, 1983, pp. 46–48; Massimi, 2004, p. 39). This argument is aimed at blocking that line of reasoning along which realists infer the truth of a theory from its predictive success. According to the underdetermination argument, any theory can have at least one empirically equivalent rival, whilst in terms of the postulated causal mechanisms (i.e. the unobservable realm) they are incompatible. In other words, even though these theories share the observable consequences, they differ in their ontologies regarding the unobservables. If we have some hypotheses about the unobservables and derive some observable implications to subject to empirical tests, even a close consonance would be an insufficient ground for inferring that the observable implications entail the hypotheses. All we can say on the basis of the empirical record is that our theories are reliable predictors. As a consequence, it may make sense to admit that alternative theories with identical empirical consequences possibly coexist (Quine, 1975). As these theories are equivalent in empirical terms, observational evidence supporting one is equally supportive of its rivals; realists can thus commit themselves to neither ontology. Given this, theory choice is insufficiently determined by data. Empirical performance cannot serve as an adequate basis for ontological inferences as two or more ontologically incompatible theories cannot be valid at the same time. The underdetermination reasoning is particularly effective as it is not an external threat: it is realists themselves who cannot choose. Even if one of the rival theories is true, realists cannot find it.

The problem of empirically equivalent models concerned Lucasian macroeconomics in an intriguing episode. Via his island models, Lucas drew attention to the fact that central banks may lose their ability to control real output if decision-makers make efforts to systematically exploit the trade-off between inflation and unemployment. The more variable nominal demand is, the steeper the Phillips curve goes and hence the narrower the real economic potential of economic policy becomes. According to new Keynesian economics, variable nominal demand drives agents to revise nominal variables more often. The higher the rate of inflation is, the faster the nominal adjustment is, and the smaller impacts inflation exerts on the real economy. Both theories have a (near) vertical Phillips curve and a paralyzed monetary policy in real terms as some empirical consequences (Ball, Mankiw, & Romer, 1988, p. 3).

The underdetermination argument rests upon Duhem's (1954, pp. 183–188) suggestions. Duhem argued that whenever an experiment is conducted in physics, it is not an isolated hypothesis that is in use to generate numerical outputs for empirical tests. In such cases rather groups of hypotheses are in action. When predictions are not in line with the observations, a researcher normally infers that (at least) one of her hypotheses is unacceptable and ought to be modified. And this is the core of the problem for the experiment tells her nothing about where the problem in her system lies. Amongst the possible modifications there may be multiple options that render the theoretical system empirically adequate. Quine (1951/2009) draws similar conclusions (we shall return to his arguments in another context in Section 1.5.3). The rationale widely known as the Duhem–Quine thesis (or holism thesis) is closely related to the thesis of empirical underdetermination. If a theory can be modified in various ways in the face of adverse observations, then all possible observations are likely to fail to uniquely determine the theory; thus holism thesis is a strong point in favour of the underdetermination thesis (Quine, 1975, p. 313).

Considering the different formulations of Newtonian mechanics, Roger Jones (1991) also argues that empirical equivalence may entail radically different ontological, explanatory, and theoretical commitments. Realists thus do not know what deserves their realist beliefs for only on empirical grounds such ontological or explanatory problems cannot be settled. Jones argues that even a non-critical realist would be confused whenever it comes to choosing the only (approximately) true theory. Jones effectively undermines the realist position: even one who wants to be a realist may have problems preferring a theory to its rivals; realism is thus no more than an insufficiently grounded belief. In his rejoinder, Musgrave (1992) highlights the role non-empirical considerations play in theory choice. For Musgrave, it is only a positivist or anti-realist prejudice to think that empirical considerations must be the sole ground for choosing a theory as such a problem is impossible to solve on empirical grounds only. This impossibility is a consequence of Gödel's incompleteness theorem. Loosely interpreted, there may occur problems within a formal axiomatic system that are unresolvable inside the system. Analogously, we cannot answer all scientific questions on empirical grounds. As a consequence, we need to find other pillars for science. Empirically equivalent rival theories are explanatorily inequivalent, and on metaphysical grounds theory choice is always feasible. Scientists do need metaphysics in order to choose from experimentally undecidable alternatives. As realists are not averse to metaphysics taken as a constituent part of rational science, it is always possible for them to find a 'best' theory on such grounds. If one refrains from constraining science to empirical considerations and allows non-empirical aspects to be a part of the game, the underdetermination problem does not arise at all.

According to the pessimistic meta-induction, the history of science fails to support realists' claims about the truth of theories. As scientific developments testify, there existed some empirically successful theories we mistakenly used to believe to be true. On what ground could thus we infer the truth of our current theories? If past theories are not approximately true regarding unobservable entities and causality (i.e. some past theories failed to latch onto the structure of the world and/or had theoretical terms that failed to refer), then present theories are also likely to be untrue: this is what a generalization of the past record sounds like. The argumentation does not address the statement that currently successful theories may happen to be truth-like but undermines the explanatory connection between empirical success and truth-likeness. On this account, truth-likeness cannot explain empirical success (Psillos, 1999, pp. 96–98). This argument is easy to block, so it is not as powerful as the underdetermination argument, since it only amounts to a pessimistic inference about the future drawn on the basis of some past failures of science. Past failures, however, do not imply future miscarriages, so we have no rationale for extrapolating past defeats into the future. Even if it is true that some past theories proved to be wrong, we are still justified to believe such mistakes will not re-emerge and expect science to converge towards the whole truth. On such grounds we thus have no serious reasons for doubts to be cast on the progress or developments of science (Devitt, 2007, p. 787). It also follows that scepticism over the achievements of science is getting less and less justified. Pessimistic meta-induction would only apply if adherents showed not only that past science had failed but also that current and future science cannot get rid of such mistakes. At this point, the underdetermination argument is of course an effective basis for the anti-realist.

Selective realisms surveyed in Chapter 3 constitute a further defence strategy against the pessimistic meta-induction. They all highlight that in spite of theory changes past theories did have some elements that can still be regarded as true. In other words, if we are willing to make do with partial or approximate truth instead of the whole truth, and the historical record of theories leaves us no other options, the pessimistic meta-induction goes empty. The purpose of such selective strategies is to fit the fact of occasionally radical theory changes into a refined realist stance, so these strategies are attempts to find a realist position that resists being undermined by the pessimistic meta-induction (Worrall, 1989, p. 99) and that regards predictive success as no miracle (Psillos, 1995, pp. 16–17). However, some 'miracle' seems to remain a part of the selective accounts (Resnik, 1994). Admittedly, a reference to partial or approximate truth is a double-edged sword. If the notion of approximate truth is applied in too generous a way, the refutation of the pessimistic meta-induction goes trivial and hence ineffective.

1.3.4 Then what is scientific realism?

A brief but comprehensive characterization of scientific realism is uneasy if not impossible to provide. It is not an overstatement to conclude that there are as many versions of scientific realism as scholars. As a further difficulty, critics do their best to paint scientific realism as disadvantageous as possible in order to suggest efficient counterarguments. To this end, opponents tend to attribute some views to realists they are unlikely to have. Instead of sound expositions, as a consequence, critiques sometimes show up as overdone caricatures. For instance, in the debates with anti-realists, the reductio ad absurdum strategy oftentimes arises when anti-realists attack some ontological inferences realists allegedly draw from predictive performance. Pinpointing an empirically successful model built upon an ontological nonsense, an anti-realist bursts out saying that the model has good empirical record; thus you as a realist cannot but believe it to be true. Needless to say, even the mere idea is absurd.

Scientific realism is either faulty or correct; though if the latter, as the controversies show, it comes with supportive arguments that require some refinements (Boyd, 1983, pp. 50–51). Even though some considerations beyond empirics still play a fundamental role in the realist practice of science, current scientific realism is confined to a properly specified area where refraining from forming some realist commitments seems irrational. Constrained by the objections mentioned above, realists' arguments are highly unlikely to convince the anti-realist camp. As we shall see in Section 1.5.2, theorists believing in dissimilar sets of scientific norms and principles are extremely difficult to persuade to accept or even to consider each other's world views. Anti-realists with their way of thinking deeply rooted in the empiricist tradition regard realists' non-empirical considerations as only some superfluous and vague metaphysical speculations. At the same time, realists cannot even imagine doing rational science without such considerations. For a scientific realist, physics informs metaphysics and metaphysics informs physics. Contrary to anti-realist scepticism, realists have solid beliefs since they count their beliefs as justified as these beliefs are formed by what realists believe to be a reliable belief-forming process (Goldman, 1979, p. 18). A basic question of the controversy over realism thus regards whether realists' belief-forming process is really reliable or not. As anti-realists argue, this problem is a dead end as we have no ways to check the relationship between knowledge and mind-independent reality. As a consequence, such problems as underdetermination signify that seeking objective truth is doomed to failure. For the realist camp, however, realist beliefs and commitments are justified in cases where we have good reasons for believing or at least we have no specific reasons for dubitation. By contrast, as anti-realists argue, we always have reasons for calling the truth of theories into question (Fine, 1991). Perhaps it is impossible to have a description of the realist stance more instructive than Jones's (1991, p. 186) account:

> [realists] share the general hope that the scientific enterprise has the capacity to provide accounts of [the] nature-of-things-itself that are true. [...] Indeed, such classical realists [...] claim that theories in the "mature" areas of science should already be judged as "approximately true", and that more recent theories in these areas are closer to the truth than older theories. [...] These claims are all closely linked to the claim that the language of entities and processes—both "observational" and "theoretical" [i.e. unobservable] ones—in terms of which these theories characterize the-nature-of-things-itself genuinely refers. That is, there are entities and processes that are part of the nature-of-things-itself that correspond to the ontologies of these theories.

> [...] [Realism] envisions mature science as populating the world with a clearly defined and described set of objects, properties, and processes, and progressing by steady refinement of the descriptions and consequent clarification of the referential taxonomy to a full-blown correspondence with the natural order.

As it is shown, scientific realism is a positive-optimist epistemic attitude towards the abilities of science. Realists conceive unobservable structures and entities hidden behind the phenomena as knowledgeable. Making room for metaphysical considerations, modern scientific realism draws some ontological inferences about the areas of reality where the withdrawal of realist commitments is irrational and weird. This is how the realist optimism manifests itself: theory choice is always feasible on non-empirical grounds; and having left the initial failures behind, science has stepped into a mature phase of its history and, as a consequence, it is only some hostile pessimism that still doubts the ability of science to understand reality. Scientific realists want to grasp and understand the world, which even at the level of words is far more than the simple predictive-pragmatist goals of anti-realists. Aspirations are some key parts of the realist commitments. As compared to realism, anti-realism is particularly passive and nihilist: here the potential of science is severely limited, and its history is nothing but a sequence of failures. When questing for the occurrences of realism, over and above our possible anti-realist beliefs it is thus indispensable to take into account the declared goals of the disciplines and the considerations theorists have made about the development and the potential of science. This line of inquiry may be a most powerful additional point in favour of scientific realism. Perhaps it is an optimistic reliance in the capacity and achievements of science that helped science to grow into a more efficient instrument of understanding reality, contrary to the bizarrely pessimistic beliefs.

1.4 Uskali Mäki's realist philosophy of economics: A quick overview

The project Uskali Mäki has initiated in the philosophy of economics is meant to fill the lacuna left by a methodological framework customized to the needs and peculiarities of economics. Economic methodology had already existed even before Mäki came up with his ideas, though it is the general philosophy of science that served as its frame of reference, so authors made efforts to apply to economics some philosophies elaborated on the basis of the natural sciences. As there have been some significant differences between, on the one hand, the ways economics as a social science and the natural sciences work and, on the other, their basic approaches, and as their fields of study (society and nature) radically differ, these philosophies of science could not show how economics exactly works and what economics is exactly like, Mäki argues. If, furthermore, the picture such philosophies paint about economics is so distorted as it is alleged to be, this flaw would inevitably strengthen the position of the anti-realist camp. The dominance the anti-realist reading enjoyed, however, was expected to lead to scepticism over our discipline and, as a consequence, fatal distortion of the self-image cutting-edge economists entertained. The anti-realist interpretation claimed less than economics is really capable of.

It is positivism as an interpretive framework the effects of which Mäki (2009a, pp. 69–70) has conceived as particularly detrimental since, even though Friedman placed his methodological recommendations on a positivist footing and even though with time there emerged a considerable consensus that Friedman's methodology really underlines the way modern economics looks at reality, in fact it has exerted no profound effects on the evolution of economics. In lieu of any forms of anti-realism it is rather realism, a carefully designed economic realism that can best describe the scientific routine of economics. In order to suggest a fruitful realist interpretation, Mäki has reversed the usual approach of economic methodology, so instead of employing a pre-given and ready-made framework in a top-down way, he has designed his 'realistic realism' along a bottom-up thread to describe the actual theorizing habits of economics (Mäki, 2005a). The main purpose of Mäki's realist philosophy is thus to understand how economics works in the real world and not to paint an idealized picture. At the same time he has suggested a comprehensive and general philosophy of science that is sensitive enough to take into account the specialities of the various disciplines (Mäki, 1996, 1998). So there must be a non-physics-based scientific realism that does not need to be customized to the needs of the social sciences ex post. This is a particularly promising idea as it does not require one to dismiss physics as an analogy. As a matter of fact, Mäki when discussing the case of economics loves citing examples taken from physics. In spite of the dissimilarities of physics and economics, as there works a circular feedback loop between society and social theories, assumptions of physics shed light on the drives of economic theorizing (Mäki, 1989, 2009a, pp. 70–71; Mäki, 2012b, p. 10).

A prerequisite of forming effective arguments for realism is to block the arguments for anti-realism. Mäki (2002b) provides a systematic overview on the specialities of the methodology of economics, and argues that none of its elements can convincingly be conceived as manifestations of anti-realist tendencies. Mäki's central thesis regards the unrealisticness of economic models and hence the nature of the way economics attaches to reality. Even though assumptions do not mirror directly experienced reality for various reasons and in different ways, such assumptions and the theories they carry are capable of conveying some forms of truth notwithstanding. Both the realist and the anti-realist camps apply unrealistic assumptions; unrealisticness thus by no means implies the abandonment of striving towards truth. In this respect suffice it to show how unrealistic assumptions can be reconciled with truth.

To do so, the different meanings of unrealisticness and hence the different ways unrealistic assumptions are unrealistic are to be clarified. In spite of their unrealisticness in terms of mere similarity, unrealistic assumptions can still be referentially and representationally realistic in cases where the entities they refer to exist and they represent features the referents have. Instantaneous price adjustment, for instance, is such an assumption: it has a referential relationship to real-world prices, which are undeniably existents, and prices do have the ability of adjusting to changes in supply and demand conditions. At the same time this assumption is veristically unrealistic as it always takes prices some time to adjust, so as a matter of fact no real price has the ability of instantaneous adjustment. As an assumption it is the result of a powerful distortion of reality where the effects responsible for the prolonged nature of price adjustment are sealed off the setting. Veristic unrealisticness as an aspect simply refers to the complexity of reality: there is always more to reality than we can include in theories (Mäki, 1992b, pp. 319–329).

By making assumptions economists attribute certain properties to some elements of the surrounding reality. Such properties cannot be found in reality as they show up in theories, whilst the theoretical entities that such inexistent properties describe successfully refer to certain objects inhabiting socio-economic reality (Donnellan, 1966). In spite of the lack of verisimilar assumptions directly reflecting reality, the possibility of gaining knowledge about reality is still given.

The next step to take in the argumentation is to demonstrate that instead of implying anti-realism, the theorizing methods of economics actually serve realist purposes. One of the most common aims of the use of unrealistic assumptions is isolation: economists by means of such assumptions carry out powerful selections in reality. Unrealistic assumptions are thus best regarded as strategic falsehoods, so when assessing assumptions and models one ought to take into account the purposes any system of assumptions serves. Every social phenomenon is complex; experienceable outcomes thus stand under the joint influence of a plethora of causal effects. Due to this complexity, the whole causal structure is impossible to comprehend, so the best bet for an economist is to focus upon some certain chosen aspects of phenomena and to aim to understand certain facets of the complex causal structure (Mäki, 2011). The point of isolation is the theoretical removal of the influence of certain elements in order that complexity could be simplified and the theorist could focus upon the mechanisms she regards as of central importance. As a result, we could have access to such layers and mechanisms of reality that are hidden behind the veil of everyday experience (Mäki, 1990b). Powerful isolation, however, further strengthens the unrealisticness of economic models as some elements of reality are abstracted away to be excluded from the analysis, whilst the included factors may be referred to via some fictitious assumptions. Even though our models seem to be useful fictions only, they have the chance of being partially true. A model contains truth by grabbing a mechanism

that is known or assumed to be in operation in reality. Theoretical isolations are like experimental designs widely applied in natural sciences:
they are constructed to highlight some mechanisms working as a part of
reality. Following Lucas (1980a), p. 696), Mäki (2005b) goes so far as to
conceive models as mentally run laboratories set up for carrying out experiments with factors that cannot be controlled in reality. Models are thus
experiments and vice versa.

Distinguishing various concepts of truth is a path to disentangling the
paradox of the realism of unrealistic assumptions. For Mäki (1994c) it is a
mistake to conflate the different kinds of truth as the merits of unrealistic
theories are dependent upon what concept of truth one has in mind. The
one is *the whole truth*: judged by this measure unrealistic economic models
necessarily fail. As models omit some selected parts of reality, models by
no means can provide us with the whole truth. The truth of models can
be of partial at best. Another notion is *nothing but the truth*. This is also too
much to expect from economic models as in the pursuit of truth isolative
models may have assumptions which on account of attributing properties
to entities they do actually not have are untrue, whilst the untruth of such
assumptions is only of secondary importance as they are instrumental
in preserving truth (Mäki, 2002b, p. 96). The assumption that goods on
markets are perfectly divisible is untrue, though it helps us to draw the
continuous supply and demand curves in the Marshallian cross in order
to state the basic law of the market, which is widely conceived to be true.
In spite of violating the whole truth and nothing but the truth, however,
a model may still convey some truths about that facet of reality it is about
(Mäki, 2013).

When it comes to associating truth with unrealistic models, some discretion is needed as the use of unrealistic assumptions is not exclusive to
realist models. To make matters clear, Mäki suggests his key dyad to distinguish *surrogate* and *substitute* systems. Models as surrogate systems are
representations of specific targets so that one by directly manipulating a
model can have indirect epistemic access to reality. The lessons one learns
about the properties and dynamics of a surrogate system are informative
about the target of the model. Even though such surrogate systems are
built upon unrealistic assumptions, they are still attached to reality via
strategic resemblance relations. Mäki definitely links surrogate systems
to causal considerations, so on his account such models aid theorists in
drawing causal inferences about how (some facet of) the world works. By
contrast, substitute systems having no targets are manipulated and analyzed for their own sake, that is, without the hope or purpose of learning
anything about reality (Mäki, 2012c). Plainly put, substitute systems are
non-representations. As usual, Mäki is generous to allow for substitute
systems to be turned into surrogate systems in cases where substitute systems are far but not cut entirely adrift from reality—or they are, but only

temporarily, for the sake developing some settings to be attached to reality at a later stage. Quite surprisingly, however, he treats the extensive use of mathematics as a pressure towards conceiving models as substitute systems only (Mäki, 2009a, pp. 79–79 and especially p. 86).

His related taxonomic work cannot be left unnoticed. Mäki (2000) has devoted a copious amount of work to resolving the confusion over the various forms of unrealistic assumptions. As they serve diverse purposes, such assumptions ought not to be treated on equal footing, so their unrealisticness is to be assessed with care. Core assumptions play a key role in theorizing by reflecting our basic approach through which we turn towards reality. The rationality postulate is an outstanding example as many economists conceive rationality and the efforts to act rationally as a key constituent of human drives. Even if not taken at face value, such assumptions are supposed to be true. By contrast, some of our unrealistic assumptions are simply false. These early-step or peripheral assumptions are replaced later or used only to help economists to focus upon the key assumptions reflecting the essential features of phenomena, so their ontological consequences are negligible. As a general rule, unrealistic assumptions are not allowed to significantly or permanently distort the worldview theorists entertain. When a direct contradiction occurs, ontological commitments ought to take priority over tractability considerations or elegance, or else the embedding model inevitably starts converging towards the set of mere substitute systems. As long as models contain truth, even it is not the whole truth and even if there are elements which are simply untrue, models remain in sufficient touch with reality and provide truths, even though such truths may sometimes (or rather usually) be small. Mäki (1994b, p. 248) underlines that it does not make much sense to evaluate in itself how unrealistic the assumptions of a model are. The genuine methodological issue regards how unrealistic assumptions can isolate the supposedly essential and inessential facets of a phenomenon and whether the embedding theory supports surrogative reasoning.

1.5 A case study: Some methodological aspects of the controversy between neoclassical orthodoxy and institutionalism

Neoclassical economics is the same age as its critique. Either the ways socio-economic reality is represented or theory-based economic policy recommendations are considered, neoclassical orthodoxy seems to meet the scientific and economic policy needs of its adherents only. Even though it is a demanding task, a list is possible to compile on those urgent macro-social problems to which neoclassical economics has no answers at all (Knoedler & Underwood, 2003; Mearman, 2007). At the same time, such a list would provide a comprehensive negative description of the theory, 'negative' taken in the sense of portraying with incapabilities, the most important feature of which to underline here is the purpose of conducting formal analyses of highly abstract macroeconomic structures whilst neglecting the vast majority of the institutional, behavioural, and historical factors of real-world societies (Csaba, 2009a, 2009b). As it is argued below, mathematical formalism is a paramount albeit non-distinguishing hallmark of neoclassical orthodoxy as it is exactly to the analysis of social institutions that some recent currents in the institutionalist approach apply mathematics.

Simultaneously, institutional economics having emerged as an opposite of neoclassical economics chose a much more evident way of understanding reality. As a consequence, in most cases institutionalists regard the level of abstraction applied by neoclassicals as unnecessarily excessive (Csaba, 2017, p. 92). The founding masters of institutional economics admittedly paid a profound attention to methodological considerations, but no matter how strong interests they showed in methodology, this curiosity is directed towards finding the answers to their own methodological problems. This development can hardly foster the communication between the currents. Even though the approach applied by the arch-rival is thoroughly analyzed, investigations are always built upon the methodological foundations the institutionalists prefer. A reconciliation between the schools is still hindered by the institutionalists' lack of any willingness to tolerate the epistemological strategy underlying neoclassical economics. As we shall see, both sides can adequately be characterized by a definite intention of rejection.

In this respect, John Dewey's methodological recommendations are most interesting. Dewey (1941/1988, p. 179) rejects the whole body of the correspondence theory of truth for its inherent subjective–objective distinction of fundamental importance. As a physical heritage, correspondence theory serves as the very fundament of neoclassical economics. According to Dewey's critique, neoclassical theorists neglect the fact that the object of the analysis (i.e. society itself) also changes objectively (Dewey, 1938, p. 161). As a response, he set out his own methodological pole labelled as conjugate correlation, according to which both sides of the relation take part in human experience (Bush, 1993, pp. 65–68). It is not justified to claim, however, that the recognition of this peculiarity is completely missed by neoclassicals. Put in a formalized way and on individualistic (or even atomistic) methodological grounds, the point of the Lucas critique is to highlight the ability of macro-economies to change and adapt to economic policy (Galbács, 2015, pp. 175–216). An endless process of change would of course render the quest for timeless economic laws unreasonable. Perhaps it is this idea that most clearly characterizes the institutionalist stance and that gives them a ground for rejecting neoclassical economics.

Neoclassical orthodoxy seems to do particularly and permanently badly which foreshadows an inevitable and overdue paradigm shift. This, however, is delayed. What is more, it is not an overstatement to say that its chance is getting lower and lower as time passes by. This weird process is difficult to explain and can at best be traced back to the stubborn resistance of the already discredited neoclassical theory. In this narrative of critical vein, surprising as it is, scientific circles appear to do their best to help an outdated theory to survive. However, even in the case of such an explicit support of anti-realism as F53 (M. Friedman, 1953/2009), it remains contentious whether it is possible to permanently deprive a discipline of the ambition to understand reality. Friedman's recommendations are regarded as puzzling and opaque even in the neoclassical camp. Even though some attempts have been made to reconcile Friedman's emphasis upon predictive success with the aim of revealing and understanding causal structures, taken as the core idea of scientific realism (Hammond, 1990, 1996; Hoover, 2009a; Mäki, 2009b), in order to re-establish the respect and the authority of neoclassical economics, as it is argued in Chapter 4, it is still the instrumentalist reading that is conceived as the standard interpretation[9] (Boland, 2010; Mariyani-Squire, 2017; Reiss, 2010). At the same time, it may also be reasonable that the transition between Friedman and Lucas took place along the relationship to reality as a major dimension, so theory change has also involved a change in this relationship (Galbács, 2017). And this is the central thesis of the present book: to highlight that Lucas, in spite of the extensive use of isolation, established a firm and powerful realist connection to socio-economic reality.

This section is devoted to an analysis of how neoclassical orthodoxy and its institutionalist critique are related in order that the main reasons for the delay of a paradigm shift could be identified. Institutional economics seems to be particularly appropriate to feature in such a comparison.

---

[9] The controversy between the various forms of realism and anti-realism is one of the most intense and intriguing debates of contemporary philosophy of economics. Taking the risk of oversimplification, we can say that economic realism scrutinizes the feasibility of theories that bear some resemblance to real macro-systems to be exploited in causal terms. In such a case, theorists set up surrogate systems by the analysis of which causal knowledge regarding the target systems is achievable (Mäki, 2009a). As antirealists argue, by contrast, such ambitions are pointless or even impossible, and we had better make do with good predictions. The controversy also has a descriptive dimension. Here the question regards what chapters of the history of economic thought can be sorted under the realist label. If the long-term performance of neoclassical orthodoxy is at stake, this aspect ought not to be neglected. Judged by the achievements of physics, mathematical formalism does not imply the abandonment of the purpose of causal understanding (Popper, 1962). What is more, as Weinberg (2015, chap. 1) argues ('we do not take the beauty of a theory as convincing evidence of its truth'), some arguments for anti-realism are rather philosophical mistakes, whilst the very purpose of science is still providing true theories of the world.

In spite of the theoretical and methodological heterogeneity, the institutionalist movement is such an on-going project that since its inception has continuously been successful in solving problems neoclassical economics neglects. On account of this achievement, institutional economics is outstanding amongst the further heterodox approaches which are either diminished or considerably younger.

The comparison below rests upon three sets of arguments. First, the methodological discrepancies are highlighted. In his recent book, Epstein (2015) draws attention to the fact that how we know something determines what we know and whether we know anything at all. Accordingly, the content of knowledge is dependent upon our pre-made methodological decisions. What is more, our questions and the methodology we apply when forming the answers form a close-knit unity. We always ought to choose our methodology with an eye kept on the problems under scrutiny. As a consequence, the complementarity of approaches (i.e. model pluralism) emerges, which may be the key to settling the debates unnecessarily dividing economics. The idea is getting more and more dominant in the literature that any social phenomenon is possible to be analyzed in various alternative models.

As alternative models serve different purposes, such goals are not necessarily substitute but complementary. This fact in itself calls into question whether the time has really come for a paradigm shift in economics. Not only would such a fundamental change require the emerging new approach to provide answers to the questions the reigning framework came a cropper with but also to excel at dealing with the majority of the already settled riddles (Kuhn, 1962, p. 169). Because of the complementarity, however, this requirement is expected not to be met. A further argument against a full-fledged paradigm shift is the fact that multiple rival and also complementing approaches challenge the neoclassical orthodoxy simultaneously. It is also a complicating factor that neoclassical economics itself, albeit very slowly, changes to incorporate certain achievements of the competing theories.

Second, a demarcation emerging at the fundamental level of scientific languages is characterized. As we shall see, research traditions have their own conceptual matrices which the followers regard as completely adequate for describing reality. For this reason, any dialogue between opposing traditions is almost impossible. As a consequence, the possibility of convincing the members of the rival camps, which would be a prerequisite of a paradigm shift, is not given. It is thus not accidental that a paradigm shift takes place with the extinction of the old approach (Planck, 1950, pp. 33–34), but only if there emerges a single framework to embrace the vast majority of the young generation of scholars. Lingual demarcation, however, is unable to impede a paradigm shift until the end of time, so it is not an overwhelming case for the 150-year sway of neoclassical economics.

And third, some theorizing strategies neoclassical economics apply to protect its key theorems are scrutinized. These strategies are also characteristic of natural sciences, as aptly analyzed by the philosophy and the sociology of science. Of these three aspects (methodological and lingual demarcation, and efficient self-defence) it is the methodological enclosure that has the most profound effects and that would be sufficient on its own to hamstring paradigm shifts. Even in the absence of mutual understanding and even if the reigning paradigm can effectively defend itself against the attacks from the competing approaches, complementarity undermines the possibilities for bearing away the bell in this conflict. As it is argued below, it is the chosen methodological strategy that prevents institutionalism with its ambitions to emerge as a rival of neoclassical orthodoxy from completing a paradigm shift. On the basis of these considerations it is possible to provide a bird's eye review on the epistemological prerequisites of a full-fledged paradigm shift.

1.5.1 A methodological demarcation

Some basic questions of the institutionalist methodology

The German historical school led by Gustav Schmoller exerted the strongest influence on institutional economics. The paths of neoclassical orthodoxy and institutionalism diverged as early as in the 19th century, even before the emergence of institutional economics, as an immediate result of the *Methodenstreit*. In this debate, Menger defended the stance of the later neoclassical orthodoxy as the right method of economic theorizing, even though in his time he showed an interest in institutions and evolutionary logic far more intense than the later neoclassical orthodoxy did (Jackson, 2009, pp. 54–55). Contrary to formal neoclassical theorizing underpinned by abstract and idealization-based concepts, Schmoller suggested comparisons between certain unique constellations and emphasized the evolutionary character of both the development of institutions and economic processes. Generally speaking, Schmoller underlined the importance of the historic and cultural aspects of economic research (Richter, 2015).

Old institutional economics openly admitted this relationship by eulogizing Schmoller for his strong emphasis upon particular data and minutiae through which, as it was argued, some refined generalizations much more sensitive to contextual details could be achieved (Veblen, 1901, pp. 79–81). It is from the German historical school that institutionalists inherited their special worldview, according to which every society has its own characteristic institutions. It is strongly believed that taking the evolution and functions of such institutions into account, that is, studying economies in their own social and historical contexts is the only research strategy that can result in genuine achievements in economics. Through these efforts, institutional economics defines itself as a discipline of reality (Parada, 2001, p. 48), whilst it has deprived neoclassical orthodoxy of all its relevance. Not only has institutional economics been conceived as having made more efforts to unveil a multitude of mechanisms of the complex causal structure, but it has also been regarded as engaged more deeply in analyzing and supporting operative economic policy (Yonay, 1998, p. 63) as compared to the neoclassical orthodoxy.

Institutional methodology is a description of the preferred way of looking at socio-economic life. Here an economist is given a lot of flexible principles that can be put into practice in various ways. The evolution of the schools raised fundamentally different methodological problems. Neoclassical economics shows great concern about both the way of connecting with reality and the importance of this connection. The issue of relevance arises in a special way. As time was passing by, justifying the claim that general economic laws can convey relevant causal knowledge about any particular macro-economies has become a special challenge. At the same time for institutionalism showing a more intense interest in the fine details of socio-economic reality the problem has been to find some generalizable content elements that can be referred to as 'theories' at all. Distortion is also a major concern for institutionalism. In order that models could preserve a considerable level of descriptive quality it is necessary to find the appropriate level of abstraction and idealization to separate the important from the unimportant. This constraint has caused a lot of problems especially for old institutional economics. Nowadays new institutional economics, as it is highlighted below, is getting at peace with a number of epistemological achievements provided by the neoclassicals.

Today the dialogue between the neoclassical orthodoxy and institutionalism is an exception rather than a rule. Any exchange of ideas is further hindered by the fact that for institutionalists questioning the scientific status of neoclassical economics seems to be a compulsory cliché, a thunderous proclamation to announce in order to give proof of one's basic theoretical stance.[10] Working at a lower level of generalization, old institutional economics has not established a coherent and well-formalized theoretical system, which has been a standard for neoclassical orthodoxy from the very beginning. This is not a failure, of course, only a peculiarity that stems from a unique interest and some methodological decisions. Upon its birth, institutional economics did not show any interest in abstract deductive systems. Instead, most institutionalists still try to capture some historical trends experienced in real societies and some country-specific social

---

[10] At the same time, neoclassical economics tends to resort to passive resistance. In his famous 'Economics', Paul Samuelson did not even devote a single word to institutionalist achievements (Tsuru, 1993, p. 59). However, as it is highlighted below, it is not too difficult for one to find examples for an open attitude towards institutionalism.

phenomena emerging under the influence of complex causal structures (Veblen, 1898). It is much more than a simple interest in social determinants[11] (i.e. the broadly conceived institutions) that neoclassical economics puts under the care of sociology and psychology (Keizer, 2007, p. 10) or even social psychology.[12] Members of the old institutionalist camp positioned their interests to another area. They denied individual and social behaviour being controlled by timeless economic laws, so they categorically rejected formalism which proved to be very effective in discovering what consequences can be derived from some sets of premises and axioms (Rutherford, 1994, p. 9). On the basis of their concepts they made efforts to understand particularities rather than general features. The ultimate purpose was to understand historically and socially determined constellations and evolutionary processes tied to unique places and periods. Such an ambition obviously requires a methodology radically different from neoclassical formalism.

Whilst neoclassical economics has evolved under the influence of physics, old institutional economics has shaped by Darwinian evolutionary logic (Hodgson, 1998, p. 168). Even though Darwinian evolution does not provide a full explanation for macro-social phenomena, it can still serve as an ontology and as a general albeit less abstract theoretical framework on the basis of which the emergence and evolution of social institutions can adequately be described. The absence of efforts towards reductionism was also regarded as a positive feature (Chavance, 2009, p. 72). On this basis, it became possible to break up with the worldview of disciplines put on a Newtonian footing, where world was conceived as of static nature (Atkinson, 1998, pp. 33–34). Hodgson (2004, pp. 143–153) also highlights that Darwinian evolutionary logic was essential for Veblen for the possibility of sequential causal analysis or cumulative causal sequence. Even though the evolution of a particular organization (be it either a biological or a social organization or institution) is governed by general laws, every evolutionary process is closely embedded in a context that can and ought to be uniquely characterized. Thus for old institutional economics specific laws and law-like tendencies are indispensable to take the preferred path of understanding (Veblen, 2007, p. 126). Whilst in neoclassical

---

[11] Such as habits, norms, rules and their evolution. These factors jointly control human behaviour, the working and the evolution of real societies and economic sub-systems. By today, new institutional economics has arranged these social institutions into a complex, multi-level hierarchy (Williamson, 2000).

[12] Consequently, inter-disciplinarity has different meanings for both of the schools. Neoclassical economics expects related branches of knowledge to succeed in exploring their own territories, so answering certain questions is transferred to these disciplines. By contrast, the institutionalist purpose is an active utilization of the achievements of the related social and human sciences (Brousseau & Glachant, 2008, p. 5).

economics, for instance, the description of price dynamics is placed upon the well-known physicalist footing, i.e. the formalization of the interplay between opposing market forces, price in institutionalism is conceived as determined by social institutions. Price is a social convention that can reflect even sectoral differences and its dynamics is affected by routine as well as by the individual act of valuation. Collecting and processing information and communication of market agents also have effects to take into account. Likewise, some effects are assigned to the forms and norms of the concentration of power inside and between economic units; to the legal rules of market interaction or even to political arrangements that establish both the source of discretion over market processes in the social hierarchy and the set of privileged social groups (Tool, 2003). In the institutionalist tradition neither price itself nor expectations are the outcomes of impersonal market forces, but rather the results of calculation processes influenced by innumerable social institutions. Any explanation of pricing is thus supposed to be incomplete unless institutions affecting prices are all taken into consideration.

Therefore the key idea of institutionalism is leaving abstractness for concreteness. According to this worldview, general theories have only limited descriptive capacities for leaving out a large number of determinants of particular macro-social constellations. Generality is thus a major concern. It is only the understanding of unique constellations that can catapult economists towards theories that sufficiently describe the working of particular institutions or classes of institutions. The ultimate purpose is to understand the evolution of societies and economies, which is always specific and hence lacks any general validity independent of time and space.

In order to explain unique phenomena, institutional economics has recently started paying attention to the 'Grounded theory' approach elaborated in sociology (Yefimov, 2004, pp. 1–2). Grounded theory is widely conceived as an appropriate mix of description and theorizing. In this framework, empirical research is not emphasized for the sake of testing hypotheses previously gained through abductive reasoning. Rather, data are processed so as to carefully ground concept formation, theories, and hypotheses. Grounded theory as a methodology thus refers to data-based theory formation. This hypothesizing strategy is contrasted to the neoclassical way of thinking, which is supposed to be deductive and rather speculative, even if this contrast seems to be unreasonably sharp (Glaser & Strauss, 1967; Martin & Turner, 1986). Admittedly, modern economics interprets data via some previously postulated theories (Hoover, 2009a, pp. 309–310) and this theorizing strategy is also typical of natural sciences. A genuine question regards whether with no pre-given theories it is possible at all to 'let the data speak' (apropos of the Lucas–Sims debate we shall return to this problem in Section 2.2.4).

As a matter of fact, neoclassical economics grounds its creatively postulated laws and law-like tendencies upon the observation of unique cases and constellations (Carnap, 1931, p. 434), so formal deductions always have experience-based foundations. Likewise, considering any consequences of postulations also requires institutional thinking to extensively apply deductive logic. Induction and deduction walk hand in hand in both theorizing traditions,[13] and abductive logic of hypothesis formation is also indispensable for both of them (Marshall, 1920/2013, pp. 24 and 638–639). By now gestalt psychology, with Michael Polanyi's (1958/2005) sociology of science as an example, has aptly underlined the presence of such cognitive acts in creating scientific knowledge that cannot be described with formal rules of thinking. Starting from the data, hypotheses are impossible to form on the sole basis of inductive logic as even establishing the set of relevant variables requires some pre-given hypotheses (Hempel, 1966). The critique institutionalists keep pushing seems to have the promise of overcoming the basic forms of human thinking, which, however, is not a feasible option.

Some methodological compromises in institutionalism

For the old institutionalist school, a completely different way of connecting with reality became the standard. Trying to answer a different set of questions they rejected to approve of the extremely abstract neoclassical theories claiming any form of realism or relevance (Vromen, 1995, pp. 13–15). It is also true that institutionalists could pay attention to unique constellations only at the cost of a considerable loss in universal validity. It is exactly this particularity that can help us to realize: neoclassical economics and institutionalism have never been rivals. Both camps have discrepant interests; and seek answers to discrepant questions that require discrepant methodologies. Both traditions entertain dissimilar ideas about science and hence believe in opposing ways of approaching reality (Mirowski, 1987).

The heterogeneity of research directions naturally affects methodology in the new institutional case (Menard, 2001). In order to achieve more explicit, more formalized theories, some modern currents in the institutional tradition have become ready to take over certain elements of neoclassical methodology (Yefimov, 2004). This is exactly the central issue in the old institutionalist critique against new institutional economics, a direct consequence of the methodological pluralism tearing not only institutionalism as a whole but also its subset, new institutional economics. Today there exist some efforts in new institutional economics that directly echo the formalism of neoclassical orthodoxy (e.g. game theory or agency theory),

---

[13] As in other sciences, Marshall regarded this fact as an effective argument for taking physics as a proper ideal for economics.

whilst some attempts still insist on plain verbalism. At the same time, efforts to overcome the constraints embedded in the neoclassical worldview are still of primary importance (Brousseau & Glachant, 2008, p. 4).

Simultaneously, some institutionalist achievements have considerably permeated the neoclassical worldview (Keizer, 2007, p. 5). Conceiving macro-systems as deprived of social institutions is no longer accepted even in neoclassical economics. What is more, institutions are apprehended as forming a structure that can enhance efficiency. The same idea naturally occurs in new institutional economics as well (Furubotn & Richter, 2005, pp. 20–21). In this context it is interesting that Lucas (1981, p. 9) designates institutionalist Wesley C. Mitchell as one of those who inspired his theory. The recurrent character of business cycles; or the characteristic that economic agents try to react to the nominal signs of real changes; and the errors of this adaptation taken as the factors that trigger off business cycles—these are the elements that Lucas found in the vast pre-Keynesian literature. Lucas revised this unformalized framework and put it under the label of "signal processing".

Furthermore, one can hardly neglect the theory of political business cycles (Nordhaus, 1975) when summarizing both the interests neoclassical orthodoxy and institutional economics share on one hand and the institutionalist influences on neoclassical orthodoxy on the other. It is one of our most important conclusions here that the traditions under scrutiny primarily differ in their methodological, epistemological, and ontological views, and not in terms of problems for analysis. Some questions that are of central importance for institutionalists are neglected in neoclassical orthodoxy, as due to the preferred methodology it is more palpable not to pay attention to them. But if so, they have been treated on the basis of their own methodology; thus there are some shared questions, approached via characteristic methodologies. It is contentious, of course, whether looking into a given problem via discrepant methodologies scholars really scrutinize the same puzzle. We can say that both Keynes and Lucas studied the problem of large-scale macroeconomic fluctuations, whilst the ways they addressed the question were so radically different that we are justified to say that they were working on different problems (see Section 1.5.2 for more on how Lucas assessed Keynes's achievements).

As a consequence of methodological pluralism, the controversy over the desired level of formalism also crumbles new institutional economics (Kasper, Streit, & Boettke, 2012, p. 43). Game theory or some agency models are highly formalized, a case where new institutional economics directly returns to neoclassical orthodoxy. It follows that self-interested rationality and the exaggeration of the cognitive capabilities of the individual as assumptions; the high level of isolation and formalism; explicit microfoundations; and the axiomatic-deductive scheme have all re-emerged (Rutherford, 1994, pp. 21–22). Levinthal (1988) explicitly refers to these agency models as 'neoclassical', calling attention to the fact that formalism seriously circumscribes validity and applicability. In his view all these achievements will prove useful outside mathematical economics only if empirical connections can be found.

Mirowski (1986, pp. 252–254) draws similar inferences about new institutional game theory. On account of the constancy assumptions, these models are clearly incapable of describing institutional changes. The constancy of humans and human nature, rules, objectives, and the environment must be stipulated for the sake of formalism. However, such assumptions recall the well-defined models of the neoclassical orthodoxy, and abstracting away the peculiarities of agents directly leads us back to the idea of the representative neoclassical agent.

On these grounds one cannot but realize that focusing upon particular puzzles and setting up the research instruments accordingly have also deprived institutional economics of the possibility of analyzing some specific problems. This was true not only of old institutional economics that hardly made any efforts towards forming universal statements but also of formalized new institutional economics that by aspiring a higher level of generality has drifted back to neoclassical orthodoxy. The currents within new institutional economics that succeeded in abandoning neoclassical postulates and in providing comprehensive descriptions of institutional environment and evolution are the least formalized attempts (Nelson & Winter, 1982, p. 22). However, rigour or the application of the formal deductive method of seeking and analyzing laws has rendered even institutionalism blind to some particularities of the institutional environment. Strange as it is, owing to its compromises institutional economics could not avoid approving of the ways of neoclassical orthodoxy. It is not about regarding formalism as an end in itself. Rather, new institutional economics has turned to problems where the neoclassical way of formalism has proved to be highly efficient. Simultaneously with the rise of the new institutionalist movement, from the end of the 1980s, old institutional economics developed under the influence of Veblen has also got some fresh intellectual injections thanks to Geoffrey Hodgson[14] (Chavance, 2009, pp. 71–72).

In the case of new institutional axiomatic-deductive models, neoclassical influences primarily consist in the intention of analysing the emergence

---

[14] Rutherford (1994, pp. 1–4) calls attention to the fact that demarcating old and new institutional theories is oversimplifying. Old institutional economics has consisted of two major currents at least (the Veblen–Ayres tradition vs. the Commons-led way). New institutional economics is far more heterogeneous. What is more, there are similar disagreements between old and new institutionalisms on some atheoretical efforts and the holistic approach, or excessively applied isolation and formalism, and sneaking back the rationality postulate. For this reason, there is no direct and close continuity between the old and new institutional approaches either.

of some institutions, where such institutions are conceived as outcomes of the optimizing behaviour of rational individuals (Keizer, 2007, pp. 4–6). In new institutional economics thus the evolution of institutions is described in the framework of non-Darwinian evolutionary processes, where selection is based upon rational decisions, as self-interested members of societies are supposed to consider the expected consequences of their decisions as well (Menard & Shirley, 2005, pp. 21–22). Micro-oriented new institutional economics seeking the laws governing societies has thus drifted far from the macro-oriented old institutional approach. In old institutional economics having shown interest in large-scale historical processes and evolution, institutions are not supposed to be the outcomes of optimizing behaviour but rather culturally embedded pillars that reflect norms and values. They are not created by rational individuals. Rather, they are the fundaments that underpin societies in an unintended way.

1.5.2 Scientific languages and the impossibility of mutual understanding

It is argued above that the competing approaches have neither thoroughly disentangled nor accepted the methodological foundations of their counterparts. Instead, both try to absolutize their own methodological standards. This attitude, however, can hardly lead to a consensus and the recognition of complementarity. This process, albeit unfavourable, is far from surprising. Rather, it inherently belongs to the way science as a social institution works. Competing ideas do not make efforts to launch dialogues but driven by the firm belief in the appropriateness of their own worldviews they commit themselves to their own visions of reality, which naturally separates the camps. Becoming an adherent of a research tradition or a research programme we devote ourselves to scrutinizing certain problems and looking at things in certain ways. Any tradition can be defined with its conventional methods, the rules that underlie the preferred techniques and the theoretical assumptions they require (Leijonhufvud, 1994/2005, p. 144). Systems are stable, since any of them can explain the relevant facts and can justify why other facts are to be neglected. This is the reason why it seems as if external complements are not needed at all.

A worldview, the way of turning to reality and of positing questions, amounts to a methodology that defines a research tradition. Such conceptual schemes are separated from any other alternative systems that are based upon dissimilar approaches to reality. Theoretical systems become utterly different languages used for describing reality. Settling down in any of them we expect other languages not to be able to describe efficiently that facet of reality we address. It is a well-known phenomenon linguistics has thoroughly analyzed: by learning a language one inevitably obtains specific knowledge of reality. World as a system of things, properties, and relations is always apprehended via languages. One looking at reality is always guided by a language. The world one conceives has already undergone the formative work of the language she speaks (Benveniste, 1966, p. 6). Languages exert influence even on our experiences. If I say 'I am watching a table', it only happens because my mind recognizes the observed thing as a table. We cannot see anything in ways other than the way the language we speak makes us see. And if it is the case, lingual differences direct us to see the world in specific ways, since languages as mediums or frames of reference stand between us and the world. It is particularly true of scientific theories that provide us with both the problems to solve and the concepts, established viewpoints or preconceptions needed for problem-solving (Kuhn, 1962, pp. 35–42). People speaking different languages and especially theorists thinking in different frameworks experience the world in different ways. As Whorf (1956, p. 214) puts it,

> We are thus introduced to a new principle of relativity, which holds that all observers are not led by the same physical evidence to the same picture of the universe, unless their linguistic backgrounds are similar, or can in some ways be calibrated.

Such differences are differences in worldviews as any (scientific) language implies a specific perspective. As the theory of linguistic relativity (or the Sapir–Whorf hypothesis) argues, linguistic categories influence (but do not entirely determine) perception and cognition, that is, '[n]o two languages are ever sufficiently similar to be considered as representing the same social reality. The worlds in which different societies live are distinct worlds, not merely the same world with different labels attached' (Sapir, 1929, p. 209). Only those speaking the same language experience the world in the same way as 'higher levels of thinking are dependent on language' (Chase, 1956, p. vi). Mutual understanding between languages is still achievable if calibration is possible: if the conceptual differences are rendered explicit and the conceptual background of one language can be expressed and conceived via another (Whorf, 1956, pp. 57–58; Ressler, 2013, pp. 161–162).

Considering the relevance of the competing systems does not take place at all as it would require an act of self-modification. A scholar would be led to conclusions she abhors now. Formal reasoning is insufficient, as exhorting the opponents to become converted (or at least to accept the basic relevance of an alternative approach) requires us by speaking their languages to make them repudiate the systems they cherish. And it never happens as nobody makes an attempt.[15] Only the efforts remain to make

---

[15] It is hardly accidental that De Vroey (2016, pp. 141–142) appraising Lucas's performance emphasized such conversions. Impressed by Lucas's high impact papers in the early 1970s a number of economists abandoned their previous research agendas in order to join him as followers.

the competing approaches appear ineffective or nonsense. As the opposing camps hope, such efforts may still trigger conversions and, at the same time, can justify why scholars themselves refuse to enter other traditions (Polanyi, 1958/2005, pp. 158–161). These debates bear close resemblance to theological controversies in which mutual excommunications are heard instead of some tolerant claims conveying mutual acceptance (Silvestri, 2017, pp. 6–11).

It is exactly the drives towards conversion and the risk of a subsequent confusion that are ruled out by protecting the hard core of a theory. As Backhouse (1992, p. 78) analyzes the Hahn–Kaldor debate, such controversies are impossible to win unambiguously, and the parties do their best to lock up in their distinctive traditions. The Kornai–Hahn episode of the neoclassical-institutionalist debate can similarly be considered. Kornai (1971) did not put forward a critique against neoclassical orthodoxy, but disapproved of its scientific status. In his reply Hahn (1973) did the same thing to Kornai, highlighting those epistemological and methodological foundations that can demonstrate the scientific status and merits for the neoclassical camp.[16] On these grounds, however, an outsider standing on different scientific principles can hardly be convinced as, like Kornai, she is likely to ignore these maxims. This is the reason why the respective camps regarded both Hahn and Kornai as winners of the debate, and this is the reason why by highlighting some epistemological considerations neoclassicals cannot convince the members of the institutionalist camp of even the basic level of relevance.

Lucas's views on Keynes and Keynesian economics are fraught with similar tensions. Lucas was ready to express his appreciation of Keynes, though his laudatory remarks were mixed with harsh critique. Lucas aimed his negative appraisal at Keynes as a theoretical economist. Whilst Lucas (1980b, p. 501) admitted that the 'General theory' was a work of high ideological impact, he regarded it as dispensable in theoretical and educational terms[17] (Snowdon & Vane, 2005, pp. 275–276;

---

[16] The literature abounds in enthusiastic suggestions authors form to delineate the shortcomings of the approaches they reject. Such statements can easily be regarded as milder versions of excommunications.

[17] Lucas loved reciting this verdict. In both his lecture at Ohio State University and his Marion O'Kellie McKay Lecture at the University of Pittsburgh (both held in 1980) it is a recurrent idea of his that the 'body of work stemming from J.M. Keynes' <u>General theory</u>, though contributing immeasurably to our theoretical and statistical equipment, has contributed nothing to our stock of useful substantive knowledge' (Hand-written notes. Lucas papers. Box 13. 'Lectures notes, 1979–80' folder). In spite of these invectives against Keynes, Lucas kept him on the problem sets, with minor emphasis and a critical point of view though (Problem 2 for Econ 331. Winter, 1977. Lucas papers. Box 35, 'Macro problems, 1977–1979 and undated' folder).

Lucas, 2005). Keynes as a political or ideological activist did a lot for the re-establishment of the reputation of economics by emphasizing: crises can be settled within the capitalist socio-economic order. As an economist, however, Keynes with his 'General theory' put economics off its beaten path. By incorporating cyclical phenomena into economic equilibrium theory, pre-Keynesian business or trade cycle theorists had the hopes of understanding why large-scale economic fluctuations are all alike.[18] Keynes, by contrast, turned to the much simpler problem of the determination of output at a point in time. By so doing, he abandoned the efforts to explain or understand cyclical fluctuations and hence, plainly put, provided no theories of business cycles (Lucas, 1977, pp. 7–8; Lucas, 1981, pp. 215–216). Theoretical failure was accompanied by a failure of application as applied Keynesian models disregarded agents' behavioural changes (we shall return to some methodological aspects of the Lucas critique in Chapter 4).

In this vein, Lucas repeatedly called into question the scientific status of Keynesian economics, and he did so in spite of the fact that Keynesian macroeconomic models meaning the Klein–Goldberger version (De Vroey, 2016, p. 164) were the first to attain the aspired level of good empirical performance of models by imitating as closely as possible the time series behaviour of actual macro-economies (Lucas, 1977, p. 11; Lucas, 1981, p. 219; Lucas & Sargent, 1979, p. 4). But did Keynesians have a model at all? Lucas argued they did not. And if we bear in mind the fact that for Lucas model and theory were interchangeable terms (De Vroey, 2016, p. 177), it is an explicit denial of Keynesian economics as a scientific theory:

> The term "model" carries a great deal more weight inside the profession than outside. Keynesians used to challenge Milton Friedman's policy position by asking him to "show us your model." This was the rhetorical equivalent to flashing a cross at a vampire, though it never seemed to have quite the effectiveness. A purely sociological consequence of the advent of rational expectations has been a turning of this rhetorical table: now Keynesians are on the defensive about their models (or lack of them). (Typed notes. Lucas papers. Box 13. 'Directions of macroeconomics, 1979' folder)

Keynesian economics and Friedmanian monetarism made the same mistake: both failed to understand business cycles as both of them devoted all their intellectual resources to the pointless controversy they had.

---

[18] In other words: 'all peacetime "cycles" look alike in sense that pattern of co-movements among series [is] the same from boom to boom, depression to depression. [...] It is this empirical finding which leads us to think of a business cycle as a thing, as a coherent event occurring in much the same way, over and over'. (Hand-written notes. Lucas papers. Box 13. 'Lectures notes, 1979–80' folder.)

By quoting Lucas's related thoughts we get an insight into the heated debate. Writing with a vitriolic pen, both his ironic rhetorical profile and his intellectual power are maxed out:

> To a degree unmatched by another area of economic theory, the study of business cycles is characterized by a curious mixture of dogmatic adherence to particular policy prescriptions and an embarrassing lack of coherent explanation for the main phenomena themselves. Keynesians and monetarists alike review history with the aim of demonstrating that, had their policy prescriptions been followed in the past, the amplitude of business cycles would have been much reduced. Whether one judges these accounts to be persuasive or not, one is struck by the lack of curiosity they display about the events they describe. Granted, for the sake of discussion, that under alternative monetary arrangements major depressions and inflations could have been avoided; why should <u>existing</u> monetary arrangements have resulted in sizeable fluctuations in employment and real output? Or, granted that government fiscal policy could have counteracted fluctuations in private demand for goods, why should the demands of thousands of individuals spontaneously shift together in one direction or another?
>
> One can, indeed, caricature the neoclassical synthesis of Paul Samuelson and the monetarism of Milton Friedman in almost the same language: Alright, we admit that capitalist economies have an unfortunate habit of throwing large numbers of people out of work from time to time, and we admit that we really don't know why. <u>But</u>, if governments will only adopt these very simple, aggregative remedies then the free market will take care of the rest (or, anyway, most of the rest). It is easier still to caricature the attitude of pre-world war I economists: Business cycle? <u>What</u> business cycle? (Typed notes. Lucas papers. Box 18. 'Equilibrium search and unemployment, 1970s' folder)

Lucas hurled the most powerful invective against Keynesian economics in his 'After Keynesian economics' paper co-authored by Tom Sargent (Lucas & Sargent, 1979). The initial reception of the famously virulent study was far from encouraging. The first, rather disappointed reactions are also recorded in the correspondence:

> Dear Tom:
> The conference was a real depressant. It will take a while for me to figure out the sense in which such occasions are "good for us."
> I was particularly unhappy with my poor showing following Ben[jamin M. Friedman]'s comments—especially since you had done such a good job with your half hour. It wasn't until I was on the plane on the way home that I realized that Ben hadn't taken issue with <u>any</u> of the substantive contentions in the paper! I think a brief rejoinder on our part would be useful, if they will permit it.
> As to a revision, my views were influenced by the fact that I was responsible for the more rhetorical parts of the paper,[19] but that you were stuck with the task of defending them. I didn't—and don't—want to stick you with a posture which you are uncomfortable with. On the other hand, having reviewed the paper again, I don't

---

[19] The reason for the offensive and straightforward rhetoric is Lucas and Sargent's desire to keep the distance from their Keynesian oriented audience (Snowdon & Vane, 2005, p. 282).

think we overstated anything, or falsified anything. By the standard Solow set on both days, I think we were rather subdued. So I am willing to let things stand as they are.[20]

There are a number of other things I had thought we might discuss, but which we didn't have a chance to. First, I sent the paper to Orley Ashenfelter. I can't locate his reply, and will have to ask him for a copy, but its main features were: his conference is on, in London, for sometime in 1979. He mentioned January, but nothing is fixed yet. He will pay the honorarium mentioned before, plus both our transportation. (For my part, I doubt very much that I can go.)

As to the paper, he liked it, but hoped we could play down the econometric portions and build up the responses to critics.[21] I am uneasy about this, since a discussion without using the econometric background we provided [...] gets too sloppy to be useful. Also, each revision is a lot of work. Anyway, we can do what we want—including saying take-it-or-leave-it.

[...] (Lucas's letter to Thomas J. Sargent. June 19, 1978. Lucas papers. Box 3. '1978, 4 of 4' folder)

The debate mentioned in the letter took place at the conference entitled 'After the Phillips curve—Persistence of high inflation and high unemployment', organized by the Federal Reserve Bank of Boston in Edgartown, Massachusetts, in July 1978. In the debate invited discussant Benjamin M. Friedman (1978) called into question that the differences between, on the one hand, equilibrium business cycles framework suggested by Lucas and Sargent and, on the other, Keynesian macro-economics they played down are really as sharp as they claimed. An emphasis upon optimizing behavioural foundations was also typical of Keynesian models of the 1950s, whilst equilibrium business cycle theory was not free of some arbitrary assumptions either, as he argued. Lucas's assessment in the letter was accurate. Friedman did not even devote a single word to the fact that Lucas put forward his microfoundations project in order to identify the genuinely invariant behavioural rules (i.e. behavioural parameters). What

---

[20] For the context, see Solow (1986, pp. 191–192). Here Solow regards Keynes as the most important economist of the 20th century and as the inventor of macroeconomics. Referring to Pigou's assessment, Solow argues that Keynes established a single formal scheme in which he could analyze all the factors of macroeconomic performance in a coherent way. Lucas later found this statement dubious, and not only for his negative opinion on Keynes. Even though he thought high of Solow, he did not admit Keynes's influence on Solow's theory (Snowdon & Vane, 2005, p. 275).

[21] Ashenfelter's informal invitation, dated on May 18, 1978, can be found in the archives right next to Lucas's letter. Ashenfelter was supportive of the tone of voice of the paper, though in other respects his reactions were rather lukewarm. As far as the London conference is concerned, he asked Lucas and Sargent for a paper that would pay more attention to unemployment policy issues and de-emphasize the econometric considerations regarding Keynesian models. In the end, the conference was held in Cambridge, England, in July 1981 (Layard, 1982). As Lucas foretold in the letter, he refused to travel to the event, and Sargent did not attend it either. The Review of Economic Studies published the papers in its 'Special Issue on Unemployment' in 1982.

is more, Ben Friedman outlined an erroneous interpretation of the island models and the signal extraction problem. As a summarizing description he told a story in which the temporary real effects of inflation stem from the peculiarity that producers experience the rise in product prices sooner than the rise in input prices. From this pattern Friedman inferred that the real effect of inflation in the island models is only a result of an ungrounded assumption that establishes a unique sequence how agents experience price changes (B. M. Friedman 1978, p. 76). However, this mechanism cannot be found in Lucas's models. The rejoinder Lucas hoped for in the letter was born and published. In this response, Lucas and Sargent (1978), insisting on the high rhetorical profile Friedman objected to, regarded his comments as off the mark for which they blamed nobody but themselves as they apparently failed to initiate a meaningful debate on business cycle models.

In a broader context we can say that both sides in the controversy of Lucas and the Keynesians disputed each other's scientific merits and theoretical capabilities. Lucas conceived the rational expectations revolution and dynamic business cycle theory as milestones that rendered classical theory able to provide adequate answers to some questions Keynes missed addressing (not mentioning the plain fact of fluctuations), and all this on correct theoretical foundations and after identifying the right questions of course (see Section 3.1.2 for more on the differences in theoretical questions between Keynes and Lucas):

> The value—or general equilibrium—theory emerging in the 1930's and '40's seemed a finished, or soon-to-be finished, product. It viewed equilibrium in terms closely modelled on physical analogues, as a position of "rest", or as a position which once attained, would tend to be maintained. Since the observed economic system is certainly not at rest, particular[ly] so if one is concentrating on business cycles, there seemed ample scope for grafting a variety of dynamic hypothes[e]s onto the equilibrium structure provided by value theory. It was not unreasonable to hope that one such structure might capture some of the phenomena which led Keynes to abandon the special (that is, traditional value) theory without going so far as to discard those elements of the special theory which seemed to enjoy some empirical success. (Typed notes. Lucas papers. Box 13. 'Directions of macroeconomics, 1979' folder)

That the economy is unsettled during cycles does not mean that general equilibrium as an analytical framework is inadequate (Lucas, 1980a, pp. 701–702; Lucas, 1981, p. 278). To explain macroeconomic fluctuations Keynesian disequilibrium theory was no longer needed. All in all, Lucas found Keynes's theory inferior to general equilibrium economics successful in numerous fields, from growth theory to financial economics (Lucas, 2005, pp. 22–23). It is no surprise at all that Lucas rejected to subscribe to the Keynesian framework when it came to outlining his own approach and research programme.

Settling down in a research tradition makes it impossible for the followers to accept the relevance of the competing approaches (Kuhn, 1962, pp. 109–110). Arguments accumulated during the decades-long controversy do not help to judge the relevance of the alternative approaches by their own merits. The same rejection forced John Dewey to make attempts to work out his own philosophy of science. Frustrating as it is, debates between the major currents are paralyzed by the lack of a common language. As it is our theories that establish the way we look at the world, no ultimate and theory-independent reference scheme is available upon which anyone could win the debate in a way the rivals admit.

The lack of mutual understanding amongst the alternative approaches to reality is an emphatical part of Kuhn's (1962) comments on paradigm shifts. Theories are segregated logical and conceptual units and the transition from one to the next is never smooth or gradual but sudden and erratic. Differences between the accepted theoretical frameworks emerge at as deep as the level of perceptions. It is thus not an overstatement to say that researchers working in dissimilar traditions experience dissimilar worlds. Incompatible theoretical systems are incommensurable: theorists looking at the world in discrepant ways grind in two mills (or more). Even if there is a shared subset of the problematic phenomena, each approach tries to address them by following its own methodology and conceptual matrix. Kuhn (2000, p. 28) describes paradigm shifts as changes in the way theoretical terms attach to reality and in the set of phenomena and entities with which terms are connected.

The incommensurability thesis is widely conceived as a hindrance to the realist interpretations of natural sciences. If the subsequent paradigms are unable to understand each another, the alternative systems cannot be true descriptions of the one and only reality (Boyd, 1983, pp. 45–47). By contrast, schools in economics, if they aspire to do so, all contribute to the understanding of the complex causal structure by highlighting certain facets of the mechanisms. Competing economic theories are not genuinely incommensurable as on account of their basic complementarity they are compatible, even if no significant intellectual resources are devoted to reconciliation (the neoclassical synthesis comes up as an example). One would say they are rather felt incompatible, but this stems from the massive lip service the followers pay to their controversies. Incommensurability is thus not the same as selectivity. The behaviour of fluids, for instance, can be described as the interaction of solid particles. On this showing, water is a mass of water molecules rolling over each other, so water shows up as a liquid only from a distance. There, whilst disregarding the interplay of its elementary parts, water can adequately be characterized as a fluid.

Bearing this in mind, the conflict between institutional economics and neoclassical orthodoxy is the aftermath of an incomplete paradigm shift. Both systems have advantages, their own problems and norms, whilst on account of selectivity and complementarity neither of them is capable of providing satisfactory answers to the problems the competing approach effectively analyses, so neither of them is justified to conceive as a better way of looking at things. A paradigm shift is thus impossible to complete. All the different albeit genuine ways of turning towards reality place both approaches in the realist tradition (Lewens, 2005, p. 569) as theories formed with realist purposes and having some epistemic grip on reality can get on with one another within the borders of realist science. This results in the emergence of mutually true[22] hence compatible theories, as realist descriptions of reality are feasible even via radically different concepts (Putnam, 1975c, p. 269; Manicas, 2006, p. 43). Neoclassicals and institutionalists working in different and competing frameworks talk about the same thing, the same social reality or even its same facet, describing it in dissimilar ways (Resnik, 1994, p. 399).

1.5.3 Safeguarding a theory against empirical evidence

From laws to fragmentary analyses

It is a commonplace in the history of economic thought that economics inherited the extensive reliance upon mathematics from natural science. The appropriateness of mathematics in economics is still a hotly debated topic. Certain problems can hardly be analyzed with formal theories, or only inefficiently at best. However, there are theoretical problems in the case of which formalism ensures high precision and hence high depth. Just for the sake of good order, a comprehensive exploration of a complex causal structure underlying a phenomenon is not deep. By contrast, here depth refers to an exhaustive and consistent analysis of a well-isolated part or facet of the mechanisms in a complex causal structure in order to pay attention to a wide range of consequences.

The intention of applying celestial physics to terrestrial social conditions causes a lot of serious methodological problems to neoclassical economics. In order to employ the physics of heavenly bodies to our highly complex social world, it is necessary to disregard all the (social, institutional, and cultural) conditions that interfere with the fundamental economic laws. Paying no attention to a lot of social determinants, however, may deteriorate empirical performance and imply the fact that one can only infer the presence of a law underlying social phenomena from dubious numerical evidences at best.

Perhaps it is the most important message of Popper's (1962, p. 97) commentaries that in celestial physics realist purposes lead to simpler and more accurate models, whilst in economics to more complex representations as the more realist a model is (i.e. the more mechanisms of a real causal

---

[22] Here truth only means approximate truth comprehended on the basis of one's own epistemological principles.

structure are preserved), the more complex it is. As a consequence, doubt is oftentimes cast upon the realism of abstract neoclassical models as, following physics, models rest upon assumptions as few and simple as possible. In order to by-pass the debates over the gradualness of realism, clear-cut methodological guidelines are in use on the basis of which approximate truth in the relevant aspects is the norm (Psillos, 1999, p. 98) both in neoclassical orthodoxy and in physics. This is exactly the crucial point in the institutionalist critique: the belief that only something complex can be realist. Tendencies to judge by this ungrounded belief have not even been eased by the fact that neoclassical theorists oftentimes highlight that it is their explicit causalist purposes that lie behind the fragmentary or piecemeal character of their models (Phelps, 2006). In the realist neoclassical orthodoxy, as in physics (Fine, 1984, p. 87), confirmation of a suitable theory has been interpreted as the sign of an approximately true ontology.

It is a fact of life that if we are interested in universal laws we need to disregard the contingencies interfering with them (Chakravartty, 2007, pp. 212–234). Neoclassical orthodoxy is always legitimate to criticize for its blindness to some problems or for its mistakenly postulating fairly stable laws. However, it is contentious whether neoclassical economics really got into bad ways by assuming its fundamental laws to be of mathematical character. The genuine question regards not whether such laws or law-like tendencies exist but whether they can adequately be analyzed in a highly formalized way. Here we thus face two questions. The first regards whether there exist such things as economic laws, whilst the second is about their very nature. Both questions are of ontological character, though it is only the latter that takes the existence of laws for granted. Opening a debate over the nature of economic laws and hence the appropriateness of the use of mathematics in economics makes sense only if the first question is answered in the affirmative. Institutionalist by answering it in the negative have subscribed to a distinct ontological line, where the nature of laws is not a concern. Pushing formalism cannot be disapproved of by denying the existence of fundamental economic laws. Subscribing to the idea of the non-existence of stable social laws one inevitably moves to an ontological platform where the nature of laws cannot be problematized at all. Neoclassicals and 'anti-neoclassical' institutionalists live in such dissimilar worlds that the adequate reply in their arguments is always 'Who cares?' on both sides.

If such laws exist, by all appearances they can be put into mathematical form. It is hard to believe that through a loose and anti-formalist institutional reasoning the real effects of changes in the money supply or, for instance, the nature of business cycles triggered by information deficiencies could have been analyzed in comparable precision and depth to the neoclassical achievements (Mäki, 1992b, p. 321). Formalism of modern macroeconomics is never a superfluous ornament or a characteristic we drag along out of sheer habit or because of the inertia of our scientific thinking. It is rather an instrument that renders it possible for us to answer certain questions in higher depth and with higher consistency than in any other approaches.

Admittedly, deductive reasoning does not necessarily require formalism. Rutherford (1994, p. 8) mentions Austrian economics as an example, where deductive reasoning has been performed not on grounds of symbolic logic or mathematics. This example, however, is rather in line with the details mentioned above. Even though careful deductive reasoning can be carried out in verbal form, the optimal rate of the growth of money or the slope of the Phillips-curve can hardly be calculated without any numerical data and formalism.

Formalism has its price, of course. This is the high level of isolation, to which scrutinizing some institutions and the historical context falls victim. However, these puzzles can be analyzed along other methods by which one could only clumsily enter the territory of neoclassical economics. As long as the complementarity of approaches is unrecognized and as long as we keep having debates over the primacy of certain necessarily incomplete approaches, no synthesizing achievements can be expected to occur in economics. Any specific problem requires a specific methodology the shortcomings of which we should be aware of all the time. If methodology has a message for all the schools of economics at all, then it is exactly this idea. Salvation does not come with a unique and universally applicable methodology having advantages only.

Protecting the core in a research tradition

The scheme of explanatory and predictivist science that McMullin (1984) labels as T-science is a constituent part of the heritage of neoclassical economics from physics. For economics Hahn (1973, pp. 323–324) clearly underlines the methodological analogies. One of the achievements of 18th century natural sciences was the introduction of hypothetical or consequential (ex suppositione) reasoning, in which it is from the consequences or effects experienced at the phenomenal level that one tries to infer the causes (Marshall, 1885, p. 21). The point of the new method mutually shaped by Descartes and Bacon is to form particular causal hypotheses on the basis of the effects (i.e. a phenomena); then to test them through experience. In other words, it is the comparison of the empirical statements generated from the hypothesis and the underlying axioms on one hand and reality on the other[23] (Hempel, 1965, p. 3; Hempel & Oppenheim, 1948,

---

[23] As some hidden layers of reality can only be accessed through hypotheses, and as we need to confirm our hypotheses, in this procedure explanation and prediction are two inseparable sides of the same coin. The only rare exception is the case of rational plausibility (Weber, 1968/1978, p. 11) when no empirical confirmation is required as one can evidently assume the causal mechanism highlighted in the hypothesis to work in reality (Mäki, 1992b, p. 346).

p. 138). A phenomenon under scrutiny obtains an explanation by being sorted under a general law or tendency. If our efforts are successful, it is confirmed by the accordance of the model outcomes with the data. This method is fraught with difficulties, however, since we need to give account of some experienced phenomena on the basis of some unexperienced entities and causal mechanisms. It is only by forming and testing hypotheses that this invisible world (of which consumers' preference systems or Friedmanian permanent income are all constituents) can approximately be approached.

The immediate result of inferring unexperienceable causes from experienced effects is a theory (so 'T' in McMullin's T-science refers to this need for theories). In such a theory, realists hypostatize a plausible causal mechanism that they expect to have real existence (van Fraassen, 1980, p. 36). On this ground, some consequences are deduced from the premises to be compared to reality. However, it is unnecessary for one to intuitively admit the plausibility of assumptions, whilst this lack of intuitive admittance by no means implies inconsistency with reality—inconsistency one openly suggests or makes do with as a compromise. Realism is always a question of taste, so any assumed causal mechanism may seem simply implausible for some. As a consequence, modern macroeconomics and, eventually, neoclassical orthodoxy as such are oftentimes blamed for this lack of direct and evident plausibility (Kornai, 1971). As it is argued, for instance, it is totally absurd to analyze an 'evidently' disequilibrium situation through an equilibrium approach.

The problem hidden in this stance is that general equilibrium environment, rational expectations, or utility maximization as postulates belong to the economic calculus as axioms, and not to the set of premises. They are not data. Premises support the testing process. They are inputs to a theory: the data from which we can draw inferences in order to confirm a theory. General equilibrium or the rationality of expectations, however, does not mean inputting directly experienced reality into our models. The lack of direct evidence does not imply either any inherent and inevitable contradiction to reality or even anti-realism if the purpose is to highlight a plausible mechanism underlying the causal structure. If a modeller cannot generate from the data (premises) some outcomes that are in line with the facts more or less, then she concludes that her theory is inappropriate. The only thing she is justified to say is that the causal mechanism she hypothesized is absent in reality, and not, exactly like in physics, that her premises proved to be inappropriate (Carnap, 1939, pp. 57–61). The institutionalist critique rejects general equilibrium as an axiom, and no other sensible option is available. However, a theory, such as a disequilibrium macro-model, built upon an alternative system of axioms is not a refutation. Affine geometry and absolute geometry both extractable from Euclid's 'Elements' constitute two systems of the same rank (MacDonald Coxeter, 1969, p. 175). It is exactly this relationship that characterizes the whole equilibrium–disequilibrium battle.

In the disequilibrium approach the disequilibrium axiom has the same status as equilibrium in the equilibrium tradition: it is a constituent part of the key terminology that shapes how theorists see the world (Kuhn, 1962, pp. 131–132). One of the major issues in the conflict between neoclassical economics and its institutionalist critique consists in the peculiarity that in the latter direct observability is advanced to be the criterion for selecting the axioms. This is the reason why it has become the most oft-voiced institutionalist counterargument that neoclassical assumptions are inadequate for they cannot directly be seen in reality; they thus contradict common sense. Institutionalists still believe neoclassical models to be refutable on this ground.[24] The absence of direct descriptive relevance, however, does not necessarily result in inconsistency with reality.

Axioms and hypotheses make up a two-layer system, in which the axioms are situated in the core, surrounded by testable hypotheses (theories) conceived as a protective belt. When comparing our theories to reality, it is the hypotheses that we test, not the axioms. If we cannot find considerable concordance between predictions and reality, we can only reject the hypotheses, not the axioms. Axioms cannot be refuted within the system and can only be judged by the purposes of the embedding theory. In other words, the only question that makes sense is whether the axioms are appropriate for achieving the purposes.

We should bear in mind the fact that it is exactly the privileged position of equilibrium in equilibrium economics that exempts it from direct comparison to reality and rejection. Any theory impinges upon experience only at some parts of it, so comparing its non-descriptive parts (that is, which are not required to save some phenomena) directly to reality is not a relevant aspect.[25] Parts of a theory that touch upon experience can always be modified so that assumptions remote from the experiential periphery can be kept intact (Quine, 1951/2009, p. 421). Reder (1982, pp. 12–18 and 21) characterizes Chicago economics in the same way. Equilibrium is such a component that is not subject to direct tests. Observed prices and quantities are conceived as good approximations to the theoretical long-term equilibrium coordinates. Even if some signs of market imperfections

---

[24] In the theory of scientific representation the precise description of how we can draw valid and sound inferences from representations distorting reality is still a vivid and exciting question. As Shech (2015) argues, for instance, political caricatures deliberately misrepresenting reality aid in drawing sound inferences. See Section 3.4 for more on this.

[25] Even though neoclassical rationality can hardly be regarded as an obvious feature of real-world economic agents, some experimental results detected it as active albeit affected by a number of omitted variables (Smith, 1991). The scope of scientific realism thus goes well beyond the case of direct evidence or descriptivism.

emerge, they have nothing to do with assumptions hidden in the hard core. In case of inconsistency between theory and observation, theorists make attempts to reconcile the phenomenon with the theory in one way or another or distrust the report of incompatible event, or, as a last resort, regard it as an intriguing anomaly to be looked into later, but keep the hard core intact. What is more, they modify even the protective belt to a minor extent only, which is a far cry from a fundamental revision of a research tradition. Small changes amount to a high level of permanence.

Actual scientific practice is more complicated. As neoclassical economic models abound in isolation and ceteris paribus clauses, they are far simpler than the complex social phenomena to be explained, empirical failures rarely lead to the rejection of a plausible and theoretically fruitful hypothesis (Hausman, 1992, pp. 221–223). Axioms are even more protected, as along with other elements of the methodology they define the research programme itself (Boland, 1992, p. 18). On account of studying the violations of the ceteris paribus clauses, or of the comprehensive exploration of the causal structure, institutional economics gives an all-embracing complement to neoclassical economics. As long as, however, the intention of unravelling the causal structure is present, any direct comparison of neoclassical models to reality to assess the underlying assumptions or the applied methodology is completely futile. For neoclassicals, the central question of an empirical test regards whether a postulated mechanism can be detected as a part of real-world social conditions and not that whether such a postulated mechanism exhausts the complex causal structure. These tests have mainly been successful. As a consequence, a line of the institutionalist critique is not aimed at calling these numerical results into question but at underlining the simple and well-known fact that such a highlighted mechanism cannot reflect the complete causal structure— which, however, has never been a purpose.

Axioms constitute the inner protected core not because the research tradition has arbitrarily chosen them for this role. Rather, the reason is that testing axioms directly, i.e. without any theory, is infeasible. If it is always through a theory that an axiom bears only an indirect relation to reality, it cannot be tested directly by confronting the embedding theory with reality. However, it does not exclude the possibility of treating an axiom of a theory as a testable hypothesis in another system. It was exactly the case with rational expectations hypothesis suggested by Muth (1961, p. 316). As the econometric tests had considerably confirmed the hypothesis, Lucas (1973) could later apply it as an axiom. However, the moment a hypothesis is placed amongst the axioms, it loses its testability. This is in complete consonance with Carnap's (1939, p. 59) arguments. It is the same process as what was described by Lakatos (1968, pp. 168–176) analyzing the evolution of modern natural science. Thanks to the positive heuristics and negative heuristics, the testable protective belt built around the hard core prevents the most characteristic and most stable system of theories and assumptions from the critique and from any modifying efforts (Blaug, 1992, p. 193). The neutrality of neoclassical orthodoxy against the institutionalist critique does not only stem from an instinctively followed scientific strategy. We should not forget about the fact that modern macroeconomics after Keynes has never made efforts to set up general theories.[26] It is exceptionally true of Friedman who worked along an eclectic methodology and was not even worried about some occasional inconsistencies between his partial theories.[27] However, it also applies to the subsequent Lucas–RBC-line that has always been directed at analyzing only certain individual mechanisms of the complex causal structure. Such occasionally conflicting efforts have all been built around a set of basic axioms to be kept intact.

1.5.4 A critique of the critique

To complete a paradigm shift the institutionalist critique should demonstrate the failure of neoclassical economics. This could be carried out in two ways. First, critics would need to shed light on the inefficiency of neoclassical economics in applying its preferred methods. In other words, the effects of some factors neoclassical orthodoxy consistently neglects could prove to be analyzable in a formalized way and in the neoclassical depth along with and in addition to the traditional problems (i.e. in the same model/theory). In this case, it would be clear that neoclassical economics has erroneously narrowed down its scope. The most part of institutional economics, however, categorically rejected this kind of formalism. In most cases, institutionalists have regarded the level of depth formalism provides as dispensable to understanding.

Institutionalists do their best to replace the allegedly abortive neoclassical methodology with the approach they favour. As institutionalism mainly refuses to admit the possible advantages of formalism, its own, less formal methods appear to have benefits only. At the same time, such non-formal efforts of institutional economics have played down the gains from the development of mathematical methods.[28] In this respect, formalized efforts

---

[26] Keynes was far from the level of complexity that is the ideal for institutional economics. De Vroey (2016, p. 74) quotes a passage where Friedman writes that his esteem to Keynes was raised by Keynes's focus upon a small number of key variables.

[27] As Friedman and Schwartz (1991, pp. 41–42) argue, we have no ultimate and absolute concepts. The economic content of variables must always be established on the basis of the problems at hand. This is also true of the question of endogeneity and exogeneity to be settled on a case-by-case basis.

[28] The fact that neoclassical economics can gradually (albeit slowly) outdo some of its traditional postulates is an immediate result of the development of mathematical and empirical methods.

of new institutional economics have abandoned the initial institutionalist purposes. By contrast, those research directions that ambitioned to reject the standard neoclassical assumptions were hostile to formalism as well. Here man is not analyzed as the homo oeconomicus, but as an actual social being, and instead of preserving depth, anti-formalist institutionalists intend to provide more comprehensive descriptions of causal structures. Unfortunately, the price of arriving at lower levels of formalism is giving up analytical depth (Williamson, 1985, p. 386), and it is exactly the consequence institutionalism tends not to pay attention to.

It is worthy of note that preferring comprehensiveness to depth is only a question of taste (Mitchell, 1913, pp. 449–450; Marshall, 1920/2013, p. 643). A researcher always follows her own interest when deciding on how large a slice of reality she would like to study. As a matter of fact it is the only decision she can make as definite methods making efficient analyses feasible appertain to any chosen problem. Methodologies come along with problems. Narrow formalism that can provide higher degrees of depth, and comprehensive but non-formalist institutionalist approach that cannot claim to have considerable depth are the endpoints of a continuum which abounds in an array of intermediate positions (Morrison, 2000, pp. 19–20; Brakman, Garretsen, & van Marrewijk, 2001, p. 323).

In the context of analytical depth and comprehensiveness it is worth attention how Giere (1988) in his overview on classical mechanics discusses the relationship between idealization and the truth of physical laws. Classical mechanics does not describe real-world mechanical systems as it neglects a number of real properties. The motion of a real swing does not abide by the theoretical description of ideal swings. Equations contain some circumstances that are only approximations to real-world conditions. Only ideal systems can completely meet the conditions the equations imply. If laws of motion are regarded as empirical claims of universal validity (i.e. claims with direct observability), they will prove to be false. Laws are thus true only in cases where reality is like the theoretical conditions. By taking more and more factors into account, that is, by enhancing complexity, reality can gradually be approached. Specifications may be rather imprecise or highly precise, though neither of them can be wholly accurate. Efforts towards higher and higher levels of precision, however, inevitably heighten complexity, whilst complete truth as an ideal is unlikely to be achievable. For scientific practice, moreover, the literal truth of laws is irrelevant. The purpose is not the whole truth but approximate truth only. In this process the extent to which reality is approached is dependent upon scientific objectives. At the end of the day, it is two dissimilar attitudes that are confronted in the neoclassical-institutionalist controversy, from which it is impossible to choose on logical grounds. Choice is solely dependent upon preferences and taste. This recognition cannot but render the debate entirely pointless and unfruitful.

Second, institutional (or any other) approach would need to demonstrate that by abandoning formalism the problems neoclassical economics analyzes could be scrutinized more thoroughly and by doing so, some new insights could be revealed. It would be an increase in analytical depth. To achieve it, some non-formalist approaches would be needed that are still capable of getting to higher degrees of depth as compared to formal methods. However, it is contentious how economics could enhance depth without the inferential rules and logic mathematics facilitates. Such an institutionalist critique would thus be efficient only if the range or length of the comprehended causal mechanisms was increased whilst other things are kept equal, that is, whilst the level of formalism would be maintained; or formalism itself would prove to be insufficient in increasing the depth of analysis. As we have seen, increasing the number of factors treated in a model necessarily leads to a drop in the level of formalism, and its price is a decrease in depth. The circumstance that institutionalism succeeds in scrutinizing some problems neoclassicals neglect with methods neoclassicals do not apply meets none of these options. Furthermore, the fact that some institutionalist problems can also be effectively analyzed in a formal way (and in separate models, which is of crucial importance for the discussion here) is rather a point in favour of the neoclassical approach. It is no surprise that De Vroey and Pensieroso (2016, pp. 17–18) explicitly ascribe the convergence of some institutionalist researches towards mainstream economics to the efficiency and the attraction of mainstream methodology.

1.6 Conclusions: Why is methodology so important?

So far it has been argued that methodology and the content of our knowledge are inseparable. The strategy for gaining knowledge we choose directly determines the extent and dimensions of our knowledge. However, the overall setting is more complex as we prefer methodologies on the basis of our pre-given beliefs on the possibilities of cognition. This chapter was devoted to the analysis of two ongoing conflicts, and it is the joint lesson of both the realism–anti-realism debate and the neoclassical-institutionalist controversy that the connection between methodology and what one knows is reciprocal. If we believe that in order to gain knowledge about reality we cannot refrain from considerations beyond empirics, then we build our theories accordingly. When it comes to forming the terms referring to fundamental entities, we apply abstraction and idealization with a view to latching onto the relevant properties of the real counterparts even in the unobservable realm. Our ontological views shape our epistemological considerations regarding the possibilities of science. What we believe to be existent or inexistent informs our ideas on what can be known about reality. To make matters more complicated, of course there is a feedback from epistemology towards ontology. Not all conclusions from epistemology to ontology are warranted, though. Chapter 3 discusses the various forms of ontic structural realism which is widely conceived as the result of some unjustified ontological inferences drawn on epistemological grounds.

Likewise, a realist regards her models as capable of grabbing unobservable causal mechanisms, so she refrains from drawing causally empty generalizations. The neoclassical-institutionalist conflict has provided a similar lesson. The way abstraction and idealization are utilized is dependent upon the extent they ought to be applied in order that we could achieve the knowledge we prefer. As we have seen, institutionalists conceive neoclassicals' knowledge as 'no knowledge', and the reason for this alleged failure is identified in the neoclassical way of theorizing and model building institutionalists refuse to accept. In other words, by criticizing neoclassical knowledge institutionalists criticize neoclassical methodology: a methodology that cannot result in knowledge institutionalists are willing to approve of. The failure of theory is a failure of methodology (theory stems from methodology), though the methodology we choose is in line with our ideas about 'good' knowledge (we choose methodology on the basis of the knowledge we aspire). What is more, theoretical knowledge inevitably affects our ontological and epistemological principles. The knowledge we have determines our ideas about both reality and the achievable forms of knowledge (Fig. 1.2).

So why is methodology important? The methodology we choose on the basis of some ontological principles and their epistemological consequences or bases, as there is a circularity here, directly shapes our theories, and no theory can be thoroughly analyzed without scrutinizing these

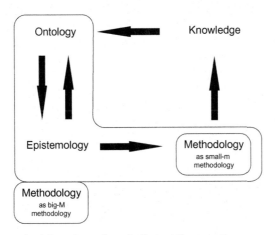

FIG. 1.2 How methodology depends and affects at the same time.

underlying considerations. Such meta-theoretical reflections form some constituent parts of the broadly conceived theories. Superficial knowledge of these considerations inevitably leads to superficial knowledge of the narrowly conceived theories. Recalling the realist–anti-realist debate, theories have dissimilar contents in cases where they are regarded as useful predictive instruments only or as useful and true at the same time. In the former case, theory rests upon a correlation of uncertain longevity and reliability. In the latter case, by contrast, the theory is aimed at unravelling (a part of) the hidden causal structure. These cases drastically differ in terms of the connections with reality, that is, in terms of the ontological status of theories. But for making these considerations explicit, assessment cannot but remain incomplete. This is the reason why methodology is especially important to the historiography of economic thought.

If this cycle is reversed, via methodology we get back to epistemology and ontology. Neoclassical orthodoxy is built upon a shared methodology. The use of highly abstract and idealized models, where descriptive realisticness of assumptions is not required, became the norm about two centuries ago. As a matter of fact, however, various kinds of knowledge may stem from such devices of poor descriptive performance. Adherents of both anti-realist instrumentalism and realism see eye to eye on regarding descriptive accuracy of the underlying assumptions as unnecessary. Thus realist and anti-realist methodologies bear some resemblance (for both, plainly put, theoretical terms are to be unrealistic in descriptive terms), whilst in referential or ontological terms these methodologies lead to dissimilar results. One might say that similar methodologies reflect dissimilar ontological and epistemological principles, or that similar methodologies can be reconciled with dissimilar ontological and epistemological principles. Methodologies thus have a superficial similarity only as simple (or descriptive) unrealisticness perfectly fits the realist purpose of unravelling the hidden causal structure of the world. The content of the statements an economist makes about reality, whether she enters the unobservable realm or not, is dependent upon her epistemological principles, the underlying ontology, and the methodology she applies to forge a theory. All these questions belong to the scope of big-M methodology.

Suggested readings

Scientific realism is a hotly debated topic, so it is uneasy to pinpoint the best sources to start with, though the compilation by Leplin (1984) seems to be a good first choice. Chakravartty (2017) gives a recent survey. To nurture familiarity with the problems of realism in economics, it is the best bet to start with Mäki's (2009a, 2012b) accounts. The criticism against neoclassical economics started as early as with the Methodenstreit in the late

19th century. Häuser (1988), Bostaph (1998), and Louzek (2011) provide some detailed overviews. Sometimes leading economists such as Leontief (1971), Tobin (1972), or Solow (1980) also voice their concerns about the unhappy state of economics. Galbraith's (1967, 1973) dissatisfaction with the neoclassical orthodoxy is well known and widely cited. Today it is World Economics Association and its journal 'Real-World Economics Review', and the Post-Autistic Economics Movement that serve as major forums of scepticism towards neoclassical economics.

References

Arthur, W. B. (2015). *Complexity and the economy*. Oxford: Oxford University Press.
Atkinson, G. (1998). An evolutionary theory of the development of property and the state. In W. J. Samuels (Ed.), *The founding of institutional economics* (pp. 33–46). London: Routledge.
Backhouse, R. E. (1992). The constructivist critique of economic methodology. *Methodus, 4*(1), 65–82.
Backhouse, R. E., Hausman, D. M., Mäki, U., & Salanti, A. (Eds.), (1997). *Economics and methodology. Crossing boundaries*. Houndmills: Macmillan.
Ball, L., Mankiw, N. G., & Romer, D. (1988). The new Keynesian economics and the output-inflation trade-off. *Brookings Papers on Economic Activity, 19*(1), 1–82.
Benveniste, É. (1966). *Problèmes de linguistique générale. (Vol. 1)*. Paris: Gallimard.
Berry, B. J., Kiel, L. D., & Elliott, E. (2002). Adaptive agents, intelligence, and emergent human organization. Capturing complexity through agent-based modeling. *Proceedings of the National Academy of Sciences of the United States of America, 99*(3), 7187–7188.
Blanchard, O. J. (2017, January 12). *The need for different classes of macroeconomic models*. Retrieved July 22, 2018, from Peterson Institute for International Economics, https://piie.com/blogs/realtime-economic-issues-watch/need-different-classes-macroeconomic-models.
Blaug, M. (1962). *Economic theory in retrospect* (1st ed.). Homewood: Richard D. Irwin.
Blaug, M. (1980). *The methodology of economics or how economists explain* (1st ed.). Cambridge: Cambridge University Press.
Blaug, M. (1992). *The methodology of economics or how economists explain* (2nd ed.). Cambridge: Cambridge University Press.
Boland, L. A. (1979). A critique of Friedman's critics. *Journal of Economic Literature, 17*(2), 503–522.
Boland, L. A. (1992). *The principles of economics. Some lies my teachers told me*. London: Routledge.
Boland, L. A. (2010). Review of "The methodology of positive economics. Reflections on the Milton Friedman legacy, ed. Uskali Mäki". *Economics and Philosophy, 26*(3), 376–382.
Boland, L. A. (2016). Philosophy of economics versus methodology of economics. *Studia Metodologiczne, 36*(1), 17–26.
Bonabeau, E. (2002). Agent-based modeling. Methods and techniques for simulating human systems. *Proceedings of the National Academy of Sciences of the United States of America, 99*(3), 7280–7287.
Bostaph, S. (1998). The Methodenstreit. In P. J. Boettke (Ed.), *The Elgar companion to Austrian economics* (pp. 459–464). Cheltenham: Edward Elgar.
Boumans, M., & Davis, J. B. (2016). *Economic methodology. Understanding economics as a science* (2nd ed.). London: Palgrave.
Boyd, R. N. (1983). On the current status of the issue of scientific realism. *Erkenntnis, 19*(1/3), 45–90.
Brakman, S., Garretsen, H., & van Marrewijk, C. (2001). *An introduction to geographical economics. Trade, location and growth*. Cambridge: Cambridge University Press.

Brousseau, É., & Glachant, J. M. (2008). *New institutional economics. A guidebook.* Cambridge: Cambridge University Press.

Bush, P. D. (1993). The methodology of institutional economics. A pragmatic instrumentalist perspective. In M. R. Tool (Ed.), *Institutional economics. Theory, method, policy* (pp. 59–108). Boston: Kluwer.

Caldwell, B. J. (1990). Does methodology matter? How should it be practiced? *Finnish Economic Papers, 3*(1), 64–71.

Caldwell, B. J. (1994). *Beyond positivism. Economic methodology in the twentieth century* (Revised edition). London: Routledge.

Carnap, R. (1931). Die physikalische Sprache als Universalsprache der Wissenschaft. *Erkenntnis, 2*(1), 432–465.

Carnap, R. (1939). *Foundations of logic and mathematics.* Chicago: The University of Chicago Press.

Chakravartty, A. (1998). Semirealism. *Studies in History and Philosophy of Science Part A, 29*(3), 391–408.

Chakravartty, A. (2007). *A metaphysics for scientific realism. Knowing the unobservable.* Cambridge: Cambridge University Press.

Chakravartty, A. (2013). Dispositions for scientific realism. In R. Groff & J. Greco (Eds.), *Powers and capacities in philosophy. The new Aristotelianism* (pp. 113–127). London: Routledge.

Chakravartty, A. (2017). Scientific realism. Letöltés dátuma: 2019. August 31, In Zalta, E. N. (Ed.), *Stanford encyclopedia of philosophy.* https://plato.stanford.edu/archives/sum2017/entries/scientific-realism/.

Chase, S. (1956). Foreword. In B. L. Whorf & J. B. Carroll (Eds.), *Language, thought, and reality* (pp. v–x). Cambridge, MA: The MIT Press.

Chavance, B. (2009). *Institutional economics.* London: Routledge.

Colander, D. (2008). *Complexity and the history of economic thought.* Middlebury College economics discussion paper no. 08-04. Middlebury: Department of Economics, Middlebury College.

Colander, D., Holt, R. P., & Rosser, J. B. (2004). *The changing face of economics.* Ann Arbor: University of Michigan Press.

Csaba, L. (2009a). Orthodoxy, renewal and complexity in contemporary economics. *Zeitschrift für Staats- und Europawissenschaften, 7*(1), 51–82.

Csaba, L. (2009b). *Crisis in economics? Studies in European political economy.* Budapest: Akadémiai Kiadó.

Csaba, L. (2017). Comparative economics and the mainstream. *Economics and Business Review, 3*(3), 90–109.

Davis, J. B., Hands, D. W., & Mäki, U. (Eds.), (1998). *The handbook of economic methodology.* Cheltenham: Edward Elgar.

De Vroey, M. (2016). *A history of macroeconomics from Keynes to Lucas and beyond.* Cambridge: Cambridge University Press.

De Vroey, M., & Pensieroso, L. (2016). *The rise of a mainstream in economics.* Discussion paper no. 2016-26, Leuven: Institut de Recherches Économiques et Sociales de l'Université catholique de Louvain.

Devitt, M. (2007). Scientific realism. In F. Jackson & M. Smith (Eds.), *The Oxford handbook of contemporary philosophy* (pp. 767–791). Oxford: Oxford University Press.

Dewey, J. (1938). Logic. The theory of inquiry. *The later works 1925–1953 Volume 12: 1938.* Carbondale: Southern Illinois University Press.

Dewey, J. (1941/1988). Propositions, warranted assertibility, and truth. In J. Dewey (Ed.), *The later works, 1925–1953. Volume 14: 1939–1941* (pp. 168–188). Carbondale: Southern Illinois University Press.

Donnellan, K. S. (1966). Reference and definite descriptions. *The Philosophical Review, 75*(3), 281–304.

Duhem, P. (1954). *The aim and structure of physical theory.* Princeton, NJ: Princeton University Press.

Epstein, B. (2009). Ontological individualism reconsidered. *Synthese, 166*(1), 187–213.

Epstein, B. (2014). Why macroeconomics does not supervene on microeconomics. *Journal of Economic Methodology, 21*(1), 3–18.

Epstein, B. (2015). *The ant trap. Rebuilding the foundations of the social sciences.* Oxford: Oxford University Press.

Ericsson, N., & Irons, J. (1995). The Lucas critique in practice. Theory without measurement. In K. D. Hoover (Ed.), *Macroeconometrics. Developments, tensions, and prospects* (pp. 263–312). Heidelberg: Springer.

Esfeld, M. (2009). The modal nature of structures in ontic structural realism. *International Studies in the Philosophy of Science, 23*(2), 179–194.

Fine, A. (1984). The natural ontological attitude. In J. Leplin (Ed.), *Scientific realism* (pp. 83–107). Berkeley, CA: University of California Press.

Fine, A. (1991). Piecemeal realism. *Philosophical Studies, 61*(1–2), 79–96.

Friedman, B. M. (1978). Discussion. In F. E. Morris (Ed.), *After the Phillips curve. Persistence of high inflation and high unemployment* (pp. 73–80). Boston, MA: Federal Reserve Bank of Boston.

Friedman, M. (1953/2009). The methodology of positive economics. In U. Mäki (Ed.), *The methodology of positive economics. Reflections on the Milton Friedman legacy* (pp. 3–43). Cambridge: Cambridge University Press.

Friedman, M., & Schwartz, A. J. (1963). *A monetary history of the United States, 1867–1960.* Princeton, NJ: Princeton University Press.

Friedman, M., & Schwartz, A. J. (1991). Alternative approaches to analyzing economic data. *The American Economic Review, 81*(1), 39–49.

Frisch, R. (1933). *Propagation problems and impulse problems dynamic economics.* Oslo: Universitetets Økonomiske Institutt.

Fullbrook, E. (2007). The Rand portcullis and post-autistic economics. In E. Fullbrook (Ed.), *Real world economics. A post-autistic economics reader* (pp. 13–25). London: Anthem Press.

Furubotn, E. G., & Richter, R. (2005). *Institutions and economic theory. The contribution of the new institutional economics.* Ann Arbor, MI: University of Michigan Press.

Galbács, P. (2015). *The theory of new classical macroeconomics.* New York: Springer.

Galbács, P. (2017). Realism in economics. The new classical case. *Acta Oeconomica, 67*(2), 257–279.

Galbraith, J. K. (1967). *The new industrial state.* Boston, MA: Houghton Mifflin Company.

Galbraith, J. K. (1973). *Economics and the public purpose.* Boston, MA: Houghton Mifflin Company.

Galilei, G. (1632/1967). *Dialogue concerning the two chief world systems—Ptolemaic & Copernican.* [S. Drake, Trans.]. Berkeley, CA: University of California Press.

Giere, R. N. (1988). *Explaining science. A cognitive approach.* Chicago: The University of Chicago Press.

Gilboa, I., Postlewaite, A., Samuelson, L., & Schmeidler, D. (2014). Economic models as analogies. *The Economic Journal, 124*(578), F513–F533.

Glaser, B. G., & Strauss, A. L. (1967). *The discovery of grounded theory. Strategies for qualitative research.* Chicago: Aldine Publishing Company.

Goldman, A. I. (1979). What is justified belief? In G. S. Pappas (Ed.), *Justification and knowledge. New studies in epistemology* (pp. 1–23). Dordrecht: D. Reidel Publishing Company.

Grüne-Yanoff, T., & Marchionni, C. (2018). Modeling model selection in model pluralism. *Journal of Economic Methodology, 25*(3), 265–275.

Hacking, I. (1982a). Experimentation and scientific realism. *Philosophical Topics, 13*(1), 71–87.

Hacking, I. (1982b). Language, truth and reason. In M. Hollis & S. Lukes (Eds.), *Rationality and relativism* (pp. 48–66). Cambridge, MA: The MIT Press.

Hahn, F. H. (1973). The winter of our discontent. *Economica, 40*(3), 322–330.

Hammond, D. J. (1990). Realism in Friedman's essays in positive economics. In D. E. Moggridge (Ed.), *Vol. 4. Perspectives on the history of economic thought* (pp. 194–208). Aldershot: Edward Elgar.

Hammond, D. J. (1996). *Theory and measurement. Causality issues in Milton Friedman's monetary economics.* Cambridge: Cambridge University Press.

Hands, D. W. (2001). *Reflection without rules. Economic methodology and contemporary science theory.* Cambridge: Cambridge University Press.

Hands, D. W. (2015). Orthodox and heterodox economics in recent economic methodology. *Erasmus Journal for Philosophy and Economics, 8*(1), 61–81.

Häuser, K. (1988). Historical school and 'Methodenstreit'. *Journal of Institutional and Theoretical Economics, 144*(3), 532–542.

Hausman, D. M. (1981). *Capital, profits, and prices. An essay in the philosophy of economics.* New York: Columbia University Press.

Hausman, D. M. (1992). *The inexact and separate science of economics.* Cambridge: Cambridge University Press.

Hausman, D. M. (2001). Tendencies, laws, and the composition of economic causes. In U. Mäki (Ed.), *The economic world view. Studies in the ontology of economics* (pp. 293–307). Cambridge: Cambridge University Press.

Hausman, D. M. (2009). Laws, causation, and economic methodology. In H. Kincaid & D. Ross (Eds.), *The Oxford handbook of philosophy of economics* (pp. 35–54). Oxford: Oxford University Press.

Hausman, D. M. (2012). In E. N. Zalta (Ed.), *Philosophy of economics.* Retrieved August 12, 2018, from Stanford Encyclopedia of Philosophy, https://plato.stanford.edu/archives/fall2018/entries/economics/.

Hempel, C. G. (1965). *Aspects of scientific explanation and other essays in the philosophy of science.* New York: The Free Press.

Hempel, C. G. (1966). Recent problems of induction. In R. G. Colodny (Ed.), *Mind and cosmos. Essays in contemporary science and philosophy* (pp. 112–134). Pittsburgh: University of Pittsburgh Press.

Hempel, C. G., & Oppenheim, P. (1948). Studies in the logic of explanation. *Philosophy of Science, 15*(2), 135–175.

Hodgson, G. M. (1998). The approach of institutional economics. *Journal of Economic Literature, 36*(3), 166–192.

Hodgson, G. M. (2004). *The evolution of institutional economics.* London: Routledge.

Hoover, K. D. (1995). Facts and artifacts. Calibration and the empirical assessment of real-business-cycle models. *Oxford Economic Papers, 47*(1), 24–44.

Hoover, K. D. (2001). Is macroeconomics for real? In U. Mäki (Ed.), *The economic world view. Studies in the ontology of economics* (pp. 225–245). Cambridge: Cambridge University Press.

Hoover, K. D. (2008a). Econometrics as observation. The Lucas critique and the nature of econometric inference. In D. M. Hausman (Ed.), *The philosophy of economics. An anthology* (pp. 297–314). Cambridge: Cambridge University Press.

Hoover, K. D. (2008b). Does macroeconomics need microfoundations? In D. M. Hausman (Ed.), *The philosophy of economics. An anthology* (pp. 315–333). Cambridge: Cambridge University Press.

Hoover, K. D. (2009a). Milton Friedman's stance. The methodology of causal realism. In U. Mäki (Ed.), *The methodology of positive economics. Reflections on the Milton Friedman legacy* (pp. 303–320). Cambridge: Cambridge University Press.

Hoover, K. D. (2009b). Microfoundations and the ontology of macroeconomics. In H. Kincaid & D. Ross (Eds.), *The Oxford handbook of philosophy of economics* (pp. 386–409). Oxford: Oxford University Press.

Hoover, K. D. (2012). Microfoundational programs. In P. G. Duarte & G. T. Lima (Eds.), *Microfoundations reconsidered. The relationship of micro and macroeconomics in historical perspective* (pp. 19–61). Cheltenham: Edward Elgar.

Jackson, W. A. (2009). *Economics, culture and social theory.* Cheltenham: Edward Elgar. https://doi.org/10.4337/9781849802116.

Jones, R. (1991). Realism about what? *Philosophy of Science, 58*(2), 185–202.

Kasper, W., Streit, M. E., & Boettke, P. J. (2012). *Institutional economics. Property, competition, policies*. Cheltenham: Edward Elgar.

Keizer, P. (2007). *The concept of institution in economics and sociology, a methodological exposition*. Tjalling C. Koopmans Research Institute discussion paper no. 07-25. Utrecht: Utrecht School of Economics.

Keynes, J. M. (1936). *The general theory of employment, interest and money*. London: Macmillan.

Kincaid, H. & Ross, D. (Eds.), (2009). *The Oxford handbook of philosophy of economics*. Oxford: Oxford University Press.

Kirman, A. P. (1992). Whom or what does the representative individual represent? *Journal of Economic Perspectives, 6*(2), 117–136.

Knight, F. H. (1935/1999). Statics and dynamics. In F. H. Knight & R. B. Emmett (Eds.), *Vol. 1. Selected essays* (pp. 149–171). Chicago: The University of Chicago Press.

Knoedler, J. T., & Underwood, D. A. (2003). Teaching the principles of economics. A proposal for a multi-paradigmatic approach. *Journal of Economic Issues, 37*(3), 697–725.

Kocherlakota, N. (2010). Modern macroeconomic models as tools for economic policy. *The Region, 23*(1), 5–21.

Kornai, J. (1971). *Anti-equilibrium. On economic systems theory and the tasks of research*. Amsterdam: North-Holland.

Kuhn, T. S. (1962). *The structure of scientific revolutions* (3rd ed.). Chicago: The University of Chicago Press.

Kuhn, T. S. (2000). What are scientific revolutions? In T. S. Kuhn, J. Conant, & J. Haugeland (Eds.), *The road since structure. Philosophical essays, 1970–1993, with an autobiographical interview* (pp. 13–32). Chicago: The University of Chicago Press.

Kuorikoski, J., & Lehtinen, A. (2018). Model selection in macroeconomics. DSGE and ad hocness. *Journal of Economic Methodology, 25*(3), 252–264.

Kydland, F. E., & Prescott, E. C. (1977). Rules rather than discretion. The inconsistency of optimal plans. *Journal of Political Economy, 85*(3), 473–492.

Ladyman, J., & Ross, D. (2007). *Every thing must go. Metaphysics naturalized*. Oxford: Oxford University Press.

Lakatos, I. (1968). Criticism and the methodology of scientific research programmes. *Proceedings of the Aristotelian Society, 69*(1), 149–186.

Latsis, S. J. (Ed.), (1976). *Method and appraisal in economics*. Cambridge: Cambridge University Press.

Laudan, L. (1981). A confutation of convergent realism. *Philosophy of Science, 48*(1), 19–49.

Lawson, T. (2006). The nature of heterodox economics. *Cambridge Journal of Economics, 30*(4), 483–505.

Layard, R. (1982). Special issue on unemployment. *The Review of Economic Studies, 49*(5), 675–677.

Leijonhufvud, A. (1994/2005). Hicks, Keynes and Marshall. In H. Hagemann & O. F. Hamouda (Eds.), *The legacy of Sir John Hicks. His contributions to economic analysis* (pp. 143–158). London: Routledge.

Leontief, W. (1971). Theoretical assumptions and nonobserved facts. *The American Economic Review, 61*(1), 1–7.

Leplin, J. (Ed.), (1984). *Scientific realism*. Berkeley, CA: University of California Press.

Levinthal, D. (1988). A survey of agency models of organizations. *Journal of Economic Behavior and Organization, 9*(2), 153–185.

Lewens, T. (2005). Realism and the strong program. *The British Journal for the Philosophy of Science, 56*(3), 559–577.

Lewin, R. (1992). *Complexity. Life at the edge of chaos*. New York: Collier-Macmillan.

Louzek, M. (2011). The battle of methods in economics. The classical Methodenstreit— Menger vs. Schmoller. *The American Journal of Economics and Sociology, 70*(2), 439–463.

Lucas, R. E. (1973). Some international evidence on output-inflation tradeoffs. *The American Economic Review, 63*(3), 326–334.

Lucas, R. E. (1976/1981). Econometric policy evaluation. A critique. In R. E. Lucas (Ed.), *Studies in business cycle theory* (pp. 104–130). Oxford: Basil Blackwell.

Lucas, R. E. (1977). Understanding business cycles. In K. Brunner & A. H. Meltzer (Eds.), *Stabilization of the domestic and international economy* (pp. 7–29). Amsterdam: North-Holland.

Lucas, R. E. (1980a). Methods and problems in business cycle theory. *Journal of Money, Credit and Banking, 12*(4), 696–715.

Lucas, R. E. (1980b). The death of Keynesian economics. In R. E. Lucas & M. Gillman (Eds.), *Collected papers on monetary theory* (pp. 500–503). Cambridge, MA: Harvard University Press.

Lucas, R. E. (1981). *Studies in business-cycle theory.* Oxford: Basil Blackwell.

Lucas, R. E. (2005). My Keynesian education. In M. De Vroey & K. D. Hoover (Eds.), *The IS/LM model. Its rise, fall and strange persistence* (pp. 12–24). Durham, NC: Duke University Press.

Lucas, R. E., & Sargent, T. J. (1978). Response to Friedman. In F. E. Morris (Ed.), *After the Phillips curve. Persistence of high inflation and high unemployment* (pp. 81–82). Federal Reserve Bank of Boston: Boston, MA.

Lucas, R. E., & Sargent, T. J. (1979). After Keynesian macroeconomics. *Federal Reserve Bank of Minneapolis Quarterly Review, 3*(2), 1–16.

MacDonald Coxeter, H. S. (1969). *An introduction to geometry.* New York: John Wiley & Sons.

Maddala, G. S., & Lahiri, K. (2009). *Introduction to econometrics* (4th ed.). New York: Wiley.

Mäki, U. (1989). On the problem of realism in economics. *Ricerche Economiche, 43*(1–2), 176–198.

Mäki, U. (1990a). Scientific realism and Austrian explanation. *Review of Political Economy, 2*(3), 310–344.

Mäki, U. (1990b). Mengerian economics in realist perspective. In B. J. Caldwell (Ed.), *Carl Menger and his legacy in economics* (pp. 289–310). Durham, NC: Duke University Press.

Mäki, U. (1992a). Friedman and realism. In W. J. Samuels & J. E. Biddle (Eds.), *Vol. 10. Research in the history of economic thought and methodology* (pp. 171–195). Bingley: JAI Press.

Mäki, U. (1992b). On the method of isolation in economics. In C. Dilworth (Ed.), *Intelligibility and science* (pp. 317–351). Amsterdam: Rodopi.

Mäki, U. (1994a). Methodology might matter, but Weintraub's meta-methodology shouldn't. *Journal of Economic Methodology, 1*(2), 215–231.

Mäki, U. (1994b). Reorienting the assumptions issue. In R. E. Backhouse (Ed.), *New directions in economic methodology* (pp. 237–256). London: Routledge.

Mäki, U. (1994c). Isolation, idealization and truth in economics. In B. Hamminga & N. B. De Marchi (Eds.), *Idealization in economics* (pp. 147–168). Amsterdam: Rodopi.

Mäki, U. (1996). Scientific realism and some peculiarities of economics. In R. S. Cohen, R. Hilpinen, & Q. Renzong (Eds.), *Realism and anti-realism in the philosophy of science* (pp. 427–448). Dordrecht: Kluwer.

Mäki, U. (1998). Aspects of realism about economics. *Theoria, 13*(2), 301–319.

Mäki, U. (2000). Kinds of assumptions and their truth. Shaking an untwisted F-twist. *Kyklos, 53*(3), 317–335.

Mäki, U. (Ed.), (2001). *The economic world view. Studies in the ontology of economics.* Cambridge: Cambridge University Press.

Mäki, U. (Ed.), (2002a). *Fact and fiction in economics. Models, realism, and social construction.* Cambridge: Cambridge University Press.

Mäki, U. (2002b). Some nonreasons for nonrealism about economics. In U. Mäki (Ed.), *Fact and fiction in economics. Models, realism, and social construction* (pp. 90–104). Cambridge: Cambridge University Press.

Mäki, U. (2005a). Reglobalizing realism by going local, or (how) should our formulations of scientific realism be informed about the sciences? *Erkenntnis, 63*(2), 231–251.

Mäki, U. (2005b). Models are experiments, experiments are models. *Journal of Economic Methodology*, *12*(2), 303–315.

Mäki, U. (2009a). Realistic realism about unrealistic models. In H. Kincaid & D. Ross (Eds.), *The Oxford handbook of philosophy of economics* (pp. 68–98). Oxford: Oxford University Press.

Mäki, U. (2009b). Unrealistic assumptions and unnecessary confusions. Rereading and rewriting F53 as a realist statement. In U. Mäki (Ed.), *The methodology of positive economics. Reflections on the Milton Friedman legacy* (pp. 90–116). Cambridge: Cambridge University Press.

Mäki, U. (2011). Models and locus of their truth. *Synthese*, *180*(1), 47–63.

Mäki, U. (Ed.), (2012a). *Philosophy of economics*. Amsterdam: North Holland.

Mäki, U. (2012b). Realism and antirealism about economics. In U. Mäki (Ed.), *Philosophy of economics* (pp. 3–24). Amsterdam: North Holland.

Mäki, U. (2012c). The truth of false idealizations in modeling. In P. Humphreys & C. Imbert (Eds.), *Models, simulations, and representations* (pp. 216–233). New York: Routledge.

Mäki, U. (2013). On a paradox of truth, or how not to obscure the issue of whether explanatory models can be true. *Journal of Economic Methodology*, *20*(3), 268–279.

Mäki, U., Gustafsson, B., & Knudsen, C. (Eds.), (1993/2005). *Rationality, institutions and economic methodology*. London: Routledge.

Manicas, P. T. (2006). *A realist philosophy of social science. Explanation and understanding*. Cambridge: Cambridge University Press.

Mariyani-Squire, E. (2017). Critical reflections on a realist interpretation of Friedman's 'Methodology of positive economics'. *Journal of Economic Methodology*, *24*(1), 69–89.

Marshall, A. (1885). *The present position of economics*. London: Macmillan and Co.

Marshall, A. (1920/2013). *Principles of economics* (8th ed.). New York: Palgrave Macmillan.

Martin, P. Y., & Turner, B. A. (1986). Grounded theory and organizational research. *The Journal of Applied Behavioral Science*, *22*(2), 141–157.

Massimi, M. (2004). Non-defensible middle ground for experimental realism. Why we are justified to believe in colored quarks. *Philosophy of Science*, *71*(1), 36–60.

Matthews, R. (2000). Storks Deliver Babies (p = 0.008). *Teaching Statistics*, *22*(2), 36–38.

McMullin, E. (1984). The goals of natural science. *Proceedings and Addresses of the American Philosophical Association*, *58*(1), 37–64.

Mearman, A. (2007). *Teaching heterodox economic concepts*. Bristol: The Economics Network.

Menard, C. (2001). Methodological issues in new institutional economics. *Journal of Economic Methodology*, *8*(1), 85–92. https://doi.org/10.1080/13501780010023243.

Menard, C., & Shirley, M. M. (2005). *Handbook of new institutional economics*. New York: Springer.

Mirowski, P. (1984). Physics and the 'marginalist revolution'. *Cambridge Journal of Economics*, *8*(4), 361–379.

Mirowski, P. (1986). Institutions as solution concepts in a game theory context. In P. Mirowski (Ed.), *The reconstruction of economic theory*. (pp. 241–263). Dordrecht: Kluwer-Nijhoff Publishing. https://doi.org/10.1007/978-0-585-26879-8_7.

Mirowski, P. (1987). The philosophical bases of institutionalist economics. *Journal of Economic Issues*, *21*(3), 1001–1038. https://doi.org/10.1080/00213624.1987.11504695.

Mitchell, W. C. (1913). *Business cycles*. Berkeley, CA: University of California Press.

Morrison, M. (2000). *Unifying scientific theories. Physical concepts and mathematical structures*. Cambridge: Cambridge University Press.

Musgrave, A. (1992). Discussion. Realism about what? *Philosophy of Science*, *59*(4), 691–697.

Muth, J. F. (1961). Rational expectations and the theory of price movements. *Econometrica*, *29*(3), 315–335.

Nelson, R. R., & Winter, S. G. (1982). *An evolutionary theory of economic change*. London: Belknap Press.

Nelson, R. R., & Winter, S. G. (2002). Evolutionary theorizing in economics. *Journal of Economic Perspectives, 16*(2), 23–46.

Nordhaus, W. D. (1975). The political business cycle. *The Review of Economic Studies, 42*(2), 169–190. https://doi.org/10.2307/2296528.

Parada, J. J. (2001). Original institutional economics. A theory for the 21st century? *Oeconomicus, 5*(3), 46–60.

Phelps, E. S. (2006). *Biography of Edmund S. Phelps*. Retrieved September 17, 2017, from Nobelprize.org, https://www.nobelprize.org/nobel_prizes/economic-sciences/laureates/2006/phelps-bio.html.

Planck, M. (1950). *Scientific autobiography and other papers*. London: Williams & Norgate.

Polanyi, M. (1958/2005). *Personal knowledge. Towards a post-critical philosophy*. London: Routledge.

Popper, K. (1962). *Conjectures and refutations. The growth of scientific knowledge*. New York: Basic Books.

Psillos, S. (1995). Is structural realism the best of both worlds? *Dialectica, 49*(1), 15–46.

Psillos, S. (1999). *Scientific realism. How science tracks truth*. New York: Routledge.

Psillos, S. (2011). Choosing the realist framework. *Synthese, 180*(2), 301–316.

Putnam, H. (1975a). What is "realism"? *Proceedings of the Aristotelian Society, 76*(1), 177–194.

Putnam, H. (1975b). *Mathematics, matter and method*. Cambridge: Cambridge University Press.

Putnam, H. (1975c). *Mind, language and reality*. Cambridge: Cambridge University Press.

Quine, W. O. (1951/2009). Two dogmas of empiricism. In T. McGrew, M. Alspector-Kelly, & F. Allhoff (Eds.), *The philosophy of science. An historical anthology* (pp. 412–423). Oxford: Wiley-Blackwell.

Quine, W. O. (1975). On empirically equivalent systems of the world. *Erkenntnis, 9*(3), 313–328.

Ramanathan, R. (2002). *Introductory econometrics with applications* (5th ed.). San Diego: Harcourt College Publishers.

Reder, M. W. (1982). Chicago economics. Permanence and change. *Journal of Economic Literature, 20*(1), 1–38.

Reiss, J. (2010). The methodology of positive economics. Reflections on the Milton Friedman legacy. *Erasmus Journal for Philosophy and Economics, 3*(2), 103–110.

Resnik, D. B. (1994). Hacking's experimental realism. *Canadian Journal of Philosophy, 24*(3), 395–412.

Ressler, M. (2013). *The logic of relativism*. Morrisville: Increasingly Skeptical Publications.

Richter, R. (2015). Bridging old and new institutional economics. Gustav Schmoller, the leader of the younger German historical school, seen with neoinstitutionalists' eyes. In R. Richter (Ed.), *Essays on new institutional economics* (pp. 135–160). New York: Springer.

Rodrik, D. (2015). *Economics rules. Why economics works, when it fails, and how to tell the difference*. Oxford: Oxford University Press.

Rolnick, A. (2010, June 15). *Interview with Thomas Sargent*. Retrieved July 23, 2018, from Federal Reserve Bank of Minneapolis. https://www.minneapolisfed.org/publications/the-region/interview-with-thomas-sargent.

Rosenberg, A. (1976). *Microeconomic laws. A philosophical analysis*. Pittsburgh: University of Pittsburgh Press.

Rosenberg, A. (1992). *Economics. Mathematical politics or science of diminishing returns?* Chicago: The University of Chicago Press.

Ross, D., & Kincaid, H. (2009). Introduction. The new philosophy of economics. In H. Kincaid & D. Ross (Eds.), *The Oxford handbook of philosophy of economics* (pp. 3–32). Oxford: Oxford University Press.

Rosser, J. B. (1999). On the complexities of complex economic dynamics. *Journal of Economic Perspectives, 13*(4), 169–192.

Rudebusch, G. D. (2005). Assessing the Lucas critique in monetary policy models. *Journal of Money, Credit, and Banking, 37*(2), 245–272.

Rutherford, M. (1994). *Institutions in economics. The old and the new institutionalism.* Cambridge: Cambridge University Press.

Sapir, E. (1929). The status of linguistics as a science. *Language, 5*(4), 207–214.

Schmidt, M. (2010). Causation and structural realism. *Organon F, 17*(4), 508–521.

Schumpeter, J. A. (1911/1934). *The theory of economic development. An inquiry into profits, capital, credit, interest, and the business cycle.* New Brunswick: Transaction Books.

Shech, E. (2015). Scientific misrepresentation and guides to ontology. The need for representational code and contents. *Synthese, 192*(11), 3463–3485.

Silvestri, P. (2017). *Disputed (disciplinary) boundaries. Philosophy, economics and value judgements.* CESMEP working paper 1/2017. Torino: University of Torino, Department of Economics and Statistics.

Smith, V. L. (1991). Rational choice. The contrast between economics and psychology. *Journal of Political Economy, 99*(4), 877–897.

Snowdon, B., & Vane, H. R. (2005). *Modern macroeconomics. Its origins, development and current state.* Cheltenham: Edward Elgar.

Solow, R. M. (1980). On theories of unemployment. *The American Economic Review, 70*(1), 1–11.

Solow, R. M. (1986). What is a nice girl like you doing in a place like this? Macroeconomics after fifty years. *Eastern Economic Journal, 12*(3), 191–198.

Sugden, R. (2002). Credible worlds. The status of theoretical models in economics. In U. Mäki (Ed.), *Fact and fiction in economics. Models, realism, and social construction* (pp. 107–136). Cambridge: Cambridge University Press.

Tesfatsion, L. (2003). Agent-based computational economics. Modeling economies as complex adaptive systems. *Information Sciences, 149*(4), 262–268.

Tobin, J. (1972). Inflation and unemployment. *The American Economic Review, 62*(1–2), 1–18.

Tool, M. R. (2003). Contributions to an institutionalist theory of price determination. In G. M. Hodgson (Ed.), *A modern reader in institutional and evolutionary economics* (pp. 3–25). Cheltenham: Edward Elgar.

Tsuru, S. (1993). *Institutional economics revisited.* Cambridge: Cambridge University Press.

Van Fraassen, B. (1980). *The scientific image.* Oxford: Clarendon Press.

Veblen, T. (1898). Why is economics not an evolutionary science? *The Quarterly Journal of Economics, 12*(4), 373–397.

Veblen, T. (1901). Gustav Schmoller's economics. *The Quarterly Journal of Economics, 16*(1), 69–93.

Veblen, T. (2007). *The theory of the leisure class.* Oxford: Oxford University Press.

Vromen, J. J. (1995). *Economic evolution. An enquiry into the foundations of new institutional economics.* London: Routledge.

Waldrop, M. M. (1992). *Complexity. The emerging science at the edge of order and chaos.* New York: Simon & Schuster.

Walras, L. (1926/1954). *Elements of pure economics or the theory of social wealth.* [W. Jaffé, Trans.]London: George Allen and Unwin.

Weber, M. (1968/1978). In G. Roth & C. Wittich (Eds.), *Economy and society. An outline of interpretive sociology.* Berkeley, CA: University of California Press.

Weinberg, S. (2015). *To explain the world. The discovery of modern science.* New York: Harper Collins.

Weintraub, E. R. (1989). Methodology doesn't matter, but the history of thought might. *The Scandinavian Journal of Economics, 91*(2), 477–493.

Whorf, B. L. (1956). In J. B. Carroll (Ed.), *Language, thought, and reality.* Cambridge, MA: The MIT Press.

Williamson, O. E. (1985). *The economic institutions of capitalism.* New York: The Free Press.

Williamson, O. E. (2000). The new institutional economics. Taking stock, looking ahead. *Journal of Economic Literature, 38*(3), 595–613.

Wong, S. (1973). The "F-twist" and the methodology of Paul Samuelson. *The American Economic Review*, *63*(3), 312–325.

Wong, S. (1978). *The foundations of Paul Samuelson's revealed preference theory*. Boston: Routledge & Kegan Paul.

Woodford, M. (1999). *Revolution and evolution in twentieth-century macroeconomics*. Princeton, NJ: Princeton University Press.

Worrall, J. (1989). Structural realism. The best of both worlds. *Dialectica*, *43*(1–2), 99–124.

Wren-Lewis, S. (2018). Ending the microfoundations hegemony. *Oxford Review of Economic Policy*, *34*(1–2), 55–69.

Yefimov, V. (2004). *On pragmatist institutional economics*. MPRA paper no. 49016, München: MPRA.

Yonay, Y. P. (1998). *The struggle over the soul of economics. Institutionalist and neoclassical economists in America between the wars*. Princeton, NJ: Princeton University Press.

Archival sources

Lucas R.E., Unpublished papers, 1960–2004 and undated. Archival material stored at the David M. Rubenstein Library, Duke University.

2

Standing on the edge: Lucas in the Chicago tradition

There are three men on a train. One of them is an economist and one of them is a logician and one of them is a mathematician. And they have just crossed the border into Scotland (I don't know why they are going to Scotland) and they see a brown cow standing in a field from the window of the train (and the cow is standing parallel to the train).
And the economist says, "Look, the cows in Scotland are brown."
And the logician says, "No. There are cows in Scotland of which one at least is brown."
And the mathematician says, "No. There is at least one cow in Scotland, of which one side appears to be brown."
And it is funny because economists are not real scientists, and because logicians think more clearly, but mathematicians are best.
Mark Haddon: The curious incident of the dog in the night-time.

Not that I believe in being over-fussy about what we say: as long as we speak as clearly as we can, yet do not pretend that what we are saying is clearer than it is, and as long as we do not try to derive apparently exact consequences from dubious or vague premises, there is no harm whatever in occasional vagueness, or in voicing every now and then our feelings and general intuitive impressions about things.
Karl Popper: Conjectures and refutations.

The central problem for this chapter is the identification of Lucas's place in the Chicago tradition in terms of his theory and methodology. By approaching the issue from various aspects we examine how much Lucas can be regarded as a Chicagoan and to what extent certain elements in his system put him outside the Chicago conventions.

The first aspect of the analysis is the subtle transformation process of Chicago economics as a research and education programme. The emergence of modern 'Chicagonomics' was the result of a three-decade evolution the outcomes of which were the establishment of price theory as

77

a firm analytical framework and its extension to a vast array of social actions. Stigler and Becker initiated to study a wide range of social phenomena in a choice-theoretic framework. It is argued that these developments paved the way for Lucas, who also placed his theory of business cycles on a choice-theoretic footing. By so doing, Lucas himself has also contributed to the extension of neoclassical choice theory treated as a unified framework. The possibility of the explanation of some macroeconomic phenomena in choice theory, that is, understanding large-scale fluctuations as a result of individual decisions has considerably strengthened the position of the theory. In this respect Lucas has been a hard-core Chicagoan economist. It is also worthwhile to pay attention to the idea suggested by Stigler and Becker that the price- and choice-theoretic framework provides realistic assumptions for the analysis of social phenomena, which is a strong point in favour of Lucas's realism. Later we shall see that Lucas insisted on choice theory as an analytical tool kit for he conceived individual decisions as the real sources of macro-level phenomena, or at least as significant factors behind macro-dynamics.

There is another aspect in which the evaluation is expected to be more problematic and less obvious. Rejecting Friedman's Marshallian inclination, Lucas established his system as a piece in neo-Walrasian economics. In consequence, the existing literature oftentimes locates him outside the boundaries of Chicago's Marshallian tradition. However, an investigation into the Marshall–Walras divide, i.e. Marshall's strong anti-Walrasian attitude, the NBER-Cowles controversy, and the Sims-Lucas debate, three emergences of the same conflict, calls attention to some essential similarities co-existing with the differences. Underlining these similarities is instrumental in the clarification of the relationship between Friedman and Lucas on the one hand and between Lucas and Chicago economics on the other. As we shall see in what follows, by reacting to Walras's empirical claims through a data-oriented turn in neo-Walrasian economics Lucas rendered his theory highly similar to the ideal Friedman entertained on the basis of his Marshallian empiricism. Lucas's emphasis on empirical testing drifts him close to the Chicago tradition, in spite of his Walrasian attitude. However, an important discrepancy also comes up. The analysis below also highlights Friedman's neglect of causal understanding which, as a scientific strategy, was alien to the Walrasian wing of Chicago economics. Thus the relationship between Friedman and Lucas can be regarded as a tense difference or sharp demarcation only at the price of some rhetorical hyperboles.

In terms of similarities and differences the third aspect of the comparison focused on the theoretical switch from Friedman's orthodox monetarism to Lucas's neo-Walrasian economics does not hold the promise of an easy answer either. The central issue of the switch was to provide a consistent theoretical solution to Hume's surmise on the short-run non-neutrality of money. Even though Lucas was dissatisfied with the explanation Friedman suggested, it is still true that by placing rational agents in a Walrasian choice-theoretic framework Lucas was engaged in a problem Friedman had also extensively studied. In other words, behind the differences in answers and in the scientific strategies leading to these answers the same problem lies. This is the reason why 'a follower', 'a reformer', or 'a revolutionary terminator' of Friedmanian monetarism are equally appropriate labels for characterizing Lucas's achievements.

2.1 Changing Chicago economics

As an aspect of the investigation into the methodological and theoretical switch between Friedman and Lucas it is intriguing to overview the way Chicago economics, the institutional and educational background for Friedman's and Lucas's academic careers, changed from the 1930s to the 1950–60s: from Friedman's years as a student to Lucas's times. Posing this question is justified by the fact that it is Chicago where both Friedman and Lucas even as students were exposed to profound intellectual influences, not to mention the 30 years that passed between Friedman's MA in economics (1933) and Lucas's PhD degree (1964). However, Friedman's connections to Chicago prior to his appointment as a professor of economics (1946) were rather weak. After completing his MA he left the university (years earlier he obtained his BA at Rutgers University), but he returned as an assistant to Henry Schultz as soon as in 1934/35. Later he spent a longer period at Columbia, where he received his PhD in 1946. Accompanying George Stigler, Friedman also showed up at the University of Minnesota in 1945. For Friedman, after all the early influences, Chicago turned into his intellectual home at the beginning of his professorship in 1946 (Friedman, 1976a; Taylor, 2007).

Comparing to Friedman's case, Lucas's presence in Chicago was more intense. He received both his BA in history (1959) and his PhD in economics (1964) at the University of Chicago, and in the meantime, he left the university only for a very short time. After receiving his BA he took a short detour (University of California, Berkeley), but he returned in the same academic year (1959/60). Having completed some graduate and undergraduate courses he started his graduate studies in economics in 1960 (Lucas, 1995). However, there is a story to tell. As we shall see, Chicago economics was both a theoretical framework and an educational concept with Milton Friedman as one of its most dominant formative minds. Lucas as a student encountered this Friedmanian version of Chicago economics: a mature but continuously developing academic endeavour. By telling this story we shall see how the empirical orientation of Chicago economics as a distinctive feature emerged and evolved through time. This empirical focus proved to be a minimum requirement that the subsequent generations of Chicagoans tried to meet along different methodologies.

2.1.1 Continuity through breaks: A strong price-theoretic tradition

The Department of Economics at the University of Chicago has never been a uniform academic community but rather a mixed bag both in theoretical and political terms (Stigler, 1962/1964?, p. 2). Thus, here a mainstream or, in other words, a common intellectual foundation laid by the leaders of the educational and scientific activity is meant by Chicago economics. Membership in the 'school' is not a measure of or a prerequisite for academic success. Nobel laureate Ronald H. Coase, for instance, could hardly be labelled as a member of the price-theoretic tradition. The Department of Economics has been a scientific community with its members not necessarily belonging to the Chicago school (Stigler, 1977, p. 4).

Alan Ebenstein (2003, p. 166) emphasizes the role Friedman's intellectual dominance played in reinforcing Chicago economics. Accordingly, he dates the completion phase of the school's development to the late 1960s and the 1970s. Hamowy (2008) and Miller (1962, p. 64), seeing eye to eye on these dates, add George Stigler to the story, whilst they still discuss the theoretical and methodological foundations of the school in terms of Friedman's theory and methodology. The systematic assessment of Stigler's contribution has just started, so for the time being we have only some initial conclusions. As far as the establishment of the microeconomic foundations for Chicago economics is concerned, Stigler's impact is comparable to Friedman's influence in macroeconomics only (Becker, 1993b, p. 762). Nik-Khah (2011) cites an abundance of laudatory remarks where the impact and importance attributed to Stigler outgrow those of Friedman. In the context of such an evaluation its date and aspects thus deserve special attention. As for monetary macroeconomics, our focus here, Friedman's leading role is unquestioned in the literature. Simultaneously, Stigler had a vital role in triggering a development process, consummated later by Becker, the outcome of which was the rational behavioural extension of price theory in order to explain economic agents' choices (Medema, 2011).

Friedman as a domineering character of post-war Chicago economics

A belief in the functioning, pervasiveness, ubiquity, ineradicableness, and allocative efficiency of a free and individualistic market economy (Stigler, 1988, p. 164) and a bias towards market solutions, whilst neglecting some of the consequences of the resulting power structure (Samuels, 1976a, p. 382); favouring neoclassical economics and extending it to cover a diverse set of individual and social phenomena (Samuels, 1976b, pp. 3–4); a strong scepticism against Keynes's ideas, bringing to the fore the relationship between macroeconomic fluctuations and money-supply dynamics and, at the same time, focusing on the money stock as the instrument to stabilize the economy or, as the other side of the same coin, regarding significant contractions as phenomena triggered by drops in the money supply; and adding a strong empiricist flavour to economics (Hammond, 2011, p. 38), meaning the placing of theory in an empirical context: Chicago economics was organized around dogmas Friedman very effectively advocated. On this showing the question remains open whether Friedman was 'the' founder or 'the' best-known adherent of the school. No doubt, for the public he became the face of Chicago economics (Ebenstein, 2015, pp. 122–123; Becker, 1991, p. 146). Even though all the assessments on Chicago economics can be regarded as attempts to answer the questions over the exact date of establishment, the names of the leader and the members, and the list of tenets, all commentators agree that Chicago economics has been a theory underpinned by a distinguishing methodology and, at the same time, a resulting economic policy stance or even a philosophy.[1]

A list is always easy to draw up, whilst it may be difficult for us to come to an agreement on its content. A component of Miller's catalogue of features is Chicago and Friedman's alleged equating actual and ideal markets. It is highly unlikely that anyone would neglect drawing the distinction, even if this charge against all versions of neoclassical economics is voiced time and again. The problem stems from the positivist methodology, where Friedman (1953/2009) regards neoclassical models as ideal types, which, in spite of Weber's objections, are easy to interpret as objects of desire or as ideals to strive for. This is exactly the misstep Wilber and Wisman (1975) take. If (1) our model is built upon the assumptions of perfect competition and market clearing, and (2) we conceive competition as beneficial to real societies, then it is easy to take a further step and jump to the conclusion that the model's abstract environment and reality are identical. To complete this amalgamation, however, one needs a further statement. Thus Miller added a third claim to the previous two. Accordingly, (3) real markets are supposed to work along the rules of

---

[1] Here the focus is on those features of Chicago economics that are the most significant as far as the Friedman–Lucas transition is concerned. In both theoretical and methodological terms the school was far more comprehensive. For instance, thanks to T.W. Schultz and D. Gale Johnson there also existed a noticeable agricultural economics wing that is disregarded here. This narrow focus, as well as being arbitrary, neglects a lot of important personal and institutional relationships. Such a detail is the connection between agricultural economics and econometrics in the 1950s (Emmett, 2011, p. 101) or some developments around labour economics in the research group of which (Research Group in Labor Economics and Industrial Relations) in Lucas's graduate years Leonard A. Rapping also showed up as a research fellow—that Rapping with whom Lucas established a close-knit collaboration in the years prior to his island models of the 1970s (The University of Chicago Announcements, Graduate programs in the Divisions for sessions of 1961–1962, pp. 251–252). However, this collaboration started later at Carnegie Tech.

perfect competition. Advocating economic freedom and market mechanisms does not lead to mixing up 'there is' and 'there should be' nevertheless. To be specific, (1) does not imply (2) and (2) does not imply (3) either. The charge is thus empty.

In the background of the amalgamation argument, however, there also stands an implicit methodological consideration, according to which the elements of reality omitted and distorted by the model of (1) are so negligible that their existence (or rather their almost non-existence) does not prevent us from intermingling. In the opposite case, the obvious presence of abstraction and idealization would certainly stop us from putting the sign of equality even when (1) and (3) are true. In other words, on the basis of some sober methodological considerations we would by no means regard model and reality as identical even if perfect competition known from theory ruled the actual markets.

This latter conclusion is important as it leaves open the question of the ontological status of perfect competition (it is only an assumption and limiting concept or a dominant and perceivable component of reality). Thus the charge of intermingling is rejected not on the ground of what Chicago economics and Friedman thought of the degree of freedom of real markets. Due to the presence of abstraction and idealization in theorizing these two settings cannot be regarded as identical in any sensible way. Moreover, the question of the ontological status cannot be answered without doubts. What does it mean that for Chicago economics 'the power of business and personal wealth in the market is greatly exaggerated by critics' (Samuels, 1976b, p. 9)? Is it that monopolies do exist, however, they are unimportant (Stigler, 1988, p. 164)? Or that their overall impact on consumers is rather beneficial (Van Horn & Mirowski, 2010, p. 198 and pp. 204–205)? A similarly contentious issue would be the neutrality of money, which holds in reality, but only in the long run. Instead, the argument underlining the nature of abstraction and idealization is placed on a methodological footing. This problem recurs in Chapter 4, where in addition to some brief remarks on the neoclassical founding fathers Lucas's models are introduced as cases of an accurate separation of reality and theory. This short detour, however, is insignificant in terms of the main thread of the present discussion.

As it was Friedman who dominated the school in the 1950s (besides him and George Stigler, Aaron Director's and Allen Wallis's contributions stand out), everybody in his academic environment was eager to be absorbed in his ideas. Thanks to his intellectual power, at Chicago he usually encountered agreement (Reder, 1982, p. 32). Martin Bronfenbrenner (1962), by defining post-war Chicago economics with reference to Friedman's economic policy suggestions (associating economic freedom with allocative efficiency, whilst neglecting the distributional effects of economic policies) and methodological recommendations (disregarding descriptive realism), also emphasizes Friedman's impact. Samuelson (1991, p. 538) refers to the post-war developments as the 'Friedman Chicago school', contrasting it with the 'Knightian Chicago school' that was of fundamentally different nature in terms of its ideas on economic and social policy or political philosophy. All in all, Friedman's dominance is a recurrent element in the narratives.

Miller (1962) placed a huge emphasis upon Friedman's position whilst kept away from the trap of characterizing Chicago economics as a Friedmanian one-man show. He applied the formulas 'Friedman and others' and 'other economists in the school' or 'Friedman and other modern Chicagoans' for description. At the same time, he could also avoid rushing into tedious battologies. And he is admittedly right: Friedman being left to his own devices, so to speak, would have never been able to transform general economic thinking. Stigler (1977, pp. 2–3) explained this fact along arguments taken from the sociology of science. Any science at any time consists of dogmas that are more stable than a single scholar could considerably change the doctrinal composition of her discipline. This explanation establishes a harmony between Friedman and the members of the school by emphasizing the integral role of the latter. In many respects, and in contrast with a professor-disciples relationship, this role is equal in rank. A school of scholars of equal academic status has the power to exert long-lasting effects on the body of science.

It is interesting to note that Stigler (1962, p. 71) as an insider disapproved of these proposed definitions of Chicago economics. It is especially the emphasis upon Friedman's dominance that evoked his objection[2] ('[Friedman] has not been ignored at Chicago, but I believe that his influence on policy views has been greater elsewhere than here'). On the one hand, he had reservations about the label 'Chicago economics' obscuring some essential disagreements. As Chicago economists have always been divided along diverse and serious differences of thought even in one

---

[2] Stigler's views on Friedman's role were far from definite. In an unpublished work from the same period he wrote the following: 'The chief source of this increased attention to the school is its dean, Milton Friedman. [...] only blind enmity could lead anyone to question either his extraordinary analytical brilliance or the deep impact he has had upon the thought and work of contemporary economists, including the non-believers' (Stigler, 1962/1964?, p. 1). Almost three decades later he was pleased to admit Friedman's leading role in establishing Chicago economics, particularly in policy terms (Stigler, 1988, pp. 150–157). In another text he refers to the period after 1946 as 'the Friedman era', making some laudatory remarks, such as 'Friedman is perhaps the only economist since Keynes to establish a world reputation as both a scholar and a participant in the public discussion of economic policy' (Stigler, 1977, p. 16). We ought not to have doubts. Such evaluations are always born under the influence of the scholar's self-image. There is a letter in Stigler's correspondence the sender of which disapproved of Stigler's eulogistic sentences on Friedman for Stigler had seemed to play down 'his own work'.

generation, let alone intergenerationally, for him it made no sense to talk about a uniform camp. And on the other hand, as he argued, the views attributed to Chicago economics failed to define Chicago economists. The vast majority of these ideas were shared by a lot of non-Chicagoan professionals. As a consequence, Stigler regarded these suggested definitions only as some precarious attempts to identify Chicago economics with Friedman's framework—which, however, does not preclude that such definitions are true. More than a decade after Miller's provocative and oft-debated paper Friedman was still widely believed to be the defining character of Chicago economics. For instance, Wilber and Wisman (1975) agreed to study the methodological principles of Chicago economics in terms of Friedman's methodology.

Intriguing as it is, Friedman (1974, p. 11) himself explicitly approved of the earlier theory- and methodology-based definitions.[3] Not only did he mention the extension of neoclassical theory or the quantity-theoretic interpretation of monetary policy as some elements of Chicago economics' distinctive approach, but he also underlined the unity of theory and facts or empirical data. The latter, however, is not a distinctive feature of Chicago economics for the Chicago school of sociology also emphasized this integrity. Thus Friedman did not narrow the label 'Chicago school' to economics, but extended it to pragmatic philosophy, sociology, or even political science. In other words, Chicago economics seems to have been a constituent part of a comprehensive Chicago school of social sciences. All the characteristics that well describe Chicago economics (or sociology) can be related to a broader field of Chicagoan social scientific thinking.

Taking into account the huge emphasis upon Friedman's contribution, the mature form of Chicago economics had not emerged before Friedman's time (Emmett, 2008; Ebenstein, 2015, pp. 100–101). As far as the chronological order is concerned, the first 'official' reference to Chicago economics comes from 1947 in Aaron Director's 1947 preface to Henry Simons' 'Economic policy for a free society' published in 1948 (Ebenstein, 2003, p. 166), where Director (1947/1948) labelled Simons as the head of the school notwithstanding. Stigler (1988, pp. 148–150) also argued in favour of this genealogy: he dated the foundation to the post-war years and the wide professional acknowledgement of the school's existence to the mid-1950s.[4] Jacob Viner was in two minds about the birth of the school, whilst he also reported on its well-organized operation from 1946, not sorting himself amongst the members (Jacob Viner's letter to Don Patinkin.

---

[3] It is Mishan (1975) who draws attention to this text in his extended paper on the market views of Chicago economics.

[4] In his thorough analysis, Medema (2014) via the 'Chicago plan' on a 100% reserve requirement for banks traces the 'Chicago economics' label back to the early 1930s.

November 24, 1969. George Stigler papers. Box 14. 'The Chicago school of economics, 1979' folder). Similarly, Emmett (2015) dates the formation period to the late 1940s and early 1950s.

The ultimate foundations of Chicago economics, however, are to be found earlier, and this fact raises the issue of continuity with the inter-war period. As the history of modern Chicago economics started in the interwar years, it is by no means astounding that in his review on the pre-history Friedman (1974, pp. 14–15) denies all forms of conformity and a closed or uniform orthodoxy. For Friedman the Department of Economics was a leading centre of economic heterodoxy, where disputes formed an integral part of education. Rutherford (2010) describes the period prior to the modern school as the years of powerful heterodoxy. This heterodoxy was of course not independent of the general heterodoxy having characterized interwar economic thinking in America, which ceased to exist by the post-war period, and did so not only in Chicago. Reder (1982, p. 3) refuses to relate the adherents of heterodoxy to the members of the post-war Chicago school. On this account the history of Chicago economics was a shift from heterodoxy towards neoclassical orthodoxy. This shift did not lead to the extinction of heterodox views, though these ideas have lost their dominance over orthodox thinking.

Dwelling upon the nature of interrelations, in his reconstruction Emmett (2006a, 2015) emphasizing Frank H. Knight's role suggests a continuity interspersed with dramatic changes and breaks, and so does Reder (1982). Miller (1962, pp. 64–65) also accepts the idea of a special mix of continuity and breaches. However, some commentators disagree on the narratives about continuity and Knight's alleged central role. Bronfenbrenner (1962, pp. 72–73) discusses two separate factions, and with reference to the interwar school he underlines the impact of Jacob Viner and the Knight-protégé Henry Simons. In terms of the evolution of the Department of Economics the idea of continuity can be emphasized only at the price of some serious distortions. To weaken the plausibility of the continuity-based narratives further, for Coats (1963) the appearance of the Knight–Viner–Simons gang also resulted in a break. Van Horn and Mirowski (2009, 2010) arguing against the 'conventional' narrative regard the emergence of the Chicago school as an endeavour in neoliberal political philosophy and emphasize the role played by Henry Simons, Aaron Director and Hayek. As 'the policy and scientific views interact' (Stigler, 1979, p. 6), or as '[t]he relationship between a school's scientific work and its policy position is surely reciprocal' (Stigler, 1977, p. 8), probably both narratives are correct: Chicago economics can easily be identified 'by its characteristic policy position' (Stigler, 1962/1964?, p. 1). It is a fact of life that different facets of the same development may be dominated by different personalities. Reciprocity stands in the fact that policy views require scientific underpinning and any social scientific theory has policy implications. An accentuation of the political philosophy thread can at best uncover some facets the narratives focused on theoretical developments underplay.

A minor albeit illuminative detail: in Section 2 of his paper on Viner, Samuelson (1991) devotes most of the space to Knight, introducing Viner's personality and his role at the Department through Knight's personality and role. Indeed, the post-war development of the school was controlled by names who were members of the 'Knight circle' or 'Knight affinity group' back in the 1930s (Emmett, 2009, p. 146). This is the reason why Henderson (1976) also underlines Knight's contribution. He was the founder and the teacher in one person surrounded by students.[5] The only exception is Theodore William Schultz, who responding to some department initiations launched the workshop system that later proved to be so vital to the school's success (see Section 2.1.2).

As far as the success of the modern school is concerned, the most important achievement of the interwar era was the establishment of the strong price-theoretic tradition (Van Overtveldt, 2007, pp. 76–81). On Emmett's account of the process the school was founded in the 1920–30s and it was of course Knight and Viner who by their teaching activity laid the foundations of modern price theory for the school of the 1950s. Hammond (2010) agrees on this periodization. Price theory took its place in the curriculum as a framework necessary but not sufficient for understanding social actions and for analyzing individual behaviour taken in a broad sense: as a discipline of limited relevance[6] (Emmett, 1998a, 2009, pp. 148–149).

Towards the imperialism of economics

Post-war Chicago school, however, turned into something Knight rejected—and this is the reason why we ought to give credit to the idea of a mix of continuity and breaks and new beginnings. As it is argued in Chapter 4, Knight insisted on neoclassical price theory, though had serious qualms about its scope and applications. If, on the one hand, the emphasis is upon continuity, some apparent disagreements come up as a problem to tackle. But if, on the other hand, it is upon the breaks (Hirsch & Hirsch, 1976; Hodgson, 2001), the idea of continuity inevitably weakens, and it seems as if post-war Chicago economics had emerged out of the blue. Moreover, as Medema (2011, pp. 154–155) highlights it, the second generation dominated by Friedman and Stigler was also heterogeneous in

---

[5] To straight the facts over the foundation of the school and a possible establishment of a paradigm, Henderson thought it necessary to have a powerful theoretical framework as well. As it is argued below, this is exactly the point where Knight's relationship to his disciples is obscured.

[6] The issue of Knight's comparative social science and its Weberian foundations is addressed in Chapter 4.

theoretical terms. Even though Friedman significantly departed from the tenets of the old school, it is still true that his classical Marshallian attitude located him closer to the original conception than the 'imperialist' Stigler and later Becker were.[7] All these considerations render it highly contentious whether post-war Chicago economics was the direct continuation of the interwar era.

Reading the assessments it is difficult to identify the main thread of the tension between the old and the new Chicago schools. If we euphemistically regard the direct empirical applications of neoclassical economics suggested by Friedman (1953/2009) only as problem orientation and a manifestation of intellectual responsibility for the society, or as a ground for social policy discussions, it is not an idea in itself Knight would have rejected (Patinkin, 1973, p. 790; Emmett, 1999, pp. ix–xii; Hammond, 2010, p. 15; Ebenstein, 2015, p. 93). Friedman (1946a, p. 4), however, found Knight's empiricism insufficient.

Friedman's explicit empirical turn had forerunners. Becker (1994, p. 349) and Friedman (Hammond, 1988, p. 12) trace the emphasis upon testing theories on data back to Viner[8]; though it remains true that Friedman's strong empiricism 'was wholly without precedent at Chicago' (Stigler, 1977, p. 17). Friedman's statement in his 'Price theory', according to which '[e]conomics is the science of how a particular society solves its economic problems', would have been to Knight's liking, whilst Knight would certainly have disapproved of the idea embedded in the next sentence where Friedman narrowed down the scope of economics to the problems of managing scarce resources; or the one from a few pages later where Friedman cancelled debates over purposes from the problem set of economics (Friedman, 1976b, pp. 1 and 7). For Friedman, the questions of should, i.e. psychological or ethical concerns regarding the formation and the evaluation of preferences, respectively, were not problems of economic nature.

Due to his idea of man as a social and cultural creature (Knight, 1948/1956, pp. 282–283), Knight did not regard the basic question of managing scarce resources as a social problem, and consequently its systematic analysis as a social science.[9] For him, managing scarce resources was

[7] Surprising as it is, the term 'economic imperialism' comes directly from Becker (1971, p. 2).

[8] Viner (1925) examines how it can be measured in practice through prices whether a market is competitive or not. Some essays (e.g. Price policies; Taxation and changes in price levels) in his 'The long view and the short' (Viner, 1958) also demonstrate how theory ought to be applied to explain concrete market problems. In another text he discusses some methodological issues of induction and deduction with a view to arguing for setting up a direct link between theory and reality (Viner, 1917). Viner's approach to price theory contributed to the formation of the Marshallian inclination of Chicago economics to a considerable extent (Medema, 2011, p. 154).

[9] Friedman (1976b, p. 1) defines a radically different economics when he puts: 'If the means are not scarce, there is no problem at all.'

subject to mere instrumental rationality which is pre-social and inherently individualistic in itself (McKinney, 1975, pp. 782–783). In order that a mechanistic science could study this managing problem, homo oeconomicus was to be created as deprived of all social relations. The economic man, consequently, never faces genuine social problems, Knight argued. Theoretical economics, for Knight, focused upon such facets or layers of the human personality that only rarely dominate the behaviour of men as social animals. Thus the relevance of neoclassical theory is highly limited (this is a recurrent topic in Chapter 4). For Knight, even goals and purposes are of societal nature in large part, and debates over goals and purposes are integral parts of human rationality (Knight, 1925/1935, p. 102; Emmett, 1994b). Individuals are both determined and constrained by their social environment (Samuels, 1976c). As it is the society that shapes the circumstances for human choices, one cannot analyze or understand such choices whilst disregarding society. Critics conceived Chicago economics built upon an extremely individualistic methodology to be unable to draw conclusions applicable to real societies.

As Friedman argued, one faces an economic problem every time she on the basis of her preferences allocates scarce resources between alternative ends in order to maximize her utility.[10] And for this reason there is no need for us to draw a principled distinction between the allocation problems of Robinson Crusoe's single-agent economy and those of the highly complex capitalist economic organization (Friedman, 1976b, pp. 2–3). Even though the way Friedman phrased on these pages anticipated the 'imperialist' turn of economics, Friedman refrained from taking this significant step. It is only Stigler and Becker who finally implemented this extension in a consistent way. For them, almost all the decisions of human life could be traced back to the basic economic allocation problem (Becker, 1971, p. 1; Stigler, 1976, p. 1212, 1979, p. 4) and there was no theoretical distinction between important and unimportant decisions or between choices regarding most distant areas of human life (e.g. discrimination against minorities or decisions concerning marriage and divorce).

Thus at the end of the day human decisions are economic decisions by their very nature: allocating scarce resources between alternative uses in order to maximize welfare in a subjective sense, which may mean even the maximization of pain if the individual is masochistic. This is something different from the way Marshall (1920/2013, p. 1) defined the scope of economics. For him, not everything is economics: economic considerations,

---

[10] Friedman here does not refer explicitly to the preferences of economic agents, his phrasing, however, suggests a preference-based decision problem of the individual: 'an individual is dealing with an economic problem when he decides how to allocate his leisure time between alternative uses' (Friedman, 1976b, p. 2). This is not a market-level allocation problem.

just like religion, are important, but that is all to it. In the 'new' economics, by contrast, anything that can be regarded as a constraint may come up as a scarce resource (e.g. income, time, even our lifetime, imperfect memory, or calculative capacities), and the preference system weighs the alternative uses (Becker, 1993a). There is no principled restriction regarding the things related to preferences: they are simply conceived as 'objects of choice', so we hardly have a decision irreducible to the comparison of costs and benefits.[11] And if the scientific problem only consists in man's maximizing utility on condition of given preferences and limited resources (Becker, 1976, pp. 13–14), then this approach provides a highly realistic description of the core of human behaviour (Stigler, 1946, pp. 13–14, 1979, p. 3).

In methodological terms it is particularly interesting how strongly Stigler/Becker and Friedman disagreed on the ontological status of neoclassical price theory. Whilst for Friedman (1953/2009) assumptions of the theory connect with reality only in an as-if way and good empirical performance is the sole criterion for model selection, Stigler in the cited texts writes about price theory as a system that has 'realistic explanatory power'—and for him, quite surprisingly, it was Friedman who recognized this power. In Stigler's interpretation the model is successful *not* for its ability to mimic agents' behaviour at the phenomenal level, but for the model adequately grabs the core of agents' decision-making procedures. It was a huge and highly conscious step towards tracing social phenomena back to individual decisions. By taking this step, Stigler and Becker implicitly raised the possibility of a micro-founded macroeconomics to be conceived as a social science of certain monetary phenomena. As it is argued in Chapters 3 and 4, it is the programme Lucas's economics perfectly fits into. It is exactly for its reduction to individual decisions (Becker, 1993b, p. 402) that this macroeconomics claims to be *realist* according to the new principles.

As mentioned above, Friedman (1953/2009) accentuated predictive performance as the criterion for model selection. The paper by Stigler and Becker (1977) on the stability of preferences proved to be a further step along the road Friedman paved.[12] If good economics means empirically

---

[11] Marshall (1920/2013, p. 27) discusses the decision problem economists face when transforming a statement of tendencies into a law. The problem regards whether they refer to a relationship so often that the benefits of formulating a law (i.e. the comfort for scientific discourse) outgrow the damage resulting from the implementation of an additional technical name. In this decision the simplicity of scientific discussion and its beauty are the objects of decision. While by introducing a new technical term they deteriorate beauty, they do enhance comfort. Economists thus move along an indifference curve. In other words, they compare the loss from forgoing beauty (as a cost) with the benefits from increased comfort.

[12] It is interesting to call attention to the fact that for Stigler and Becker (1977, p. 76) this assumption of stable preferences is to be preferred to other options in cases where it provides economists with 'more useful results', as they say. This assumption thus follows from some performance-based considerations.

successful economics, then explanation is to be constrained to the scope of scientific economics narrowly conceived as neoclassical choice theory (Emmett, 2006b). If there were a large number of external, non-economic variables listed as factors of human behaviour, then their effects would always be understood as disturbances to the economic laws. As a consequence, empirical performance would inevitably deteriorate. Thus all 'non-economic' factors ought to be excluded from the mechanisms of social reality. The key to good empirical performance is the extension of neoclassical choice theory by sorting a vast array of individual and social phenomena under the jurisdiction of neoclassical economics.[13] Stigler and Becker suggested assuming that people have similar and stable tastes in order to prevent economics from unfruitful debates as such debates on taste are non-scientific and to be cancelled from economics (Becker, 1976, pp. 5 and 14; Emmett, 2009, p. 152). Any changes in behaviour are traced back to changes in incomes and prices, broadly conceived. Consequently, economics catalogizes as 'exogenously given' a vast array of 'fundamental factors' the long-run changes in which a complex social science conceives as significant factors of social actions. For Knight (1924/1999, pp. 36–37) the stability of such factors can be a short-run assumption at best. What is more, the stability assumption precludes the possibility of rational debates on them (Emmett, 1994a).

Friedman might have agreed on assuming a considerable similarity and stability of tastes. It may be a clue that Friedman discussing the relationship of positive and normative economics suggested attributing the differences of opinions on economic policy to some ambiguities of positive economics rather than to some fundamental differences in the basic value judgements (Friedman, 1952). Accordingly, economic policy debates are possible to mitigate as people are unlikely to show signs of serious disagreement on questions of basic values.

On the strict price-theoretical foundations Chicago economics disregarded social or individual objectives and focused instead on finding the most efficient way of achieving given purposes—in the Chicagoan reading it was exactly the task of economics that has social responsibility (Friedman, 1967, pp. 85–86). This attitude relegated the debates over objectives (and tastes; see above) from scientific-positive economics to find their new home in normative economics (Friedman, 1953, p. 2; Gramm, 1975, p. 758). It is possible to have discussions over objectives, but economists can start working only after objectives are well-defined and fixed.

---

[13] Morgan and Rutherford (1998, pp. 13–14) understand the imperialism of neoclassical economics as achievements of economists having applied neoclassical formalist 'tool-kit economics' to diverse unusual problems during the war and as early as the Great Depression. This sense of achievement has boosted their confidence in both the techniques and the ideas underlying the tool-kit.

For the post-war school, price theory was no more in the need of outside disciplinary support in understanding and controlling individual and social actions.[14] The result was a policy-focused applied science.

The methodology and the world view along which the new generation rendered economics problem-oriented thus fundamentally differed from the principles of the preceding generation. Even though economics opened up to a larger area of individual and social life, it did so through a focused and rational approach.[15] Consequently, mankind in the new setting was deprived of its social existence, or at least, more specifically put, from the previously conceptualized form of social existence. Whilst Knight was in support of the idea of direct real-world relevance of social science, he did not expect neoclassical theory alone to live up to this requirement. In Friedman's hands, however, theory and data analysis formed a close-knit unity, and he thus supposed economics to live on its own (Hammond, 2010, p. 9). Social life turned into a series of decisions made along a clear-cut single principle where the adjective 'social' only referred to the effects of decisions on fellow agents. The birth of Chicago economics took place as a radical redefinition of man as a social animal.

Instead of a complex social science, economics grew into an objective,[16] unified, and extended discipline to explain all forms of social and economic phenomena, and the key to its extension lies in its unification.[17] Economics was able to solve in its unique framework a plethora

---

[14] If the market is so efficient in coordinating social processes beyond the family levels, why would it not be possible to extend the scope of price theory to cover the family-level events and changes? As Miller (1962, p. 66) puts it, 'it is not a caricature to imagine some modern-day Chicagoans hard at work on the problem of introducing the price system into the family organization.' At this point, however, it is unclear whether Miller refers to the price system as an effective interpretive framework, or as an impersonal mechanism so that prices should coordinate the achievement of individual goals even at the family level.

[15] This is not the assumption of Muthian–Lucasian rational expectations, but the basic idea that human beings like the prototypical economic man rationally consider allocating available resources between known ends; or in other words, the idea that rational individuals compare the expected returns and costs of their actions (Stigler, 1979, p. 4).

[16] Assessing empirical performance is always fraught with subjective judgements. As Friedman (1953/2009, p. 30) says, '[t]here is never certainty in science, and the weight of evidence for or against a hypothesis can never be assessed completely "objectively."' Fantastic as it is, this inevitable 'human factor' does not exert principled influence on the objectivity of economics (Friedman, 1967, p. 86).

[17] Emmett (1997) well describes that for Knight abstract price theory and reality gradually became two separate worlds with no passage in between. Assuming a lack of a connection through successive approximations renders the direct and exclusive empirical applications of the theory highly dubious (Emmett, 1994a).

of problems taken over from other branches of social sciences. Having these new achievements in the bag, economists took pride in the diversity of new applications of price theory. As Stigler (1979, p. 3) puts it, '[t]he development of price theory and its extension to areas where it had not previously been used became the hallmark of Chicago economics'. According to the new social science, every problem is an economic problem if someone needs to allocate scarce resources of whatever nature between alternative uses of whatever nature (Friedman, 1976b, p. 3). The task was to find and understand a common and unified basis that reduced societies into a single pre-social set of individualistic individuals, or, as it is argued in Section 3.1, that created primitive societies by the multiplication of the single Lucasian representative agent. In order to apply the methods of the natural sciences as consistently as possible, economics reshaped its ideas on the social organization, but for Knight such conglomerates ceased to be societies (Medema, 2011, pp. 153–154).

In Samuels' (1976b, pp. 4–5) words, Chicago economists were striving towards conquering the territory of prior institutional-heterodox analyses. On this showing, the core of the break between the old and the new schools resulted from the new approach of solving the problem of complexity with either omission (economics was kept away from the question of value problems) or the extension of neoclassical tool-kit economics (loosely put, everything else was regarded as diverse manifestations of the one and only decision problem). In spite of the direct empirical applications, however, this technical science connected with reality only in a highly indirect and abstract way. Applying descriptively realistic assumptions was not a requirement (very wisely), and describing or even paying attention to various facets of social development seemed to be equally inappropriate. These problems may be interesting to study, but not for economics (Bronfenbrenner, 1962, p. 75). And the way Emmett (1999, pp. x–xi) depicts Knight's dissatisfaction with neoclassical economics renders it highly reasonable to conceive the continuity between the interwar and post-war traditions as a series of breaks.

This disapproval of the new, technical, and performance-oriented science had a lot in common with the transition of interwar American economics to the post-war period. By the end of the war the abstract, formal-technical, and more general and objective economics gradually surpassed the pluralistic and descriptively more realistic heterodoxy and its real-world focus (Morgan & Rutherford, 1998, pp. 6–7). This new economics was deliberately designed to provide reliable predictions to control economic behaviour (Stapleford, 2011, pp. 4–6). The connection with reality persisted, though it re-emerged in a different way. Even though it resulted in a new economic theory, direct empirical relevance remained a high-ranked aspect. For Friedman, there was

The real distinction was not making price theory the focal point of the graduate curriculum. [...] The fundamental distinction is treating economics as a serious subject versus treating it as a branch of mathematics, and treating it as a scientific subject as opposed to an aesthetic subject [...]. [...] The fundamental difference between Chicago at that time and let's say Harvard, was that at Chicago economics was a serious subject to be used in discussing real problems, and you could get some knowledge and some answers from it. For Harvard, economics was an intellectual discipline on a par with mathematics, which was fascinating to explore, but you mustn't draw any conclusions from it. It wasn't going to enable you to solve any problems, and I think that's always been a fundamental difference between Chicago and other places. MIT more recently has been a better exemplar than Harvard. (Hammond, 1988, p. 17)

Transformation of economics fitted in the comprehensive social reorganization in the course of which social interests gradually turned away from the economics of ethical reforms to a technical, value-free, sound, and sober science (Bateman, 1998; Goodwin, 1998; Hammond, 2011). Analyzing old and new versions of Chicago economics Gramm (1975) draws similar conclusions. Going over the methodologies and the views of society the faculty members of the Chicago Department of Economics entertained he infers that the modern school subscribed to a world view the figures of the interwar period openly rejected. Consequently, breaks emerge in the narrative again to dilute the idea of a simple and unproblematic continuity. For the old or early school, the individual is of social nature: there exist both an interdependence and a mutual constraint between man and society. Individuals are not atomistic members of a simplified society conceived as a mere summary of its members. Even though Gramm does not mention the island models, it is easy to identify the Lucasian islanders with his hyper-individual, ultra-rational, selfish, and amoral individuals dissociated from real societies. Markets still served as the stage for interaction; however, ideas on mankind and its actions and on the relationship of man and society were so radically different that the interwar school would certainly have doubted the new scientific standards.[18] Gramm places the

---

[18] Similar objections have emerged in the debate between institutional economics and neoclassical orthodoxy (see Section 1.4). It is unclear whether it really makes sense to draw too sharp a distinction between classical and neoclassical theories or between the interwar and post-war generations of the Chicago school. Gramm realizes a direct relationship between the early school and Smith, Marshall, or Menger, and so did Friedman (1974), though Gramm belittles the idea of continuity. Chapter 4 provides an analysis on Max Weber's rationality-based methodological individualism. There it is argued that Weber's recommendations bear close resemblance to Lucas's extreme version of methodological individualism both in theoretical (social actions are the sums of individual actions as it is only the individuals who can take actions) and methodological terms (ideal types based upon abstraction and idealization). Of course, this resemblance is not a point in favour of Lucas's direct Weberian reading. It is also argued in Chapter 4 that economics has remained a social science in spite of this minimalist social concept.

blame on Friedman for deleting the discussion of moral concerns from the agenda and for forcing economics to follow a unique methodological path. Instead of the eclectic and 'complexicist' methodology of the early Chicago school, Friedman suggested the idea of treating natural and social sciences on equal footing.

In the following chapters it is argued that Lucas had a similar attitude towards the relation of theory to socio-economic reality. He also subscribed to the idea of explaining macro-economic phenomena in the neoclassical choice-theoretic framework, to which he added rational expectations as a unique flavour.[19] In this context it is interesting to realize how Lucas, in order to preclude extra-economics considerations, designed and applied his theory to look into phenomena and mechanisms that seemed to lie outside the scope of economics. To pay attention to the complexity of social phenomena Lucas was precise to underline the role of social institutions in affecting individual decisions. Accordingly, Lucas and Rapping (1972, pp. 186–190) argued that their 'hypothesis accounts for much, but not all, of the observed labor-market rigidity' and their 'theory postulated lags in the adjustment of price-wage expectations as the only source of "rigidity" or of the persistence of unemployment. In fact, other important sources of rigidity were present in the Great Depression'. Or in a similar vein and from the same period: 'Implausible that all or even most unemployed workers are actively engaged in search—so that theory of search [is] not likely to provide full theory of unemployment. But [it] seems certain that such a full theory will include elements of search.' (Hand-written notes. Lucas papers. Box 20. 'Equilibrium search and unemployment, 1973' folder) Omission also concerns the decision problem, since their 'analysis will be restricted to the household decision problem involving the choice between market work and leisure. This is admittedly an oversimplification of a more complex decision problem involving choices amongst market work, leisure, homework, and schoolwork' (Lucas & Rapping, 1969, p. 726). However, social factors do not affect social processes from the outside or in a deus-ex-machina way for these institutions and agreements reflect the decisions of agents (B. M. Friedman, 1978, p. 78). Who carry the social institutions if not the individuals forming societies?

Lucas thus approved of the basic view of Chicago economics that admitted the existence of complex legal and moral rules in any economy, but that traced back these rules to comparisons of (not necessarily economic or monetary) costs and benefits (Samuels, 1976b, p. 11). In Lucas's own words:

---

[19] In his early models co-authored by Rapping, Lucas assumed an adaptive expectations framework.

> Understanding employment fluctuations must involve [...] understanding how this choice is made or what combination of preference characteristics and changing opportunities gives rise to the patterns we observe. [...] [T]here is no question that social convention and institutional structures affect these patterns, but conventions and institutions do not simply come out of the blue, arbitrarily imposing themselves on individual agents. On the contrary, institutions and customs are designed precisely in order to aid in matching preferences and opportunities satisfactorily. Taking into account theoretically [...] the complicated arrangements we observe in actual labor and product markets would not be a step toward constructing an *alternative* model to the one Rapping and I used [in (Lucas & Rapping, 1969)], but toward an extension or elaboration. (Lucas, 1981, p. 4)

Or in other words:

> Labor market "institutions", like wages and hours, are market-determined and their features must be attributable to the nature of technology and employer and worker preferences. Today's apparent mistakes are not <u>explained</u> by saying that agents committed themselves to making them yesterday.[20] (Typed and hand-written notes. Lucas papers. Box 18. 'Labour supply, undated, 1 of 2 folder')

Thus the choice-theoretic framework for Lucas was more than a productive assumption or a useful interpretive framework. As it is argued in Chapter 4, the road to the understanding of the interplay between information deficiencies and large-scale fluctuations (or in other words, between inflation and unemployment) leads through the understanding of decisions for the simple fact that agents really make decisions to adapt to any changes in the environment. Individual decisions serve as the ultimate fundament for all social phenomena, and modelling this dependency is the key to successful explanations and good empirical performance. Going over Lucas's arguments in Chapter 4 it is argued that his applying the choice-theoretic framework is a strong point in favour in his realism.

By these considerations Lucas at the same time responded to those theoretical challenges that tried to derive certain labour-market phenomena from contract-induced rigidities (see Section 2.3.3). Lucas had serious reservations about these attempts for their alleged failure to explain anything. Normally, testable outcomes in models follow from the set of assumptions and hypotheses via mathematical deduction. However, as Lucas argued, corroboration makes no sense in cases where the outcomes are built in the models at the assumptions level. A similar objection may emerge to SVAR models for the dubious link they have between the micro- and macro-levels (see Section 2.2.4).

---

[20] The original and more sarcastic sentence, crossed and corrected in ink, was the following: 'Today's apparent stupidity is not <u>explained</u> by saying it was determined yesterday.'

2.1.2 Chicago economics as an education programme: From a battle against ignorance to analytical rigour

Chicago economics as an education programme was born in the debates over appropriate education taken place in the first three decades of the 20th century. These debates also concerned the nature of scientific economics. Prior to World War I, the university education programme for both the undergraduate and graduate levels the progressivists advocated was aimed at eradicating ignorance, and the levels differed only in the length of time to be devoted to acquiring general erudition. In those years highbrow scientific activity did not mean specialization as science was striving towards understanding and resolving social problems in a comprehensive way.

The reorganization of scientific education at the University of Chicago started in the interwar period, one of the outcomes of which was the formal separation of general education and graduate training, the latter with an explicit focus on specialized research methods[21] (Frodin, 1992, p. 63). These changes also affected the responsibilities of the Department of Economics as the College took over the whole undergraduate education programme (The University of Chicago Announcements, The College and the Divisions, Sessions of 1942–1943, pp. 4–8). On account of a tension between the College and the Divisions, in 1953 the Department resumed some courses at the undergraduate level[22] (Orlinsky, 1992, p. 65). These

---

[21] Some faculty members at the Divisions were unhappy with the changes. The Committee on Social Thought, an academic unit still active since its establishment in 1941, offered a pluralistic graduate programme in interdisciplinary specialization, which as an alternative was appealing to graduate students and faculty members frowning at increasing disciplinary specialization. The foundation of the Committee was heavily related to the prior debates over general education (Emmett, 2010a, 2013). The founders were especially concerned about, first, depriving social sciences of their moral and normative aspects and, second, the sharp separation of the disciplines: the changes the Department of Economics also implemented during the specialization process.

[22] In academic year 1952–53 the College as usual awarded 'The Bachelor of Arts degree with general scholastic honours' for the completion of the general education programme. Studies in the Divisions were optional. Students applied for admission to one of the Divisions or Schools in order to follow their interests or to prepare for subsequent higher studies (The University of Chicago Announcements, The College, Sessions of 1952–1953, pp. 4–10). In academic year 1953–54 it is highlighted that the College 'joins with the Divisions in offering programs leading to the Bachelor of Arts and the Bachelor of Science degrees which combine general studies in the College with specialized study in a Division' in addition to the usual Bachelor of Arts degree in general education (The University of Chicago Announcements, A General Statement, Sessions of 1953–1954, p. 4). In the new system a College student had the option of taking specialized courses in one of the Divisions, generally in her last year at the College (The University of Chicago Announcements, Undergraduate Programs 1954–1955, pp. 28–29).

were the so-called intermediate courses inviting those completing their work for the Bachelor's degree and for others preparing for advanced training in economics. There existed a programme combining general studies with specialized work in one of four fields (humanities, biological sciences, physical sciences, and social sciences including economics) and leading to the degree of Bachelor of Arts in the case of the Humanities or the Social Sciences, or Bachelor of Science in the case of Biological Sciences or the Physical Sciences. In this framework, the Department of Economics, over and above its responsibilities in graduate training, offered programmes for upper-division students at the undergraduate level for the Bachelor of Arts degree with specialization in Economics. In this division of labour, education at the College provided the Department of Economics with students having profound knowledge of the basic texts in social sciences, which served as an excellent basis for training economic researchers (Emmett, 1998b, p. 140; The University of Chicago Announcements, Undergraduate Programs 1954–1955, p. 28). As a further aspect to highlight, in this setting the Department had the opportunity of focusing on the joint responsibility of graduate training and research.

Bringing the Cores to the fore

As early as between 1926 and 1930 built the Department of Economics its education programme upon three core sequences: price theory; money and banking; and the history of economic thought (Emmett, 2015). The structure of the Cores changed under T.W. Schultz's chair (1946–1961) to take the current form: price theory, monetary theory, and econometrics[23] (Emmett, 2010a). The more regulated post-war degree programme rested on a strictly defined structure of coursework with a sharpened focus. Students were required to acquire a creative and firm command in price theory and advanced statistic-econometric methods: these were the essential theoretical and empirical competencies. This was the way price theory as an empirical-applied, objective (at least less subjective) policy science and as a distinctive feature of the Chicago approach has emerged in education. Strong theoretical monism (the sets of both the problems and the acceptable answers were constrained) and analytical rigour (there were standard ways of addressing scientific problems) characterized the graduate education programme at the Department.[24] In the case of monetary

---

[23] The names might also have changed. In the current framework, the three Cores are: price theory; the theory of income, employment and the price level; quantitative methods.

[24] This description clearly reflects Kuhn's (1962) paradigm concept and his description of the way a normal science works. The characteristics of neoclassical economics that the heterodox (excluding new institutional economics) critique objects to are the necessary means for a discipline to have a paradigm. Keeping in mind that the maintenance of a paradigm is partly dependent upon the reproduction of followers it is no wonder that Chicago economics also worked as a successful education programme.

economics the aim was to study the monetary factors of business cycles (as the Announcements of 1952–53 and 1953–54 described Friedman's Workshop in money and banking). Theoretical results tell more than this general statement. Assuming long-run neutrality the basic problem was to explain through the quantity equation Hume's surmise on the short-run non-neutrality of money. All of Friedman's significant theoretical work on the role and effects of money took shape in the workshops[25] (Lothian, 2009). The book 'Studies in the quantity theory of money' edited by Friedman (1956a) summarized the theoretical and methodological foundations of Friedman's subsequent work and provided an overview on the accomplishments of some young researchers (Lothian, 2016), who as members of Friedman's workshop completed their PhD degrees in 1954 (Cagan, Lerner, and Selden) and 1955 (Klein). Cagan (1956), John J. Klein (1956), Lerner (1956), and Selden (1956) applying the framework Friedman suggested studied the connection between the money supply, the price level, and real macroeconomic performance on episodes taken from international economic history.

In the time of Lucas's graduate studies (1960–64) the programme for PhD in economics consisted of five parts. First, students were required to take advanced courses in the core of economics: price theory and monetary theory and banking (a. 1); further courses in statistics, economic history, and the history of economic thought[26] (a. 3); and elective courses in economics (a. 4). Students also had to choose two fields of specialization (a. 2). Second, students had to pass written examinations both in the core work (b. 1) and in the two fields of specialization (b. 2). Third, during the first year, students were also bound to demonstrate their good command of mathematics and of a foreign language (c). Fourth, students had to elaborate a dissertation plan and to have a discussion about it in the Department's thesis seminar (d. 1). And fifth, after a departmental

---

[25] As a reminder, Chicago economics has been much more than monetary macroeconomics and also covered international trade, labour economics, agricultural economics or industrial organization.

[26] Henderson (1976) provides a detailed explanation why the history of economic thought played a crucial role in the formation of the Chicago school of economics. Even though Viner's and Knight's motivations and approaches fundamentally differed, which renders their disagreement almost legendary (Patinkin, 1981, p. 7; Medema, 2014, p. 4), and even though Viner did not run courses in the history of economic thought, both of them contributed to the emergence of the tradition that applied the history of economic thought as an instrument for the advancement of economic theorizing. Emmett (1998b, p. 135) also mentions the critical attitude towards the economics profession (this is the so-called disciplinary self-critique) as a distinctive feature of Chicago economics. In other words, the history of economic thought served as a ground for students to learn how to avoid past mistakes. In the Chicago economics education programme thus economic theory and the history of economic thought were combined in a unique way.

approval of the completed thesis (d. 2), as a final step students had to show a satisfactory performance in a final oral examination in the field of the thesis (e). Graduate education consisted of two distinct phases. First, students acquired theoretical knowledge and in the core exams they attested to their good command in using the analytical tools. And second, students learned how to apply the acquired tools to a specific field of research.

The curriculum officially published in the Announcements of the University of Chicago summarizes the structure of subjects in a sample programme[27] in the following way (Table 2.1):

The 'core' courses (a. 1) were common to the programmes of the great majority of students. Likewise, advanced courses in statistics, economic history, and the history of economic thought (a. 3) were also common to most PhD programmes, but the students had freedom to deviate from courses listed in the sample programme. Courses in the fields of specialization (a. 2) and elective courses (a. 4) depended upon individual choices, of course. For each student a part of the second and the third year of studies was to comprise research on the doctoral thesis topic as a member of research workshops. The length of the programme was dependent upon the expertise of the student. For instance, a student with little or no undergraduate training in any of the subjects needed to spend her first year repairing these deficiencies. Subjects formed a system in which students after acquiring theoretical knowledge of the tool kit gradually gained introduction to empirical applications in a real research milieu only to prepare for conducting individual research. The curriculum was specified for training researchers.

The Department organized the subjects it offered into 12–13 sequences. In academic year 1960–61 in addition to the 'Basic courses' these were Price theory (not the same as the basic course 'Price theory'; see below); Monetary theory and banking; Economic history; Econometrics and statistics; History of economic thought; Agricultural economics; Government finance; International economic relations; Economics of consumption; Labor economics and industrial relations; Industrial organization; Economic

---

[27] With the grid of subjects remaining the same, for 1960 the Announcements published a different, whilst equivalent structure. The ingredients of a successful thesis defence were listed as: (1) satisfactory performance in a written core examination covering the theory of prices, resource allocation, money, income, and employment; (2) satisfactory performance in two other written preliminary examinations, one of which, with the approval of the Department, might have been in a field outside economics; (3) a well-rounded command of the subject matter of the major fields of economics; (4) effective reading knowledge of a foreign language approved by the Department; (5) completion of an approved programme of study in mathematics or effective reading knowledge of a second foreign language; and (6) acceptance of the candidate's thesis prospectus. In addition, students had to have their completed theses approved at the Department and to successfully take a final oral examination.

TABLE 2.1   Sample graduate programme at the Department of Economics, the University of Chicago. Announcements, Graduate programs in the Divisions for sessions of 1962–1963, pp. 254–256.

First year

Autumn quarter	Winter quarter
(a. 1) Econ 301: Price Theory (a. 1) Econ 331: Money (a. 2) *Econ 350: Economic Organization for Growth (with particular reference to agriculture)*	(a. 1) Econ 302: Price Theory (a. 1) Econ 332: The Theory of Income, Employment, and the Price Level (a. 2) *Econ 351: Economic Organization for Stability (with particular reference to agriculture)*
Spring quarter	*Summer quarter*
(a. 2) *Econ 352: Income, Welfare and Policy (with particular reference to agriculture)* (a. 3) Econ 325: History of Economic Thought (a. 3) Econ 334: The Development of Monetary and Financial Institutions	(b. 1) Written core examination (b. 2) *Written examination in agricultural economics*

Second year[28]

Autumn quarter	Winter quarter
(a. 2) *Econ 340: The Labor Movement* (a. 3) Econ 311: Principles of Statistical Analysis (a. 4) *Econ 370: Monetary Aspects of International Trade*	(a. 2) *Econ 341: The Labor Market* (a. 4) *Econ 361: Public Finance in the American Economy* (d. 1) Econ 450: Seminar: Agricultural Economics (beginning preparation of thesis prospectus)
Spring quarter	*Summer quarter*
(a. 2) *Econ 342: Labor Economics* (d. 1) Econ 450: Seminar: Agricultural Economics (Working on thesis prospectus)	(b. 2) *Written examination in labor economics* (d. 1) Completion of thesis prospectus and preparation to Thesis Seminar

Third year

(d. 2) Completion of PhD thesis

(e) Final oral examination

In this sample plan the student specialized in 'Agricultural economics' and 'Labor economics and industrial relations'. Elective courses and courses of specialization are in italics.
Published with the permission of the Special Collections Research Center, the University of Chicago.

[28] By the end of the second year the student would have completed requirements for the master's degree and all requirements for the PhD degree except for the thesis and final examination (The University of Chicago Announcements, Graduate programs in the Divisions for sessions of 1960–1961, p. 234).

development, complemented after 1954 by workshops and research groups as compulsory-elective courses (Emmett, 2011, pp. 104–105). The fateful course 'Econ 301' (Price theory) combined with some courses (302: Price theory; 331: Money; 332: The theory of income, employment, and the price level) laid the foundations for advanced studies. These courses are listed in the Announcements as 'Basic courses' amongst the 'Advanced courses' in a slightly confusing terminology. In his Nobel bio Lucas (1995) was ready to admit the significance and the fame of the sequence.[29] A sophisticated system of prerequisites interlinked the subjects. The vast majority of these prerequisites were detailed in the Announcements, whilst in some cases, especially as for research courses, their specification was left to the consents of instructors.

Friedman's Price theory sequence

Laudatory remarks on Friedman's Price theory sequence are recurrent elements in both the recollections and the descriptions of Chicago economics. On account of the high importance attributed to the subjects, their subject matters and requirements reveal a lot about how the Chicago economics education programme worked as an intellectual environment. As far as Econ 301 and 302 are concerned the primary focus was upon the pricing of final products, with Econ 302 paying some attention to the problems of pricing of the factors of production. The theory of distribution was accordingly treated as a special case of the theory of pricing; and value and distribution theories were unified under price theory (Friedman, 1951/1960, p. 2). According

---

[29] Friedman was not the sole instructor of the sequence (Becker, 1991, p. 141). Whilst Friedman ran Econ 301 in the Autumn and Econ 302 in the Winter quarter, Econ 301 was assigned to Zvi Griliches in the Winter and Econ 302 to David Gale Johnson in the Spring quarter in academic year 1960–61. According to the records thus there was a group Friedman taught along the Autumn and Winter quarters. This is the group relevant to Lucas, since, as he puts it in his Nobel bio, 'In the fall of 1960, I began Milton Friedman's price theory sequence.' It is noteworthy that the Department's Announcements fail to provide full information on teaching assigments. For instance, in his Nobel bio, discussing his graduate years in Chicago, Lucas mentions a mathematical economics course taught by Donald Bear, an assistant professor from Stanford. However, for neither 1960 nor 1961 was Bear's name listed in the Announcements. Salvation comes with the archives. As a departmental record testifies, 'Donald Bear of Stanford [was] offered an assistant professorship in the area of mathematical economics and econometrics' (Minutes. January 18, 1961. University of Chicago. Department of Economics Records 1912–1961. Box 41. Folder 2). What is more, in another record ('Tentative plans for 1961–62 in the Math-Econ-Metrics Area') we can find the detail that in academic year 1961–62 Econ 306 'Linear economics' together with Econ 307 'Economic Dynamics or Special Topics' were assigned to Bear (Undated memorandum. University of Chicago. Department of Economics Records 1912–1961. Box 41. Folder 11), but Econ 307 is not listed the Announcements for 1961–62 at all. Officially, Econ 306 was assigned to J. Denis Sargan for 1961–62.

to the copies of final examinations and problem statements available from the first half of the 1960s, the problem sets of Econ 301 belong to today's standard microeconomics. The types of exercises were diverse. True or false tests, filling in the missing terms in short statements, brief discussions, mathematical optimization problems, and essays: forms still widely used. The exercises, however, reveal a complex and comprehensive approach. There was huge emphasis upon the functioning of markets (e.g. the relationship of marginal revenue and output, the effects of taxation on prices and output, income flexibility, various problems of individual demand, cost functions of the firms and their relations, the characteristics of monopolies), but the preference-based analyses of consumer behaviour also arose. Problem orientation is a prominent feature. Students recurrently had to provide theoretical explanations to 'everyday' economic problems sketched in excerpts from newspapers or high literature, such as translating quotations into economics (Economics 301, Final examination. December 1960. Milton Friedman papers. Box 77. Folder 2), or analyzing particular business practices discussed in the excerpts, or suggesting tests of the outlined explanations (Final exam. Winter, 1964). In the exams, and presumably during the courses as well, Friedman did not prefer sophisticated mathematical reformulations. Rather, the emphasis seems to have been upon acquiring profound theoretical knowledge, with or without mathematics.[30]

The problems for Econ 302 are beyond the scope of standard microeconomics. However, problem orientation remained the same: graduate students had to discuss the market and social effects of some real or real-like economic events. It is noteworthy that the single-product island models with agents having identical production functions turned up in the problems, so did the model of the firm that adjusts to changes in consumer demand through its inventories to be kept at a desired level (Economics 302, Final examination. March 15, 1961. Milton Friedman papers. Box 77. Folder 3). Later Lucas (1972, 1975) also applied these frameworks in his island models. As an extended application of price theory, in Econ 302 a distinguished problem was the analysis of business cycles in terms of wage changes and unemployment, assuming that the hypothesis of a stable Phillips curve is invalid (Economics 302, Problem for reading period. Due March 15, 1961. Milton Friedman papers. Box 77. Folder 3). Plainly put, the curriculum was aimed at instilling the dogmas of Chicago economics in graduate students. As it has just been mentioned, when studying the Phillips curve, the approach suggested by Phillips (1958) was swept away at the assumptions level. In the context of monopolistic competition Friedman discussed Stigler's approach in like manner. The reading lists were of demoralizing length, to say the least. In addition to the thick volumes of basic works

---

[30] Becker (1991, p. 143) was explicitly disappointed with the insufficient emphasis upon general equilibrium analysis and mathematical economics.

in economics the three-and-a-half-page lists were cluttered up with compulsory assignments. Friedman was unbiased to make his selection. In spite of his well-known Marshallian attitude (see Section 2.2), he could avoid being dogmatic, though the students extensively read Marshall's 'Principles of economics'. Friedman's approach was quite Marshallian (Hammond, 2010, p. 12) and so was the whole Chicagoan Price theory framework (Patinkin, 1981, p. 7; Hammond, 1988, p. 12; Emmett, 2007, p. 182). Over and above some lengthy passages from Marshall, the two Keyneses (Neville's 'The scope and method of political economy' and Maynard's 'The general theory of employment, interest and money'), Hayek, his own methodological paper (Friedman, 1953/2009), his works on the Marshallian demand function (Friedman, 1949) and the consumption function (Friedman, 1957), works from Knight, Viner, Harberger, and Stigler, together with Walras's 'Elements of pure economics' were also on the list. Readings on imperfect competition[31] are also noteworthy (Economics 301 and 302, Reading assignments by M. Friedman. October, 1960. Milton Friedman papers. Box 77. Folder 4).

The courses used Friedman's mimeographed, less than 130-page-long, letter format, double-spaced notes as textbook, jointly distributed under the title 'Notes on lectures in price theory' (Friedman, 1951/1960). Here Friedman re-emphasized some elements of his approach: the problem of scarce resources, a suggestion pointing towards imperialism, a focus upon the economic problems of real societies or the basic identity of Robinson and the capitalistic economic organization facing the same allocation problems.

The next subjects in the sequence were Econ 331 'Money' and Econ 332 'The theory of income, employment, and the price level'. In Lucas's early graduate years these subjects were not assigned to Friedman. His name as instructor appears neither on the exam papers and reading lists stored at the Hoover Institution Archives nor in the Department Announcements (Econ 331 and 332 were assigned to Martin Jean Bailey, David Gale Johnson, Carl Finley Christ, and David Meiselman). In academic year 1963–64 (this was Lucas's last year as a graduate student) Friedman taught both courses, but in 1962–63 even Don Patinkin showed up as an instructor of Econ 331. In the second half of the 1970s and in the early 1980s Lucas was also involved[32] in teaching both Econ 331 and 332 (Problems for Econ 331 and 332. Lucas papers. Box 35. 'Macro problems, 1977–1979 and undated' folder).

---

[31] Paying attention to imperfect competition was not Friedman's invention. Patinkin (1973, p. 788) also mentions it with reference to Knight's and Viner's Econ 301 courses.

[32] He was not the only instructor: names of Robert J. Barro, Larry Sjaastad, and Allan Drazen also appear. By this time the curriculum underwent some changes. Econ 331 was placed under the title 'The theory of income, employment and the price level' and Econ 332 under 'Dynamic models of growth, inflation and cycles' (Lucas papers. Box 38. 'Reading lists, 1975–1983' folder).

In Lucas's graduate years the reading list for Econ 331 was divided into six broad topics: the supply of money; classical quantity theory and the rate of interest; the Keynesian revolution; the wake (or afterlife) of the revolution (with the names of Hicks, Modigliani, or Patinkin referring to the neoclassical synthesis); the demand for money and general equilibrium theory; the monetary standard and international monetary adjustments. The exam papers we have from the late 1950s and the early 1960s reveal that macro-level monetary phenomena and the operations of commercial banks comprised a single problem set. Money supply, budgetary policy, and the relationship between national income and prices were under scrutiny; the monetary system was thus regarded as an integral part of the national economy (Econ 331, Reading list and Preliminary examination. Autumn, 1961 and Summer, 1959, respectively. Milton Friedman papers. Box 77. Folder 8).

Econ 332 kept on conjoining theory and applications. The focus was upon the problems of compiling and interpreting macro-level statistics and on the interconnections of variables with a special emphasis on the relationship between the supply of and the demand for real cash balances and their relations to the interest rate and investment. Multi-equation national income models and Walrasian general equilibrium models served as the framework, but not exclusively: Friedman's permanent income hypothesis was also in use (Economics 332, Final examination. Spring, 1962. Milton Friedman papers. Box 77. Folder 9). All in all, the legendary Price theory sequence was designed to imbue graduate students with neoclassical economics and especially the Chicago dogmas and to prepare them for creative applications.

Workshops for research training

Chicago economics as an education programme, however, would have been incomplete without installing an institution to integrate education and research. As one of the distinctive features of Chicago economics was faculty members' keen interest in collaborative research (Reder, 1982, pp. 1–2) and as the purpose of graduate education was research training, the idea of socializing students into the research environment almost naturally emerged as the most efficient solution. The purpose to achieve by setting up the workshop system was to render social scientific research similar to the practice of natural sciences as closely as possible. Harold Gregg Lewis well described the later system in broad terms in an undated memorandum sent (presumably) to T.W. Schultz. Emmett (2011) dates the memo to the late 1940s or the early 1950s. If the latter is correct, it can be the very early years at best, as the department minute on the discussion of the formal proposal is dated to April 4, 1951 (Minutes. April 4, 1951. University of Chicago. Department of Economics Records 1912–1961. Box 41. Folder 2). According to the idea, senior researchers would have run laboratories with a few research assistants, and doctoral candidates would have acquired the necessary practical skills in the course of research projects in the laboratories. Consequently, the completion of serious laboratory work would have drawn the demarcation between the master's and the PhD degrees (Typed note from H.G. Lewis. University of Chicago. Department of Economics Records 1912–1961. Box 41. Folder 1).

The workshop system, the hallmark of Chicago economics, has put this idea into practice. After some initial attempts made at the end of the 1940s, the workshop framework started its regular operation in 1954. By setting the scene the Cowles Commission also gave inspirations (Patinkin, 1981, pp. 15–16; Christ, 1994, p. 31). The Cowles Commission moved to the University of Chicago in 1939: in a time when workshops served only as some complementary forums to graduate education and research activity at the Department. Soon thereafter active student collaboration in workshops progressively grew into an explicit requirement of graduation, so the conjoining of education and research was complete. According to the formal requisites, students had to acquire the practical applications of theoretical knowledge by working in workshops. By launching the workshop system, an innovation that crucially contributed to building the school's reputation, the post-war school could considerably cut itself adrift from the interwar period. Key figures of the interwar era played only marginal roles in this infrastructure at best (Emmett, 2009). Workshops transformed inspiring scientific debates and joint thinking to be the basis of graduate training. In this framework, training and research formed an integrated unity as the institutional infrastructure of workshops was built upon an effective and powerful fundament constituted by price theory, monetary theory, statistics, and econometrics.

Formally, the Economics Research Center as an academic unit was responsible for co-ordinating research and research training taking place at the Department and for assisting in the organization of research seminars and various working groups. The Center published the book series 'Studies in economics', devoted to the major research output of the Department.[33] Each of the research groups was small, consisting of one or more faculty members, one or more research associates, and a few advanced students (there existed a few workshops where no research fellows are listed). These members worked together on closely related individual and joint research projects. Student members received individual instructions and attended the regular research seminars and staff meetings of the group (The University of Chicago Announcements, Graduate programs in the Divisions for sessions of 1959–1960, p. 218). The first mention of the Center[34] comes from academic year 1955–56, which was the year the Cowles Commission left

---

[33] The series was active from 1956 to 1973 and contains 10 published works. Amongst its volumes we can find Friedman's 'Studies in the quantity theory of money' (1956) or Gary Becker's 'The economics of discrimination' (1957). The last hit is H. Gregg Lewis' 'Unionism and relative wages in the United States. An empirical inquiry' (1973).

[34] Under a very similar name (Economic Research Center) a research centre has been in operation at the Department since 2001.

Chicago. Until 1955 the Cowles Commission is listed in the Announcements as an affiliated Department unit responsible for managing the workshop system. The number of workshops fluctuated. Workshops being in operation in Lucas times[35] (1960–61) are the following (Table 2.2):

TABLE 2.2　Workshops under the Economics Research Center, 1960–61, as listed in the 'Announcements, Graduate programs in the Divisions for sessions of 1961–1962', pp. 251–252.

Research group in mathematical economics and econometrics
Faculty: Carl Finley Christ and Zvi Griliches
Research fellow: Jon Cunnyngham
Projects: (1) Bayesian statistical inference in econometrics. (2) Economics of technical change

Research group in the history of economic growth and development
Faculty: Earl Jefferson Hamilton
Research fellow: Jacob Philip Meerman
Project: Long-term problems in economic development in important periods and areas.

Workshop in money and banking[36]
Faculty: Milton Friedman and David Meiselman
Research fellows: Arthur L. Broida, Edgar L. Feige, and George R. Morrison
Project: The role of monetary and banking factors in economic fluctuations

Research group in labor economics and industrial relations
Faculty: Harold Gregg Lewis, Albert Everett Rees, Simon Rottenberg, Joel Seidman, George P. Schultz, and Arnold R. Weber
Research fellows: Harry J. Gilman and Leonard A. Rapping
Projects: (1) Hours of work and the demand for leisure. (2) Investment in humans. (3) The white-collar labor market. (4) Studies of unions and collective bargaining. (5) The impact of unfair labor practice decisions. (6) Differential unemployment in the labor force. (7) Economics of casual labor. (8) The anti-sweating movements. (9) Occupational licensing

Office of agricultural economics research
Faculty: Zvi Griliches, David Gale Johnson, Arcadius Kahan, Theodore William Schultz
Research fellows: Gladstone Bonnick, David H. Boyne, John M. Davis, Winston A. Dummett, Lyle P. Fettig, Robert S. Firch, John E. Floyd, Herman W. Isenstein, Raj Krishna, Hans W. Popp, Nilakantha Rath, Lucio Graciano Reca, Adam Z. Runowicz, Ezra Sadan, and Alfred D. Stament
Projects: (1) Comparative studies of the contribution of agriculture to economic growth. (2) Soviet agriculture. (3) Economics of technology. (4) Agricultural factor markets. (5) Supply of agricultural products

[35] For academic years 1961–62, 1962–63, and 1963–64, workshops and other research groups were not placed under the Economics Research Center. Instead, research groups and their faculty members are listed in the subject grid, under the label 'Seminars and research'. In 1962–63 and 1963–64 their number varied around 8. Econometrics, Money and banking, Labor economics and industrial relations, Agricultural economics, Government finance and Industrial organization were still active. However, the Workshop in urban studies proved to be ephemeral (1962–63); by 1963–64 the Research group in the history of economic growth and development ceased to exist, whilst Latin-America as a topic made a comeback. The system of workshops was in continuous dynamism, with a few stable and long-living groups.

TABLE 2.2   Workshops under the Economics Research Center, 1960–61, as listed in the 'Announcements, Graduate programmes in the Divisions for sessions of 1961–62', pp. 251–252—cont'd

Research group in government finance
Faculty: Martin Jean Bailey and Arnold Carl Harberger
Research fellows: Yoram Barzel, Gloria Begue, James Holmes, Pedro Maal, Robert Noble, and Larry A. Sjaastad
Projects: (1) Empirical research on those areas of the economy where the impact of government economic policy, including fiscal policy, is greatest. (2) Studies in the valuation of government services to determine optimal expenditures

Research group in economics of consumption
Faculty: Margaret G. Reid
Projects: (1) Trends in and factors determining consumption levels. (2) The distribution of income in the United States and other countries

Research group in economic growth and development
Faculty: Mary Jean Bowman, Zvi Griliches, Bert Frank Hoselitz, Arcadius Kahan, Margaret G. Reid, and Theodore William Schultz
Research fellow: Alan Fechter
Projects: (1) Economics of human wealth with special emphasis on education. (2) Non-economic institutions in economic growth. (3) Reporting of some projects of the Office of Agricultural Economics Research

Research group in the economic development of Latin America (with special emphasis on Chile)
Faculty: Martin Jean Bailey, Arnold Carl Harberger, Reuben A. Kessel, Harold Gregg Lewis, Simon Rottenberg, Theodore William Schultz; in Chile: James Oscar Bray, John S. Chipman, and Tom Edward Davis
Research associate: Wade F. Gregory (in Chile)
Fellows: Luis A. Alcazar, Pablo Baraona, Rodolfo Castro, Mario Corbo, Leoncio Durandeau, Ricardo French-Davies, Luis Arturo Fuenzalida, Dominique Hachette, Rolf Luders, Juan Naveillan, Sergio Munoz, Hans W. Stein, Kurt Ullrich, and Gert P. Wagner
Projects: Problems in the economic development of Latin America, with special emphasis on Chile

Workshop in the economics of South Asia
Faculty: W. David Hopper
Fellows: Muzaffer Ahmad, Rajani Godbole, Mallampally T.R. Sarma, H.K. Manmohan Singh, and Koichi Tanouchi

Workshop in industrial organization
Faculty: Aaron Director, Reuben A. Kessel, John S. McGee, Lester G. Telser, and George Stigler
Research fellows: James M. Ferguson, John C. Hause, Yehuda Kotowitz, and J. Ralph Winter
Project: Survey of basic problems in the field of industrial organization. Some attention will be paid to problems of government regulation of economic activities

Published with the permission of the Special Collections Research Center, the University of Chicago.

[36] Friedman was the first to start a workshop in 1951–53 that was up to the later standards. According to Emmett's (2011, pp. 103–112) overview, the workshop was still in operation at the end of the 1970s and, what is more, even today. Surprising as it is, Lucas did not attend Friedman's workshop. His interests drew him to econometrics and Harberger's group on government finance (McCallum, 2007, pp. 60–61).

The importance of the workshop system is a contentious issue. It is noteworthy that Stigler showing great interest in the history of Chicago economics paid no attention to the workshops. It is also typical that others also understand the success story of the Chicago school as 'an assembly of great minds having great ideas'. As a consequence, a strange case has emerged in which everyone feels that Chicago was 'something different', but no one knows what this difference consisted in. According to Ross Emmett (2008, 2011), however, the workshop system was the key to the academic success of the Chicago school, as price theory made its way right in this framework to be an applied policy discipline, and workshops served as the socializing environment for students into highbrow science. Any other explanations emphasizing geographical position, the outstanding working ethic, or academic excellence fall short of suggesting a feature that was unique to Chicago economics. The only candidate is the system of workshops.

As the emphasis upon the contribution made by the workshop system is a recent development in the history of economics (Emmett, 2007), we know only a little about the everyday life of workshops. Only a few systematic accounts of Friedman's workshop have come out, though Becker (1991) reveals a lot of tiny details. Lothian (2016, p. 1094) adds that students had to merit their membership in the workshop with a passing grade in the tough preliminary exam in money and banking. Thanks to Lucas we also know that workshops typically operated on an invitation basis (McCallum, 2007, p. 61). In the Latin-America workshop it is the students who generally chaired the sessions (Valdés, 1995, p. 143). It is also certain that work in workshops followed some well-defined rules. There existed some generalities or common minimums all workshops shared, whilst besides them workshops had a lot of individual characteristics. Members assembled at least once a week (Friedman's workshop gathered twice a week) to discuss papers, one at a time. Attendees were supposed to read the paper in advance in order to devote as much time to discussion as possible. Discussions were substantive and intense. Presenters never received polite pats on the back, though the tone of voice was never rude or offensive. Invited visitors for presentations frequently showed up, and the remaining time was devoted to discussions on presentations by students and faculty members. There were some differences in the length of presentations: Friedman kept it very brief. Discussion was allowed over any issues a paper raised. However, these facts are only some minutiae. Hopefully, Ross Emmett's 'Chicago oral history project' will keep broadening our understanding of the inner life of the workshops.

2.2 The Marshall–Walras divide

The history of economic thought regards Friedman's strong Marshallian inclination as a fact of life. Friedman was ready to admit his admiration to Marshall (Hammond, 1988, pp. 11–12; Taylor, 2007, pp. 119–120 and p. 132). As Hammond (2010, 2011) argues, it is Friedman's desire to live up to Marshall's methodological recommendations that governed both his whole academic career and his job as an applied statistician. Marshall's approach, an effective methodology for observation-based concept formation routine and theorizing, guaranteed Friedman a connection with reality in terms of both the location of problems and the practical usefulness of answers. All aspects of Friedman's empirical orientation: focusing upon actual social problems, taking theory and data as a close-knit unity, understanding economics as an empirical science: all of them can be traced back to Marshall's methodological principles.

Friedman time and again contrasted practical-empirical economics with neo-Walrasian mathematical economics allegedly devoid of all practical content. When rejecting the application of complex economic models, he directly cites Marshall (1925, p. 427):

> Translate your results into English and then burn the mathematics. I think there's too much emphasis on mathematics as such and not on mathematics as a tool in understanding economic relationships. I don't believe anybody can really understand a 40-equation model. Nobody knows what's going on and I don't believe it's a very reliable way to get results. (Taylor, 2007, p. 132)

This is an if-then association (the more maths, the less truth), which is not necessarily true. The Marshall–Walras divide as a debate was over the nature of proper theorizing in economics and grew into one of the most serious inner conflicts of the Department of Economics. Friedman turned his critique against the neo-Walrasian economics of Arrow and Debreu (Hammond, 1988, p. 12), a highly abstract framework a long way away from directly experienced reality, but his conclusions cannot be generalized. Just like Friedman, Lucas also consulted socio-economic reality and data in order to set up and test his models. The way of looking at things, the theorizing strategy admittedly changed. This change, however, does not imply the termination of connections with reality. What is more, as it is also argued in Chapter 4, Friedman's instrumentalist methodology deprived him of the possibility of sound causal understanding, whilst Lucas through his microfoundations project re-established the connections between theory and reality Friedman previously cut off.

2.2.1 Characterizing Marshall's methodology: Simplicity in mathematics to build connections with reality

The suggestions Marshall (1920/2013) made on good economics imply the tasks of good economists. The vast majority of his methodological recommendations are located in Book I of the 8th edition of his 'Principles of economics', but some important additions are in Appendix C (The scope and method of economics) and D (Uses of abstract reasoning in economics) and in the prefaces to the 1st and 8th editions. Friedman (1949) works on a wider textual basis.

The starting point for Marshall was the lack of a fundamental difference between economics and physics as both are law-seeking disciplines. Economists using the laws can infer the causes of some known events and the effects of some known circumstances. However, laws in physics and economics are only general propositions or statements of tendencies that hold only under specific circumstances as some external factors may disturb the precise operation of laws.[37] In economics, these factors are sorted under the 'economic' and 'non-economic' labels.[38] Accordingly, an economic law describes the behavioural patterns the members of an industrial group are expected to show under specific circumstances (Marshall, 1885, pp. 18–19).

Marshall, however, always relates an economic law to given space and time, laws are thus not timeless generalizations. Economics must study the economic aspects of man's political, private, and social life, so theorizing must rest upon relevant facts.[39] Development tendencies of societies

---

[37] The orbit of Jupiter is easier to calculate than the dynamics of ebbs and flows. Even though both are under the influence of general gravity, contingencies of weather considerably affect ebbs and flows. There are no principled differences between physics and economics, though laws of human action are more difficult to grab than gravity is in the simple case of Jupiter.

[38] Here it is only of marginal importance that Marshall regarded the measure of value function of money as a point in favour of measurability in economics. Thanks to measurability, economics could be more exact than other social sciences. Economics by using money can measure the force of our driving motives, since the money one pays to satisfy her needs is proportional to the intensity of her desire, he argued. The monetary reward of an action is also a good measure. However, measuring in economics is not entirely exact, which contributes to the malleability of economic laws. This is the reason why economics faces more difficulties than physics when describing laws. By these considerations Marshall also circumscribed the scope of economics. For him, economics dealt with measurable desires and measurable behavioural implications.

[39] Marshall warns that direct empirical relevance, if ill-used, is an inadequate basis for managing science. Upon the birth of significant thoughts later successful applications are rarely predictable. The same principle in Friedman's (1953, p. 1) words: 'If we really knew enough in advance to know that a particular piece of research is worth doing, it would be unnecessary to do the research.'

manifest themselves as changes in behavioural patterns. As long as these patterns are intact, society remains the same for the economist. Phenomena of societies uniform in terms of an underlying behavioural pattern are explainable by the law describing this behaviour. However, if similarity does not hold, laws must reflect this diversity. Under such conditions, economists whilst seeking laws shoot a moving target, which makes their job highly problematic (Marshall, 1885, pp. 13–14). Too broad generalizations are not solutions to the problem. In this case, economists would be on the lookout for generalizations that hold in societies considerably diverse in the relevant aspect. As an economic law describes the common core of behavioural patterns, a core they share, the more diverse behavioural patterns economists try to squeeze under a law, the less similar these patterns are. Consequently, the law that grabs the tiny common core can explain only a tiny section of the real behaviour.[40] Striving towards too broad generalizations is thus a mistake Marshall regarded as an obstacle to understanding real societies. Instead of empty generalizations the scope of good economics is shaped in order to take more concrete details into account. Such details are indispensable when it comes to analyzing the discrepancies between laws and phenomena, though this phase of research can be completed only if the relevant economic laws are known. In such comparisons, economists must consider all the factors that have regular effects on the behaviour of members of society: even morals, if morals exert considerable influence on the differences between the normal behaviour of rational business men or city men (here 'normal' means the patterns neoclassical economics regards as normal) and the actual behaviour of the group.[41] It is easy to imagine societies impossible to analyze by the laws based upon rational economic calculation (Marshall, 1885, pp. 15–16).

The difference between good economics and bad economics seems to consist in the quantity of mathematics applied; however, this falls short of a principled distinction between the two scientific strategies. Mathematical statistics and simple charts to depict the co-movements of variables were adequate analytical tools for Marshall. He regarded his own problem-oriented economics as good economics, which happened to be based upon a moderate amount of mathematics. Practicality, however, is not the consequence of little mathematics, even if Marshall suggests this idea. Little mathematics surely has one consequence at least: it leads to increased clarity and mutual understanding. This objection, however, may only be appealing to an academic environment the members of which are rather unfamiliar with hardcore calculus and econometrics.

---

[40] The same idea emerges again in the context of Max Weber's methodology of ideal types (see Section 4.1.1).

[41] This, of course, does not amount to suggesting economists should make moral statements.

Practicability and little mathematics as such are independent characteristics that do not imply each other. For Marshall, problem orientation, when theory becomes 'applied' and data-based, stems from empirics, which, however, has nothing to do with the quantity of mathematics. It is rather a qualitative issue. Strongly formalized economics can only be abundantly applied and empirical when mathematics and empirical methods are advanced enough to make this happen. Thus there may admittedly be a trade-off between the quantity of mathematics and applicability, but only in cases where the quality of mathematics cannot facilitate its extensive use in applications. Plainly put, Marshall did not possess the mathematics upon which he could have placed his economics to keep it as applied and empirical as he desired. Thus his insistence on little mathematics as a prerequisite for an adequate level of empirics follows from the inappropriateness of his complex mathematics.

Even though Marshall criticizes long chains of deductive reasoning, he admits that turning back to data and facts can place even such economics back on track. These suggestions of his mitigate the idea of a categorical demarcation between Marshallian and Walrasian economics. This is a crucial point in understanding that Marshall did not object to Walrasian general equilibrium economics as such, he only preferred focusing on partial problems. One can admittedly represent a national economy with a simultaneous equations system, but it is unnecessary for her to approach the entirety of the problem, as Marshall argues. When looking into concrete problems, the system has parts which are not under direct scrutiny. Walrasian general equilibrium economics, however, is too general to be used in unravelling specific truths. Thus economists ought to apply Walrasian economics only as a background knowledge whilst concentrating on particular problems in the forefront (Friedman, 1949, pp. 490–491).

Jaffé also underlines the similarities of the approaches in a translator's note. Here he mentions as a significant discrepancy that Walras was consistent to tell apart pure theory and applied theory, whilst Marshall neglected this distinction (Walras, 1926/1954, p. 542). For Walras (1926/1954, p. 40), his pure economics of pricing behaviour shown under the hypothetical conditions of perfectly free competition has a meaning similar to Marshall's economics of social laws wrapped up in ceteris paribus clauses (i.e. placed under equally hypothetic circumstances). But Walras had an additional point to make. Simultaneous equations make it possible for the economist to cut down on ceteris paribus clauses and the isolation of causal mechanisms. Multi-equation models can treat causal structures in higher complexity.

In the Preface to the fourth edition of his 'Elements of pure economics', Walras (1926/1954, pp. 47–48) dwells upon the distinction between pure economics and applied economics.[42] Walras conceived pure economics as necessarily written in mathematics, upon which applied economics is based. Other options are dissatisfying: either ungrounded applications *sans* pure theory, or bad pure economics *sans* mathematics (or worse, based upon bad mathematics). Here Walras does not preclude applications, he makes no objections. Quite on the contrary, he discusses pure economics as the basis for applied economics. However, he made this distinction only to highlight some negative examples. Walras's positive examples are astronomy and mechanics: on an appropriate mathematical basis, each discipline as a pure science could grow into an empirical discipline. For Walras, as a consequence, a pure theory is *not* a system torn apart from empirics. Even though he distinguished pure theory and applied science, he suggested *not* separating them (Friedman, 1971). In Walras's own assessment, his economics is an empirical science laid on proper (pure) theoretical foundations. He really thought that through his system he was able to grab the real pricing mechanism of markets (Blaug, 1992, p. 162). In spite of the considerable distance between his model and reality thus he attributed firm empirical content to his theory that he believed to describe the core around which real prices oscillate (Schumpeter, 1954/2006, p. 965; Donzelli, 2007, pp. 101–102, 108–109, and p. 127). Accordingly, Lucas's 'empirical' neo-Walrasian economics can still be regarded as a pure theory (Galbács, 2015) on account of the general Newtonian or Euclidean axiomatic-deductive scheme it employed (Hahn, 1984; Blaug, 1992, pp. 52–53; Montes, 2006a, pp. 247–248; Montes, 2006b, pp. 102–103).

Marshall (1885, p. 25) also applies his distinction of good science vs. bad science to physics. Good physics refuses to make do with general analyses based on no data. Here, however, there is no trace of a statement like 'good physics applies little mathematics'. Consequently, the quantity and quality of mathematics in theories are rather dependent upon the complexity of the problem under scrutiny. The nature and the complexity of the problem Walras (1926/1954, pp. 43–47) examined compelled him to apply tough mathematics. Reductions in the isolation of a real causal mechanism cannot but make the 'simple' mathematics Marshall preferred more complex. Describing the trajectory of Jupiter in astrodynamics and calculating the highest point of a tide on a given day and at a given shore demand very different amounts of mathematics, even if both problems fall under the rules of gravity, thus even if the theoretical framework is the same. By preferring little mathematics Marshall could not avoid constraining economics to simple problems, which is rather dissonant for Marshall oftentimes suggested that economists paying attention to other social sciences ought

---

[42] The first two books (Book one: 'The elements of pure economics'; Book two: 'The elements of applied economics') of the 1st edition (1874) highlight the same distinction.

to treat the causal structures in complexity.[43] However, it is impossible to complete with little mathematics. Given this, the only way leads to an economic science being afraid of using complex calculus that has proved to be a significant factor underlying the rapid development of post-war economics (Lucas, 1980, p. 697). Advances in mathematical economics facilitated the proper and consistent discussion of certain problems:

> I think that the remarkable extension in the scope of the idea of "equilibrium" which Arrow, Debreu and others have brought about means that many problems which seemed, in the 1930's, to be outside the scope of Walrasian theory can now be treated within it. This is clearly true for many of the informational problems which interested Hayek. (Lucas's letter to Gerald P. O'Driscoll, Jr. November 23, 1977. Lucas papers. Box 3. '1977, 1 of 2' folder)

For Marshall, however, widening the scope of theory inevitably involves some loss of clarity, and clarity is always to be preferred to complexity, even at the price of excessive simplicity.

Marshall emphasized data to place the difference between good economics and bad economics on a principled basis. This thought was of fundamental importance to Friedman. The contrast of the two traditions manifests itself in the purposes: problem orientation stands against generality and mathematical elegance. As the distinctions between 'much' and 'little' mathematics or 'appropriate' and 'too long' deductions are hopelessly ambiguous and dependent on tastes,[44] the most effective argument seems to be an emphasis upon the allegedly ineffective data basis to deprive bad economics of its scientific status. Bad economics is not economics at all, but rather pure mathematics, as Marshall argues. This is exactly the same discrediting strategy that has already emerged in Chapter 1. Mathematicians do these intellectual exercises to demonstrate how useful mathematical methods are in economics and other disciplines. However, reality-based economics is *per definitionem* empirical. As a matter of fact, in the history of economic thought there has existed a tendency with only scant empirical connections. Weintraub (1983) analyzing the post-1930 history of neo-Walrasian general equilibrium economics points out

---

[43] Marshall (1885, p. 36) places a huge emphasis upon cutting problems into parts and isolating the causal structure. This is the strategy that also led physics to success. Disregarded factors are hidden behind the caveat 'other things equal'. However, this does not force economists to tackle simple problems which abound in ceteris paribus clauses (Friedman, 1949, p. 470). It only means that simple problems must precede complex problems. The question remains, notwithstanding, how one can complete this task by applying little and simple mathematics.

[44] Recall the Sorites paradox as known as the paradox of the heap. Analogously, where does a distinct and generally accepted line lie between too much mathematics and an adequate level of formalism?

that empirical work made no contributions to theoretical advancements. However, this still does not amount to a complete separation of theory from practice, since theory remained economic theory, and this connection must have its roots somewhere. And it certainly has: theorists in pure economics rely upon a set of pre-given concepts and theories which they select in the expectation that such concepts and theories have proper roots in reality. However, as Friedman argues, this stance is difficult to accept on Marshallian grounds.

On the basis of this argument Marshall was unable to hurl a sufficiently grounded and permanently valid invective against highly formalized economics. Marshall's arguments come to nothing the moment Walrasian economics faces data. Lucas (1972, 1973, 1975) by completing the empirical turn of Walrasian general equilibrium economics (De Vroey, 2016, pp. 193–194) neutralized this objection at one blow.

2.2.2 Friedman's interpretation of Marshall: Neglecting causal complexity

Friedman articulated his Marshallian methodological views in a series of papers. These papers considerably contribute to clarifying the alleged differences between Marshallian economics and Walrasian general equilibrium theory. Friedman's interpretations of Marshall also shed some light on his own methodological stance, of course. His positivist methodology (Friedman, 1953/2009), widely regarded as his only or most important methodological paper, is only one piece in this sequence. Certainly, this is the only work Friedman entirely devoted to methodology, even if he loved to dwell upon methodological issues by hiding his additional methodological considerations in further writings. As far as his Marshallian attitude is concerned, however, these works are more informative than his positivist methodology usually discussed in itself in the context of causal understanding. Even though Hammond (1996) and Hoover (2009) have made attempts to interpret Friedman's positivist methodology in the full context of his Marshallianism, their plausibility is far from obvious. Friedman's ideas on causal understanding are particularly obscure, and this obscurity may undermine even the widely held views on his strong Marshallian inclination. In these terms, Hoover's argumentation is especially vulnerable. For him the strongest point in favour of Friedman's causal realism is Friedman's strong Marshallian attitude. Accordingly, just like Marshall, Friedman is supposed to have been a causal realist. This line of argument, however, is easy to walk from the opposite direction. In this case Friedman does not seem to be a consistent Marshallian for he gave up causal realism taken as the purpose according to which theories ought to be aimed at unravelling the real and mind-independently existing causal mechanisms. Here and in the next section it is argued that

Friedman turned away from the idea of complex causal understanding, which may be an explanation to his vicious antipathy towards Cowles Commission's causally focused econometric practice.

Friedman regarded the purposes of the Marshallian and Walrasian traditions as fundamentally distinct. Mathematical economics succeeded in developing a formal language for theory. In order to confirm hypotheses, however, economics needs testable results, and this is the point where Walrasian economics falls short (Friedman, 1949, p. 491). Theoretical work makes sense only if price theory takes a Marshallian shape. Accordingly, theory ought to result inductively from generalizations based on abundant observations and to produce testable consequences in a second, deductive phase (Marshall, 1885, pp. 12–13; Friedman, 1946a, pp. 4–5). Thus there emerges a cyclical loop between data and theory: concrete facts underlie the theory from the very first step, and it is also the facts that govern the later modifications of or additions to the theory.[45] In this tradition economics is supposed to keep having adequate links to reality. However, in order to have this link both phases are necessary: realistic assumptions do not free the theory from empirical tests. Only empirical tests provide a firm basis for theory choice (Friedman, 1953/2009). The purpose of Marshallian economics is 'the discovery of concrete truths' in practical problems (Marshall, 1885, p. 25). Economists ought to address these problems at a low level of generalization and to define all the concepts of a theory in the context of a concrete problem. What is more, applications make it possible for concepts and theories to reveal themselves (Friedman, 1949, pp. 469–479).

Some empirical connections also exist in Walrasian economics, but Friedman rejects them as insufficient cases. His review on Lange (1944) abounds in the related objections (Friedman, 1946b). Admittedly, Lange's system incorporates some functions (his excess demand functions) the general characteristics of which are not in conflict with the widely held views based on observations.[46] Friedman, however, claims that Lange in this framework of a general theory of economic equilibrium established a comprehensive scheme. Its concrete forms that Lange regards as realistic show up only as special cases, so his theory can be specified to any possible

---

[45] Even though Friedman regarded himself as a stranger to general philosophy of science (Hammond, 1988, pp. 6–8), in his Lange-recension (Friedman, 1946b, pp. 617–618) he provides a very effective summary of the 'underdetermination of theory by data' objection (see Section 1.3.3). Even though one can place various incompatible theories upon an available empirical basis, the empirical (meaning: empirically testable) consequences will hopefully show some differences. The deductive phase is important for it might be possible to choose from the rival theories on an empirical basis.

[46] For instance, any demand for goods implies a supply of money, any supply of goods implies demand for money; or that Lange (1944, pp. 5–6) characterizes the market for labour force through a Marshallian cross.

world. Thus, as Friedman argues, the theory was ready before data could play any role whatsoever. Admittedly, in Lange's work there are no clues of the extensive datasets of later macroeconometric practice, and there are no testable consequences in the game on account of this marginal role of data. Even though Lange tries to rectify this shortcoming by ruling out some prominently unrealistic specifications, this is not a way out. Friedman cannot help thinking that Lange established a flexible abstract formal structure the specification of which to reality failed.

Whilst making definite statements about reality, Lange (1944, p. 83) cites the facts in a very loose way: in terms of a relevant period, there are good reasons for believing in equilibrium mechanisms, price flexibility holds, etc. However, there are neither data nor clear-cut confirmation strategies involved, so there are no proper grounds for checking the validity either. The allegedly plausible or factual statements Lange makes ought to be tested empirically one by one. Interestingly, Lange also devotes the Appendix to lengthy formal deductions, and he does not even give a single hint to data. His empirical statements are confusing for the very reason that their factual basis is unknown. Neither the too general initial link[47] nor the subsequent specification of dubious value can result in a convincing connection with reality. Economics deprived of empirical content produces taxonomic knowledge at best, Friedman agues. Such a theory cannot help us solve specific problems or design economic policies.

All in all, Friedman claims that Lange formed a flexible general scheme rather than a theory. And if a framework is this general, then inconsistencies with reality cannot occur, not even as possibilities. All potential realities cannot but confirm the theory. Consequently, if a system implies a boundless array of possible specifications, each specification is highly superficial and devoid of details. One may suggest that Lange did not try to solve specific problems, but to provide such theoretical knowledge that can later be applied in solving specific problems, but Friedman rejects this option as well.

Two comments come up. First, Friedman voiced his critique in the early 1950s, years before the first English edition of Walras's 'Eléments d'économie politique pure' came out and years before a series of papers suggested the Arrow-Debreu-McKenzie variant of Walrasian economics. The latter, of course, could hardly have convinced Friedman of the problem

---

[47] Friedman disapproving of the use of pre-given knowledge in theorizing explicitly applies double standards. In the last paragraph of his Lange-recension he says: 'A man who has a burning interest in pressing issues of public policy, who has a strong desire to learn how the economic system really works [...] is not likely to stay within the bounds of a method of analysis that denies him the knowledge he seeks. He will escape the shackles of formalism, even if he has to resort to illogical devices and specious reasoning to do so' (Friedman, 1946b, p. 631). Friedman thinks he knows the acceptable results even prior to having the theory. Simply put, he assesses the results on the basis of his pre-given knowledge.

orientation of neo-Walrasian economics.[48] Thus Friedman's knowledge of Walrasian economics was rather superficial. In the recension he wrote on the English edition (Friedman, 1955) his opinion is less repulsive, though in broad terms it remained the same. The paper was an opportunity for him to repeat all his previous objections to Lange. Here Walrasian general equilibrium economics grows from inherently bad economics into a preparatory-initial theorizing phase, a classificatory scheme, which may be highly useful when it comes to checking the logical consistency, but which, at the same time, is only form without substance. Substance is peculiar to Marshallian economics. Friedman was partly right—Walrasian economics is a powerful logical device. Characterizing Walrasian simultaneous equations systems, Tinbergen (1940, p. 81) suggests some logical strengths, such as consistency or the explicitness of differences of theories.

Second, there is a fly in Friedman anti-Walrasian ointment for he regarded the version of general equilibrium economics he knew as descriptively more realistic than Marshallian economics (Friedman, 1946b, 1949), whilst at the same time he denied its connections with reality. Friedman complains that there are no testable implications in spite of the more realistic descriptions. Thus, plainly put, he probably found the connection with reality ill-positioned and misdone, as in Lange's case. This seems to be the same principle Friedman (1953/2009) re-emphasized in his positivist methodology: theories are not to be judged by the realisticness of their assumptions (Friedman, 1953, p. 3). For Friedman, it is the lack of empirical implications that rendered Walras's economics inferior. As he argued, Walras solved the problem of general economic equilibrium in general terms only. Delineating and algebraically solving the equations on the one hand and finding concrete numerical values to the constants in the equations on the other are distinct problems. It is argued in Chapter 4 that two decades later Lucas by confronting his equilibrium cycle models with data filled this lacuna. On the one hand, the way Lucas placed his theory upon a choice-theoretic framework helped him to establish the connections between reality and his assumptions. In these terms, due to the lack of empirical implications, Friedman rejected Lange's superficial solution. Thus in itself this step would have been insufficient to produce a Walrasian theory to live up to Friedman's requirements. Realistic assumptions do not substitute for empirical consequences. So, on the other hand, Lucas's economics came to have the testable-measurable implications Friedman (1955, p. 906) called for. It is also argued in Chapters 3 and 4 that Friedman, however, failed to realize a connection of crucial importance between the truth of assumptions and the truth of empirical implications or the possibility of causal understanding.

[48] At the end of the 1980s, from the term 'neo-Walrasian economics' Friedman associated to these authors (Hammond, 1988, p. 12).

At the bottom line, the Walrasian economics Friedman criticized is a model-building principle, according to which the proper way of representing economies is to put simultaneous equations forward whilst playing down the importance of concrete empirical applications. This principle, however, says nothing about the theoretical content or origin of the equations, and it does not preclude the possibility of empirical applications once and for all. As we shall see in the next section, Lawrence Klein (1950), for instance, filled Keynesian stuffing into the empty Walrasian form. By contrast, Lucas filled the form with equations derived from a firm neoclassical choice-theoretic framework and subjected the resulting models to empirical tests. In spite of the simultaneous equations form thus it is fair to say that thanks to Lucas's strong empirical interest he rendered economics in many respects a system Friedman had always been looking for: a theory placed upon sufficient empirical footing.

2.2.3 Friedman's Marshallian empiricism

Walras's definition of pure economics renders the debate between the approaches partly of terminological nature. As it is argued above, neither the interest in general equilibrium nor the emphasis upon concrete empirical implications drives an enduring wedge in between. The level of generality, the amount of mathematics each approach applies, and the connections with reality (induction vs. deduction) are the aspects upon which Marshall and Walras tried to build a clear-cut demarcation. Along these lines, unfortunately, one cannot go too far. However, the empirical applications of Marshallian and Walrasian theories are still impossible to mix up, so here a real and straightforward distinction may emerge. Some caution is still needed, of course.

Cherrier (2011, pp. 350–351) relates Friedman's methodology to the descriptivist statistical methodology of the National Bureau of Economic Research (NBER) and Walrasian economics to the econometric research the Cowles Commission conducted. The Marshall–Walras divide, a debate Friedman also did his best to stir up, re-emerged as a conflict between these research institutions so that this controversy became one of the dimensions of the theoretical opposition. Again, a principled distinction, the relationship of theory and empirics, is uneasy to define: there arose some arguments in the debate both parties applied.[49] Moreover, Epstein (1987, p. 64) and Hammond (1996, p. 23) draw attention to the fact that

---

[49] Friedman (1940, p. 659), for instance, played out the same card against Tinbergen's theoretically founded model that his critics put forward against his instrumentalist and allegedly atheoretical analyses: statistical correlations cannot be expected to remain intact in the long run. This fact served as a starting point for Lucas (1976/1981) to formulize his well-known Lucas-critique. We shall return to this topic in Chapter 4.

the institutions contended for the same research funds, so Epstein and Hammond ascribe the (over)emphases on the differences to this rivalry and the strong desires to be unlike the other. But still, the purposes of the Cowles Commission to represent economies with simultaneous equations systems in a Walrasian fashion and to enhance causal understanding to provide government interventions with reliable theoretical backgrounds, and the fact that Friedman consistently rejected these purposes make it relatively easy for us to distinguish the opposite approaches. However, as it is argued below, at the fundamental level they had something in common: to establish the unity of quantitative and qualitative analyses, which they wanted to accomplish along different strategies though. It is worthwhile, therefore, to consider this 'institutional' contention in the context of scientific excommunications (see Section 1.4.2 for more on this).

The National Bureau of Economic Research

From 1920, the foundation of NBER, through 1945 Wesley C. Mitchell served as the first research director of the institution. Mitchell's methodology well characterizes the NBER research method for he was one of the defining figures during the formative years (Fabricant, 1984). Mitchell laid down the foundations regarding the research style and scientific standards with which the NBER set out to operate. It is also Mitchell's (and Burns') methodology through which Koopmans (1947) criticized the NBER as a case of 'measurement without theory'. Admittedly, Mitchell approached the phenomena and the theories of business cycles from a unique direction. He provides some brief summaries of the descriptivist analysis he suggests on the one hand in section 'The method of investigation' of Part I and in sections 'Framework' for Part II and III of his 'Business cycles' (Mitchell, 1913) and on the other hand in section 'Plans for future work' of his 'Business cycles—The problem and its setting' (Mitchell, 1927). Further methodological considerations are embedded in section 'Working plans' of Chapter 1 in his 'Measuring business cycles' co-authored by Arthur F. Burns (Burns & Mitchell, 1946). A recurrent element in these overlapping statements is Mitchell's emphasis upon the empirical-factual side of business-cycle research.[50] Through this interest the NBER joined Marshall's programme of direct problem orientation (Hammond, 1996, p. 25).

Mitchell's explanation to his keen interest in empirical facts was a concern of his. On account of the complexity of the problem, in his time various theories of the business cycles were available. These theories were

---

[50] Fabricant (1984, pp. 2–3) describes the NBER research principles in five points three of which (a focus on facts; a preference for knowledge of quantitative character; a refrainment from making economic policy recommendations) are explicitly present in Mitchell's methodology.

partly or entirely inconsistent with one another and doing justice to them on logical grounds was impossible. As these theories were aimed at explaining some empirical facts, it is upon an observational basis that professionals should have chosen from them, whilst theories had no adequate empirical footings to support this choice. It is worthy of note that Mitchell, referring to some kind of scientific efficiency, did not want to apply the theories, and he himself did not intend to set up a closed and well-defined neoclassical-style business cycle theory either. In other words, it is not indirectly, it is not through a theory to be tested that he intended to appeal to observation, to the analysis and systematization of the phenomena and facts of business cycles. Rather, Mitchell placed the blame on economic theorists for approaching reality only indirectly, via some invented and speculative concepts. Through his attitude, Mitchell explicitly undertook the charge of having no theory. He was aware of the rival theories, though he had nothing to do with them. In his endeavour, he planned to collect data directly and objectively, not influenced by any theories. On the basis of the available and well-known theories, he drew up a catalogue of the phenomena to be observed, but that is all to his business with theories. In his critique, by contrast, Koopmans (1947) underlined that atheoretical empirics, like Mitchell's, with no hypotheses is inevitably hopeless, lengthy, and potentially useless.

Of Marshall's dyad, theorizing and empirical work, Mitchell places his emphasis upon the latter, though he rejects the need to choose. Consequently, he does not object to theorizing efforts. Quite on the contrary, he regards theoretical work as indispensable (Mitchell, 1925); however, theorizing seems to him to be feasible only in cases where data are available in appropriate quantity and quality. Collecting and processing empirical facts must thus precede theorizing as theorists are only allowed to postulate co-movements of variables where such co-movements are factually detected (Vining, 1949, p. 85). Mitchell regards his own data-based approach as a promise of a more grounded way of forming hypotheses and an easier way of choosing from them. He explicitly relates these hopes to the current and future development of statistical methods. An elimination of the demarcation between qualitative and quantitative economic theories, however, is a prerequisite: qualitative analysis must include quantitative work, instead of using quantitative analyses as post-theorizing tests. To this end, theoretical work must be freed from the trap of concepts and unrealistic assumptions.

Here a special duality lies between the lines. Even though Mitchell refrains from calling into question the authority of neoclassical economics (whilst he cruelly attacks neoclassical economists of the past eras), he is also unwilling to insist on it and calls for fundamental reforms which he wants to complete on ground of his quantitative analysis suggested to re-invent economics in a form which it was always supposed to have.

Thanks to his statistical turn, theory may grow into an objective science of reality, making theories of the past of no interest. In this new quantitative economics, as one of the most important consequences, variety and particularity will replace sameness and generality, probability will take the place of certainty, and approximation will hold instead of invariant laws. Irrespective of these high ambitions, in their reviews both Knight (1928) and Schumpeter (1930) found that Mitchell was unable to get rid of Marshall's theory. Raw empirical work raised the suspicion that Mitchell and the NBER disregarded causal connections, but Somers (1952) tried to refuse these accusations.

Mitchell's interest in theories was still more intense than Mills', a colleague of his at the NBER. In his 'The behavior of prices', Mills (1927) takes an extremely atheoretical stance. He cancels theories off his scientific radar screen in a literal sense. He is neither unsatisfied with theories, nor does he intend to reform them, and nor does he suggest a statistical turn: he just ignores all theories. In his descriptivist analyses in price dynamics he considers no theoretical explanations. Neoclassical price theory dawns on the horizon only to the extent that prices in capitalist economies admittedly play a crucial role and form a complex system of interrelations. Retaining such a minimal background, Mills was thus unable to dispense with all theories. Doing so, he created an odd situation for he grabbed prices out of their context, even if the price system has a multitude of interrelations to the surrounding economy as a whole (Viner, 1929).

Mills focused his first and foremost interests on the trends and co-movements of time series, the problem of lags, and the amplitudes of fluctuations. The considerable stability of such tendencies, if it is given, facilitates short-run forecasts. The accuracy of data, seasonal adjustment, and the various preliminary calculations to make the data comparable occurred as distinct concerns for Mitchell. However, he did his best to stay away from drawing causal inferences and using causal terminology as statistical methods form an inappropriate ground for thinking in causal terms, he argued. The circularity of causal links, the danger of infinite regress, and the complexity of the causal structure underlying social phenomena deteriorate the chance for meaningful causal analyses.

Friedman's empirical Marshallian methodology takes him close to these NBER traditions. The background for his connections to the institution is biographical. Friedman was a student of NBER researchers Arthur Burns (1931–32) and Wesley Mitchell (1933–34) then worked as an assistant to statistician Henry Schultz (1934–35) and from 1937 as a research fellow at the NBER. Even though his magnum opus, the 'Monetary history' (Friedman & Schwartz, 1963) contains neither a methodological introduction nor a methodological summary, the statistical techniques he applied (e.g. index numbers, comparisons of growth rates, measuring dynamics through simple charts, publishing lengthy and detailed tables, moving-average trending) bear direct resemblance to the NBER methods. In another text he was pleased to explicitly admit the similarities (Friedman & Schwartz, 1982, pp. 73–97). Consequently, Friedman's empirical work faced the same critical reception as the NBER method did.

Regarding it as insufficient, Friedman's critics rejected the theoretical work he put forward to underpin his empirics (Hammond, 1996, pp. 26–27). For a whilst Friedman succeeded in defending the NBER methodology by advocating the out-of-sample forecast performance[51] as a measure (Friedman, 1940, p. 659; Patinkin, 1981, p. 16). Judged by this standard, Cowles-style simultaneous equations systems kept failing even in the 1950s (Christ, 1994, pp. 45–47). By the end of the 1970s, however, one-equation models could no longer hold out against the complex approach. Simplicity turned out to be a shortcoming (Brainard & Cooper, 1975, pp. 169–170 and pp. 173–174). What is more, a most important empirical consequence of the Lucas critique (Lucas, 1976/1981) was an emphasis upon the poor out-of-sample predictive performance of the then existing models (Sargent, 1984, p. 409). Pushing it as his main argument in the debate over empirical success, Friedman underlined that simultaneous structural equation systems failed to outperform single-equation naïve models and given this fact he saw no point in constructing complex models. However, as it is argued below, Cowles modellers were motivated by the purpose of sound causal understanding, so there is much more to this debate than the number of equations. By this statement of his, Friedman inevitably subscribed to the stance of belittling the importance of complex causal structures underlying socio-economic reality, and this is a stance that is difficult to reconcile with the idea of causal realism. Friedman placed his sole focus on empirical performance, whilst the Cowles Commission desired good empirical performance and theoretical clarity in causal terms at the same time. In Chapter 4 this thread of Friedman's reasoning re-emerges as an aspect of his instrumentalism.

The Cowles Commission

The underlying idea that called the Cowles Commission into existence in 1932 was a different combination of theory and application. A part of this mix was an emphasis upon a special kind of formalism that pushed the institution towards the Walrasian polar of the Marshall–Walras dyad. Cowles researchers regarded economic theory as the appropriate basis for empirical work. This theoretical background belongs to our pregiven knowledge, which, given this, is prior to econometric work. In the literature this knowledge is widely referred to as a priori or aprioristic, which is misleading. In their original meaning, these adjectives describe

---

[51] This is a variant of empirical performance Friedman (1953/2009) suggested in his positivist methodology as a criterion for model selection.

knowledge independent of experience, such as the sense of causality, space and time, or tautologies (Kant, 1781/1998, 1783/1997). However, economic theory subjected to econometric tests is not like this. As it is argued in Chapters 3 and 4, Lucas related his basic concepts to reality, or in other words, he kept an eye on reality during theorizing, and he is the rule in science, not the exception (Weinberg, 2015). The nature of inductive logic generally applied in economic theorizing precludes characterizing this knowledge as aprioristic in the correct sense. It is a better option to regard this knowledge as pre-given, meaning a knowledge we have prior to the deductive phase. As we shall see it in Section 2.2.4, the Lucas-Sims debate was pointless in a sense for both of them strongly relied upon empirics prior to theorizing.

Based on this, the Cowles Commission aimed at reconciling economic theory, statistical methods, and observed data. The enhancement of both the potential of economic policy interventions and the overall macroeconomic performance on the one hand and complex causal understanding[52] on the other emerged as a declared purpose at the very beginning (Loveday, 1939, p. 9; Tinbergen, 1940, pp. 73–76). In this philosophy the case of multiple causes, thanks to multivariate correlation analysis, does not emerge as a combination of previously isolated causes: complex models constitute the framework from the very first step. Accordingly, the Cowles personnel regarded the Mitchell approach as an unfruitful early attempt to be swept away (Tinbergen, 1939, p. 12). Epstein (1987, pp. 61–62) argues that placing emphasis upon economic policy consequences was inevitable. A desire to control the endogenous variables naturally emerges if the equations describing behavioural rules and facilitating economic policy interventions are available.

A characteristic feature of the 'Cowles Commission method' from the Marschak era (1943) was the extensive use of simultaneous stochastic difference equations in a Walrasian fashion in order to represent complete macro-economic systems. According to the core idea, macroeconomic phenomena are products of agents' simultaneous interactions (the individuum is the ultimate source of social events); thus the most effective

---

[52] Infinite regress is an obstacle to causal understanding as any cause can be traced back to further causes. It was the excuse Friedman found to avoid applying the causalist terminology (Hammond, 1988, pp. 1–3). His objection reflects a real problem but fails to underpin the abandonment of causal thinking and the limitation of theoretical discussions to 'proximate' causes. Through his theory of gravity Newton provided a causal explanation to the riddle of planets orbiting the Sun, whilst he refused to address the issue of 'the' cause of gravity. It is thus unnecessary to walk down the route implied by the causalist approach and to find the ultimate causes (Manicas, 2006, pp. 14 and 23). Friedman kept struggling with the problem throughout his academic career. In order to keep away from the use of the whole causalist vocabulary, he resorted to diverse euphemisms (Hoover, 2009, p. 306). For instance, he talked about 'underlying factors' instead of causes in general.

strategy to understand these phenomena is treating them as they are by sorting agents into quite homogenous clusters (Haavelmo, 1943). Epstein (1987, pp. 66–68) clearly points out the parallelisms between the Cowles Commission method and methodological individualism. The approach is flexible, so it is consistent with another conception according to which actions are not simultaneously determined but sequences of mutual reactions. Under certain conditions the tension of these two approaches (simultaneous determination vs. sequences of reactions) does not necessitate the dismissal of the simultaneous equations framework. In broad terms, simultaneous or interdependent models can be regarded as good approximations to recursive models as long as the available data correspond to a time interval much longer than the response time of agents (Strotz & Wold, 1960).

As Cowles researchers let pre-given economic theories draw up the catalogue of relevant variables and describe the way they are interconnected and specify the restrictions on them (Tinbergen, 1939, pp. 11–12), the focus was on the staff's elaborating the right estimation methods, and their running and improving the estimations. Not an overstatement is it to say that Cowles-style empirical work received ready-made equations from economic theory;[53] thus the selection of variables was not a problem (Hildreth & Jarrett, 1955, p. 7; Christ, 1994, p. 33). In a specific case of company-level modelling, for instance, the problem regarded the mathematical steps of turning the economic theory into an estimatable form, the set of the relevant production processes at the given company, or the set of measurable inputs in the assumed production function. By this framework the Cowles Commission rendered the relationship between theory and data unidirectional in a characteristic way. An output of the Cowles estimations could point to the good or bad empirical performance of a theory (Epstein, 1987, p. 64), but they left the following revision to the discretion of theorists (Klein, 1950, p. 1). On the basis of empirical results, theoretical economists were free to change the models, though this step did not belong to the scope of econometrics. Later, Lucas with his neo-Walrasian models did a lot to cease this separation of theorizing and empirics.

The dissociation of these phases, however, does not imply theory's disinterest in empirical results. On the contrary, Klein's preface might have gained even Marshall's liking:

---

[53] In theoretical terms the Cowles Commission had an explicit Keynesian inclination (Sims, 2011, p. 1190) and it is in this orientation that Christ (1994, p. 35) identifies one of the reasons for Friedman's harsh antipathy towards the Cowles method. Friedman's anxiety fitted into the decade-long conflict between the 'Knight wing' of the Department of Economics and the Cowles Commission (Reder, 1982, p. 10).

> The stated attempt here is to estimate laws of human behavior in economic life. If we reach the goal of discovering autonomous behavior patterns, we should expect them to hold under a variety of circumstances—for example, under both prewar and postwar conditions. Although I believe that the models presented in the ensuing pages give a reasonably good description of the prewar economic process, they do not carry over in all respects to the postwar situation. (Klein, 1950, p. vii)

Two essential elements of Marshall's methodological programme appear here: economics as a law-seeking science the purpose of which is to identify some laws or tendencies that can change in time.

Hammond (1996, p. 25) sorts the work done under the aegis of the Cowles Commission into two separate streams, and in comparison to the theoretical-mathematical econometric research activities he strongly belittles the empirical part, mentioning Larry Klein's (1950) Keynesian model as the only example. This account is rather distorted, though econometric-theoretical work certainly had a special emphasis. Prior to any empirical applications the staff needed to 'create' econometrics and to fix the problems around ordinary least-squares estimations by developing alternative estimations techniques (Marschak, 1950, pp. 39–41; Hurwicz, 1950; Koopmans, 1950; Haavelmo, 1953; Girschick & Haavelmo, 1953; Chernoff & Divinsky, 1953) that took enormous theoretical efforts. These results served as the notional ammunition in Klein's models and Koopmans' NBER critique. However, Christ (1994, p. 45) lists further empirical works. Marschak and Andrews (1944) modelled company production, whilst Hildreth and Jarrett (1955) studied the manufacturing of livestock products with simultaneous equations. Through production function estimations Borts (1952) looked into the problem of increasing return to scales in the railway industry. Allen (1954) modelled the market for agricultural products with linear stochastic equations.

In the context of empirical work Epstein (1987, pp. 101–103) refers to the underdetermination of theory by data and highlights the insufficiency of economic theory. Data supported a variety of mutually acceptable structures, so empirical work became ambiguous. Tinbergen (1939, p. 12) foresaw this danger. There was a huge gap between the theory of individual behaviour and aggregate-level data: the theoretical issue of tracing macro-level phenomena back to individual agents was unresolved then. This theoretical problem set emerged as a hindrance to successful empirical work and added to the need of inventing the proper mathematic-econometric methods. Thus in 1952 even 'theory construction in economics' appeared amongst the declared purposes of the Cowles Commission, which is far more than testing some ready-made theories (Cowles Commission, 1952, p. 2 and p. 47).

In 1955, however, the Cowles Commission, deferring to the pressure from the Department of Economics, left Chicago for Yale University to involve James Tobin as their new research director. Consequently, the

Cowles Commission could not exert direct influence on Lucas in his graduate years, but still, a mix of firm neoclassical theorizing and extended empirical work became the pillars of Lucas's subsequent economics. Triggered through different channels though, the beginnings of Lucas's keen interest in both mathematical economics and econometrics and his suspicion of Marshall are dated back to his early graduate years in Chicago. It is Samuelson's 'Foundations of economic analysis' and the influence by Dale Jorgenson that he himself highlighted in this context. By 1963, the time of his assistant professorship at Carnegie Tech, he had already been committed to the mix of theory, econometrics and measurement. Exposed to Edward Prescott's and Edmund Phelps's (and to some further external) influences, there did he start elaborating his rational expectations neo-Walrasian general equilibrium economics (Lucas, 2001). Through this framework Lucas joined a research tradition placing him outside the Chicago school (Emmett, 2009, p. 151). As it is argued above, however, some caution is needed as Stigler and Becker's realist interpretive efforts or Lucas's strong empirical commitment are powerful arguments against his 'extra-Chicagoan' position. By the time he returned to Chicago in 1975 his work later awarded the Nobel prize had already been done. His efforts towards both causal understanding (a point to make in Chapters 3 and 4) and the unification of theory and empirics, accompanied by his neo-Walrasian approach, drove him along the Cowles methodological path. It must be noted, however, that by the Lucas critique (Lucas, 1976/1981; Lucas & Sargent, 1979) he considerably weakened the position of Cowles-style econometrics (Boumans, 2005, p. 96).

2.2.4 The Marshall–Walras divide in a new guise: Sims on the need for 'atheoretical' VARs

The Marshall–Walras or the NBER-Cowles divide was a debate in the subsequent rounds of which each party failed to recognize those points in the analytical toolkit of the rival approach through which the methods could have been reconciled (Christ, 1994, p. 53). Both approaches have genuine scientific merits, even though they emphasize distinct phases of the same social scientific research endeavour. By the copious amounts of raw data, the Marshallian NBER approach supports the inductive stage to have meaningful generalizations. On the other hand, the Walrasian Cowles Commission approach can be regarded as the phase of deductive theorizing and empirical testing. On this showing, the Marshall–Walras divide regarded the primacy of the equally essential steps of scientific research. Friedman, however, placed emphasis on theorizing and testing, so he could overcome Mitchell's atheoretical empiricism. The Cowles Commission could not avoid getting involved in indictive theorizing either, thus the once allegedly distinct approaches merged into one another.

Even though econometric methodology and the use of simultaneous equations systems may ground a principled distinction, Friedman (1970) also elaborated a three-equation model. Here his sole purpose was to provide a theoretical background for empirics; thus he performed no Cowles-style econometric estimations.

At the end of the 1970s the Marshall–Walras divide surfaced in a further field: time-series models to macroeconomics. Then Thomas Sargent and Christopher Sims together raised the need for a macro-modelling technique which was supposed to be free of any pre-given theoretical background in order to let the data speak (Sims, 1980a). The episode of suggesting vector autoregressive (VAR) models was a fresh re-emergence of the Marshallian methodology. Letting the data speak as a modelling and theorizing philosophy explicitly has its roots in Marshall's approach:

> Experience in controversies [...] brings out the impossibility of learning anything from facts till they are examined and interpreted by reason; and teaches that the most reckless and treacherous of all theorists is he who professes to let facts and figures speak for themselves, who keeps in the back-ground the part he has played, perhaps unconsciously, in selecting and grouping them, and in suggesting the argument *post hoc ergo propter hoc*. (Marshall, 1885, p. 44)

Soon afterwards Sargent lost his interest in this modelling approach, so Sims alone kept the pot boiling (De Vroey, 2016, pp. 205–206).

Sargent and Sims (1977) mounted a frontal offensive against the characteristic theories of the age. They objected to economists' turning to data only through some arbitrary assumptions of theories. The inevitable consequence is an alleged ignorance of certain co-movements between variables. What is more, as their argument was going on, theoretical assumptions oftentimes are only of ad hoc character the sole purpose of which is the reconciliation of theory with data, but all this is done in a way where the real features of agents are disregarded (as it is argued in Chapters 3 and 4, a keen interest in the properties of real agents was one of the most essential characteristics of Lucas's scientific strategy). So instead of having a bad theory we had better keep the role pre-given theories play to a minimum.

They proposed an atheoretical statistical approach to aim at studying interrelated time series by looking for significant lags (Sargent, 1979, p. 8; Sims, 1996, p. 117) in the general form

$$X_t = \alpha_0 + \alpha_1 X_{t-1} + \ldots + \alpha_4 X_{t-4} + \alpha_5 Y_{t-1} + \ldots + \alpha_8 Y_{t-4} + \alpha_9 Z_{t-1} + \ldots + \alpha_{12} Z_{t-4} + u_t$$
$$Y_t = \beta_0 + \beta_1 Y_{t-1} + \ldots + \beta_4 Y_{t-4} + \beta_5 X_{t-1} + \ldots + \beta_8 X_{t-4} + \beta_9 Z_{t-1} + \ldots + \beta_{12} Z_{t-4} + v_t$$
$$Z_t = \gamma_0 + \gamma_1 Z_{t-1} + \ldots + \gamma_4 Z_{t-4} + \gamma_5 X_{t-1} + \ldots + \gamma_8 X_{t-4} + \gamma_9 Y_{t-1} + \ldots + \gamma_{12} Y_{t-4} + w_t$$

$$(2.1)$$

specified for three endogenous variables (X, Y, and Z) and four lags (i.e. as a fourth-order autoregressive structure), where u, v, and w are error terms. As the example shows, it is not some pre-given theories but the data themselves that suggest the significant interrelations of variables. Theorizing cuts in only in the next stage, when after the empirical phase co-movements ought to receive systematic explanation.[54] Lucas, accordingly, regarded time series models as the initial stage of theorizing (Lucas & Sargent, 1979, pp. 5–6; Friedman, 1978, p. 75). For Sims, by listening to what the data say modellers can avoid the theory-led restrictions on some variables. The assumed relations between time series exclusively depend on the strengths and directions of the detected connections: data dictate what the theorists should pay attention to. Sargent and Sims explicitly related their own approach to the NBER methodology. By so doing, they could not but oppose the theory-led methodology of the Cowles Commission (both in its traditional simultaneous equation and the subsequent DSGE forms). Amongst the predecessors Sims (1996, p. 117) emphasizes Friedman and Schwartz's achievements as well. One of the manifestations of this intellectual connection is Sims's way of presenting his empirical results in the NBER fashion. His focus is on co-movements of variables and on the qualitative and quantitative features of dynamics. As another emergence of the Mitchell-Burns approach, Sims (1980a, pp. 32–33) suggests VAR models for testing the rival theories.

A further point of connection to the NBER methodology could be the following of Mitchell's idea that diverse phenomena emerging during a business cycle ought to be traced back to a few or even one ultimate cause as a single index (Sargent, 1979, p. 12). This is the logic and the terminology behind the label 'index models' for VARs. According to Sims's (1980b, 2011, p. 1197) results, the past values of the interest rate well explain money supply dynamics, whilst the interest rate is predictable on past values of industrial production. An explicit focus upon a single assumed cause, however, is also a key element in Lucas's theory, also referring to Mitchell. In Lucas's theory, shocks to the money supply as triggering fluctuations through price dynamics due to the repeated mistakes of agents served as this ultimate single cause (Lucas, 1981, pp. 7–16).

Sims's approach cannot exclude all pre-given theories or theoretical considerations. At a minimum, pre-given knowledge is applied in identifying the relevant set of variables and perhaps in setting the maximum lag length. As far as the latter is concerned, Sims (1980a, p. 15) resorts to

---

[54] It must be emphasized again that the characterization of economic theories as mental constructs torn apart from reality is seriously distorted. Natural and social sciences per definitionem have some bearing on reality. With a few special exceptions, there exists no science without connections to reality. The frequent case against such theories refers to highly abstract formal models. Loosely put, pure mathematics and formal logic without social or natural implications can be characterized as disciplines unconnected to reality. Sims's caricature neglects the fact that induction and deduction cooperate in theorizing.

an arbitrary solution when he sets such a long lag structure that longer cases would be implausible. As a further instance for the presence of theoretical background in general, Sims in his VARs mentions the functions of demand for and supply of money or the Phillips curve equation (Sims, 1986), and occasionally refers to consistencies or inconsistencies between theories and data.[55] In the case of a VAR model, in the background there stands a theory in the realist sense of the word; thus VARs ought not to be built upon relationships such as the one between the number of storks and birth dynamics, not even in cases where such a model performed well. This seems to be a huge leap forward after Friedman's instrumentalist philosophy, where mere explanatory power might have governed the selection of variables.[56] A system emerges the form of which takes after theory-based models but which is free of theoretical assumptions and interpretations of dubious value (Sargent, 1984). All the co-movements and their characteristics are clearly visible, but their theoretical interpretations are still missing.

Results from VARs are the inputs for theorizing: Sims (1986, pp. 12–15) makes efforts to inductively fit a theory to his numerical results. VAR models deliver the facts with which a good theory ought to be in consonance (Sims, 2011, p. 1197). Sims restricts the set of variables in advance, orders them into equations and, consequently, establishes their interrelations, studies the numerical results, and offers plausible stories as explanations. By so doing, however, he cannot but hit a kind of the problem of underdetermination of theory by data he himself highlights (Sims, 1980a, p. 15, 1996, p. 107). Numerical results change according to the set of included variables. Even though in all cases there is a story to tell (if not, that is not a relevant case), no one knows which the true theory is. Thus the modeller (or theorist?) compels herself to take a random walk. It can be avoided in two ways. First, she chooses from the theories on a plausibility basis. In this case, however, she needs the most plausible theory only, but it is known even before the empirical phase. This is a return to the case of traditional pre-given theories (see Section 1.3.1). Or second, she regards

---

[55] Sometimes Sims is very careful to phrase. Sargent and Sims (1977, p. 66) regard the negative trade-off between inflation and unemployment as the "Phillips curve" (in quotation marks!) which for them is only an empirical regularity called the Phillips curve in theory. All the expressions referring to a theoretical background or an interpretation are cancelled from the primary vocabulary to suggest: this is what a theoretical economist *would* say.

[56] Even though Friedman had problems using the causalist terminology, he is highly unlikely not to have regarded the changes in money supply as the real causes of changes in nominal income. His instrumentalist philosophy manifests itself in the idea that in terms of empirical performance and the set of variables the 'real' causal structure is indifferent (see Section 2.2.3 and Chapter 4).

the explanatory power as the foremost aspect of model selection. In this case, however, no theorizing is needed, and at the end of the day she gets to Friedman's instrumentalism where she might want to consider using the number of storks as an explanatory variable of birth dynamics. If these options are not satisfying, the modeller needs to make do with a random walk and hoarding theories of equal merit.

The conflict between Lucas and Sims reached its peak in the debate over the Lucas critique that also hit Sims's VAR models (Sargent, 1984, pp. 408–409). A change in policy affects some parameters of the equations, irrespective of whether there is an underlying theory or not. If we take it as given that agents adjust their behaviour to policy and behaviour has effects on macroeconomic phenomena, then parameters must change even in a theory-free system should the modelled economy itself change. To be more specific, not having rational expectations hypothesis in the background, one cannot but neglect the effects of policy changes on rational agents. On this ground an atheoretical approach is a shortcoming as the modeller fails to recognize an important aspect of her target system.

For Sims (1982a, p. 112), however, Lucas's rational expectations hypothesis would be acceptable only if statistical results proved its real existence; the assumption must thus be empirically underpinned. As a response Sims (1982a) suggests the idea that the public regard economic policy changes as random steps even if policy makers do not take random actions. There is no distinction between agents forming the public and policy makers: policy is made by simple rational individuals. Policy decisions are not sudden or surprise actions with long-run consequences. There are no stable rules policy can permanently change. Policy makers showing up in a sequence cannot compel their successors to follow the prior decisions. This is the reason why optimizing economic policy actions seem to be random changes to the public. If agents perceive policy actions as random steps, they cannot respond through systematic changes in their behaviour, not even in Lucas's world, Sims argued. Thus Sims proposed VAR models the parameters of which follow random walks. This way he expected to avoid spurious behavioural stories behind parameter changes and to place rational expectations on a firm statistical basis.

The debate was open and recorded in Lucas's correspondence. In the summer of 1982, Lucas and Sims clarified their stances in two long letters. These pieces are so precise in phrasing that they are worth quoting at full length:

> Dear Chris:
> It was good to see you in Cambridge last week, and as always, I found your paper stimulating.
> I hope (but am not at all sure) that I didn't come across as unsympathetic to the work you are doing with VAR's. I think this, as did your earlier work with index models, is helping us to look at time series in new ways, and will (really, already has)

stimulate theoretical developments. Certainly I agree with you that the fact that interest rates "knock out" the effects of money innovations is basic, and has to be dealt with. I also agree that in the absence of any theory, natura non facit saltum is about all we have to go with.

But the idea that constructing structural models with "controversial" identifying restrictions is not the best research route to take, which you seemed to me to be advancing, does not seem to me borne out by observations on at least the better developed areas of applied economics.

On the way home, I fixed on your use of "controversial" as a pejorative. I don't think you really believe this, and you certainly have stimulated your own share of controversy with your work. Really, there is never going to be such a thing as an uncontroversial way to settle disputes over economic policy, nor do I see why one would hope for such a state of affairs. It seems to me that our job is to try to make controversy useful, by focusing it on discussable, analyzeable issues. In Taylor's first paper, for example, contract length was selected arbitrarily (hence "controversially") and was central to the operating characteristics of the model. But labor contracts are something we can collect independent evidence on (as John did) or theorize about (as many people are not doing). Work like this is productive not because it settles policy issues in a way that honest people can't disagree over but because it channels controversy onto potentially productive tracks, because it gets us talking and thinking about issues that our equipment may let us make some progress on. (Lucas's letter to Christopher A. Sims. July 15, 1982. Lucas papers. Box 5. '1982, 1 of 2' folder)

In response Sims highlights that ungrounded theorizing inevitably injects speculative elements into models, which makes it impossible for theorists to approach the ideal of objective knowledge. Consequently, such speculation is undesirable. We ought to keep in mind the fact that the letters are from 1982: the year when Sims rejected rational expectations hypothesis as an ungrounded assumption. Accordingly, his tone of voice is not particularly conciliatory:

Dear Bob:

Thanks for your letter of July 15. I think you did come across as rather unsympathetic to use of loosely structured models for policy evaluation. Some may have had the impression you were unsympathetic to loosely structured analysis of data in general, but I didn't think you intended that.

I don't mean to be using "controversial" as pejorative. I do mean to be using it as a kind of opposite to "objective", occupying a position much like "subjective". There is a research style which always approaches data with a tightly structured model, treating such a model as if it were the same kind of universally acceptable framework for discussion as a corresponding physical probability model in engineering or biological experiments. Approaching data with such a model can, undeniably, be useful. But the air of objective precision surrounding conclusions which treat such a model as true hinders real scientific discussion and our efforts to get the lay public to understand that there is something approaching objective knowledge allowing us to keep subjective or controversial hypotheses separate from the mundane smoothness and limited time dependence assumptions which I think have something closer to objective status.

I don't regard the kind of policy analysis I did at the end of the paper as "way inside the frontier". With a heavier dose of a priori knowledge, much sharper conclusions about available policy choices would be possible. But I doubt that one can dig very much deeper into the bag of our a priori knowledge without coming up with material that is controversial. I would not take the position that one should not dig into the bag at all because of that – in fact, in a heuristic way I do entertain some controversial hypotheses in discussing the results. The point is only that to the extent that the paper's analysis does succeed in getting conclusions about a policy projection without resting heavily on a controversial framework of maintained hypotheses it is doing something which is on the frontier.

Enclosed is a copy of my Rotterdam paper, which you might not have seen, in which I ramble on at some more length on these themes.[57]

As I see it, the position you have taken has led to many economists' thinking that there is no hope for obtaining useful conclusions about policy in a model which is not fully identified using rational expectations assumptions. The practical thrust of my counterargument is that we can get useful conclusions with identifying assumptions that fall far short of explicit behavioral interpretation of every equation in a model, and that this is lucky because otherwise it might be a long time before we could get any conclusions in a believable model of reasonable size.

I enjoyed our discussion in Cambridge, as usual. It might have been more enlightening for all concerned if we hadn't been so hot and tired, but there was no time for a really thorough discussion anyway. The discussion we had seemed to have raised interest in this kind of issue in the audience, which is most of what could have been hoped for. (Christopher A. Sims's letter to Lucas. July 26, 1982. Lucas papers. Box 5. '1982, 1 of 2' folder)

However, as we have just seen, Sims was unable to keep his methodology away from theorizing. His ideas on agents and economic policy constitute a theory, and not just some heuristic speculations, of the structure of socio-economic reality. What is more, a theory that challenged Lucas's economics at the microfoundations level (Sims, 2011, p. 1202). From his atheoretical VAR models Sims gradually moved towards structural vector-autoregressive (SVAR) systems that applied theory-based restrictions to prove useful in economic policy analysis (Sims, 2011, p. 1199). Ironically, in order to defend his theory-free statistical methodology, Sims also needed to form an underlying theory. It had some derived consequences that could be in consonance with reality, thus deductive logic accompanied inductive theorizing. The two seemingly different methodologies merged into one another again, leaving room only for some subtle theoretical discrepancies.

Sims, it must be noted, interconnected the micro- and the macro-level in a highly loose way, which, as the correspondence informs us, he took as a great merit. He shaped his micro-theory in order not to establish an explicit connection between the levels. His macro-level equations do not explicitly stem from the agent-level assumptions. On the contrary, through the assumptions he assigned such characteristics to his agents that he

---

[57] Sims presented his paper entitled 'Scientific standards in econometric modeling' (Sims, 1982b) at the conference held in honour of the 25th anniversary of the Econometric Institute, Netherlands School of Economics, at Erasmus University, Rotterdam, in January 1982.

could avoid taking this formal and explicit deductive step. As it is argued in Chapters 3 and 4, Lucas's approach radically differed in these terms. In his case there existed an explicit relationship (embedded in traceable deductive algebraic steps) between the levels. For Lucas the relevance of the general choice-theoretic framework was unambiguous, and he filled this frame with a substance he distilled from the observed behaviour of real agents. Admittedly, there was an axiomatic link in his chain of thoughts: macroeconomic phenomena ought to be traced back to individual decisions. SVAR models also applied the same assumption, though the agents, due to their characteristics, remained hidden.

2.3 The transition in theoretical terms: Money, monetary and fiscal policy

2.3.1 Friedman on money and monetary policy

Friedman placed his oeuvre upon some constantly evolving ideas; thus a review is supposed to be both easy and complicated at the same time. It is easy as the relation between nominal money supply and nominal income, Friedman's central tenet, is highly straightforward to summarize. However, it is also difficult as Friedman's ideas were far from coherent. In the field labelled as 'the quantity theory of money' he relocated the focus of his interest for several times over his long academic career. Even though his foremost interest was in the macroeconomic effects of money, his views on its real effects considerably changed. In the beginning Friedman was unclear how a change in nominal national income splits between inflation and the rate of real economic growth. Studying the co-movements of inflation and unemployment through the Phillips curve, he suggested a temporary trade-off and later a straight relation. Blaug (1992, pp. 193–194) discusses the successive versions of Friedman's monetarism, ranging from the reformulation of the quantity theory of money through empirical investigations into the demand for money in the economic history of the United States to the debates with Keynesians over the possibilities of discriminating between competing models on empirical grounds. De Vroey (2016, pp. 66–70) labels Friedman as a single-idea economist whilst distinguishing three separate albeit overlapping periods in Friedman's professional career. These accounts do not seem to be in contradiction, though they eminently underline the fact how difficult it is to provide a comprehensive summary of Friedman's theory. Did Friedman have a single idea and unique theory at all? Even if we take he did, its reconstruction requires careful interpretation and may still obscure or even distort some meaningful elements in order to create a presumed coherence (Skinner, 1969, pp. 16–17). Accordingly, neglecting the problems of periodization and changing emphasis, the focus here is, first, on how Friedman conceived the relationship between the quantity of money and nominal income dynamics and, second, on how he understood the way the changes in nominal income could be divided into inflation and real economic growth. The result, hopefully, is a picture that can be coherent at the price of the least possible distortions.

Friedman positioned his theory between the simple quantity theory of money (that assumes the constant velocity of money) and the simple Keynesian income-expenditure theory. The latter was built upon the idea of non-monetary price determination and traced back nominal income dynamics to changes in real output. This was the theory Friedman rejected on empirical grounds, whilst he remained more gracious to the former. The stability of velocity (relative to the nominal stock of money or nominal income) was a strong point in favour of the simple quantity theory (Friedman & Schwartz, 1982, pp. 622–624). For Friedman the demand for money was not simply stable (i.e. constant) but a stable function of some variables (Friedman & Schwartz, 1963, p. 679). When velocity changes (Friedman & Schwartz, 1965, p. 43), this change can easily be traced back to changes in the determinants of demand (e.g. inflation expectations), and the whole process is well-predictable. Friedman provides detailed numerical accounts of the changes in the demand for money and in velocity, and relates these changes to income dynamics. When real income grows at a steady rate, velocity slightly lowers for money is a luxury commodity. During cyclical fluctuations, however, changes in velocity follow income dynamics as changes in permanent income have effects on expenditures (Friedman, 1958/1969, 1959). Changes in the demand for money and in velocity complicate the relationship between the stock of money and prices.

It is the stable demand for money that establishes the positive relationship between nominal money supply and nominal income; the quantity theory of money is thus the theory of the demand for money (Friedman, 1956b), though the relationship is fraught with short-run fluctuations and disturbances. In the expansion phase of a cycle, prices are on the increase, whilst they drop in the contraction phase (that is, prices and income move together), accompanied by higher or lower growth rates of the money stock in the expansion or contraction phase, respectively. Only in severe depressions may the absolute quantity of money drop instead of its growth rate. In the long run the relationship between the quantity of money and the price level is even clearer. This is due to the fact that it is not the changes in the determinants of demand for money (e.g. rates of interest) that establish the close co-movements of nominal income and nominal money supply. Rather, money has effects on nominal income;[58] at least in most cases, as there may occur feedbacks from income to the quantity of money. The main connection, however, leads from money to income; thus such feedbacks do not reverse the relationship. At the phenomenal level the theory bears resemblance to the simple quantity theory of money, though it takes into account the fact that demand for money is under the joint influence of multiple factors.

Friedman applies both the classical

$$MV = Y = Py \qquad (2.2)$$

and the

$$M = kPy \qquad (2.3)$$

Cambridge forms of the quantity theory (where M stands for the stock of money; V is the average number of times per period that the money stock is used in making income transactions; Y is the nominal national income; P is the price index implicit in the estimations of national income at constant prices—plainly put, the price level; y is the national income measured in constant prices; and k is the ratio of money stock to income, or simply the reciprocal of V). The Cambridge form more directly expresses the relationship between the demand for and the supply of money on the one hand and the way these two variables determine the price level on the other hand. Friedman derives both equations from the demand functions for money of agents (taken as both the ultimate wealth holders and, at the expense of some minor reinterpretation of variables, business enterprises).

According to Eq. (2.3), demand for money is dependent upon real income, the price level, and some further factors squeezed into k (Friedman, 1970, pp. 200–202). In a more detailed specification, the demand function for money takes the

$$M = f\left(P_1 r_b - \frac{1}{r_b}\frac{dr_b}{dt}; r_e + \frac{1}{P}\frac{dP}{dt} - \frac{1}{r_e}\frac{dr_e}{dt}; \frac{1}{P}\frac{dP}{dt}; w; \frac{Y}{r}; u \right) \qquad (2.4)$$

form, where the demand for money stands under the influence of six variables (the real return of bonds; the real return of equities; the real return of physical goods; the ratio of non-human to human wealth as the

---

[58] There may be further variables the dynamics of which follow the behaviour of the economy. Instead of the monetary theory of business cycles we may subscribe to the pin theory of business cycles if the production of pins reflects the dynamics of general business. However, we could hardly find a channel through which the production of pins may lead to changes in the course of general business. In other words, the monetary theory of business cycles is more plausible than its rivals. The more so as money supply changes can be traced back to specific historical circumstances, thus we cannot say that money income is the prime mover of the money stock (Friedman & Schwartz, 1965, pp. 48–50).

conversion of one form into the other necessitates the use of money; total wealth; and some variables, including income and expectations about economic stability, affecting tastes and preferences towards the services rendered by money—respectively, separated by semicolons). From this multivariable demand function, Friedman (1956a) gets to the simpler

$$M_0 = P \times l\left(y_0; r\right) \tag{2.5}$$

form, and then to the well-known

$$M = \frac{Py}{V} \tag{2.6}$$

version. Eq. (2.6) uniquely establishes P if the real economy is supposed not to respond to money supply changes, if velocity is constant and if prices are entirely flexible. If not, a change in nominal income will be a mix of inflation/deflation and a change in real output.[59] Thus the relationship between the quantity of money and the price level holds, even if it is not direct or mechanically rigid. According to Eqs (2.4), (2.5), Friedman accepts the interest rate elasticity of the demand for money, though he supposes this influence to be weak, at least definitely weaker than that would be necessary for the Keynesians' liquidity trap (Friedman, 1966/2007). It is also true of inflation that only high rates have effects on the demand for money (Friedman, 1958/1969). These channels do not considerably disturb the connection between the money supply and price dynamics.

Separating the changes in nominal income into real output changes and inflation is still ambiguous. The simplest case is pure inflation. Friedman, however, leaves room even for a negative connection between money supply and real output. An anticipated growth in the quantity of money increases the price level, which increases the costs of holding money; thus velocity also rises, with reference to the fact that in an expansion velocity usually gets above its trend (Friedman & Schwartz, 1963, p. 682). In the resulting situation the growth rate of nominal income is higher than would be necessitated by the growth of nominal money supply. In this case the rise in nominal income is accompanied by a drop in real output (so the rate of inflation outnumbers the growth rate of nominal income), as the higher costs of holding money drive producers to reallocate their resources, which deteriorates production efficiency (Friedman, 1970, pp. 229–231). This is the case of a reverse Phillips curve and slumpflation (i.e. higher rates of inflation occur with higher rates of unemployment) that Friedman sometimes attributed to a decline in the informativeness of

---

[59] Friedman (1968, p. 8, 1970, p. 219), without further explanation, relates real income to Walrasian general equilibrium and, at the same time, separates it from the equations of demand, investment, demand for and supply of money.

prices (due to a higher level of noise and distortions of relative prices), frictions in markets, and a drop in market efficiency one of the consequences of which is a rise in the unemployment rate (Friedman, 1977, pp. 465–468). A further case is a Phillips curve which is negatively sloped in the short run and vertical in the long run (Friedman, 1968, p. 11). Here an unanticipated rise in the growth rate of money modifies the growths of prices and wages, and some ambiguities over the interpretation of price and wage dynamics trigger real output to temporarily increase beyond its trend (see Section 4.1.2 for more on Friedman's Phillips curves).

The one thing we can claim with considerable certainty is that changes in the growth rate of money have effects on the rate of inflation, whilst short-run real consequences are ambiguous. Long-run monetary dynamics and long-run real economic growth are largely independent. Economic growth may occur even with prices declining, but in such a case price dynamics must be foreseeable and steady. Real economic performance is rather dependent upon natural resources, innovation, technology, or the accumulation of capital. Output is only affected by short-run changes in the money supply (Friedman & Schwartz, 1965, p. 53). The most one can say thus is that money supply instability accompanies real income instability. By relating real output drops to declines in the stock of money Friedman and Schwartz (1963) in their studies in economic history suggested further instances for real effects of money (Friedman, 1968, p. 3).

No matter what distribution emerges, through the revision of adaptive expectations the whole system moves towards a new equilibrium. Here the new higher and stabilized rate of money growth results in a higher rate of inflation only; thus it does not affect anything real in the long run. Due to these troubles it is more prudent to relate changes in the money supply to nominal income dynamics, and one had better neglect how the change is divided between prices and the real economy. This approach is preferable to both the simple quantity theory of money as it takes real output as given and the changes in nominal income as the direct inflationary consequences of changes in the money stock; and to the simple Keynesian income-expenditure theory as it takes prices as given and relates real economic fluctuations to changes in the money supply. Compared to these options, Friedman's theory more flexibly adjusts to the conditions as it supposes none of the $Y = Py$ determinants of nominal income to be stable or given (an advantage); however, Friedman could provide only some vague suggestions about how to divide changes in nominal income between inflation/deflation and changes in real output (a shortcoming).

As the stock of high-powered money proves to be the major force behind the changes in the stock of money (Friedman & Schwartz, 1963, p. 684), and as it is the stock of money that triggers changes in nominal and real income and in the price level, monetary policy has some power to affect these variables (Friedman, 1968, p. 3). The distribution of effects is the question again. Thus views on the potential of monetary policy are related to the views on the interrelations of macroeconomic variables. Even if monetary policy through an unanticipated money increase makes an attempt to reduce unemployment below its natural rate (it is a separate problem that finding the natural rate is highly problematic due to its variability), unemployment will remain under the natural rate only temporarily: it lasts until expectations are revised and the correct perception of agents on price and wage dynamics is restored.[60] Assuming adaptive expectations monetary policy can easily surprise the agents, and it is such recurrent surprises that are necessary to permanently keep unemployment at a low rate. This is the case of continuously accelerated inflation that achieves some seemingly beneficial real effects at the price of destructive price dynamics. Its application in macroeconomic control is thus strongly inadvisable. For Friedman, monetary policy can influence but cannot control. Due to a highly complex transmission mechanism even the price level is out of a direct and close control. All the beneficial real consequences are ephemeral and imply detrimental side effects. What is more, monetary policy efforts to control may easily result in some negative outcomes: it is far easier to trigger something negative than to achieve the desired positive results. As Friedman (1968, p. 12) says, 'Every [...] major contraction in this country [including the Great Contraction] has been either produced by monetary disorder or greatly exacerbated by monetary disorder. Every major inflation has been produced by monetary expansion.' As a consequence, Friedman argues that monetary policy ought to avoid being a cause of macroeconomic shocks and to maintain a stable background for the economy. Both objectives can effectively be pursued by applying the rule of a constant growth rate of money supply; hence the scope of discretionary monetary policy ought to be curbed as much as possible.

2.3.2 Lucas and new classical macroeconomics on money and monetary policy

One of Friedman's achievements in monetary economics was an explicit consideration of expectations through which he drew attention to both the neutrality of money and its limitations. As long as expectations are fulfilled, that is, as long as changes in the money supply are anticipated, monetary policy can trigger nominal adjustments only. Lucas with his rational expectations hypothesis kept narrowing the real economic potential of monetary policy. Although anticipated economic policy actions are ineffective in Lucas's theory as well, except for his 1975 island model

---

[60] Friedman (1968, p. 11) estimated the time necessary for this initial effect to unfold at 2–5 years, whilst it takes the system decades to get back to the prior unemployment rate.

(Lucas, 1975, 1981, pp. 179–214), assuming rational expectations and completely flexible nominal variables monetary policy still has some scope for surprises, whilst this scope is narrower than before. In other words, as Lucas argued, it is even more difficult for monetary policy to generate systematic errors in expectations formed by employees and employers; monetary neutrality is thus more extended.

This stems from the discrepancies of the expectation formation mechanisms Friedman's and Lucas's theories postulate. Friedman's adaptive scheme can well be characterized with an operator according to which an expectation on macroeconomic variable x in period t is dependent upon past expectations (more specifically, past expectations on the past values of the same variable) and expectations errors. In algebraic terms,

$$x_t^e = x_{t-1}^e + \beta\left(x_{t-1} - x_{t-1}^e\right) \qquad (2.7)$$

where x_t and x_{t-1} are the values of x in periods t and $t-1$, index e refers to the expected value and $\beta > 0$. If expectations are incorrect, agents are supposed to adjust their prior expectations according to the error. An underestimation triggers an upward correction. In a more sophisticated operator an expectation on x is the weighted average of past figures with decreasing weights (Friedman, 1970, pp. 228–229; Galbács, 2015, pp. 229–240), as in

$$x_t^e = \beta_1 x_{t-1} + \beta_2 x_{t-2} + \beta_3 x_{t-3} + \ldots + \beta_k x_{t-k} \qquad (2.8)$$

meaning that in expectation formation past values are taken into account with lower and lower weights so that $\beta_1 > \beta_2 > \beta_3 > \ldots > \beta_k$. Most importantly, agents in the adaptive scheme form expectations *only* on the basis of past values in a rather mechanical way. Thus the only requisite for an economic policy surprise is a shift of the target variable from its previous trend. This simple instrument is available for economic policy interventions at any time as, according to the assumptions, agents cannot consider any information beyond past dynamics. Any change is unforeseeable and unpredictable.

Monetary policy as the source and absorber of shocks

Presuming rational expectations the scope of surprises is radically narrower. In Friedman's theory systematic economic policy could easily trigger temporary real effects by derailing the target variable off its trend. It follows from the fact that Friedman failed to distinguish systematic and unanticipated-surprise economic policy actions. For him, any change was a surprise, even systematic actions. Rational agents, however, harness all available information including past data and the knowledge of the future (Sargent & Wallace, 1975, pp. 246–247). As economic policy is usually situation-related (i.e. systematic), agents by observing economic policy actions taken under different circumstances can map the future steps. Of policy changes all the systematic steps become predictable, whilst these steps were regarded as surprises in the adaptive scheme. Rationally formed expectations build a high barrier around economic policy. Agents are capable of learning the rules of any systematic economic policy; thus they can in advance adjust their behaviour to future economic policy actions. It is only random (i.e. unpredictable) steps that can bring about real effects. It is questionable, however, whether randomized economic policy makes any sense.

To Friedman's idea of the long-run neutrality of money Lucasian new classical macroeconomics has added the dogma of short-run neutrality (Gordon, 1979, pp. 1–2), which, however, does not imply the inability of all changes in the money supply to trigger temporary real effects. Money in both Friedmanian monetarism and new classical macroeconomics is neutral only if its changes are fully anticipated and if both these changes and their nominal consequences are correctly perceived. This short-run neutrality is thus incomplete, since it only regards the ineffectiveness of rationally foreseeable but adaptively unforeseeable actions. There is still, however, a small set of monetary policy actions having real consequences: these are the rationally unforeseeable steps. The signal processing problem Lucas (1972, 1973) postulated in his island models successfully highlights that due to the noises of price signals and the ambiguities of interpreting price dynamics agents may mistakenly respond to purely monetary shocks by changing their output and labour supply. Monetary policy by generating excess inflation can deceive agents; however, this potential gradually weakens with time. A supplier acting on an isolated market compares her expectations about the general price level with the price she perceives on her local market in order to distinguish real shocks (stemming from changes in local demand) and nominal shocks (triggered by monetary policy). Local price dynamics reflects two separate shocks, whilst agents are unable to distinguish. Agents thus need to speculate about the relative weights of the shocks (Lucas, 1973, pp. 327–328, 1981, pp. 133–134). By so doing, any agent considers her experience about the past differences between her local price and the general price level she expected. If σ^2 is the variance of shocks having deviated the price level from its expected level and τ^2 is the variance of shocks having deviated local prices from the price level, then the

$$\theta = \frac{\tau^2}{\sigma^2 + \tau^2} \tag{2.9}$$

ratio shows how real shocks affected local prices in the past. If τ^2 is relatively small, so if real shocks were negligible and nominal shocks predominated in the past, agents will attribute any increase in the local prices to a monetary expansion. The greater the share nominal shocks had in past price dynamics is the more the trade-off between inflation and unemployment fades away—Phillips curve tends to be vertical even in the short run.

An increase in the money stock thus may have temporary real effects, though effects gradually shift towards pure inflation. In other words, the more the monetary policy tries to utilize the Phillips curves in short-run control, the less it can successfully do so. Short-run Phillips curves do exist but gradually disappear; thus monetary policy cannot exploit them to systematically influence real variables (more specifically, monetary policy actions cannot exhort agents to boost their supply in the long run). Whilst for Friedman such systematic control was possible in spite of the detrimental side effects, Lucas drastically curtailed the set of deceiving policies.

Thus for Lucas money is still non-neutral in the short run if monetary policy can temporarily surprise rational agents, but only in this case and no systematic policy can be built upon this limited potential. A related question is whether monetary policy can be efficient in countercyclical smoothing. The answer is again in the negative. Based on Lucas (1973), Sargent and Wallace (1975, p. 242) introduce a surprise production function:

$$y_t = \alpha_1 k_{t-1} + \alpha_2 \left(p_t - {}_{t-1}p_t^e \right) + \varepsilon_t \tag{2.10}$$

where period t output (y_t) is dependent upon the capital stock available in the previous period (k_{t-1}), current price level (p_t), expectations about the current price level formed in the previous period (${}_{t-1}p_t^e$), and an unpredictable white noise term (ε_t) independent of price expectations so that $E(\varepsilon)=0$ and both $\alpha_1 > 0$ and $\alpha_2 > 0$ (all terms are in natural logarithmic forms). The white noise term is an aggregate level real shock introduced to facilitate the study of its neutralization by monetary policy. So in this framework, as opposed to Lucas's (1972, 1973) island models, it is not only the central bank that is capable of generating aggregate level shocks. The capital part on the right ($\alpha_1 k_{t-1}$) can be referred to as the natural level of output (y_t^*), so Eq. (2.10) is equivalent with the simpler

$$y_t - y_t^* = \alpha \left(p_t - p_t^e \right) + \varepsilon_t \tag{2.11}$$

surprise production function (Begg, 1982, p. 135). If y_t^* is exogeneous, output gap is dependent upon the expectations error and the white noise term. According to Eq. (2.11), equilibrium is not guaranteed even in cases where expectations are correct ($p_t - p_t^e = 0$). Expectations may be fulfilled, but unpredictable shocks to the macro-system can still generate unpredictable fluctuations in the overall performance of the economy. Monetary policy can trigger surprises; it can thus achieve dissatisfaction of expectations, though by so doing it is unable to systematically neutralize unpredictable shocks. As the central bank has no information about period t shock in advance, it cannot design eliminative actions either. Any activist strategy is inadvisable as an intervention may even contribute to the exacerbation of a negative shock. Given this information structure, no successful counter-cyclical policy is feasible. Non-systematic actions (surprises) are still possible, though the resulting overall macroeconomic effects are dependent upon unpredictable conditions. Even though money is non-neutral in the short run, upon this basis monetary policy is unable to establish systematic control over the economy, not even in the short run. The elimination of shocks through monetary policy as a goal is void of sense. The argument for the passivity of monetary policy emerges again.[61]

It is also worthy of note that no central bank can keep the money stock under close control. Begg (1982, p. 138) suggests a simple operative target for the central bank in the

$$m_t = \gamma_1 m_{t-1} + \zeta_t \tag{2.12}$$

form, where m_t stands for the money stock interpreted as one of the monetary aggregates in period t (in logarithmic terms), γ_1 is the monetary policy rule describing the money growth rate, and ζ_t is another white noise term. As Eq. (2.12) shows, if price-level dynamics is related to the money stock, price level is unpredictable even if the monetary policy rule is known and consistently followed: as monetary policy is inevitably fraught with noises. In this case, however, inflation expectations may be incorrect in Sargent and Wallace's (1975) production function even without the purpose of monetary policy to deceive. This circumstance further erodes both the probability of an emergence of macroeconomic equilibrium and the systematic countercyclical efficiency of monetary policy. Results are similar for money multiplier φ between monetary aggregates M_0 and M_1 and white noise term η_t:

$$M_{1,t} = \varphi M_{0,t} + \eta_t \tag{2.13}$$

If a close relation between M_1 and the price level is assumed, even rational agents cannot avoid inflation expectations errors, so on the right side of Eq. (2.11)

$$p_t - {}_{t-1}p_t^e = \eta_t' \tag{2.14}$$

---

[61] The information structure of Lucas's island models is a topic for analysis in Section 4.2.3. It is argued there that Sargent and Wallace's and Lucas's islands are dissimilar in terms of the origins of shocks. In Sargent and Wallace's world agents are exposed to aggregate shocks irrespective of the monetary policy. This is the reason why studying the elimination of shocks by monetary policy emerges as a problem. On Lucas's islands, on the contrary, the only source of aggregate shocks is monetary policy. Local shocks stem from the distribution of supply and demand over the islands.

stands, though these errors are not triggered by the central bank. As monetary policy cannot predict white noise $\eta_t{'}$, it cannot eliminate its effects through discretionary actions. At the end of the day Eq. (2.11) takes the

$$y_t - y_t^* = \alpha\eta_t{'} + \varepsilon_t \qquad (2.15)$$

form. Output gap is under the joint influence of two white noise terms. Monetary policy has neither information nor instruments to neutralize these effects.

Disentangling Hume's surmise

Friedman's and Lucas's monetary theories were aimed at clarifying Hume's monetary ideas.[62] Their models provide characteristic answers why the effects of a rise in the money stock split between inflation and output growth in the short run and why monetary policy has no potential to control real income in the long run. In his famous essays from 1752, 'Of money' and 'Of interest', Hume (1752) suggested the long-run neutrality of money, which has become the basic dogma of modern monetary economics. Whilst Hume emphasized the nominal effects of changes in the money stock, he left some room for temporary real effects. For Hume the long-run neutrality of money stems from the rationality of agents, and he just raised but did not solve the enigma of the short-run real effects of money neutral in the long run. Hume did not go farther than committing to paper the plain observation that before the state of the neutrality of money sets in, there is a period in which money may have real effects. If money is neutral in the long run and if agents are rational, however, money is also supposed to be neutral in the short run, which would be a case in contradiction to Hume's experiences. In Lucas's words:

> Perhaps he simply did not see that the irrelevance of units changes from which he deduces the long-run neutrality of money has similar implications for the initial reaction to money changes as well. [...] If everyone understands that prices will ultimately increase in proportion to the increase in money, what force stops this from happening right away? (Lucas, 1995/1996, p. 663)

---

[62] Lucas discusses his relation to Hume in his Nobel lecture at greatest length (Lucas, 1995/1996). It is a recurrent theme, though with no reference to Hume's name: 'Useful to know that inflation rate [is] dictated [...] by [the] rate of money growth. This is 18th century knowledge, but no less true and useful today. Useful also to know that removal of monetary instability could remove much of real instability – a 20th century finding.' (Hand-written notes. Lucas papers. Box 13. 'Lectures notes, 1979–80' folder) Friedman refers to Hume's two essays as the progressive forerunners of his own theory (Friedman & Schwartz, 1982, p. 623).

Refinements to Hume's early monetary theory were necessitated by his neglect of the mechanisms along which the long-run neutral money can have short-run real effects. Taylor (1998, p. 2) tried to trace Hume's explanation back to the sticky wages and prices assumptions, though Lucas regarded these presumptions as implicit at best. Friedman placed the transitory real effects upon an implausible expectation formation mechanism and further problematic presumptions. In Section 4.1 these assumptions re-emerge as instances for Friedman's instrumentalist methodology. Lucas proposed to solve the puzzle in a rational expectations framework where rational agents have incomplete information on aggregate-level price dynamics. This was his strategy to avoid the trap of introducing temporary real effects at the price of relaxing rationality in the short run, which would have been an explanation inevitably flawed. By so doing, Lucas provided a theory consistent with both the natural rate hypothesis (Friedman, 1968) and the case of monetary-induced real fluctuations Friedman and Schwartz (1963) documented.

2.3.3 New Keynesian modelling: Contributions to clarifying the limitations to the inefficiency of monetary policy

New Keynesian models count as significant contributions to the theoretical developments ranging from orthodox monetarism to new classical macroeconomics. New Keynesian authors considerably broadened our understanding of the conditions under which systematic and anticipated monetary policy is not ineffective even if rational expectations are assumed. Although some empirical results suggested that nominal prices and wages were not fully flexible, traditional Keynesian economics was unable to underpin these typical Keynesian assumptions with an appropriate theory. If these assumptions hold, they establish the channels through which nominal shocks can generate real adjustments. However, if these rigidities are no more than some arbitrary assumptions applied only to ensure real adjustments in the theory, the new classical inefficiency theorem of monetary policy can be saved on the basis of flexibility, underlying rationality, and optimizing behaviour. The most exciting contribution of new Keynesian modelling is the clarification of the reasons why the presence of nominal rigidities does not contradict the axioms of rationality and optimizing behaviour (Ball, Mankiw, & Romer, 1988, pp. 1–2).

Several strategies are available to introduce nominal rigidities. Fischer (1977) studies what happens when flexible adjustment of nominal variables is hindered in a rational expectations framework. In his model the controlling potential of monetary policy stems from a special kind of information deficiency. Fischer draws attention to such non-indexed nominal wage contracts the validity period of which is longer than the time monetary policy needs for reacting to changing conditions. These contracts cause temporary wage rigidity and, consequently, create an opportunity for monetary policy to stabilize the real economy through anticipated (i.e. non-surprise) actions. Employers and employees cannot take new information into account after concluding the contracts. If some conditions emerge which were unforeseen during the negotiation process but monetary policy can react to, output control is feasible even through systematic monetary steps. On the part of agents expectations errors occur, and monetary policy simply plays on them. If rationality holds, however, such temporary wage rigidity cannot ensure a potential of monetary policy to control in the long run as the structure of economy adjusts to policy changes, as Lucas argues. If monetary policy intends to systematically play on temporary wage rigidities, then agents re-open the contracts to re-conclude them on the basis of this information. Phelps and Taylor (1977) analyzing the case of contract-based price rigidities receive similar results. Monetary policy taking advantage of inflexibility is able to control real output even with fully anticipated and systematic actions.

Other cases of staggered price and wage setting explain why the time needed for aggregate adjustment of prices is longer than the frequency of individual price adjustments, resulting in price-level inertia that leads to large and long-lasting real effects. If agents adjust their prices at different moments, then they tend to do small modifications in order to avoid significant real price realignments (Taylor, 1979). When modifying the contracts agents may negotiate whilst having other contracts to be taken into account and this also leads to rather minor adjustments. Agents rather replicate each other's nominal variables (Taylor, 1980). Aggregate price adjustment thus slows down, and nominal shocks have prolonged real effects.

A related question regards the reasons why staggered price and wage setting emerges at all. Ball and Romer (1987) suggest that some market failures lead to staggering. Ball and Cecchetti (1987) explain staggering with information deficiencies: having inadequate information agents imitate others' pricing decisions. Price stickiness may also stem from menu costs. There are costs to flexible and instant price adjustments and as long as the benefits of modification do not outgrow these costs, price re-setting is delayed. On this showing, price stickiness is the result of some rational considerations (Mankiw, 1985). However, stickiness may equally result from a lack of complete rationality when such sub-optimal behaviour has low costs. If the benefits from perfect rationality are small, agents will take on the small costs and make do with non-maximizing behaviour (Akerlof & Yellen, 1985/2005). Menu costs and staggering wage and price setting mutually reinforce one another. When nominal rigidities stemming from menu costs hold, a staggering structure slows down price-level adjustment (Ball et al., 1988, p. 12).

Taylor (1975) studies possible monetary policy actions in a setting where agents after a structural shift in monetary policy can temporarily predict future policy actions with distortions only. As long as expectations are not rational, monetary policy can surprise agents even with systematic actions for its new policy rule is unknown yet. Monetary policy can well be characterized with the variance and the mean or expected value of inflation. After a structural shift, the public is uncertain about the mean, and during the transition taken as a learning process new information is mixed with old beliefs. Before agents become familiar with the new expected value they need to resort to the past mean. As a consequence, until rational expectations and unbiased predictions re-emerge (i.e. the new expected value becomes known), expectations are formed as if the public followed an adaptive scheme. During the transition from one monetary policy regime to the next the public switches from a factually adaptive scheme to rational expectations. If the time necessary for regaining the ability to form rational expectations is also taken into account, temporary real effects emerge even with optimizing agents. Just as in Fischer's model, this policy efficiency does not amount to a rehabilitation of systematic monetary policy. Retarding the public in building up rational expectations may have detrimental side effects.

2.3.4 Curtailing the potential of fiscal policy

Friedman (1957) had serious reservations about the potential of fiscal policy to control aggregate demand just as he regarded activist monetary policy as of dubious value. To argue against fiscal policy interventions he suggested a new framework, his permanent income hypothesis, in which some of the concerns about monetary policy (policy responds with considerable lags) still hold (Friedman, 1968, p. 3).

Permanent income is a simple annuity into which an optimizing agent calculates her expected disposable income. If households are assumed to decide on consumption expenditures on the basis of their permanent income, the resulting theory can, on the one hand, explain the discrepancy between statistically smooth aggregate consumption and strongly fluctuating current income and, on the other hand, eliminate the reliable link traditionally supposed to relate consumption to current income. In the lack of the latter, however, the simple Keynesian case for fiscal policy control over aggregate demand comes to nothing. For a stimulation of consumption a change in permanent income is needed (Houthakker, 1958, pp. 397–398).

As far as the limitations of fiscal policy are concerned, expectations are of high importance as it is the expectation formation mechanism that determines what information set agents utilize when forming expectations about their permanent incomes. Consequently, expectation formation illuminates how current income ought to change to modify permanent income estimations. According to Friedman's adaptive scheme, permanent income calculations rest upon past information (Holbrook & Stafford, 1971). Permanent income is assumed to be the weighted average of past current incomes with decreasing weights. Even if current disposable income increases, there are only minor instantaneous corrections to permanent income. In other words, current consumption expenditures are dependent upon past incomes to a large extent (Friedman, 1957, p. 238).

This is a serious limitation to fiscal policy. In order to significantly stimulate consumption, policy needs to trigger a significant upward revision in permanent income. With adaptive expectations a long-lasting level shift in disposable income generates a gradual convergence of permanent income. Thus the adjustment or revision process is slow. The effect of a one-time fiscal stimulus is slight and temporary, whilst a long-lasting stimulus can exert influence only gradually (Galbács, 2015, pp. 229–240). In consequence, the stimulative potential of fiscal policy weakens, though does not fall through. In Friedman's adaptive scheme, any change in disposable income drives agents to recalculate their permanent incomes.

With rational assumptions assumed the relevant information set is broader. Agents under such conditions may revise their permanent incomes even before current incomes change, and permanent income may remain fixed even in spite of changes in current incomes. The Barro-Ricardo equivalence theorem taken as a rational expectations extension of Friedman's permanent income hypothesis thus sets further limits on the possibilities of fiscal stimulation (Barro, 1974; Seater, 1993). The underlying story is simple. Fiscal policy cuts lump sum taxes (the story remains the same with an increase in transfer payments), whilst it tries to keep government expenditures on the previous path. The resulting tension between unchanged expenditures and lower tax revenues compels the government to cover the deficit with bond issuance in a sum equal to the tax cut. The government plans to pay the bond debt out of a subsequent tax increase timed to the maturity date.[63] The equivalence theorem studies whether this fiscal mix has effects on consumer expenditures. The answer is unaffirmative. Agents forming rational expectations do relate the promise of a subsequent tax increase to the mix of tax cut and bond issuance and, as a consequence, refuse to spend the money from tax cut

---

[63] The tax cut is the present value of the subsequent bond debt and, equivalently, the tax increase is the future value of tax cut, so between the end points there is a single rate of interest applying to both the public and the government. As a further assumption, government expenditures are equal to tax revenues and borrowing in each period. It follows that the present value of taxes can change only if the present value of expenditures changes (Barro, 1989).

on consumption. If they decide to purchase bonds out of the increase in disposable income, the equivalence is perfect. Agents save up to cover the tax increase they expect.

Equivalence theorem is a far cry from a categorical denial of fiscal control as inefficiency rests upon a crucial assumption of unchanged government expenditures. In other words, the debt-tax swap is ineffective only if expenditures are kept intact. Several further factors weaken the exact equivalence. Such a factor is the prohibition of monetization: the debt-tax swap is inefficient only if economic policy refrains from covering the bond debt with running the money printing press. If it does not, the tax cut will have transitory real effects, even if monetization does not take rational agents by surprise. After aggregate demand has risen, output and inflation dynamics is dependent upon supply and price reactions. With rational expectations the only question regards the timing of real effects. Fiscal policy can modify its previous decision to substitute monetization for the expected tax increase: real effects emerge when the government makes this decision. Real effects also occur when the government levies consumption taxes to cover its debt (Cullis & Jones, 2009, pp. 321–325).

Prolonging the debt service is a further option of triggering real adjustments. In such a case, the government rolls over the bond debt for an extended period by covering debt services with issuing new bonds time and again. When fiscal policy, by contrast, does not or cannot continue postponing the payments and decides on a tax increase, a negative shock will offset the prior favourable real effects. In this case, the public spend the monies from tax cut on consumption. As a prerequisite, agents must believe prolongation to be maintainable until the end of time or at least until the death of the currently active generation, but no dynastic inter-generation connections via transfers are allowed (Blanchard, 1985). If so, utility of a generation is partly dependent upon the utility of their descendants. In consequence, any generation regards their descendants as their own extensions and tries to free the children from an expected tax burden via savings. Altruism expands the time horizon of finitely living agents to infinity; thus the sequence of finitely living individuals gives way to a single, infinitely living dynastic family taken as a representative agent (Bernheim & Bagwell, 1988). There are exceptions, of course, such as some intergeneration transfers aimed at influencing the inheritors in behavioural terms and not at saving up for future tax burdens (Bernheim, Shleifer, & Summers, 1985). If subsequent generations are connected via mutual altruism (children are concerned about their parents' well-being and vice versa), equivalence does not hold again (Kotlikoff, Razin, & Rosenthal, 1990). Uncertainties over expected lifetime further erode the equivalence (Levhari & Mirman, 1977; Yaari, 1965).

All this leads to the conclusion that under some precisely specified conditions countercyclical fiscal policy is ineffective. Even though uncertainty of lifetime, altruism, or preferences may well erode the equivalence, a basic question of economic policy consequences still regards the effects of changing budgetary expenditures. But for changes in government outlays, agents would refuse to modify their consumption paths; thus any attempt of fiscal policy to countercyclically stimulate the real economy would be doomed to failure. Structural reforms to government expenditures and improvements to public sector efficiency, however, have real effects, though not in a countercyclical way but via affecting the long-run growth potential (Galbács, 2015, pp. 258–271). By introducing rational expectations, theoretical developments after Friedman kept weakening fiscal policy potential for systematic demand management.

2.4 Conclusions: Arguments for dampening the contrast between Friedman and Lucas

Having studied the complex relationship between Lucas and Chicago economics, one definite conclusion emerges: there are no clear-cut inferences to draw. Any such attempts or efforts would inevitably lead to some oversimplifications. The aspects reviewed above are points in favour of a connection fraught with tensions.

This connection shows its most powerful facet in the emphasis Lucas placed upon the choice-theoretic framework. Chicago economics as a research and education programme rested on the extended and consistent use of neoclassical price theory. The transition of economics into an objective and unified science has gradually taken place. First, the scope of economics has considerably shrunk to exclude debates over values and purposes and to become a focused discipline. This new economics was aimed at solving the technical problems of allocating scarce resources between alternative but pre-set uses. The taking of this step was mostly Friedman's achievement. Second, this focused technical economics has drawn more and more diverse social phenomena to its territory to perform systematic analyses. At the bottom line, according to Stigler and Becker's hypothesis, a vast array of individual actions are decisions regarding the alternative uses of some broadly interpreted scarce resources. Irrespective of the objects of decisions, agents compare expected costs and expected benefits. Subscribing to this approach Lucas traced back the multi-faceted phenomena of large-scale macroeconomic fluctuations to individual decisions and, by so doing, he joined the Chicago tradition.

Lucas, however, broke up with Chicago's strong Marshallian inclination. As it is argued above, his reasons are biographical. Samuelson had already been an influence on Lucas before he was exposed to Marshallian economics in Friedman's price theory sequence. After his graduation he left Chicago for a decade. Carnegie Tech was the institution where Lucas fruitfully responding to the intellectual impressions established his most influential theoretical contributions. Amongst these impressions it is his taking the rational expectations hypothesis and Walrasian general equilibrium economics seriously that took him away from the Chicago traditions to a distance. An assessment, however, ought to be careful enough to take into account the scientific standards along which Lucas breathed new life into neo-Walrasian economics. Even though the high level of abstraction was probably not to Friedman's liking, Lucas with his emphasis upon empirical testing and out-of-sample considerations met some of Friedman's objections to anti-empiricist Walrasian theory.

Friedman's Marshallianism and Lucas's Walrasianism, so to speak, render their relationship an episode of the Marshall–Walras divide. In consequence, it is inevitable to emphatically scrutinize the dissimilarities. The Marshall–Walras divide as an academic debate regards the appropriate way of theorizing, the use of mathematics, and the desired level of abstraction. As a matter of fact, it is rather some rhetoric achievements than references to some principled discrepancies that occasionally dominated the subsequent episodes of the debate. Some artificially incited conflicts, however, could not endow these approaches with unique characteristics. Efforts to exclusively utilize either induction or deduction failed to prove to be feasible theorizing options. Even though the emphases can change, deductive logic needs inductive theorizing in order to maintain connections with reality, and inductive theorizing alone similarly fails if the outcome is supposed to be a theory with some testable implications deduced from the set of assumptions. Due to the contributions by Lucas and the Cowles Commission, the differentiation based on the empirical implications was also ineffective. The emphasis upon some rhetorical origins of the differences dampens the contrast between Friedman and Lucas.

Studying the theoretical transition between Friedman and Lucas does not lead to unambiguous answers either. This transition gave birth to a theory that explained monetary short-run non-neutrality and long-run neutrality, Hume's age-old surmise in monetary economics, in a unified framework with no spurious assumptions. The pre-Lucasian suggestions, including Friedman's monetarism, providing answers to only one of the issues were dissatisfying. Assuming rationality away either partially or wholly cannot be a viable option for it is rationality that explains long-run neutrality. Lucas formulized his answers in a theory that had a lot in common with Friedman's analytical framework. Both the taking of expectations into account and the idea of a vertical long-run Phillips curve are such shared elements that discourage us from interpreting their relationship as a radical break-up. As it is argued in what follows, another aspect of this relation can be more readily regarded as a drastic opposition. Lucas's reality-based choice-theoretic framework is the point where he definitely turned against Friedman's neglect of causal understanding.

Suggested readings

Some comprehensive works (Emmett, 2010b; Van Horn, Mirowski, & Stapleford, 2011) on Chicago economics are the best choices to start with when one wants to nurture in-depth knowledge about the history of the school. Van Overtveldt (2007) and Ebenstein (2015) provide intriguing and popular summaries which are full of stories to introduce the personalities standing behind the great minds of Chicago. McGrath (1948) and MacAloon (1992) give assessments on the general educational programme of the University of Chicago and other institutions. De Vroey (1999, 2004, 2009) has a series of publications devoted to the problem of the Marshall–Walras divide. Leonard J. Savage compiled an anthology of Milton Friedman's papers on economics (Friedman, 2007). Robert Lucas's 'Studies in business-cycle theory' (Lucas, 1981) and 'Collected papers on monetary theory' (Lucas, 2013) are exhaustive selections of his works in monetary dynamics and business-cycle theories. Galbács (2015) offers a systematic overview on Friedman's monetarism and Lucas's new classical macroeconomics.

References

Akerlof, G. A., & Yellen, J. L. (1985/2005). A near-rational model of the business cycle, with wage and price inertia. In G. A. Akerlof (Ed.), *Explorations in pragmatic economics* (pp. 410–423). Oxford: Oxford University Press.

Allen, S. G. (1954). Inventory fluctuations in flaxseed and linseed oil, 1926–1939. *Econometrica*, 22(3), 310–327.

Ball, L., & Cecchetti, S. G. (1987). *Imperfect information and staggered price settings.* NBER working paper no. 2201, Cambridge, MA: National Bureau of Economic Research.

Ball, L., & Romer, D. (1987). *The equilibrium and optimal timing of price changes.* NBER working paper no. 2412, Cambridge, MA: National Bureau of Economic Research.

Ball, L., Mankiw, N. G., & Romer, D. (1988). The new Keynesian economics and the output-inflation trade-off. *Brookings Papers on Economic Activity*, 19(1), 1–82.

Barro, R. J. (1974). Are government bonds net wealth? *Journal of Political Economy*, 82(6), 1095–1117.

Barro, R. J. (1989). The Ricardian approach to budget deficits. *Journal of Economic Perspectives*, 3(2), 37–54.

Bateman, B. W. (1998). Clearing the ground. The demise of the social gospel movement and the rise of neoclassicism in American economics. In M. S. Morgan & M. Rutherford (Eds.), *From interwar pluralism to postwar neoclassicism* (pp. 29–52). Durham, NC: Duke University Press.

Becker, G. S. (1971). *Economic theory.* New York: Alfred A. Knopf.

Becker, G. S. (1976). *The economic approach to human behavior.* Chicago: The University of Chicago Press.

Becker, G. S. (1991). Milton Friedman. In E. Shils (Ed.), *Remembering the University of Chicago. Teachers, scientists, and scholars* (pp. 138–146). Chicago: The University of Chicago Press.

Becker, G. S. (1993a). George Joseph Stigler. January 17, 1911–December 1, 1991. *Journal of Political Economy*, 101(5), 761–767.

Becker, G. S. (1993b). The economic way of looking at behavior. Nobel lecture. *Journal of Political Economy*, 101(3), 385–409.

Becker, G. S. (1994). George Joseph Stigler (17 January 1911–1 December 1991). *Proceedings of the American Philosophical Society*, *138*(2), 348–354.

Begg, D. K. (1982). *The rational expectations revolution in macroeconomics. Theories and evidence.* Oxford: Philip Allan.

Bernheim, B. D., & Bagwell, K. (1988). Is everything neutral? *Journal of Political Economy*, *96*(2), 308–338.

Bernheim, B. D., Shleifer, A., & Summers, L. H. (1985). The strategic bequest motive. *Journal of Political Economy*, *93*(6), 1045–1076.

Blanchard, O. J. (1985). Debt, deficits, and finite horizons. *Journal of Political Economy*, *93*(2), 223–247.

Blaug, M. (1992). *The methodology of economics or how economists explain* (2nd ed.). Cambridge: Cambridge University Press.

Borts, G. H. (1952). Production relations in the railway industry. *Econometrica*, *20*(1), 71–79.

Boumans, M. (2005). *How economists model the world into numbers.* Abingdon: Routledge.

Brainard, W. C., & Cooper, R. N. (1975). Empirical monetary macroeconomics. What have we learned in the last 25 years? *The American Economic Review*, *65*(2), 167–175.

Bronfenbrenner, M. (1962). Observations on the "Chicago School(s)". *Journal of Political Economy*, *70*(1), 72–75.

Burns, A. F., & Mitchell, W. C. (1946). *Measuring business cycles.* New York: National Bureau of Economic Research.

Cagan, P. (1956). The monetary dynamics of hyperinflation. In M. Friedman (Ed.), *Studies in the quantity theory of money* (pp. 25–117). Chicago: The University of Chicago Press.

Chernoff, H., & Divinsky, N. (1953). The computation of maximum-likelihood estimates of linear structural equations. In W. C. Hood & T. C. Koopmans (Eds.), *Studies in econometric method* (pp. 236–269). New York: John Wiley & Sons.

Cherrier, B. (2011). The lucky consistency of Milton Friedman's science and politics, 1933–1963. In R. Van Horn, P. Mirowski, & T. A. Stapleford (Eds.), *Building Chicago economics. New perspectives on the history of America's most powerful economics program* (pp. 335–367). Cambridge: Cambridge University Press.

Christ, C. F. (1994). The Cowles Commission's contributions to econometrics at Chicago, 1939–1955. *Journal of Economic Literature*, *32*(1), 30–59.

Coats, A. W. (1963). The origins of the "Chicago School(s)"? *Journal of Political Economy*, *71*(5), 487–493.

Cowles Commission. (1952). *Economic theory and measurement. A twenty year research report, 1932–1952.* Chicago: The University of Chicago.

Cullis, J., & Jones, P. (2009). *Public finance and public choice. Analytical perspectives* (3rd ed.). Oxford: Oxford University Press.

De Vroey, M. (1999). The Marshallian market and the Walrasian economy. Two incompatible bedfellows. *Scottish Journal of Political Economy*, *46*(3), 319–338.

De Vroey, M. (2004). The history of macroeconomics viewed against the background of the Marshall–Walras divide. *History of Political Economy*, *36*(AS1), 57–91.

De Vroey, M. (2009). A Marshall–Walras divide? A critical review of the prevailing viewpoints. *History of Political Economy*, *41*(4), 709–736.

De Vroey, M. (2016). *A history of macroeconomics from Keynes to Lucas and beyond.* Cambridge: Cambridge University Press.

Director, A. (1947/1948). Prefatory note. In H. C. Simons (Ed.), *Economic policy for a free society* (pp. v–vii). Chicago: The University of Chicago Press.

Donzelli, F. (2007). Equilibrium and "tâtonnement" in Walras's "Eléments". *History of Economic Ideas*, *15*(3), 85–138.

Ebenstein, A. (2003). *Hayek's journey. The mind of Friedrich Hayek.* New York: Palgrave MacMillan.

Ebenstein, L. (2015). *Chicagonomics. The evolution of Chicago free market economics.* New York: St. Martin's Press.

Emmett, R. B. (1994a). Frank Knight. Economics versus religion. In H. G. Brennan & A. M. Waterman (Eds.), *Economics and religion. Are they distinct?* (pp. 103–120). Boston: Kluwer.

Emmett, R. B. (1994b). Maximizers versus good sports. Frank Knight's curious understanding of exchange behavior. *History of Political Economy, 26*(S1), 276–292.

Emmett, R. B. (1997). "What is truth" in capital theory? Five stories relevant to the evaluation of Frank H. Knight's contributions to the capital controversy. In J. B. Davis (Ed.), *New economics and its history* (pp. 231–250). Durham, NC: Duke University Press.

Emmett, R. B. (1998a). Frank Knight's dissent from progressive social science. In R. P. Holt & S. Pressman (Eds.), *Economics and its discontents. Twentieth century dissenting economists* (pp. 153–164). Cheltenham: Edward Elgar.

Emmett, R. B. (1998b). Entrenching disciplinary competence. The role of general education and graduate study in Chicago economics. *History of Political Economy, 30*(S), 134–150.

Emmett, R. B. (1999). Introduction. In F. H. Knight & R. B. Emmett (Eds.), *Vol. 1. Selected essays* (pp. vii–xxiv). Chicago: The University of Chicago Press.

Emmett, R. B. (2006a). Frank Knight, Max Weber, Chicago economics and institutionalism. *Max Weber Studies, 7*(1), 101–119.

Emmett, R. B. (2006b). De gustibus est. disputandum. Frank Knight's reply to George Stigler and Gary Becker's "De gustibus non est disputandum" with an introductory essay. *Journal of Economic Methodology, 13*(1), 97–111.

Emmett, R. B. (2007). Oral history and the historical reconstruction of Chicago economics. *History of Political Economy, 39*(S1), 172–192.

Emmett, R. B. (2008). How should we think of the success of the Chicago school of economics? In W. J. Samuels, J. E. Biddle, & R. B. Emmett (Eds.), *Vol. 26A. Research in the history of economic thought and methodology* (pp. 47–57). Bingley: Emerald.

Emmett, R. B. (2009). Did the Chicago school reject Frank Knight? Assessing Frank Knight's place in the Chicago economics tradition. In R. B. Emmett (Ed.), *Frank Knight and the Chicago school in American economics* (pp. 145–155). London: Routledge.

Emmett, R. B. (2010a). Specializing in interdisciplinarity. The Committee on Social Thought as the University of Chicago's antidote to compartmentalization in the social sciences. *History of Political Economy, 42*(S1), 261–287.

Emmett, R. B. (Ed.), (2010b). *The Elgar companion to the Chicago school of economics.* Cheltenham: Edward Elgar.

Emmett, R. B. (2011). Sharpening tools in the workshop. In R. Van Horn, P. Mirowski, & T. A. Stapleford (Eds.), *Building Chicago economics. New perspectives on the history of America's most powerful economics program* (pp. 93–115). Cambridge: Cambridge University Press.

Emmett, R. B. (2013). *Frank H. Knight and the Committee on Social Thought. Contrasting visions of interdisciplinarity in the 1950s.* Unpublished working paper, East Lansing: Michigan State University, James Madison College.

Emmett, R. B. (2015). *Frank H. Knight and the Chicago school. Conference presentation, 'The legacy of Chicago economics', 5 October 2015.* Chicago: The University of Chicago.

Epstein, R. J. (1987). *A history of econometrics.* Amsterdam: North Holland.

Fabricant, S. (1984). *Toward a firmer basis of economic policy. The founding of the National Bureau of Economic Research.* New York: National Bureau of Economic Research.

Fischer, S. (1977). Long-term contracts, rational expectations, and the optimal money supply rule. *Journal of Political Economy, 85*(1), 191–205.

Friedman, B. M. (1978). *Discussion.* In *After the Phillips curve. Persistence of high inflation and high unemployment* (pp. 73–80). Boston: Federal Reserve Bank of Boston.

Friedman, M. (1940). Review paper. Business cycles in the United States of America, 1919–1932 by J. Tinbergen. *The American Economic Review, 30*(3), 657–660.

Friedman, M. (1946a). Some correspondence on methodology between Milton Friedman and Edwin B. Wilson. In R. Leeson & C. G. Palm (Eds.), *The collected works of Milton Friedman.* Stanford: Hoover Institute.

Friedman, M. (1946b). Lange on price flexibility and employment. A methodological criticism. *The American Economic Review, 36*(4), 613–631.

Friedman, M. (1949). The Marshallian demand curve. *Journal of Political Economy, 57*(6), 463–495.

Friedman, M. (1951/1960). *Notes on lectures in price theory*. Chicago: Mimeo, Distributed by the Department of Economics, the University of Chicago.

Friedman, M. (1952). Comment on "Methodological developments" by Richard Ruggles. In R. Leeson & C. G. Palm (Eds.), *The collected works of Milton Friedman*. Stanford: Hoover Institution.

Friedman, M. (1953). Comment on "Some contemporary tendencies in economic research". In R. Leeson & C. G. Palm (Eds.), *The collected works of Milton Friedman*. Stanford: Hoover Institution.

Friedman, M. (1953/2009). The methodology of positive economics. In U. Mäki (Ed.), *The methodology of positive economics. Reflections on the Milton Friedman legacy* (pp. 3–43). Cambridge: Cambridge University Press.

Friedman, M. (1955). Leon Walras and his economic system. *The American Economic Review, 45*(5), 900–909.

Friedman, M. (Ed.), (1956a). *Studies in the quantity theory of money*. Chicago: The University of Chicago Press.

Friedman, M. (1956b). The quantity theory of money. A restatement. In M. Friedman (Ed.), *Studies in the quantity theory of money* (pp. 3–21). Chicago: The University of Chicago Press.

Friedman, M. (1957). *A theory of the consumption function*. Princeton: Princeton University Press.

Friedman, M. (1958/1969). The supply of money and changes in prices and output. In M. Friedman (Ed.), *The optimum quantity of money and other essays* (pp. 171–187). Chicago: Aldine.

Friedman, M. (1959). *The demand for money. Some theoretical and empirical results*. Cambridge, MA: National Bureau of Economic Research.

Friedman, M. (1966/2007). Interest rates and the demand for money. In M. Friedman & L. J. Savage (Eds.), *Milton Friedman on economics. Selected papers* (pp. 120–134). Chicago: The University of Chicago Press.

Friedman, M. (1967). Value judgements in economics. In S. Hook (Ed.), *Human values and economic policy. A symposium* (pp. 85–93). New York: New York University Press.

Friedman, M. (1968). The role of monetary policy. *The American Economic Review, 58*(1), 1–17.

Friedman, M. (1970). A theoretical framework for monetary analysis. *Journal of Political Economy, 78*(2), 193–238.

Friedman, M. (1971). A monetary theory of nominal income. *Journal of Political Economy, 79*(2), 323–337.

Friedman, M. (1974). Schools at Chicago. In the Midwest they have flourished without threatening the University's traditional heterodoxy. *The University of Chicago Magazine, 67*(1), 11–16.

Friedman, M. (1976a). *Biography of Milton Friedman*. Retrieved Sept 27, 2018, from Nobelprize. orghttps://www.nobelprize.org/prizes/economics/1976/friedman/auto-biography/.

Friedman, M. (1976b). *Price theory*. Chicago: Aldine.

Friedman, M. (1977). Inflation and unemployment. Nobel lecture. *Journal of Political Economy, 85*(3), 451–472.

Friedman, M. (2007). In L. J. Savage (Ed.), *Milton Friedman on economics. Selected papers*. Chicago: The University of Chicago Press.

Friedman, M., & Schwartz, A. J. (1963). *A monetary history of the United States, 1867–1960*. Princeton: Princeton University Press.

Friedman, M., & Schwartz, A. J. (1965). Money and business cycles. In NBER (Eds.), *The state of monetary economics* (pp. 32–78). Cambridge, MA: National Bureau of Economic Research.

Friedman, M., & Schwartz, A. J. (1982). *Monetary trends in the United States and the United Kingdom. Their relation to income, prices, and interest rates, 1867–1975*. Chicago: The University of Chicago Press.

Frodin, R. (1992). Very simple, but thoroughgoing. In D. N. Levine (Ed.), *The idea and practice of general education* (pp. 25–99). Chicago: The University of Chicago Press.

Galbács, P. (2015). *The theory of new classical macroeconomics*. New York: Springer.

Girschick, M. A., & Haavelmo, T. (1953). Statistical analysis of the demand for food. Examples of simultaneous estimation of structural equations. In W. C. Hood & T. C. Koopmans (Eds.), *Studies in econometric method* (pp. 92–111). New York: John Wiley & Sons.

Goodwin, C. D. (1998). The patrons of economics in a time of transformation. In M. S. Morgan & M. Rutherford (Eds.), *From interwar pluralism to postwar neoclassicism* (pp. 53–81). Durham, NC: Duke University Press.

Gordon, R. (1979). *New evidence that fully anticipated monetary changes influence real output after all*. NBER working paper no. 361, Cambridge, MA: National Bureau of Economic Research.

Gramm, W. S. (1975). Chicago economics. From individualism true to individualism false. *Journal of Economic Issues, 9*(4), 753–775.

Haavelmo, T. (1943). The statistical implications of a system of simultaneous equations. *Econometrica, 11*(1), 1–12.

Haavelmo, T. (1953). Methods of measuring the marginal propensity to consume. In W. C. Hood & T. C. Koopmans (Eds.), *Studies in econometric method* (pp. 75–91). New York: John Wiles & Sons.

Hahn, F. H. (1984). *Equilibrium and macroeconomics*. Cambridge, MA: MIT Press.

Hammond, J. D. (1988). An interview with Milton Friedman on methodology. In R. Leeson & C. G. Palm (Eds.), *The collected works of Milton Friedman*. Stanford: Hoover Institution.

Hammond, J. D. (1996). *Theory and measurement. Causality issues in Milton Friedman's monetary economics*. Cambridge: Cambridge University Press.

Hammond, J. D. (2010). The development of post-war Chicago price theory. In R. B. Emmett (Ed.), *The Elgar companion to the Chicago school of economics* (pp. 7–24). Cheltenham: Edward Elgar.

Hammond, J. D. (2011). Markets, politics, and democracy at Chicago. Taking economics seriously. In R. Van Horn, P. Mirowski, & T. A. Stapleford (Eds.), *Building Chicago economics. New perspectives on the history of America's most powerful economics program* (pp. 36–63). Cambridge: Cambridge University Press.

Hamowy, R. (2008). Chicago school of economics. In R. Hamowy (Ed.), *The encyclopedia of libertarianism* (pp. 135–137). Los Angeles: SAGE.

Henderson, J. P. (1976). The history of thought in the development of the Chicago paradigm. In W. J. Samuels (Ed.), *The Chicago school of political economy* (pp. 341–361). East Lansing: Michigan State University.

Hildreth, C., & Jarrett, F. G. (1955). *A statistical study of livestock production and marketing*. New York: John Wiley & Sons.

Hirsch, E., & Hirsch, A. (1976). The heterodox methodology of two Chicago economists. In W. J. Samuels (Ed.), *The Chicago school of political economy* (pp. 59–78). East Lansing: Michigan State University.

Hodgson, G. M. (2001). Frank Knight as an institutional economist. In J. E. Biddle, J. B. Davis, & S. G. Medema (Eds.), *Economics broadly considered. Essays in honour of Warren J. Samuels* (pp. 64–93). London: Routledge.

Holbrook, R., & Stafford, F. (1971). The propensity to consume separate types of income. A generalized permanent income hypothesis. *Econometrica, 39*(1), 1–21.

Hoover, K. D. (2009). Milton Friedman's stance. The methodology of causal realism. In U. Mäki (Ed.), *The methodology of positive economics. Reflections on the Milton Friedman legacy* (pp. 303–320). Cambridge: Cambridge University Press.

Houthakker, H. S. (1958). The permanent income hypothesis. *The American Economic Review*, *48*(3), 396–404.

Hume, D. (1752). *Political discourses*. Edinburgh: Fleming.

Hurwicz, L. (1950). Prediction and least squares. In T. C. Koopmans (Ed.), *Statistical inference in dynamic economic models* (pp. 266–300). New York: John Wiley & Sons.

Kant, I. (1781/1998). In P. Guyer & A. W. Wood (Eds.), *Critique of pure reason*. Cambridge: Cambridge University Press.

Kant, I. (1783/1997). In G. Hatfield (Ed.), *Prolegomena to any future metaphysics that will be able to come forward as science*. Cambridge: Cambridge University Press.

Klein, J. J. (1956). German money and prices, 1932–44. In M. Friedman (Ed.), *Studies in the quantity theory of money* (pp. 121–159). Chicago: The University of Chicago Press.

Klein, L. R. (1950). *Economic fluctuations in the United States, 1921–1941*. New York: John Wiley & Sons.

Knight, F. H. (1924/1999). The limitations of scientific method in economics. In F. H. Knight & R. B. Emmett (Eds.), *1. Selected essays* (pp. 1–39). Chicago: The University of Chicago Press.

Knight, F. H. (1925/1935). Economic psychology and the value problem. In F. H. Knight, M. Friedman, H. Jones, G. Stigler, & A. Wallis (Eds.), *The ethics of competition and other essays* (pp. 76–104). Freeport: Books for Libraries Press.

Knight, F. H. (1928). Homan's contemporary economic thought. *The Quarterly Journal of Economics*, *43*(1), 132–141.

Knight, F. H. (1948/1956). Free society. Its basic nature and problem. In F. H. Knight, W. L. Letwin, & A. J. Morin (Eds.), *On the history and method of economics* (pp. 282–299). Chicago: The University of Chicago Press.

Koopmans, T. C. (1947). Measurement without theory. *The Review of Economics and Statistics*, *29*(3), 161–172.

Koopmans, T. C. (1950). The equivalence of maximum-likelihood and least-squares estimates of regression coefficients. In T. C. Koopmans (Ed.), *Statistical inference in dynamic economic models* (pp. 301–304). New York: John Wiley & Sons.

Kotlikoff, L. J., Razin, A., & Rosenthal, R. W. (1990). A strategic altruism model in which Ricardian equivalence does not hold. *The Economic Journal*, *100*(12), 1261–1268.

Kuhn, T. S. (1962). *The structure of scientific revolutions* (3rd ed.). Chicago: The University of Chicago Press.

Lange, O. (1944). *Price flexibility and employment*. Bloomington: The Principal Press.

Lerner, E. M. (1956). Inflation in the Confederacy, 1861–65. In M. Friedman (Ed.), *Studies in the quantity theory of money* (pp. 163–175). Chicago: The University of Chicago Press.

Levhari, D., & Mirman, L. J. (1977). Savings and consumption with an uncertain horizon. *Journal of Political Economy*, *85*(2), 265–281.

Lothian, J. R. (2009). Milton Friedman's monetary economics and the quantity-theory tradition. *Journal of International Money and Finance*, *28*(7), 1086–1096.

Lothian, J. R. (2016). Milton Friedman's monetary economics. In R. A. Cord & J. D. Hammond (Eds.), *Milton Friedman. Contributions to economics and public policy* (pp. 178–197). Oxford: Oxford University Press.

Loveday, A. (1939). Preface. In J. Tinbergen (Ed.), *Statistical testing of business-cycle theories. A method and its application to investment activity* (pp. 9–10). Geneva: League of Nations.

Lucas, R. E. (1972). Expectations and the neutrality of money. *Journal of Economic Theory*, (2), 103–124.

Lucas, R. E. (1973). Some international evidence on output-inflation tradeoffs. *The American Economic Review*, *63*(3), 326–334.

Lucas, R. E. (1975). An equilibrium model of the business cycle. *Journal of Political Economy*, *83*(6), 1113–1144.

Lucas, R. E. (1976/1981). Econometric policy evaluation. A critique. In R. E. Lucas (Ed.), *Studies in business cycle theory* (pp. 104–130). Oxford: Basil Blackwell.

Lucas, R. E. (1980). Methods and problems in business cycle theory. *Journal of Money, Credit and Banking, 12*(4), 696–715.

Lucas, R. E. (1981). *Studies in business-cycle theory*. Oxford: Basil Blackwell.

Lucas, R. E. (1995). *Biography of Robert E. Lucas, Jr.* Retrieved Sept 27, 2018, from Nobelprize. org, https://www.nobelprize.org/prizes/economics/1995/lucas/auto-biography/.

Lucas, R. E. (1995/1996). Monetary neutrality. Nobel lecture. *Journal of Political Economy, 104*(4), 661–682.

Lucas, R. E. (2001). *Professional memoir*. Mimeo.

Lucas, R. E. (2013). In M. Gillman (Ed.), *Collected papers on monetary theory*. Cambridge, MA: Harvard University Press.

Lucas, R. E., & Rapping, L. A. (1969). Real wages, employment, and inflation. *Journal of Political Economy, 69*(5), 721–754.

Lucas, R. E., & Rapping, L. A. (1972). Unemployment in the Great Depression. Is there a full explanation? *Journal of Political Economy, 80*(1), 186–191.

Lucas, R. E., & Sargent, T. J. (1979). After Keynesian macroeconomics. *Federal Reserve Bank of Minneapolis Quarterly Review, 3*(2), 1–16.

MacAloon, J. J. (Ed.), (1992). *General education in the social sciences. Centennial reflections on the College of the University of Chicago*. Chicago: The University of Chicago Press.

Manicas, P. T. (2006). *A realist philosophy of social science. Explanation and understanding*. Cambridge: Cambridge University Press.

Mankiw, N. G. (1985). Small menu costs and large business cycles. A macroeconomic model of monopoly. *The Quarterly Journal of Economics, 100*(2), 529–537.

Marschak, J. (1950). Statistical inference in economics. An introduction. In T. C. Koopmans (Ed.), *Statistical inference in dynamic economic models* (pp. 1–50). New York: John Wiley & Sons.

Marschak, J., & Andrews, W. H. (1944). Random simultaneous equations and the theory of production. *Econometrica, 12*(3/4), 143–205.

Marshall, A. (1885). *The present position of economics*. London: MacMillan and Co.

Marshall, A. (1920/2013). *Principles of economics* (8th ed.). New York: Palgrave MacMillan.

Marshall, A. (1925). In A. C. Pigou (Ed.), *Memorials of Alfred Marshall*. London: MacMillan and Co.

McCallum, B. T. (2007). An interview with Robert E. Lucas, Jr. In P. A. Samuelson & W. A. Barnett (Eds.), *Inside the economist's mind. Conversations with eminent economists* (pp. 57). Oxford: Blackwell.

McGrath, E. J. (Ed.), (1948). *Social science in general education*. Dubuque: W.M.C. Brown Company.

McKinney, J. (1975). Frank H. Knight and Chicago libertarianism. *Journal of Economic Issues, 9*(4), 777–799.

Medema, S. G. (2011). Chicago price theory and Chicago law and economics. A tale of two transitions. In R. Van Horn, P. Mirowski, & T. A. Stapleford (Eds.), *Building Chicago economics. New perspectives on the history of America's most powerful economics program* (pp. 151–179). Cambridge: Cambridge University Press.

Medema, S. G. (2014). *Identifying a 'Chicago school' of economics. On the origins, diffusion, and evolving meanings of a famous brand name*. Unpublished working paper, Denver: University of Colorado.

Miller, H. L. (1962). On the "Chicago school of economics". *Journal of Political Economy, 70*(1), 64–69.

Mills, F. C. (1927). *The behavior of prices*. New York: National Bureau of Economic Research.

Mishan, E. J. (1975). The folklore of the market. An inquiry into the economic doctrines of the Chicago School. *Journal of Economic Issues, 9*(4), 681–752.

Mitchell, W. C. (1913). *Business cycles*. Berkeley: University of California Press.

Mitchell, W. C. (1925). Quantitative analysis in economic theory. *The American Economic Review, 15*(1), 1–12.

Mitchell, W. C. (1927). *Business cycles. The problem and its setting.* New York: National Bureau of Economic Research.

Montes, L. (2006a). On Adam Smith's Newtonianism and general economic equilibrium theory. In L. Montes & E. Schliesser (Eds.), *New voices on Adam Smith* (pp. 247–270). London: Routledge.

Montes, L. (2006b). Adam Smith. Real Newtonian. In A. Dow & S. Dow (Eds.), *A history of Scottish economic thought* (pp. 102–122). London: Routledge.

Morgan, M. S., & Rutherford, M. (1998). American economics. The character of the transformation. In M. S. Morgan & M. Rutherford (Eds.), *From interwar pluralism to postwar neoclassicism* (pp. 1–26). Durham, NC: Duke University Press.

Nik-Khah, E. (2011). George Stigler, the Graduate School of Business, and the pillars of the Chicago school. In R. Van Horn, P. Mirowski, & T. A. Stapleford (Eds.), *Building Chicago economics. New perspectives on the history of America's most powerful economics program* (pp. 116–147). Cambridge: Cambridge University Press.

Orlinsky, D. E. (1992). Not very simple, but overflowing. A historical perspective on general education at the University of Chicago. In J. J. MacAloon (Ed.), *General education in the social sciences. Centennial reflections on the College of the University of Chicago* (pp. 25–76). Chicago: The University of Chicago Press.

Patinkin, D. (1973). Frank Knight as teacher. *The American Economic Review, 63*(5), 787–810.

Patinkin, D. (1981). *Essays on and in the Chicago tradition.* Durham, NC: Duke University Press.

Phelps, E. S., & Taylor, J. B. (1977). Stabilizing powers of monetary policy under rational expectations. *Journal of Political Economy, 85*(1), 163–190.

Phillips, A. W. (1958). The relation between unemployment and the rate of change of money wage rates in the United Kingdom, 1861–1957. *Economica, 25*(100), 283–299.

Reder, M. W. (1982). Chicago economics. Permanence and change. *Journal of Economic Literature, 20*(1), 1–38.

Rutherford, M. (2010). Chicago economics and institutionalism. In R. B. Emmett (Ed.), *The Elgar companion to the Chicago school of economics* (pp. 25–39). Cheltenham: Edward Elgar.

Samuels, W. J. (1976a). Chicago doctrine as explanation and justification. In W. J. Samuels (Ed.), *The Chicago school of political economy* (pp. 363–396). East Lansing: Michigan State University.

Samuels, W. J. (1976b). The Chicago school of political economy. A constructive critique. In W. J. Samuels (Ed.), *The Chicago school of political economy* (pp. 1–18). East Lansing: Michigan State University.

Samuels, W. J. (1976c). Further limits to Chicago school doctrine. In W. J. Samuels (Ed.), *The Chicago school of political economy* (pp. 397–457). East Lansing: Michigan State University.

Samuelson, P. A. (1991). Jacob Viner, 1892–1970. In E. Shils (Ed.), *Remembering the University of Chicago. Teachers, scientists, and scholars* (pp. 533–547). Chicago: The University of Chicago Press.

Sargent, T. J. (1979). Estimating vector autoregressions using methods not based on explicit economic theories. *Federal Reserve Bank of Minneapolis Quarterly Review, 3*(3), 8–15.

Sargent, T. J. (1984). Autoregressions, expectations, and advice. *The American Economic Review, 74*(2), 408–415.

Sargent, T. J., & Sims, C. A. (1977). *Business cycle modeling without pretending to have too much a priori economic theory.* Minneapolis: Federal Reserve Bank of Minneapolis.

Sargent, T. J., & Wallace, N. (1975). "Rational" expectations, the optimal monetary instrument, and the optimal money supply rule. *Journal of Political Economy, 83*(2), 241–254.

Schumpeter, J. A. (1930). Review paper. Mitchell's business cycles. *The Quarterly Journal of Economics, 45*(1), 150–172.

Schumpeter, J. A. (1954/2006). *History of economic analysis.* London: Routledge.

Seater, J. J. (1993). Ricardian equivalence. *Journal of Economic Literature, 31*(1), 142–190.

Selden, R. T. (1956). Monetary velocity in the United States. In M. Friedman (Ed.), *Studies in the quantity theory of money* (pp. 179–257). Chicago: The University of Chicago Press.

Sims, C. A. (1980a). Macroeconomics and reality. *Econometrica, 48*(1), 1–48.

Sims, C. A. (1980b). Comparison of interwar and postwar business cycles. Monetarism reconsidered. *The American Economic Review, 70*(2), 250–257.

Sims, C. A. (1982a). Policy analysis with econometric models. *Brookings Papers on Economic Activity, 13*(1), 107–164.

Sims, C. A. (1982b). Scientific standards in econometric modeling. In M. Hazewinkel & A. H. Rinnooy Kan (Eds.), *Current developments in the interface. Economics, econometrics, mathematics* (pp. 317–337). Dordrecht: Springer.

Sims, C. A. (1986). Are forecasting models useable for policy analysis? *Federal Reserve Bank of Minneapolis Quarterly Review, 10*(1), 2–16.

Sims, C. A. (1996). Macroeconomics and methodology. *Journal of Economic Perspectives, 10*(1), 105–120.

Sims, C. A. (2011). Statistical modeling of monetary policy and its effects. *Nobel lecture The American Economic Review, 102*(4), 1187–1205.

Skinner, Q. (1969). Meaning and understanding in the history of ideas. *History and Theory, 8*(1), 3–53.

Somers, H. M. (1952). What generally happens during business cycles—and why. *The Journal of Economic History, 12*(3), 270–282.

Stapleford, T. A. (2011). Positive economics for democratic policy. Milton Friedman, institutionalism, and the science of history. In R. Van Horn, P. Mirowski, & T. A. Stapleford (Eds.), *Building Chicago economics. New perspectives on the history of America's most powerful economics program* (pp. 3–35). Cambridge: Cambridge University Press.

Stigler, G. J. (1946). *The theory of price.* New York: MacMillan.

Stigler, G. J. (1962). On the "Chicago school of economics". Comment. *Journal of Political Economy, 70*(1), 70–71.

Stigler, G. J. (1962/1964?). *The non-Chicago school.* Unpublished paper, Box 17, 'The non-Chicago school, 1964' folder. George Stigler papers. Special Collections Research Center The University of Chicago Library.

Stigler, G. J. (1976). The successes and failures of Professor Smith. *Journal of Political Economy, 84*(6), 1199–1213.

Stigler, G. J. (1977). *Schools in science.* Unpublished paper, Box 15, 'Schools in science, 1977' folder. George Stigler papers. Special Collections Research Center, The University of Chicago Library.

Stigler, G. J. (1979). *The Chicago school of economics.* Unpublished paper, Box 14, 'The Chicago school of economics, 1979' folder. George Stigler papers. Special Collections Research Center, The University of Chicago Library.

Stigler, G. J. (1988). *Memoirs of an unregulated economist.* New York: Basic Books.

Stigler, G. J., & Becker, G. S. (1977). De gustibus non est. disputandum. *The American Economic Review, 67*(2), 76–90.

Strotz, R. H., & Wold, H. A. (1960). Triptych on causal chain systems. *Econometrica, 28*(2), 417–463.

Taylor, J. B. (1975). Monetary policy during a transition to rational expectations. *Journal of Political Economy, 83*(5), 1009–1021.

Taylor, J. B. (1979). Staggered wage setting in a macro model. *The American Economic Review, 69*(2), 108–113.

Taylor, J. B. (1980). Aggregate dynamics and staggered contracts. *Journal of Political Economy, 88*(1), 1–23.

Taylor, J. B. (1998). *Staggered price and wage setting in macroeconomics.* NBER working paper no. 6754, Cambridge, MA: National Bureau of Economic Research.

Taylor, J. B. (2007). An interview with Milton Friedman. In P. A. Samuelson & W. A. Barnett (Eds.), *Inside the economist's mind. Conversations with eminent economists* (pp. 110–142). Malden, MA: Blackwell.

Tinbergen, J. (1939). *Statistical testing of business-cycle theories. A method and its application to investment activity*. Geneva: League of Nations.

Tinbergen, J. (1940). Econometric business cycle research. *The Review of Economic Studies, 7*(2), 73–90.

Valdés, J. G. (1995). *Pinochet's economists. The Chicago school in Chile*. Cambridge: Cambridge University Press.

Van Horn, R., & Mirowski, P. (2009). The rise of the Chicago school of economics and the birth of neoliberalism. In P. Mirowski & D. Plehwe (Eds.), *The road from Mont Pélerin. The making of the neoliberal thought collective* (pp. 139–178). Cambridge, MA: Harvard University Press.

Van Horn, R., & Mirowski, P. (2010). Neoliberalism and Chicago. In R. B. Emmett (Ed.), *The Elgar companion to the Chicago school of economics* (pp. 196–206). Cheltenham: Edward Elgar.

Van Horn, R., Mirowski, P., & Stapleford, T. A. (Eds.), (2011). *Building Chicago economics*. Cambridge: Cambridge University Press.

Van Overtveldt, J. (2007). The Chicago school. In *How the University of Chicago assembled the thinkers who revolutionized economics and business*. Agate: Chicago.

Viner, J. (1917). Some problems of logical method in political economy. *Journal of Political Economy*, (3), 236–260.

Viner, J. (1925). Objective tests of competitive price applied to the cement industry. *Journal of Political Economy, 33*(1), 107–111.

Viner, J. (1929). Review paper. Mills' Behavior of prices. *The Quarterly Journal of Economics, 43*(2), 337–352.

Viner, J. (1958). *The long view and the short. Studies in economic theory and policy*. Glencoe: The Free Press.

Vining, R. (1949). Koopmans on the choice of variables to be studies and the methods of measurement. *The Review of Economics and Statistics, 31*(2), 77–86.

Walras, L. (1926/1954). *Elements of pure economics or the theory of social wealth*. W. Jaffé, Trans.London: George Allen and Unwin.

Weinberg, S. (2015). *To explain the world. The discovery of modern science*. New York: Harper Collins.

Weintraub, E. R. (1983). On the existence of a competitive equilibrium, 1930–1954. *Journal of Economic Literature, 21*(1), 1–39.

Wilber, C. K., & Wisman, J. D. (1975). The Chicago school. Positivism or ideal type. *Journal of Economic Issues, 9*(4), 665–679.

Yaari, M. E. (1965). Uncertain lifetime, life insurance, and the theory of the consumer. *The Review of Economic Studies, 32*(2), 137–150.

Archival sources

Department of Economics Records 1912–1961. Archival material stored at the Special Collections Research Center, University of Chicago Library.

Friedman M., Unpublished papers, 1931–2006. Archival material stored at the Hoover Institution Library & Archives, Stanford University.

Lucas R.E., Unpublished papers, 1960–2004 and undated. Archival material stored at the David M. Rubenstein Library, Duke University.

3

Agents and structures

The paradox is now fully established that the utmost abstractions are the true weapons with which to control our thought of concrete facts.
Alfred North Whitehead

There is a pattern and structure to all things. Only we can't see it. Our job is to discover that pattern and structure and work within it, as a part of it.
Richard Flanagan: The narrow road to the Deep North

Lucas and his microfoundations project did not come out of the blue. Seeking the ultimate foundations of some macroeconomic phenomena at the level of individuals emerged as early as in the period of classical economics. The basic idea of the microfoundations programme is straightforward. As real macroeconomic systems consist of agents acting and interacting, at a minimum one can say that macro-level phenomena may not be independent of the way market participants behave. Some connection between macroeconomic outcomes and agents is thus very plausible to exist. In their theories, economists endow this connection between the levels with varying strength, though they have never eliminated it completely, not even in those times when defining explicit microfoundations for macroeconomics was not regarded as the best way of doing good economics. The emergence of the microfoundations programme was thus a long historical process before Lucas in the early 1970s put forward the revolutionary idea pointing towards a complete elimination of macroeconomics to the micro. For him the only way of understanding macro-level phenomena was to represent any macroeconomic system as a set of well-defined agents and to regard these phenomena as the outcomes of actors' interactions. In broad terms, this hard-core version of the microfoundations project set itself the task of building systems out of interacting agents and other entities.

Doing microfounded macro is a crucial concern of the transition between Milton Friedman and Robert Lucas. The way Friedman established the notion of his agents is highly typical of his own theorizing habit, though its typicality of the microfoundations project as a whole is far from obvious. One of the key aspects of the economic methodology he suggested is the complete neglect of the descriptive performance of models. Plainly put,

Friedman (1953/2009, pp. 16–30) by playing down the importance of real entity properties argued that theoretical entities do not need to bear any resemblance to their real counterparts.[1] However, entity properties still seem to play an important role in making up structures. Even the simplest market settings are structures where, for instance, buyers have a taste for a thing, so through the market they connect with its producers, and not with other agents on the supply side. Technology, together with demand conditions, determines what kind of labour force is needed and in what quantities. Preference systems, endowments, productivity, or technology are such entity properties that underlie how market participants contact and hence how a social structure emerges. As there is expected to be an intimate connection between parts and a resulting whole, intuitively one expects the properties of parts to determine the properties of their system. If this account is plausible in broad terms at least, the adequacy of a microfounded model then exclusively depends on the assumptions that define the interrelated entities. In this case, untrue descriptions of entity properties (such as propositions, beliefs, or theories about them) cannot but ground non-existent structures or causal mechanisms, so Friedman's definitely anti-realist entity assumptions deprived him of the possibility of enhancing causal understanding.

To look into this question, first, it is necessary to discuss whether macroeconomic systems can be reduced exclusively to micro-level entities, or something else is needed. Here two categories emerge. *Supervenience* in this context means that macro-level properties stem from micro-level properties; thus any change at the macro-level results from some accordant change in the micro.[2] By contrast, *reducibility* concerns the possibility of tracing everything emerging at the macro back to micro-level entities and properties. The importance of these two aspects is dissimilar. If supervenience holds, reductions to micro-level entities may be feasible and meaningful; supervenience is thus a necessary but not sufficient condition for reducibility. Micro-level entities in the lack of reducibility may be insufficient on their own to underpin the macro-level. Only if supervenience applies to macroeconomics is it sensible to consider the role of entity properties in establishing the structures of agents.

After sorting out the problems of supervenience and reducibility, a general framework is needed to scrutinize the relationship of entity properties and the properties of their structures. In the general philosophy of science

---

[1] In physics and philosophy of physics the term 'theoretical entities' refers to unobservable objects. In the present context the homo oeconomicus, the prototypical, abstract agent having characteristic cognitive capabilities is meant by the postulated theoretical actor or entity of economics. Manicas (2006, p. 84) applies the term 'theoretical entity' in this vein: it is an abstract and typical (observable or unobservable) object of a discipline. Friedman's agents forming adaptive and Lucas's agents forming rational expectations are contrasting incarnations of the theoretical agent of economics.

[2] The opposite statement, according to which any change in the micro results in an according change in the macro, does not hold as multiple micro-states may lead to a single macro-state.

and philosophy of physics and mathematics it is some recent results in structuralism that emerged as a melting pot of some divergent and occasionally opposing ideas on this relationship. As we shall see, not only is it implausible to assume the compatibility of untrue descriptions of entity properties with true hence causally exploitable structural representations but it is exactly the entity properties that constitute structures and do the work of causation. The knowledge of a structure cannot be cut adrift from the knowledge of its constituent parts; structural realism thus entails entity realism and vice versa. On this showing, in economics any causally useful representation of a structure must rely upon the causally active properties of the agents and other entities. As there is no point in preserving features playing no role in a given causal mechanism, this activity sets some limits on making assumptions in models[3] and highlights why mere similarity, interpreted as the sharing of a subset of properties by two or more distinct entities (Suárez, 2002, p. 5), is insufficient as a requirement for describing abstract theoretical entities. To a certain extent every single thing is similar to every other thing in every respect (Giere, 1988, pp. 78–81), even if it is to no appreciable extent. By contrast, the emphasis upon how to preserve causally active entity properties via abstraction and idealization helps both to distinguish causal adequacy and descriptive performance of models and to explain how descriptively minimalist theories can still be causally adequate. Instead of a simple and vague general similarity, this approach highlights that even abstraction in itself is not a guarantee for causal adequacy, which is something to establish through selecting those properties that carry a causal mechanism under scrutiny.

These properties of entities are oftentimes unobservable and undetectable though still open to experience. On the one hand, it is easy to argue for the key position of real causal properties in economic theorizing,[4] but,

---

[3] Even though it is possible to distinguish 'model' and 'theory', Lucas (1980, pp. 696–697) treated them as synonyms and interchangeable terms (Hand-written notes. Lucas papers. Box 27. 'Adaptive behavior, 1985—1986, 1 of 2' folder). Accordingly, models are theories and theories are models below. Equating them, however, is not generally accepted, and there exist various ways of distinction. Sometimes theory is conceived as containing a set of related models. As Bailer-Jones (2003, pp. 61–62) argues, theories are not about the empirical world, while models are. On this account, theories are pointed at abstract objects, so in order to be used in modelling about specific empirical phenomena they need to be customized accordingly. In this vein, in Section 2.2.1, Lucas's system was referred to as a pure theory ready for empirical applications in a Walrasian fashion.

[4] To make this point, suffice it to refer to the differences in the outcomes if agents find it rational to hoard money or they do not. In the first case, Say's law holds and there is no room for widespread excesses of supply. In the second case, the propensity to save may be so much stronger than the drive to invest that it creates a substantial barrier to 'full' investment and may be an obstacle to full employment (Viner, 1936, p. 152). Here Viner relates rationality to some properties in the setting: '[i]n static equilibrium analysis, in which perfect price flexibility is assumed and monetary changes are abstracted from, there is no occasion for consideration of hoarding'.

on the other, if these properties are hidden and we have no epistemic access to them, then causal adequacy can be no more than an unachievable desire. Introspection and commonsensibles offer a short cut. One may have experiences of some of her own properties, the details, and components of her mental processes and other states of mind without the possibility of detection or observation taken in the everyday sense. In so far as it is justified to assume that human minds are alike in broad terms, so the way one makes her decisions is approximately true of any other fellow human being's decision-making process, the experience of one's own mind inevitably widens to be a general picture of economic agents. Saving, consuming, comparing various goods, our preferences, our everyday habits: all these unobservable and undetectable properties are some elements of our common-sense reality ready to serve as a basis for causally adequate theorizing. What is more, as Manicas (2006, p. 17) argues, introspection (taken as experiencing our own actions as causes) aids in identifying causal mechanisms.

3.1 Microfoundations in the Friedman–Lucas transition: Some basics

By the modern era a wide conviction emerged that conceived economics as having the adequate model of individual behaviour. The rational individual as a constrained maximizer was a perfect candidate for the role of the ultimate foundation of all macro-level phenomena and hence the basis of macro-structures (Kirman, 1992, p. 119). However, the earliest ambitions of seeking the microfoundations date back to Adam Smith, Bernard Mandeville or David Ricardo connecting social welfare to individual welfare. The 17–19th history of economic thought can well be described by considering how the schools understood the central explanatory role shifting between individuals and supra-individual categories, moving to one of the extremes or taking intermediate positions. Hoover (2012) sorts even Keynes amongst the early forerunners of modern microfoundations for his apparent emphasis in the 'General theory' upon the behaviour of heterogeneous agents[5] and firms (Casarosa, 1981; Chick, 2016). Economics in the 1930s was typically microeconomics. This was the environment in which Keynes came up with a theory intended to be macroeconomics as such albeit with connections to microeconomics (as it is mentioned in Section 1.2.1, it is not Keynes who coined either micro- or macroeconomics). Whether it is the firms' decisions to invest on the basis of their long-

---

[5] This heterogeneity is perhaps best exemplified by how Keynes (1936, pp. 46–51 and pp. 147–164) treats expectations.

term expectations (Keynes, 1936, pp. 135–164) or the liquidity preference (Keynes, 1936, pp. 165–174 and pp. 194–209) or the consumption function (Keynes, 1936, pp. 89–112), Keynes was prone to build upon a relation between the choices of firms or individuals and the related macroeconomic outcomes. It holds even if Keynes did not systematically examine the interrelations between the micro- and the macro-levels (Hoover, 2008, pp. 316–318; De Vroey, 2012, pp. 180–182). Keynes, treading in Marshall's footsteps, did macroeconomics whilst making efforts to preserve the lines towards the micro-level. For Keynes and his early followers the problem of interrelatedness regarded whether aggregate relationships were compatible with microeconomics, but they hardly intended to formally deduce the aggregate level from agent-level premises (Hoover, 2014, p. 14). Later Lucas problematized this reducibility as his definitive programme. After Keynes's time, reconciling Keynesian macro with standard neoclassical microeconomic theory received special emphasis (Klein, 1949, pp. 56–90 and 258–265; De Vroey, 2012, pp. 182–183; De Vroey, 2016, pp. 55–64 and 117–118; Visco, 2014, p. 613).

3.1.1 Friedman and the microfoundations: The problem of the underlying properties

Amongst the forerunners of the Lucasian microfoundations project Hoover (2008, p. 318; 2012, pp. 41–44) mentions Friedman as one of those seeking the microfoundations for some macro-level phenomena (consumption, demand for money or investment) in the post-war years (Friedman, 1956). Hoover focuses on Friedman's consumption function and permanent income hypothesis (Friedman, 1957), arguing that Friedman based his account upon microeconomic, utility-maximizing theory. In a similar vein, Friedman (1968, 1977) made efforts to trace his Phillips-curve mechanisms back to the microeconomic properties of employers and employees.[6] When Friedman outlined his expectations-augmented Phillips curves, he cited how employees and employers form expectations, observe prices, and process the available information, and how employees try to optimize. Accordingly, the well-known shape of his Phillips curve is grounded upon the way individual workers on the market for labour force mispercept the price and wage dynamics and believe the rise in their nominal income to be a rise in their real income, and upon the way employers make good use of this situation. Thus his Phillips curve models are instances for founding some macro-level mechanisms upon some microeconomic notions.

---

[6] Interestingly, Friedman contrasted the seeking of microfoundations with the use of multi-equation models (Taylor, 2007, pp. 121–122), a standard for economics after Friedman.

Friedman's positivist methodology (Friedman, 1953/2009) perfectly fits into these efforts. In this paper Friedman applies some microeconomic examples to describe the methodology he suggests. Unfortunately, he runs into some ambiguities over his instances for theoretical assumptions. Through his examples Friedman argues that theories are not supposed to be judged by the descriptive realism of their underlying assumptions. His starting point is the formula $s = \frac{1}{2}gt^2$ taken from physics, the law of falling bodies that describes the distance (s) a body dropped in vacuum travels during time t, where g is the constant acceleration due to gravity. This formula assumes vacuum that does not necessarily hold in reality; therefore in most cases, one of the crucial assumptions of the theory is not met. One may infer that the theory is flawed for it only applies under unrealistic circumstances. However, as Friedman argues, the formula performs fairly well in many cases in spite of its descriptive and factual inaccuracy. Whilst one can modify the formula in order to give account of the disturbances to the basic law (e.g. air pressure or the shape of the body), for the most part it is unnecessary as real bodies usually fall as if they fell in vacuum. Thus, even if its assumptions are descriptively unrealistic, the formula performs well in empirical terms. Along these lines Friedman argues for assumptions not holding in reality, whilst he leaves open the question of the exact nature of their unrealisticness and the cognitive-methodological source of assumptions. Are they based upon some existent properties or are they completely of fictitious character? In any case, comparing theoretical assumptions to reality is senseless for, regardless of differences, a theory may work well for some purposes. His recommendation is simple: its use ought to be constrained to cases where a theory proves useful.

After dwelling upon this case coming from physics, in order to illustrate the right way of theorizing Friedman delineates some instances from social sciences. Here stands his famous case of a model for estimating the density of leaves on a tree. If in a set of alternative models one stands out empirically, the one that assumes leaves to be rational utility maximizers, this is the model to prefer to its rivals. As Friedman argues, one does not need to assume that real leaves rationally calculate the amount of incident sunlight. Instead, suffice it to assume that leaves 'behave' in a way as if they were rational utility maximizing agents. When it comes to assessment, like in model selection, it is irrelevant to consider the characteristics of real leaves. Accordingly, the only purpose of a modeller is to find an assumption upon which a theory can save the phenomena (here: the density of leaves on a tree). By so doing, the modeller can successfully describe the 'behaviour' of leaves, and that is all to this problem. She does not need to pay attention to the actual characteristics of leaves.

Similarly, if the purpose is to model the shooting 'behaviour' of a billiard player, it is sensible to assume him to plan the trajectories in a way as if he knew all the formulas describing the optimal courses. Thus Ronnie O'Sullivan is playing as if he made mathematical calculations in advance to plan the paths of his colourful snooker balls and as if his success was dependent upon his proficiency in putting such theoretical trajectories into practice. Such an assumption works well because Mr. O'Sullivan's shots are in consonance with our predictions, irrespective of the way he actually plans. Mr. O'Sullivan can rightly be considered as one of the greatest players in the history of snooker for he consistently achieves the same results as if he played using complex formulas.

Friedman's last example is the microeconomic theory of companies regarded as profit maximizers. According to the theory, entrepreneurs act as if their behaviour was governed by the purpose of rational profit-seeking and as if they had all the necessary information to act rationally. Thus by assuming that an entrepreneur knows both her company's demand and cost functions and the marginal revenue and marginal cost functions her decision implies, and that she sets the output to equalize marginal revenues and marginal costs we have a theory that well saves the phenomena: a theory with satisfying empirical performance. Upon assessment the real information structure of agents or their object functions as properties are to be disregarded, just like previously. Success results from the fact that market competition compels entrepreneurs to act as if they were rational microeconomic agents. Even if their success is due to mere luck, at the level of phenomena this success is in accordance with the outcomes of our rationality-based theory. The real motives of actions are irrelevant as long as behaviour looks like the outcome of rational calculations.

Friedman's argumentation, however, is flawed as all his three examples connect with reality in dissimilar ways. Friedman's postulates are thus the products of some contrasting conceptualizing strategies. The clearest case is the tale of the leaves. Here Friedman assumes something non-existent. Leaves have no rationality in any form; thus based upon the rationality postulate, a theory can provide good approximations to their spatial positions only at the phenomenal level. This is an extreme case, so when Friedman argues for the irrelevance of how closely assumptions describe reality, he is ready to make do with fictitious properties. It amounts to the condition when non-descriptive assumptions are made up of non-existent properties.

The tale of a billiard player calculating as a physicist is a disparate case. To say how, it is helpful to cite Michael Polanyi's philosophy of science and his account of tacit knowledge. As Polanyi argues, our knowledge contains some elements and in our actions we rely upon skills we only unconsciously or tacitly know. In cases where such skills are applied, there is no focal awareness upon them. Of his several examples the story of a cyclist and her balancing on a bike is a case in point (Polanyi, 1958/2005, p. 51). There is a simple rule every cyclist obeys. When a cyclist starts falling to the right she turns the handlebars to the same direction so that the path of her bike is deflected along a curve towards the right. This manoeuvre triggers off a centrifugal force pushing the cyclist to the left and thus offsets the gravitational force dragging her down to the right. This correction throws the cyclist off balance to the left, which she needs to counteract by turning the handlebars to the left. The cyclist can keep herself in balance by manoeuvring along a series of appropriate curves. The path the cyclist ought to follow can simply be described in mathematical terms: for a given angle of unbalance the curvature of each winding is inversely proportional to the square of the speed at which the cyclist is proceeding. The cyclist thus really applies a physical rule and this is the reason why we can well describe her actions with the appropriate formula. Her awareness of the formula is subsidiary. Even if she is familiar with the physical background of her action, riding her bike is not supported by a constant conscious calculation process. Moreover, if her focal awareness was directed at the physical rule and its constant application, this would inevitably result in her crashing into a tree. Thus describing the behaviour of a snooker player with a mathematical formula is accurate, both in descriptive and cognitive terms. The feasibility of such an epistemological strategy of ours is underpinned by the very structure of human knowledge we want to model.

The notion of profit-seeking companies is a case where some existent entity properties are preserved to be applied in providing a theoretical description of firms in general, or firm as a theoretical entity (Chakravartty, 2007, pp. 187–192). In such a case, quite informally, we can say that a theoretical entity is endowed with properties that either characterize its real counterpart (the theoretical entity has existent properties that can be found in reality) or refer to some of its characteristics (inexistent properties are used to represent existent characteristics). Doing either way, some selected features of a real entity are preserved in theory (in Section 3.4, these techniques are described as abstraction and idealization). Bearing in mind the theoretical and practical problems around the objectives of companies (Jensen, 2001), standard microeconomics boils down the company objective function to profit maximization (Varian, 2010, pp. 347–348). Assuming maximum profit as a company objective implies our disregarding further motives (e.g. fairness or job satisfaction), whilst what we assume can be found as a constituent part in socio-economic reality (Reiss, 2010, pp. 107–108).

Of Friedman's three examples two can easily be reconciled with the characteristics of real agents. The behaviour of a successful billiard player can exactly be described with some physical formulas; his play is thus factually built upon the unconscious application of physical laws. Likewise, profit maximization as a drive belongs to the motives of firms as real market participants, so assuming profit orientation in theory by no means involves assuming inexistent properties. Judged by the case of his rational leaves, however, Friedman is highly unlikely to have suggested insisting on such existent properties. By contrast, his point in the leaf parable is to save macro-level phenomena (e.g. the density of leaves on a tree) on the basis of some micro-level assumptions (e.g. the rationality of leaves) which are not only descriptively inaccurate but also completely inexistent.[7] More likely thus he just might have chosen some inappropriate and mutually inconsistent examples to underpin his main thread. At the same time, the tale of the leaves is an example of a two-layer world where some macro-level phenomena (the distribution of leaves) stem from the properties and interactions of micro-level entities (utility maximizing leaves). On this showing, in his version of the microfoundations project the sole focus was on macro-level phenomena to save on whatever grounds. Microfoundations are good to have, but their role is only to facilitate satisfactory macro-level predictions. This seems to be the only requirement for micro-level theorizing. In Chapter 4 his positivist methodology re-emerges as a topic to be further analysed in this vein.

Surprising as it is, Hoover (2009a) analyzing Friedman's epistemological stance in his positivist methodology suggests a case for causal realism. As Hoover argues, Friedman's methodology is to be free of sophisticated philosophical interpretations for Friedman discussed methodology as an economist, not as a philosopher. Placing the positivist methodology in the broader context of Friedman's oeuvre, Hoover claims that Friedman and Schwartz (1963, 1965) devoted economics to the purpose of causal understanding. It is a contentious issue whether it is relevant to consult Friedman's oeuvre when analyzing his positivist methodology (Boland, 2010, pp. 379–380), whilst it is also unclear how well his positivist methodology mirrors the methodology he factually applied as an economist. However, Hoover's rendition is worth a thorough consideration as it problematizes the possibility of combining causal understanding and the neglect of entity properties in the microfoundations project. If Friedman with his economics strove towards the understanding of macro-level causal connections, then in his positivist methodology he tried to clarify how to set up agent-level assumptions in order to reach this aim. And if so, then Hoover's causal realist Friedman may be reconciled with Friedman as an anti-realist regarding agent-level assumptions. What is more, Hoover's point amounts to the claim that causal connections of entities can be represented via untrue entity-level propositions as assumptions. Thus at the end of the day entity properties seem not to matter at all in the big picture. One can, however, pose the same question in a broader context. What kind of agent-level assumptions does the causal understanding of macroeconomic

---

[7] To make things more complicated, his opening example of the formula from physics is indecisive. Taken at face value, the law of freefalling bodies when applied to non-vacuum conditions assumes something inexistent. However, the contribution of air pressure is easy to interpret as the effect of a factor that disturbs the basic law which is admittedly true.

mechanisms require? How should we set up the properties describing our theoretical entities in order to answer the causal questions of macroeconomics? These are questions that lie far beyond the scope of simple statistical correlations.

3.1.2 Microfoundations *á la* Lucas: Choice-theoretic framework, general equilibrium, and voluntary unemployment

Even though it is Lucas who started the modern era of the microfoundations project, the forerunners of this programme, as it is argued above, emerged well before his time (Hands, 2015, p. 63). Lucas and new classical macroeconomics 'only' emphasized and gave new impetus to a then existing idea (Hoover, 2008, p. 315). Hoover (2012) mentions three dissimilar albeit overlapping coherent programmes in the modern times. As he argues, these projects were aimed at different scientific goals. The central problem of the *aggregation programme* was checking whether the 'behaviour' of macroeconomic aggregates was consistent with individual economic behaviour. It is typical how Klein (1949, pp. 57–58), for the sake of simplicity, built his model upon aggregates whilst paying attention to proper aggregation methods to establish the formal analogies between micro- and macro-level variables (Klein, 1946a, 1946b). Given this, aggregates were alleged to consistently substitute for micro-level data. The *general equilibrium programme* was aimed at constructing disaggregated, general equilibrium models out of formally conceived individual agents to mimic some characteristic features of the economy at the macro-level and to foster the understanding of how spontaneous coherence emerge from interactions of agents (Arrow, 1974; Düppe & Weintraub, 2014, p. 13; Madden, 1989; Townsend, 1987). These first two approaches can jointly be labelled as chapters in the *non-eliminative microfoundations programme* as both of them approved of doing macroeconomics. These lines of research posed the question how some genuinely macroeconomic phenomena can be traced back to the microeconomic level of individual behaviour. But there is a third programme, the project of *eliminative microfoundations*. Of these three versions it is only the third one having led to the currently domineering representative-agent project that belongs to Lucas, and it is also the one that follows the others in time. Lucas's purpose was to elaborate a theory that would render it unnecessary to distinguish microeconomics and macroeconomics as all economic phenomena could be understood in the sole theory of economics by deriving all results from microeconomics, that is, from the understanding of individual choice, taking taste and technology as given (Hoover, 2014, pp. 14–15).

Lucas's papers from the 1970s consistently draw attention to the importance of giving account of macro-level phenomena upon the fundament of a proper micro-economic theory (a re-emerging topic in Chapter 4).

To this end, as we have seen, Lucas suggested a choice-theoretic framework taken as the core of the problem of understanding some macro-dynamics (Phelps, 1970, p. 2). It is noteworthy, however, that Lucas's microfoundations project is not an accomplished endeavour. In the 1980s (having completed his most powerful models in the first half of the 1970s) Lucas (1987, pp. 107–108) discusses in future conditionals

> the reincorporation of aggregative problems such as inflation and the business cycle within the general framework of 'microeconomic' theory. If these developments succeed, the term 'macroeconomic' will simply disappear from use and the modifier 'micro' will become superfluous. We will simply speak, as did Smith, Ricardo, Marshall and Walras, of *economic* theory.[8]

In a broader context, in his Nobel lecture he is very modest to conceive his whole monetary economics as only an initiation having only the hopes of leading us towards satisfactory answers in the future (Lucas, 1995/1996, p. 661).

Lucas's interest in the problem of microfoundations dates back to the years when he was not an ardent enemy of Keynesian economics. In his early papers co-authored by Rapping (Lucas & Rapping, 1969, 1972) his aim was not the questioning or rejecting of Keynesian orthodoxy, but rather providing the theory with firm microfoundations in the wage-price sector (Lucas, 2005, p. 20). Lucas and Rapping addressed the problem by reconciling neoclassical growth theory with the labour supply ideas of short-run Keynesian theory. By assuming short-run labour market equilibrium they resorted to the equilibrium approach as their framework. By so doing, whilst this assumption did not imply the assuming away of unemployment as such and was in consonance with observable labour market fluctuations, Lucas and Rapping could avoid measured unemployment entering into the model. This way they received a conceptually clearer theory. The interpretation of unemployment raised some problems in those days as unemployment was inevitably regarded as involuntary, which was an idea Lucas and Rapping rejected. In Section 4 of their 1969 paper, suggesting a difference between current wage and normal wage, they provided an alternative interpretation of the government's employment survey. The model was intended to give account of the dynamics of unemployment conceptualized as of voluntary character.

---

[8] Some years earlier Becker (1971, p. viii) exerted similar views, saying that 'there is only one kind of economic theory, not separate theories for micro problems, macro problems, nonmarket decisions, and so on. Indeed, the most promising development in recent years in the literature on unemployment and other macro problems has been the increasing reliance on utility maximization and the other principles used to study micro problems'. Becker took over Econ 301 from Friedman in 1976 and here he also preferred the label 'Economic theory' to 'Price theory' (Van Overtveldt, 2007, pp. 107–108).

Rationalizing the employment decisions of households and firms on equal footing with consumption and investment decisions seemed to Lucas to be of fundamental importance. He argued that clarifying the choice-theoretic background ought to precede any other approaches or theorizing attempts. His basic idea regarded households making labour supply decisions on the basis of information about perceived current and future wages and prices. As Lucas believed, expectations have effects on decision-making and these effects detectably contribute to employment dynamics. Lucas made efforts to understand the real decision problems of real economic agents: '[u]nderstanding employment fluctuations must involve [...] understanding how this choice is made or what combination of preference characteristics and changing opportunities gives rise to the patterns we observe' (Lucas, 1981, p. 4). The decision problem for an agent lies in her changing the hours she supplies in response to changes in the real interest rate or real rate of return. Prices enter into the setting for inflation expectations influence behaviour. Rising inflation reduces the real return on labour supplied, which reduces planned future consumption expenditures. Lucas thus regarded the changes in employment as the results of individual decisions made on the basis of intertemporal substitutability of labour (Lucas, 1981, pp. 2–5).

Lucas's emphasis upon the fact that expectations contribute to decision-making means that economic models are not supposed to grab the whole causal structure. Lucas time and again highlights in his texts that his models only analyze some aspects of phenomena, and that the omitted variables are likely to deteriorate the empirical performance (Lucas & Rapping, 1972, p. 190; Lucas, 1981, p. 63). Regarding unemployment as voluntary by no means implies the assumption that unemployment as a real-world phenomenon is entirely voluntary. This assumption only highlights how and why voluntariness contributes to unemployment dynamics, right in the same way as we can learn a lot about the different properties of water by approaching its various properties via some incompatible assumptions (Teller, 2004, p. 439). Labour supply responds to changes in the real wage, though this relationship may work along several mechanisms. Real wage affects child-bearing decisions and, indirectly, the size of the population; it also influences participation rate and the number of hours people on the market for labour force offer. Of the possible channels Lucas and Rapping scrutinized two: hours supplied and participation rate (Lucas & Rapping, 1969, p. 726; Lucas, 1981, p. 24). This model, however, elaborated to study the so simplified setting aids in understanding labour supply dynamics and separating short- and long-term responses of labour supply to real wage changes. For Lucas, in general, placing the blame on an abstract-idealized model for its partiality or because it omits some details of reality amounts to the simple misunderstanding of economics (Lucas, 1980, p. 700; 1981, p. 277).

By the 1970s the problem received a more comprehensive treatment. It is Phelps,[9] then already working in a general equilibrium framework, who drew Lucas's interest towards general equilibrium economics. Thanks to his provocative impressions Lucas started treating the decision problem as an information problem. From that time his basic problem concerned whether information deficiencies could serve as the channel or mechanism leading from the shock to the emergence of cycles. Accordingly, Lucas's (1972) strategy was to place Lucas-Rapping households[10] in a monetary economy in order to scrutinize the way they respond to stochastic shocks to the money supply. It is also Phelps's achievement that Lucas started theorizing in the island model framework that proved to be adequate for the mathematical representation of informationally incomplete macroeconomic environment.[11]

The explicitness of Lucas's microfoundations has changed in time. The elaboration has its peak in his 1972 island model (Lucas, 1972). In this version, informationally isolated agents living on two islands taken as separated markets try to optimize by reacting to confusing signals coming either from the government or from relative shifts in demand (or both). Rational agents make decisions on the basis of relative prices, though they do not have the adequate information to distinguish *relative* and *general* price movements. For Lucas, this model was the proof of the feasibility of his programme. As it turned out, it was possible to construct a disaggregated general equilibrium model out of agents (who were fundamentally alike) to account for the systematic relation between the rate of change in nominal prices and the level of real output (i.e. the Phillips curve). In the 1973 model (Lucas, 1973) the island metaphor remained in use and agents inhabited a large number of markets, instead of two, and Lucas kept referring to the microfoundations in order to derive his surprise aggregate supply function. Whilst he applied the 1972 version to provide the Phillips curve with firm microfoundations, he aimed the 1973 model at deriving an aggregate supply function to be tested on international data.

An explicit reference to the islands as informationally separated markets is also present in the 1975 model (Lucas, 1975). However, the discrepancies from the 1972 version are prominent. There Lucas traced back the whole problem of current consumption, current labour supply, and future consumption to as deep as the common utility function describing the preference systems of individual agents (Lucas, 1972, pp. 106–109;

---

[9] See Phelps's introduction to Phelps (1970).

[10] More technically, households facing the decision problem defined by Lucas and Rapping (1969).

[11] The island model as a general framework is very easy to customize. In his unpublished papers there is a version in which 12 islands are situated around a clockface and only the neighbouring islands are allowed to have trade connections. As an exercise, students were required to prove the existence of a barter equilibrium (Problem 4 for Economics 332. Spring, 1977. Lucas papers. Box 36. 'Monetary theory, 1978–1981 and 1983, 2 of 2' folder).

Lucas, 1981, pp. 69–72), but in the later versions he skipped this step. Taking the problem of explicit microfoundations solved, Lucas turned his attention to deriving testable implications and introducing serially correlated (non-white-noise) fluctuations into the system. The choice-theoretic framework was getting more and more implicit. Hoover (2012, pp. 49–50) places the blame on the new classical texts for being devoid of direct and explicit references to the microeconomics of individual optimization. In his narrative the Lucasian microfoundations programme seems to have been rather a lip service. This assessment, however, is far from obvious as an intentional neglect of explicating the ultimate choice-theoretic foundations time and again ought to be considered rather as a firm scientific strategy. In lieu of completing the same task over and over, which is hardly necessary once a scientific problem is satisfyingly resolved, it is possible to extend a theory to new directions. Proceeding in science requires theorists to have faith in and to build upon the results they already have (Kuhn, 1962, pp. 46–49; 1977, pp. 233–234).

One of Lucas's central concepts is voluntary unemployment which he needed to regard the state of being out of work as the outcome of decisions. Accordingly, agents rationally prefer other activities to work if they perceive their current wages to be temporarily lower than normal (Lucas & Prescott, 1974, p. 188; Lucas, 1981, p. 156). Situational awareness is fraught with information deficiencies. An unemployed person does not know her exact current wage rate. In order to find it out, she enters a job seeking process in which she will regard her normal wage rate as a guide. Her idea on her normal wage rate is under the joint influence of several information sources: typically, her and others' labour market experiences. When a job seeker is convinced that her normal wage is lower than she previously expected, she will reduce her wage demands. As information is incomplete and costly, and as acting accordingly to the information (moving or retiring) takes considerable investment, labour supply only gradually changes (Lucas & Rapping, 1972, p. 736; Lucas, 1981, p. 31). As long as the worker remains unemployed during this searching and revision process, her unemployment is of voluntary nature. However, voluntary unemployment explains only a part of the perceived labour market rigidities (Lucas & Rapping, 1972, p. 186; Lucas, 1981, p. 59). Compared to this account, the Keynesian approach is severely simplifying. Workers are willing to take jobs even at their current wage rates (whatever it is), and if they cannot, they are regarded as involuntarily unemployed. However, coining involuntary unemployment is unscientific for it is something to explain, not to assume:

> the postulate of "involuntary" unemployment is not an ingredient of an economic theory of employment changes, but rather a confession that such a theory has yet to be discovered. In a discipline such as ours, in which one rarely admits that any phenomenon is unexplained, one would expect such a confession to come only under extreme duress. [...]

Can observed fluctuations in employment be explained as the rational responses of households to observed fluctuations in wages and prices? Keynes began the General Theory with the frank confession that he could not do so, disguised (as confessions often are) as a scornful attack on anyone who might pretend he could. It is a testimony to the force of this attack that for some thirty years following the publication of the General Theory, the determination of aggregate employment levels [was] generally discussed as though the decision as to whether or not to spend the day working at the most attractive available job was made not by the worker in question, but rather by some mysterious and un-named external force.

Events since 1970 have painfully illustrated the fact that codifying the behavior of mysterious and un-named forces over a particular sample period does not lend any insight as to how they may be expected to behave in the future. (Typed notes. Lucas papers. Box 18. 'Labour supply, undated, 2 of 2' folder)

Lucas and Rapping's workers act in a different setting. Their approach also takes into account the circumstance that it takes some time for a worker to become aware of her current wage rate. As long as her expectations are not revised, she is unemployed, but she is voluntarily so. The worker would take a job at her normal wage, but until she receives it (i.e. until her current wage rate is not lower than her normal wage rate), she voluntarily rejects job offers. Lucas and Rapping's workers refuse to work at the current wage rate if it is lower than the normal (i.e. expected) wage. Thus at any current wage rate the market for labour force is assumed to be in equilibrium in each period (Lucas & Rapping, 1969, p. 736; Lucas, 1981, p. 31). For Lucas and Rapping (1969, p. 748; Lucas, 1981, p. 42) measured unemployment therefore refers to people regarding their current wage rates as too low, so strictly speaking they choose to be unemployed. Being unemployed is of course not to their liking.[12] Workers are actively seeking jobs, but they are unwilling to get back to work as their expectations and experiences are not yet in consonance. But unemployment may be a prolonged state, and it seems to be difficult to explain on the basis of the concept of voluntary unemployment. The unemployed in this framework just appear to be stubborn to recognize their real situation on the market for labour force (Rees, 1970). However, Lucas and Rapping showed that during the Great Depression wages and prices were below their normal values. Households kept correcting their expectations, so normal wages and prices were on the decrease during the crisis, though they changed slower than the factual data (Lucas & Rapping, 1972, p. 189; Lucas, 1981, p. 62), leading to long-lasting unemployment.

---

[12] Voluntary unemployment does not mean that workers treat the periods of unemployment as leisure time to enjoy or an economic downturn as a fortunate event. Lucas's (1977, p. 18; 1981, p. 226) example is a food market in equilibrium. Hunger is easily reconcilable with the equilibrium state and we do not need to think people enjoy starvation.

Lucas presents the mature form of the equilibrium approach in his island models. General equilibrium is the framework through which Lucas could study how individual decisions contribute to large-scale employment and output fluctuations. Assuming an equilibrium environment is the point where Lucas suggested the sharpest break with the preceding Keynesian theory. Instead of making efforts to explain business cycles Keynes sought the institutional sources of instability, and he did so in the hope that by identifying these sources he could provide a remedy and that some appropriate institutional changes would contribute to their elimination. In Lucas's account, Keynes focused on the policy options to place the economy back on track, whilst he completely neglected the way it derailed. Lucas characterizes himself with his efforts to abandon this belief. He strongly disagreed on regarding the study of countercyclical policies as the only justified purpose of economics, even if his results have effects on the potential of countercyclical policies (Lucas, 1977, p. 8; Lucas, 1981, p. 216).

The choice-theoretic framework and voluntary unemployment, his general equilibrium economics and rational expectations hypothesis comprise Lucas's key conceptual matrix. The assumption that unemployment is chosen led to the concept of voluntary unemployment. On this showing, unemployment is the outcome of agents' optimizing efforts. The distinction between voluntary and involuntary forms of unemployment urged Lucas to find a more comprehensive, dynamic macroeconomic framework in which he rendered the general state of the economy dependent on individual optimization. By applying the general equilibrium framework Arrow and Debreu handed down, Lucas could break an association consistently worked until his time—the idea where macroeconomic equilibrium was static, and fluctuations were consequently regarded as disequilibrium situations.[13] As a conducive step, Lucas utilizing Muth' (1961) hypothesis provided a mathematically tractable solution to the problem that information is not common but differs amongst traders.[14]

---

[13] The Arrow-Debreu version of neo-Walrasian modelling assumed money away, which was a problem for Lucas he solved by refurbishing this variant (Hahn, 1965). Citing Hahn (1980, p. 285), Lucas emphasized that '[i]f "we want to model a monetary economy" [...] the Arrow-Debreu framework must be replaced with one which contains an explicit role for money' (Typed notes. Lucas papers. Box 19A. 'Drafts, undated' folder). And as Mehrling (1998, p. 296) puts it, '[m]onetary Walrasianism thus turned out to be an oxymoron at best and at worst a Procrustean bed' in the beginning.

[14] Rational expectations hypothesis, the Arrow-Debreu-McKenzie version of general equilibrium theory, and the island model framework appeared in Lucas's analytical tool-kit roughly at the same time (Lucas, 2001, pp. 12–16; Snowdon & Vane, 2005, p. 280), between 1963 (his assistant professorship at Carnegie Tech) and 1969 (the conference leading to the Phelps volume, 'Microeconomic foundations of employment and inflation theory'). This is interesting as Lucas and Rapping (1969) assumed adaptive expectations, though Lucas thanks to Zvi Griliches became aware of Muth's rationality hypothesis yet in Chicago before 1964 (McCallum, 2007, p. 61).

By so doing, Lucas related dynamic general equilibrium analysis with the tradition Mitchell (1913) started that some speculative elements and agents' inappropriate reactions to imperfect signals played a key role in the emergence of business cycles (Lucas, 1980, pp. 706–708; Lucas, 1981, pp. 284–286). As he says in a letter:

> I have certainly never argued that the "islands" parable can be retold within the Arrow-Debreu complete markets framework. This is clear from "Expectations and Neutrality of Money." The relationship between that model and the A[rrow]-D[ebreu] framework is as alluded to in the last paragraph of p. 285 in my book. [Studies in business-cycle theory] [...] The point is that one can use the contingent-claim set-up, as I did in "Expectations...", to study incomplete market situations as well as complete ones. (Lucas's letter to Axel Leijonhufvud. October 28, 1982. Lucas papers. Box 5. '1982, 1 of 2' folder)

His 1972 island model comprises all the three key components of Lucasian macroeconomics: representative agents with optimizing behaviour and rational expectations, and a general equilibrium framework.[15] He placed rational expectations amongst the assumptions in order to maintain both the rationality and the expectation errors of agents in an incomplete market setting leading to fluctuations. As rationality does not assume away expectations errors, agents can only optimize with making some mistakes and there are no ways available for them to perfectly hedge against uncertain outcomes. It was a solution different from the way uncertainty was treated in the Arrow–Debreu framework. In the complete contingent claim framework of pre-Lucasian neo-Walrasian economics, uncertainty comes from the fact that agents do not know in advance which state of the world will actually hold. Thus optimizing agents are interested in making all their decisions prior to any state in fact prevails. In all possible states the same physical commodity is considered as economically different commodities; thus the static general equilibrium framework is reinterpreted to account for future outcomes. The notion of ordinary commodities is replaced by contingent commodities, i.e. promises to buy or sell a given commodity on condition that a certain state of the world sets in later. In this case contingent prices are on the market. No matter what outcomes eventually occur, agents are prepared by buying and selling contingent claims (Arrow, 1968, p. Sect. 8; Arrow, 1973, pp. 39–40; Arrow, 1974; Debreu, 1959). As a result, optimal allocations emerge (Arrow, 1964). However, if markets are incomplete, as in the Lucasian case, resource allocation may be sub-optimal (Geanakoplos & Polemarchakis, 1986). Here optimal outcome is only a purpose.

---

[15] In assembling all these components, his 1971 paper with Prescott (Lucas & Prescott, 1971) was a milestone.

As Lucas realized, associating equilibrium with stability was nothing but a theory-inflicted reflex. It was unnecessary to interpret dynamic large-scale fluctuations, the changes in output and prices, as dislocations from general equilibrium. After Lucas had introduced his general equilibrium approach, macroeconomics came to be divided into a trichotomy in terms of a basic approach. Whilst the neoclassical founding fathers considerably heightened our knowledge of the prerequisites and conditions of static macroeconomic equilibrium, Keynes responding to the urging unemployment problems of his age simply relocated the issue. By changing the fundamental approach, Keynes tried, on the one hand, to identify the institutional factors having effects on the equilibrium tendencies of macroeconomies and, on the other hand, to find the reasons for the tendency of economies to get stuck in troughs of waves. Keynes was uninterested in the nature of waves themselves (Lucas, 1980, p. 704; Lucas, 1981, p. 282). He just wanted to find a way economic policy could drive an economy back from its plight. Lucas transformed the then twofold view (*neoclassical static equilibrium* vs. *Keynesian disequilibrium fluctuations*) into a trichotomy by studying whether some of the real (i.e. non-institutional) factors neoclassicals scrutinized in the static equilibrium framework could contribute to the emergence of large-scale fluctuations. For Lucas it seemed plausible that some sources of instability could be found right in the equilibrium system. Plainly put, Lucas suggested the idea that optimization does not necessarily lead to optimal allocation as agents cannot but act on the basis of the available information. However, the information set is incomplete, so they do not do the same as they would if they had full knowledge. As a consequence, fluctuations occur even in spite of general equilibrium (Lucas, 1972, p. 103; Lucas, 1981, p. 66). On this showing, at the phenomenal level both Keynes and Lucasian macroeconomics studied the same thing: the cyclical fluctuations of macroeconomic systems.[16] Keynes focused on the institutional factors neoclassicals intentionally neglected, whilst Lucas highlighted that business cycles are not necessarily disequilibrium situations for they might result from the individuals' optimization strategies whilst the majority of the traditional postulates keep intact (Sargent, 1977).

Without overemphasizing the similarities between Keynes and Lucas, it is interesting to realize that business cycles in both approaches are regarded as oscillations about a trend (see Fig. 3.1).

---

[16] As it should go without saying, this claim by no means entails that in other respects (e.g. in methodological terms) there were no discrepancies. This statement only underlines the simple fact that Keynes and Lucas studied the same phenomenon, though they did so through dissimilar methodologies and drew dissimilar theoretical and economic policy conclusions.

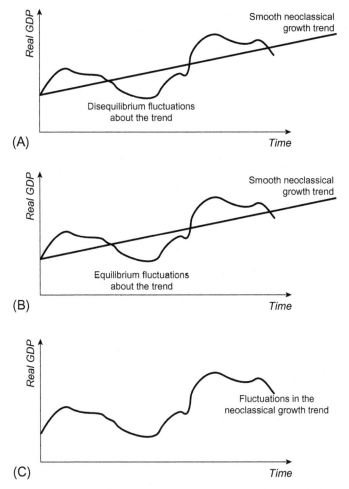

FIG. 3.1 A schematic overview of how Keynes (A), Lucas (B), and real business cycle theorists (C) conceptualized the relationship of large-scale short-run fluctuations in real GDP and its long-run trend (vertical axis) in time (horizontal axis).

Fluctuations are temporary departures from a smooth trend described by neoclassical growth theory. In terms of the mutuality of short-run cycles and the trend, Lucas (1980, pp. 699–700; Lucas, 1981, p. 275) talks about two selves of Keynes. The one is the Keynes (1930) of the 'Treatise'. In this early book of his, Keynes aimed to understand fluctuations around a secular trend, where real magnitudes were described by neoclassical value theory and where prices were regarded as driven by the quantity theory of money. The other Keynes (1936) is the Keynes of the 'General theory': the great depression turned Keynes away from supplementing the static neoclassical theory with some short-run dynamics, undertaken in the 'Treatise'. The endeavour Keynes initiated in the 'General theory' was to give an account of how and why capitalist economies can remain in non-full employment situations for prolonged periods of time (Hoover, 2012, p. 19). Later, by using the neoclassical growth model for interpreting short-term fluctuations, real business cycle (RBC) theory eliminated this earlier difference between trend and cycles. For RBC theorists, it is the trend itself that fluctuates (Snowdon & Vane, 2005, pp. 300–303).

3.1.3 Some critiques: Supervenience and reducibility

The most dangerous critique for the microfoundations project was the DSM theorem directed against the core connection between the micro- and the macro-levels. The DSM theorem (named after its elaborators, Gerard Debreu, Hugo Sonnenschein, and Rolf Mantel) called the feasibility of microfounded macroeconomics into question. The starting point was the relationship of aggregate demand functions to the demand functions of individuals (Rizvi, 1994, 2006). For the macro-analysis, it is the aggregate demand function that had importance, though the microfoundations project urged theorists to reduce it to the postulated characteristics of agents (individual utility function, initial endowments, and the resulting excess demand curves) in one way or another. This task seemed to be easy: at the bottom line, the demand function of the whole society emerges as the sum of individual excess demand functions. The papers underlying the DSM theorem (Debreu, 1974; Mantel, 1973; Sonnenschein, 1972, 1973), however, pointed out that no matter how precisely one establishes the micro-level conditions and characteristics, these features do probably not constrain the shape of aggregate excess demand functions—or they do, but under very narrow conditions.

An aggregate excess demand function only receives three features from the micro-level: continuity; that Walras's law holds; and that the price level is indifferent (no changes in the price level affect aggregate demand). An aggregate demand function having the appropriate characteristics can only be derived from the micro-level under highly specific circumstances. Mathematically it is a satisfying solution if in a model there is a representative agent assumed with a homothetic utility function. In case of a single representative agent homotheticity implies that she has a linear Engel curve, whilst in the case of multiple agents their Engel curves are parallel straight lines at the same prices. In the latter case, individual indifference systems generate a unique community indifference map (Gorman, 1953). For some it is highly contentious, however, whether straightforward economic analyses are possible at all as these strong restrictions push our models farther and farther from reality (Hoover, 2015, p. 707). As Hoover (2012, pp. 53–54) argues, postulating a single representative individual fails to restore the interlevel connections in itself, it is rather only a witty way of bypassing the problem. The price of mathematical cleanness is thus increasing abstraction. In Kirman's (1992) description, the DSM theorem confronts microfoundations theorists with a harsh dilemma. An aggregation problem emerges when connecting the macro-level with heterogeneous agents or, to avoid it, identical agents are to be postulated with appropriate (i.e. homothetic) utility functions, which for some is too restricting an assumption. The most destructive consequence of the DSM theorem is the lack of an analogy between the micro-level of heterogeneous agents and the macro-level.

The microfoundations project mainly neglected the DSM theorem (Rizvi, 1994). Hahn (1975, p. 363) was one of the few who explicitly emphasized the danger the DSM theorem raised against neoclassical orthodoxy. Lucas addressed the DSM aggregation problem by modelling the macro-level with a single representative unit (see Fig. 3.6) such as a household (Lucas & Rapping, 1969) or by postulating identical agents in a generation[17] (Lucas, 1972). Lucas's (1972, pp. 104–106; 1981, pp. 68–69) identical agents maximize according to a common utility function, and he carries out the representation of the whole economy in per capita terms. Hoover (2008, p. 329) argues that Lucas by so doing does not solve but only ignores the problem of aggregation. As all the painful consequences of the DSM theorem hold, the whole macroeconomic system has to be characterized with one agent's behaviour. Even though Hoover (2012, p. 51) claims that the adherents of the microfoundations movement, including Lucas, did probably not know about the inherent dangers, Lucas himself was apparently aware of the problems representative agent modelling raised:

> A satisfactory theoretical account of the determination of <u>average</u> employment (say, hours per household per year) and of cyclical fluctuations in average employment can be obtained by using the fiction of a representative household. Under this abstraction, a ten per cent employment reduction is treated as though it involved each household choosing to supply ten percent fewer hours. At the level of <u>individual</u> behavior, however, any theory which predicts a continuous labor supply response to wage movements is decisively rejected by the zero-one character of many observed employment changes. It would be more (though not perfectly) accurate to view a ten percent employment decrease as being effected by ten percent of households withdrawing all of their labor, the rest withdrawing none.
>
> For the purpose of aggregative theory, it is unclear whether this observation is of central or peripheral importance. After all, in a given year some people buy one new car and others none, yet we model aggregate automobile demand as though it arose from a representative household continuously adjusting its consumption of "automobile services". In this case, we know that the more abstract aggregative theory can be reconciled with the individual observations by averaging over households. In the case

---

[17] The single-agent optimization problem and placing many (representative) agents in a general equilibrium framework are two distinct stages in the evolution of Lucas's modelling technique (Hoover, 2012, p. 47).

of labor supply behavior, however, a suspicion persists that something fundamental is lost by such averaging. The observation of one worker being laid-off while another apparently identical worker continues to work full time is taken to imply not simply a need for a finer theory of equilibrium behavior for application at the individual level but rather the impossibility of finding <u>any</u> equilibrium account of labor supply behavior. (Typed notes. Lucas papers. Box 18. 'Labour supply, undated, 1 of 2' folder)

As Hoover (2015, p. 693) underlines, the usual argument renders these allegedly flawed attempts as only the first steps towards a satisfying solution. In spite of the misgivings he voiced in these fragments, as a matter of fact, Lucas insisted on his representative agent. Here he made efforts to attribute observed discontinuities in labour supply to the same kind of lump sum or fixed cost elements as that render it uneconomic for the individual to adjust her consumption of automobile services on a day-to-day or a year-to-year basis.

By placing the DSM argument on metaphysical grounds, recently Brian Epstein (2014) argued against the supervenience of macroeconomics on microeconomics. In his metaphysics, microeconomic properties fail to exhaustively determine macroeconomic properties, supervenience thus does not hold. For him, individuals and their properties and relations fail to determine social facts (Epstein, 2009). Epstein places his reasoning upon the nature of interdisciplinary connections to emphasize that it makes no sense to talk about the supervenience of macroeconomics on microeconomics until the domain of microeconomics is specified. The problem requires a careful analysis for if microeconomic properties are too broadly conceived, then supervenience becomes trivial. If everything macro is dependent upon is sorted under microeconomics, macro becomes inevitably supervenient upon micro. But if, on the contrary, the scope of microeconomics is conceived as too narrow, the result may be an empty theory. It is only a tin macroeconomics that such a void and depleted micro can underpin. Epstein's strategy is to elaborate a supervenience test through which it can be analysed whether microeconomic 'situations' with identical properties may generate dissimilar macroeconomic features. If so, macroeconomics is not supervenient on microeconomics for there must be something else over and above the micro-level properties to define the macro-level. Here Epstein resorts to a case of rule-based budgeting in order to demonstrate: different levels of government expenditures induced by different environmental outcomes trigger different macro-situations, whilst the micro-level remains the same.

In a series of papers Kevin D. Hoover exerted a far more balanced critique. Whilst Epstein denies both supervenience and reducibility, Hoover only rejects reducibility, but subscribes to supervenience. As he claims, the entities of macroeconomics cannot exist without individual agents, so supervenience holds. Hoover points out that reducibility to the micro-level is associated with two distinct things. The first is *methodological individualism*:

according to this principle, social scientific explanations are adequate only if social phenomena are understood in terms of individual properties, attitudes, beliefs, actions, and decisions (Blaug, 1992, p. 44). This principle, as Hoover (2001, p. 227) suggests, sets economists a highly arduous and complex task, and this is the reason why solutions are rather unsuccessful and dissatisfying. From this Hoover infers that methodological individualism[18] must be underpinned by a firm belief in *ontological individualism*, according to which only individual agents exist and all collective or supra-individual phenomena are derived from individuals' decisions (Blaug, 1992, p. 45). Manicas (2006, p. 75 and 92) provides a moderate version of ontological individualism. For him, persons are the dominant causal entities in societies, so agents must be the fundamental units in the social sciences, which in itself is a strong point in favour of the eliminative microfoundations project. In their rough forms Hoover characterizes both methodological individualism and ontological individualism as troublesome, even though several social scientists (including Blaug himself or Hayek) share a firm belief in ontological individualism. This belief, however, does not render methodological individualism more achievable. An ontological individualist thus may easily say that what she believes in as a scientist is methodologically infeasible. But in any case, ontological individualism entails the view that macroeconomic aggregates are not fundamental but only of secondary, derivative, and epiphenomenal units of economic reality, and this is the view Hoover challenges.

He argues that certain macroeconomic facts are irreducible to the choices or properties of individual economic entities, even though such facts are supervenient on microeconomics at the end of the day. For Hoover the relationship between the levels stands Epstein's supervenience test. If two worlds have the same micro-level properties, then they cannot but have the same macro-structure. In other words, their implied macro-structures are identical (Hoover, 2009b, p. 390). Hoover conceives macroeconomics as having an ontological anchor in the individual (i.e. in microeconomics), whilst there exist causally interacting macroeconomic entities (e.g. some aggregates). Plainly put, some entities of the macro-level cannot be in existence without individuals, whilst such entities are still ontologically distinct. This is only a weak form of reductionism. This argumentation perfectly fits into the recent literature of analytic philosophy where the exact relationship between supervenience and reducibility is extensively analyzed. Even if domain A is supervenient on domain B, it does not follow

---

[18] Reductions to the object level do not define the social sciences as the natural sciences have similar ambitions and similar problems as well. Theories in the natural sciences also have details irreducible to the fundamental objects (Hoover, 2008, pp. 319–320). The case of natural sciences is a strong point in favour of Hoover's objections to the reducibility of macroeconomics.

that every A-property is entailed by a B-property. Thus to define domain A something more is needed. If reduction is conceived as entailment, then supervenience fails to suffice for reducibility (Kim, 1990; McLaughlin, 1995).

Hoover's main point against reducibility is the fact that macroeconomic theorizing or even thinking about the macro involves some genuinely macroeconomic categories irreducible to the micro. Real economic agents cannot avoid relying on macroeconomic concepts, and so doing they directly deal with the macro-level. Broadly speaking, macroeconomics forms an inherent part of the microeconomic universe (Hoover, 2009b, p. 391), which fails to undermine Manicas's arguments for the individual regarded as the dominant causal entity in economics. As Hoover argues, a part of macro can successfully be reduced to micro-entities, but there is another part what is not and cannot be. At these points macroeconomics refers to irreducible macroeconomic entities (Hoover, 2001, p. 244). This is a fact no theory can escape if its purpose is to give an account of the behaviour of individual agents and other micro-level entities in a macro setting.

Through these statements Hoover perfectly describes the strategy Lucas applied, which, however, is a far cry from a lethal blow. Lucas's agents sometimes neglect the micro-level and directly focus upon the macro-level (Hoover, 2008, pp. 323–324). Lucasian islanders are tied to the macro as a matter of fact: they err as for global price dynamics, their rational expectations are identified with the outputs of an overall macro-model (Hoover, 2012, p. 20), and the budget constraint for the representative agent is the national income (Hoover, 2001, p. 228), though in per capita terms (Lucas, 1972, pp. 105–106; Lucas, 1981, pp. 68–69). It is contentious, however, whether this irreducibility and the constant presence of macro made up an impassable constraint to Lucas or it was a quality he actively exploited when seeking the informational sources of business cycles. In effect, Lucas (1972) intentionally emphasized this tension between the levels. The signal processing problem in Lucas's island models rests upon the agents' confusion when they are unable to distinguish local and global price dynamics. Here a genuinely macroeconomic level plays a key role in triggering large-scale fluctuations in a microfounded model.

At the bottom line, even though along dissimilar arguments, Epstein and Hoover see eye to eye on the failure of the microfoundations project as agents and their properties in themselves cannot define the macro-level. According to their main thread, macroeconomics in itself fails to rest exclusively upon microeconomics for macroeconomics contains a lot of elements that cannot be derived from the micro. In a strict reading it follows that if a model contains 'things' other than agents and their properties, then microfoundations are insufficient. But what are these 'other things' in Lucas's models? A well-defined setting taken as the environment. A playground that imposes also well-defined restrictions upon the interactions of agents, with a government and some institutions that can implicitly be regarded as created and carried by individuals. Such an institution in the island models is the agreement to control social-level division of labour, according to which members of the young generation are employed to produce whilst the elderly are retired to consume out of government transfers. Some of these elements may not be reduced to the agents but, as Hoover argues, socio-economic reality also contains some non-individualistic concepts and entities.

According to the criticism, these non-individualistic elements are redundant and unjustified parts in a truly microfounded model. But what would such a genuinely microfounded macro-model be like, a model free of all 'superfluous' elements to live up to Hoover and Epstein's standard? Nothing but agents, properties, and interactions, all placed into a vacuum expressing the lack of environment. Such a microfounded model would not contain anything that renders a set of agents a macroeconomy. To live up to this standard would be a further and highly drastic step along the road of making economics more abstract, idealized, and unreal. Not only would taking this step deteriorate applicability to real societies but would also render it dubious whether the resulting theory is still economics or social science. If the high level of abstraction and idealization is a concern, this standard hardly improves the acceptability of modern macroeconomics. This is a road back to a theory regarded as form without content, and Friedman's (1946, 1949, 1955) oft-voiced objections to Walrasian economics would be relevant again (see Section 2.2 for more on this). It might thus be unjustified to call the island models 'microfounded' in a strict sense, but at the same time these models, right for these non-individualistic elements, can provide more realistic representations than strictly and narrowly conceived microfounded models could. On this showing the irreducibility argument becomes only of terminological nature (is 'microfoundations' a proper qualifier to describe the project?), whilst neglects the line of its own reasoning. If macroeconomics cannot be reduced to the micro, as Hoover aptly argues, then there must be something non-micro in the models. Giving way to such elements in a theory can hardly be a failure.

Agents in the island models attach to this non-individualistic setting, monitor and interpret their environment, respond to its changes, and manipulate some other non-individualistic entities, such as money tied directly to the supra-island government hence to the macro. This setting triggers changes in the actors' statuses and vice versa: the government may consider giving monetary shocks to the system to which the agents need to respond. To carry out this response, agents may design institutions, such as a rule-based budget in Epstein's (2014) example. His case is a story of a national economy where budgetary expenses, similarly to an insurance scheme, change according to the weather. Epstein argues that such changes are changes right in the macro, so micro-level assumptions cannot exclusively define the macro-level. However, his example is off the mark. Passive (rule-based) responses to stochastic events like changes in weather fail to lead to changes in the structure of an economy. Weather outcomes do not establish differing macro-level settings, rather possible reactions to changes in weather are embedded or coded in the structure. Structure remains the same, it is only its state that changes under the contingencies. All this also applies to Lucas's theory. As parts of the environment, nominal shocks to the economy may emerge as unsystematic monetary-fiscal turbulences. Their source is not the narrowly conceived structure taken as a net stretched by agents alone, but the environment of this structure to which agents need to adjust. By constructing the model, Lucas highlighted in a mathematically tractable way that economic agents need to make decisions under conditions that change before they could collect and process all the necessary information. Environment is unsettled, so agents are incapable of placing their decisions upon an adequate information basis. In reality, this strain can be eased by purchasing additional information, though this detail does not significantly modify the relevance of Lucas's models (Lucas, 1975, pp. 1113 and 1120, fn. 8; Lucas, 1981, pp. 179 and 212, fn. 8).

Whilst the supervenience and reducibility problem regards the exclusiveness of micro-level assumptions in building macro, Hoover (2009a) analyzed a distinct albeit related question: the way a system emanates from its parts, irrespective of these parts being purely micro or partly macro. Here Hoover argues that causal realism is achievable through assumptions selected with a view to predictive performance (as a reminder, in Section 3.1.1 above Friedman's definitely micro-level assumption of rational leaves is analyzed as a pure case of performance-driven theorizing to disregard the real nature of the target). If macro is supervenient on micro, a real causal system cannot but consist of real entities and their characteristics as reality is identical to itself. In this context, irreducibility only underlines that beyond micro any 'microfounded' macroeconomic theory must contain some entities inherently of macroeconomic nature (as reality itself does), and all these components are to be placed into the theory via assumptions. Hoover (2009a), however, argues that the *same* real causal mechanism can also be represented via untrue and purely fictitious entity-level propositions that are not supposed to preserve real entity properties (Section 3.4 details the ways real-world entity properties can show up in theories). It follows that a macro-structure can stem from at least two dissimilar micro-levels: a real-like micro (such as $micro_1$ in Fig. 3.2) and a cooked-up micro ($micro_2$ in Fig. 3.2), a macro-level causal mechanism of reality is thus alleged to be able to live on unreal micro. Fig. 3.2 summarizes Epstein's and Hoover's criticisms over the microfoundations project in terms of supervenience and reducibility.

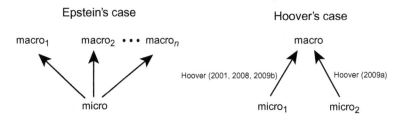

FIG. 3.2   Supervenience and reducibility in Epstein's and Hoover's accounts.

In Epstein's case, one micro may result in various macro-levels, but any macro can uniquely be reduced to the micro. By contrast, in Hoover's case various micro-levels lead to the same macro-level causal structure. More specifically, Hoover argues for the independence of macro as various micro-levels seem to determine the same macro which is far from obvious. Interestingly, neither Epstein nor Hoover raises the possibility of a one-to-one relationship between the levels. To be on the safe side, it must be mentioned that all this is not the problem of multiple realization of macro, mentioned above. Multiple micro-levels may lead to the same macro, though in such a case all micro-levels are real. By contrast, Hoover's claim amounts to the case for the possibility of building the same causal structure upon untrue sets of entity-level propositions, such as the causal analysis of the density of leaves via assuming rational utility-maximizing leaves. However, it is contentious whether on the basis of Friedman's rational leaves one can answer the questions regarding the real causal structure underlying the position of real leaves, even if rational leaves may save the phenomenon. The intuitive answer is in the negative. Dwelling upon the parables of the leaves, all we know is that leaves have a given density on a tree because their 'behaviour' looks as if they were rational optimizers, whilst they are obviously not. This (not only descriptively) false assumption forces us to rotate in inferential circles whilst it is impossible to gain knowledge about the real causes of the phenomenon.

Generally speaking, the debates over the microfoundations of macroeconomics concern the way parts combine into a larger whole. Hoover's (2009a) arguments highlight that the relationship between a whole and its constituent parts is unclear as it is conceived to be possible to represent a system through some parts alien to it. If a system is regarded as consisting of parts, it is dubious at a minimum whether other parts having unreal characteristics can form the same system, or parts of a system are typical of it and without them a concrete structure cannot emerge either in reality or on the scratch pads of social scientists. More specifically, if a system or structure is to be similar somehow to its real counterpart in order that a sound causal analysis could be performed at the structural level, it is at least plausible that its parts are also to bear some resemblance to their real counterparts. All this boils down to the assumptions issue of economics as it is the theorist who establishes a structure representation via entity assumptions, regardless these entities are micro-level objects or genuinely belong to the macro. If it turns out that entity properties and structures form a close-knit unit, as they presumably do, this relationship will work as a constraint to or a minimum requirement for making assumptions. In this case any partial macro-level causal analysis must rest upon real entity properties, which still does not imply the purpose of precise description.

In the general philosophy of science and philosophy of physics, structuralist accounts are entirely devoted to looking into this problem, the problem of parts building a system or structure. They thus promise to serve as an appropriate general framework for the analysis of the relationship between parts and wholes. Entity realism and the different forms of structural realism, the extreme views, all claim that knowledge of structures and knowledge of entities are separable somehow. And they ought to be as reality has zones where we had better withdraw our realist commitments, so both these views are rather ambitious to 'radically reform intuitive realist presuppositions about theories' (Chakravartty, 1998, p. 406). By emphasizing the implausibility and the epistemic unviability of these radical cases, a moderate version has emerged very recently. Not only does Anjan Chakravartty's 'semirealism' argue that structures are unconceivable without putative relata, so entity realism and structural realism entail and contain one another (Chakravartty, 2007, pp. 42–43), but it also places entity properties into a central position in terms of underpinning the emerging structures and hence causal relations. According to the basic idea of semirealism, there are 'properties which entities satisfying particular structural relations [...] must possess, for it is in virtue of these [...] properties that entities partake in [...] structural relations in the first place' (Chakravartty, 1998, p. 400). This is the missing one-to-one relationship between entities and causal structures mentioned above.

By contrasting structural realism and entity realism below the purpose is to highlight that any concrete structure is inseparably tied to its relata and their characteristics, which is a constraint any representation must take into account. Even though structural realism is the result of some recent debates in the philosophy of physics, the application of this framework to social sciences leads neither to the distortion of socio-economic reality nor to the reduction of economics to physics. As Witt (2008) argues, this framework Aristotelian by origin was intended to provide a causalist framework applicable to both the natural and the social sciences. As far as causation is considered, natural and social sciences can thus be treated on equal footing. However, it by no means implies the assumption of the reducibility of human characteristics to physical theories (Manicas, 2006, p. 23 and 43). Even though there is an ontological regress across the disciplines along which macroeconomics and other social sciences are allegedly reducible even to the behaviour of subatomic particles, the basic objects in economics are still our well-known agents and other non-individual entities. This claim stops the ontological regress halfway through in order that economics could remain economics. Thus the contrast of structural realism and entity realism is only intended to draw attention to the fact that economic entities have properties and these properties are of crucial importance in establishing connections and carrying the structure they are embedded in. This can easily be taken as a special 'natural ontological attitude' to understand societies as formed by identifiable agents having intrinsic properties (Witt, 2008, p. 136).

3.2 Realism in trouble: The need for selectivity

Chapter 1 provided a bird's eye review on those arguments emerged in the philosophy of science that weakened the position of scientific realism. As these arguments could hardly be ignored, realism is compelled to act on the defensive. Bearing both the arguments and the counterarguments in mind, even though theories are oftentimes successful in predictive terms, scientific realism is best regarded as a belief or a hypothesis in the literal sense the ultimate fundaments of which sceptical anti-realists can undermine (Putnam, 1978, p. 4 and p. 19). For the realist camp this belief is properly grounded as it does not go beyond a healthy epistemic caution (Berenstain & Ladyman, 2012, p. 152), but these grounds do not seem to be strong enough to convince an anti-realist to abandon her faith.

The realist–anti-realist conflict is about the extent of the realist commitment. Whilst a realist firmly believes that human knowledge can be achieved even in the unobservable region, anti-realists constrain this conviction to the observables. For an anti-realist, causality which she regards as inherently unobservable lies beyond the territory of science and belongs to the realm of mere metaphysical speculations or worse.[19] Instrumentalism–anti-realism thus makes do with saving the phenomena. As any commitment to the realism of causality and other unobservable 'things' is problematic and difficult to prove, paying attention to scientists' realist ambitions and efforts ought to be a crucial aspect in any research in the history of science and methodology. Being a realist is plausibly accompanied by one's ambition to be a realist—a prominent aspect of her intentional background the importance of which is aptly studied in the literature (Suárez, 2002, p. 4). This emphasis upon the realist's ambitions by no means amounts to defining scientific realism by aims.

---

[19] This is only an anti-realist prejudice. Manicas (2006, p. 17) convincingly argues that in many cases causality is open for direct observation. On this ground, it is easy to presume that causality works in the unobservable region as well.

Even though the idea has a growing literature (van Fraassen, 1980, pp. 8–9; Lyons, 2005, 2017), it is far from convincing that neglecting scientific achievements to conceive scientific realism in terms of aims still leads to a variant of scientific realism (Chakravartty, 2017d). However, in the present context ambitions and aims are telling. As we shall see in Chapter 4, in his methodology Friedman openly neglected any concerns beyond empirical performance, a key constituent of his instrumentalism, whilst Lucas highlighted some key aspects of realist theorizing, so paying attention to aims here is necessitated, first, by the sharp dissimilarities in Friedman's and Lucas's ambitions and, second, by the suspicion that achievements are likely to appear in combination with aspirations. See Section 5.3 for more on the mitigated versions of scientific realism.

Narrowing down the focus of realist aspirations to a limited territory constitutes an effective defence for realism. In this context, Fine (1991) suggests a special piecemeal realism by which the weaknesses of the arguments for an overall realism can be overcome. He argues that it is necessary to examine on a case-by-case basis which hypotheses and entities seem to be irrational to doubt. As another example, the common reference to the approximate truth of our best theories[20] (Worrall, 2012) also stems from this strategy. Strictly speaking, our theories are highly likely to be false whilst they may admittedly contain some parts that are worth realist commitment for being close to the truth (Laudan, 1981; Leeds, 2007; Chakravartty, 2017b, p. 14). The discourse over mature and ad-hoc theories is also aimed at identifying the theories that deserve realists' adherence. For instance, it is only in the case of generally accepted, long-living, and predictively successful (in short: mature) theories that Worrall (1989, pp. 113–114; 2012, p. 82) accepts the realist arguments for approximate truth. A mature theory has stood falsifying tests for a long time (Chakravartty, 2007, p. 28) and, what is more, such a theory predicts some phenomena which are not written into it: phenomena which were unobserved the time the theory was born; thus it could not have been formulated with the aim of saving them.[21] This is prediction in the literal sense of the word. A phenomenon a theory predicts becomes observable thanks to this prediction.

---

[20] Or 'being true in some respects', as French and Ladyman (1999) put it. The vocabulary is colourful. Referring to the abundance of false propositions applied in theorizing, Bailer-Jones (2003, p. 64) talks of 'a weakened version of truth for scientific models'. Following Popper (1962), Niiniluoto (1977) and Oddie (1986), Teller (2004, p. 434) delineates a more diverse vocabulary including verisimilitude, closeness to the truth and truthlikeness.

[21] Mäki (2011, p. 5) conceives this narrow focus on mature theories as too stringent a criterion for it threatens to screen out economic theories as immature attempts. His minimal formulation of scientific realism entails no definite commitment to the truth of a theory. For him it is enough that a theory might be true or false. Accordingly, the purpose of scientific realism is not a commitment to true theories but to decide whether a theory can be true or it is false.

Psillos (1999, pp. 105–107) distinguishes truth-like constituents and idle components of theories. It is the truth-like constituents that mainly support the empirical success of theories that deserve realist commitments. Realists thus take responsibility only for some parts of their cherished theories.[22] As a consequence, good empirical performance serves as an argument for the verisimilitude of not the whole bulk of a theory but only its key parts. It is only its parts and not a whole theory that is intended to be true. In the meantime, no claim for the realisticness of idle components emerges, so in this respect there is no need for empirical underpinnings.

A crucial shortcoming of these approaches is their fundaments being composed of highly vague concepts. Neither approximate truth (Worrall, 1989, p. 104; Teller, 2001, p. 403) nor maturity has generally accepted definitions, so these conceptions work well at an intuitive level at best.[23] The efficiency of defence can be improved by pinpointing those characteristics and elements of our theories that genuinely deserve fine-tuned realist commitments. Theories contain a plethora of untrue statements; however, some parts are still worth realists' adherence.

Entity realism and structural realism are also the products of this specialized strategy. In spite of the crucial differences, they have something in common. Both put forward the assertion that even our best theories are untrue if taken at face value, but they still contain something the real existence of which, together with the (approximate) truth of some related statements, cannot plausibly be questioned. A chief dissimilarity between these philosophies stands, on the one hand, in where they place the demarcation lines between the realistically acceptable and unacceptable parts and, on the other, in the way the followers provide a principled guide to choose from the candidate theories.

3.2.1 Entity realism

Entity realism embraces a conviction that some unobservable entities our theories postulate exist in the mind-independent reality. Its main adherent, Hacking (1982) tried to identify the entities regarding which scientists must be realist or cannot reasonably be anti-realist at least. He suggested the set of objects and their properties which are applied as instruments in experiments. Manipulability[24] may come in various forms

---

[22] It is far easier to identify such truth-like elements or working posits post hoc than ex ante (Chakravartty, 2017d, p. 3382). In order to find them we need causal understanding of phenomena.

[23] As an example from the history of economic thought, RBC theorists regarded the stochastically disturbed neoclassical growth model as an established theory (Prescott, 2006, p. 204), while in his assessment De Vroey (2016, p. 304) rejects this view and harshly criticizes RBC models on this ground (as well).

[24] Conditions more permissive than manipulability can also be formulized. For instance, Dorato (2000a) puts forward measurability as a possible ground for existence claims.

and includes the capability of systematically employing an entity; the use of entities with the aim of intervening in phenomena involving other, less understood entities or causal mechanisms; or the application of entities as causes of phenomena described in causal explanations (Chakravartty, 2017b, p. 18). It is exactly the most significant achievement of entity realism that it called attention to the direct relationship between the possibility of realist commitments and causal understanding (Chakravartty, 2008b, pp. 154–155). The manipulation of objects and the execution of experiments they underlie are facilitated by the knowledge of objects' causal properties, so for Hacking entity realism stems from what one can do with objects as causal instruments. If it is possible to precisely trigger something by using a then hypothetic entity, what the electron also used to be, then it makes no sense to doubt its real existence. Before accepting its reality, an unobservable entity must be hypothetical. However, the ability to manipulate may be different in different cases, the strength of realist commitments thus varies accordingly (Chakravartty, 2008b, p. 156).

Some scepticism about theories, the approximate descriptions of the way the world works permeates Hacking's reasoning. Even if a theory provides a good explanation to a phenomenon, the truth of the theory does not follow. However, similar misgivings about objects are pointless, since by exploiting their well-documented causal properties expected outcomes are achievable. Hacking regards causal understanding as a prerequisite for realism.

One of the most significant consequences of Hacking's arguments is the alleged separability of the knowledge about entities' causal properties from the truth of theories describing entities' behaviour and relations. It is of course dubious whether this separability is plausible, which is a question that also regards structural realism. As theories also contain entities, it may be more accurate to say that entities conceived to be existent form those parts or aspects of theories the truth of which is irrational to doubt. Accordingly, even if the causal properties are known, this is argued to be insufficient to ground the realism of the related theories.

The limits of observability and hence the knowledgeability of entities emerge in economics in a unique way. As it is argued in Section 3.4.3, economics relying upon introspection has epistemological grip in some fields beyond the realm of physically observables. What is more, economics normally works with a lot of observable entities and their properties. However, for instance, Friedman's theoretically postulated and unobservable permanent income is a different case. Friedman's consumption theory based on the permanent income hypothesis successfully explains why consumer expenditures are less volatile than the national income (Galbács, 2015, p. 224). But this achievement, as Hacking's reasoning suggests, fails to provide a sufficient ground for a belief in the existence of permanent income. Even if the theory is successful, agents may only behave as if they adjusted consumption to an assumed permanent income. Seeking the ground, turning to the limits permanent income theory sets on economic policy is a good bet.[25] For instance, by a simple increase in disposable income fiscal policy is unexpected to boost consumption expenditures. Households' conviction that the change in disposable income is permanent is a prerequisite for an effective fiscal stimulus. This is a peculiarity especially emphasized by the rational expectations extension of permanent income theory (Bilson, 1980; Bird & Bodkin, 1965; Shea, 1995) and the Barro–Ricardo equivalence theorem (Barro, 1974; Buchanan, 1976). The theory thus distinguishes successful and unsuccessful fiscal stimuli and, consequently, success and failure come to be unambiguously predictable. If fiscal policy by utilizing these causal properties can smoothly stimulate consumption expenditures whilst another policy neglecting these concerns falls through, following Hacking's logic the existence of permanent income is irrational to doubt.

Hacking's ideas are contentious. As it is underlined above, Hacking's philosophy addresses the causal roles entities play. Causal understanding of the world in the lack of theories, however, is difficult to imagine. A belief in the simple existence of entities can hardly serve as an efficient support. As Chakravartty (2007, p. 31) puts it, one 'cannot have knowledge of the existence of entities in isolation', that is, isolated from the knowledge of what they are like and how they behave. A theory voiceless about the behaviour of entities can at best be a set of assertions aiding in seeking entities but on the basis of manipulability alone the question of existence remains unanswerable. As a consequence of separation an entity realist may regard the entities of some already falsified theories as existent. This situation, if found undesirable, is only avoidable by constraining the sources of possible existents to theories conceived as true. Accordingly, Elsamahi (1994) boils entity realism down to theory realism as exploiting the causal functions of entities (i.e. manipulation) is impossible without a reliable theoretical background.

It is thus the content and extent of knowledge that determine whether it is reasonable to regard the entities of a falsified theory as real. One may suggest a theory of storks delivering new-born babies to be statistically tested on birth rates and the size of stork populations. Even when this theory is falsified, the entities it assumes (storks and human babies) can still be conceived as existents. If our ontological claims are limited to mere existence, it is no problem if entities of an already falsified theory are still supposed to be real. Storks exist even if they do not bring babies. However, it also makes sense to say that storks as the theory conceives them are

---

[25] These limits were further elaborated by the studies that specified the numeric values for propensities to consume on certain income categories Friedman suggested (Holbrook & Stafford, 1971; Laumas & Mohabbat, 1972).

inexistent. The theory is about some funny creatures called 'storks' and having large wings and a friendly attitude towards babies, but they are not like the black-and-white birds we are all familiar with in experience. As knowledge about the causal roles of entities is far more than belief in existence, and as this knowledge yields theories, if a theory is falsified, assumptions about the causal roles may also be invalidated. However, existence claims may still hold. To make matters worse, even in such a case falsification may happen not to undermine knowledge of the causal roles of certain entities. Theories may err about some entities but not necessarily about others. In general, falsified theories might be approximately true and might deserve realist commitments.

3.2.2 Structural realism

Hacking's entity realism subscribes to the meagre belief in the existence of experimentally utilized objects and in the possibility of knowing some of their causal properties. The purpose of describing entity properties belongs to theories, but these theories as a matter of fact change from time to time. We know that the Earth exists, even though we used to conceive it as flat, so the idea of the Earth as a globe is only a quite recent development. According to entity realism, one can be certain of the existence of certain entities; however it is contentious whether the flat Earth and the spherical Earth are the one and same object (Chakravartty, 2007, p. 32). Entity realism is problematically flexible. If entity realists claim that they still believe in the same entity regardless of the significant changes in its descriptions, they can never err. In this case realism goes trivial (Chakravartty, 2008b, p. 154). No statement about an entity can be wrong as any statement is empty.

By contrast, structural realism suggests the idea of realism about relations and structures,[26] the 'web of relations' (in Cassirer's words) whilst withholds any knowledge of entities. Structural realism thus takes the other extreme. Whilst it is sceptical about the existence (let alone the nature) of unobservable entities, it remains realist about the structure of the unobservable world and about the theories describing this structure. Structural realists regard the relations as real, but beyond the structure they deny the possibility of knowledge of the underlying nature of reality (Chakravartty, 2004, p. 151). The content of our knowledge of entities, if there are such things as entities at all, changes, but theories with their equations well describe the structure. Even though structural realism on some influential accounts seems to be relevant only to formal mathematical sciences, it does not imply an exclusive commitment to mathematical

---

[26] Informally put, various forms of structural realism refer to structure as systems of relations.

models. Mathematics has no monopoly over describing the structure of a facet of reality. Set theory and formal logic have the same consistency as mathematics when it comes to representing the qualitative characteristics of structures, and the structure is always conceived as more than pure logico-mathematical structure. Instead, structure is meant to be theoretically informed structure (French & Ladyman, 2003a, p. 32; French, 2007).

It is Worrall's (1989) seminal paper that catapulted the idea of structural realism or syntactic realism to fame in modern times.[27] Even though the ongoing debate regards the ontological status of unobservable theoretical entities in physics, economics may also benefit from some implications. What is at stake is the relationship of objects and the structure they form, which is the physical analogy of the relationship between agents in microfounded macroeconomics and their relations.

Worrall studies whether there are some parts of theories that with some modifications survive the radical changes in science. Empirical performance may keep inconsistent theories alive, so it is better to scrutinize predictive success and theoretical developments in isolation. One of Worrall's several examples regards the Newton–Einstein transition in physics. In multiple cases the predictions are indistinguishable, whilst the theories are radically different. On this ground he argues that science at the empirical level develops cumulatively (successful predictions are preserved), whilst in theoretical terms sharp changes occur. Phenomena may thus be saved upon dissimilar theoretical grounds. These changes in science, however, are far from comprehensive, so there is a middle case between a preservation of mere empirical content and a preservation of the whole theoretical background. This is the preservation of form or structure on the basis of which a limited realism remains tenable and all the troublesome consequences of theoretical switches seem to be blocked. This is a conception which is in line with both the no-miracles argument (see Section 1.3.2); thus empirical success can still be regarded as a sign of truth (approximate structural truth at least), and the pessimistic meta induction (see Section 1.3.3) as theories may turn out to be false (Worrall, 2012, pp. 77–78).

Worrall tries to perfectly separate structures and entities: the former is the form, whilst the latter is the content that describes the entities filling the structure. Based on his examples taken from the history of science he infers that it is possible to provide a true description of the structure of the world by a theory that misses the real nature of entities. Equations express

---

[27] Following Worrall's explicit references, Morganti (2004, p. 81) tracks structural realism down to Pierre Duhem and Henri Poincaré's distinction between relations and the things standing in relations. Seeking the roots of epistemic structural realism Chakravartty (2007, p. 33), partly based on Gower's (2000) arguments, provides a longer list including Russell, Cassirer, and Carnap as well.

relational structures and causal relations (Psillos, 1995, p. 23; Morganti, 2004, p. 81) and they survive exactly for the relations they describe are real. At the same time, further knowledge of the entities is unnecessary and unachievable. One knows how objects are related and in order to know it there is no need for her to know what they are or what they are like. Relations and structures of mathematical nature constitute the only accessible level of reality.

As a matter of fact, Worrall's claim is meagre and vague. His only reference is the alleged observation that in the history of science some structural statements of some theories in modified forms might have re-emerged in some subsequent theories. Worrall, however, defines the structural aspects of theories in such broad terms that they cannot be more than some highly general statements about structures (Stanford, 2003, p. 571). No wonder that some continuity occurs. Depicted with a wide brush, everything is similar to everything else.

A crucial consequence of Worrall's reasoning is the alleged possibility of providing true descriptions of structures with entities remaining obscure and hidden. For Worrall, to be more specific, a structure can correctly be described even if a theory intentionally errs on the entities. In other words, even if theoretical entities are deprived of real properties on purpose. The fact that science in history was for many times in the wrong about the nature of entities may suggest that it is unnecessary to have even approximately true entity descriptions. As a striking consequence, it follows that theoretical entities can be hypothesized in order to act in a certain, theoretically postulated mechanism and to this end they are not supposed to bear any resemblance to their real counterparts. Theories can describe real causal mechanisms as structures composed of wholly fictitious entities. This is Friedman's stance in Hoover's (2009a) account. These useful fictions only serve to 'express' the structure, and in other respects we have nothing to do with them. Structure is only a logical form, a system of connections, and the same structure may be compatible with various ontologies (Psillos, 1995, pp. 20–24).

Followers of Worrall's original idea shortly broke into two camps. To point out the differences, Ladyman (1998) coined the terms *epistemic structural realism* (ESR) and *ontic structural realism* (OSR). Discussing *restrictive structural realism* (meaning ESR) and *eliminative structural realism* (meaning OSR) Psillos (2001) suggests a similar distinction. ESR is the milder version. Here structure is representable even if there are errors about the entities. There may be something beyond the structure (objects probably exist), but it is only the structure we can have knowledge about. Over and above structure the nature of the physical world remains hidden (French, 2006). Entity descriptions usually turn out to be false because we only assume that the best way of understanding the world necessarily leads through our understanding the objects. According to the radical variant, OSR, there is a reason more fundamental than the limits of observations for keeping away from entity descriptions. OSR philosophers simply call the existence of putative relata into question. For them, there is only structure without entities (Morganti, 2004, p. 82). Whilst ESR admits that there is probably something 'out there' beyond the structure to which we have no epistemic access, OSR claims there is nothing but structure (Psillos, 2001, p. S18). Objects (entities) only play a heuristic role. Their only purpose is to facilitate the introduction of structures that carry the ontological weight (Busch, 2003, pp. 215–220; Psillos, 2006). The moment the structure is ready, however, objects can be rubbed out of the picture (French & Ladyman, 2003a, p. 42). In order to describe relations, here a structure is not necessarily in need of the relata having the underlying properties.

Epistemic structural realism

ESR believes that the objective world consists of entities amongst which some are probably unobservable. Entities are characterized by some properties and relations, whilst we can only have knowledge of relations and hence the structure. Plainly put, the nature of entities standing in structures is unknown. ESR does not eliminate the entities, though solely refers to them through the structure (Ladyman, 1998, p. 413). Accordingly, ESR is nothing but an epistemologically corrected or limited version of traditional full-blown realism: there stands an epistemological obstacle in the way of our having knowledge about the entities (Chakravartty, 2003a, pp. 867–868). It is only the structural aspects of reality that we can have knowledge of. French and Ladyman (2011, p. 27) distinguish two forms of ESR. According to one of them, individual but unobservable objects do exist, but they are completely hidden for us. They reject to be known (ESR_1). The other form (ESR_2) leaves this question open: individual objects may exist, but human knowledge is so constrained that we can never know this for certain (French & Ladyman, 2011, p. 27). It is a highly debated issue which version of ESR Worrall launched in deed.

It is rather difficult to imagine a structure that leaves entities hidden, let alone to conceptualize that. A lot depends on the definition of structure. If one succeeds in finding a definition that is empty enough, structural similarity (or similarity of structures) may emerge as a relation between theories and in this case there is no need to know anything about objects. Theories can preserve and share the same structure, so the main tenet of structural realism automatically holds. The careful definition Russell (2009, p. 224) provides is a most instructive example: 'a class α ordered by the relation R has the same structure as a class β ordered by the relation S, if to every term in α some one term in β corresponds, and vice versa, and if when two terms in α have the relation R, then the corresponding terms in β have the relation S, and vice versa'. However, as Chakravartty

(2007, pp. 36–37) underlines, the so interpreted structural similarity may apply to relations between radically different theories. Here, as a matter of fact, to know anything about the properties of relata is unnecessary for interpreting the structure. The problem is that the so conceived structure claims absolutely nothing about the relata beyond their simple cardinality. Any two sets can bear structural similarity to each other if each contains as many elements as the other. The concept of structure here is completely empty. On this conception, any knowledge of structure beyond cardinality is aprioristic (Demopoulos & Friedman, 1985, pp. 627–629). Structure in this framework can provide only trivialities.

One of the possible completions of ESR is the application of Ramsey sentences. Ramsey sentences represent structures so that the place of each unobservable entity is filled by a 'thing' that can be whatever fitting into a given structure. We thus only know that entities exist and stand in a certain (well-described) structure, whilst we have no knowledge of their nature. The knowledge of entities is purely structural, and the properties of entities play no role in building the structure. Theorizing in Ramsey sentences implies that all the referentially suspect terms are omittable from the phrasing; theories can thus be approximately true even when the remaining terms fail to have determinate referents (French, 2007; Papineau, 2010, p. 377). Consequently, realism stays tenable even in cases where there are no determinately referring terms, so successful reference (i.e. the approximate truth of theoretical description of the nature of entities) is no longer a precondition for established realist claims.

As an advantage, the debate over the assumed entity properties does not emerge, so it is not a question whether the flat Earth and the spherical Earth are the same Earth or not. If entities are not omitted, it is always debatable whether a referred entity satisfies some set of theoretical descriptions.[28] The strategy is not aimed at defending untrue theories[29] but rather at dismissing 'successful' reference, whatever 'successful' means, as a standard for building or assessing theories. Here reference is not a ground for judging the approximate truth of theories, and the referential status of

---

[28] Appropriate definitions of abstraction and idealization on the one hand and denotation and representational codes on the other hand ease his tension. Abstraction is a justified tool for a realist if it aids her in selecting from the real properties of objects. Realistically idealizing some real characteristics requires a representational code to facilitate the interpretation. See Section 3.4.1 for more on this.

[29] As in entity realism, a diluted reference standard or reference requirement has some bizarre consequences. Even an untrue theory can meet a generous enough definition of reference. In such cases some wholly misdescribed entities are regarded as successfully identified. It is of course contentious how an entity can be identified in the lack of an at least partly adequate description. Along this line any theory can be true. In this vein, for instance, Hardin and Rosenberg (1982) argue that aether successfully refers to the electromagnetic field.

any theoretical term is irrelevant. There is no need for a theory either to postulate existing entities or to provide approximately true descriptions of them (Cruse & Papineau, 2002). The novelty of this approach stands in the possibility of creating theories being true without reference: true in a structural sense. According to the idea, the places of entities can remain empty in a structure representation; structures can thus be described even with ignoring the nature of entities. Ramsey sentences, however, also raise the critique by Demopoulos and Michael Friedman mentioned above (Chakravartty, 2007, pp. 37–38).

Ontic structural realism

ESR holds that objects and their properties are unimportant as we can hardly have any knowledge of them. ESR only hides entities behind a veil of ignorance whilst does not reject their existence. The more radical version of structural realism, OSR makes efforts to completely eliminate the objects and conceives theories to be capable of revealing the relations only. In contrast with ESR's partiality, OSR emerges as a complete realism for it draws some ontological inferences from an epistemological obstacle ESR highlights. As OSR argues, the supervenience of relations on relata (subatomic particles, molecules, or even human beings) does not seem to be a metaphysical necessity. One can thus imagine ontologies where relations do not rest upon related objects and their properties. In such a case, in a purely relational ontology, objects can be the bundles or nodes of relations at best, without any enduring individuality or identity (i.e. haecceity). If objects are eliminated, the problem of the epistemological grip on them will never emerge. If it is only structures that exist, then structural realists have complete knowledge of the world, and there is no need for ambiguous details (French, 2010, p. 91; Esfeld, 2013). For this reason, ESR believers find OSR excessively radical and call for more caution about cancelling objects from amongst the existents just because in some special cases some ambiguity over their ontological status emerges. Their non-existence is equally dubious. Epistemic inaccessibility does not imply definite non-existence.

Morganti (2004, p. 102) argues that OSR reverses the traditional Aristotelian object-based ontology that dominated Western human thinking until recently. In this ontology, the ultimate building blocks of reality are the entities as individual objects with intrinsic properties,[30] and relations are of derivative character only (Chakravartty, 2012, p. 190).

---

[30] In broad terms, an object instantiates an intrinsic or non-relational property whether or not the object stands in relations to other objects. By contrast, extrinsic or relational or relationally determined properties belong to objects because of the relations objects are involved in. It is noteworthy, as it is argued in what follows, that intrinsic properties may ground relations, so they have relational aspects.

Consequently, traditional scientific realism is also said to require a fundamental revision for it rests upon the object-based ontology OSR rejects. ESR is in consonance with this world view in broad terms, the only conflict stems from ESR's efforts to ignore the nature of entities (French, 2006, p. 171). This is the reason why OSR denies to regard ESR as a real alternative to traditional scientific realism: ESR making some refinements is alleged to support and not to revise the ontological consequences of conventional scientific realism. Accordingly, OSR blames ESR for fading into this old-fashioned idea. An important distinction still holds, however. Traditional realism reaches far beyond the structural properties of the objects, whilst ESR approves of structural knowledge only (Ladyman, 1998, pp. 411–418).

OSR reverses this relationship and renders the structures primary. As everything beyond structures is ambiguous, our best bet when studying reality is not to postulate superfluous existents. By so doing, we can form a purely structural conception of reality. Structure for OSR is not simply privileged but ontologically autonomous. Structure is primary over and prior to the objects, and relata themselves are conceived to be ontologically eliminable. This is a definite top-down approach, starting from the structural level, instead of the bottom-up, object-based world view (French, 2012, p. 20). According to OSR, structure is primitive and ontologically subsistent, and structures are not supervenient on the existence and properties of entities, so the structural approach does not imply a further belief in metaphysically robust objects (Ladyman, 1998, p. 420). Even in the cases where OSR openly admits the existence of objects, they are conceptualized only structurally, so objects and properties are derivative at best. There exists nothing beyond the structures in the unobservable realm. Objects are primary in the traditional ontology, where they have certain properties and get in relations to other objects.[31] By contrast, OSR starts from the level of structure and suggests talking about 'objects' as the derivatives of relations, strictly in quotation marks[32] (French & Ladyman, 2003a, pp. 39–40). OSR implies an extremely thin notion of objects at a maximum. Objects are regarded as superfluous and dismissible concepts forced by our irrational insistence on the conventional object-based ontology.

Philosopher of mathematics Stewart Shapiro provides a highly instructive description of the idea of structures ontologically primary over objects. In a Platonist fashion, Shapiro (1997, p. 9) suggests *ante rem* (i.e. before-the-thing) structuralism, according to which structures exist without systems

---

[31] This is the standard picture in which entities have 'non-derivative ontological status' (Chakravartty, 2017a, p. 2278).

[32] While OSR asserts the dependence of relata on relations, this dependence is not of ontological nature but rather mere conceptual dependence, since here there are no relata at all. Relata are concepts having no counterparts in physical reality (Chakravartty, 2017a, p. 2279).

of objects exemplifying them (Landry, 2012, p. 40). Shapiro's examples are the natural-number structure, the real-number structure, and the set-theoretic hierarchy that exist regardless there are objects standing in such structures. Even though there exist no objects that can act as relata, structures as systems of relations can still be in existence. Busch (2003, p. 213) discusses the idea in the context of universals and particulars. Universals exist independently of their instances; structures are thus conceived to be existent even with no instances. By contrast, the Aristotelian conception of structures can be labelled as *in re* (i.e. in-the-thing) structuralism (Shapiro, 1997, p. 84), where in order for a structure to exist objects are to precede the structure. In this framework, without objects it makes no sense even to try to imagine a concrete structure.[33] It is worthy of note that here there are two statements, however. Claiming that structures exist regardless they are instantiated by objects is not the same as arguing for the sole existence of structures. The strong reading of OSR suggests the latter view. Even if one claims that it is only (the representation and understanding of) structures that matter in science, it does not follow that only structures exist.

As OSR is intimately related to quantum mechanics (French, 1998, pp. 94–107) that has problems with the traditional concept of individual objects, it seems as if the epistemological consequences of quantum mechanics (in the quantum domain we may have access to the structural properties only) had driven OSR believers to some excessive and hardly conceivable ontological inferences (it is only structures that exist). Quantum objects reject to be regarded as individuals with identity in the standard metaphysical sense (Castellani, 1993). Quantum mechanics is conceived to have undermined the identity or individuality of quantum particles. More specifically, quantum mechanical state functions attribute the same properties to distinct particles; thus elementary particles in the quantum domain seem to be indistinguishable (Busch, 2003, p. 212). As a consequence, these entities emerge as non-individuals and non-identities in the OSR ontology (French & Ladyman, 2011, pp. 26–28) and are completely dissolved in structure. In other words, some theories have an embedded metaphysical underdetermination as for the nature of objects (i.e. we do not exactly know what they are), so it is the simplest to dispense of them (Ladyman, 1998, p. 419). However, on the basis of the alleged rejection of the quantum domain to be conceptualized in the object-based ontology, OSR takes a further and highly contentious step to suggest a

---

[33] It holds even if Landry (2012, pp. 41–42) claims that objects in both the *ante rem* and *in re* versions of structuralism have structural properties only, and there are no properties to objects that stand independently of the structural properties. Psillos (2006) is more permissive, leaving open the possibility that objects may have characteristics other than structural properties. It is most difficult to find a fix point in the controversies over structuralism.

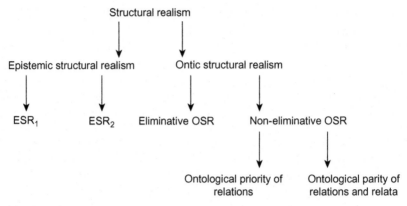

FIG. 3.3   An overview of the different forms of structural realism.

similar rejection regarding objects in the non-quantum domain (Ladyman, 2008). For this reason, Busch (2003, p. 221) finds OSR a viable option only as an epistemological and not as an ontological stance.

OSR also comes in two forms and under even more names (Fig. 3.3 aids the reader in making heads or tails out of the various ways of putting structural realism). One of them is the original form, which gets rid of objects (eliminative OSR), whilst the other (non-eliminative OSR) preserves a very thin concept of entities[34] (Saunders, 2003; Cao, 2006, p. 41; Stachel, 2006; Ladyman, 2007). The purpose of non-eliminative OSR is to dispose of some hardly acceptable ideas of the radical version whilst maintaining the achievements of the structuralist ontology. It is far from easy to identify what the different versions mean by structure. Busch (2003, p. 211) argues that the eliminative or strong version takes structures to have ontological primacy over objects, whilst the non-eliminative or weaker version conceives structures and objects to independently exist alongside one another. It is uncertain, however, whether the nodes the eliminative variant suggests are not conceptionally identical to the thin objects of the more cautious version (French & Ladyman, 2011, p. 30).

The non-eliminative form may seem to be a viable alternative in the object-based ontology thanks to its more permissive attitude towards objects. Here structures have relata, so this approach may be able to avoid the trap or paradox of the idea of structures without putative relata. The point here, however, is again an ontological priority of the relations of objects and the properties of relations over objects which creates an untenable mix. All we have is a subtler phrasing, since for non-eliminative OSR structures have greater priority than objects, or structures are more basic and fundamental than objects. Moderate OSR is willing to accept

---

[34] Schmidt (2010, p. 510) distinguishes *radical OSR* and *moderate OSR*.

a minimalist concept of objects in which objects have relational properties only. Schmidt (2010, pp. 513–514) is neat to underline the ontological problems of non-eliminative OSR. If structure is the source of causation, then we do not need objects, which is a bizarre ontological commitment. But if objects are allowed to have causal powers (Witt, 2008), then objects in themselves possess causal properties,[35] regardless of relations, which is unacceptable in all versions of OSR. Due to its more tolerant attitude towards objects, non-eliminative OSR is even less tenable and more puzzling than the eliminative form. If objects are causally passive (i.e. structures are the source of causation), then objects are unnecessary and their alleged presence in a structure is only an unwanted compromise to appease the believers of the object-oriented ontology. As Psillos (2012, p. 169) puts it, 'Ontic Structuralists are happy to "mimic" talk of non-structure, or objects in particular, but they hasten to add that this mimicking does not imply any serious metaphysical commitment to them'.

Placing an emphasis upon structures when there are no objects at all is as problematic as the case where there are thin objects having so little substance that it requires an explanation. What exactly does it mean when Ladyman and Ross (2007, p. 131) claim that 'there are objects in [the non-eliminative structuralist] metaphysics but they have been purged of their intrinsic natures, identity, and individuality, and they are not metaphysically fundamental'? The non-eliminative approach argues that the natures and identities of such thin objects are exclusively determined by the relations in which they show up. Here we have entities, though they are dependent upon their relations in every respect. This is the sense in which Ladyman (2007) talks about contextual individuation or Saunders (2003) suggests the term 'non-reductive relationalism'.

All this means that the understanding of the natures of related objects is allegedly possible on the basis of their extrinsic features. Even if there are intrinsic properties, we have no knowledge of them and we are not even in need of them for understanding. These are objects that beyond their relations have no knowledgeable identifying properties or intrinsic features. It seems possible to kill two birds with one stone: there are objects, though they are properly identified by their relations. In this sense, structure is more fundamental than relata and this is what is meant by the ontological priority of structures. However, Chakravartty (2012, p. 197) argues that an object having no intrinsic features is not an object at all, the moderate, non-eliminative version of OSR thus turns out to be reducible to the eliminative version. Extrinsic characteristics cannot do the job of

---

[35] Here it is beside the point, though worthy of note that the relationship between properties and powers is rather opaque. It is usually conceived that entities have powers thanks to their properties (powers stem from properties, so they are distinct albeit related), while Mumford (2008) argues that properties are simply powers.

either the identification of objects or causation in the way intrinsic properties do. The non-eliminative version also fails to plausibly relocate the ontological emphasis between relata and relations.[36] Even if it is possible for an object to have extrinsic identity, this way only an object existent and identifiable prior to and independently of a structure can be placed into a certain system of relations. Not even now does the object gain its identity structurally as its existence is prior to the structure. In this context Chakravartty (2012, p. 205) sets as an example the relationship of a member of the species *Homo sapiens* to the species *Homo sapiens*. He argues that what renders a *Homo sapiens* a *Homo sapiens* is a particular relation of descent the given individual bears to a hominid ancestor of her. Here it is this ancestor–descendant relationship that constitutes extrinsic identity as a human being. However, even in this case there must be a well-identifiable object (such as Indiana Jones) as an extrinsic property can only be attributed to something that stand in the relevant relation and that is ontologically grasped prior to gaining extrinsic identity (as Henry Jones's son).

However, it is contentious whether reality beyond the quantum territory can or should also be reconceptualized in a purely structuralist fashion. It is probably unnecessary in spite of OSR's suggestions. What is more, it is far from obvious whether there is any field where we ought to abandon our basic ontological commitment to the existence of objects, not even in quantum mechanics. OSR itself is also in two minds about the ontological status of objects in the non-quantum domain. Subatomic particles satisfy almost all of our criteria that underlie our realist commitments in the non-quantum domain (Chakravartty, 2017a, p. 2277). For the current purposes, however, the debate over the nature of the quantum domain is of secondary importance, so here there is no need to resolve these conflicts. The fundamental question for a structuralist interpretation of economics regards not that whether there are well-definable entities in economics (there are) but rather the role the individual properties of entities (mainly agents) play in shaping our ideas on structure. In other words: is a realist structure representation feasible through non-realistic (anti-realist) entity descriptions? Analyzing OSR in this context is indispensable to making the point that in the realm of well-definable and individuated entities there is no need for a structuralist ontology that questions the existence of entities. As microfounded macroeconomics

---

[36] Non-eliminative OSR itself can be divided into two camps. The one supposes the existence of objects to be derivative of their relations but not vice versa, thus asserting the ontological priority of relations over entities. The other conceives the existence of both entities and their relations as mutually derivative, thus asserting ontological parity of relations and relata (Brading & Skiles, 2012, pp. 111–112; Chakravartty, 2017a, p. 2279). Nounou (2012, pp. 121–122) delineates even more versions of OSR.

with its agents is in consonance with the conventional object-based ontology, the conditions to justify a structuralist ontological switch do not hold (Chakravartty, 2003a).

Cao (2006, pp. 41–42) argues that such a purely structuralist reconceptualization is needless indeed if our objects are epistemically accessible to us. On this account, OSR's territory is thus constrained to cases similar to the quantum domain. Ross (2008, p. 742) seems to be talking about a twofold ontology. On his account, there is a zone of reality where the structuralist ontology is proper, whilst in other zones we have no reasons to give up the object-based world view; we thus have a twofold ontology. For Sklar (2003) and Teller (2004) even a manifold or pluralistic ontology seems acceptable, stemming from the methodological pluralism of the sciences. Given the fact that theories as explanatory schemes come with a plurality of referents and assumed properties, our best bet is to admit the idea of world showing up in a plurality of ontologies. In this vein, Brading and Skiles (2012) argue that the problem of metaphysical underdetermination ought to be solved by leaving open the question of individuals and non-individuals, and we may need a threefold ontology made up of individuals, non-individuals and further entities the natures of which are inaccessible hence undetermined. It is thus a distinct question when objects can or should be structurally dissolved or reconceptualized (Nounou, 2012, p. 118). As Ross argues, it is senseless to question the existence of observable objects, whilst these entities cannot act as good models of fundamental reality. OSR claiming that there are no objects at all, however, is particularly radical at this point. It is questionable whether different territories of reality demand different ontologies. Even if one admits that in the quantum-domain there is no need for the object-based ontology and from this she infers that it is also erroneous in the macroscopic world, this way of argumentation may also be a strong point against the object-free ontologies for this route of reasoning can also be travelled in the opposite direction. From the inappropriateness of the object-free ontology in the non-quantum domain one can infer its inappropriateness in the quantum region. In this vein, Castellani (1993, p. 106) argues that our traditional concept of objects may need a revision in order to make room for quantum particles conceived as objects in a very general definition established even on a case by case basis. Admittedly, if both observable and unobservable objects are conceived to be experienced via their causal roles and properties, an insistence on the object-based ontology may turn out to be justified even in the quantum domain (Chakravartty, 2004, p. 159). The most significant consequence here is that different ontologies are not consistent with every structure (Chakravartty, 2007, p. 67). In the object-based sphere of the world the traditional, object-based ontology is still an adequate interpretive framework (French & Ladyman, 2003a, p. 41). If we have objects, the structure is to be derived from them.

Before moving on, it is worthwhile to highlight some dilemmas OSR faces. Even though its basic idea is to subject entities to a metaphysical decomposition in a structuralist sense, as OSR is in need of an object-free ontology, its feasibility is far from obvious. Is it possible at all to conceptualize a structure without relata? The key question for OSR regards the natures, the properties, and the causal roles of objects. Are objects indispensable to understanding the structure of the world? OSR argues in the negative: the constancy of a relation is insufficient for us to infer that it has constant carriers (French & Ladyman, 2011, p. 34). If, accordingly, there are no individuated objects, the ontology resting upon them also fails to be adequate for modern physics. Quantum mechanics calls the very concept of individual objects into question and OSR is aimed at providing a supportive metaphysical background for this endeavour. OSR throws away object orientation and the whole entity-based ontology, and it is also in this framework that OSR reconceptualizes the physical objects. Entities for an ontic structuralist are idle and otiose metaphysical components (French, 2006, p. 172). Individual objects only show up as some aspects of the underlying structure. Here the world is understood wholly as of structural character. OSR tries to completely eliminate the hidden properties ESR is ready to tolerate. Objects are only the nodes of structure, the intersections of relations (French & Ladyman, 2003a, p. 39). In the case of physics OSR may prove to be an adequate ontology as sometimes it is really difficult to decide whether terms of physics refer to veiled individuals or to non-individuals. Referents are ambiguous. OSR solves this problem with a single blow. Casting away all the objects is admittedly a simpler albeit radical and contentious response.

3.2.3 A critique of selective realisms: The way to semirealism

In a series of books and papers Anjan Chakravartty suggested his semirealism as the most systematic critique of entity realism and structural realism. He argues that entity realism and structural realism, most plausibly construed, lead to the same conclusions regarding the existence and properties of entities. Entity realism and structural realism thus collapse into each other. Chakravartty does not reject either of the stances but aims to provide a unified and consistent account built of the two.

The emergence of semirealism as a structuralist philosophy was necessitated by the debates slashing the realist camp. Whilst both entity realism and structural realism in themselves provide effective answers to the anti-realist arguments, the debate they conduct against each other is rather detrimental to their positions (Chakravartty, 2013a, pp. 116–117). The arguments entity realism and structural realism have elaborated are incompatible, which further undermines the status of scientific realism. It cannot mature into a coherent epistemic attitude until its refined versions stop fighting and a commonly acceptable platform emerges to bring the hope of a consensus, which is further hindered by the rather opaque and unclarified terms, including scientific realism itself, the parties use (Berenstain & Ladyman, 2012, p. 151). One of the purposes of semirealism is thus to bring the inner debates of the realist camp to an end by suggesting a synthesis that preserves the most progressive insights of both alternatives whilst eliminating their shortcomings. By refining the key concepts and ideas of these approaches, semirealism as a unified and metaphysically grounded epistemology intends to fly in the face of anti-realist efforts. As the anti-realist criticism suggests, a unified realist philosophy of science is infeasible, a successful synthesis in itself would thus be an effective response to anti-realists' scepticism.

Semirealism aimed at finding those parts of reality where scepticism is irrational is a more grounded form of selective scepticism as it concentrates on well-detectable (causal) properties. The key message of semirealism is the intuitive idea that the causal knowledge of entities is closely interwoven with the knowledge of structures, and structural knowledge cannot even be imagined without either a warranted belief in the existence of some kinds of entities or the admittance of the knowledge of some entity properties. These two kinds of realism entail each other. Causal properties of entities and the dispositions[37] for relations these causal properties confer form a basis upon which entity realism and structural realism emerge as two reconcilable sides of the same semirealism. It is typical of science that semirealism failed to soothe the debates in the realist camp. Thus as a grotesque manifestation of a synthesis the parties in controversy have found a new common enemy to combat (Stathis Psillos's reluctance[38] is particularly interesting for his stance regarding structural realism is close to Chakravartty's position). Chakravartty (2013b) gave a thorough response to the objections by French (2013), Ghins (2013), and Psillos (2013) in the same issue of Erkenntnis.[39]

As semirealism argues, one of the major problems of entity realism is its minimalism. According to entity realism, as we have seen above, the belief in the mere existence of unobservable entities is the only justified

---

[37] Other terms standing for 'disposition' in more or less synonymous ways are capacity, propensity, or tendency (Chakravartty, 2017c). All these terms describe the idea that dispositions determine how entities behave and react under various circumstances (Ellis, 2008).

[38] Busch (2003, p. 211) mentions Psillos as an explicit opponent of structural realism.

[39] The critiques are diverse. French as a structural realist does not reject semirealism but urges its structuralist refinement through which we could retain its virtues while its alleged pitfalls would not deteriorate its plausibility. Ghins casts doubts on the way semirealism establishes the relationship between objects and laws. Psillos attacks semirealism for its Aristotelian roots.

knowledge of ours. As Resnik (1994) points out, however, entity realism could have successfully separated existence claims and structural knowledge only if knowledge of or belief in an object was possible without having certain knowledge of its characteristics. It is a radical distinction between existence and knowledge. Resnik's critique aptly highlights that studying the causal roles in a Hackingian way inevitably yields knowledge reaching far beyond mere existential claims. The knowledge of a certain class of entities requires a theory, and if one is certain of an object's existence and causal properties, she inevitably has a theory that describes the relations of objects and the causal mechanisms they are involved in.

In order to avoid some absurd consequences of rejecting theories (reductio ad absurdum, believing in something without knowing anything about it), entity realists resort to a rather lame distinction between global or fully fledged theories and low-level generalizations. Clarke (2001, pp. 704–705) argues that a plausible version of entity realism can live on the latter. However, it is dubious whether the knowledge of the causal roles some entities play can be regarded as low-level generalizations or it is massive structural knowledge. This is the reason why it is so difficult to reconstruct what entity realists believe in. Clarke's reasoning clearly shows the incoherence of entity realism. He insists on entity realism's maintaining realism about causal explanation, so rejects Musgrave's (1996, p. 20) caricature. For Musgrave, entity realism is when one believes in hobgoblins without knowing or thinking anything about what they are like. This is an empty conviction with no details. Clarke strongly disagrees, and to argue that entity realism is something different he cites causal understanding. Then, for the sake of demonstration, he modifies Musgrave's hobgoblin parable. Here he conceives entity realists to also know that hobgoblins are little, creepy, and disposed to do the housework. These are thus the causal properties entity realists claim to know. If knowledge is genuinely of causal character, it must embrace more.

Following Resnik, Massimi (2004) suggests empirically equivalent entities and further dilutes the viability of the entity realist stance. Manipulability is inefficient for various causal entities may trigger the same phenomenon; manipulability thus fails to lead to sound causal knowledge. On the basis of experiments alone it is impossible to decide what entity to regard as real. This is the same conclusion again: causal knowledge reaches beyond the mere existence of entities.

As Chakravartty (1998) underlines, it is the roles entities play in causal chains that ground our belief in their existence. Objects step into causal mechanisms and processes via their causal properties (Chakravartty, 2003b). Any concrete structure is understood as consisting of the relations between the properties the objects have, so a structure in semirealism cannot be conceived without objects[40] and their properties (Chakravartty, 2007, p. 119). A concrete structure thus has as its relata the first-order properties of objects and not directly the objects themselves.[41] These properties are of intrinsic nature, but they have a relational quality. As objects connect via their properties, the way the objects are related is determined by the way their properties are related (Chakravartty, 2007, p. 40 and pp. 89–90). Objects connect in a correlated manner. For all these reasons, all knowledge of structure contains a plethora of information about the intrinsic natures of objects (Chakravartty, 2004, p. 156).

The reasoning rests upon the idea that we never perceive entities in themselves but via the behaviour they show in causal interactions. Objects instantiating some properties can trigger changes in the properties other objects instantiate, produce other objects or other properties in objects (Esfeld, 2009). Entities are structured and can play causal roles in structures via their properties. It is thus the properties that determine the causal relations, and these properties reveal themselves in causal interactions. We can infer the properties of entities from the causal processes and connections describing the objects' interactions.[42] Causal regularities thus

---

[40] The exact nature of objects is contentious and hotly debated. As Chakravartty (2012, p. 189) argues, structuralism suggests too narrow a conception of objects to exclude count nouns and to include mass nouns only, such as plasma or kinetic energy, that cannot be counted but quantified. By contrast, semirealism suggests a more comprehensive concept of objects to include anything that possesses some properties bound together in a spatiotemporal locus. As a consequence, individuality is not a prerequisite of objecthood. Water in the glass on my desk meets the criterion of being an object in the semirealistic approach, though it is a far cry from an individual. Individuals are of course objects notwithstanding. See Section 3.4.2 for more considerations on how individuality and objecthood are related.

[41] Chakravartty (2004, p. 155; Chakravartty, 2007, p. 40) distinguishes concrete structures and abstract structures. He relates to the latter those structure representations that regard structures as properties of relations (i.e. higher order properties). Various concrete structures can instantiate an abstract structure, which is a formal or mathematical system making it possible for various concrete structures to exemplify it. As a concrete structure is conceived to be carried by first-order properties of objects, the dilemma of entity realism and structural realism can easily be re-formulized in the context of abstract and concrete structures. Is it true that theories only provide knowledge of abstract structures? Or is it also possible to gain knowledge about concrete structures and hence first-order entity properties? Semirealism argues for the latter.

[42] Experiences on causal roles in the observable and the unobservable realms emerge in different ways. Accordingly, amongst the features of unobservable objects Chakravartty (1998, p. 394) highlights the special detection properties. These are the characteristics upon which the detection of causal regularities rests in the unobservable region (Dorato, 2000b, pp. 1615–1624). In the case of observable entities, however, gaining knowledge about causal properties is far less problematic.

rest upon causal properties, so these causal properties must be observable or detectable at least—in short, experienceable. It is noteworthy, however, that not all properties are experienceable. Even though some of them may be causal, no knowledge of them is possible. By contrast, experienceable properties are necessarily of causal nature. If we are aware of the existence of an entity, it is because we know the interactions in which the entity is involved. Thus we must have knowledge of the properties that establish the behaviour the entity shows in its relations.[43] The knowledge of entities is facilitated by their experienceable behaviour and this knowledge involves the knowledge of some properties that lie within the jurisdiction of theories. The beliefs entity realism implies, if it is able to convey genuine knowledge of causal properties, thus reach far beyond mere existence.

Structural realism is similarly infeasible in itself. It denies the distinction between nature and structure or form and content; it thus makes no sense for the adherents to think that objects have nature beyond the way they are structured (Landry, 2012, pp. 29–30 and 36–37). In semirealism, by contrast, it is also undoubted that nature and structure are close-knit, though structure is not conceived as a substitute for nature. Any theory when describing a structure inevitably tells something about the entities as well. It is highly difficult if not impossible to separate theoretical statements on structure and statements on the nature of entities (Stanford, 2003, p. 570). Structural realism believes that the nature of an entity is over and above the embedding structure. Structure is knowable, but the nature of any entity is transcendent. However, when we talk about the nature of an entity, then in effect we talk about the behaviour it shows in relations (Psillos, 1995). Since a structure consists of relations, no structure can thus be understood without knowing how the entities behave in these relations. Knowledge of entities and knowledge of structure cannot be separated (Morrison, 1990), since it is the entities' structural properties that inform us about how entities act in the structure. Entity realism places structural realists' causal knowledge to the entity level which in itself is an argument against the plausibility of structure-level causal knowledge. Any of these weakened versions of all-or-nothing realism, entity realism and structural realism, seem to be inviable without the other and the answer to this difficulty must be some combination of the two.

As structurally active characteristics of objects reveal themselves simultaneously as structural knowledge develops, structural knowledge is the same as the knowledge of structural properties of objects (Psillos, 2001,

---

[43] It is not an attempt to restore full-blown realism since selectivity remains in the game. A distinction between the parts worthy and unworthy of realist commitment holds. It is rational to pledge to experienceable causal properties and their relations (i.e. the structure the properties carry).

p. S17). Entities play certain causal roles, and it is exactly on the basis of these causal roles that we have knowledge of entities. Consequently, ESR's assumed distinction between objects and structure proves invalid. The knowledge of structures and the causal order yields knowledge of the entities, in the same way as the knowledge of entities' causal roles yields structural knowledge. Here the world consists of entities, their properties, and relations; thus an integral part of this world view is an ontological commitment to the existence of objects. Standing upon this vision it seems unnecessary to dissolve entities in the structures (French & Ladyman, 2003b).

The relation-relata dependence is both an ontological and a conceptual dependence; it is thus simply problematic to suggest a structure without relata. As Busch (2003, p. 213) says, 'a relation might take *anything* as its relata, but it always takes *something*'. A structure interrelates some things, and without such things a structure rejects to be conceptualized (Chakravartty, 2003b). The 'big question' for structural realism regards the content what is supposed to be 'out there' beyond the structure but not to be known. What are the parts or aspects of reality that ESR regards as inaccessible and that OSR tries to completely eliminate? ESR-style relation descriptions provide less information than property descriptions could do. A relation description in a structuralist fashion specifies how the entities connect whilst leaving any other characteristics in the shade. However, Psillos (2001, p. S20) argues that relation descriptions unavoidably contain some property descriptions. For instance, the relation description 'A is the father of B' implies that A is male. There is thus no epistemological gap between relational properties and first-order properties. If we have entities, a focus on relations is not a way out from paying attention to entity properties. Such properties render it possible for the instantiating entities to stand in certain relations, as to be a male carries the disposition for someone to be a husband of a female someone else.

At this point it is worthwhile to return to Shapiro's structuralist ideas. As he argues,

> Define a *system* to be a collection of objects with certain relations among them. A corporate hierarchy or a government is a system of people with supervisory and co-worker relationships; a chess configuration is a system of pieces under spatial and 'possible move' relationships; a language is a system of characters, words, and sentences, with syntactic and semantic relations between them; and a basketball defence is a collection of people with spatial and 'defensive role' relations. Define a *pattern* or *structure* to be the abstract form of a system, highlighting the interrelationships among the objects, and ignoring any features of them that do not affect how they relate to other objects in the system. (Shapiro, 2000, p. 259)

It is a subtle but certainly unradical way of putting that structure representations can do without the properties inactive to the way entities are structured. Semirealism does not claim more either. The key difference is whether structural properties come from the structure itself or it is the first-order causal properties of objects that determine the way objects stand in relations. As Chakravartty argues, structure cannot be separated from objects' own, intrinsic, first-order causal properties. If there are features determining the way of being structured, such features are the features of something. Objects emerge as the natural owners and carriers of properties. Structures cannot establish the nature of things, but structures do stem from objects' own characteristics. In other words, the notion of objects cannot plausibly be replaced with the concept of placeholders in structures (taken as empty holes not filled by objects) and such placeholders cannot plausibly be defined by properties exclusively coming from structures. Even if the idea of relations without specific relata seems to work in the case of some physically non-existent abstract entities like numbers, it is dubious whether it can sensibly cover objects having physical existence:

> The essence of a natural number is its *relations* to other natural numbers. The subject matter of arithmetic is a single abstract structure, the pattern common to any infinite collection of objects that has a successor relation with a unique initial object and satisfies the (second-order) induction principle. The number 2, for example, is no more and no less than the second position in the natural-number structure; 6 is the sixth position. Neither of them has any independence from the structure in which they are positions, and as places in this structure, neither number is independent of the other. The essence of 2 is to be the successor of the successor of 0, the predecessor of 3, the first prime, and so on. (Shapiro, 1997, p. 72)

The core of the problem thus regards, on the one hand, the way entity and structure can be separated and, on the other hand, the distinction between the knowledge of entities and the knowledge of structure. As it is argued, we have epistemological access to entities via their causal properties and it is these properties that form the structure and hence the causal relations (see Fig. 3.4). These entities are not necessarily human beings or

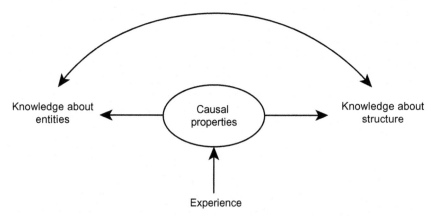

FIG. 3.4 Why the knowledge of causal properties implies the knowledge of both entities and structure.

representative agents as money or commodities in economics are also specific entities having definite causal properties. Structural knowledge implies the knowledge of parts and the way they are interrelated. A structure consists of relations: the relations of its parts. Structural realism makes efforts to describe structure in a way where the related things are regarded as of secondary importance or as non-existent. For Chakravartty (1998, p. 399), however, the neglect of structural realism on relata is inconsistent. The least we can know is that the related entities are existent.

But structural knowledge implies more as a matter of fact since it entails the knowledge of first-order entity properties underlying the causal connections. Entity realism thus implies structural realism since structures open up for knowledge through the properties of the related entities. If a structure is known, then both the causal properties and the objects having these properties must also be known. Whilst semirealism has primary ontological commitment to the detectable causal properties, a belief in objects carrying these properties is only a minimal extension of this commitment (Chakravartty, 2013b, p. 45). A belief in entity propertics whilst withholding another belief in the objects would seem an untenable option. Structural knowledge thus stems from the same source as the knowledge of entities. Experienceable causal properties convey information on both. We have knowledge of both the structure and the entities or neither of them. As structural knowledge is inseparable from the knowledge of entities, Demopoulos and Michael Friedman's critique is invalid here (Chakravartty, 2007, p. 41) (Fig. 3.5)

This connection works in two directions (Chakravartty, 1998, p. 400). If we believe in the existence of some entities, this belief rests upon our knowledge of some of their properties, but these are the properties that underlie their relations (Clarke, 2001, p. 702; Resnik, 1994). It is the relations that facilitate the knowledge of entities, so structural realism implies entity realism. ESR argues that knowledge cannot reach beyond the truth of relations. By contrast, semirealism emphasizes that relations also contain a plethora of entity-level information. These pieces of information describe what features entities have: features crucial for getting related and interacting. Structural realism makes itself believe to have adequate relation representations via an emphasis on structures and on the neglect or even the dismissal of entities. If a structure rests upon entities and their relations, however, then entity properties open up simultaneously as the structure reveals itself. In Chakravartty's (1998, p. 402) words: 'relations and thus structures are not meaningful concepts in the absence of actual things [i.e. relata, entities, objects, etc.] which are putatively related according to the structures considered'. Entities and structures are separable at a metaphysical level at best, in epistemological terms; however, they are close-knit and imply each other. In their primitive forms neither entity realism (where existence claims are based upon causal roles of entities,

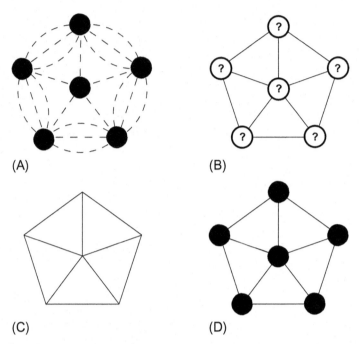

(A) (B)

(C) (D)

FIG. 3.5 How entity realism (A), epistemic structural realism (B), ontic structural realism (C), and semirealism (D) conceive the same structure.

though realist commitments to structures are withdrawn) nor structural realism (where structures are conceived as having no putative relata or based upon too thin a concept of objects) is tenable.[44] Properly construed, they imply each other and semirealism as the refined form emerges (Chakravartty, 1998, p. 392).

Consequently, if one studies a facet of reality that she can adequately describe in the object-based ontology, then what she needs are true propositions about entity properties in order to represent a structure and hence a causal mechanism in which entities are involved. If we have entities and if these entities are individuated and known through the causal roles they play, like in economics, it makes no sense to think either that first-order properties are unknowable as such properties underlie the causal functions, or that structures can be represented via untrue entity-level propositions about properties. These properties can be dismissed in case of objectless structures at best, if such structures exist at all.

---

[44] Due to the emphasis upon the primacy of objects, Chakravartty's semirealism is oftentimes conceived as a form of neo-Aristotelianism. Chakravartty (2008a) clarifies the antique roots of semirealism.

3.3 Causation and structures

At some point in the last section a discussion on causality and structures emerged just out of the blue, so it is about time to look into the problem set for more details. To begin with, there is no consensus in the structuralist literature over how causality and structure are related. Structures in structural realism are usually conceived as displaying a primitive form of modality (Ladyman & Ross, 2007, pp. 258–297; Psillos, 2012, p. 170). Modal relations cover possibility, necessity, and impossibility, so considerations about modality convey information on how things could, must, or could not have been (Berenstain & Ladyman, 2012, p. 153); structures thus may give an account of causal relations. The existing literature of OSR, however, fails to provide a clear-cut description of the concrete content and extension of this modality. There are multiple ways to understand the connection between causality and entity-free structures. Structures need to be causally efficacious or else we would be unable to detect them. The other option is to regard structures as ante rem existents, independent of concrete manifestations. In this case, however, we would have no factual knowledge of them; thus their existence would be an assumption in the strict sense (Busch, 2003, p. 220). As French and Ladyman (2003a, p. 46) put it,

> there are mind independent modal relations between phenomena (both possible and actual), but these relations are not supervenient on the properties of unobservable objects and the external relations between them, rather this structure is ontologically basic.

If structures do not rest upon objects, then causal mechanisms are not supposed to be traced back to entities. In the lack of objects, relations themselves must be causally empowered and such causal powers are conceived as inherent to the emerging relations (French & Ladyman, 2011, pp. 31–40). Esfeld (2009), accordingly, definitely regards OSR-style structures as of causal nature in themselves. As a consequence, we need no underlying causal properties of objects to establish their causal relations. Esfeld thus plants causal properties and dispositions into the structure itself in order that structures could give account of causation and be detectable (Schmidt, 2010, p. 509). Structures for him are causal structures by which he intends to overcome the initial vacillations of OSR theorists. Esfeld argues that it is unclear what exactly a primitive modality consists in. As a response, he explicitly makes a stand for the causal interpretation of structures. Ladyman and Ross (2007) at the same time reject to conceive causation as a fundamental physical feature, whilst Psillos (2012, pp. 170–172) rejects the idea how ontic structuralists implant causality into relations. Without entities having causal properties a causally empowered structure cannot but be mysterious.

It is not necessarily a plausible solution if the locus of causation is placed into the structure itself (Chakravartty, 2017a), so in the object-free structures the conceptualization of causation is fraught with difficulties. Everything depends on how one interprets the structures. Chakravartty (2007, pp. 41–42) argues that relations stand between objects' causal properties (or, in other words, causally active properties or causally efficacious properties). As properties also determine objects' interactions, these properties and their relations produce causal activity of objects. Causation 'works' along the lines of a particular or concrete structure,[45] where a structure is determined by dispositions, conferred by causal properties (Chakravartty, 2004, p. 156). Concrete structures are thus inherently causal structures, though the source of causation is not the structure itself. Causal properties endow the objects with specific dispositions; thus objects in virtue of their causal properties (the properties they possess, instantiate, exemplify, etc.) behave in structures in specific ways. As Chakravartty (2003c, p. 394) puts it, 'to say that an object has a particular causal property is to say that it is disposed to behave in particular ways in particular circumstances, and that all objects having this same property are likewise so disposed'. Causal properties are many-faceted; thus a causal property attracts multiple dispositions, though dispositions do not always manifest causal connections, which does not mean that a causal property confers different dispositions under different conditions. Dispositions are invariantly associated with causal properties. Air has the disposition for forcing a cube to fall at a rate slower than a spherical object being of the same volume and made of the same material; or the mechanism how hydrogen and oxygen combine to form water stems from the properties of hydrogen and oxygen. Likewise, being hot, an object has disposition for melting ice or causing burn on one's skin (Hawthorne, 2001, p. 361), though ice to be melted must be exposed to that. Being hot as a property is not the cause of ice melting. Some relation is needed in which hotness of an object can act as a cause of ice melting. If something is water-soluble, it needs to be exposed to water to be dissolved (Ellis, 2008, p. 81). Entities can exert their causal effects only under specific conditions, such as the exposure to or the interactions with other entities, and entities in these interactions behave as dictated by their causal properties. Causal effects are thus dependent upon the conditions (Manicas, 2006, pp. 22–23; Witt, 2008, p. 132; Mumford, 2008, p. 142).

The problem of manifestation does not mean that relations take priority over causal properties. Even though an object can only be related through relations (with no relations an object cannot stand in structure), it is conceived to have causal properties regardless of manifested relations.

---

[45] As a consequence, the problem of abstract structures does not emerge in the discussions over causation.

The identity of an object is determined by its potential for relations, and not by the relations themselves. It is thus not the relations that endow the objects with properties—as opposed to what non-eliminative OSR claims (Chakravartty, 2012, p. 196). Even if relations may be required so that a property could come into being, this fact does not entail either that such a property is of purely relational nature or that a property is not carried by an object. One needs to be something in order to be structured in a certain way. Properties may remain the same in spite of changes in relations: they are still of intrinsic nature (Chakravartty, 2013b, p. 44). In order for an entity to stand in relations and to play certain roles, it must have certain properties, whilst these properties never come from the structure. These properties are the intrinsic characteristics of the entity as they remain the same even when the entity quits the structure. Causal properties are the prerequisites for any entity to be structured; structure thus cannot be the source of entity properties.

In these terms, a crucial question regards what relations are manifested under specific conditions. Causal properties are only dispositions for certain relations but do not imply the relations themselves (Chakravartty, 2004, p. 157). Manifestation is dependent upon the conditions (the environment), on what other objects an object having certain dispositions meets and what dispositions these other objects have. A causal property is not necessarily accompanied by relations, though dispositions are prior to their possibly implied relations. This, however, does not undermine the idea that a manifest relation always rests upon a corresponding causal property. Relations obtain only if the things (properties and their carriers) they relate exist (Chakravartty, 2003a, pp. 401–404). In this context it is worthy of note that Psillos argued against the separability of entities and structures in a similar vein, though Chakravartty's and his trains of thought are not identical. Psillos finds the distinction blurred. By contrast, Chakravartty (2007, p. 43) maintains the distinction between the natures of particulars and structural relations since objects do not always realize all the relations to which properties dispose them. A structure emerges only if there are relations, but relations do not necessarily follow from properties. This does not overwrite the principle that the knowledge of a structure implies the knowledge of objects' properties. Even though a structure presupposes some properties, this inference fails to work the other way round. Even if a property holds, this does not necessarily trigger a relation. Berenstain and Ladyman (2012, pp. 149–150 and 157) undermining the latter's position make some efforts to understand the disagreement between Chakravartty and Psillos by regarding Chakravartty as an anti-Humean and Psillos as a Humean scientific realist.

In spite of some disagreements and in spite of OSR's indeterminacy over causation, both the various forms of structural realism and semirealism thus try to give account of causality in structural terms. Consequently, causal realism seems to be discussable in a structural realist framework.[46] A key discrepancy regards the role objects are conceived to play in the conceptualization of structures. We may have to abandon playing on the causal properties of individual objects only under specific conditions, especially in the scope of quantum mechanics. It is admittedly possible that in the quantum domain the nature of the world is such that structure is describable even without individuated objects and their properties. If, however, the existence of objects is out of question, structure stems from their structural-structuring properties. We may need to wholly abandon our belief in the existence of objects and hence the object-based ontology, but if not, an insistence on objects implies an insistence on their properties. What is more, in the object-based ontology we must insist on them as structures rest upon such properties. As far as our everyday world is considered, the initial threefold menu (ESR vs. OSR vs. semirealism) has been narrowed down to semirealism by now. If we have objects, ESR cannot be a considerable alternative: when a concrete structure is known in the object-based ontology, the involved objects are also known. By the same token, OSR is fundamentally alien to the ontology of the microfoundations project.

It is thus the role objects play in a structure that is decisive whether their properties carry the structure, or the structure may be conceived and represented without objects. If objects are dismissible, their properties are also superfluous.[47] If, by contrast, a structure stems from individuated entities, the structure rests upon the entities' characteristics. Individuated objects and their properties come in one package. Realist representations of structures thus require realist assumptions on the causal properties. In this case causality cannot be explained at the level of structures. Chakravartty (2003c) argues that objects with properties are of central importance in causal explanations. Such entities form the ontological resource of and the key conceptual basis for causal explanations. Without appropriately characterized entities in a structure an explanatory gap emerges between subsequent states of any process along the same causal chain.

As semirealism suggests, the idea of relations resting on causal properties is to replace the traditional notion of event-based causal mechanisms (Chakravartty, 2005). As it is the causal properties that stand in

---

[46] As a reminder, in the present context it is a highly important achievement for Hoover (2009a) interprets Friedman as a causal realist.

[47] This is not a rejection of the object-based ontology, which gives the reason for the conditional in the sentence. If entities are not involved in establishing a structure, then the structure is really describable without entities and entity properties. The present reasoning leaves open the question of fundamental ontology, just to be on the safe side. The focus here is on that aspect of reality where any efforts to eliminate entities and the rejection of the supervenience of structure on entities would be a bizarre idea.

relations, events cannot play the main role in causal chains. Their role is only illusory. On this account, the reference to events in the causalist context only serves as a relief for everyday communication, but in fact causal properties and their relations do the work of causation. Events show up as causes and effects (an event is the cause of a resulting event) for objects having causal properties act in these happenings. Causal properties endow the entities with behavioural dispositions, so these properties exert causal effects through the interactions. This is the way the causal processes emerge in the semirealist account. Events only act as frames for the property-determined causal connections. Events happen to objects because they have certain properties. As Chakravartty (2007, pp. 111–112) says,

> causally efficacious events incorporate objects with property-conferred disposi-tions, and the occurrence of subsequent effects can thus be understood in terms of manifestations of the relevant dispositions of the objects involved.
> [...] Objects with causal properties are disposed to behave in certain ways when in the presence or absence of other objects with properties of their own. Causal phenom-ena are produced by the ways in which property-conferred dispositions are linked to one another, and noting this may be the best causal realists can do.

In reality cause-events never trigger effect-events. Causal interactions always take place between causal properties and, indirectly, between the objects having these properties. Along these lines, Chakravartty (2007, pp. 89–118 and 120) gets as far as to natural and social laws (including causal laws), since if objects due to their properties get involved in causal pro-cesses and if other objects also possess the same properties under similar circumstances but in different spatiotemporal settings, then regularities and laws emerge as the recurring occurrences of the same singular causal processes (Chakravartty, 2003a, pp. 393–394). Every individual causal chain is thus an instantiation of a certain causal law (Chakravartty, 2005, p. 25). It is one of the main advantages of the epistemology or the metaphys-ics of dispositional or causal properties that singular and general (law-like or regular) causation can be unified (Chakravartty, 2017c).

As any event in the object-based ontology happens to things and their properties, and events emerge as the consequences of interactions of en-tities with certain properties (Harré, 1970, p. 35), it is exactly things and their properties that any causal analysis in this ontological framework ought to rest upon. As causal connections are regarded as stemming from objects' characteristics, causal understanding requires the knowledge of these relations and the underlying entity properties, and these properties uniquely determine the causal connections. In order to provide a causal explanation, one needs to have knowledge of the entities' causal prop-erties and this knowledge yields the desired explanation. By contrast, in cases where a theoretical description of objects postulates nothing but missing or non-existent properties not referring to real entity properties in one way or another (Section 3.4 dwells upon how non-existent properties can be applied in theories to refer to existent properties found in reality), only non-existent or fictitious causal processes can emerge the generalizations of which cannot but result in vacuous laws. Good predictive performance is not a compensation for such a lack of causal understanding rendered impossible by the exclusive use of vacuous laws, and the partiality of theoretical descriptions is not an obstacle to carrying out adequate causal analyses. What matters is that a causal analysis must rest upon (at least a subset of) entity characteristics that underlie a causal mechanism chosen for analysis. If one succeeds in preserving some entity properties carrying a causal structure, her causal analysis is adequate as it grabs (a part of) an existent causal mechanism. Vacuous laws, however, work in fictitious worlds only. As the underlying theoretical entities are not described via propositions that are either true or untrue albeit referring to real properties, their structure cannot be real either. Such fictive laws on their own never contribute to the causal understanding of reality, even though there are intermediate cases where referring and non-referring idealizations and abstractions are mixed in the picture. The extent to which causal understanding is paralyzed is dependent upon how approximately true a theory is made.

What seemed at the beginning of the chapter as a ludicrous enterprise has proved by now the only tenable strategy. If the purpose is the causal understanding of some socio-economic phenomena emerging at the macro-level as the outcome of the interactions of agents and other entities, the microfoundations project of modern macroeconomics can do the job. A careful argumentation is needed here, though. In itself, micro-founding cannot guarantee causal adequacy. Accordingly, it is not argued that any allegedly microfounded model is the 'best of all worlds'. Instead, the Friedmanian project is conceived here as a faulty attempt for Friedman is suspicious of making do with some untrue entity-level propositions. As it has been just argued, the extent to which real entity properties are disregarded, causal understanding is corrupted, and it is exactly the negligence towards what entities are like in reality that Friedman suggested in his F53. The role of the Friedmanian version of the microfoundations endeavour in the present analysis is only to highlight the traps hidden in building macroeconomics on microfoundations of dubious value.

3.4 Representing structures

It is one of the key lessons of the discussion in the preceding sections that in order for causal relations to emerge, entities must have certain characteristics. Entities can enter causal mechanisms if they possess the necessary causal properties. As relations cannot be separated from the properties of entities, a relation representation requires the representation of the underlying entity properties in one way or another. Entity properties form crucial parts of the mechanism: but for their contribution the mechanism would never emerge and work. And in the opposite direction: if entities must have non-existent properties in order for a causal mechanism to be described in a theory that structure cannot be existent either. As a consequence, a realist representation of a structure cannot make do with some non-existent cooked-up properties introduced as assumptions exactly for carrying a structure under scrutiny. Assumed causal properties, be they real or unreal, inevitably carry some causal mechanisms, but when representing a real causal mechanism the underlying real properties are essential. A realist structure representation bearing appropriate similarity to the real structure rests upon realist entity representations bearing appropriate resemblance to the corresponding properties of real entities. Under such circumstances, the approximate truth of the theory is guaranteed.

3.4.1 A quick overview on how to use abstraction and idealization in representing structures

Realist structure representations thus rest upon the successful representations of real entity properties. As truth about every single phenomenon is many-faceted and as theories are rarely meant to provide all-embracing descriptions, some selection is needed. Selection is carried out via various isolative strategies of which abstraction and idealization are the most commonly applied and known.[48] The set of properties to be represented, the degree of abstraction, and the extent of idealization are all dependent upon scientific interests and the intentions of users. When preparing for abstraction and idealization a theorist separates the active causal properties directly relevant, less relevant (hence potentially omittable), and irrelevant in terms of the problem under scrutiny (Katzner, 2016). Thus 'causally active' and 'relevant' are terms *not* to use interchangeably. There exist relevant and irrelevant subsets of causally active properties where 'relevant' means 'supposed to be relevant in terms of the problem under scrutiny' (Giere, 1999). Plainly put, the practice of partial representations in the sciences implies that reality is always divided into relevant and irrelevant facets or zones. Theorists choose the sets of relevant and irrelevant factors for given purposes, so what is relevant for one may be irrelevant for others as a factor's contribution may seem negligible for one, whilst fundamental for others. Sometimes subjective choices or judgements of relevance are conceived as dependent upon the intention of model users (Bailer-Jones, 2003, pp. 67–71). Relevance considerations are always to be interpreted in the context of scientific interests.

[48] In what follows term 'isolation' is thus used to refer to abstraction and idealization.

Every scientific problem establishes the relevant causal relations and the corresponding causal properties; we thus have nothing to do with the causal properties playing no role or simply being uninteresting. It is a multi-step process where the basic approach provides an initial orientation to the problem, as choosing the choice-theoretic framework for addressing the problem of large-scale fluctuations did in Lucas's case. Causally active properties, the properties via an object enters causal relations, have a relevant set beyond which a theorist does not need to look, given her current analysis on a causal mechanism. Every causal property may take part in more than one casual process, but if one is uninterested in some of these chains, casual properties involved only in the causal processes not under scrutiny are ignorable. The resulting picture may be still highly complex, so the need for further abstraction may arise to distinguish between the still overly populous set of relevant properties. Representations are thus normally partial (Giere, 1999). This fact opens the door for regarding the relationship amongst alternative theories as complementary since they highlight different aspects of the same phenomenon (Bailer-Jones, 2003, p. 66; Teller, 2004, p. 434).

The trade-off between the depth and the comprehensiveness of a scientific approach suggested in Chapter 1 holds here. It means that in order to deepen her analysis a theorist needs to abandon some parts of the initially relevant set of causally active properties. Further abstraction may be needed to squeeze an already abstract setting into a mathematically tractable form and to perform the partial analyses at the highest possible consistency and precision.[49] The price of mathematical consistency and precision is a drop in the cardinality of the included entity properties. Given this, any abstract structure representation can be successful only if the core causal properties are identified and preserved. The stronger an abstraction is, the more likely there are items in the set of the omitted properties and relations that have considerable effects on the causal mechanism the theory isolates. An abstract representation of a causal structure implies its being grabbed out of an infinitely complex setting for closer scrutiny. By representing some causal properties, theories can highlight the corresponding causal relations,[50] though some relations to the omitted

---

[49] Abstraction is unavoidably subject to the possibility of error and ignorance. Via abstraction inexperienced and unknown causal properties and mechanisms may also be omitted.

[50] Interestingly, Chakravartty (2010c, p. 407) relates the partiality of models to the very nature of scientific observation and detection. Scientific observation and detection are limited and partial in scope, so even our best and most accurate and comprehensive models cannot but be abstractions (Teller, 2001, p. 393; Suárez, 2002, p. 3). As we are unable to experience all the aspects and details of reality, abstraction and idealization are inevitable parts of theoretical representation.

parts inevitably cross the borderline. These relations are cut through in order that their effects on the analyzed structural unit could be disregarded. Even though the omitted objects, causal properties, and their relations influence whether a highlighted causal process emerges in reality (due to omission, empirical performance and descriptive accuracy of a model are likely to deteriorate), via pure abstraction (i.e. via preserving existing causal properties as they are in reality) it is possible to correctly represent the corresponding relations. Partial representations obviously have the ability of leading to causal adequacy (Chakravartty, 2007, pp. 148–149). In spite of the partiality of the picture, such a structure representation is correct or causally adequate if no idealization distorts the way the included causal properties are described (Chakravartty, 2001, p. 328).

A direct consequence of partial and concentrated realisticness of abstraction is descriptive falsity. Descriptive similarity, as Chakravartty (2010a, pp. 200–207) claims, 'is clearly unnecessary for representation in many cases'. Abstraction is aimed at omitting some factors admittedly or at least likely having some effects on the causal process a related theory isolates, and without them the represented causal process runs its own way. As a consequence, theoretically generated outcomes cannot be real, though the theory is still true. Models are far simpler than reality. Correctness of pure abstraction thus does not reach farther than correct representation of some isolated relations and the related causal properties. As Chakravartty (2010c, p. 407) puts it, pure abstract models tell the truth without telling the whole truth. Even though the representation contrasted with the target system is incorrect for there are a lot of omitted details, the included parts are correctly described.[51] The parts grabbed and highlighted in abstraction are definitely 'out there', even if due to omission the representation as a whole is not like reality itself.

Therefore descriptive similarity is not a prerequisite for causal adequacy. Scientific representation is always successful if a representing vehicle (or, in other words, the source of representation) aids in drawing causally sound inferences regarding a target system or object (Suárez, 2002, pp. 2–3). Pushing descriptive similarity inevitably leads to piling up causally less relevant or even irrelevant (or causally inactive) properties,

---

[51] In this context, Mäki (2002, p. 96) says that such abstract theories give nothing-but-true accounts without providing the-whole-truth. As he also underlines, this commonly applied 'slicing' approach rests upon the conviction that reality can be understood in parts. There is a contrasting ontological belief, however, according to which the universe is a giant organism with parts tied together by unbreakable relations. If one understands reality in this way, the unit of scientific investigation must be the whole universe itself. However, even if we believe the world to be accessible to partial scientific investigations, this belief by no means entails an anything-goes attitude. The way we split the universe and its entities into pieces must be justified by sound realist scientific standards. Idealization also ought to support theorizing in seeking the truth.

whilst, quite paradoxically at first sight, descriptive dissimilarity does not imply the vehicle bearing no resemblance to the target. Some form of similarity may still seem to be required. Identifying the exact form and locus or even deciding upon its genuine necessity, however, is highly problematic as a useful vehicle bears resemblance to the target so that they are descriptively dissimilar at the same time. There are aspects in which the resemblance holds (and must hold) even if it is only partial and not extended enough for implying descriptive accuracy or even similarity. Resemblance in a non-descriptive sense means that a model bears specific representational relations to its target; thus we ought to talk of resemblance in the relevant aspects. In other words, a thing via a representational relationship can bear resemblance to another thing without being similar to it. Therefore 'similarity' and 'resemblance' or 'being similar to' and 'bearing resemblance to' and the related expressions are not used here as interchangeable terms, and 'similarity' is meant to have a definite descriptivist connotation. As a key to causal adequacy, at the end of the day, a theory must preserve nothing but a carefully defined subset of the entity properties the causal mechanism under scrutiny rests upon. A proper representational relationship ensures that theories can convey approximately true knowledge even at the entity level with no descriptive similarity in the game as theoretical entities are built, at least partly, to preserve real entity properties.

Abstraction can always be criticized for its partiality on a twofold ground. First, abstractions oftentimes are regarded as overly excessive. Sometimes factors are omitted that allegedly have crucial effects on the real outcomes under scrutiny. This objection is easy to block along the arguments of Section 1.3 suggesting a trade-off between depth and comprehensiveness. Omitted parts can always be theorized about in alternative models (Bailer-Jones, 2003, p. 67). Second, sometimes it is also argued that abstraction in certain cases cannot successfully be applied as some parts of some causal mechanisms cannot be left out. These parts are conceived as belonging to the 'core' of a phenomenon. How can the operation of a restaurant be modelled whilst disregarding the contributions of the kitchen? Or that of a car whilst disregarding the contribution by its wheels? These two objections are the same as a matter of fact, the second argument only elevates to a principled level the critique the first one articulates with a reference to individual taste and dissatisfaction. So 'impossible' replaces 'dislike' to suggest a seemingly more powerful and hence more dangerous complaint. Theorizing success wholly depends upon the nature of the case in point and upon whether a theorist can identify the key causal properties. Even the omission of the most fundamental variables may be justified if their causal contribution is known and clarified. In other words, if abstraction does not imply ontological consequences such as the denial of the existence of some causal properties and mechanisms. In such a case, one would erroneously say what she does not deal with is inexistent. By contrast, consistent abstraction implies the intentional neglect of something the existence and operation of which is known (if not, there is no ground for a critique). In this vein, for instance, Marshall (1920/2013, p. 636) masterly brushes aside the complexity objection to abstract theorizing. As he argues, social phenomena are too complex to be studied without extended abstraction. The objection if reversed also works which is hardly a point in favour of its strength. Along the same thread Rodrik (2015, pp. 85–86) argues that a car broken down is supposed to be checked part by part. Even though every component contributes to proper functioning, the whole system can only be examined in parts.

This is the point where the case of ceteris paribus law statements comes to be relevant. These regularities emerge under real conditions only if some omitted variables do not disturb the theoretical law (Chakravartty, 2017c). Ceteris paribus laws work right because such partial representations are correct: the parts isolated in pure abstraction do work in reality, but oftentimes disturbed by the omitted factors:

> If correct, *ceteris paribus* law statements are accurate representations of possible relations between specific causal properties. The presence or absence of objects with other causal properties will determine whether the outcomes predicted by law statements for concrete cases of causation are manifested, but such occurrences are irrelevant to the question of whether *ceteris paribus* expressions correctly map *some* possible relations. The relations they describe may be laws of nature regardless. (Chakravartty, 2003c, p. 409)

Using the parts of reality (more specifically, existing entity properties) to distil ceteris paribus law statements is the warrant for the applicability of these laws to non-isolated conditions. A part of the practice in both the natural and the social sciences is the export of knowledge obtained from abstract law statements to the world in general (i.e. into non-abstracted or non-idealized conditions) in order to causally understand everyday natural and social processes. Such an export, however, would be unsuccessful and pointless without ceteris paribus laws being related to real entity properties.

Idealization raises more problems, and in its case the commitment to realism is inevitably weaker. Realisticness of idealizing models is not so obvious as that of pure abstraction. It is for idealization and abstraction as processes are of completely dissimilar nature. The differences, however, are usually implicit and intangible as their simultaneous applications make their own effects blurred and inseparable (Chakravartty, 2007, pp. 221–222). As we have seen, abstraction leads to representations that may even appear in reality if the omitted variables do not interfere with the theoretically isolated causal process, licensing not only valid but sound inferences.[52] When idealizing, by contrast, a theorist provides distortions to depict some elements of causal chains in a way they cannot ever appear in reality. Strictly speaking, she assumes something inexistent. As a consequence, similarity at the entity level as a necessary condition for successful representation and causal adequacy at the supra-entity level gets out of the picture. In the case of idealization, the differences between the representing vehicle and reality do not stem from omissions but rather from the incorporation of 'factors that cannot exist as represented given the actual properties and relations involved' (Chakravartty, 2007, p. 191 and 221; Chakravartty, 2010b, p. 39).

Chakravartty's example clearly shows how abstraction and idealization are interwoven sometimes to form an inseparable unit. Chakravartty interprets the usual assumption of classical mechanics that the mass of an object is concentrated at an extensionless point as an idealization for it portrays things in a way that contradicts our usual visions on the concentration of mass. However, the idea of the extensionless physical point can also be regarded as an abstraction. If all the individual characteristics of all existent objects are disregarded, a physical point with no extension and with infinite density emerges as the common abstract core of all objects. A thing that manifests the characteristic all objects have in common and into which all objects in the world collapse when deprived of their individual characteristics, except for one: their elementary objecthood.

Via abstraction a set of causal properties are selected to be included in a model and these factors may be subject to idealization. In such a case, idealization is aimed at distorting these preserved elements with a view to further simplification or for tractability reasons. Whilst pure abstraction faithfully represents the involved parts (though due to omissions the resulting picture is still not descriptively accurate), idealization when applied in the next step transforms these parts into something non-existent. As long as, however, theorizing starts from the existent causal properties of objects, as Teller (2001, pp. 397–401) and Katzner (2016) emphasize, both abstraction and idealization guarantee causal adequacy even at the lowest levels of descriptive accuracy (Chakravartty, 2001, p. 329; Contessa, 2007). Katzner (2016, pp. 82–83) places the blame on the tension between primary and secondary assumptions for rendering models more and more unrealistic. Whilst primary assumptions via abstraction grab the key properties as they are, for the sake of tractability, simplification, or consistency, secondary assumptions are needed. Such secondary assumptions are typically idealizations, oftentimes applied to modify the primary assumptions, albeit still point towards real entity properties. Reality is in the game all along the theorizing process. It is thus a mistake to call

---

[52] Quite informally, an inference is valid if it can be validly drawn in a model, while it is sound as well only if it is true of the target (Contessa, 2007).

idealizations simple 'fictions'. They are admittedly fictitious, whilst they are aimed at telling some truth by preserving some existing or real properties of the entities inhabiting the target system. To make this fact explicit, Teller (2004, pp. 445–446) suggests using the terms 'veridical fictions' or fallible veracities'. Needless to say, it is up to the theorist whether she applies idealization to refer to existing properties. Via idealization it is easy to 'steal' some non-existent and merely 'cooked-up' properties into our models. In any case, idealization does not entail similarity, not even partial similarity at the entity level, beyond the basic level of similarity that everything is similar to every other thing to a certain extent (see Section 4.2.2 for more on how to consider similarity in economic modelling).

This connection with existent causal properties is obvious in the case of abstraction, but how does this work for reality-based idealization? How is it possible to preserve something in cases where the whole idealizing process is aimed at distortion carried out by assuming non-existent properties? Even though they go in different ways, both abstraction and idealization result in caricatures (Chakravartty, 2001, p. 327); hence both render the theories descriptively false, and, if appropriately used, both can guarantee causal adequacy. As for abstraction, as we have seen, identifying and preserving a subset of causally active properties in abstract form guarantees causal adequacy. By contrast, the representational relationship of an idealization-based theory to reality is something to establish, and in these terms denotation can do the job (Chakravartty, 2007, p. 226). Denotation places a fictional property into a referential relationship to an existent characteristic. In denotation a fictitious property is related to a real entity feature through a reference or referential relationship the modeller lays down.

Successful denotation, a case where surrogative inferences[53] can be drawn, presupposes some additional elements. In this context, Shech (2015, pp. 3469–3471; Shech, 2016, p. 314) highlights the role of representational codes as a prerequisite. On closer scrutiny, denotation taken as mere stipulation (Suárez, 2004) on its own may only be a simple labelling process that amounts to statements like 'the red pen stands for a tanker' on a map whilst 'the eraser for a battleship'. Specifically, labelling declares what a part of a model stands for, but it provides no clear-cut set of inferential rules. It may remain unclear what inferences are sensible to draw. To spell this out, a representational code is needed, as neither the relations within a denotator nor its properties can obviously be used

---

[53] The term 'surrogative reasoning' is coined by Chris Swoyer (1991) to label the cases where on the basis of a representation taken as a surrogate we can draw sound causal inferences about the thing it represents. Swoyer's account is most important here for he explains the possibility of surrogative reasoning with structural similarity between vehicle and target.

to learn about the denotatum. In some extreme cases, denotation implies no possibility for surrogative inferences. For instance, based on the London Underground logo, nobody can plan their route from Heathrow to London City Airport. By contrast, a representational code establishes a functional connection between a sign and its target. In such a case, idealization is related to some existent parts of reality. Even though strong idealization taken at face value is highly uninstructive, the code for deciphering the hidden information is available (Chakravartty, 2010b, pp. 38–39). Given this, on the basis of the relations and the properties of the denotators, surrogative inferences regarding the target system are possible to draw.[54] To make it happen, it is always reality that is to be distorted in or referred to via idealization, which is a far cry from assuming non-existent (cooked-up) properties.

In this context, Hughes (1997) places his emphasis on interpretation, whilst Suárez (2002, p. 22) on the representational force of the representation set towards the target. In order to provide surrogative reasoning via formal deductions in a model, it needs to be interpreted in terms of its target system and in line with the intentions of the user (Contessa, 2007). Based on her judgement and background knowledge, a competent and informed user always knows what inferences she is justified to draw (Suárez, 2004), even if this knowledge of hers does not always elevates to explicitness. In the case of pens on a sheet of paper, users actively utilize the rules of mapping a 3D-space into two dimensions and, on this basis, how a spatiotemporal position of a real object can be represented on a 2D map and how to extrapolate the trajectories pens show to infer the positions of ships on the sea. Even though, for instance, the string of a swing in theory is assumed to be massless, we ought not to infer that strings of actual swings are massless as it would be an unsound inference.[55] This set of standards clearly explains why and how such highly formalized theories as the oft-criticized Arrow–Debreu framework can remain within the boundaries of the causally adequate social sciences.

---

[54] Apropos of Picasso's Guernica, Chakravartty (2007, p. 229) argues that models and artworks are not required to be descriptively accurate for imparting valid and smashing information about reality. It is widely albeit not generally believed that scientific and artistic representation, conceived as manifesting the same kind of relationship between representations and targets, can be treated on equal footing (Suárez, 2002, p. 30; Shech, 2016).

[55] It is worthy of note that representational force and the reference to informed users form not too strict a standard as it can be met even by a simple instrumentalist model. Keeping in mind that her model is silent about the causal structure, one can easily predict the birth rate on the basis of her model built on the simple statistical correlation between the number of storks and the birth rate. Background knowledge breaks in to tell her to refrain from saying anything about the causes. Highlighting real entity properties to carry a causal structure forms a more stringent approach.

As French and Ladyman (1999, p. 107) say, there is an analogy taken as a specific representational relationship between model and target to establish, and it is on the basis of this analogy that surrogative reasoning can take place. Analogy stems from denotation combined with interpretation or a representational code that fixes what aspects (properties and relations) of the vehicle can aid in learning about (what properties and relations in) the target system. To do so, quite paradoxically, no similarity is needed at the entity level, so even a reality-based idealization can do the job on its own, provided it insists on some key causal properties.[56] The feasibility of surrogative reasoning may be given even in the case of idealization, even if a model is unfaithful and misrepresents[57] its target at the entity level in every respect. But interpretation or a proper representational code renders it possible for the vehicle to preserve some existent properties, which via ensuring partial structural similarity establishes the potential for surrogative inferences.

Proper denotation and representation codes are pivotal in determining whether one is justified to endow an idealizing model with her realist commitment. If denotation and representation codes are missing or unspecified, we enter the instrumentalist case. By contrast, with a clearcut representational code in the bag, playing on how Friedman assumed some non-existent properties in his F53 would be an insufficient ground

---

[56] There is a basic level of similarity between things that can hardly be avoided. For instance, both the pen and the tanker may be red, both of them may be made up of steel, but, at a minimum, both are objects. Dimensions of similarity at the entity level, however, play no role in representation. Even a green pen or any other object can successfully represent a tanker. We do not need more but objects standing in well-established representational relationships. As everything is similar to every other thing in some respects, similarity cannot make a difference between representations and non-representations. See Section 4.2.2 on how Lucas built upon the idea that everything can be a representation of something.

[57] Misrepresentation also preserves truth content, so misrepresentation is not to be mistaken for non-representation. In broad terms, the distinction between representation and misrepresentation refers to the distinction between correct and incorrect, accurate, and inaccurate or faithful and unfaithful (or even partially faithful) representations. Incorrect and inaccurate representations entail weaker descriptive performance for certain, though it is also argued that in order for a representation to be completely faithful, such as an up-to-date London underground map, it does not need to be a replica of its target. A misrepresentation represents with properties the target does not have. It is worthwhile here to recall the case of political caricatures which are misrepresentations of reality, while it is still some real properties that are distorted in meaningful ways. There is a scope for each representation within which it leads to valid and sound inferences. Such inferences can be drawn from maps, but maps are by no means replicas of the world (Contessa, 2007). To turn back to the theory of swing for a moment, the mass of strings is outside the representational scope, so there is no ground for sound inferences in this respect.

for arguing for his instrumentalism. If representational codes are available, inexistent properties are still in the game, whilst it is an idealization worthy of realists' adherence as idealized properties in the vehicle refer to some existent features of the target and carry (a facet of) the causal structure. To make this happen a representational relationship is to be established between existent and inexistent properties to spell out what is preserved and how. Friedman, however, refused to provide such a code. Instead, as we have seen, he did his best to avoid any discussions about real entity properties. He paid attention to them inasmuch as he clarified the fact that his assumptions had nothing to do with real entity properties. The only slight possibility of a realist commitment lies in his insistence on expectation errors playing a crucial role in triggering large-scale fluctuations. A significant part of Chapter 4 is devoted to clarifying that the way Friedman theorized about expectation errors, that is, his abandoning the real properties of employers and employees, places his Phillips curves into the category of causally inadequate instrumentalist models.

As for Lucas's case, for instance, assuming market clearing and individual optimization taken as intertemporal optimization between work and leisure in time (Lucas & Sargent, 1979, p. 7) renders it possible to study whether optimizing behaviour contributes to the emergence of large-scale fluctuations. It is exactly this programme declaration that provides the representational code thanks to which the idealization-based concept of general equilibrium fits into a realist albeit not descriptively realist economic theory. Whilst general economic equilibrium is not a descriptive conception (Snowdon & Vane, 2005, p. 281), so it is not a sensible question whether real economies are in equilibrium or not, general equilibrium analysis enhances knowledge of reality. The island models provide further examples for realist idealizations where the highly unrealistic framework of separated islands and randomly allocated agents can successfully represent the process how real agents try to optimize in an incomplete information setting. As it is shown in Fig. 3.6, surrogative inferences are possible to draw even from the extremely abstract framework inhabited by Lucas's single representative agent.

To sum up, in the semirealist approach to structure representation it is the relevant set of active causal entity properties that are conceived to carry the structure represented, thus representing a structure requires the representation of existing entity properties in one way or another. This is a twofold relationship: partial structural similarity between a vehicle and its target (Sklar, 2003, p. 426), i.e. the case of representing an aspect of a real structure, requires and presupposes preserving via abstraction and idealization that set of entity properties that establish the facet of a concrete causal structure one is currently interested in. Selectivity means that representing a part of a causal structure in a simplified form still contributes to the understanding how a complex structure works. In the meantime,

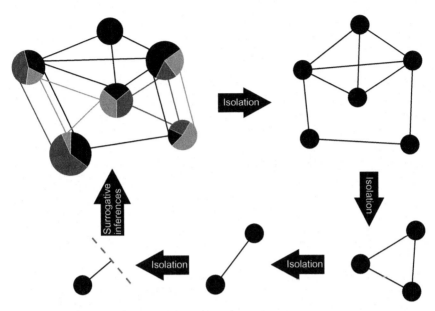

FIG. 3.6 Establishing partial structural similarity between target and model by preserving the relevant causal properties.

similarity at the level of entity properties is not required as via proper idealization some existent entity properties can be referred to via some non-existent properties. This is the basis for surrogative reasoning where having started from real entity properties a model is constructed for demonstrative purposes and with a view to turning back to reality again. Preserving real entity properties is the key to this two-direction epistemological play, from reality to model and then back to reality again (Hughes, 1997; Suárez, 2002, p. 7).

3.4.2 Some arguments against an OSR-based reconstruction of economics

Kincaid (2008) and Ross (2008) argue for an OSR-based interpretation of economics, as defended by Steven French (2010, p. 107) later. Both of them interpret the extensive use of the homo oeconomicus having no concrete individuality as a strong point in favour of the proposed structuralist reconceptualization of the individual as an object of economics. This OSR-based interpretation is allegedly facilitated by the fact that modern economics is formulated in a highly formal mathematical language. Along these lines, economics could reach so high a level of formalism that is appropriate to express a set of standard theories. This is the reason why some other social sciences (e.g. sociology) rejecting mathematical formalism do not fit into structuralist reinterpretations, even if sociology is aimed at studying social structures instead of individuals.

In contrast with Ross, Kincaid (2008, p. 722) does not constrain the structuralist approach to formal economic theories. He sets Marx for demonstration. Kincaid underlines that Marx regarded social structure as a system of interrelated social positions, statuses, and roles instead of individuals. From this fact Kincaid infers that social sciences interpret structure in consonance with the ideas of OSR and commonly regard any object as anything that can fit into a given structure. Positions or statuses are socially determined. It still holds, however, that relata can only be humans who have personal characteristics enabling them to act in the social structure in certain ways. In spite of the impersonal nature of market relations (Simmel, 1900/2005) our societies remain human societies and it is still the individual who carries the properties she needs to fulfil others' role expectations by possessing some individual qualities (Schütz & Luckmann, 1973).

Émile Durkheim's social theory, however, is a framework that may sensibly be subject to an OSR-based interpretation. For Durkheim (1895/1982, pp. 34–47; 1897/2005), society is a system that has some independence of individuals in that it can perform actions (i.e. social actions) even against them. The Hart-Devlin debate taken place in legal theory is highly instructive as for Durkheim's ideas (Cane, 2006; Feinberg, 1973; Hart, 1989). Patrick Devlin echoing Durkheim's views regarded morals as the integrating norms of societies. Individual actions infringing social rules are against social interests, and in such cases society has the right to protect itself by enforcing norms by law. However, even Durkheim took it for granted that conceptually the egoistic individual capable of acting stands against society's collective consciousness (Allan, 2010, p. 102). Individuals are not dissolved in society; it is rather a conflict of the two.

Demonstrative references from outside the neoclassical orthodoxy thus fail to heighten OSR's acceptability as an interpretive framework for economics. As Ross (2008, p. 734) himself admits, if the purpose of economics is taken as the prediction of the behaviour of everyday entities, OSR fails to hold its ground. To apply the OSR approach, it would be necessary to reduce directly observable existents (consumers, producers, goods, and services) to structures, whilst this step contradicts our common-sense world view. But still, the idea of our representative agent raises the possibility of an ontic structuralist account. Ross argues that individuals are only interesting for economics to the extent of their places in the social structure. Accordingly, models attribute as many characteristics to individuals as are necessary for them to play their assigned roles. It means to him that the homo oeconomicus radically different from man as a biological-social-cultural being is wholly dissolved in the structure (Ross, 2005, pp. 213–265; 2006). OSR thus regards the structure as the source of

the individuals' roles and the individual as a structurally determined minimalist set of her roles. What economics claims about the individual (e.g.
preference system, production possibility frontier, the circumstances of
market interactions) are conceived as external properties handed down
by the roles she plays in the structure.

Here it is worth quoting Ross (2008, p. 742) at length:

> The thin concept of agency in economic science identifies agents with the gravita-
> tional centers of consistent preference fields. The theory incorporates no thesis about
> which empirical entities implement such roles. Nor does it entail anything about how
> long their embodiment typically persist. Agents may be as transient as a modeler likes;
> so although agents may not change their preferences and remain the same agents,
> people may do so and can simply be modeled as successions of economically related
> agents. [...] ([A]mong organisms) insects, because their preferences don't change, are
> better exemplars of basic economic agency than people [...].

This angry invective bears close resemblance to Kornai's (1971) critique
of neoclassical mainstream economics. There Kornai on the basis of the
failure of general equilibrium theory in descriptive terms refuses to ac-
knowledge it as a real science, i.e. as a discipline related to or having any
epistemological grip on socio-economic reality.

Ross's reasoning skids onto thin ice when he draws some ontological
inferences from the theorizing-epistemological habit of economics and the
sciences. The notion of the representative economic agent is abstracted
and idealized from the actual human beings taken as market agents.
Normally, neither abstraction nor idealization is supposed to change the
nature of a referent (e.g. *Homo sapiens*). Physics works in the same way
(Castellani, 1993, pp. 105–106). Theoretical entity *Fe* as a chemical element
is constructed on the basis of experiencing concrete *Fe* atoms, so it incorporates those properties the possession of which renders an element *Fe*.
This is a two-way process, as there is a way back from the theoretical entity to any concrete *Fe* atom having individuating properties, including
spatiotemporal features. What we know of the theoretical entity directly
applies to all *Fe* atoms (Manicas, 2006, pp. 84–85). Theory starts from the
concrete and leads to the typical but has a way back to the concrete again.
Stepping into the abstract is not a ground for depriving the homo oeconomicus of its ability to be concrete again. In general, objecthood does not
require individuality (Brading & Skiles, 2012, pp. 104–106; Nounou, 2012,
pp. 118–120). Under the burden of this point the argument that theoretical
agents of economics have no individuality hence ought to be subject to a
structuralist decomposition immediately collapses. This lack of individuality stems from our everyday theorizing strategy, whilst the real counterparts of the homo oeconomicus always have individuality and our related
theoretical knowledge is always ready for individuation. In the case of
social sciences it is typical how Weber (1968/1978, pp. 3–62) insisted on

constructing the typical agent of neoclassical economics out of the properties of everyday market participants and how he applied theoretical outcomes in individual cases to consider the extent to which theoretically assumed properties governed actual human behaviour (see Section 4.1.1 for further reflections on this). Other entities of economics, such as goods, money, or natural resources, all fall into the category of objects without individuality, like water in a glass. It follows that neither the homo oeconomicus nor our further theoretical entities provide sufficient reasons for us to reconceptualize economics in a structuralist way.

Economics admits of human complexity and individuality; thus it only disregards some individual properties for tractability or relevance reasons. These are details that are of secondary importance as for its defining theoretical purposes. Discussions in economics over the typical or representative agent do not imply the abandonment of the intention of preserving some existent entity properties or gaining knowledge about individual entities. As semirealism argues, it is exactly the fact that multiple objects may have the same causal property and they consequently tend to behave in the same way under similar conditions that renders it possible for us to make generalizations. As a consequence, the emerging causal regularities and tendencies in the behaviour of individual entities can be traced back to individual properties. If multiple entities possess the same characteristic, this characteristic is typical of them so it defines a set of objects—the set of objects having a property in common. Thus, if theorizing is carried out with the aim of preserving this common feature whilst neglecting others to separate the wheat from the chaff in an analysis, the result is a theoretical entity that successfully refers to every individual entity in the given set.

As a result of abstraction, individual differences admittedly disappear for the theory. Man in economics is reduced to the easily multipliable homo oeconomicus. However, it is still the individual who is the referent. By contrast, Don Ross argues that our discussions about a typical electron instead of concrete electrons or about the homo oeconomicus instead of concrete human beings inevitably lead to a structuralist decomposition of entities. Individuality is alleged to be dissolved in structure. Ross thus apparently takes abstraction as a theorizing technique and the structuralist reconceptualization of objects on equal footing. Abstraction, however, does not eliminate the notion of individual objects or call their existence into question (abstract concepts successfully refer), only highlights some causal properties of central importance. These properties still belong to the individual in reality.

3.4.3 Commonsensibles in economics

The problems of unobservables in economics emerge in the context of commonsensibles. Uskali Mäki and Daniel M. Hausman are the two who have made the most important contributions to the clarification of the role commonsensibles play in economic theorizing. Even though they disagree on the applicability of realism to economics, they see eye to eye on regarding most of our concepts as commonsensibles.

Mäki highlights that economics postulates a lot of unobservable entities; however, these are of different nature as compared to the electrons or quarks of physics. Physics' unobservable waves or elementary particles suggest a radical ontological departure from our common-sense world. On the basis of this common-sense world view modern theoretical physics is unconceivable as its ontic furniture radically differs from our everyday experience. The realm of modern physics is populated by entities to which we have access only through subtle theories as these entities are well beyond the boundaries of our ordinary experience (i.e. our unaided senses). Unobservables in economics are not of this kind. There is no ontological jump here. These things belong to our common-sense world. From preferences to expectations, from choices to costs: all our economic concepts come from the common-sense realm of familiar things (Mäki, 1996, pp. 433–434). As a consequence, unobservability is not a major concern for economics as unobservable entities here are associated with things we are familiar with from our everyday life (Hands, 2012, p. 159).

This common-sense world of course has a plethora of observable entities (Mäki, 2000, p. 111), even though there is no definite demarcation between observables and unobservables. Whilst our fellow agents as physical creatures are observables, their preferences belong to the unobservable albeit common-sense or everyday realm.[58] So when an economist talks of unobservables in the strict sense of the word, she applies such concepts that are also accessible to a pre-theoretic attitude. Mäki (2011, p. 8) suggests the term 'folk objects' to express the circumstance that economic commonsensibles are identified by our common-sense or everyday experience. And this has a lot to do with the ontological status of economics. One of the most crucial pillars for economic realism is the compatibility between economic theories and common-sense experience (Mäki, 1996, p. 428).

This accessibility remains a fact of life even though scientific economics modifies these objects of folk economics via abstraction, omission, idealization, and other forms of conceptualizing acts. Economics assumes well-behaving preferences whilst at the same time it is commonly known what 'preferring coffee to tea' means as a mental state (Hands, 2012, p. 167) regardless whether ourselves or others are considered (Mäki, 2009a, p. 87).

---

[58] There is no consensus whether preferences are observables or unobservables. Hands (2012, p. 159) regard them as unobservables, while for Mäki (2002, p. 95) they are observables. It is relatively easy for one to draw up a sketch about her choices regarding two commodities at given income levels, other things equal. She can thus imagine her preferences though cannot observe them in the everyday sense.

Similarly, Friedman's permanent income hypothesis emerges as a plausible story describing the everyday money management of households. As a consequence, it is out of question that basic economic concepts refer, and the referents are in existence. Abstract-theoretical representation of preferences does indeed refer to the real tastes of real economic agents. Mäki suggests a three-step system ranging from *general folk views* through *folk economics* to *scientific economics*. By walking along this path, economists still discuss the same things, but at higher and higher levels of abstractness and formalism of language. In other words, in economics, rearranging and modifying the elements available to us in common-sense experience, we theoretically represent our common-sense economic entities. Even though there are various ways to isolate the theoretically relevant and irrelevant and to approach the selected parts in scientific terms,

> none of [these operations] accomplishes a major departure from the ontic furniture of the ordinary realm. No new *kinds* of entities or properties are introduced. Only the ordinary entities and properties are modified. (Mäki, 1996, p. 435)

It means that the vast majority of the concepts in scientific economics are only the modified versions of economic folk views. However, this does not amount to the obvious and evident truth of economic theories. Such theories may also occur that rearrange and re-relate some everyday objects of economic reality in an untrue way. Using commonsensibles like employers, employees, prices, or wages is not a guarantee even for approximate truth if these commonsensible theoretical entities have some key properties obviously not shared by their real counterparts (see Chapter 4 for more on this). But as long as theories conceptualize upon the real properties of real agents via abstraction and meaningful idealization, economics is capable of drawing sound causal inferences. Economic realism is thus far from evidently given (Mäki, 2000, p. 119). According to the selective realist arguments presented above the way we represent or misrepresent economic reality ought to be accomplished with a view to the truth or close-to-truth. For semirealism and the semirealistic approach to economics this problem boils down to isolating the relevant causally active properties of entities. Giving them up inevitably takes us away from the realm of commonsensibles as Mäki's analysis on commonsensibles also suggests. But if our theories keep postulating existing entities and real properties (bearing in mind the indispensability of representational codes), then we can stay in the commonsensibles realm and there is a clear ground for realist commitments.

Hoover (2001, pp. 229–230) underlines that Mäki's commonsensibles interpretation is more cogent for some concepts of economics than for others. For instance, everyday people of folk economics have problems understanding such concepts as the 'real GDP' or 'the general price level'. Hoover distinguishes *natural aggregates* and *synthetic aggregates*. For him, only natural aggregates can be conceived as commonsensibles for these simple sums or averages as measures have the same dimensionality as their individual components. Total unemployment or the average rate of interest can easily be interpreted on the basis of our everyday experience. However, synthetic aggregates consist of components in a way that modifies the dimensionality of the parts; thus no easy or analogous interpretation is available. For instance, the price of a commodity is easy to understand; however, in the case of the general price level one compares current-period dollars to base-period dollars (Hoover, 2009b, p. 390). Such synthetic aggregates are too closely related to complex economic theories for being open to common-sense interpretations.

Interesting as it is, Arrow (1974, pp. 253–254) discusses economic equilibrium in the same vein. In the everyday, normal experience laymen can easily interpret a situation in which the quantity supplied is equal to the quantity demanded. However, this understanding is not so thorough as to cover the understanding of how the interplay of the underlying mechanisms (i.e. the reallocation of production inputs or interactions between shifts in technology and the allocation of the labour force) can lead to general economic equilibrium. As another example, Hands (2012) suggests contemporary revealed preference theory as a radical departure from this standard of commonsensibles. Thus, for him, it is unjustified to say economics *as such* operates exclusively with commonsensibles. Some qualifications are needed, though Mäki's common-sense realism still holds as a normative standard.

In spite of the apparent problems, we do have commonsensibles in economics. Citing Robbins (1935/1984, pp. 75–79), Hands (2008) argues for the key role of introspection in economic theorizing. Over and above obvious empirical facts such as scarcity (which can also be conceived as a commonsensible), some economic concepts of fundamental importance (e.g. preferences or permanent income) do not come from experiments or observation but from self-knowledge. Any individual knows by self-observation or inner everyday experience that different things have different importance to her and in terms of importance things can be arranged in a certain order. We all have clear mental pictures, which we can render even clearer by apt theorizing, of how economic agents think, decide, or act. For the present argumentation suffice it to underline that there is no confusion in our ideas regarding the fundamental properties of economic agents. We can easily judge whether a theoretical description of a 'typical' agent corresponds to our views on ourselves. Considering the success of isolation by making such an intuitive comparison is an undemanding job in most cases.

Mäki and Hausman's disagreement is only of definitional nature. Hausman argues that the central problem for the realism of natural sciences regards the ontological status of unobservables such as electrons

(Mäki, 2000, pp. 117–118). For him, scientific realism is a warranted stance only when we have appropriate epistemic grip on unobservables. Similarly, the various isolative strategies of scientific realism are all motivated by the purpose of finding those parts of reality whose existence is undeniable, or at least are irrational to call into question. The conflict between realism and anti-realism regards the unobservables, whilst even anti-realists refrain from undermining the belief in the visible world (in so far as they are free from the radical forms of Cartesian doubt). From the fact that unobservables are central to scientific realism Hausman infers that it is inapplicable to economics as economics has little to do with unobservables. As he says, 'the ontological, semantic, and epistemological issues separating realists from anti-realists and from some instrumentalists are largely irrelevant to economics. The reason is simple: economic theories for the most part do not postulate new unobservable entities' (Hausman, 1998, p. 196). By contrast, Mäki (2011, p. 4) highlights that the issue about unobservables is not a defining feature of scientific realism as it is only one aspect of the realist controversies (Psillos, 2011, p. 302). There is thus no hindrance to discussions about economics under scientific realism, at least in a version which is customized to make room for the peculiarities of economics (Hands, 2012, p. 156).

3.5 Conclusions for economics: Distinguishing descriptive accuracy and causal adequacy

Having completed this lengthy struggle through concepts and approaches in general philosophy of science, it is about time to draw some brief conclusions regarding the methodological analysis of the Friedman-Lucas transition in macroeconomics. One of the most lingering debates of economic methodology regards the performance aspects of unrealistic models. What knowledge can such models impart? And based on them, what can we know at all? It is exactly to these questions that the analysis of abstraction and idealization as theorizing strategies provided some preliminary answers above.

As far as the potentials of abstract-idealized models are considered, there exist two extreme views in economic methodology. According to one of them, these models are only heuristic devices constructed to save the phenomena but saying anything about the causal structure underlying socio-economic reality is well beyond their scope. In this regard, Røgeberg and Nordberg's (2005) account on abstract-idealized (in their terminology: 'absurd') theories in economics is outstanding. In spite of their positive attitude towards the extensive use of 'absurd' and 'bizarre' assumptions in economics, they exert a rather negative criticism. They understand these models as some inevitable devices of human thinking which we create to minimize the cognitive burdens the organization of experiences places on us. For them, causality is not a concern; models are only shorthand summaries of observed facts, not theories in the strict sense. Moreover, watching causality into phenomena in a Kantian way seems to be a common feature of our thinking; thus we ought to avoid taking our causal accounts too seriously. Causal thinking is conceived only as an unfavourable by-product of the human mind. This line of reasoning can easily be traced back to constructive empiricism and economic instrumentalism where the only layer of reality to take into account is the level of observable phenomena. Everything else is regarded as unwarranted and ungrounded metaphysical speculation. It is only the empirical regularities we ought to focus on.

The other extreme is Uskali Mäki's realist philosophy of economics (Mäki, 2009a). Mäki launched an overall and powerful attack to suggest a realist interpretation of economics. His distinction between surrogate systems and substitute systems was exactly aimed at clarifying what kind of models can legitimately be expected to unravel the causal structure. It is only members of the former set that have the promise of supporting us in seeking causal understanding. A related and similarly intriguing question regards the way descriptively unrealistic models as surrogate systems are to be set up: models which are still realistic somehow so that they can provide indirect epistemic access to reality. As the analysis of abstraction and idealization suggests, descriptive falsity is not a hindrance to isolative models' capability of supporting causal understanding. In other words, causally adequate models, models having the quality of latching onto the causal structure of socio-economic phenomena do not need to be descriptively realistic.

What is more, by setting the standard of approximate truth, realist philosophers of science and scientists themselves have abandoned the idea of descriptive realisticness (Worrall, 2012, p. 79). Selectivity and the resulting complementarity of models in themselves entail a rather poor descriptive performance. Even the case of pure abstraction, when no distortion is in the game, results in descriptively false models as some facets of reality are disregarded, so the resulting picture cannot be correct in descriptive terms, whilst they still convey relevant and meaningful information about the target (Teller, 2004, p. 436). Our theories if taken at face value are oftentimes untrue, which renders it highly unlikely for them to perform well in descriptive terms. An indirect cognitive access to reality, however, may still be given, even if it is still a possibility only. It does not necessarily follow that any unrealistic model has causal adequacy, so descriptive falsity fails to unconditionally imply causal adequacy.[59] On the basis of the

---

[59] Admittedly, if one starts arguing for the (causal) realism of some (descriptively) unrealistic models, it may be very difficult for her to reject the temptation of making the case for the realism of unrealistic economics as such. Maybe this was the reason for Mäki's efforts to provide a realist account of Friedman's antirealist methodology (Mäki, 2009b).

semirealistic approach to economics it is argued that causal adequacy is something to be established via proper theorizing intended to be realist, and the key is a focus on the relevant causally active properties of entities involved in the causal mechanism under scrutiny.

Everything is thus dependent upon the underlying purposes of a theorists and the theorizing strategy as a part of the methodology she applies. It is not excessively difficult to draw a principled distinction. In pure abstraction there are some omitted parts of reality but with no additions to it (Mäki, 2012). Depending on the extent of abstractness, the result may be either verisimilar or 'bare' models. However, abstraction still guarantees that models are causally adequate in either case. The same is true of idealization provided that the model has a representational code or a proper interpretation in terms of the target to fix which existing part of reality it is that the model represents in a non-existing (distorted) way. In all such cases, models remain descriptively false, whilst they retain causal adequacy even at the lowest levels of descriptive accuracy. In other words, we may need to distinguish *realisticness* (to refer to the level of descriptive performance) and *realism* (to refer to the capability of revealing some facets of a causal structure) of models. It means that the realism of a theory by no means requires realisticness. Scientific models despite their unrealisticness do have much to do with truth. In other words, realist models are usually descriptively false, whilst they still deserve realist commitments for latching onto (some parts of) a causal structure. By contrast, instrumentalist models, equally inaccurate in descriptive terms, have nothing to say about truth beyond the phenomenal level, so figuring out whether a model is worthy of realist commitment to its partial causal truths requires us to dig down to the underlying interpretations, representational codes, and the ambitions the modeller sets herself. Considering only descriptive performance is a primitive, misleading, unfruitful, and rather out-dated form of theory assessment.

Suggested readings

When it comes to reading up on the theory of representation, it pays to start with some entries in the Stanford Encyclopedia of Philosophy. Frigg and Nguyen (2018) survey and compare the various standards of scientific representation. Chakravartty (2017e) discusses the major problems of scientific realism with a special emphasis upon structural realism and entity realism. Ladyman (2019) gives a comprehensive overview on the diverse versions of structural realism with a detailed bibliography. The basic creed and the vocabulary of semirealism can be found in Chakravartty's (2007) seminal book. Chakravartty (2017f) provides further considerations regarding the relationship of ontology, metaphysics, and modern science.

Beni (2019) examines structural realism in the context of scientific representation. Hanami (2003) shows how the term 'structural realism' is used outside the field of natural sciences.

References

Allan, K. (2010). *Explorations in classical sociological theory. Seeing the social world*. London: Pine Forge Press.

Arrow, K. J. (1964). The role of securities in the optimal allocation of risk-bearing. *The Review of Economic Studies, 31*(2), 91–96.

Arrow, K. J. (1968). Economic equilibrium. In R. K. Merton & D. L. Sills (Eds.), *Vol. 4. International encyclopedia of the social science* (pp. 376–388). London and New York: Macmillan & The Free Press.

Arrow, K. J. (1973). *General economic equilibrium. Purpose, analytic techniques, collective choice*. Cambridge, MA: Harvard University Press.

Arrow, K. J. (1974). General economic equilibrium. Purpose, analytic techniques, collective choice. Nobel lecture. *The American Economic Review, 64*(3), 253–272.

Bailer-Jones, D. M. (2003). When scientific models represent. *International Studies in the Philosophy of Science, 17*(1), 59–74.

Barro, R. J. (1974). Are government bonds net wealth? *Journal of Political Economy, 82*(6), 1095–1117.

Becker, G. S. (1971). *Economic theory*. New York: Alfred A. Knopf.

Beni, M. D. (2019). *Cognitive structural realism. A radical solution to the problem of scientific representation*. Heidelberg: Springer.

Berenstain, N., & Ladyman, J. (2012). Ontic structural realism and modality. In E. M. Landry & D. P. Rickles (Eds.), *Structural realism. Structure, object, and causality* (pp. 149–168). New York: Springer.

Bilson, J. F. (1980). The rational expectations approach to the consumption function. A multi-country study. *European Economic Review, 13*(3), 273–299.

Bird, R. C., & Bodkin, R. G. (1965). The National Service life-insurance dividend of 1950 and consumption. A further test of the "strict" permanent-income hypothesis. *Journal of Political Economy, 73*(5), 499–515.

Blaug, M. (1992). *The methodology of economics or how economists explain* (2nd ed.). Cambridge: Cambridge University Press.

Boland, L. A. (2010). Review of "The methodology of positive economics. Reflections on the Milton Friedman legacy, ed. Uskali Mäki". *Economics and Philosophy, 26*(3), 376–382.

Brading, K., & Skiles, A. (2012). Underdetermination as a path to structural realism. In E. M. Landry & D. P. Rickles (Eds.), *Structural realism. Structure, object, and causality* (pp. 99–115). New York: Springer.

Buchanan, J. M. (1976). Barro on the Ricardian equivalence theorem. *Journal of Political Economy, 84*(2), 337–342.

Busch, J. (2003). What structures could not be. *International Studies in the Philosophy of Science, 17*(3), 211–223.

Cane, P. (2006). Taking law seriously. Starting points of the Hart/Devlin debate. *The Journal of Ethics, 10*(1–2), 21–51.

Cao, T. Y. (2006). Structural realism and quantum gravity. In D. Rickles, S. French, & J. Saatsi (Eds.), *The structural foundations of quantum gravity* (pp. 40–52). Oxford: Clarendon Press.

Casarosa, C. (1981). The microfoundations of Keynes's aggregate supply and expected demand analysis. *The Economic Journal, 91*(1), 188–194.

Castellani, E. (1993). Quantum mechanics, objects and objectivity. In C. Garola & A. Rossi (Eds.), *The foundations of quantum mechanics. Historical analysis and open questions* (pp. 105–114). Dordrecht: Kluwer.

Chakravartty, A. (1998). Semirealism. *Studies in History and Philosophy of Science Part A, 29*(3), 391–408.

Chakravartty, A. (2001). The semantic or model-theoretic view of theories and scientific realism. *Synthese, 127*(3), 325–345.

Chakravartty, A. (2003a). The structuralist conception of objects. *Philosophy of Science, 70*(5), 867–878.

Chakravartty, A. (2003b). Book review. The reality of the unobservable. Observability, unobservability and their impact on the issue of scientific realism. *The British Journal for the Philosophy of Science, 54*(2), 359–363.

Chakravartty, A. (2003c). The dispositional essentialist view of properties and laws. *International Journal of Philosophical Studies, 11*(4), 393–413.

Chakravartty, A. (2004). Structuralism as a form of scientific realism. *International Studies in the Philosophy of Science, 18*(2–3), 151–171.

Chakravartty, A. (2005). Causal realism. Events and processes. *Erkenntnis, 63*(1), 7–31.

Chakravartty, A. (2007). *A metaphysics for scientific realism. Knowing the unobservable.* Cambridge: Cambridge University Press.

Chakravartty, A. (2008a). Inessential Aristotle. Powers without essences. In R. Groff (Ed.), *Revitalizing causality. Realism about causality in philosophy and social science.* London: Routledge.

Chakravartty, A. (2008b). What you don't know can't hurt you. Realism and the unconceived. *Philosophical Studies, 137*(1), 149–158.

Chakravartty, A. (2010a). Informational versus functional theories of scientific representation. *Synthese, 172*(1), 197–213.

Chakravartty, A. (2010b). Truth and representations in science. Two inspirations from art. In R. Frigg & M. C. Hunter (Eds.), *Beyond mimesis and convention. Representation in art and science* (pp. 33–50). New York: Springer.

Chakravartty, A. (2010c). Perspectivism, inconsistent models, and contrastive explanation. *Studies in History and Philosophy of Science Part A, 41*(4), 405–412.

Chakravartty, A. (2012). Ontological priority. The conceptual basis of non-eliminative, ontic structural realism. In E. M. Landry & D. P. Rickles (Eds.), *Structural realism. Structure, object, and causality* (pp. 187–206). New York: Springer.

Chakravartty, A. (2013a). Dispositions for scientific realism. In R. Groff & J. Greco (Eds.), *Powers and capacities in philosophy. The new Aristotelianism* (pp. 113–127). London: Routledge.

Chakravartty, A. (2013b). Realism in the desert and in the jungle. Reply to French, Ghins, and Psillos. *Erkenntnis, 78*(1), 39–58.

Chakravartty, A. (2017a). Particles, causation, and the metaphysics of structure. *Synthese, 194*(7), 2273–2289.

Chakravartty, A. (2017b). Case studies, selective realism, and historical evidence. In M. Massimi, J. W. Romeijn, & G. Schurz (Eds.), *EPSA15 selected papers. The 5th conference of the European Philosophy of Science Association in Düsseldorf* (pp. 13–23). Heidelberg: Springer.

Chakravartty, A. (2017c). Saving the scientific phenomena. What powers can and cannot do. In J. J. Jacobs (Ed.), *Putting powers to work* (pp. 24–37). Oxford: Oxford University Press.

Chakravartty, A. (2017d). Reflections on new thinking about scientific realism. *Synthese, 194*(9), 3379–3392.

Chakravartty, A. (2017e). In E. N. Zalta (Ed.), *Scientific realism.* Letöltés dátuma: 2019. August 31, Stanford encyclopedia of philosophy https://plato.stanford.edu/archives/sum2017/entries/scientific-realism/.

Chakravartty, A. (2017f). *Scientific ontology. Integrating naturalized metaphysics and voluntarist epistemology.* Oxford: Oxford University Press.

Chick, V. (2016). On microfoundations and Keynes' economics. *Review of Political Economy, 28*(1), 99–112.

Clarke, S. (2001). Defensible territory for entity realism. *The British Journal for the Philosophy of Science, 52*(4), 701–722.

Contessa, G. (2007). Representation, interpretation, and surrogative reasoning. *Philosophy of Science, 74*(1), 48–68.

Cruse, P., & Papineau, D. (2002). Scientific realism without reference. In M. Marsonet (Ed.), *The problem of realism* (pp. 174–189). Aldershot: Ashgate.

De Vroey, M. (2012). Microfoundations. A decisive dividing line between Keynesian and new classical macroeconomics? In P. G. Duarte & G. T. Lima (Eds.), *Microfoundations reconsidered. The relationship of micro and macroeconomics in historical perspective* (pp. 168–189). Cheltenham: Edward Elgar.

De Vroey, M. (2016). *A history of macroeconomics from Keynes to Lucas and beyond*. Cambridge: Cambridge University Press.

Debreu, G. (1959). *Theory of value. An axiomatic analysis of economic equilibrium*. New Haven, CT: Yale University Press.

Debreu, G. (1974). Excess demand functions. *Journal of Mathematical Economics, 1*(1), 15–21.

Demopoulos, W., & Friedman, M. (1985). Bertrand Russell's the analysis of matter. Its historical context and contemporary interest. *Philosophy of Science, 52*(4), 621–639.

Dorato, M. (2000a). Measurability, computability and the existence of theoretical entities. In E. Agazzi & M. Pauri (Eds.), *The reality of the unobservable. Observability, unobservability and their impact on the issue of scientific realism* (pp. 207–217). Dordrecht: Kluwer.

Dorato, M. (2000b). Substantivalism, relationism, and structural spacetime realism. *Foundations of Physics, 30*(10), 1605–1628.

Düppe, T., & Weintraub, E. R. (2014). *Finding equilibrium. Arrow, Debreu, McKenzie and the problem of scientific credit*. Princeton, NJ: Princeton University Press.

Durkheim, É. (1895/1982). *The rules of sociological method* [S. Lukes, Ed., & W. D. Halls, Trans.]. New York: The Free Press.

Durkheim, É. (1897/2005). *Suicide. A study in sociology* [G. Simpson, Ed., J. A. Spaulding, & G. Simpson, Trans.]. London: Routledge.

Ellis, B. (2008). Powers and dispositions. In R. Groff (Ed.), *Revitalizing causality. Realism about causality in philosophy and social science* (pp. 76–92). London: Routledge.

Elsamahi, M. (1994). Could theoretical entities save realism? *Proceedings of the Biennial Meeting of the Philosophy of Science Association, 1994*(1), 173–180.

Epstein, B. (2009). Ontological individualism reconsidered. *Synthese, 166*(1), 187–213.

Epstein, B. (2014). Why macroeconomics does not supervene on microeconomics. *Journal of Economic Methodology, 21*(1), 3–18.

Esfeld, M. (2009). The modal nature of structures in ontic structural realism. *International Studies in the Philosophy of Science, 23*(2), 179–194.

Esfeld, M. (2013). Ontic structural realism and the interpretation of quantum mechanics. *European Journal for Philosophy of Science, 3*(1), 19–32.

Feinberg, J. (1973). *Social philosophy*. Englewood Cliffs, NJ: Prentice Hall.

Fine, A. (1991). Piecemeal realism. *Philosophical Studies, 61*(1–2), 79–96.

French, S. (1998). On the withering away of physical objects. In E. Castellani (Ed.), *Interpreting bodies. Classical and quantum objects in modern physics* (pp. 93–113). Princeton, NJ: Princeton University Press.

French, S. (2006). Structure as a weapon of the realist. *Proceedings of the Aristotelian Society, 106*(1), 169–187.

French, S. (2007). *The limits of structuralism*. Mimeo: British Society for the Philosophy of Science presidential address.

French, S. (2010). The interdependence of structure, objects and dependence. *Synthese, 175*(S1), 177–197.

French, S. (2012). The presentation of objects and the representation of structure. In E. M. Landry & D. P. Rickles (Eds.), *Structural realism. Structure, object, and causality* (pp. 3–28). New York: Springer.

French, S. (2013). Semi-realism, sociability and structure. *Erkenntnis, 78*(1), 1–18.

French, S., & Ladyman, J. (1999). Reinflating the semantic approach. *International Studies in the Philosophy of Science, 13*(2), 103–121.

French, S., & Ladyman, J. (2003a). Remodelling structural realism. Quantum physics and the metaphysics of structure. *Synthese, 136*(1), 31–56.

French, S., & Ladyman, J. (2003b). The dissolution of objects. Between Platonism and phenomenalism. *Synthese, 136*(1), 73–77.

French, S., & Ladyman, J. (2011). In defence of ontic structural realism. In A. Bokulich & P. Bokulich (Eds.), *Scientific structuralism* (pp. 25–42). New York: Springer.

Friedman, M. (1946). Lange on price flexibility and employment. A methodological criticism. *The American Economic Review, 36*(4), 613–631.

Friedman, M. (1949). The Marshallian demand curve. *Journal of Political Economy, 57*(6), 463–495.

Friedman, M. (1953/2009). The methodology of positive economics. In U. Mäki (Ed.), *The methodology of positive economics. Reflections on the Milton Friedman legacy* (pp. 3–43). Cambridge: Cambridge University Press.

Friedman, M. (1955). Leon Walras and his economic system. *The American Economic Review, 45*(5), 900–909.

Friedman, M. (1956). The quantity theory of money. A restatement. In M. Friedman (Ed.), *Studies in the quantity theory of money* (pp. 3–21). The University of Chicago Press.

Friedman, M. (1957). *The theory of the consumption function*. Princeton, NJ: Princeton University Press.

Friedman, M. (1968). The role of monetary policy. *The American Economic Review, 58*(1), 1–17.

Friedman, M. (1977). Inflation and unemployment. Nobel lecture. *Journal of Political Economy, 85*(3), 451–472.

Friedman, M., & Schwartz, A. J. (1963). *A monetary history of the United States, 1867–1960*. Princeton, NJ: Princeton University Press.

Friedman, M., & Schwartz, A. J. (1965). Money and business cycles. In NBER (Eds.), *The state of monetary economics* (pp. 32–78). Cambridge, MA: National Bureau of Economic Research.

Frigg, R., & Nguyen, J. (2018). In E. N. Zalta (Ed.), *Scientific representation*. Retrieved August 31, 2019, from Stanford Encyclopedia of Philosophy https://plato.stanford.edu/archives/win2018/entries/scientific-representation/.

Galbács, P. (2015). *The theory of new classical macroeconomics*. New York: Springer.

Geanakoplos, J. D., & Polemarchakis, H. M. (1986). Existence, regularity and constrained suboptimality of competitive allocations when the asset structure is incomplete. In W. P. Heller, R. M. Starr, & D. A. Starrett (Eds.), *Uncertainty, information and communication. Essays in honor of K.J. Arrow* (pp. 65–95). Cambridge: Cambridge University Press.

Ghins, M. (2013). Semirealism, concrete structures and theory change. *Erkenntnis, 78*(1), 19–27.

Giere, R. N. (1988). *Explaining science. A cognitive approach*. Chicago: The University of Chicago Press.

Giere, R. N. (1999). Using models to represent reality. In L. Magnani, N. J. Nersessian, & P. Thagard (Eds.), *Model-based reasoning in scientific discovery* (pp. 41–57). Boston, MA: Springer.

Gorman, W. M. (1953). Community preference fields. *Econometrica, 21*(1), 63–80.

Gower, B. (2000). Cassirer, Schlick and "structural" realism. The philosophy of the exact sciences in the background to early logical positivism. *The British Journal for the History of Science, 8*(1), 71–106.

Hacking, I. (1982). Experimentation and scientific realism. *Philosophical Topics, 13*(1), 71–87.

Hahn, F. H. (1965). On some problems of proving the existence of an equilibrium in a monetary economy. In F. H. Hahn & F. R. Brechling (Eds.), *The theory of interest rates* (pp. 126–135). London: Macmillan.

Hahn, F. H. (1975). Revival of political economy. The wrong issues and the wrong argument. *The Economic Record, 51*(3), 360–364.

Hahn, F. H. (1980). Unemployment from a theoretical viewpoint. *Economica, 47*(187), 285–298.

Hanami, A. K. (Ed.), (2003). *Perspectives on structural realism*. New York: Palgrave Macmillan.

Hands, D. W. (2008). Introspection, revealed preference and neoclassical economics. A critical response to Don Ross on the Robbins-Samuelson argument pattern. *Journal of the History of Economic Thought, 30*(4), 453–478.

Hands, D. W. (2012). Realism, commonsensibles, and economics. In A. Lehtinen, J. Kuorikoski, & P. Ylikoski (Eds.), *Economics for real. Uskali Mäki and the place of truth in economics* (pp. 156–178). Oxford: Routledge.

Hands, D. W. (2015). Orthodox and heterodox economics in recent economic methodology. *Erasmus Journal for Philosophy and Economics, 8*(1), 61–81.

Hardin, C. L., & Rosenberg, A. (1982). In defense of convergent realism. *Philosophy of Science, 49*(4), 604–615.

Harré, R. (1970). *The principles of scientific thinking*. London: Palgrave Macmillan.

Hart, H. (1989). *Law, liberty and morality*. Oxford: Oxford University Press.

Hausman, D. M. (1998). Problems with realism in economics. *Economics and Philosophy, 14*(2), 185–213.

Hawthorne, J. (2001). Causal structuralism. *Philosophical Perspectives, 15*(1), 361–378.

Holbrook, R., & Stafford, F. (1971). The propensity to consume separate types of income. A generalized permanent income hypothesis. *Econometrica, 39*(1), 1–21.

Hoover, K. D. (2001). Is macroeconomics for real? In U. Mäki (Ed.), *The economic world view. Studies in the ontology of economics* (pp. 225–245). Cambridge: Cambridge University Press.

Hoover, K. D. (2008). Does macroeconomics need microfoundations? In D. M. Hausman (Ed.), *The philosophy of economics. An anthology* (pp. 315–333). Cambridge: Cambridge University Press.

Hoover, K. D. (2009a). Milton Friedman's stance. The methodology of causal realism. In U. Mäki (Ed.), *The methodology of positive economics. Reflections on the Milton Friedman legacy* (pp. 303–320). Cambridge: Cambridge University Press.

Hoover, K. D. (2009b). Microfoundations and the ontology of macroeconomics. In H. Kincaid & D. Ross (Eds.), *The Oxford handbook of philosophy of economics* (pp. 386–409). Oxford: Oxford University Press.

Hoover, K. D. (2012). Microfoundational programs. In P. G. Duarte & G. T. Lima (Eds.), *Microfoundations reconsidered. The relationship of micro and macroeconomics in historical perspective* (pp. 19–61). Cheltenham: Edward Elgar.

Hoover, K. D. (2014). *Reductionism in economics. Causality and intentionality in the microfoundations of macroeconomics*. CHOPE working paper no. 2014-03 Durham, NC: Center for the History of Political Economy, Duke University.

Hoover, K. D. (2015). Reductionism in economics. Intentionality and eschatological justification in the microfoundations of macroeconomics. *Philosophy of Science, 82*(4), 689–711.

Hughes, R. I. G. (1997). Models and representation. *Philosophy of Science, 64*(2), S325–S336.

Jensen, M. C. (2001). Value maximization, stakeholder theory, and the corporate objective function. *Journal of Applied Corporate Finance, 14*(3), 8–21.

Katzner, D. W. (2016). The stages of model building in economics. *Studies in Microeconomics, 4*(2), 79–99.

Keynes, J. M. (1930). *A treatise on money*. New York: Hartcourt Brace and Co.

Keynes, J. M. (1936). *The general theory of employment, interest, and money* (1964 ed.). New York: Harcourt Brace Jovanovich.

Kim, J. (1990). Supervenience as a philosophical concept. Selected philosophical essays. In J. Kim (Ed.), *Supervenience and mind* (1993 ed., pp. 131–160). Cambridge: Cambridge University Press.

Kincaid, H. (2008). Structural realism and the social sciences. *Philosophy of Science, 75*(5), 720–731.

Kirman, A. P. (1992). Whom or what does the representative individual represent? *Journal of Economic Perspectives, 6*(2), 117–136.

Klein, L. R. (1946a). Macroeconomics and the theory of rational behavior. *Econometrica, 14*(2), 93–108.

Klein, L. R. (1946b). Remarks on the theory of aggregation. *Econometrica, 14*(4), 303–312.

Klein, L. R. (1949). *The Keynesian revolution* (1966 ed.). London: Macmillan.

Kornai, J. (1971). *Anti-equilibrium. On economic systems theory and the tasks of research*. Amsterdam: North-Holland.

Kuhn, T. S. (1962). *The structure of scientific revolutions* (3rd ed.). Chicago: The University of Chicago Press.

Kuhn, T. S. (1977). *The essential tension. Selected studies in scientific tradition and change*. Chicago: The University of Chicago Press.

Ladyman, J. (1998). What is structural realism? *Studies in History and Philosophy of Science Part A, 29*(3), 409–424.

Ladyman, J. (2007). On the identity and diversity of objects in a structure. *Proceedings of the Aristotelian Society, 81*(1), 23–43.

Ladyman, J. (2008). Structural realism and the relationship between the special sciences and physics. *Philosophy of Science, 75*(5), 744–755.

Ladyman, J. (2019). In E. N. Zalta (Ed.), *Structural realism*. Letöltés dátuma: 2019. August 31, The Stanford encyclopedia of philosophy https://plato.stanford.edu/archives/fall2019/entries/structural-realism/.

Ladyman, J., & Ross, D. (2007). *Every thing must go. Metaphysics naturalized*. Oxford: Oxford University Press.

Landry, E. M. (2012). Methodological structural realism. In E. M. Landry & D. P. Rickles (Eds.), *Structural realism. Structure, object, and causality* (pp. 29–57). New York: Springer.

Laudan, L. (1981). A confutation of convergent realism. *Philosophy of Science, 48*(1), 19–49.

Laumas, P. S., & Mohabbat, K. A. (1972). The permanent income hypothesis. Evidence from time-series data. *The American Economic Review, 62*(4), 730–734.

Leeds, S. (2007). Correspondence truth and scientific realism. *Synthese, 159*(1), 1–21.

Lucas, R. E. (1972). Expectations and the neutrality of money. *Journal of Economic Theory, 2,* 103–124.

Lucas, R. E. (1973). Some international evidence on output-inflation tradeoffs. *The American Economic Review, 63*(3), 326–334.

Lucas, R. E. (1975). An equilibrium model of the business cycle. *Journal of Political Economy, 83*(6), 1113–1144.

Lucas, R. E. (1977). Understanding business cycles. In K. Brunner & A. H. Meltzer (Eds.), *Stabilization of the domestic and international economy* (pp. 7–29). Amsterdam: North-Holland.

Lucas, R. E. (1980). Methods and problems in business cycle theory. *Journal of Money, Credit and Banking, 12*(4), 696–715.

Lucas, R. E. (1981). *Studies in business-cycle theory*. Oxford: Basil Blackwell.

Lucas, R. E. (1987). *Models of business cycles*. Oxford: Basil Blackwell.

Lucas, R. E. (1995/1996). Monetary neutrality. Nobel lecture. *Journal of Political Economy, 104*(4), 661–682.

Lucas, R. E. (2001). *Professional memoir*. Mimeo.

Lucas, R. E. (2005). My Keynesian education. In M. De Vroey & K. D. Hoover (Eds.), *The IS/LM model. Its rise, fall and strange persistence* (pp. 12–24). Durham, NC: Duke University Press.

Lucas, R. E., & Prescott, E. C. (1971). Investment under uncertainty. *Econometrica, 39*(5), 659–681.

Lucas, R. E., & Prescott, E. C. (1974). Equilibrium search and unemployment. *Journal of Economic Theory, 7*(2), 188–209.

Lucas, R. E., & Rapping, L. A. (1969). Real wages, employment, and inflation. *Journal of Political Economy, 77*(5), 721–754.

Lucas, R. E., & Rapping, L. A. (1972). Unemployment in the great depression. Is there a full explanation? *Journal of Political Economy, 80*(1), 186–191.

Lucas, R. E., & Sargent, T. J. (1979). After Keynesian macroeconomics. *Federal Reserve Bank of Minneapolis Quarterly Review, 3*(2), 1–16.

Lyons, T. D. (2005). Toward a purely axiological scientific realism. *Erkenntnis, 63*(2), 167–204.

Lyons, T. D. (2017). Epistemic selectivity, historical threats, and the non-epistemic tenets of scientific realism. *Synthese, 194*(9), 3203–3219.

Madden, P. (1989). General equilibrium and disequilibrium and the microeconomic foundations of macroeconomics. In J. D. Hey (Ed.), *Current issues in microeconomics* (pp. 179–208). New York: Macmillan.

Mäki, U. (1996). Scientific realism and some peculiarities of economics. In R. S. Cohen, R. Hilpinen, & Q. Renzong (Eds.), *Realism and anti-realism in the philosophy of science* (pp. 427–448). Dordrecht: Springer.

Mäki, U. (2000). Reclaiming relevant realism. *Journal of Economic Methodology, 7*(1), 109–125.

Mäki, U. (2002). Some nonreasons for nonrealism about economics. In U. Mäki (Ed.), *Fact and fiction in economics. Models, realism, and social construction* (pp. 90–104). Cambridge: Cambridge University Press.

Mäki, U. (2009a). Realistic realism about unrealistic models. In H. Kincaid & D. Ross (Eds.), *The Oxford handbook of philosophy of economics* (pp. 68–98). Oxford: Oxford University Press.

Mäki, U. (2009b). Unrealistic assumptions and unnecessary confusions. Rereading and rewriting F53 as a realist statement. In U. Mäki (Ed.), *The methodology of positive economics. Reflections on the Milton Friedman legacy* (pp. 90–116). Cambridge: Cambridge University Press.

Mäki, U. (2011). Scientific realism as a challenge to economics (and vice versa). *Journal of Economic Methodology, 18*(1), 1–12.

Mäki, U. (2012). Realism and antirealism about economics. In U. Mäki (Ed.), *Philosophy of economics* (pp. 3–24). Amsterdam: North Holland.

Manicas, P. T. (2006). *A realist philosophy of social science. Explanation and understanding.* Cambridge: Cambridge University Press.

Mantel, R. R. (1973). On the characterization of aggregate excess demand. *Journal of Economic Theory, 7*(3), 348–353.

Marshall, A. (1920/2013). *Principles of economics* (8th ed.). New York: Palgrave Macmillan.

Massimi, M. (2004). Non-defensible middle ground for experimental realism. Why we are justified to believe in colored quarks. *Philosophy of Science, 71*(1), 36–60.

McCallum, B. T. (2007). An interview with Robert E. Lucas, Jr. In P. A. Samuelson & W. A. Barnett (Eds.), *Inside the economist's mind. Conversations with eminent economists* (p. 57). Oxford: Blackwell.

McLaughlin, B. P. (1995). Varieties of supervenience. In E. E. Savellos & Ü.D. Yalçin (Eds.), *Supervenience. New essays* (pp. 16–59). Cambridge: Cambridge University Press.

Mehrling, P. (1998). The money muddle. The transformation of American monetary thought, 1920-1970. In M. S. Morgan & M. Rutherford (Eds.), *From interwar pluralism to postwar neoclassicism* (pp. 293–306). Durham, NC: Duke University Press.

Mitchell, W. C. (1913). *Business cycles.* Berkeley, CA: University of California Press.

Morganti, M. (2004). On the preferability of epistemic structural realism. *Synthese, 142*(1), 81–107.

Morrison, M. (1990). Theory, intervention and realism. *Synthese, 82*(1), 1–22.

Mumford, S. (2008). Powers, dispositions, properties or a causal realist manifesto. In R. Groff (Ed.), *Revitalizing causality. Realism about causality in philosophy and social science* (pp. 139–151). London: Routledge.

Musgrave, A. (1996). Realism, truth and objectivity. In R. S. Cohen, R. Hilpinen, & Q. Renzong (Eds.), *Realism and anti-realism in the philosophy of science* (pp. 19–44). Dordrecht: Springer.

Muth, J. F. (1961). Rational expectations and the theory of price movements. *Econometrica, 29*(3), 315–335.

Niiniluoto, I. (1977). On the truthlikeness of generalizations. In R. E. Butts & J. Hintikka (Eds.), *Basic problems in methodology and linguistics* (pp. 121–147). Dordrecht: Springer.

Nounou, A. M. (2012). Kinds of objects and varieties of properties. In E. M. Landry & D. P. Rickles (Eds.), *Structural realism. Structure, object, and causality* (pp. 117–133). New York: Springer.

Oddie, G. (1986). *Likeness to truth*. Dordrecht: D. Reidel Publishing Company.

Papineau, D. (2010). Realism, Ramsey sentences and the pessimistic meta-induction. *Studies in History and Philosophy of Science Part A, 41*(4), 375–385.

Phelps, E. S. (1970). *Microeconomic foundations of employment and inflation theory*. New York: Norton.

Polanyi, M. (1958/2005). *Personal knowledge. Towards a post-critical philosophy*. London: Routledge.

Popper, K. (1962). *Conjectures and refutations. The growth of scientific knowledge*. New York: Basic Books.

Prescott, E. C. (2006). The transformation of macroeconomic policy and research. Nobel lecture. *Journal of Political Economy, 114*(2), 203–235.

Psillos, S. (1995). Is structural realism the best of both worlds? *Dialectica, 49*(1), 15–46.

Psillos, S. (1999). *Scientific realism. How science tracks truth*. London: Routledge.

Psillos, S. (2001). Is structural realism possible? *Philosophy of Science, 68*(3), S13–S24.

Psillos, S. (2006). The structure, the whole structure, and nothing but the structure? *Philosophy of Science, 73*(5), 560–570.

Psillos, S. (2011). Choosing the realist framework. *Synthese, 180*(2), 301–316.

Psillos, S. (2012). Adding modality to ontic structuralism. An exploration and critique. In E. M. Landry & D. P. Rickles (Eds.), *Structural realism. Structure, object, and causality* (pp. 169–185). New York: Springer.

Psillos, S. (2013). Semirealism or neo-Aristotelianism? *Erkenntnis, 78*(1), 29–38.

Putnam, H. (1978). *Meaning and the moral sciences* (2010 ed.). London: Routledge & Kegan Paul.

Rees, A. (1970). On equilibrium in labor markets. *Journal of Political Economy, 78*(2), 306–310.

Reiss, J. (2010). Review of "The methodology of positive economics. Reflections on the Milton Friedman legacy, ed. Uskali Mäki". *Erasmus Journal for Philosophy and Economics, 3*(2), 103–110.

Resnik, D. B. (1994). Hacking's experimental realism. *Canadian Journal of Philosophy, 24*(3), 395–412.

Rizvi, A. T. (1994). The microfoundations project in general equilibrium theory. *Cambridge Journal of Economics, 18*(4), 357–377.

Rizvi, A. T. (2006). The Sonnenschein-Mantel-Debreu results after thirty years. *History of Political Economy, 38*(S1), 228–245.

Robbins, L. (1935/1984). *The nature and significance of economic science*. London: Macmillan.

Rodrik, D. (2015). *Economics rules. Why economics works, when it fails, and how to tell the difference*. Oxford: Oxford University Press.

Røgeberg, O., & Nordberg, M. (2005). A defence of absurd theories in economics. *Journal of Economic Methodology, 12*(4), 543–562.

Ross, D. (2005). *Economic theory and cognitive science. Microexplanation*. Cambridge, MA: The MIT Press.

Ross, D. (2006). The economic and evolutionary basis of selves. *Cognitive Systems Research, 7*(2–3), 246–258.

Ross, D. (2008). Ontic structural realism and economics. *Philosophy of Science, 75*(5), 732–743.

Russell, B. (2009). *Human knowledge. Its scope and limits*. London: Routledge.

Sargent, T. J. (1977). *Is Keynesian economics a dead end?* Working paper no. 101 Minneapolis, MN: University of Minnesota and Federal Reserve Bank of Minneapolis.

Saunders, S. (2003). Indiscernibles, general covariance, and other symmetries. The case for non-reductive relationalism. In J. Renn, L. Divarci, & P. Schröter (Eds.), *Revisiting the foundations of relativistic physics* (pp. 151–173). Dordrecht: Kluwer.

Schmidt, M. (2010). Causation and structural realism. *Organon F, 17*(4), 508–521.

Schütz, A., & Luckmann, T. (1973). *The structures of life-world*. Evanston: Northwestern University Press.

Shapiro, S. (1997). *Philosophy of mathematics. Structure and ontology*. New York: Oxford University Press.

Shapiro, S. (2000). *Thinking about mathematics. The philosophy of mathematics.* Oxford: Oxford University Press.

Shea, J. (1995). Union contracts and the life-cycle/permanent-income hypothesis. *The American Economic Review, 85*(1), 186–200.

Shech, E. (2015). Scientific misrepresentation and guides to ontology. The need for representational code and contents. *Synthese, 192*(11), 3463–3485.

Shech, E. (2016). Fiction, depiction, and the complementarity thesis in art and science. *The Monist, 99*(3), 311–332.

Simmel, G. (1900/2005). Individual freedom. In G. Simmel & D. Frisby (Eds.), *The philosophy of money* (T. Bottomore, & D. Frisby, Trans., pp. 283–356). London: Routledge.

Sklar, L. (2003). Dappled theories in a uniform world. *Philosophy of Science, 70*(2), 424–441.

Snowdon, B., & Vane, H. R. (2005). *Modern macroeconomics. Its origins, development and current state.* Cheltenham: Edward Elgar.

Sonnenschein, H. (1972). Market excess demand functions. *Econometrica, 40*(3), 549–563.

Sonnenschein, H. (1973). Do Walras' identity and continuity characterize the class of community excess demand functions? *Journal of Economic Theory, 6*(4), 345–354.

Stachel, J. (2006). Structure, individuality, and quantum gravity. In D. Rickles, S. French, & J. Saatsi (Eds.), *The structural foundations of quantum gravity* (pp. 53–82). Oxford: Clarendon Press.

Stanford, P. K. (2003). Pyrrhic victories for scientific realism. *The Journal of Philosophy, 100*(11), 553–572.

Suárez, M. (2002). *The pragmatics of scientific representation.* Centre for Philosophy of Natural and Social Science (CPNSS) discussion paper series, DP 66/02 London: CPNSS/London School of Economics.

Suárez, M. (2004). An inferential conception of scientific representation. *Philosophy of Science, 71*(5), 767–779.

Swoyer, C. (1991). Structural representation and surrogative reasoning. *Synthese, 87*(3), 449–508.

Taylor, J. B. (2007). An interview with Milton Friedman. In P. A. Samuelson & W. A. Barnett (Eds.), *Inside the economist's mind. Conversations with eminent economists* (pp. 110–142). Malden, MA: Blackwell.

Teller, P. (2001). Twilight of the perfect model. *Erkenntnis, 55*(3), 393–415.

Teller, P. (2004). How we dapple the world. *Philosophy of Science, 71*(4), 425–447.

Townsend, R. M. (1987). Arrow-Debreu programs as microfoundations of macroeconomics. In T. F. Bewley (Ed.), *Advances in economic theory* (pp. 379–428). Cambridge: Cambridge University Press.

van Fraassen, B. C. (1980). *The scientific image.* New York: Oxford University Press.

Van Overtveldt, J. (2007). *The Chicago school. How the University of Chicago assembled the thinkers who revolutionized economics and business.* Agate: Chicago.

Varian, H. R. (2010). *Intermediate microeconomics. A modern approach.* New York: W.W. Norton & Company.

Viner, J. (1936). Mr. Keynes on the causes of unemployment. *The Quarterly Journal of Economics, 51*(1), 147–167.

Visco, I. (2014). Lawrence R. Klein. Macroeconomics, econometrics and economic policy. *Journal of Policy Modeling, 36*(4), 605–628.

Weber, M. (1968/1978). *Economy and society.* Berkeley, CA: University of California Press.

Witt, C. (2008). Aristotelian powers. In R. Groff (Ed.), *Revitalizing causality. Realism about causality in philosophy and social science* (pp. 129–138). London: Routledge.

Worrall, J. (1989). Structural realism. The best of both worlds. *Dialectica, 43*(1–2), 99–124.

Worrall, J. (2012). Miracles and structural realism. In E. M. Landry & D. P. Rickles (Eds.), *Structural realism. Structure, object, and causality* (pp. 77–95). New York: Springer.

Archival sources

Lucas R.E., Unpublished papers, 1960–2004 and undated. Archival material stored at the David M. Rubenstein Library, Duke University.

Realism and instrumentalism along the Friedman–Lucas transition

Go back and look at what's on the page [...].
Forget the other reading for next week. You have to read what's on the page.
Jonathan Franzen: The discomfort zone.

Histories of modern macroeconomics have in common the view that descriptive inaccuracy, the hallmark of modern economics, is a feature that precludes all forms of realism. However, this view rests on an undifferentiated and oversimplified rendition of economic-scientific realism that regards a significant degree of descriptive realism as a precondition of realism as such. In this framework any element in any theory claiming to be realist must bear considerable similarity to its target.

In Chapter 3 it was highlighted that descriptive performance is only one and, what is more, not the most important dimension of realism, and that descriptive capabilities are to be assessed independently of the causal understanding purposes and achievements of scientific realism. It was argued that descriptively inaccurate models can still be adequate and hence realist in causal terms. However, as long as we refuse to draw this distinction and if based on some favourable examples we tend to overemphasize the causal adequacy of descriptively minimalist models, we shall inevitably argue for the causal adequacy of descriptively minimalist models in general. It is highly likely that such uncritical efforts have resulted in some realist interpretations of Friedman's (1953/2009) 'The methodology of positive economics' (abbreviated as F53 hereafter). Even the recent literature suggests some accounts that take for granted *en bloc* the causal realism of models performing poorly in descriptive terms (Aydinonat, 2018).

If through isolation we can preserve a relevant subset of causally active properties of entities, our models devoid of details can effectively support us in striving towards sound causal understanding. At the same time, it remains true that some assumptions may endow our theoretical entities with some inexistent properties. Such assumptions form a constituent part of the general practice of science (Laudan, 1981, p. 27). To ensure causal adequacy, it is required to adjust our models to the problem under scrutiny and hence to preserve the features we regard as relevant in terms of our concrete scientific problem. As it was argued in Chapter 3, causal connections stem from entity properties; therefore the problem under scrutiny implies what features ought to be conceived as active. It follows that judging causal adequacy stands in judging on the one hand whether a postulated causal mechanism is plausible and on the other hand whether it is possible to trace the assumed causal connections back to some real features of entities. If the answer to the first question is affirmative, these entity properties must be existent, though it fails to imply their being successfully grabbed at this stage. After identifying the underlying active entity properties, a relevant subset of theirs is to be preserved. Entities and through them the represented structure and hence the causal mechanism have properties that are indispensable to the analysis. If the postulated causal connections are based upon entity-level assumptions (and in the object-based ontology they are), it is unnecessary to have further presumptions at this level, so minimalist entity and structure representations are highly efficient and economical (concentrated) vehicles of surrogative reasoning. Tractability and other theorizing concerns may compel us to resort to some further assumptions, of course. Irrelevant and omitted entity properties may naturally hide some facets of the complex causal structure: facets that may be highly important to the analyzed phenomenon, thus descriptively minimalist models are always easy to criticize for assuming some mechanisms away. As we have seen in Chapter 1, however, there is a trade-off between the depth and the comprehensiveness of any scientific analysis. As the most significant advantage, descriptive minimalism facilitates the enhancement of analytical depth.

Built upon the general considerations over scientific realism performed in Chapter 3, this chapter is aimed at drawing a sharp methodological distinction between Friedman and Lucas by discussing the dynamics of descriptive accuracy and causal adequacy along the transition between their systems of ideas. As a first attempt, a contrast aids in achieving a deeper understanding of Friedman's methodological stance as so far we only have had some half-baked arguments about his use of assumptions in F53 and the potential of his alleged causal realist aspirations. Friedman's use of the Weberian[1] term 'ideal type' in his F53 raises the possibility of a Weberian line in Friedman's methodology. This would be an interesting problem

---

[1] It is Georg Jellinek, the German historian, and not Weber who coined the concept of ideal types. However, thanks to Weber's refinements today ideal types are commonly regarded as a constituent part of Weber's methodology (Ringer, 1997, pp. 110–111; Bruun, 2007, p. 215).

in itself; however, for lack of Friedman's explicit references to Weber we only have speculations regarding this intellectual connection. For various reasons detailed below it is highly unlikely that Friedman directly read Weber, though it is equally unlikely that as a member of Knight's circles he could get away with no Weberian influence. Knight's Weberian methodology is reviewed below as it was Knight through whom Weber became a constituent part of the Chicago intellectual environment. Beyond this purely speculative historian thread Weber's and Knight's methodologies serve as an interpretive framework. Using some conclusions of the discussions presented in Chapter 3, Weber's and Knight's social scientific methodologies emerge as some positive examples effectively highlighting the compatibility of descriptive inaccuracy and causal adequacy. Through a comparison Friedman's methodological stance is interpreted as a case of causal inadequacy hence instrumentalism. This methodological comparison is independent of any historical speculation; it is thus applicable regardless one gives credit to the historical account.

Next, as a second attempt, we turn to Friedman's Phillips curves regarded below as the exact manifestations of the instrumentalist methodological principles laid down in F53. It is argued that his instrumentally designed theoretical entities in his Phillips curves could not help him to achieve the causal adequacy of the structure they are embedded in. Friedman neglected the properties of real entities that deprived him of the possibility of causally adequate modelling. In this narrative below his purpose is understood as an ambition to derive a series of short-run negatively sloped Phillips curves to make the case for the natural rate of unemployment and he drew up the catalogue of his agents' properties with the sole purpose of achieving these desired and presupposed outcomes, no matter what properties real agents have.

Lucas's methodology is interpreted as a radically different case. Whilst emphasizing his oft-mentioned extreme descriptive minimalism it is argued that Lucas when laying down the microfoundations paid particular attention to preserving some causally active entity properties underlying the causal connections. As it is argued, he regarded the microfoundations as the apparatus of establishing the realist connections with socioeconomic reality. Like Friedman, Lucas also took predictive performance of models as a high-ranked aspect, though he refrained from rendering empirical success the sole or even the most important aspect of model selection. Whilst insisting on descriptive inaccuracy and minimalism Lucas thus was able to achieve a high level of causal adequacy. By so doing, he distanced himself from Friedman's instrumentalist methodology. This demarcation, however, rests upon the level of the fundamental assumptions and the connections with reality which lies deeper than the roots of the Marshall–Walras divide. As a consequence, a strikingly realist Lucas emerges: a picture that would seem bizarre but for the arguments taken from general philosophy of science.[2] As we shall see, whilst real entity properties were nothing for Friedman, for Lucas they were everything. Friedman refused to establish a representational relationship between the real properties of leaves and the rationality postulate he applied to describe the behaviour at the phenomenal level; therefore real entity properties played no role in his methodological recommendations.

4.1 Friedman's case: Descriptive inaccuracy and causal inadequacy

4.1.1 The first attempt: Friedman's instrumentalism in a Weberian reading

Knight's social scientific methodology and its Weberian roots

Frank H. Knight is a central character of Weber's reception in America that rendered the University of Chicago one of the American centres of Weberianism (Scaff, 2011, p. 199). As Emmett (1999, pp. vii–viii) and Scaff (2014, p. 274) aptly document, the source of Knight's keen interest in Weber is autobiographical. Knight was born and raised in a strict protestant family[3] thanks to which he sensitively responded to Weber's idea of an intimate relationship between worldly action and religious life.[4] Even though the time when Knight first encountered Weber's works is shrouded in mystery, by the time he returned to Chicago in 1928 from his tenured position at the University of Iowa, he had nurtured an in-depth knowledge of Weber's social scientific methodology and comparative historical

---

[2] The adjective 'realist' is applied below in consonance with the considerations of Chapter 3. Lucas's abstract-idealized and descriptively false models are unrealistic representations of reality. However, these models are designed to convey sound causal knowledge of their target systems. As it is argued in Chapter 3, these models are realist in causal terms, whilst descriptively unrealistic. This distinction is rendered explicit by the rather informal use of the words *realist* and *realistic* or the distinction between descriptive (in)accuracy and causal adequacy.

[3] Emmett (2015b) enumerates further details about how Knight's family wavered between the Methodist and Congregational Churches and how the austere religious family background affected Knight's later critical attitude towards religion.

[4] In 'The protestant ethic and the spirit of capitalism', his most important and genuine work, Weber studies how Protestantism contributed to the emergence of capitalism as an economic and social order (Weber, 1930; Bruun, 2007, p. 236; Whimster, 2007, p. 134). This work widely regarded as a mature application of his method of ideal types introduces the protestant working ethic as an antecedent of capitalism. By contrast, in his general economic history (Weber, 1927) he analyzed the objective and technological prerequisites of capitalism. Thanks to Knight's achievements as a translator, this was Weber's first book to be published in English.

sociology in addition to the works of the German historical school. Emmett (2006, pp. 106–107) dates the beginnings of Knight's Weberian interests to the period between 1913 and 1919.[5] Knight kept paying intense attention to Weber even up to the 1940s and used Weber's tenets a fundament upon which he built his own complex social scientific approach. Even though his explicit references to Weber were rather scarce, especially from the 1930s, Weber for Knight remained the most influential intellectual authority throughout his career. Today the history of economic thought, mainly thanks to Ross Emmett, regards the close intellectual connection between Knight and Weber as a fact, though this connection is almost invisible at the level of Knight's references to Weber. Knight very scarcely cites Weber: he refuses to mention Weber's name even when directly reflecting upon his thoughts (Noppeney, 1997, p. 328). Likewise, we cannot find a single reference to Weber in his methodological works analyzed below. In his correspondence, however, he was always ready to admit his deep respect for Weber (Emmett, 2006, p. 101). This tacit relationship is typical of the way Weber was judged later. Chicago's attitude towards Weber became particularly ambivalent after political philosopher Leo Strauss arrived in 1949. Strauss harshly criticized Weber and through his scholarly power he could successfully bias the public opinion. As a consequence, Weber's ideas gradually became freely citable. Such implicit and often unconscious references to Weber render it extremely difficult and contentious to trace the spreading of his ideas. Knight was greatly reliant upon Weber in understanding the formation of capitalism, in redefining economics in methodological terms and in the economic interpretation of history (Emmett, 1999, pp. xiii–xv).

Knight's most interesting methodological tenets concern the relationship between neoclassical economics and the broadly interpreted social sciences. He gave utterance to his methodological views in a series of publications one of the recurrent thoughts of which is that physics-based neoclassical orthodoxy with its mechanical analogies has only highly limited relevance. On its carefully circumscribed territory, however, it meets the standards of modern science (Noppeney, 1997, p. 334). For Knight, economics deals with ideal concepts which are as universal for instrumentally rational economic behaviour as ordinary geometry; thus its territory covers the rational core of human actions under abstract-ideal conditions. However, theoretical economics is not to be applied for describing actual behaviour or events in concrete time and space (Knight, 1935, pp. 277–279; Weber, 1968/1978, p. 24). Treading in Weber's footsteps and arguing for the irrelevance of neoclassical economics outside its scope, in these texts Knight identifies the genuine scope of the theory.

Reviewing and summarizing Weber's social scientific methodology is far from easy. The available literature abundantly discusses how Weber's

[5] The earliest point is marked by Knight's journey to Germany in 1913, whilst the other endpoint is his first appearance at the University of Chicago in 1917–19.

methodology fits into his oeuvre. Even though there have been some efforts to reconstruct his methodology as a unified framework, Weber himself did not seem to strive towards a consistent social scientific methodology of general validity. As a consequence, it is not too difficult to find some inconsistencies appearing intertextually or even within a given work. These discrepancies are not satisfyingly resolved for the time being, though a fully consistent methodology may not be to Weber's liking either (Bruun, 2007, pp. 4–6 and pp. 207–208).

Weber describes the conceptualizing strategy of neoclassical economics by the methodology of ideal types. Weber, however, attributed a more comprehensive validity to the methodology of ideal types. Ideal types can be applied in theorizing outside economics, but a consequence of the diversity in applications is a less consistent account of how ideal types are used in social sciences in general. Accordingly, it has remained a highly contentious issue whether Weber meant one thing by his ideal types or there is a subtle structure of possible interpretations. The concept 'ideal type' itself has a changing emphasis in his texts. The original form gradually became superseded to give way to the simple 'types'. Some regard this shift as either a significant change in meaning or a diversity of conceptualizing strategies Weber associated with his ideal types. To ease this tension, Bruun (2007, pp. 46–47) takes the inconsistencies between the different versions of ideal types as a simple fact to highlight but not to eliminate. However, the issue of the conceptualizing strategy of neoclassical economics can be discussed without surveying these controversies in the literature.

For economics, creating ideal types is a means of seeking laws. Ideal types aid in understanding the considerably stable tendencies underlying the causal structure of socio-economic reality. An ideal type in economics by definition summarizes the forms of human behaviour that would occur as strictly instrumentally rational actions under hypothetic and hence not real-world conditions (Bruun, 2007, p. 236). Ideal types for social science, interpreted in a broad sense to include both economics and sociology (Weber, 1968/1978, pp. 18–19), ought to serve as bases for comparison. Real-world actions, events, and behavioural patterns in this framework show up as deviations from the ideal types[6] (Weber, 1917/1949, pp. 43–45; 1968/1978, pp. 6–30; Bruun, 2007, p. 44 and p. 216; Whimster, 2007, p. 111). There is a plethora of factors distorting the ideal typical patterns theorists may consider.

---

[6] A comparison is aimed at registering and causally explaining these deviations of reality from model outcomes and not at underpinning the model with data. Drawing a direct contrast between model and reality (when one is looking for the similarities and not the discrepancies) is fraught with dangers as it may lead to the distorting of reality in order to substantiate the relevance and real manifestations of a highly abstract concept. It is exactly this danger that renders it indispensable for theory to use modern econometrics in detecting causal mechanisms. Weber denied that reality always unique was explainable by general laws only (Bruun, 2007, p. 130).

In understanding, Weber placed his emphasis upon some mental factors of irrationality (Bruun, 2007, pp. 227–230), whilst economists working in the institutional tradition or transitology may show interest in the effects legal environment, culture, or history exert. At the same time, Weberian irrationality emerging due to incomplete information is still a relevant factor.

Rationality-based ideal types ought to be regarded only as methodological devices but not as the manifestations of a world view. The extensive use of the homo oeconomicus built upon rational actions does not imply the assumption of complete rationality of real market agents. Abstract ideal types economics applies are thus not descriptive terms, whilst rationality is highlighted as an element of the real motivational structure (Bruun, 2007, pp. 208–209). Rationality is neither tangible nor visible though still highly important. Neoclassical economics of ideal types never describes reality in a direct way as our concepts fail to reveal anything about how real-world actions obey complete rationality and other assumptions, whilst the extent of discrepancy can be considered only by comparisons between ideal types and reality. Declaredly one-sided ideal types are unable to comprehend the infinite complexity of reality, though this obscurity could never be penetrated and interpreted without them. Against ideal typical economics there is an oft-made point emphasizing that real economic agents never show complete rationality and events in socio-economic reality radically differ from the outcomes of pure economics. The most powerful case for these models is undoubtedly the fact that such a claim could never be put forward without the thorough knowledge of economic rationality and its consequences, and this knowledge stems from the use of ideal types. Instead of rendering neoclassical economics senseless or irrelevant, the institutional-historical approach actively (albeit presumably in an unconscious way) presupposes abstract models. Lucas resorts to this line of reasoning when he highlights that considering the effects of market institutions does not require alternative models but the extensions or further elaborations of the basic Lucas-Rapping framework (Lucas, 1981, p. 4).

The laws and tenets of neoclassical "pure" economics thus constitute no more than the rational core of a mass phenomenon. Resting on some postulated law-like tendencies, neoclassical economics built upon abstract ideal types can thus only highlight some mechanisms from the infinity of causal relations of the narrowly conceived economic events and institutions[7]

---

[7] Weber (1904/1949, pp. 64–65) so circumscribes the scope of neoclassical economics (1). Here he applies a threefold typology to correctly draw a division of labour between social sciences. Accordingly, we need to distinguish (2) economically relevant phenomena and institutions not of economic nature and (3) economically conditioned phenomena and institutions also not of economic nature. The latter may cover even arts, so the range is wide. A broadly conceived economic interest may focus on the institutions disturbing the fundamental laws, though they lie outside the scope of neoclassical economics.

working in real socio-economic systems (Bruun, 2007, pp. 127–128). Both the concepts and the mathematical laws resting upon complete economic rationality are hypothesized to consider what the economic dimension of our societies would look like if the assumptions of theory held in reality. These are the theorems of economics built upon the neoclassical way of theorizing that emerge as the completely rational limiting concepts of the market actions performed by the selfish agents considering their fellows' expected behaviour as conditions. Unambiguity of the results is ensured by our clear-cut definitions and presumptions and the consistent application of mathematical deduction.

To this extent, using abstract ideal types is a necessary methodological step, whilst the complex act of social scientific understanding should obviously amount to much more than constructing ideal concepts. In this view, the effects of the social-historical-institutional factors that modify or distort the rational core framework can only be comprehended by contrasting reality with the theoretically generated formal and rational outcomes. This methodological approach is thus built upon an explicit distinction between hypothetic and actual actions. Accordingly, abstract ideal types are not directed at the purpose of describing real-world actions. The ultimate goal is to make contrast and the more sharply the hypothetic outcomes differ from real situations, the easier it is to complete this comparison. At the end of the day, it is a definite advantage of an ideal type if it does not look like real entities.

Weberian ideal types are the instruments[8] of causal realism. Either the rational core or the distorting factors is considered (Weber, 1968/1978, pp. 20–21), the purpose in both cases is to reveal the causal structure underlying real social processes. Mechanisms highlighted in ideal types somehow contribute to the emergence of actual processes. Weber (1968/1978, pp. 10–11) also interpreted Gresham's law in this way. Some of the causes lying behind the phenomena are summarized in ideal-typical theories, whilst other causes are comprehended as the effects triggering the differences between actual processes and ideal-typical outcomes. Weber regarded this comparison as the essence of understanding. It raises some problems, however. How does rationality manifest itself in actual market actions and how does the absence of this rationality emerge? As the rational core framework has to be adequate as for the causal structure, the differences from these hypothetic outcomes also require sound causal explanations. In the simplest Marshallian cross a rise in the price is regarded as a real cause of a drop in demand (Marshall, 1920/2013, p. 28; Hoover, 2009a, pp. 309–310), whilst the complex understanding of market processes requires a wider range of causal factors to be considered beyond

---

[8] Ideal types are instrumental in understanding (Bruun, 2007, p. 214), though they are far from the results of a Friedmanian instrumentalist conceptualizing habit.

price dynamics. Bruun (2007, p. 112) describes the disputes between the German historical school and neoclassical economics to make it clear: the efforts of economics towards causal understanding were widely admitted. Rather, the debate was over whether the theory with its narrow focus could lead to sensible results at all if actions under scrutiny are under the influence of a plethora of neglected causal factors.

Ideal-typical concepts are intentionally deprived of real and directly experienceable existence as they are all built upon the intended selective distortion of the entities experienced in reality (Weber, 1968/1978, p. 9). As a consequence, their adequacy cannot empirically be either proven or refuted: they have a utopian status (Bruun, 2007, p. 209 and p. 229). The same is true of the consequences derived from the economic laws postulated via ideal types. The validity of abstract economic models is not a question of empirical performance. To be more specific, confirming a theory is not necessarily possible through confronting it with the data. This is the case of rational plausibility Weber (1968/1978, p. 11) suggests. Accordingly, a theorist even before formulizing her theory clearly knows the causal structure that is supposed to be underlying the situation she analyzes. So, without empirical evidence her best bet is to entertain a belief that the description of a social action is causally adequate. Our last resort is the adequacy with respect to meaning between surmised causes and their effects.

Giving a comprehensive description of reality is impossible. Economists are thus forced to make selections, so they need to decide which hidden mechanisms they want to reveal. But for this discretion, they would be compelled to give immense descriptions of reality that would not be clearer or better organized than reality itself. Selection and simplification are necessary, and for this purpose it is constructing abstract ideal types that is the most effective option in a twofold sense. First, such ideal types can be used for highlighting laws and, second, for comparisons supporting causal explanations. Bringing certain laws to the fore is dependent upon the theorist herself (Weber, 1904/1949, pp. 81–82) as social reality is always approached from specific points of view,[9] and when making this decision she is under the influence of some social factors (Whimster, 2007, pp. 112–113).

First of all, she is influenced by the scientific environment in which she has become socialized,[10] but it is also clear that the "big questions"

---

[9] This specificity can also be extended to the considerations over neoclassical economics. Following classical mechanics, it has set the task of seeking laws, which is nothing else but a specific interest. Applying this train of thought, we can easily clear the neoclassical orthodoxy of the charge of having too narrow a focus.

[10] Similar traditions worked regarding the causal role of money. Lucas as a Friedmanian monetarist (De Vroey, 2016, p. 197) regarded this role as evident—an idea not shared by the subsequent RBC-theory. See Section 4.3.3 for more on this.

troubling the theorist's broader social environment also make an impression on her (Bruun, 2007, p. 47). This is the reason why schools of economic thought emerge at all. Even though it is always the individual who serves as a direct articulator, the directions of interest and the ways how a theorist puts forward her questions are established by the ultimate foundations rooted in her scientific-social environment. As a matter of fact, creating ideal types becomes a question of identity as ideal types make it explicit what elements of reality both the community and the individual scholar regard as most important for systematic analyses. There is only *one* reality, however diverse it is, whilst there is an infinite number of possible approaches. This is the ultimate reason for theorists to conceive new models to understand the one and only (albeit changing and many-faceted) reality (see Section 5.3 on the complementarity of theories).

On these grounds Knight suggested an analytical framework in order to take into account the fact that social reality is never like the highly abstract ideal types of neoclassical economics. By so doing, he drew attention to the necessity of complex causal analyses to make allowance for the very nature of the social phenomena under study. Of the content and the form of economic actions, as Knight argued, formal economic laws can grab the static form only. Through these considerations Knight could precisely circumscribe neoclassical economics as the theory of perfect instrumentally rational individual behaviour that is easily describable with laws (Knight, 1972, p. 7), and that works in a framework the elements of which (opinions, beliefs, attitudes, and institutions) are in constant development. For Knight, mechanical analogies did not seem to be appropriate to describe this large-scale evolution as the process itself renders it impossible. He regarded the extensive use of ceteris paribus clauses as justified only in cases where the effects of such 'other things' assumed to be equal were really negligible, which defines a highly limited scope for economics (Knight, 1935/1999, pp. 166–168). As Knight (1922/1935, p. 20) argued, the tension between dynamics and statics is only imperfectly resolvable within the theory. Neoclassical economics aids in identifying the static laws and the key variables of the economic sphere of societies but analyzing the evolution of the dynamic framework is far beyond the formal theory. Knight so highlighted that as far as the understanding of real social phenomena is considered neoclassical economics is in need of historical analyses describing the development of institutions (Knight, 1972, p. 6; Noppeney, 1997, pp. 322–323) as this is the only way to analyze the differences between theoretical predictions and real outcomes (Knight, 1944, pp. 308–310).

Knight was ready to admit neoclassical theory imparting true knowledge of reality in its territory (Knight, 1935, p. 286), even if Knight regarded its scope as rather limited. Due to the neglect of complexity, of course, these truths can be partial at best. Neoclassical laws have general validity whilst they are unable to provide complete causal analyses.

Consequently, their descriptive performance is expected to be weak. Even though the circumstances under which formally deduced economic laws can perfectly emerge in reality are unlikely to set in, which would be undesirable in social-political terms (Knight, 1956, p. 270; Bruun, 2007, p. 214), Knight (1924/1999) regarded the behavioural tendencies, the fundamental laws, and the assumptions underlying the ideal type of homo oeconomicus as some evidently existent properties of social reality (Knight, 1944, pp. 293–305): as something that are hidden behind the complex and chaotic socio-economic reality as fundamental tendencies (Knight, 1921, pp. 4–5).

Knight took the stance of methodological pluralism, in which the interpretation of economic actions exhorts us to utilize all the social scientific disciplines (Knight, 1972, p. 10). In this context neoclassical economics served as only one of the suggested approaches. Knight's ultimate purpose was to establish a complex interpretative social science in which theoretical economics was complemented by other approaches including both the humanities and the entire field of social disciplines. As a consequence, actions could be analyzed in the broader context of social reality (Fu-Lai Yu, 2002, p. 4). He expected the involvement of these approaches to enhance both the complexity of causal understanding and the predictive success beyond the possibilities of neoclassical theory (Knight, 1940/1999).

Friedman's instrumentalism in the context of descriptive accuracy and causal adequacy

Knight's intellectual power and his influence on Friedman are very difficult to portray. Consequently, it is highly difficult if not impossible to reconstruct the channels through which Friedman might have been exposed to some Weberian effects. Friedman himself denied his proficiency in philosophy, so he was highly unlikely to have a systematic reading in economic methodology (Hammond, 1988, pp. 7–8). A possible channel was Knight's formal and informal environment, for instance the dinners in his home on Sunday evenings. Friedman is reported to have been a member of this eminent intellectual circle (Emmett, 2015a). Highlighting the significance of Knight's circle is possible only at the price of dubious speculations, though. However, it is Knight's personal impact that Reder (1982, p. 6) underlines as the main channel of his influence.

From the middle of the 1930s Stigler (1985, p. 2) reports a Weber seminar of Knight he himself attended. According to Edward Shils's commentaries, the seminar took place in 1936, built on the close reading of the original German edition of Weber's 'Economy and society', a highly important text in methodological terms (Scaff, 2011, p. 209). Friedman also attended the seminar, however, Shils (1981, p. 184) reports him to have lost his interest in Weber and consequently he began to show up only sporadically. It is less probable that Friedman acquired his Weberian insights in this seminar as he regarded his German erudition as superficial: 'I can read a little bit of German, but it's beyond me really, so I never read anything in original German' (Hammond, 1988, p. 8). This episode renders the intellectual connections between Weber and Friedman doubtful and implausible. In this context, however, Hoyningen–Huene draws attention to Knight's compilation published in 1935 (The ethics of competition), co-edited by Friedman. From this fact and the text of the editorial introduction, Hoyningen-Huene (2017, p. 12) infers that Friedman was likely to know Knight's 'Economic theory and nationalism' thoroughly and hence to be indirectly exposed to some Weberian effects.

This paper of Knight is commonly regarded as his most famous methodological work (Emmett, 2006, p. 113). By placing neoclassical economics into a broader social scientific and social political context, here Knight deprives the theory of the purpose of describing events taking place in concrete spatiotemporal settings. Concepts of the theory are of ideal typical character. Here, for Knight, applying such ideal types in economics is an explicit requirement. By meeting this requisite, theory gets far from reality, though at the same time acquires universal validity where mechanical analogy is justified to apply. However, as real economic actors and economic actions differ from their theoretical counterparts, caveats about the limited applicability still hold. Even though Knight provides no explicit references to Weber, it is Weber (1917/1949, pp. 43-44) Knight echoes when describing neoclassical theory as a framework built from ideal types. In Weber's phrasing,

> Pure economic theory, in its analysis of past and present society, utilizes ideal-ty[p] e concepts exclusively. Economic theory makes certain assumptions which scarcely ever correspond completely with reality but which approximate it in various degrees and asks how would men act under these assumed conditions, if their actions were entirely rational? It assumes the dominance of pure economic interests and precludes the operation of political or other non-economic considerations.

Despite all the restrictions, Knight (1935, pp. 277–284) still believed neoclassical theory to be highly useful and relevant in understanding real societies.

The text being highly brief and complex, not only is it difficult to analyze, but its careful reconstruction also requires us to be cognizant of both Knight's oeuvre and Weber's related ideas. Even though it results from Knight's line of reasoning that making the theory bear close similarity to reality (i.e. realistic in descriptive terms) is a methodological fault (Emmett, 2006, p. 114; 2015a), we ought to bear in mind the fact that Knight identified real behavioural patterns in economic laws (Knight, 1924/1999, p. 29). This is the reason why Knight is implausible to have abandoned elements of reality as the building blocks of theorizing. On the contrary, Knight following Weber drew attention to how economists could be causal realists via forming descriptively unrealistic assumptions. For Knight, through its ideal types neoclassical economics describes not real behaviour but patterns deduced under ideal-utopian conditions. This is necessary in order that economics could focus on the core behavioural patterns uninfluenced by social changes and preserve its practical relevance. These considerations are particularly important as Friedman's methodology is characterized below as an abandonment of the causal properties of real agents.

Due to the ambiguities mentioned above any intellectual connections between Weber and Friedman are dubious. Drawing attention to the Weberian roots of Friedman's methodology is not novel in itself, even if it has remained an under-scrutinized problem in the history of economics. To the best of my knowledge, thus far Eric Schliesser (2011) has made the only systematic efforts to point out a relationship. Schliesser tries to identify some Weberian influences on Friedman without arguing for Friedman's direct Weberian reading. He traces Friedman's Weberian reminiscences back to Parsons to whom there exists an explicit reference in Friedman's personal notes on Viner's Econ 303. Moreover, through Friedman, Schliesser extends these Weberian effects even to Stigler. It is thus likely that the connection between Weber and Friedman was indirect and superficial with Friedman not having actually read Weber's texts. However, it is still a contentious issue whether Friedman acquired his Weberian insights from Parsons. Doubly so as Schliesser does not point out that Friedman had anything by Parsons in his hands. Based on the available literature Frank H. Knight appears to have been the most probable diffuser. It is difficult to imagine that Friedman could be a student of Knight without encountering Weber's social theory, even if this encounter is likely to have been superficial.[11] However, even without some clearly identifiable connections Weber's methodology is still applicable as a framework to highlight some features of Friedman's instrumentalism.

Friedman's F53 is an epigrammatic and widely debated summary of his methodological tenets (Friedman, 1953/2009). In the text Friedman applies the very Weberian term 'ideal type' for seven times. Of these instances, there are six clear cases, whilst in one case he mentions ideal and real entities, which bears close resemblance to the rather informal fashion Knight (1935, pp. 277–278) discusses ideal concepts and ideal behaviour. In addition to the Weberian terminology it is also worth attention that

---

[11] In a conference paper, Emmett (2015a, p. 5) also intimates an indirect connection between Weber and Friedman, with Knight as the mediator. As he puts it, '[Knight's] Weberian methodology led him to emphasize the relevance of basic economic principles to real world analysis, while denying the necessity of providing theory with realistic assumptions—an argument that Friedman maintained albeit with an instrumentalist defence'.

Friedman characterizes the relationship between economic models and reality in a Weberian fashion. Here his account is in consonance with Weber's ideas. For Friedman economic models built upon ideal types 'are aimed at abstracting essential features (i.e. 'only the forces that the hypothesis asserts to be important') of complex reality' (p. 9) some elements and mechanisms of which are omitted from models—elements and mechanisms that can disturb the functioning of the ideal-typical core. The purpose of ideal-typical models is by no means description. By contrast, hypotheses underlying significant theories 'will be found to have "assumptions" that are widely inaccurate descriptive representations of reality, and, in general, the more significant the theory, the more unrealistic the assumptions (in this sense).' 'A theory or its "assumptions" cannot possibly be thoroughly "realistic" in the immediate descriptive sense so often assigned to this term'. 'Any attempt to move very far in achieving this [highly descriptive] kind of "realism" is certain to render a theory utterly useless'. Friedman rephrases Weber (1904/1949, p. 80) when explaining: 'A hypothesis is important if it "explains" much by little, that is, if it abstracts the common and crucial elements from the mass of complex and detailed circumstances surrounding the phenomena to be explained. [...] To be important, therefore, a hypothesis must be descriptively false in its assumptions'. Consequently, descriptive accuracy is unnecessary for 'a simpler theory' to work 'well enough'[12] (pp. 14–32).

Along these lines, Friedman provides an analysis of the modelling strategy of Marshallian neoclassical economics (pp. 35–37). Neoclassical theory assumes perfect competition without regarding it as a manifest characteristic of reality. If we give credit to the suggestion that models are not for describing reality, abstract economic theory becomes uncriticizable on such grounds. Equilibrium and complete rationality are only "engines" in the Weberian sense, constructed to analyze the world. By highlighting some relevant facets of reality by ideal types we render it possible to analyze a chosen facet or mechanism as an element of the complex causal structure. Here lies the most striking puzzle of this model-building

---

[12] Lucas agreed on the prohibition of building theories upon descriptively well-performing axioms: 'the axioms on which any body of theory [is] built will not serve as a "foundation" in any empirical sense. [...] [T]he idea that one can verify a set of axioms empirically, and then know the truth of a body of theory derived from these axioms without having to test the latter, seems to me just fantasy'. (Types notes. Lucas papers. Box 27. 'Adaptive behavior, 1985–1986, 2 of 2' folder) It is also clear that Lucas placed emphasis upon the empirical performance highlighted by Friedman. In the same folder Lucas highlights as a criterion of model selection the capability of theories to generate predictions being in considerable consonance with observations. However, as it is argued below, this agreement on empirical performance implied a dissimilar methodology on Lucas's part as he suggested a strict resemblance connection between descriptively minimalist models and reality to ensure causal adequacy.

strategy as theorists are to bring some aspects of reality to the fore so that their models could be adequate as to the problem under scrutiny (p. 42). By applying this strategy, we can answer the question whether a postulated causal mechanism contributes to the emergence of some social phenomena. This is exactly the reason why we need to carry out empirical tests. Socio-economic reality is full of entities differing in a multitude of aspects, though we invent ideal types to accentuate both certain properties real entities have in common and mechanisms they are involved in.

Over and above the view reflecting Weberian tenets we can find some passages in F53 where Friedman echoes Knight's critique on neoclassical economics. In such a statement, Friedman suggests as an obstacle to objective economics the fact that economics regards the connections and interactions of agents, and that the investigator belongs to the subject of her study in a way which is more intimate than in physics (p. 4). Here Friedman directly adduces Knight's parable on a drawer drawing a picture on himself in the act of drawing, which would entail a troublesome and infinite regress[13] (Knight, 1935, p. 280). It is also Knight whom Friedman resounds in his short discussion on the shortcomings of dynamic monetary macroeconomics. Here Friedman refers to the problems of analyzing how the economy adjusts to the changing conditions (p. 42). It is exactly the line along which Knight (1935/1999, p. 154), whilst drawing attention to the limits of the mechanical analogy, circumscribed the territory of neoclassical economics.

These parallelisms, however, are not to be overemphasized. Even though for both Knight and Weber neoclassical orthodoxy was only one approach in the broader context of social sciences, paying attention to the possible contributions of other disciplines was not a concern for Friedman. Placing his unique emphasis on the empirical performance of economics, he was uninterested in the social sciences in terms of either providing more in-depth causal understanding or enhancing the predictive performance of the theory. The Chicagoan efforts towards the imperialism of economics rendered it senseless to keep in touch with other social scientific disciplines (see Section 2.1.1 for more on this).

Moreover, Weber advocated a theorizing practice in which models conceptually heighten certain aspects (i.e. existent properties) of reality. Abstract ideal types are to be constructed with regard to realities (Ringer, 1997, pp. 111–119). Weber's causal concept was analogous to causal responsibility in a court of law. As a causalist, Weber's primary interest was to provide sound causal analyses to find out why and how social phenomena are caused (Bruun & Whimster, 2012, p. xxvi). In this framework, entity characteristics and the selected causal mechanisms are abstract-idealized

---

[13] Thanks to Whimster (2007, p. 265), this idea of a social scientist not being a fix point of the social environment she analyzes can also be traced back to Weber.

forms of prior descriptive accounts. Economists depict such mechanisms and relationships and entity properties in abstract-idealized forms that are either visible or evident parts of the social facts (Weber, 1904/1949, p. 90). Here 'visible' refers to mechanisms and relationships that are open to experience in one way or another, whilst 'evident' to the ones undeniably working (Knight, 1940/1999, pp. 378–381). In other words, only characteristics and mechanisms that work in reality can be used as elements in extremely simplified forms in the model-constructing process, whilst being an evident part of reality does not necessarily entail detectability. In modern parlance, models as analogue systems must bear resemblance to reality in the relevant aspects. This is how Weber (1906/1949, p. 173) clarifies the relationship of economic models to reality. Weber's conclusive argument is worth quoting at length:

> [abstract economic theory] is like a *utopia* which has been arrived at by the *analytical accentuation* of certain elements of reality. Its relationship to the empirical data consists solely in the fact that [in cases] where market-conditioned relationships of the type [...] are discovered or suspected to exist in reality to some extent, we can make the *characteristic* features of this relationship pragmatically *clear* and *understandable* by reference to an *ideal type*. (Weber, 1904/1949, p. 90)

Here Weber provides the selective criterion for drawing up the set of assumptions: theoretical assumptions are to be created by selecting and preserving some really existing properties of entities: this is the technique commonly referred to as abstraction (Chakravartty, 2007, pp. 190–191). Either city economy or handicraft is considered (Weber picked these concepts for demonstration), the purpose of ideal types is always to accentuate some 'existing' and 'retraceable' features of reality, and focusing on such features is the standard for creating ideal types. This crucial connection with reality also holds in the case of wholly 'fictional' ideal types. Even though it is always the theorist who decides upon the details to accentuate, these details as properties are always some existent parts of social reality (Bruun, 2007, p. 47). Weber regarded the wish to act rationally as a highly significant component of modern occidental culture.[14] Although the rational [ideal] types cannot [...] function as hypotheses, [...] their basic premises conform to what Weber believes to be a rationalistic *tendency* in the subject-matter' (Bruun, 2007, p. 230). The emphasis upon the 'fictional' character is an emphasis upon how the discrepancies between ideal types and reality support the causal analyses. This is a far cry from suggesting ad hoc assumptions through which it is also possible to create worlds

---

[14] This is a good example for the two-way epistemological play between real-world market participants and the representative agent of economics, mentioned in Section 3.4.1. The typical agent of economics is made up of existent entity properties to facilitate the application of theoretical knowledge to everyday human beings.

differing from ours. Rational ideal types of economic theory draw attention to the irrational elements dominating real-world actions.

The unrealisticness of neoclassical ideal types always means descriptive unrealisticness. Bruun (2007, p. 213) provides a highly instructive description of how Weber found it appropriate to apply descriptively inaccurate assumptions in causally relevant models. What is more, for Weber, this methodological mix was an explicit requirement ('Weber has to make certain that the concepts of the cultural sciences are defined so that *they do not correspond to any particular phenomenon in the reality from which their elements are taken*'). Ideal types in themselves are the instruments of causal understanding. Even though neoclassical ideal types are of abstract, one-sided, and unreal character (Bruun, 2007, pp. 213–215), a connection with reality still holds: the construction material for ideal types, so to speak, comes from our reality (Whimster, 2007, p. 112). The comparative function of abstract ideal types also makes it clear that they themselves underlie real causal mechanisms. Thanks to the comparison of observed behaviour to the predictions of ideal typical models some differences emerge. If such a discrepancy is significant, we can surmise the interplay of some further important causal factors. In an extreme case, the motive assumed via the ideal type may temporarily be inactive: a rational ideal type also aids us in realizing the complete absence of rationality (Bruun, 2007, p. 232). By contrast, if it is small, 'we can assume that the motives of the actual behaviour were roughly the same as the premises of the constructed [ideal] type' (Bruun, 2007, pp. 225–230). In case of such a coincidence, we would have no causal explanations if these premises were cut adrift from the real causal structure. Arbitrary assumptions alien to our social reality have no role in Weberian ideal types. As Weber (1904/1949, p. 91) says: '[Each utopia] has really taken certain traits, meaningful in their essential features, from the empirical reality of our culture'.

The purpose of abstract ideal types is thus to bring to the fore some threads of the complex causal structure hidden behind the phenomena. Just as abstract models are to be causally adequate, discrepancies between models and empirical reality also require causal analyses. This task, however, becomes senseless when our concepts and models fail to bear resemblance to reality. In such a case, we postulated some mechanisms the actual operation of which would be implausible to assume. This is the point where problems arise. Registering the discrepancies of empirical reality from causally inadequate models can never deepen our causal understanding as reality and models having nothing in common are necessarily disparate. Such models fail to accentuate certain elements of reality and it is not some existent entity properties and causal mechanisms that provide the building blocks for theory construction. And if there is no resemblance, discrepancies necessarily emerge, but now discrepancies result exactly from the theorizing practice and not from the underlying forces of social reality. No matter how good predictions a model is capable of, empirical performance cannot substitute for causal analysis (Hausman, 1992, p. 163). In such a case, predictive success cannot be a sign of successful causal understanding. The ultimate basis of scientific realism is the theorist's realist effort. It is exactly in this vein that Weber in his social scientific methodology called attention to the accentuation of existent properties and causal mechanisms.

Arguments for the instrumentalist reading of F53

Friedman's instrumentalism is contentious, though it remained the standard reading.[15] The chances of a proper and final interpretation are hindered by the fact that Friedman in F53, his methodological manifesto, phrased in an obscuring way, refused to clarify his stance and after realizing how passionate interpretive and methodological debates the paper stirred up he early chose to keep away from the battle fields.

Friedman provided multiple explanations to his reluctance. According to the one, methodology is appealing to young and early-stage researchers only. A significant part of methodological studies is not worth publishing as they easily and soon lose their relevance (Friedman's letter to Edwin B. Wilson, December 16, 1946; for the context, see (Friedman, 1946a)). Typically, Friedman agreed upon the publication of the correspondence he had with Wilson on methodology, whilst turned down the subsequent ask for comments (Stephen M. Stigler's notes on (Friedman, 1946a)). According to another explanation, by keeping away from the debates Friedman wanted to follow Marshall's example (Hammond, 1988, pp. 14–15). As a matter of fact, it is only rarely that Friedman broke this resolution. Boland (2010) reports upon the 2003 ASSA meeting where a session was devoted to F53 on occasion of the 50th anniversary of its publication. Friedman followed and commented on the talks on the phone. He explicitly approved of Boland's instrumentalist interpretation (Caldwell, 1980, p. 367; Boland, 2010, p. 377). For the most part, however, Friedman remained silent in methodological issues.

Among the contemporaries, Samuelson hurled the most powerful invective against Friedman's methodological suggestions. The ardency of Samuelson's critique was further emphasized by both his academic authority and his feisty rhetorical profile. Friedman's tenets were on the agenda of a debate on methodology at the meeting of the American Economic Association held on December 27–29, 1962 (the talks were

---

[15] Mariyani-Squire (2017) gives a brief overview on some further interpretations. Caldwell (1992) drawing a distinction between the non-cognitive and predictivist forms of instrumentalism provides a deeper analysis to highlight: Friedman simply disregarded the truth of theories whilst he admitted that theories could be either true or false. In the non-cognitive version, however, this evaluation of theories is neglected by saying that theories are only vehicles, therefore they cannot be regarded as true or false.

published next year in a special issue of the 'American Economic Review', entitled 'Papers and proceedings of the seventy-fifth annual meeting of the American Economic Association'). In the session, philosopher of science Ernst Nagel (1963) filled with mixed feelings provided a lukewarm defence of Friedman's methodology. In the discussion, however, Samuelson (1963) explicitly rejected the stance he simply regarded as F-twist after Friedman's family name. Calling into question the basic idea, according to which good predictions may come from highly unrealistic assumptions selected with a view solely to good empirical performance,[16] Samuelson argued that predictions of a model cannot be in consonance with the facts whilst its presumptions do not share the realisticness of the forecasts. Samuelson suggested building from reality, saying that '[g]ood science discerns regularities and simplicities that are there in reality' (p. 236).

Wong (1973) regarded Samuelson's methodological stance as descriptivism, which seemed just like as problematic as Friedman's, though for other reasons.[17] For Samuelson, a theory is no more than a description of experienceable reality, knowledge thus consists of observational reports and theories are to be expressed in observational language or in terms of observational statements. Wong found it contentious whether it was consistent and desirable to suggest theories directly reflect or mirror experience. Wong also pointed out that Samuelson himself, in spite of his harsh critique on Friedman, also had a tendency to resort to the F-twist. As Wong argued, Samuelson's critique was unsuccessful as he was unable to suggest an acceptable methodology in lieu of Friedman's alleged F-twist. As Wong argued, any economist interested in sound causal understanding ought to reject both methodologies. In spite of his methodological missteps, Samuelson successfully underlined that Friedman's methodology is strikingly anti-intellectual as the underlying idea, which Wong (1973, p. 314) following Popper (1962) regarded as 'instrumentalism' for the first time, relieves economists of providing mere statistical correlations with causal explanations[18] (Boland, 2010, p. 377). Unlike Friedman, Samuelson insisted upon connecting abstract models to reality even at the level of assumptions:

> Experience suggests that nature displays a mysterious simplicity if only we can discern it. [...] And unrealistic, abstract models often prove useful in the hunt for these regularities.
> [...] If the abstract models contain empirical falsities, we must jettison the models, not gloss over their inadequacies. (Samuelson, 1963, p. 236)

---

[16] Samuelson was not the first to object to the contingency of the way assumptions connect with reality. Boland (1979) provides a thorough review of F53's initial reception.

[17] Boland (2016, p. 20) identifies Wong's paper as one of the milestones of modern economic methodology for it was the first journal paper published after the 1962 debate.

[18] Hands (2018, p. 8) underlines the close unity explanation and description formed in Samuelson's methodology.

Setting aside the limitations to Friedman's instrumentalism (as Friedman argues, it is unnecessary for theories to refer to real entity properties), in itself it still proves to be a logically consistent methodology; thus its inconsistencies provide no basis for rejection (Boland, 1979). Of course, the lack of logical inconsistencies is not an appropriate basis for acceptance either; therefore the critique arriving from other methodological stances remained intense. Instrumentalism as a methodology implies a requirement as for the goals of science and on this ground F53 is still objectionable. As the scientific ideal F53 puts forward is weaker than realist scientists following their beliefs and convictions suggest, F53 remained appealing to the sceptics at best. Accordingly, Caldwell (1980) casts doubts whether prediction is the only and genuine goal of science. The moment explanation taken as providing answers to causal questions emerges as a tenable purpose, the position of instrumentalism inevitably weakens (Mantzavinos, 2014, p. 47).

This instrumentalist interpretive tradition was challenged by Mäki's (2009a) efforts to suggest a realist reinterpretation. Mäki pointed out that some parts of F53 are in consonance (or at least are reconcilable) with a realist methodological position. His attempt evoked heated reactions. The first responses labelling Mäki's endeavour as eccentric and bizarre were mainly rejective.[19] To be sceptical over this realist interpretation it is enough for one to highlight some parts of F53 that can hardly be reconciled with scientific realism (Reiss, 2010). It is Mäki's selective attention that triggered the most powerful objections. It was argued that Mäki simply disregarded those paragraphs of the text that were inconsistent with his preferred reading. What is more, the project itself, *rewriting* F53 as a realist manifesto, openly infuses the attempt to identify Friedman's genuine purposes with a suspicious creative flavour (Boland, 2010, p. 381). Accordingly, the instrumentalist interpretation as the most likely reading has remained dominant. However, Mäki's attempt is still present in the literature and keeps inflicting new reactions (Mariyani-Squire, 2017). Mäki (2018) also seems to insist on it.

Friedman's possible causal awareness can be analyzed in a context far beyond his F53. Whilst the instrumentalism embedded in F53 precludes our asking causal questions[20] (Blaug, 1992, pp. 195–196; Koopmans, 1947,

---

[19] An earlier version of Mäki's 2009 paper (Mäki, 2009a) was also in the programme of the 2003 ASSA meeting. In his comments on the presentation, Friedman found Mäki's suggestion 'silly' (Boland, 2010, p. 380).

[20] Abandonment of causality deviates Friedman's methodology from Marshall's standards in a crucial aspect (see Section 2.3). In his 'Principles', Marshall (1920/2013, p. 24 and p. 33) time and again places emphasis upon the ultimate task of economists to reveal the connections between causes and effects, which amounts to sound causal understanding. The implied difficulties can be overcome by analysing the causal mechanisms first in isolation then in combination. Friedman referring to the infinite regress of causes was reluctant to subscribe to the idea of causal analysis (Hammond, 1988, p. 1).

p. 167; Manicas, 2006, pp. 19–20; Wilber & Wisman, 1975, p. 669; Wong, 1973, p. 324) and any knowledge of the time range a simple empirical connection holds, one of the central ideas in Friedman's oeuvre is the causal connection between the money supply and nominal income (De Vroey, 2016, pp. 77–78). Hammond (1996) provides a detailed account of the related debates of Friedman with his contemporaries (the 'post hoc ergo propter hoc' fallacy), so it is admittedly possible to find some points under Friedman's pen that can be conciliated with the idea of causal understanding and scientific realism. In some cases, however, he fronted up in the scrums as an ardent antagonist of causalism, such as with his objections to the simultaneous equations approach of the Cowles Commission. This stance is easy to understand as regarding causal interests as pointless in cases where simple models with good empirical performance are available. It is worthy of note that Friedman's position may also imply that simple (single-equation) models are built upon real causal mechanisms in a highly isolated form. However, in order to identify Friedman's methodology as a case of this focused-isolative[21] strategy it would be necessary to find some passages in his texts that suggest firm causal understanding as a purpose. This would be a fairly common standpoint in which the vast majority of the complex causal structure is disregarded only to place the sole focus upon one highlighted causal mechanism.

In the present context it is worthwhile to recall that as a matter of fact by his famous example of the mathematical problem of the density of leaves on a tree[22] he inevitably subscribes to instrumentalism (pp. 19–20). Here Friedman keeps arguing that if a theory built upon a specific hypothesis has good predictive performance, then the realisticness of the underlying assumptions is of secondary importance.[23] Moreover, at the same time, he misses realizing the fact that there is an empirically equivalent hypothesis available according to which leaves with no rationality assumed adjust their position in order to maximize the amount of incident sunlight. This tiny detail helps us recognize how Friedman throughout F53 neglects the real properties of entities. As far as confirmation is considered, Friedman

---

[21] Without coining a more proper term, these adjectives refer to the extreme stance of building a model upon a highly isolated causal mechanism whilst neglecting complexity (e.g. demand function in a Marshallian cross). For the sake of good order, it must be noted that a simultaneous equations system also treats the causal structure in isolation as a comprehensive causal account is a metaphysical option at best but infeasible in practice. The extent of isolation is variable.

[22] In addition to tale of leaves, Mariyani-Squire (2017, p. 82) enumerates further examples for non-isolative theorizing. As he argues, return-maximizing entrepreneurs and billiard players following Newtonian mechanics are also fictionalizing inventions and not entities abstracted from reality. See Section 3.1.1 for more on Friedman's colourful conceptualizing practice.

[23] This is a recurrent idea of Friedman. For further considerations, see (Friedman, 1952, p. 1).

is satisfied when a hypothesis leads to predictions in line with observed phenomena. This pattern of confirmation explicitly implies no causal understanding (p. 9).

As we have seen, this instrumentalism, however, is in no accordance with Weber's neoclassical ideas (Knight, 1924/1999, p. 31). Even though Friedman saying that ideal types are constructed to highlight the characteristics that play a key role in a particular problem (p. 36) occasionally appears to argue for accentuating the existing features and mechanisms of reality, he defends the idea of an explicit inconsistency between assumptions and reality (as in his parable on leaves acting as if they were rational utility maximizers). In the latter case, however, there exists no ambition to capture some existent features in ideal-typical concepts. It is a similarly exciting example when Friedman (1953, p. 3) distinguishes descriptive realism and analytical realism. Descriptive realism is not an option for him: he rejects this position in the common way. However, it is not well-established causal understanding but a harmony between predictions and observations that he means by analytical realism. Descriptive inaccuracy for Friedman is not accompanied by the preservation of causally active entity properties. Through this strategy unrealistic representations would also have been feasible (albeit only in descriptive terms), though coming with analytical realism conceived in causal terms. This option was likely to leave Friedman cold. As a typical example, we may recall Friedman merging the purposes of causal analysis and simple predictions into one another (Hammond, 1988, pp. 5–6).

Friedman properly draws attention to the idea that assumptions of a good theory would fall far from reality (p. 32). This is true, but it is also true, though in a different way, of the realist models in which empirical performance was originally not a high-ranked aspect (Knight, 1924/1999, pp. 31–32; 1935, pp. 282–284; 1940/1999, pp. 388–394; Medema, 2011, p. 154). As Weber (1904/1949, p. 80) puts it:

> The more comprehensive the validity, – or scope – of a term, the more it leads us away from the richness of reality since in order to include the common elements of the largest possible number of phenomena, it must necessarily be as abstract as possible and hence *devoid* of content.

In other words, the most universal laws and the assumptions capturing the common cores of different kinds of things stand the farthest from the totality of our reality. We have a similar setting in the case of the assumptions underlying a realist model and their descriptive relevance. Instrumentalist assumptions are also unrealistic in descriptive terms, but in their case there is no targeted isolation in the game as the act of connecting with reality. Isolation starting from existing entities and properties is replaced by some plain pragmatist considerations. There is no ambition to connect the model to reality over and above the simplest desire for saving the phenomenon. Picking out the assumptions is driven by the utility which arises from the empirical performance of the models built upon them. The unrealisticness of instrumentalism and the unrealisticness of realism are of completely different nature. Assumptions applied in realist models have no descriptive accuracy either. However, the methodology by which these assumptions are created is not of marginal importance. Through abstraction and proper idealization we can establish presumptions that can capture some significant existing elements of reality, even if they cannot reflect their totality (Galbács, 2017).

4.1.2 The second attempt: The instrumentalist foundations of Friedman's Phillips curves

The Phillips curve as a framework has a unique position in Friedman's oeuvre. He devoted his famous presidential address (Friedman, 1968) to disentangling the mechanisms underlying the phenomenal Phillips curve, though there an explicit model played a minor role only. A few years later the Phillips curve got into the limelight: in his Nobel lecture Friedman discussed his accomplishments in the context of the Phillips curve (Friedman, 1977). The Phillips curve provided the analytical framework by which Friedman could combine his views on equilibrium (the natural rate of unemployment) with his thoughts on the limitations to monetary policy. If Friedman is taken as a single-idea economist (De Vroey, 2016, p. 66), the Phillips curve framework is no more than a possible articulation of Friedman's oft-voiced ideas. However, there is more to it. The Phillips curve provided Friedman with an efficient instrument for combating Keynesian economics[24] (De Vroey, 2001), even if the Keynesian missteps he associated with it appear to be his fantasies (Forder, 2010). In the present methodological analysis Friedman's Phillips curves are important as they aid in highlighting the problematic relationship between the faultily designed microfoundations and macro-level causal understanding.[25]

Friedman's ideas on the Phillips curve were born in the debates triggered by Samuelson and Solow's 1960 paper (Samuelson & Solow, 1960) on the guidelines for monetary policy (Taylor, 2007, p. 136). This was the study in which the authors some 2 years after the emergence of the Phillips curve used it as the analytical framework of economic policy and inflation (Schwarzer, 2013). According to the traditional narrative put

[24] It is exactly through the Phillips curve that De Vroey (2001) portrays the methodological differences between Friedman and Lucas. The importance of the Phillips curve to Friedman is properly pictured by the fact that De Vroey (2016, pp. 95–111) dedicates a whole chapter to the related papers by Phelps (1967a, 1967b).

[25] Phelps (1995, p. 17) emphasizes that the major novelty in his and Friedman's Phillips curves was to place the model upon explicit microfoundations.

forward in Friedman's Nobel lecture, Friedman and Phelps called into question the stability of the trade-off between the rate of inflation and the rate of unemployment and hence the Phillips curve. As expectations matter, by keeping inflation at a high rate it is impossible to stabilize unemployment under its natural level. The Phillips curve always shifts. Forder (2014) disapproves of Friedman's account, especially the suggestion that it is Friedman (and Phelps) who called attention to the role of expectations. When Friedman brought in these thoughts, they had already been available in the literature for a long time. As a matter of fact, Samuelson and Solow themselves were also sceptical about the stability of the curve (Hoover, 2015). At the same time the framework had crucial importance specifically to Friedman. He devoted his Nobel lecture to some theoretical problems raised by the curve whilst the economic literature of 1960–70s did not place much emphasis upon it. In those days some attention was admittedly paid to the relationship between wage and price inflation on the one hand and unemployment on the other, but Phillips's contribution was only one in the array.

As it was argued in Section 4.1.1, Friedman in his F53 by playing down the importance of the real properties of entities placed the sole emphasis upon saving the phenomena; hence he subscribed to instrumentalism.[26] Friedman's Phillips curves provide further striking examples for neglecting the purpose of causal understanding. The role ideal types play in causal understanding properly highlights how Friedman designed his entity-level assumptions in his Phillips curves in order to derive the macro-level conclusions he wished in advance. James Forder (2016) also calls attention to some confusions hidden in Friedman's AEA address. Forder places special emphasis upon the unclear phrasing through which Friedman portrayed the dissimilar flexibilities of prices and wages. In Forder's reading, that Friedman (1968) conceives prices as rising faster than wages may mean both that price and wage inflations start at different moments and that there are differences between the rates of price and wage inflations. Friedman, however, apparently neglected to resolve this confusion.

Forder regards it as a simple logical error having no crucial importance as this laxity of Friedman by no means distorted significantly the key message. However, the error is undoubtedly there, and even if we are willing to attribute it to Friedman's negligence, saying that this minor misstep proved to be neutral as for the overall impact of Friedman's theory, such a mistake inevitably has an effect on the assessment of Friedman's oeuvre. As there is no sign of Friedman's putting forward some undigested thoughts here (as Forder aptly highlights, the same mistake emerges in the drafts),

---

[26] In Chapter 1, instrumentalism is defined as a methodological stance neglecting causal understanding.

there is no reasoned ground for playing down the mistake. Instead, it is equally easy to argue that Friedman's explanation is carried by some implicit assumptions that are of crucial importance as for his conclusions. On this showing, these confusions are not logical errors but the results of some arbitrary assumptions and, accordingly, they ought to be assessed in a less generous way. Assuming that Friedman concentrated on his pre-set or pre-given conclusions whilst neglecting the way he got there, these implicit and unnatural assumptions seem to be the perfect manifestations of the instrumentalist principles of F53. At a minimum they effectively highlight how Friedman belittled the importance of careful reasoning.

The system of negatively sloped short-run Phillips curves and a vertical one to signify the natural rate of unemployment, and the possibility for the agents to switch between the curves require an image of employers and employees that cannot be reconciled with the properties their real counterparts have. In these terms the assumptions on the information background are crucial. Friedman's technique here closely obeys his causal instrumentalist stance in F53. His primary purpose was to generate predictions in line with the observations whilst there is no emphasis upon causal understanding. Hiding behind the idea of descriptive inaccuracy and unrealisticness, Friedman sneaked some suspicious entity properties into his Phillips curves: entity properties that fail to facilitate the sound causal understanding of the labour market phenomena under scrutiny. Friedman's starting point was the absence of a stable trade-off between inflation and unemployment. As he argued, this trade-off comes to nothing if expectations are taken into account (De Vroey, 2016, p. 102). It is the underlying information structure that Friedman defined via some bizarre assumptions, which is highly problematic as initially he aspired to resolve the confusions over the Phillips curve by considering the role of expectations (i.e. forward-looking behaviour and information processing).

The idea is briefly summarized in the following graphic framework (Fig. 4.1):

The basic mechanism is highly simple, even if its interpretation raises some problems. If the represented economy starts from equilibrium point C (appertaining to the natural rate of unemployment, U_N) and if inflation (π) rises from A to B for one reason or another, then the system temporarily relocates into point D and at the same time unemployment lowers below the natural rate (U_L). This state, however, is only ephemeral as the system refuses to get stuck in this favourable unemployment situation. The Phillips curve shifts from P' to P'' and the economy albeit at a higher level of inflation returns to the natural rate of unemployment (E) where after the temporary swing the system is in general equilibrium (Friedman, 1968, p. 8). In this framework the initial CD movement can be triggered by expansionary monetary policy actions that are designed to set aggregate production and employment to statuses more favourable than the

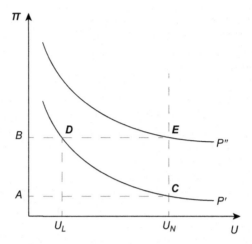

FIG. 4.1   A system of expectations augmented Phillips curves (P' and P'') showing the trade-off between unemployment (U) and inflation (π). *Redrawn from Friedman, M. (1977). Nobel lecture. Inflation and unemployment. Journal of Political Economy, 85(3), 457.*

natural level. Friedman, however, was doubtful whether it is possible to permanently reduce unemployment by monetary policy measures.

In Friedman's (1977) narrative, the narrative Forder (2014) aims to discredit, some empirical studies showed him that the actual (data-based) Phillips curve refused to behave in the way the theory predicted (Friedman, 1977, p. 451). A stable trade-off between unemployment and inflation was undetectable, that is, multiple levels of inflation might belong to the same level of unemployment. Any given rate of unemployment was accompanied by higher and higher rates of inflation.

In the beginning, Friedman came up with a story very similar to the original explanation. When making their labour supply decisions, workers take into account their expectations about inflation and real wages. Taking expectations into account does not mean that workers decide to increase labour supply just because they expect real wages to increase. By contrast, it is an expectation error, a discrepancy between observations and expectations, that triggers the overall effects. Plainly put, the increase in the labour supply is generated by a monetary policy surprise. If monetary policy wants to achieve a rate of unemployment lower than the natural level, then to this end it must boost the money growth rate and hence aggregate demand. One of the channels is the drop in the rate of interest enhancing investment demand, and the other is the higher aggregate demand directly stemming from the increase in the stock of money.

Agents (both producers and employees) in this situation of increased money growth boost their supplies as a response to higher aggregate demand. The worsening of the initial positive employment effect occurs as workers based on their experiences adjust their expectations about prices.

As a consequence, unemployment returns to the natural rate. This rebound may take place along two possible mechanisms. In the one scenario, workers finally understand real wage dynamics and as real wage remains the same all along they reduce their labour supply to the initial level. In the other, properly experienced real wages urge workers to ask for higher money wages to be compensated for the higher price level. As a result, this readjustment leads to a drop in the demand for labour force. However, Friedman left this detail unanswered.

To explain the dynamics of the system it is insufficient to refer to some nominal changes experienced as real changes. Two further assumptions are needed. One is the dissimilar reactions of prices and wages as responses to changed demand conditions. Accordingly, stimulated demand increases prices faster than wages, wages are thus stickier.[27] As a consequence, the lower rate of unemployment is the effect of dropping real wages, and the only cause of the system's returning to the natural rate of unemployment is the phase when workers regain their situation awareness which results in an adjustment process. Employees understand the actual dynamics of prices and wages and subsequently they act accordingly. The other arbitrary assumption is a special information asymmetry: what workers do not know about real wages, nominal wages, and prices is completely clear to the employers.

Friedman (1968, p. 10; 1977, p. 456) explains the rigidity of nominal variables (prices and wages) with some contracts concluded on the basis of prior expectations. These contracts hinder prices flexibly adjusting to demand. However, the assumption of dissimilar demand flexibilities of different sets of prices requires a more thorough theoretical underpinning.[28] Such contracts only form a special condition that can easily be regarded as responsible in the first place for the stickiness, though assuming their existence is far from obvious. Suggesting some contracts as a theoretical explanation to a subtle system of price changes is only a short cut and requires underpinnings. If such an underpinning is unavailable (as in Friedman's case), it is easy to assume a radically different pattern of flexibilities where it is the rise in money wages that starts earlier (it only requires the similarly arbitrary assumption that wage and price

---

[27] This is one of the two possible interpretations of the word 'faster' Forder (2016, p. 106) suggests. As far as the final effect is concerned, this detail is indifferent. A rise in prices higher than a simultaneous rise in wages inflates away money wages increasing at a slower pace. In this regard, Forder is right: the difference in meanings has nothing to do with the outcome. However, as we shall see soon, this fact does not render the story acceptable.

[28] According to Lucas (1980, p. 711; 1981, p. 290), in a Phillips curve there exists 'a parameter describing the speed with which an "auctioneer" adjusts the nominal wage to excess demands and supplies'. The auctioneer emerging as an arbitrary assumption is indispensable as these models for the sake of mathematical simplicity do not trace all macro-level events back to individual preferences. As a consequence, price and wage dynamics is not the result of agents' interactions only (Lucas, 1987, p. 16).

contracts terminate at different times). However, it is contentious whether the course of events Friedman suggested still emerges. A rise in money wages accompanied by a later increase in prices results in a growth in real wages (dissimilar rates of increase would lead to the same outcome), which leads to a rise in labour supply and, simultaneously, to a drop in the demand for labour force as employers properly perceive price and wage dynamics. Confusing nominal and real changes is still a factor as workers are ill-informed about their actual real wages. They conceive the rise in money wages as a rise in real wages, though in this case they are right. In this scenario the initial expansion of employment thus fails to happen. What is more, the opposite would occur as in case of excess supply it is demand that establishes the level of employment. Only the equilibration of the changes in prices and wages, a restoration of the initial real wages, could take the economy back to the natural rate of unemployment.

Even if for a moment it is left unnoticed that dissimilarity of price and wage flexibilities has remained unexplained, nominal contracts cannot be blamed for workers' inability to perceive correct price dynamics and hence the changes in real wages. Although wage contracts are formed to apply to a given expected rate of inflation, it is hard to infer that employees cannot perceive actual (and unexpected) inflation. Even under the contracts there is nothing that can stop employees from withdrawing their unnecessarily boosted labour supply when they experience some unexpected changes in real wages. If all it is taken into account, the beneficial employment effect triggered by excess inflation can only be ephemeral, lasting until workers realize the actual albeit unexpected changes in prices.

Lessons become particularly instructive when the same and undelayed flexibility is assumed for both prices and wages. In such a case, excess demand drives prices and wages to start rising at the same time and in the same extent. Workers again, following Friedman's assumptions, expect price dynamics to keep following the prior trend, so they unsurprisingly experience higher money wages as higher real wages. Employers, however, know that real wages have not changed. As a consequence, the system refuses to leave the natural rate of unemployment even temporarily. Only a vertical shift upwards occurs (from C directly to E). In spite of Friedman's efforts, a confusion over nominal and real changes in itself is insufficient to explain the CDE route of the economy. The dynamics Friedman suggested rests upon a special system of price and wage dynamics that he left unexplained.

Assumptions of information asymmetry and weird price and wage flexibility are necessary in order that employment effects could be explained. Mistaking nominal changes for real changes and the holding of one of the additional implicit assumptions are insufficient for the dynamics Friedman suggested to emerge. What happens if only one of the assumptions holds? In the first case, only information asymmetry applies. Accordingly, employees fail to perceive the rise in prices. At the same time, however, now wages and prices start changing simultaneously. Workers mistakenly perceive their real wages increasing. Beneficial employment effects do not occur as employers know that real wages have remained unchanged. In the second case, there is a difference only in changes in prices and wages but no information asymmetry. Employees perceiving a rise in real wages err again. However, the same happens to employers (as there is no information asymmetry), so employment can drop at best. By contrast, if assuming information asymmetry away means the correct perception of real wages on both sides, then because of the principle of the short side a boost in employment cannot occur again (for there is a drop in real wages as a matter of fact). All in all, both assumptions, information asymmetry and the flexibility of prices and wages, are indispensable to the emergence of the favourable employment effects.

There is a further case to consider where there is no need for the assumption of information asymmetry, but this is only an irrelevant option. If workers perceive a rise whilst employers a drop in real wages, Friedman's story on the expansion of employment can be told. In this case it is true that both sides are subject to mistakes, so there is no information asymmetry in the game. However, it is rather an uninteresting scenario as the story is about inflation and sticky wages. The relevant cases are thus confined to either (1) correct perception of a drop in real wages or (2) a misperception.

Friedman seems to be imprecise when saying: '[p]roducers will tend to react to the initial expansion in aggregate demand by increasing output, employees by working longer hours, and the unemployed, by taking jobs now offered at former nominal wages' (Friedman, 1968, p. 10). If workers responded to a rise in aggregate demand with increasing their labour supply at the prevailing nominal wages (that cannot result in higher real wages[29]), it would be possible only if there was involuntary unemployment in the system. This results in an obvious inconsistency with the ideas on the natural rate of unemployment regarding which Friedman (1968, p. 8) refers to Walrasian general equilibrium. A rise in employment when nominal wages remain unchanged (and when real wages remain unchanged as the best case) is possible only on a disequilibrium labour market, where there are workers willing to take jobs even at the prevailing money (or real) wages, though they cannot because of the insufficiency of aggregate demand.

Another oddity is the implicit information asymmetry underlying the mechanism Friedman suggests. It means that employees' naïve (adaptive)

---

[29] Resorting to money illusion is not a way out of this plight as Friedman discusses how employment changes at the former level of nominal wages. Supposing that nominal wages do not change, even if employees are trapped in money illusion (that is, they may even expect the former price dynamics to go on), the real wage they think they perceive cannot outgrow the former level. Involuntary unemployment is thus a relevant phenomenon the cause of which is insufficient aggregate demand.

expectations are accompanied by employers' correct perception of prices. A rise in prices inflating nominal wages away and facilitating a higher level of demand for labour force is properly perceived by employers. At the same time, on the basis of their expectations, employees acting as buyers on the same market are alleged to still experience former price dynamics living on—erroneously, of course. In terms of real wages, it is the price level of the products employees have in their consumer basket that is relevant, on the basis of which it must be easy to infer the general price level. The idea of a single centralized market, however, makes it impossible to plausibly introduce the incompleteness of information as an assumption.

Shaw (1984, p. 38) traces back this information asymmetry to some explicit assumptions. In his setting the real wage employees perceive is determined by expected inflation, whilst employers make their labour demand decisions on the basis of actual price changes. Friedman refers to this dubious assumption as an evident albeit unimportant circumstance, highlighting that

> [b]ecause selling prices of products typically respond to an unanticipated rise in nominal demand faster than prices of factors of production, real wages received have gone down—though real wages anticipated by employees went up, since employees implicitly evaluated the wages offered at the earlier price level. Indeed, the simultaneous fall *ex post* in real wages to employers and rise *ex ante* in real wages to employees is what enabled employment to increase. (Friedman, 1968, p. 10)

Confusing nominal and real changes as it is shown here is highly problematic as employees can be deprived of their basic situation awareness only arbitrarily. At the same time, employers' perception is uncorrupted. This theorizing can hardly be underpinned by the purpose of sound isolation. Friedman seems to have designed the presumptions for this mechanism in order to draw the conclusions he desired in advance. To outline a theory in which unemployment is expected to bounce back to the natural rate after an initial drop, and in which there is no stable trade-off between unemployment and inflation it was necessary for him to introduce a difference of knowledge and the inability to realize the actual real wage. In reality, employees and employers respond to changes in the real wage in different ways, properly depicted even in the simple Marshallian cross of the labour market. Plainly put, what is good for the one is disadvantageous for the other. As the basic market mechanism would never result in the employment effects Friedman wished to see, he was compelled to have a creative play with the underlying assumptions.

In the later version of the model Friedman tried to resolve the problem of information asymmetry by subjecting both sides of the labour market to mistakes (Friedman, 1977, pp. 456–459). Employers face the Lucasian signal processing problem: even though each of them perceives the rise in the price of her own product, she is unable to decide whether it comes from a rise in the general price level or from a favourable readjustment of relative prices. Judging by the possibility of a favourable change in the price structure, an individual producer tries to avoid missing profit opportunities, so she boosts her output. As it is expected, there are two cases of wage rigidity here: nominal wages are sticky and start rising later in time or the rate of growth of nominal wages is lower than the rate of inflation. Any employer when making her labour demand decision only considers the increase in the price of her own product, and on this ground the real wage she perceives is on the decrease. A rise in the demand for labour force is thus plausible. This later version could relax the problematic assumption on price dynamics: the increase in prices naturally starts earlier as this is the change that triggers labour market adjustments and the boost in production. Simultaneously, the problem raised by the confusing word 'faster' is also sorted out here.

Friedman's Marshallian framework implying one centralized market can at best insufficiently suggest the friction between local markets and the knowledge of aggregate-level dynamics. A plausible way of introducing this assumption is definitely beyond its power. Further parts of the story remained unchanged: employees realize the rise in prices with a delay and hence initially conceive higher nominal wages as higher real wages. But for an increase in labour supply, leaving the natural rate of unemployment would never emerge. The swing comes to an end when real wage dynamics becomes properly experienced. Involuntary unemployment does not need to be present in the final version either as it is the rise in nominal wages regarded as a rise in real wages by employees that triggers labour market readjustments.

The theory has remained problematic as it is unclear how the presupposed mechanism leads to a temporary drop in unemployment. The reaction employers show is reasonable. Rising prices naturally inflate nominal wages away; thus under the resulting conditions enhancing employment is possible and profitable. By contrast, the reaction of employees is difficult to understand. They are expected to be aware of their nominal wages. It is also plausible to assume them to perceive the rise in the price level as exactly those prices are considered in the story that they face as consumers on a daily basis: real wage dynamics is driven by the prices of the products they purchase. These two things together should cause employees to experience the drop in real wages. As a consequence, an increase in the labour supply is not a plausible option, whilst a rise in employment presupposes this outcome. Friedman (1977, p. 457) insists on the story that employees only gradually come to understand they have erred on real wage changes. Both sides make mistakes: employers are uncertain about relative prices (i.e. the relationship between product prices and the general price level) whilst employees are unable to realize the real wages.

Confusions worsen if employers are also allowed to show up on consumer markets as buyers. Like workers, now they must perceive the general price level as well. In such a case, neither the information processing problem nor a rise in output emerges: there are no real changes. The problem is that Friedman's agents perceive multiple prices at the same time (the price of a producer's own product, nominal wages, and the general price level as on a single market they are inevitably informed about the general price level), and even though there are multiple goods and prices in the picture, information on the general price level cannot be precluded as consumer prices are unproblematically perceived. The story is obscured in one way or another. By contrast, Lucas has placed a single-product economy on his islands where agents acting as employers and employees at the same time are plausibly deprived of information on the general price level. In his framework the general price level consists of the prices of the single product sold on separated markets.

The detail that decreasing real wages trigger a rise in the demand for labour force is clear. This amounts to a shift along the labour demand curve: a drop in real wages enhances the demand for labour. However, lower real wages ought to result in a drop in labour force supplied. To avoid this conclusion, Friedman had to prevent this mechanism from being triggered. To this end, he needed the assumption of employees not perceiving the changes in the prices of the products they consume. Employees can miss cutting down on labour supply in one way only: if they simply do not know they ought to do so. This is exactly the weakest point of Friedman's theory.

Saying that contracts hinder employees in acting and hence labour supply is constrained seems to be a way out. However, the problem lies in the fact that employees do act—they respond to excess inflation with increasing their labour supply. This cannot be explained by wage rigidity. In order for a boost in employment to emerge a boost in the labour supply is definitely needed to accompany the boost in demand as because of the principle of the short side it is always the smaller of supply and demand that determines the level of employment. If one wants to suggest a rise in employment when real wages are on the decrease, the assumed blindness of employees is indispensable—or else, the power of employers to have the discretion to set employment according to their demand for labour force. We have no other option than attributing the rise in labour supply accompanied by a drop in real wages to the workers' flawed recognition of the situation. However, this is an arbitrary assumption that efficiently highlights Friedman's 'most Friedmanian' face. No matter how hard we try to resolve the contradictions, we always encounter some new problems.

4.2 Lucas's case: Descriptive inaccuracy and causal adequacy

All the thorough methodological analyses of Lucas's lifework highlight his insistence on an extremely minimalist and descriptively inaccurate notion of agents (Vercelli, 1991, p. 141; Hoover, 1995; Boumans, 2005, pp. 92–96; De Vroey, 2016, pp. 71 and pp. 174–190). For Lucas (1986, p. S425) the superficial view on individuals and social relations is a definite merit of modern macroeconomics. Thanks to this view, theory can have meaningful predictions on human behaviour without knowing too many details on the life of the modelled individuals. This is a plan of a methodology suggested to get rid of the superfluous details and to conceptualize with a narrow focus on things. However, the extension of this minimalism has remained a contentious issue. Is it possible that keeping away from fine details is so comprehensive that it renders economic models mere fictions in the case of which any relationship with reality emerges at the level of numerical predictions only? As it is argued in what follows, powerful isolation has meant to Lucas the abandonment of details dispensable in terms of the problem under scrutiny. This is the age-old case for the abandonment of pushing descriptive accuracy, also suggested in Friedman's methodology. Discussions in Chapter 3, however, underlined the possibility of preserving causally relevant properties even in minimalist representations. Weber's social scientific methodology is a paramount example.

Perhaps the most intriguing question as for Lucas's methodology regards his attitude towards sound causal understanding. What did Lucas (1986, p. S408) have in mind when scrutinizing the conditions under which descriptively false abstractions can still be 'adequate'? Weber's, Knight's, and Friedman's methodologies effectively underline that the absence of descriptive accuracy is not necessarily accompanied by the purpose of causal understanding. Descriptive (in)accuracy and causal (in)adequacy are two quite independent dimensions of the assessment of assumptions.[30] It depends on the efforts of the modeller whether she theorizes with a view to causal understanding or makes do with mere empirical performance.[31] As it was argued in Chapter 3, macro-level causal relations forming the structure in the object-oriented ontologies root in properties of entities—as far as the microfoundations project is concerned, mainly in the properties of agents and other irreducible entities. Thus if one is

---

[30] In this respect it is illuminating how Lucas and Rapping define the decision problem the representative household faces. There is a plethora of available alternatives: work vs. leisure time; work vs. leisure time vs. job seeking; etc. According to the problem under scrutiny, any of them may be postulated. Lucas and Rapping (1969, p. 726 fn. 5; Lucas, 1981, p. 48) chose the dyad 'work vs. leisure time' as it was sufficient for the analysis of unemployment conceived as an activity (Lucas, 1981, p. 5).

[31] We do not need to address the question whether general economic equilibrium has real existence if the theoretical problem regards how optimization and the efforts towards equilibrium contribute to the emergence of large-scale fluctuations. Until the role and the nature of equilibrium are ill-understood, it makes no sense to have discussions about disequilibrium situations, especially about the allegedly evident disequilibrium of real macroeconomic systems (Plosser, 1989, p. 53).

interested in a (partial) analysis of real causal mechanisms, she needs to postulate some causal entity properties that are active in terms of the relations she wishes to represent. Reality thus cuts in. Macro-structures and hence their representations cannot be independent of the underlying properties of entities, of the properties that carry the causal connections. As a consequence, assumptions defining theoretical agents and other entities must be adequate as for the represented causal connections. Thus the question if a model is capable of providing an adequate causal analysis on the chosen facet of reality boils down to the question of the adequacy of the postulated entity properties. It may be possible that the features of Lucas's highly abstract entities support sound causal understanding.

Lucas's most productive years are characterized by an intense interest in methodology which in itself is an instructive detail in an overall assessment of his economics. Whilst in terms of the basic theoretical questions his work showed stability throughout the 1970s, his methodology determining the way of providing the answers considerably evolved through refinements (Lucas, 1981, p. 1). His methodology is even more intriguing as Lucas conceived his theory only as a slight theoretical and economic policy contribution to Milton Friedman's post-war monetarism, which is a further aspect of the relationship between Friedman and Lucas. On this showing a major novelty of Lucas's macroeconomics is to be found in his methodology as it is the fundament that made it possible for him to find new answers to some age-old questions (see Section 2.3 on how the theoretical and economic policy considerations changed from Friedman to Lucas).

Economic methodology as a field of self-reflection forms the meta-theory of economics. Even though methodology cut off from applications may turn into a waste of time, this interest of Lucas as an applied economist shows his dissatisfaction with the very fundaments of economics. Walking along the paved way with no critical concerns never raises the need for checking the directions. Lucas's efforts to clarify the ultimate grounds of economics are likely to refer to a kind of uncertainty and the desire to consolidate the discipline.[32]

4.2.1 The basic requirements and the traces of understanding

Lucas put forward some firm requirements good models must meet. One of them is empirical or predictive performance, even in the case of theories not subject to econometric parameter estimations, as Friedman also underlined. Based on the postulated mechanisms models are demanded to fairly well reproduce some observable phenomena of business cycles. The emphasis upon good empirical performance came up as

---

[32] Bruun (2007, p. 4) explains Weber's intense interest in methodology with similar reasons.

early as in his paper co-authored by Rapping (Lucas & Rapping, 1969) where they provided some econometric estimations for the equations of the postulated model. Estimations are aimed at giving partial accounts of observed events via some assumed mechanisms (Lucas & Rapping, 1972, p. 186; Lucas, 1981, p. 59). A good theory must be in line with observations (Lucas, 1976a/1981, p. 91) as, plainly put, it is always suspicious if a theory is inconsistent with the facts. For Lucas the short-run non-neutrality and long-run neutrality of money were key empirical features of modern business cycles (Lucas, 1973, p. 326; 1981, p. 131; Snowdon & Vane, 2005, p. 224) and they are all shown by the model Lucas (1972, p. 103; 1981, p. 66) constructed to derive a complex Phillips curve mechanism.

Another key principle regards the descriptive capacity of models, or rather the suggested absence of this capacity. Lucas regarded good descriptive performance of models as a superfluous property; thus in the common way good predictive capacity does not entail comprehensive description. Any emphasis on it is an obstacle to the proper use:

> One of the functions of theoretical economics is to provide fully articulated, artificial economic systems that can serve as laboratories in which policies that would be prohibitively expensive to experiment with in actual economies can be tested out at much lower cost. To serve this function well, it is essential that the artificial "model" economy be distinguished as sharply as possible in discussion from actual economies. Insofar as there is confusion between statements of opinion as to the way we believe actual economies would react to particular policies and statements of verifiable fact as to how the model will react, the theory is not being effectively used to help us to see which opinions about the behavior of actual economies are accurate and which are not. This is the sense in which insistence on the "realism" of an economic model subverts its potential usefulness in thinking about reality. Any model that is well enough articulated to give clear answers to the questions we put to it will necessarily be artificial, abstract, patently "unreal."[33] (Lucas, 1980, p. 696; 1981, p. 271)

Accordingly, Lucas's equilibrium concept is not a descriptive category (Snowdon & Vane, 2005, p. 281). Neglecting the descriptive function, drawing a sharp distinction between models and real economies is neither novel nor surprising. In this context the discussions in Chapter 3 on isolation are relevant again. Lucas's equilibrium conception is an idealization that does not reject a realist interpretation.

This precise differentiation between model and reality emerges not only in Lucas's dedicated methodological works. Elsewhere his phrasing is clearer: equations have direct empirical relevance only when the assumed features can be expected to be manifest in reality as well

---

[33] Excerpts from Lucas (1980) are reprinted from 'Journal of Money, Credit and Banking', vol. 12, Robert E. Lucas, 'Methods and problems in business cycle theory', pp. 696–715, Copyright (1980), with permission from John Wiley & Sons.

(Lucas & Rapping, 1969, p. 733; Lucas, 1981, p. 28). Even though Lucas and Rapping regard the expectations formation mechanism they postulate as plausible for the period under study (1929–65), they expect the households to abandon it if prices are systematically under- or overestimated. The assumption that labour is a freely variable input is similar. Unsurprisingly, reality is not like theory, so Lucas and Rapping dwell upon the details of this difference. For instance, companies may invest huge amounts of money in training, so they are highly unlikely to flexibly adjust employment. As a consequence, it is only a tendency towards which companies converge that the model can describe at best as there are some (omitted) factors that deteriorate market flexibility. The same principle turns up as the observation that omitted factors are detrimental to empirical performance (Lucas & Rapping, 1972, p. 190; Lucas, 1981, p. 63).

19th century founding fathers precisely drew a distinction between models and reality (Galbács, 2015, pp. 24–25). Hicks (1932, pp. 42-56) was also right to underline that a lot of factors beyond pure theory ought to be considered in order to understand real macroeconomies. Elsewhere Hicks (1946) accurately distinguished theoretical economics and institutional analysis, also taking the former as relevant in terms of understanding reality.[34] An objection to descriptive realism is also a constituent part of Friedman's instrumentalism. Some complications, however, emerge as Weber placing emphasis upon causally adequate analysis also argued against descriptivism. This paragraph by Lucas thus does not provide sufficient grounds for us to reproduce how he conceived the relationship of models and reality, and what he thought of the possibilities of and the need for causal understanding. Such brief statements as 'the progress in economic thinking means getting better and better abstract, analogue economic models, not better verbal observations about the world' (Lucas, 1980, p. 700; 1981, p. 276) reveal nothing about this relationship. This claim neither implies its reduction to mere empirical performance nor advocates the idea of sound causal understanding. However, as models are instrumental in gaining knowledge about reality, some form of this relationship must evidently exist. This is not too much as a requirement since even causally inadequate models can successfully support the evaluation of alternative economic policies (as it is put forward in the lengthy quotation above). If in such a situation we are ready to make do with simple correlations, an emphasis upon causal understanding degrades into a dispensable flounce. Sometimes Lucas does not seem to claim more:

---

[34] There are some counterexamples. De Vroey (2016, p. 4) mentions that Austrian economics responded to the crisis of 1929–33 with some completely mistaken recommendations as a result of the direct application of a similarly abstract theory to reality.

If, subjected to forces similar to those acting on actual societies, the artificial society reacts in a similar way, we gain confidence that there are useable connections between the invented society and the one we really care about. (Typed notes. Lucas papers. Box 13. 'Directions of macroeconomics, 1979' folder)

In a close reading, this excerpt requires a model to show the same reaction to the same shock as real economies do. According to this minimum requirement, usefulness of a model is underpinned by co-movements of variables bearing similarity to the patterns of observed correlations. This passage above only establishes a link between the opposite ends of a causal chain. Here Lucas demands a well-known shock to trigger a well-known effect—but that is all to it. The question of real causal mechanisms is not even mentioned. However, the connection between model and reality is important and malleable at the same time:

These notes contain examples of <u>monetary theories</u>: systems of equations which provide exact descriptions of behavior in highly abstract, fictional economies in which securities which I will label "money" play an important role. Insofar as people perceive interesting and useful connections between these fictional economies and actual economies, there will be a definite sense in which these mathematical examples constitute "good" or "successful" theories; insofar as they do not, they will be "unsuccessful". (Typed notes. Lucas papers. Box 23. 'Money, 1975–1977, 2 of 2' folder)

We are still uncertain about the grounds of the key connection. The next paragraph is more instructive about Lucas's methodological stance:

At the same time, not all well-articulated models will be equally useful. Though we are interested in models because we believe they may help us to understand matters about which we are currently ignorant, we need to test them as useful imitations of reality by subjecting them to shocks for which we are fairly certain how actual economies, or parts of economies, would react. The more dimensions on which the model mimics the answers actual economies give to simple questions, the more we trust its answers to harder questions. This is the sense in which more "realism" in a model is clearly preferred to less. (Lucas, 1980, pp. 696–697; 1981, p. 272)

The picture is more complex now, though it is still blurred. There are three words (understand, imitation, mimic) emerging above Lucas loves to use. This paragraph is easy to interpret as a point in favour of neglecting causal understanding as Lucas seems to suggest the idea that 'goodness' of models does not require more than good empirical performance. Words 'mimic' and 'imitation' fail to imply causalist efforts. As a matter of fact, 'imitation' as a requirement only refers to models (built upon endogenous and exogenous variables and stochastic/random shocks) with empirically estimatable parameters (Lucas, 1980, p. 701; 1981, p. 277). In other words, as Boumans (2005, pp. 92–94) highlights, imitation as a quantitative requirement means to Lucas the imitation of real macroeconomic dynamics with descriptively simple models.

Understanding as a requisite (together with the oft-emerging words 'explain' and 'explanation'), however, appears to play on a scientific ideal of a different kind (Manicas, 2006, pp. 12–16). According to the Webster's New World Dictionary (Agnes & Guralnik, 2007), to 'understand' means to know something thoroughly, to grasp or perceive clearly and fully the nature, the character, or the functioning of a thing under scrutiny. Similarly, to 'explain' something refers to making a thing under scrutiny clear, plain, or understandable, to finding the underlying reasons. Interestingly, in his paper emphasizing 'understanding' right in its title, Lucas (1977, pp. 7–8; 1981, pp. 215–216) attributes the same ambition to both Keynes and himself. As far as the fundamental purpose of their analyses is concerned, Lucas identifies his goal with Keynes's aim: to 'understand' something, even if it is different things that they studied.[35] Mariyani-Squire (2017, p. 83), however, points out that understanding as a purpose also emerges in F53, the word thus has an extended anti-realist record. This fact undermines the impression that the understanding of a phenomenon necessarily refers to grounded and realistic causal understanding.

The superficial characteristics of Lucas's phrasing are anything but convincing. Lucas applies the words 'explain' and 'explanation' to models in the cases of which causal understanding does not emerge even as an intention.[36] Such a case is when Lucas discusses Slutzky's (1937) model where Slutzky relates some regularities of business cycles to chaotical random shocks. As Lucas puts it,

> [t]his exercise suggested a relationship between theoretical models and the observations they are constructed to explain that differed quite radically from anything previously proposed in economics. A theoretical model was to be asked not to generate statements <u>about</u> the behavior of economic agents, statements hedged with a battery of unverifiable <u>ceteris paribus</u> clauses, but simply to generate behavior, to produce an historical record sufficiently explicit to be compared in detail to historical records produced by actual economies. (Typed notes. Lucas papers. Box 13. 'Barro, Robert, 1974, 2000, undated' folder)

Sometimes the words 'rationalize' and 'rationalization' also show up (Lucas & Rapping, 1969, p. 722; Lucas, 1981, p. 20), but in this case our intuitions are even less persuasive. In a possible meaning, rationalizing a social phenomenon refers to explaining or interpreting it on rational grounds, but being aware of the real motives of actions is not a prerequisite

---

[35] See Sections 1.4.2 and 3.1.2 for more on Lucas's attitude towards Keynes.

[36] The fact that 'explanation' is a part of the basic terminology of the causally problematic RBC models (Long & Plosser, 1983, p. 41) also contributes to the confusion.

for devising plausible explanations. The term thus rather covers guess-work about possible or plausible causes of actions.

Judged by his phrasing, Lucas still seems to occasionally subscribe to more than the simple idea of good empirical performance. As Lucas (1972, pp. 103–104; 1981, p. 67) says, features of aggregate behaviour derived in an abstract framework 'bear more than a surface resemblance to many of the characteristics attributed to the U.S. economy'. Even though it is only a slight suspicion for the time being, here it may be plausible to infer the presence of causal understanding as a purpose beyond mere empirical capacity. The proper reconstruction of Lucas's phrasing in this context, however, requires a thorough analysis of the way his models connect with socio-economic reality.

4.2.2 Imitation and some underlying considerations: How to construct 'useful' analogue systems?

Assessing the results of Adelman and Adelman (1959) Lucas (1977) places a huge emphasis upon the predictive performance of mathemat-ical economic models. Empirical success in itself is insufficient, though. This effort only underlines that the path Slutzky suggested is promising (Typed notes. Lucas papers. Box 13. 'Barro, Robert, 1974, 2000, undated' folder). His discussion on the Adelmans' results makes it clearer what he meant by 'imitation'. By multi-equation macroeconometric models it was possible as early as at the end of the 1950s to mimic or imitate the cyclical-dynamic behaviour of real macroeconomies in both quantitative and qualitative terms (the length of cycles, the length of each section of a cycle, the lists of leading, coincident, and lagging variables) and this achievement established the requirements for the studies of business cycles:

> This achievement signaled a new standard for what it means to understand busi-ness cycles. One exhibits understanding of business cycles by constructing a *model* in the most literal sense: a fully articulated artificial economy which behaves through time so as to imitate closely the time series behavior of actual economi[e]s.[37] (Lucas, 1977, p. 11; 1981, p. 219)

However, on the same page (fn. 8) Lucas also draws attention to the important fact that even a polynomial may be capable of good fit. In the main text, the purpose of understanding is present again and Lucas repeatedly confronts his theory with Keynesian models. With the latter

---

[37] Excerpts from (Lucas, 1977) are reprinted from 'Stabilization of the domestic and international economy', Robert E. Lucas, 'Understanding business cycles', pp. 7–29, Copyright (1977), with permission from Elsevier.

good predictive success was also achievable, at least in the short run. These Keynesian models, however, proved to be useless when it came to assessing the expected effects of economic policy changes. As a similar failure, Keynesian models in the time of the weak predictions of the 1960–70s also suggested some improper economic policy actions on the basis of an erroneously assumed stable trade-off (Lucas & Sargent, 1979, pp. 4–6). What is more, good empirical performance is feasible even with some Sims-style time series models having no economic theory in the background (Snowdon & Vane, 2005, p. 287). Empirical success, however, is an inadequate ground for us to be satisfied with a model. As it is pointed out below, Lucas treated as a distinct problem the plausibility of the microfoundations and the resulting micro-level empirical consistency.[38] Although the Adelman-Adelman results underline that the dynamics of macroeconomies is imitable even without some descriptively accurate accounts of the structure and the functioning of real economies (Boumans, 2005, p. 93), it is still a contentious methodological issue which parts of reality, if any, one ought to preserve in minimalist descriptions. Imitation capacity when judged by predictive success is only illusory if the microfoundations underlying the conclusions are messy:

> The rapid progress of the econometric models toward something that appeared close to imitative perfection was […] illusory. Sargent and I […] have subsequently argued in some detail that useful analogue systems will not be found among variations within the class of these pioneering econometric models. (Lucas, 1980, p. 701; 1981, p. 277)

One of Lucas's beloved terms is 'analogue system' or 'analogies'. It is a highly complex expression and Lucas time and again makes efforts to provide a clear-cut definition. At the greatest length, he deals with the conceptual issues of analogue systems in his notes prepared for his subsequent paper entitled 'Adaptive behavior and economic theory' (Lucas, 1986). Lucas in these notes returns to the tension between descriptive (un) realisticness and the relevance of a model in terms of the problem under scrutiny. When resolving this puzzle, Lucas was under the influence of the related ideas of Herbert A. Simon, so these notes also offer some insights into their intellectual connection. Elsewhere Lucas (1980, p. 697; 1981, p. 292; 1986, p. S425) only provides some brief suggestions on Simon's influence on him.

---

[38] 'The problem with that statement [i.e. the appropriate criterion for establishing the fruitfulness of a theory is the degree of empirical corroboration] is that not all empirical corroborations are equal. There are some crucial things that a theory has to account for and if it doesn't we don't care how well it does on other dimensions' (Snowdon & Vane, 2005, p. 287).

Analogy regards the nature of the relationship between model and its target. It is a kind of abstraction- or idealization-based relationship[39] that makes it possible for one to draw relevant conclusions about the modelled phenomenon on the basis of the model:

> we think of theory and phenomena as being "matched" [...], but I think the nature of the match, or the relationship between theory and observation, is one of analogy [...] which I take to mean a symmetric relationship between two things. (Hand-written notes. Lucas papers. Box 27. 'Adaptive behavior, 1985–1986, 1 of 2' folder)

Models constitute a broadly conceived concept. Lucas also sorts under this label the set of so-termed 'historical models' in the case of which we gain knowledge of a real society on the basis of observing some events in another one. The only problem of historical models is that past societies used as analogies cannot be manipulated or controlled in order that the analogy could be improved or theorists could generate some unhappened events. Under these conditions it is only on the basis of some factually happened historical episodes that we can draw inferences from historical models, and these inferences are relevant only if the society to be understood and the other society used as analogy are similar enough. In Lucas's words:

> I like to think of theories – economic and [psychological], both – as simulateable systems, analogues to the actual systems we are trying to study. From this point of view, the Wharton model, say, bears the same kind of logical relationship to the United States economy as France, say, does: It is just a different economy, or system, but one that is similar enough to the U.S. economy that we might hope to learn about the properties of one through the study of the other. If our objective is to learn what the consequences of introducing a value added tax in the U.S. might be, we might study its consequences in France or simulate the Wharton system under such a tax or, better still, do both. (Typed notes. Lucas papers. Box 27. 'Adaptive behavior, 1985–1986, 1 of 2' folder)

A related problem is the construction of artificial economies as models that can help via analogies with real societies in drawing relevant

---

[39] This is the way how Lucas conceives everything becoming the model or representations of every other thing. Anything can be a model of something if the model renders it possible for us to draw meaningful inferences regarding the target of representation. As a matter of fact, anything can be the model of anything else, even if a useless model that fails to aid in drawing relevant surrogative inferences. By contrast, an analogy can make this happen. From insights assembled when using a given chair we have good reason to infer that we can replace a light bulb whilst standing on another one. What is more, the analogy supports us in extending these positive experiences to tables. When it comes to surrogative reasoning, the most important point is to have an analogy that is useful for our specific scientific problem. As Chakravartty (2010, pp. 200–204) puts it, 'any two things are similar in *some* respects', though it does not mean 'that all pairs of things stand in representational relationships.' See Section 3.4.1 on how similarity affects the problem of representations.

conclusions. The key question thus regards the nature and the establishment of analogies. Lucas, citing Herbert Simon, argues for a minimalist connection between model and reality:

> it is clearly not a serious strategy [...] to try to model any process of decision making by codifying all that is really going on. Even the most detailed "protocols" compiled by questioning decision makers [...] about their thought processes capture, and are intended to capture, only a tiny fraction of what is in fact being thought. [...]
> Any operational model of any decision making process [...] will necessarily be highly abstract – it will leave almost everything out. (Typed notes. Lucas papers. Box 27. 'Adaptive behavior, 1985–1986, 2 of 2' folder)

Here Lucas concentrates on the problem of descriptive accuracy again. Simon distinguishes the 'inner environment' of a modelled entity (in other words, the way it works) from its 'outer' or 'task environment'. In the case of a plethora of problems, modelling is feasible with placing an emphasis upon the features of the outer environment, whilst the description of the inner environment can be kept brief and sketchy (Simon, 1969/1996, p. 8). The key to this minimalist modelling habit lies in distinguishing the properties of the target to be preserved from those to be neglected.[40] When adapting Simon's framework, Lucas needed to find and choose those limited features of reality that can be represented in successful abstract systems (Hoover, 1995, pp. 35–36). Those properties can always be neglected that are inactive and irrelevant to the problem under study, whilst at a high level of abstraction and generality the set of relevant features is highly narrow. So the purpose is not to provide a meticulous and intricate description of an agent and her behaviour by preserving all her real properties but to decide 'which [features of the target] can safely be abstracted from for the set of questions at hand' (Typed notes. Lucas papers. Box 27. 'Adaptive behavior, 1985–1986, 1 of 2' folder). All the preserved and omitted properties are the real features of real entities. Even an extremely strong abstraction is realist as long as the relevant causally active properties are maintained.[41] And as the narrowest set of the active

---

[40] When interpreting Simon's related ideas, it is advisable to take into account the paper he wrote under the banner of the Cowles Commission, in which he argued for the causalist interpretation of simultaneous equations models (Simon, 1953). Simon insisted on the possibility of traditionally conceived causal analyses, taken in the everyday sense. This may serve as an important argument for distinguishing instrumentalist and realist modelling tendencies. See Section 2.2.3 for more on the causalist efforts of the Cowles Commission.

[41] Bearing in mind the fact how profound an influence Phelps exerted on Lucas (1981, pp. 6–7) as an early-stage researcher, this kind of realism (viz. descriptively minimalist realism that implies causal adequacy though) seems to be Lucas's answer to Phelps's original program. Just as a reminder, Phelps (2006) considers himself to have been one of those economists 'who wanted macroeconomic models to have lifelike actors whose expectations and beliefs were causal forces'.

properties is to be preserved whilst everything else can be ignored, this strategy makes it clear how descriptively ill-performing models can still satisfyingly perform in empirical terms and how they can support causal understanding. The modeller highlights the analyzed mechanisms from reality by preserving the relevant properties of the objects under scrutiny. In this vein, Lucas's minimalism amounts to abandoning the (truly super-fluous) purpose of descriptivism that, at the same time, does not entail the neglect of the key entity properties:

> Trying to model explicitly this entire [decision making] process, really an entire human personality, would surely be a lunatic enterprise and I do not propose to un-dertake it. (Hand-written notes. Lucas papers. Box 27. 'Adaptive behavior, 1985–1986, 1 of 2' folder)

Lucas's insistence on the reduction of descriptive capability to a min-imum when doing powerful isolation is not intended to imply the aban-donment of causally active properties. This minimal level of descriptive performance stems exactly from the fact that it is only the narrowest set of active properties that is preserved. Macroeconomics as Lucas (1977, p. 10; 1981, p. 218) envisioned ought to focus upon the 'core' factors of large-scale fluctuations: the factors that root in the most universal laws. Every analysis has their specific aspect, and this is the reason why the same actor, mechanism, or phenomenon can be analyzed from various al-beit complementary points of view (see Section 3.4.1 for more on the com-plementarity of models stemming from their partiality). Lucas keeps the possibility of causal understanding in the game even when he discusses Slutzky's model mentioned above. The atheoretical stance Slutzky (1937) took and the empirical regularities he highlighted did not undermine the-oretically underpinned causal analyses but constituted a stage on the road to this end:

> it is clear enough [...] that the ultimate aim of the enterprise was to obtain systems that could be interpreted as reflecting some economic "mechanism of causality." [...]
> I take one of the points of the paper to be that it is possible to consider the mechan-ics of business cycles – the issue of the kind of mathematical structure one wants to cast theoretical ideas in – separately from the substance of business cycles – the eco-nomic interpretation one wants to place on "shocks" to the system and the behavior that underlies the way the system responds. This separation cannot be exactly right [...] but if it is approximately right, it is a useful idea, for it enables us to think through the positive and normative objectives of the theory at a relatively early stage, and in a relatively neutral way ideologically. (Typed notes. Lucas papers. Box 13. 'Barro, Robert, 1974, 2000, undated' folder)

The term 'substance' Lucas mentions in these notes refers to a twofold world view in which beyond form there exists a substance to be placed into the form via theoretical interpretations. However, it is causal under-standing that renders this substance accessible. Having knowledge of the substance, or at least the desire or intention to have it, implies our ability to tell why (i.e. along what mechanisms) business cycles emerge. Theoretical debates over Lucasian economics have been about this substance, as clearly highlighted by the following letter:

> I don't like the island abstraction [...]. You have not convinced me that informationally distinct markets which imply tricking are the essence of modern business cycles. In the past when there was less information I suspect this effect was more important.[42] (Edward C. Prescott's letter to Lucas. September 14, 1974. Lucas Papers. Box 13. 'An equilibrium model of the business cycle, 1974' folder)

The ultimate task of theoretical economics is to construct artificial-abstract economies the characteristics of which are established in order that these models, in spite of their artificiality, could be practically relevant. Practical relevance means that such models can possibly help us to assess the effects of policy or other changes, and the conclusions can be projected to real economies. On the basis of models and surrogative reasoning, we can learn about the target, and to make it possible, analogies between a model economy and its real counterpart are to be carefully established. An analogy is thus a theoretically exploitable connection between model and reality. Such a connection, however, ought not to be taken for granted. Its establishment is a complex act, the connection itself requires a separate analysis and 'it requires no more than [a] superficial thought to recognize that there can be no simple connection between what appears on the scratch pads of professional economists [...] and important conclusions about the way our society ought to operate'. (Typed notes. Lucas papers. Box 13. 'Directions of macroeconomics, 1979' folder) This connection as the basis of analogy rests upon isolation thanks to which a model highlights certain mechanisms only, whilst it is uninformative about the neglected facets of reality (Lucas, 1987, p. 50). There exist some entities, relations, and actions that have no counterparts in the model. Via isolation, however, it is possible to build simple artificial economies still bearing resemblance to real societies in the relevant aspects:

> Economic theory, like anthropology, "works" by studying societies which are in some relevant sense simpler or more primitive than our own, in the hope either that relationships which are important but hidden in our society will be laid bare in simpler ones, or that concrete evidence can be discovered for possibilities which are open

---

[42] Barro (1989, p. 6) criticized new classicals on similar grounds. If uncertainty over monetary aggregates and price level dynamics were really as crucial as Lucas assumed, it would be easy for the agents to have relevant information in adequate quantity and quality. This is not a well-posed critique. Lucas has never claimed that complete information is impossible to collect but emphasized the circumstance that agents may not have enough time to assemble all the necessary information before making decisions and this incompleteness contribute to the emergence of business cycles.

to us which are without precedent in our own history. Unlike anthropologists, however, economists simply invent the primitive societies we study [...]. (Typed notes. Lucas papers. Box 13. 'Directions of macroeconomics, 1979' folder)

Lucas (1987, p. 63) applies the words 'resemble' and 'resemblance' in this sense. What a model displays is similar to what we can observe in reality, though in a simplified form so much as that some meaningful analyses could be performed on the model with a view to understanding reality. This is exactly the sense how surrogative reasoning was described in Chapter 3.

Highlighting some relevant connections in a society taken as a structure catapults us far away from the causally instrumentalist attitude of F53 where even the (completely implausible) rationality of leaves might go as an entity-level assumption. For Lucas, there were some enigmatic details in the functioning of macroeconomies that had been waiting for him to come into play and that proved to be understandable only by his reductions to a choice-theoretic framework. However, this means that even the closest mimicking of macroeconomic dynamics (whilst neglecting causal understanding) is something different than understanding. As a consequence, good predictions in themselves fail to ensure the Lucasian way of understanding. It is again the case where the road to understanding leads through predictive success and good fit is a sign of successful efforts to understand, whilst models must meet some qualitative requirements as well. Referring to Lucas and Sargent's (1979) interpretation on useful analogue systems (Lucas, 1980, p. 701; 1981, p. 277), this qualitative requirement regards the microfoundations and the methodology of laying them down. But for this emphasis it is only possible to design useless analogue systems at best.

The way Lucas extends the use of models is also worthy of note. The higher number of simple problems a model offers answers to, the more trust we can have in it when addressing more complicated problems. But for successful causal understanding and realism in the relevant aspects, however, this desire would remain unjustified (Hausman, 1992, p. 168). Thus, on this showing, Lucas's ambitions may still prove to be excessive as the intention of extending the application of models does not necessarily imply some adequate grounds for it. What has he done to have a basis for this extension?

4.2.3 The information structure underlying the island models of 1972–75

As Lucas regards descriptive realism as something to avoid, the realism of Lucas's immensely abstract models cannot be judged by the realisticness of the framework taken at face value. Accordingly, in his first island model

(Lucas, 1972) the basic scheme is highly esoteric. In every period N identical agents are born on two separated islands. Their life is two-period long; thus population is always of $2N$. In the first period of life, agents act as producers (the young), whilst in the second, they consume the products of the next young generation (the elderly). Elderly people are always distributed across the islands evenly. Supra-islands government pays transfers to the elderly they spend on consumption; thus total monetary demand is also distributed evenly. Pre-transfer money stock in per capita terms (m) is known. Post-transfer money stock (m') is driven by random variable x as

$$m' = mx \qquad (4.1)$$

Agents rely upon prices when making guesswork on post-transfer money stock. The distribution of the young is stochastic. Accordingly, proportions $\theta/2$ and $1-\theta/2$ go to the islands, respectively, so that $0<\theta<2$ and the density function of θ is symmetric. Both the dynamics of the money stock and the allocation of the members of the young generation are driven by stochastic variables only the density functions of which are known. In each period three variables (m, x and θ) sufficiently describe the state of the economy. Neither information flow nor trade is allowed between the islands.

The model precisely specifies the information set each agent possesses. This way it avoids the problem of incomplete information emerging in the form Friedman so awkwardly addressed. A benefit of the information background Lucas postulated is its ability to aid in distinguishing long-term and perfectly informed decisions from short-run decisions based on incomplete information (Lucas, 1976a/1981, p. 92). Neither the present nor the future is known to the agents (Lucas, 1975, p. 1113; 1981, pp. 179–180). Assumptions define the incompleteness of information in a consistent way.[43] There are two shocks working simultaneously in the system, but agents can get a line on them on the basis of prices only. As a consequence, they are unable to distinguish the nominal effects of changes in the money stock and real effects of relative changes in supply and demand. Expectations of future prices are precise though not necessarily correct. Rational agents when making decisions rely upon relative prices only, though they act in a setting where relative and absolute price changes cannot be distinguished (Lucas, 1973, p. 327; 1981, p. 133). On the

---

[43] Lucas's (1975, p. 1138; 1981, pp. 205–206) assumed information structure is a middle-ground solution between Friedman's adaptive scheme (that wastes too much knowledge and applies a messy way of neglecting some forms of information) and the equally unrealistic assumption of perfect knowledge which is similarly unfruitful as for the understanding of business cycles. This purpose required the avoidance of both extremities. By postulating perfect knowledge Lucas was unable to derive cyclical fluctuations. His suggestion was to introduce rational expectations based upon incomplete information.

one extreme, in case of a pure real shock, when there is no confusion, the observed market price is a clear sign of the change in supply and demand conditions, whilst, on the other, money proves to be neutral in case of a pure monetary shock. As agents have only inadequate information on the whole system, they cannot but have a mixed strategy and respond with some real adjustments even to a nominal shock (Lucas, 1972, pp. 104–114; 1981, pp. 67–77). Only with some limitations can monetary policy exploit such nominal shocks to stimulate the real economy as rational agents experiencing nominal surprises start expecting systematic efforts.

As we have seen in Section 2.3.2, Sargent and Wallace (1975) introduced an error term that has an effect on macro-system dynamics independently of the public's inflation expectations. Equilibrium in that framework is not guaranteed even if expectations are correct. For Lucasian islanders, monetary policy is the only source of aggregate-level shocks. If unanticipated monetary shocks do not confuse the agents, production on each island instantly adjusts to the stable (i.e. constant or constantly growing nominal) demand. This mechanism offered itself to be tested empirically as '[t]his theory implies that the existence of a trade-off between output and inflation is conditional on economic agents misinterpreting the price movements they see. Hence, we should expect countries with widely fluctuating exogenous shocks to have a more vertical Phillips Curve than others, because their inhabitants want to react only to <u>real</u> changes in variables, and tend to improve the instrumental they use to differentiate between real and nominal changes'. (Jose L. Alberro: The Lucas hypothesis on the Phillips curve. Some further international evidence. Paper presented in the 'Money and banking' workshop, May 4, 1976. Lucas papers. Box 14. 'Output inflation tradeoffs, 1973' folder) See also Alberro (1981).

Given that monetary policy may make attempts to exert systematic stimulative shocks to the economy, an agent faces a decision problem in which she must decide whether the change in prices she has experienced stems from a nominal or a real shock and act accordingly. This dilemma is simple at the end of the day. Any agent wants to avoid both mistakenly responding to a purely nominal shock and mistakenly not responding to a meaningful real signal (Lucas, 1975, p. 1140; 1981, p. 208). This mechanism leads to the short-run non-neutrality and the long-run neutrality of money. Lucas built the model upon the (successfully preserved) characteristic of real agents always acting on their own, separated markets that they only have incomplete information on aggregate-level dynamics and that observing their local markets offers no effective remedy to this information deficiency. It is the connections with reality, put forward as a representational code, that make it possible for Lucas (1972, p. 122; 1981, p. 84) to conclude: 'the Phillips curve emerges not as an unexplained empirical fact, but as a central feature of the solution to a general equilibrium system'. His model was aimed at explaining the

Phillips curve, conceived as one of the key features of observed business cycles, as a joint consequence of shocks and optimization failed due to information problems.

His 1975 island model (Lucas, 1975) the same precisely defines information deficiencies. It still holds that each agent can only observe the market price of her own market when making inferences (i.e. forming expectations) on aggregate changes. Money stock dynamics at the aggregate level (m_t) is governed by the log-linear difference equation

$$m_{t+1} = m_t + x_t. \tag{4.2}$$

Market z receives only a proportion of the growth in the quantity of money as described by another difference equation:

$$\theta_t(z) = \rho \cdot \theta_{t-1}(z) + \epsilon_t(z), \tag{4.3}$$

where $x_t \sim N(\mu; \sigma^2)$ and $\epsilon_t(z) \sim N(0; \sigma_\epsilon^2)$. Agents do not have knowledge of shocks $\epsilon_t(z)$, $\theta_t(z)$ and x_t. The state of macro is described by capital stock k_t, money m_t and nominal government spending x_t. The situation of any market z is characterized by $u_t(z) = k_t(z) - k_t$ as its local difference from aggregate (i.e. average) capital stock and its $\theta_t(z)$ share in the growth of money. As agents wander from market to market with time, they can directly observe none of these variables. Lucas specified in a mathematically tractable way the informationally deficient setting; thus agents are not assumed to neglect some widely known facts in order that a presumed mechanism could be triggered. An agent can only observe the prices of the markets she has visited, so a price history $p_t(z)$, $p_{t-1}(z')$, $p_{t-2}(z'')$, ... emerges to her. When it comes to forming expectations on future prices, each market participant infers the state of both the macroeconomy and her local market from the price series she has registered. Agents have expectations about the economy as a whole ($\hat{k}_t$ and $\hat{m}_t$) and about both the return on capital and the return on money.[44] Households want to hold two kinds of assets: money and capital, and the demands for them are dependent upon their expected returns. The return on money is the expected deflation rate, conceived as the difference between observed current price on market z and the general price level expected for the next period. The return on capital is the expected real rental price. Lucas relates the latter to prices. Nominal rental price on market z is proportional to the local price, though this rental price is to be deflated by the expected general price level as capital income is likely to be spent on another market. In other words, market

---

[44] At this point Lucas for tractability reasons assumed that these estimates are pooled among traders, so the average values describe all agents' expectations. Lucas was highly dissatisfied with this solution and regarded it as temporary only (Lucas's letter to Edi Karni. October 18, 1976. Lucas papers. Box 3. '1976, 1 of 2' folder).

participants calculate the expected real return on capital on the basis of the local price and the general price level, both expected for the next period. As the distinction between nominal and real shocks holds, conclusions change according to the nature of shocks.

Agents respond to the changes in expected returns and think that current relative demands on local markets well indicate these changes in returns and that current price movements are informative about current relative demands. If agents react to a positive monetary shock with increasing their productive capacities, the new level of capital higher than previously does not allow the price level to adjust to the new stock of money. Expectations about aggregate variables only slowly adjust to the shock: perceptions of capital and money gradually converge to their true values. In sum, Lucas built a structure in which the largest impact does not emerge in the beginning, right after the shock. Such a case was suspicious to him as sharply inconsistent with the observed features of business cycles.

The archetypes of islanders trying to optimize in an informationally deficient framework are the workers in the Lucas-Rapping models. There the key problem regarded the relationship between labour supply and real wage dynamics as labour supply was conceived as responding to changes in real wage. This basic relationship following from the more general decision problem of households between consumption and leisure time works through multiple mechanisms. The postulated decision problem is complex as it rests upon considerations not only about current but also about expected prices. Current labour supply is dependent upon wage expectations as well. If a drop in wage a worker has experienced seems to be temporary only, she cuts down her labour supply, whilst if it is expected to be permanent, she changes her job. Accordingly, Lucas and Rapping trace the utility of the representative household to four variables: current consumption, current labour supply, future consumption and future labour supply (Lucas & Rapping, 1969, pp. 726–727; Lucas, 1981, p. 24). The household's dilemma bears close similarity to the decision problem of the subsequent Lucasian islanders. An unemployed individual is unaware of her current wage rate and her best bet to find this out is to start seeking job. A job seeker is ready to lower her wage demands (she moves or changes her profession, etc.), but only when she recognizes that her normal wage rate is below the level she expected. As information is incompletely available and expensive to collect and as acting according to information (moving or training) is also costly and requires excessive investment, labour supply only slowly changes (Lucas & Rapping, 1969, pp. 735–736; Lucas, 1981, pp. 30–31). Empirical results effectively confirmed that households were slow to revise their expectations (Lucas & Rapping, 1972, p. 189; Lucas, 1981, pp. 62–63). As far as the supply decision is concerned, the ambiguity of information, as in the subsequent island models, is of crucial importance. Any agent faces a problem she must solve having no adequate aggregate-level information.

4.2.4 Constructing descriptively false assumptions with a view to sound causal understanding

The next step for us to take is to delineate the points that reveal Lucas's insistence on causal understanding carried out via descriptively false assumptions.

The paper having put forward the Lucas critique (Lucas, 1976b/1981) is not usually mentioned as a methodological piece, even if it appropriately highlights the details of Lucas's strategy of applying descriptively false models to understand reality. The bulk of the paper is devoted to a technical description of the then conventional econometric practice. In this context Lucas argues that the widely used econometric models perform well only in short-run forecasting and that this short-term predictive success by no means underpins an ability to assess alternative economic policies. Policy evaluation rests upon simulations intended to show some macroeconomic consequences of changes in policy-controlled variables. However, as Lucas argues, economic policy interventions alter the overall structure of the economy; thus it is impossible to estimate how an economy would behave under alternative and hypothetical policies. Accordingly, he understood the conventional econometric practice as built upon an incautious presumption only. In contrast with the widely held opinion, it is irrational to expect the forms and parameters of functions not to change systematically with policy changes (Lucas, 1976b/1981, pp. 105–110). To be more specific, under alternative policies it is not the same economy that operates in different ways, but the economy itself changes according to the policies. Traditional econometric models with unchanging parameters cannot but miss the target.

Lucas suggests a couple of examples to demonstrate his point. Turning to the Phillips curve, he applies his 'standard' island model with rational agents, separated markets showing up as islands and the only signal informing about two kinds of shocks. Effects of a policy change can be forecast only if agents in advance know the key parameters describing the new policy. In cases where this assumption does not hold, changes in agents' behaviour will inevitably take place, which are unpredictable if the modellers expect this behaviour to remain settled (Lucas, 1976b/1981, p. 123).

A major originality of the paper, however, is how Lucas extends his theoretical conclusions to the behaviour of real agents. Here we can see a two-direction epistemological play in action, portrayed in Section 3.4.1 as a general case, going on in front of our eyes as Lucas demonstrates the unpredictability of real macro-dynamics with some theoretical considerations from which he thus jumps back to socio-economic reality. All the conclusions drawn from the models thus apply to real circumstances, which would be impossible with no representational relationship between theoretical assumptions and real entity properties. Rational and optimizing theoretical agents adjust to policy changes and modify their behaviour accordingly. Lucas uses this conclusion to draw another inference regarding the conventional econometric models about real-world behaviour, and this inference is the same in both settings (model and reality). In Lucas's parlance: 'given that [...] optimal decision rules vary systematically with changes in the structure of series relevant to the decision maker, it follows that any change in policy will systematically alter the structure of econometric models' (Lucas, 1976b/1981, p. 126). Real economic agents are expected to respond to changes in direction of economic policy through changing their behaviour. This second step (i.e. the extension of a theoretical conclusion to reality) would be infeasible without a first step taken on the soil of reality to theorize from real-world properties. This is the link connecting model with reality and this is the kind of realism Hausman (1992) regards as a prerequisite for meaningful extensions.

Theoretical assumptions in Lucas's models are possible to turn into descriptions of socio-economic reality. Employment in any segment of the labour market is dependent upon the demand for the related consumer goods and upon the overall state of the economy. The complementing part is responsible, first, for absorbing the unemployed from the given section and, second, for fuelling it with labour force through a two-direction flow of employees. An employee either works or not. If the latter, as unemployed she starts a search process to find a job in one of the complementing parts of the economy. This realistic description is the summary of how Lucas and Prescott (1974, pp. 190–191; Lucas, 1981, pp. 158–159) formalized the labour market. All the island models are also translatable into everyday parlance. On some occasions Lucas explicitly provides the readers with the purpose of his extreme isolations. It is nothing more than modelling in a mathematically tractable way the fact that the environment of agents is changeable, and they are thus unable to assemble the necessary information for a more careful and grounded decision making process (Lucas, 1975, pp. 1120–1122; 1981, pp. 186–188). The purpose of the models is to clarify whether this information deficiency contributes to the emergence of large-scale fluctuations. It is a similar instance when in a draft model Lucas assumed that 'each household's marginal utility for total consumption fluctuates in an unpredictable way'. Even though this presumption may seem bizarre at first sight, it is only 'intended to capture unpredictably varying "tastes", due for example, to unforeseeable medical needs or [...] to the unexpected discovery of a particularly attractive item'. (Typed notes. Lucas papers. Box 23. 'Money, 1975–1977, 2 of 2' folder) As another instructive case:

> The model sounds a little silly, but that is the way economic models are when you take them seriously, and we will see that it fits certain aspects of reality.
>
> Let's think of an economy where the same good is produced everywhere, but traded in a whole lot of markets, which are separated.
>
> Each market has a demand curve, and that demand curve is shifted by an aggregate shock, which I am going to take to be the percentage rate of change in nominal income, which affects all markets equally, and each market is also affected with a relative shock, based on shifting tastes and technologies, which differs from market to market, and which averages to zero over markets.
>
> So that is demand.
>
> Suppliers in each of these markets would like to respond to [...] relative prices. If their market is good this year, they would like to produce more. If it is bad, they would like to cut back. But they can't directly observe relative prices so they respond to perceive[d] relative prices.
>
> And to get at these perceptions, they go through some calculations which are rational. That is to say, they are utilizing their limited information in an optimum way. [...]
>
> One, people are fooled by demand movements, aggregate movements; and, two, people's decision rules are a little bit off because they have got to hedge. They don't respond as much as they should to true relative price movements because they have to hedge against the possibility that the price movements, that they are faced with, are, in fact, only nominal. (The phenomenon of worldwide inflation.[45] Transcript of a tape recording. Lucas papers. Box 2. '1974, 2 of 2' folder)

An exchange of letters with Costas Azariadis in the autumn of 1976 also reveals a lot about the connection Lucas has built between model and reality and about the representational code through which he translates elements of socio-economic reality into a formal-abstract language. In his letter of October 19, Azariadis objects to the technical particular of the island metaphor how Lucas randomly allocates producers across the markets. For Azariadis, it is nonsense to assume an agent located on a market with favourable demand conditions to be ready to leave. Instead of the spatial dimension, Azariadis offers the distribution of demand over time. In his reply Lucas defends the metaphor by providing the representational

---

[45] Lucas gave this talk in Washington on May 7, 1974 upon the invitation from the American Enterprise Institute for Public Policy Research. Lucas launched his speech with a short introduction infused with his usual sarcasm: 'In preparing, I made two guesses, and both turned out to be wrong. The first was that Ed Phelps was going to talk about [the] social costs of inflation, which he can certainly do, but chose not to. The second guess was that we would have a blackboard. So let me go ahead and discuss what I would have written on the blackboard if Ed Phelps had talked about the social costs of inflation'.

code that clarifies which part of reality is referred to by an element of the formal structure:

> One has to take my spatial set-up metaphorically or it is crazy. By "forcing" people to leave good markets, I just wanted to capture the fact (which I think is obviously present in reality) that there are transitory demand and supply shifts. (Lucas's letter to Costas Azariadis. October 25, 1976. Lucas papers. Box 3. '1976, 1 of 2' folder)

At the same time, this is a far cry from merging model and reality into each other, the alleged misstep Weeks (1989, pp. 130–131) regards as the original sin of new classicals. A sharp distinction between model and reality still holds. This, however, does not imply the lack of an epistemological-ontological-representational relationship between the two sides, a connection that places Lucas's models among Mäki's (2009b) surrogate systems. By analyzing the models, we can gain causal knowledge of reality. At the same time, this excerpt is also an instructive example for how to theorize about reality via postulating some inexistent (i.e. idealized) features in models. Here Lucas explicitly refers to some real properties of agents through a setting which cannot be found in socio-economic reality (see Section 3.4.1 for more on the use of abstraction and idealization in representing structures).

This connection of models with socio-economic reality remains preserved. Quantitative assessment of alternative policies requires us to imagine how the concerned agents would behave in some yet unobserved situations, that is, under new economic policies. To this end, it is indispensable to understand agents' past decisions and to assess how a certain change in economic policy would affect the decision rules they apply (Lucas, 1975, pp. 1113–1114; 1981, pp. 179–180). In a letter Lucas dwells upon the reasons why rationality is a good assumption in cases where the changes of decision rules are to be understood. Replying to Shiller and commenting on his forthcoming review (Shiller, 1984), Lucas turns back to Muth:

> You have got to be right [...] that "most individuals behave in accordance with simple rules of thumb which are only rarely reevaluated."[46] It has always intrigued me that Muth hit on his formulation at Carnegie Tech at the time when "behavioral" economics was at [its] peak there. In the introduction to his original paper, Muth [...] insists that his hypothesis does not assert that rationality characterizes the "scratch work of entrepreneurs." Whatever may be said of his successors, I think it is crystal clear that Muth was trying to push "rationality" to an extreme not in naive ignorance of parallel behavioral work, but in full knowledge of it, at the then current center of behavioral work in economics.

---

[46] The quoted sentence is on p. 121 of the published review.

Muth was right I think, that what promise economic theory offers is precisely guidance as to what will happen at those [rare] points at which people are compelled by events to reevaluate the rules of thumb they use. At such points, the kind of codified rules of thumb psychologists record are useless. Your point that economics is bad psychology is well taken but it does not follow that psychology is good economics. (Lucas's letter to Robert J. Shiller. February 16, 1983. Lucas papers. Box 5, '1983, 2 of 2' folder)

The rationality postulate is not a descriptive category, but still, assuming efforts towards rational behaviour aids in understanding how agents make decisions in cases where their routine procedures turn out to be useless. Here it is of real economic agents that Lucas is talking all along. Lucas highlights that in contrast with the behaviourist tendencies aimed at studying the actions of real-world agents, economists' rationality postulate provides an effective alternative when it comes to understanding the behaviour real agents show under some special conditions. It is admittedly true that under normal circumstances human behaviour rests upon a lot of non-rational automatisms (Kahneman, 2011), but if such normal conditions fail to apply for one reason or another, such as an economic policy intervention, we need to admit, first, the need for new decision rules and, second, the fact that agents will not form these new rules on the basis of the old set. In a case like this, knowledge of the abandoned rules is of no help. As Lucas argues, agents in such problematic situations devote their cognitive resources to interpreting the setting and to the proper adjustment of their behaviour—plainly put, to adaptation, which is in close concert with some results of experimental economics (Caginalp, McCabe, & Porter, 2003; Smith, Suchanek, & Williams, 1988).

An assumption not aimed at achieving descriptive purposes thus sheds light on the real causal mechanisms of phenomena. The subtle relationship between descriptive accuracy and causal adequacy explicitly occurs in the texts. In an island paper Lucas puts forward the idea that

The introduction of separate, informationally distinct markets is not a step toward "realism" or (obviously) "elegance" but, rather, an analytical departure which appears essential (in some form) to an explanation of the way in which business cycles can arise and persist in a competitive economy. (Lucas, 1975, p. 1132; 1981, p. 199)

Here Lucas rejects realism taken in the descriptivist sense. Following the age-old traditions, when setting up a model that is intended to produce fluctuations similar to some dynamic features of business cycles he does not strive towards models to precisely or even closely describe reality in its entirety. At the same time, his remonstrance also highlights that the island model framework, in contrast with a Friedmanian centralized market, populated by rationally optimizing and ill-informed agents can easily be regarded as a step towards descriptive realism.[47] As we have seen above, this statement of not pushing descriptive realism by no means implies the abandonment of causal adequacy. The case of Weber's social scientific methodology effectively highlighted that Friedman was not compelled to give up the adherence to causal adequacy on the basis of his descriptively inaccurate assumptions: a problem that deserves further scrutiny in Lucas's case. As a matter of fact, so far there have been no signs of his turning away from sound causal understanding. However, to conclude the argumentation, there is a last step to take: we need to line up some excerpts where Lucas explicitly argues for causal understanding and the application of real entity properties.

4.2.5 Microfoundations to connect analogue systems with reality

Lucas provides the most careful discussion on the connections between model and reality in one of his most powerful methodological works (Lucas, 1977). The highly complex and instructive paper is an effort to clarify how macroeconomics in line with observable facts ought to be placed upon microeconomics in line with observable facts. In this context, Lucas has made some explicit statements to identify those parts of his model that have real counterparts and that deserve realist commitments.

For Lucas (1987, p. 20), the road to the understanding of aggregate-level phenomena leads through the understanding of individual decisions. It is the Lucas critique that underlies this idea. As we cannot expect individual behaviour to remain the same after a change in economic policy or in

---

[47] Sometimes Friedman (1949, pp. 490–491; 1952, p. 2) also mentions Walrasian general equilibrium analysis as a step towards the realism of assumptions and as an opportunity to overcome the ceteris paribus clauses extensively used in Marshallian partial analyses. A complex approach to the economy renders it unnecessary to highlight too narrow a slice of reality. Friedman kept conceiving Walrasian economics as a negative case, since descriptive realisticness of assumptions entices theorists to carry out the defective test of judging the adequacy of models on this ground. Friedman consistently rejected this procedure and placed emphasis upon empirical tests instead. What is more, Friedman also touched upon the efforts not to follow where theorists describe agents in models by using surveys and other empirical results, as, again, the realisticness of assumptions is an insufficient ground for theory assessment. As it is argued in Section 4.2.5, the application of realistic presumptions gained from this survey strategy constitutes one of the key features of Lucas's approach. Elsewhere Friedman (1946b) objects to the arbitrary character of judgements about realisticness.

any parts of the setting, forecasting macroeconomic dynamics ought not to rest upon models that postulate fix decision rules. As Lucas says,

> agents' *decision rules will* in general change with changes in the environment. An equilibrium model is, by definition, constructed so as to predict how agents with stable tastes and technology will *choose* to respond to a new situation. Any disequilibrium model, constructed by simply codifying the decision rules which agents have found it useful to use over some previous sample period, without explaining *why* these rules were used, will be of no use in predicting the consequences of nontrivial policy changes. (Lucas, 1977, p. 12; 1981, pp. 220–221)

Lucas sees the chance for improvement in interpreting macro-dynamics as a consequence of individual optimizing responses to price changes. To this end, the prototypical modelling of decision making is indispensable. As Lucas goes on:

> with uncertainty, he [i.e. the typical agent] must draw up a contingency plan, saying how he will react to unforeseeable events.
> [...] [O]ne needs to imagine a fairly precise view of the future in the mind of this agent. Where does he get this view, and how can an observer infer what it is? [...] [I]t is absolutely crucial for understanding business cycles [...]. (Lucas, 1977, p. 14; 1981, p. 223)

Elsewhere Lucas also highlights the principle of economic model building according to which theorists ought to set up artificial economies in order to decide which parameters they can justifiably regard as stable:

> Empirical business cycle theory can be thought of as directed at the following problem. Given a collection of broadly representative economic time series yt [...], one would like to be able to decompose the series into an intelligible part xt and an unintelligible part ut (that is, $yt = xt + ut$). By <u>intelligible</u>, I mean parametrically describable in a way in which parameters have a clear enough economic meaning that estimates of them may be compared to evidence from other sources, and that one may arrive at some judgement as to their invariance under interesting variations of economic policy. In practice, this means that xt is accounted for either by characteristics of tastes and technology or, at an opposite extreme, by entirely unsystematic ("white") disturbances. By unintelligible, I mean the rest, but with the understanding that "the rest" be not worth bothering about, due either to quantitative unimportance or to an evident futility of efforts to account for it.[48] (Typed notes. Lucas papers. Box 13. 'Linear economy, undated' folder)

The foundations of Keynesian economics are of dubious value for Keynesians place future economic policy actions upon some statistical inferences drawn from past statistical data, whilst they expect the future

---

[48] These notes were prepared for a paper the applied part of which was based on U.S. quarterly data from the period 1947–72, thus the notes are from the early post-1972 years.

to be exactly like the past. The latter, however, is only an ungrounded assumption:

> Keynesian economics – at least in its analytically explicit and operative Tinbergenian variant, which is the form that interests me – offered a way to go from a set of sample moments (variances, covariances, autocovariances – the whole multivariate world) to policy options available to society – "trade-offs". [...] We observe that government spending and unemployment have been negatively correlated in the past (think of WW's I and II). We use this correlation to estimate the change in unemployment to be expected from an increase in government expenditure in the future. That's all there is to the multiplier – there is nothing deeper. [...]
>
> Difficulty is this: no reason to believe that correlations exhibited in past data will continue to obtain under new policies. Old correlations may contain no useful information on future trade-offs. I say "may" but situation is worse than this: now [we] know that multipliers for aggregate monetary, fiscal policy are useless. (Hand-written notes. Lucas papers. Box 13. 'Lectures notes, 1979–80' folder)

The answers are to be found in the individual's optimizing behaviour and this is the reason why macroeconomic phenomena are to be traced back to individuals and their properties. This leads us back to the central tenet of the microfoundations project. It is worthy of note, however, that Lucas suggests the precise understanding of the individual's decision problem. Accordingly, Lucas does not regard this problem and the related choice-theoretic framework as an instrumentalist basis leading to models that satisfyingly mimic some observed facts. By contrast, Lucas conceived the understanding of business cycles as an act of understanding to complete through nurturing in-depth familiarity with the way individuals make their decisions:

> To practice economics, we need *some* way [...] of understanding *which* decision problem agents are solving. (Lucas, 1977, p. 15; 1981, p. 223)

Having finished with this, Lucas turns to the minutiae of individuals' decision problem, and this is the point where he establishes the connection with real agents. Microfoundations are of crucial importance as they are the key to successful surrogative reasoning, i.e. to drawing sound causal inferences regarding reality. Lucas making some laudatory remarks on John J. McCall's (1970) labour market theory clarifies that the purpose of his microfoundations project is the understanding of individual behaviour:

> we are *thinking* about unemployment, really thinking about what it is like to be unemployed in ways that fix-price and other macroeconomic-level unemployment theories can never lead us to do. Questioning a McCall worker is like having a conversation with an out-of-work friend: 'Maybe you are setting your sights too high', or 'Why did you quit your old job before you had a new one lined up?' This is real social science: an attempt to model, to *understand*, human behavior by visualizing the situations people find themselves in, the options they face and the pros and cons as they themselves see them. (Lucas, 1987, p. 57)

Even though Lucas at this time was working in the RBC framework of Kydland and Prescott and studied the dynamics of the system with money (Lucas, 1987, p. 85), the role he intended the microfoundations to play in understanding remained the same.

It is also to micro-level behavioural patterns that Lucas traces macro-level dynamics in the island models of the 1970s. The basic question regards the response to price changes. If an agent experiences a rise in the price of his product and if he expects this rise to be long-lasting, 'we know from much evidence that he will work no harder, and probably a little less hard'. This describes the expected long-term reaction, as on this time horizon the wage elasticity of labour supply is about zero (Lucas, 1977, p. 16; 1981, p. 225). By contrast, if the change in price is transitory, the worker responds on the basis of the rate of substitutability between work today and work tomorrow. If leisure time is highly substitutable over time, the worker or producer works more on high-price days. Lucas referring to his own previous results (Lucas & Rapping, 1969) underlines that a highly elastic response is expected to be given to transitory price changes. However, the key part of Lucas's discussion here is his emphasis upon the consonance with reality. Significant supply reactions to small price changes are typical of observed business cycles (Lucas, 1977, p. 17; 1981, p. 225).

Lucas's micro-level assumptions are thus not of arbitrary character. He argued for micro-level assumptions hypothesized in line with observations and microeconomics in order that sound macro-level understanding could be accomplished. By so doing, he intended to build his models upon the strong form of microfoundations, which is a more restrictive requirement than mere theoretical consistency or the absence of inconsistencies with microeconomics (Faust, 2009, p. 53; Chari, Kehoe, & McGrattan, 2009). This was a great opportunity for him to criticize Keynes, since Lucas regarded him as one discussing involuntary unemployment as if the concept had stemmed from observations. On this showing, disequilibrium or rigid prices are no more than some unjustified presumptions as their connection with reality is unclarified (Lucas, 1977, p. 12; 1981, p. 220). For Lucas the proper way of concept formation rests upon observation and hence reality. The key to good macroeconomics is the understanding of the individual making decisions. All aggregate-level consequences are to be derived from these individual patterns of behaviour well-documented by censuses, panels, and surveys.[49] If we want to understand the reactions of the macroeconomy,

---

[49] Lucas (1987, p. 102) traces the idea of real fluctuations stemming from the misinterpretation of price signals back even to Hume.

we need to understand the reactions of the individuals.[50] By placing the agents into the well-specified setting of market conceived as a transmission mechanism, we can infer the macro-level outcomes from individual reactions and interactions, and consequently group behaviour becomes predictable which leads to good 'mimic' at the aggregate level (Lucas, 1980, pp. 709–712; 1981, pp. 288–291). With these considerations Lucas also responds to Sims's (1982) objections in advance, who argued that the assessment of the effects of policy changes on individual decisions and the according modification of the equations were based upon some speculations of dubious value (see Section 2.2.4 on the Lucas-Sims debate as a chapter in the Marshall–Walras divide).

If we browse the archives again, some notes are available where Lucas emphasizes the reduction of macro-level phenomena to the microfoundations and the exact nature of these microfoundations:

> What would it mean to <u>explain</u> [the Great Depression]? Surely not simply to fit some formula to [the dramatic decline in goods and services produced] and other facts. [...] What we <u>do</u> mean by an explanation of a unique event like the Depression is, I think, an account of how these summary figures could have been generated by a combination of individual decisions, decisions arrived at in a way that is consistent with other evidence we have about economic decision making, and perhaps unique external events or "shocks". We need, in other words, to try to see the Depression from the inside out, not to <u>label</u> the behavior the term "depression" summarizes but to be able to <u>reproduce</u> it as an intelligible response chosen by people as intelligent and informed (but not more so) as we are, to the situations they found themselves in. (Typed notes. Lucas papers. Box 13. 'Barro, Robert, 1974, 2000, undated' folder)

Now Lucas turns his attention to real economic agents' labour supply decision which he thinks is crucial in understanding business cycles. In order to understand large-scale fluctuations, it is indispensable to understand this decision problem through which an individual determines how much time to allocate to working in jobs in return for income. To this end, we need to be aware of the decision tendencies of employees, and here Lucas clearly focuses upon the preferences of real workers. All the behavioural tendencies he highlights come from observations. Such a case is the fact that, as Lucas says, rich people tend to work less hard:

> We know, in the first place, that the wealthier people are the less hard they work. This can be seen by comparing rich to poor societies, the U.S. today, say, versus the

---

[50] This observation-based understanding of individual behaviour was also a constituent part of the practice of the Cowles Commission. Roy J. Epstein (1987, pp. 101–102) reports the problems the Cowles staff faced when they were unable to decide upon some rival theories on the basis of estimations (see Section 2.2.3). The staff identified as a possible way out the method in which econometricians intended to size up the motivations and actions of real economic agents via close observations, interviews and surveys.

U.S. a century ago or versus India today. People in rich societies enter the workforce later in life, retire earlier, take longer and more frequent vacations, and work shorter weeks [than] people in poor countries. Those with large non-labor incomes work less than others in the same society with lower income from capital. Leisure – defined broadly to include all activities other than working for pay – is a normal good. (Typed notes. Lucas papers. Box 13. 'Barro, Robert, 1974, 2000, undated' folder)

In this portray of reality there is a place even for unanticipated changes relevant to understanding individual reactions to surprise monetary policy shocks:

> There is, at the same time, enormous latitude as to <u>when</u> one works. We concentrate our work effort in peak-earnings years: When leisure years are added, they are added at the beginning (a year or so of goofing off after or during college, say) or at the end (early retirement) when we aren't worth as much on the market as we are in our 30s and 40s. [...] Within the year, everyone concentrates his work effort during peak times. Workers in the construction trades substitute winter for summer vacations. People in retailing work long hours in December, short hours in July. Academic journal editors work harder in the summer, when their colleagues are free enough from teaching duties to write up and submit their results. Unpredictable peaks have the same effects as predictable seasonals. Everyone in a manufacturing establishment works long hours when a big order comes in unexpectedly: vacations are postponed, people don't get "sick" as often, overtime hours are put in [...]. (Typed notes. Lucas papers. Box 13. 'Barro, Robert, 1974, 2000, undated' folder)

As a further characteristic, employees dislike too frequent switches between different activities:

> A third feature of observed work patterns is that people like work (and leisure) time to come in chunks. We like fifteen vacation days in one three week period, not scattered through the year. We put in forty hours in five eight hour pieces, not seven six hour days, or twelve siesta-broken half days. Even within a day, we like blocks of time: writing in the morning, teaching and committee busywork in the afternoon. There are setup costs, large (like a two-hour commute or a three day drive to the Rockies) and small (like the fifteen minutes it takes to get back into a problem one hasn't thought about for a while) that make it wasteful to change activities too frequently. (It is in the allocation of time that the convexity beloved by economists is most obviously violated: no one prefers a convex combination of eating, sleeping, working and watching TV to any of the extreme points over a ten minute period, though we all do over a week and most of us would over a day.) (Typed notes. Lucas papers. Box 13. 'Barro, Robert, 1974, 2000, undated' folder)

These peculiarities are some obvious and evident parts of reality. Here Lucas explicitly refers to the commonsensibles strategy of theorizing in economics. The micro-level insights with which we feed economics are obvious and evidently given parts of the socio-economics universe around us:

> These three features of working life – the increasing demand for leisure as wealth increases, the willingness of people to substitute over time so as to concentrate work effort in high return periods, and the fixed costs of activity switching that induces in

to work and consume leisure in stretches of time – are well known to anyone who walks through the world with his eyes open. We do not need econometricians to "test" these observations. Neither do we need theorists to determine whether this sort of behavior follows from standard axioms of rational behavior: It is perfectly easy to imagine a rational agent who reacts to a windfall wealth increase by working harder, or who likes to allocate his time by engaging in hundreds of different activities every microsecond. It is the task of economic and econometric theory to help us to get from what we already know to what we would like to know and [...] not to tell us we cannot make use of what we already know. (Typed notes. Lucas papers. Box 13. 'Barro, Robert, 1974, 2000, undated' folder)

These features are present in spite of the fact that '[e]mployment reductions in depressions are clearly of a different character than [holidays and summer vacations]. They are events that happen to people, not events initiated by them, and they are generally perceived as bad events, as a worsening in opportunities'. (Hand-written notes. Lucas papers. Box 13. 'Barro, Robert, 1974, 2000, undated' folder) Plainly put, Lucas highlighted three key features of real labour markets—features he regards as apparent characteristics of labour markets and agents acting on them. What is more, these properties are easy to reconcile with the rationality postulate. Judging from this fact, the task of economics and econometrics is to aid in drawing sound conclusions regarding what we have not yet understood—that is, to guide us from the knowledge of agents to the understanding of business cycles. As Lucas concludes:

> What we do need help on [...] is in determining whether the reduction in total hours worked during the 1929-34 period can be accounted for entirely in terms of these three features of work behavior, or whether we need to invoke other aspects of behavior, not so far mentioned. Put more technically, is it possible to formulate a model of labor supply behavior, consistent qualitatively and quantitatively with the facts to which I have alluded, such that the hours reduction that occurred over this period is intelligible as a response to the changes in work opportunities that people were then confronted with? (Typed notes. Lucas papers. Box 13. 'Barro, Robert, 1974, 2000, undated' folder)

Lucas (1977) applies the same argument (i.e. the requirement of connecting with real individual behaviour) when suggesting the signal extraction problem as an assumption. In this context it is worth mentioning that Lucas (1977, p. 23; 1981, p. 237) here refers to Austrian business cycle theory as a forerunner. However, the authors he cites (Hayek, 1933, p. 139; Haberler, 1946, pp. 283–344) regard the interest rate as the source of information (in contrast with the price signals Lucas assumed) from which large-scale fluctuations can be derived only if the interest rate elasticity of investment is assumed to be higher than the actual value. This is the reason why Lucas liked these theories from a distance as they were built upon some contradictions with the facts. However, uncertainty about aggregate-level price dynamics and the erroneous guesswork about the missing information are not arbitrary presumptions:

> In the reality of a multi-commodity world [...] no one would want to observe all prices every day, nor would many traders find published price indices particularly useful. An optimizing trader will process those prices of most importance to his decision problem most frequently and carefully, those of less importance less so, and most prices not at all. (Lucas, 1977, p. 21; 1981, p. 230)

Lucas thus postulated the information background of agents on the basis of the habit real market participants follow when processing information. His island models highlight the property of real macroeconomies that the whole price system is hardly observable. As a consequence, no arbitrary assumptions are needed to assume that judgement over price changes is fraught with errors.

4.3 Conclusions: The dynamics of causal adequacy along the Friedman–Lucas transition

4.3.1 Some preliminary structuralist considerations: A reminder

When scrutinizing Friedman's alleged causal realist achievements, Hoover (2009a) relates Friedman's entity-level assumptions to realism about causal relations. In his reading, these underlying assumptions ensure that the theory could highlight some relevant causal mechanisms emerging at the macro-level. As modern structuralist philosophies highlight, causality works along the structures; thus causal realism boils down to some form of structural realism (Chakravartty, 2007; Esfeld, 2009; French & Ladyman, 2003b; French & Ladyman, 2011). Hoover's interpretation is equal to the tenet of structural realism that if one is satisfied with a model appropriately highlighting the structure of a chosen facet of reality and the related causal mechanisms, then her theory does not need to be (approximately) true in any other respects: it can be a useful fiction only (Psillos, 1995, p. 24). In this case, as Psillos (2006) argues, entities play only a heuristic role and are confined to introducing the fundamental structures in order to carry the ontological weight. Thus there is a need for the reconceptualization of entities in a purely structuralist fashion. Here structural realism and entity-level instrumentalism are alleged to go hand in hand for entities and their properties are conceived as mere fictions to underlie concrete structures. Entities can be whatever as long as a given structure emanates from them. As it is argued above, this mix describes most properly how Hoover interprets

Friedman's stance in F53 for the microfoundations project cannot dismiss entities as a fundamental building unit of social reality.[51]

This stance of playing down the importance of entities involves a strict separation of entities and structures. However, it can be a plausible suggestion only if structural realism presupposes no realism about entities (Worrall, 1989; Psillos, 1999, p. 108), which is far from obvious. Scientific realism, be it structural or entity realism, is rarely more than the intention of highlighting some relevant partial truths. If structural realism can thus do without entity realism, it amounts to abandoning the correspondence (i.e. approximate truth) between model and reality at the level of entities[52] (objects or agents and other entities in the case of economics, such as money) to be established via assumptions (Giere, 1988, p. 78). In this case, in other words, it seems possible to succeed in representing structures through models built upon entities (and their properties and the relations of these properties) described in anti-realist ways.

This question boils down to the problem whether the representation of relations can be separated from the representation of entities. Even though Worrall's (1989, p. 117) answer was affirmative,[53] it is still doubtful whether an alleged focus upon structural-causal realism can exempt us from providing reliable representational relationships to preserve some underlying entity properties. As it was argued in Chapter 3, structural realism requires at least a minimal level of entity realism. Structures in the object-based ontology cannot be represented without representing entities, so a version of structuralism detached from entities is not a viable option in economics either. Even when one wants to place the emphasis upon causal structures, she cannot make this focus exclusive: the knowledge of a structure cannot be separated from the knowledge of entities. To begin with, if structures are causal structures and we have even a very thin notion of entities acting in structures, neglecting the behaviour and properties of entities may be problematic at a minimum. By contrast, it seems

---

[51] In this context, the difficulties in interpreting F53 seem to stem from the authors' intentions of talking about entity or structural realism on the one hand, and, on the other hand, from their analysing F53 only or Friedman's oeuvre.

[52] This is not the only attempt to solve the problem raised by the referential status of theoretical terms. Following the practice of putting theories into Ramsey sentences (Chakravartty, 2007, pp. 37–38), Cruse and Papineau (2002) and Papineau (2010) argue for the possibility of an epistemological scientific realism where this referential status is irrelevant. In this framework the nature of entities is of no importance: any things fitting into a structure can be relata.

[53] According to Worrall, a structure can be properly described even if we fundamentally miss the entities. A further version of this idea is when entities in our models are designed in ways so that they could aid in highlighting some pre-given laws. This is the entity-level instrumentalism that can be regarded as the stance of F53.

to be a more plausible option to think, as Dorato (2000, pp. 1624–1625) argues, that in order for an entity to stand in specific relations, it needs to possess specific properties. Entities having other properties stand in other relations; thus properties of entities are not neutral in terms of relations. Causal properties of entities and their dispositions thus seem to be of crucial importance in forming causal relations.

In this context Chakravartty (1998, pp. 400–402; 2007, p. 134) also underlines that structural knowledge entails knowledge of the structural properties of entities: the properties that determine how entities get involved and behave in relations. Psillos (1995) obtains similar conclusions, summarized with the term 'structural properties'. Any concrete causal structure rests upon certain properties of entities, so knowledge of a structure, even if it is partial knowledge about a facet of a concrete structure, implies the knowledge of the active entity properties, and vice versa. Relations in the object-based ontology inevitably contain information about the related entities. This information describes those properties of the objects that play crucial roles in objects' getting structured and making interactions. Any concrete structure is only compatible with certain entities: those it relates (Chakravartty, 2007, p. 67). A concrete structure is thus by no means neutral regarding its relata. As a consequence, a description of a real causal structure cannot be built upon entities lacking the underlying properties of their real counterparts. Since the representation of a causal structure requires some entity-level assumptions as well (as structure penetrates the objects or emanates from them), a prerequisite for a (partial) description of real causal mechanisms is entity realism regarding (at least a subset of) the active and relevant causal properties. Structural and causal properties of objects are not transcendent to structure. As Psillos (1995, pp. 31–32) points out in his critique on structural realism, describing a structure is exactly the same as describing the way entities are related and the way entities act in these relations. Thus if one wants to describe a real structure or subject it to various isolative strategies, she needs approximately true entity descriptions.

By contrast, if there is no representational relationship in the relevant respects between our theoretical entities and their real counterparts, then our knowledge can be negative at best. Reality around us evidently differs from our notions, and such a theory provides no causal understanding of any process under scrutiny. In such a case, moreover, no causal analysis of the differences between theory and reality can be instructive as there is only one fundamental cause underlying all discrepancies: our theory erroneously conceives how the facet of reality we have chosen for analysis works.

We have another reason why mixing untrue entity descriptions with striving towards causal realism is problematic. If structures turned out to be independent of the related entities, it would be unnecessary for economists to give up entity realism and reference. Why would we need to drop approximately true entity descriptions and reference if entities play no role in carrying the causal structures? If our entities are really independent of the embedding structures, then we have no reason to draw up entity descriptions flying in the face of everyday or common-sense experience. Strictly speaking, as in such a case we would not need entities at all, representing entities by preserving some of their prominent or striking properties could be no more than a generous allowance to the usual object-based ontology. A complete dismissal of entities is admittedly too radical a position, though a more permissive option of admitting some entities playing no role in causation is nonetheless confusing.

If we conceive structures as observable and knowledgeable and entities as unobservable (Laudan, 1981, pp. 22–24; Worrall, 1989, p. 118) whilst causal adequacy at the structural level still requires some entity-level assumptions to describe how the entities are related, then it is not the limits of observability that compel us to abandon the fairly liberal concept of entity realism in economics, in contrast with physics. Even though in physics we may be uncertain of the nature of the entities beyond experience, this tenet cannot be a principled reason in economics for throwing out everything we know or can reasonably assume[54] (Psillos, 1995, p. 20; Schmidt, 2010, p. 508). Even those arguing for OSR call attention to the fact that in the realm of observable entities there is no need to relinquish their ontological priority (French & Ladyman, 2003a, p. 41). Economic agents' properties relevant in structural and causal terms do not compel us to abandon traditional scientific realism, since in their case we have the necessary epistemic grip that facilitates verisimilar entity descriptions (French, 1998, p. 422; 2006, p. 177). When Hacking (1983, p. 264) talks of some commonly shared beliefs about entities, he also refers to such properties that are accepted irrespective of the theoretical backgrounds.

When it comes to considering Friedman's alleged causal realist efforts, the genuine problem thus regards whether theorizing about a real macroeconomic causal structure is possible whilst omitting the real properties of the related economic entities. The intuitive answer is unaffirmative. To see why, suffice it to recall the case of his rational leaves. As it is the object-oriented ontology that characterizes the microfoundations project of modern macroeconomics as well, entity realism seems to be indispensable to describing a causal mechanism. Properties of objects prescribe the way objects are related. This is how entities and their properties carry the structures. Structural realism in the absence of entity realism,

---

[54] This claim is not to be mistaken for the circumstance that unravelling the casual structure always takes place on a hypothetical ground as causality is unobservable in a strict sense. However, we are still free to regard the causal structure as an objective feature of the world.

by contrast, would mean that whilst one is interested in some existent (or assumed-to-be-existent) causal relations, the related entities are only regarded as of secondary importance at best. It stands to reason that we cannot latch onto unexperienceable properties,[55] whilst in the structuralist framework we have a different claim. As it is argued, to be a causal realist in the extreme structuralist sense one would need to describe the structure at the level of the structure itself, detached from entities—the only difference stands in whether there exist objects dispensable in structural terms (ESR) or there are no such things as objects (OSR). Here we admittedly have some conflicting ontologies. However, if objects take priority (when they undeniably exist), then they are indispensable[56] (French & Ladyman, 2003b, p. 76).

As the microfoundations project embracing Friedman as well has regarded structure as supervenient on the existence and properties of individual objects (if not, why would Friedman have bothered to describe entities at all?), it can hardly be reconciled with a metaphysical foundation that eliminates (OSR) or disregards (ESR) the individual as a micro-unit in order to abandon the whole object-oriented ontology (French, 1998, p. 107). Using OSR as an interpretive framework makes sense only in cases where the individualization and the objecthood of objects are problematic (French & Ladyman, 2003a, pp. 37–38; Brading & Skiles, 2012; Nounou, 2012). However, microfounded economics is not like this. Friedman was profuse to apply assumptions defining economic agents; thus his focus upon causal connections was unlikely to drift him as far as to OSR as his stance was not to interpret agents in a purely structuralist way. On the contrary, in an ESR-like fashion, Friedman in his Phillips curves attributed some well-defined properties to his agents and built the causal structure upon (the relations of) these properties whilst disregarding the real properties of agents. However, as no causal understanding is possible on the basis of untrue or ad hoc entity-level propositions, on account of his assumptions suggested in F53 and his Phillips curves, Friedman had no chance to achieve causal understanding. To consider whether he had any chance for sound causal understanding in theories other than his Phillips

---

[55] There exist properties indescribable in structural terms (Ladyman, 1998, p. 418), but they are omittable. However, in the case of economic agents, knowledge of such properties is not corrupted.

[56] Esfeld (2009) gives an outstanding description on this. He also details a moderate version of OSR that allows structures to have embedded objects (Esfeld, 2013). However, entity description is still minimal as no entity possesses identity beyond its relations. This conception was suggested in order to block the critique according to which structures without related things cannot be conceived and in order to remain as close to the original notion of OSR as possible. In the meantime, the radical form of OSR claiming that it is only structures not the entities that are in existence is still in use.

curves ought to also be judged by the role real entity properties play there as it is the only aspect where the conclusions drawn here are of general validity.

Any analysis of any causal mechanism in the object-based ontology is to be tied to reality via entity-level assumptions, or else our knowledge proves useless when it comes to causal understanding. This is the intuitive answer to the problem of causal analyses built upon instrumentally described entities. It follows that realism about causality hence structures sets a minimum standard for entity descriptions, so some entity realism is required. Even though the common theorizing practice of economics and other sciences entails poor descriptive performance, entity properties playing a crucial role in underlying causal mechanisms are to be preserved in one way or another. The lack of entity realism cannot be complete, and our entities cannot be of ad hoc character.

Structure is a system of relations of properties, thus a structure to be represented needs to be reduced to these properties. To the properties of individual objects, of the institutions they invent, of the instruments they own and manipulate and of the environment, following the rules of abstraction and idealization. As it is argued here, this is what is meant by Lucas's microfoundations project. The fact that there are some irreducible macro-entities (Hoover, 2001, 2008, 2009b) is insufficient to overturn this account. If one analyzes the fundaments to which Lucas reduced the macro-structure and if one claims that this set of entities and properties partly lies outside a narrowly conceived microeconomic theory, then the failure of the microfoundations project inevitably follows. No matter how unfair they are, Hoover and Brian Epstein's critique (Epstein, 2009, 2014) successfully underlines that some items in Lucas's system cannot be reduced to his representative agents. But what can that must be reduced to a choice-theoretic framework the postulates of which come from the understanding of the way real economic agents make decisions. Lucas thus did not associate his microfoundations programme with a reduction to an overly narrow set of microeconomic agents and their properties. His purpose, instead, was to trace some macro-dynamics back to the causal properties of micro- and some genuinely macro-level objects, institutions and the environment.

4.3.2 Representing the structure via highlighting real entity properties

The circumstance that employers and employees perceive price dynamics in dissimilar ways constitutes a set of causally active entity properties as these properties are indispensable to the working of the causal chain Friedman put forward in his Phillips curve analysis. If a feature is missing from reality, so if it is only a cooked-up assumption (that is, it is introduced with the sole purpose of saving the phenomena via a resulting macro-level mechanism), then the underpinned causal relations cannot be real either. It is highly problematic to build a theoretical account of an observed regularity or recurrent behavioural pattern upon entity-level properties not found in reality. In such a case, some relations do emerge between the assumed properties of entities, though their real working cannot be expected. As Chakravartty (2007, p. 142) puts it, '[r]elations obtain only if the things they relate exist. Thus, specific causal laws obtain only in worlds containing the requisite casual properties'. Without existent features, i.e. in the case of missing properties, we cannot but come to vacuous laws. For sure, such laws can always be established in a model via assumptions, whilst we cannot expect them to emerge in reality. Thinking in a framework like this cannot enhance our causal knowledge about reality.

Playing on Chakravartty's terminology, Friedman's idealization starts from some inexistent properties, so it is impossible to find a representational code establishing a representational relationship between the properties of real entities and the idealized features theoretical entities are assumed to have. Friedman underplayed the importance of real entity properties, so his unrealistic assumptions are not aimed at referring via representational relationships to real features. His instrumentalism refuses to latch onto reality beyond the phenomenal level. F53-style instrumentalist assumptions constitute a special case of in-principle vacuity. This is the term Chakravartty (2007, p. 143) coins to describe situations where causal properties carrying some relations 'do not exist in the actual world for a principled reason'. In the methodology Friedman applied in his Phillips curves there is no representational relationship between the causal properties he put forward to carry some causal relations and the real properties that actually underlie the structure he wanted to understand. The principled reason for vacuity thus lies in the common-sense notion of the basic economic entities. Without entity realism, however, causal realism in the object-based ontology remains an untenable option only. Implied by its very purpose, saving the phenomena whilst neglecting the real properties of entities falls short of understanding. If a theoretical description of a causal relation is true, it contains partial truths, whilst if not, it can describe nothing in a true, sound or causally meaningful way. However, real manifestation is not guaranteed (so poor descriptive performance may hold) even when there are partial truths in the game as omitted variables may interfere with the represented relations.

As we have seen, in his methodological strategy Lucas aimed at providing a structure representation by the highlighting of some causally active and hence structurally important properties of entities, regarding the choice-theoretic framework as adequate in terms of the problem at hand (see Section 3.4.1 on the abstraction- and idealization-based representations of structures). When large-scale fluctuations are conceived as the outcomes of a decision problem, the details of how the individual make her decisions obviously come up as the relevant characteristics. Selection and partiality are in the game, though. As long as economic agents and other entities in a model have characteristics that refer to the real properties (most) relevant as for the given causal analysis, descriptive accuracy is a redundant feature and an inappropriate measure of causal adequacy.[57] As in the case of causal adequacy and descriptive inaccuracy a model contains all the relevant entity properties, the inclusion of further entity characteristics cannot enhance causal adequacy, such a hoarding is thus unnecessary. Causal adequacy and descriptive performance are two, rather independent measures of models' capabilities. Causal adequacy, if established at the desired level, cannot be improved by increases in descriptive accuracy. It is not the purpose here to argue for the causal adequacy of models in general though. The analysis of Lucas's methodological strategy has effectively underlined that it is possible to construct causally adequate models by building them upon some enormously unrealistic entities having only a few features as long as these features are constructed on the basis of the characteristics of the real counterparts. This is the reason why in the analysis above there is a special attention paid to the information background and decision problem of economic agents.

Undoubtedly, Friedman's theoretical assumptions are descriptively inaccurate hence unrealistic, as he also highlighted it in his oft-cited positivist methodology (Friedman, 1953/2009). However, whilst assumptions in Friedman's and Lucas's theories are similar in their not being found in reality (the mutual lack of descriptive accuracy), they are radically dissimilar in terms of their connections with real entity properties. As far as Friedman's anti-realist assumptions are concerned, it is unjustified to talk about their truth-likeness. He applied his assumptions only for the sake of empirical success, so causal adequacy was either a neglected aspect of his theorizing or an aspiration he was unable to achieve. As the semirealist approach to causal realism clearly shows, it is only his genuine ambitions that can be doubtful as any causal realist purposes in the object-based ontology are doomed to failure when one starts from entities defined in

---

[57] Psillos's (1999, p. 107) realist reasoning provides further nuances to describe Lucas's strategy. Psillos draws attention to the fact that oftentimes theorists themselves point out the parts and features of their theories that contribute the most to empirical success and hence that can be regarded as realistic. As a consequence, history of science is rarely compelled to seek on its own the cores of theories. This key constituent in Lucas's island models is the carefully assembled microfoundations as Lucas recurrently placed his emphasis upon its causal adequacy. Bearing in mind Psillos's exposition studied in Chapter 3, causally adequate microfoundations get on well with some idle components introduced, for instance, for tractability reasons. These idle parts do not undermine the appropriately established causal realism of the theory.

an instrumentalist fashion. As such assumptions play a crucial role in the emergence of his conclusions, they cannot easily be swept under the rug as presumptions of marginal importance. By contrast, Lucas's truth-like components, the parts of his theory mainly responsible for the explanatory success (Psillos, 1999, pp. 105–107), by virtue of precise isolation preserve what is indispensable to disentangling the problem under scrutiny and to causal understanding.

4.3.3 Technology, taste, money

It was also the intention of connecting with reality that drove Lucas to postulate monetary-induced business cycles. In his papers he was enthusiastic to declare that the pro-cyclicality of money stock and velocity convinced him not to call into question the monetary source of large-scale fluctuations (Lucas, 1972, p. 103; 1975; 1976a/1981, p. 90; 1977, p. 9; 1981, pp. 66–67 and 217; Snowdon & Vane, 2005, p. 238). Lucas (1981, p. 16) conceived as obvious that business cycles have monetary origins. If not money, what else can the source be? Elsewhere he puts the following on it:

> The idea that changes in the quantity of money (somehow defined) are an important causal factor in real economic instability is a very old one. Indeed, many nineteenth century economists <u>defined</u> business cycles to be monetary or financial "crises." […] [I]t became clear that business fluctuations were pervasive, not at all confined to the financial sectors of the economy. Nevertheless, the idea persisted that fluctuations <u>originated</u> somewhere in the financial sector.
>
> The evidence bearing on the relationship of money to real activity in the U.S. economy was assembled by Milton Friedman and Anna J. Schwartz, in their 1963 monograph, <u>A Monetary History of the United States, 1867-1960</u>, [and a] sequel, <u>Monetary Trends in the United States and the United Kingdom</u> […]. These studies show, among many other things, that major contractions in economic activity are invariably associated with contractions in the quantity of money […]. (Typed notes. Lucas papers. Box 13. 'Barro, Robert, 1974, 2000, undated' folder)

It is worthy of note that Lucas approved of Friedman's achievements in highlighting the ability of money to trigger large-scale fluctuations. However, in itself it is insufficient to establish a causally adequate theory. Even if we may be cognizant of the correlation that a thing always seems to generate another thing, it is still a far cry from having knowledge about the mechanism leading from the causes to the effects.

Lucas was also careful to apply the causalist terminology. Whilst sweeping away the problem of infinite regress not to be constrained in using the causalist terminology, he calls attention that causality is not a context-free concern:

> What are the <u>causes</u> of business cycles? This is not a very well-posed question (because "cause" is such a bad word) but it is [a] question that anyone trying to

model economic time series has to ask, in one form or another. [...] The first attempt to deal with it in the context of an explicit economic model was in Adelman and Adelman's simulations of Klein and Goldberger's econometric model of the United States.

[...]

In the Klein-Goldberger system [...] there is a definite sense in which one can say that business cycles are <u>caused</u> by "autonomous" (as we called them then) fluctuations in various components of private spending. Since the variance of the error terms in investment equations are, in models of this type, much larger than consumption errors, one can sharpen the conclusion to the statement that business cycles are caused by autonomous fluctuations in investment demand. Of course, this conclusion does not imply that such fluctuations do not themselves have more "fundamental" determinants, but only that these determinants are treated as outside the model itself. (In fact, in the Klein-Goldberger model, investment fluctuations are traced, in part, to autonomous fluctuations in business profits.) (Hand-written notes. Lucas papers. Box 13. 'Barro, Robert, 1974, 2000, undated' folder)

Models contain causal hypotheses, so in different models different variables emerge as triggers leading to business cycles. He goes on:

This substantive conclusion of Klein, Goldberger, Adelman and Adelman is, of course, of great interest [...]. Their work was also a great advance methodologically, or at least terminologically: A variable is said to <u>cause</u> business cycles (in the context of a particular, simulatable model) if setting its error variance equal to zero eliminates them in simulations. More generally, one wants to be able to speak of several causes, so in place of "eliminate" one wants to say "substantially reduces", or some similar locutions (as long as one can do this in a way that does not suggest some mindless statistical test!).

This notion of cause has the advantage of being fully operational. [...] If one can forecast the errors in the causative shock (and there is no presumption that causal variables in this sense are unpredictable), policies can be designed that will, in the context of the model, offset them. This is the Klein-Goldberger model, fluctuations in autonomous private spending flows can be offset by changes in taxes and government spending, stabilizing (though perhaps not fully) real output and employment. Of course, the prime motivation of Klein and Goldberger's work was to gain the ability to do this.

An apparent deficiency in this idea of causation is that causal relationships are properties of a particular model, not of "reality" itself. The fact that fluctuations in autonomous investment demand "cause" business cycles in the Klein-Goldberger framework, which is demonstrable, does not preclude the possibility that some quite different model can be constructed, one that fits the facts just as well, in the context of which, say, fluctuations in the money supply "cause" business cycles in an equally demonstrable way. How can economics be used to resolve disputes, to settle issues of policy in a way that all reasonable people can agree on, if this confused state of affairs is allowed to persist? (Hand-written notes. Lucas papers. Box 13. 'Barro, Robert, 1974, 2000, undated' folder)

As a consequence, no clear-cut causal inferences emerge even if a model produces real-like output or unemployment dynamics. Arguing so, Lucas sidesteps the usual realist argument that regards good empirical performance as a strong point in favour of the realism of a theory. At the same time he responds to the problem of underdetermination of theories by the common plausibility argument. Empirical performance is insufficient as a ground, so something more, plausibility and theoretical consistency, are needed. This purpose is served by the introduction of money as a trigger and the use of the choice-theoretic framework. The diversity of causes in various models is not an obstacle to discussing money as a cause of large-scale fluctuations. There can be found a multitude of factors, associated with some effects in statistical terms, playing causal roles in theories, but money is something different. It is the most probable and plausible candidate for 'the' cause of business cycles. As we have just seen, here Lucas is apt to stay away from the troubles over ultimate causes, so the causal role of money can be understood without digging deep in the further causes triggering changes in the money supply. For Lucas the causal role of money was an obvious and well-documented fact:

> There has been much scholarly dispute about Friedman and Schwartz's interpretation of the 1929-33 period, and given the difficulty of drawing causal inferences from nonexperimental data of this sort, perhaps this is unavoidable. But what are the other candidates? What possible forces, other than the well-documented monetary collapse, could have induced the millions of independent decision makers in this modern industrial economy to have reduced their joint production of goods and services by 34 percent over a four year period? If changes in the money supply did not induce these events, then something else did. What was it? (Typed notes. Lucas papers. Box 13. 'Barro, Robert, 1974, 2000, undated' folder)

There are no signs of his admitting that the *only* motivation in choosing his choice-theoretic framework was to produce macro-level outcome consistent with the data in an instrumentalist fashion. Tracing macro-level phenomena back to the decisions made by agents is not an as-if framework. Friedman and Schwartz were right in thinking that money had a triggering effect with respect to business cycles; however, it was Lucas who unravelled the hidden causal mechanism. Money triggers large-scale fluctuations through individual decisions. Lucas obviously discusses choices as the real basis of macroeconomic phenomena:

> My example of models stressing what one might call "autonomous" fluctuations in the money supply, as an alternative to the causal role played by autonomous investment spending in Klein and Goldberger's,[58] and other Keynesian, models is not,

---

[58] Here Lucas refers to the simulations Adelman and Adelman (1959) performed on the Klein-Goldberger model (Klein & Goldberger, 1955). The Adelmans first ran the model deterministically (i.e. without stochastic shocks) that resulted in a quick convergence towards an equilibrium real output. No sizeable oscillations, but a complete absence of business cycles emerged. Second, they built realistic variances upon the error terms for exogenous government spending components. Results bore close similarity to the outcomes of the deterministic session. Finally, they put realistic variances to the error terms for the private sector spending equations. In the latter case, variability in real output and employment similar to real-world fluctuations emerged. As Lucas argued, on the basis of these results it was possible to draw the ungrounded inference that business cycles can be eliminated via spending or tax policies.

of course, hypothetical. (Hand-written notes. Lucas papers. Box 13. 'Barro, Robert, 1974, 2000, undated' folder)

The strength of his conviction is clearly indicated by its direct similarity with Newton's famous principle 'hypotheses non fingo' (i.e. 'I do not feign hypotheses'):

> I have not as yet been able to deduce from phenomena the reason for these properties of gravity, and I do not feign hypotheses. For whatever is not deduced from the phenomena must be called a hypothesis; and hypotheses, whether metaphysical or physical, or based on occult qualities, or mechanical, have no place in experimental philosophy. In this experimental philosophy, propositions are deduced from the phenomena and are made general by induction. (Newton, 1713/1999, p. 943)

Newton of course formed some hypotheses (Cohen, 1969), so this claim of his ought not to be taken at face value. Rather, Newton here underlines that hypotheses in empirical sciences are to root in observations as deep as possible and to be as close to the facts as possible in order to avoid ambiguous and empirically unsupported speculations (Whewell, 1840, p. 438). In this case hypotheses can serve as pillars for theories with the highest certainty.

For Lucas thus consistency was guaranteed by the application of his choice-theoretic framework. This is the only scheme that does not split into parts the decision emerging as a single problem in reality:

> If business cycles are to be modeled as a stochastic difference equation system, one needs candidates for the "shocks" that are viewed as driving the system, as causing output and employment variability. What are the possibilities? From an old-fashioned point of view, in which stochastic errors are simply tacked on to each equation, there seem to be as many possibilities as there are equations in the system. But as soon as one thinks about the decision problems underlying these equations, the possibilities narrow quickly. Consumers cannot be thought of as facing one shock that affects their consumption decision, a second, independent shock affecting their labor supply, a third affecting portfolio choice, and so on. These are decisions simultaneously arrived at, and if the decisions taken fluctuate over time it must be because the terms of the decision problem are fluctuating. (Hand-written notes. Lucas papers. Box 13. 'Barro, Robert, 1974, 2000, undated' folder)

Notions on the role of money exerted a fundamental influence on how Lucas assessed other theories. Money is the only factor that undergoes fluctuations of an order comparable to the magnitude of real economic fluctuations. Accordingly, he was particularly critical of the RBC models (Kydland & Prescott, 1982) in which monetary shocks were replaced by technological shocks (Lucas, 1987, pp. 32–33). Lucas doubted the idea that observed business cycles can plausibly be traced back to real shocks alone. Even though both the availability and the exploitation of the factors of production are unstable, thus some variability enters real output dynamics on this account; these factors are likely not to be strong enough to trigger business cycles as they are observed.

As Lucas argued, observed business cycles could have been derived from Kydland and Prescott's model only if real shocks had been assumed to be too large for technological shocks, or the propagation mechanism[59] responsible for spreading the effects of shocks over time had had implausibly high multipliers. If it is not the fluctuations in money stock but some real shocks that are regarded as the trigger of business cycles, we are likely to face serious difficulties in finding some possible candidates for shocks in the appropriate magnitude. Kydland and Prescott sidestepped this issue by setting the variance of technological shocks in order to have generated time series consistent with observed GNP variability (Lucas, 1987, pp. 71–72). However, according to Lucas's critical remarks, Kydland and Prescott assumed some causal properties that in themselves were unable to play the role RBC models assigned to them. In reality, a technological shock cannot be large enough to be sufficient for triggering the observed macroeconomic fluctuations.

This verdict is in consonance with Lucas's neglecting technological changes in his monetary models of the 1970s.[60] It makes no sense to require pre-set parameter values in a model not to be in contradiction with available micro-level observations[61] (Kydland & Prescott, 1982, p. 1359) if the model itself seems to be inadequate in causal terms. The plausibility of RBC theory seemed to be most unsound at this point (Solow, 1988, p. 311). De Vroey (2001, p. 277) interprets the Solow residuals endowed with a causal role as a melting pot of a plethora of factors (such as even

---

[59] In RBC models, an 'impulse mechanism' serves as the shock (conceived as an exogenous shock to technology or productivity) the effect of which is expanded in time by a 'propagation mechanism' (Plosser, 1989, p. 56) in order that cycles could be long-lasting (e.g. consumption smoothing, lags in the investment process or intertemporal substitution of labour).

[60] Snowdon and Vane (2005, p. 267) suggest that the Lucas critique is possible to extend to technology. Not only decision rules, but technology or even taste may also alter in response to an economic policy change. Lucas later, in an environment of lower monetary noises, had a change of heart and came to attribute less importance to monetary shocks.

[61] Reliability of the microfoundations can underpin realist commitments (Chakravartty, 2008, p. 157) even if doing calibration raises the suspicion of instrumentalism. It is a thought-provoking problem whether Kydland and Prescott when setting *the lack of inconsistency*, instead of directly striving towards consistency, as a requirement placed themselves in a comfortable situation in terms of building the micro-foundations. At the bottom line, calibration implies parameters in line (or at least not in contradiction) with the theoretical background in cases where estimations are infeasible for one reason or another. As it was argued in Section 3.2.1, the strength of belief in the existence of entities varies as realistically acceptable entities and objects postulated for mere empirical purposes may co-exist in a theory. RBC theory whilst having some assumptions widely regarded as of instrumentalist character paid close attention to avoiding inconsistency and to the clearness of microfoundations. A realist ideal of science emerges here.

institutional changes) difficult or impossible to measure separately. This special composite character further erodes the causal role the Solow residuals can play—there is a shock generating macroeconomic fluctuations, but this is all we can know. De Vroey (2016, pp. 263–264) and Hoover (1995, pp. 40–41) relate the alleged fading away of causal understanding to the hotly debated calibration methodology. However, some are more permissive of the practice of calibration. It is easy to find opinions sounding that calibration only amounts to a simple call for the application of reliable micro-data in cases where they are available (Kuorikoski & Lehtinen, 2018). As a matter of fact, calibration does not necessarily imply ad hoc assumptions or instrumentalism as it may mean opting for data cannot be applied in any other ways.

With a single blow has RBC theory got over the age-old Human idea that set economists the task of studying the role of money in triggering large-scale fluctuations and that regarded growth theories and theories of the business cycle as distinct fields (Kydland & Prescott, 1982, p. 1345). Even though integrating growth and business-cycle theories, that is, tracing macroeconomic fluctuations back to shocks to growth factors had some precursors (Kydland & Prescott, 1996, p. 76), it has remained contentious whether some shocks to tastes, technology, or productivity, no matter how easy they are to generate in formal settings, can plausibly lead to short-run fluctuations. As far as the reliability of the data on technological shocks is considered, even the proponents themselves were hesitant. Realizing the satisfactory empirical performance of the models calibrated on these data (Kydland & Prescott, 1982, p. 1359), however, they swept their concerns under the rug. The usual argument (studied in Chapter 1) served as the ultimate foundation for their reasoning: even though we may be uncertain whether calculated productivity disturbances are good estimations for the true changes in productivity, good empirical performance should resolve the doubts. If our assumptions and data are erroneous, model outputs cannot provide good fit either[62] (Plosser, 1989, pp. 62–63). However, they were careful (and right) not to conceive real shocks as the only trigger for macroeconomic cycles (Long & Plosser, 1983, p. 68). Plainly put, these studies were aimed at figuring out whether there were further driving forces behind business cycles beyond the well-scrutinized albeit still incompletely understood role of money (Kydland & Prescott, 1996, pp. 74–75).

---

[62] As we have seen, in itself it is a weak argument even if realists are eager to regard good predictive performance as a proof of realism. Various models can produce good predictions. Realist commitment is fuelled by a belief in theories grabbing existent causal relations. If this belief is plausible, it can be further underpinned by good empirical performance. Predictive success in itself, however, is insufficient to raise our realist aspirations.

RBC theorists seem to have wanted to fulfil Lucas's programme. As he points out (Lucas, 1977, p. 10), business cycles are alike, so there must be a unified theory as a single framework for studying the shocks and the transmission mechanisms underlying fluctuations observed in capitalist economies. This is exactly the way Plosser considers RBC theory. It is regarded as the general and flexibly customizable framework in which demand-side shocks (e.g. changes in tastes Lucas regarded as given) or even the effects of monetary or fiscal policy can be scrutinized[63] (Plosser, 1989, pp. 66–71). As far as its ambitions are considered, RBC theory is meant to be the grandiose unified framework of macroeconomics. A general theory easy to customize to look into the causal factors, one by one or in combination, leading to large-scale fluctuations.

On this ground Lucas (1994, p. 13) stands up for RBC theory. Its emergence has not discouraged economists from admitting some possible monetary causes of business cycles. In Lucas's assessment, RBC theory arose in a situation where shock-free monetary policy made it possible to look for other causes of large-scale fluctuations. By contrast, monetarists had scrutinized the real effects of monetary changes in a day and age when the contribution of the Solow residuals was negligible and did not interfere with the monetary mechanisms. As early as in his island models did Lucas clarify that the causal structure underlying observed macroeconomic phenomena is far more complicated than the simplified mechanisms economists can highlight in their models. Bearing this in mind, it is not surprising at all that good empirical performance in this context meant that there was a considerable (albeit statistically not particularly strong) correlation between price dynamics and the cyclical component of real output, leaving room for some further omitted variables (Lucas, 1973, pp. 331–332; 1981, pp. 139–140).

Suggested readings

Emmett (2009) has done the most for our having a clear picture of Frank H. Knight's theory and methodology. Whimster (2007) and Bruun and Whimster (2012) provide the most current systematic overviews of Max Weber's social scientific methodology. Forder (2019) goes over Friedman's economics in the context of his biography. Forder (2018) gives further considerations on Friedman's Phillips curve theory and its reception. Forder

---

[63] Prescott (2006, pp. 203–204) goes even farther. According to his commentaries the evolution of macroeconomics has mainly proved to be an evolution of methodology, thanks to which the methodology Kydland and Prescott suggested underpins a general framework adequate for addressing all kinds of economic problems.

(2015) examines how the Phillips curve is present in university education. Some assessments of Lucas's economic methodology are available in the literature by Vercelli (1991), Boumans (2005) and De Vroey (2016). By using bibliometrics data, Andrada (2017) identifies Lucas's most significant papers and the authors who had influence on him.

References

Adelman, I., & Adelman, F. L. (1959). The dynamic properties of the Klein-Goldberger model. *Econometrica, 27*(4), 596–625.

Agnes, M., & Guralnik, D. B. (Eds.), (2007). *Webster's new world college dictionary*. Cleveland, OH: Wiley.

Alberro, J. (1981). The Lucas hypothesis on the Phillips curve. Further international evidence. *Journal of Monetary Economics, 7*(2), 239–250.

Andrada, A. F. (2017). Understanding Robert Lucas (1967-1981). His influence and influences. *Economia, 18*(2), 212–228.

Aydinonat, E. (2018). The diversity of models as a means to better explanations in economics. *Journal of Economic Methodology, 25*(3), 237–251.

Barro, R. J. (1989). *New classicals and Keynesians, or the good guys and the bad guys*. NBER working paper no. 2982. Cambridge, MA: National Bureau of Economic Research.

Blaug, M. (1992). *The methodology of economics or how economists explain* (2nd ed.). Cambridge: Cambridge University Press.

Boland, L. A. (1979). A critique of Friedman's critics. *Journal of Economic Literature, 17*(2), 503–522.

Boland, L. A. (2010). Review of "The methodology of positive economics. Reflections on the Milton Friedman legacy, ed. Uskali Mäki". *Economics and Philosophy, 26*(3), 376–382.

Boland, L. A. (2016). Philosophy of economics versus methodology of economics. *Studia Metodologiczne, 36*(1), 17–26.

Boumans, M. (2005). *How economists model the world into numbers*. Abingdon: Routledge.

Brading, K., & Skiles, A. (2012). Underdetermination as a path to structural realism. In E. M. Landry & D. P. Rickles (Eds.), *Structural realism. Structure, object, and causality* (pp. 99–115). New York: Springer.

Bruun, H. H. (2007). *Science, values, and politics in Max Weber's methodology*. Aldershot: Ashgate.

Bruun, H. H., & Whimster, S. (2012). Introduction. In M. Weber, H. H. Bruun, & S. Whimster (Eds.), *Collected methodological writings* (pp. xi–xxviii). London: Routledge.

Caginalp, G., McCabe, K., & Porter, D. (2003). The foundations of experimental economics and applications to behavioral finance. The contributions of Nobel laureate Vernon Smith. *Journal of Behavioral Finance, 4*(1), 3–6.

Caldwell, B. J. (1980). A critique of Friedman's methodological instrumentalism. *Southern Economic Journal, 47*(2), 366–374.

Caldwell, B. J. (1992). Friedman's predictivist instrumentalism. A modification. *Research in the History of Economic Thought and Methodology, 10*(1), 119–128.

Chakravartty, A. (1998). Semirealism. *Studies in History and Philosophy of Science Part A, 29*(3), 391–408.

Chakravartty, A. (2007). *A metaphysics for scientific realism. Knowing the unobservable*. Cambridge: Cambridge University Press.

Chakravartty, A. (2008). What you don't know can't hurt you. Realism and the unconceived. *Philosophical Studies, 137*(1), 149–158.

Chakravartty, A. (2010). Informational versus functional theories of scientific representation. *Synthese, 172*(1), 197–213.

Chari, V. V., Kehoe, P. J., & McGrattan, E. R. (2009). New Keynesian models. Not yet useful for policy analysis. *American Economic Journal: Macroeconomics*, 1(1), 242–266.

Cohen, I. B. (1969). Hypotheses in Newton's philosophy. In R. S. Cohen & M. W. Wartofsky (Eds.), *Boston studies in the philosophy of science* (pp. 304–326). Dordrecht: Springer.

Cruse, P., & Papineau, D. (2002). Scientific realism without reference. In M. Marsonet (Ed.), *The problem of realism* (pp. 174–189). London: Ashgate.

De Vroey, M. (2001). Friedman and Lucas on the Phillips curve. From a disequilibrium to an equilibrium approach. *Eastern Economic Journal*, 27(2), 127–148.

De Vroey, M. (2016). *A history of macroeconomics from Keynes to Lucas and beyond*. Cambridge: Cambridge University Press.

Dorato, M. (2000). Substantivalism, relationism, and structural spacetime realism. *Foundations of Physics*, 30(10), 1605–1628.

Emmett, R. B. (1999). Introduction. In F. H. Knight & R. B. Emmett (Eds.), Vol. 1. *Selected essays* (pp. vii–xxiv). Chicago: The University of Chicago Press.

Emmett, R. B. (2006). Frank Knight, Max Weber, Chicago economics and institutionalism. *Max Weber Studies*, 7(1), 101–119.

Emmett, R. B. (2009). *Frank Knight and the Chicago school in American economics*. London: Routledge.

Emmett, R. B. (2015a). *Frank H. Knight and the Chicago school. Conference presentation*. In *The legacy of Chicago economics*. October 5, 2015.

Emmett, R. B. (2015b). *Frank H. Knight before he entered economics (1885–1914)*. East Lansing, MI: James Madison College, Michigan State University.

Epstein, B. (2009). Ontological individualism reconsidered. *Synthese*, 166(1), 187–213.

Epstein, B. (2014). Why macroeconomics does not supervene on microeconomics. *Journal of Economic Methodology*, 21(1), 3–18.

Epstein, R. J. (1987). *A history of econometrics*. Amsterdam: North Holland.

Esfeld, M. (2009). The modal structure of structures in ontic structural realism. *International Studies in the Philosophy of Science*, 23(2), 179–194.

Esfeld, M. (2013). Ontic structural realism and the interpretation of quantum mechanics. *European Journal for Philosophy of Science*, 3(1), 19–32.

Faust, J. (2009). The new macro models. Washing our hands and watching for icebergs. *Sveriges Riksbank Economic Review*, 20(1), 45–68.

Forder, J. (2010). Friedman's Nobel lecture and the Phillips curve myth. *Journal of the History of Economic Thought*, 32(3), 329–348.

Forder, J. (2014). *Macroeconomics and the Phillips curve myth*. Oxford: Oxford University Press.

Forder, J. (2015). Textbooks on the Phillips curve. *History of Political Economy*, 47(2), 207–240.

Forder, J. (2016). A neglected inconsistency in Milton Friedman's AEA presidential address. *Journal of the History of Economic Thought*, 38(1), 105–112.

Forder, J. (2018). What was the message of Friedman's presidential address to the American economic association? *Cambridge Journal of Economics*, 42(2), 523–541.

Forder, J. (2019). *Milton Friedman*. London: Palgrave Macmillan.

French, S. (1998). On the withering away of physical objects. In E. Castellani (Ed.), *Interpreting bodies. Classical and quantum objects in modern physics* (pp. 93–113). Princeton, NJ: Princeton University Press.

French, S. (2006). Structure as a weapon of the realist. *Proceedings of the Aristotelian Society*, 106(1), 169–187.

French, S., & Ladyman, J. (2003a). Remodelling structural realism. Quantum physics and the metaphysics of structure. *Synthese*, 136(1), 31–56.

French, S., & Ladyman, J. (2003b). The dissolution of objects. Between Platonism and phenomenalism. *Synthese*, 136(1), 73–77.

French, S., & Ladyman, J. (2011). In defence of ontic structural realism. In A. Bokulich & P. Bokulich (Eds.), *Scientific structuralism* (pp. 25–42). New York: Springer.

Friedman, M. (1946a). Some correspondence on methodology between Milton Friedman and Edwin B. Wilson. In R. Leeson & C. G. Palm (Eds.), *The collected works of Milton Friedman*. Stanford, CA: Hoover Institute.

Friedman, M. (1946b). Lange on price flexibility and employment. A methodological criticism. *The American Economic Review, 36*(4), 613–631.

Friedman, M. (1949). The Marshallian demand curve. *Journal of Political Economy, 57*(6), 463–495.

Friedman, M. (1952). Comment on "Methodological developments" by Richard Ruggles. In R. Leeson & C. G. Palm (Eds.), *The collected works of Milton Friedman*. Stanford, CA: Hoover Institution.

Friedman, M. (1953). Comment on "Some contemporary tendencies in economic research". In R. Leeson & C. G. Palm (Eds.), *The collected works of Milton Friedman*. Stanford, CA: Hoover Institution.

Friedman, M. (1953/2009). The methodology of positive economics. In U. Mäki (Ed.), *The methodology of positive economics. Reflections on the Milton Friedman legacy* (pp. 3–43). Cambridge: Cambridge University Press.

Friedman, M. (1968). The role of monetary policy. *The American Economic Review, 58*(1), 1–17.

Friedman, M. (1977). Nobel lecture. Inflation and unemployment. *Journal of Political Economy, 85*(3), 451–472.

Fu-Lai Yu, T. (2002). The economics of Frank H. Knight. An Austrian interpretation. *Forum for Social Economics, 31*(2), 1–23.

Galbács, P. (2015). *The theory of new classical macroeconomics*. New York: Springer.

Galbács, P. (2017). Realism in economics. The new classical case. *Acta Oeconomica, 67*(2), 257–279.

Giere, R. N. (1988). *Explaining science. A cognitive approach*. Chicago: The University of Chicago Press.

Haberler, G. (1946). *Prosperity and depression*. New York: United Nations.

Hacking, I. (1983). *Representing and intervening*. Cambridge: Cambridge University Press.

Hammond, J. D. (1988). An interview with Milton Friedman on methodology. In R. Leeson & C. G. Palm (Eds.), *The collected works of Milton Friedman*. Stanford, CA: Hoover Institution.

Hammond, J. D. (1996). *Theory and measurement. Causality issues in Milton Friedman's monetary economics*. Cambridge: Cambridge University Press.

Hands, D. W. (2018). *Re-examining Samuelson's opertionalist methodology*. Unpublished working paper, version 1.2. Tacoma: University of Puget Sound.

Hausman, D. M. (1992). *The inexact and separate science of economics*. Cambridge: Cambridge University Press.

Hayek, F. A. (1933). *Monetary theory and the trade cycle*. New York: Sentry Press.

Hicks, J. R. (1932). *The theory of wages*. London: Macmillan.

Hicks, J. R. (1946). *Value and capital*. Oxford: The Clarendon Press.

Hoover, K. D. (1995). Facts and artifacts. Calibration and the empirical assessment of real-business-cycle models. *Oxford Economic Papers, 47*(1), 24–44.

Hoover, K. D. (2001). Is macroeconomics for real? In U. Mäki (Ed.), *The economic world view. Studies in the ontology of economics* (pp. 225–245). Cambridge: Cambridge University Press.

Hoover, K. D. (2008). Does macroeconomics need microfoundations? In D. M. Hausman (Ed.), *The philosophy of economics. An anthology* (pp. 315–333). Cambridge: Cambridge University Press.

Hoover, K. D. (2009a). Milton Friedman's stance. The methodology of causal realism. In U. Mäki (Ed.), *The methodology of positive economics. Reflections on the Milton Friedman legacy* (pp. 303–320). Cambridge: Cambridge University Press.

Hoover, K. D. (2009b). Microfoundations and the ontology of macroeconomics. In H. Kincaid & D. Ross (Eds.), *The Oxford handbook of philosophy of economics* (pp. 386–409). Oxford: Oxford University Press.

Hoover, K. D. (2015). *A review of James Forder's Macroeconomics and the Phillips curve myth*. CHOPE working paper no. 2015-07Durham, NC: Center for the History of Political Economy, Duke University.

Hoyningen-Huene, P. (2017). *Revisiting Friedman's F53. Popper, Knight, and Weber*. Hannover: Leibniz Universität.

Kahneman, D. (2011). *Thinking, fast and slow*. New York: Farrar, Straus and Giroux.

Klein, L. R., & Goldberger, A. S. (1955). *An econometric model of the United States, 1929–1952*. Amsterdam: North-Holland.

Knight, F. H. (1921). *Risk, uncertainty and profit*. Boston: Houghton Mifflin Company.

Knight, F. H. (1922/1935). Ethics and the economic interpretation. In F. H. Knight, M. Friedman, H. Jones, G. Stigler, & A. Wallis (Eds.), *The ethics of competition and other essays* (pp. 19–40). Freeport: Books for Libraries Press.

Knight, F. H. (1924/1999). The limitations of scientific method in economics. In F. H. Knight & R. B. Emmett (Eds.), Vol. 1. *Selected essays* (pp. 1–39). Chicago: The University of Chicago Press.

Knight, F. H. (1935). Economic theory and nationalism. In F. H. Knight, M. Friedman, H. Jones, G. Stigler, & A. Wallis (Eds.), *The ethics of competition and other essays* (pp. 277–359). Freeport: Books for Libraries Press.

Knight, F. H. (1935/1999). Statics and dynamics. Some queries regarding the mechanical analogy in economics. In F. H. Knight & R. B. Emmett (Eds.), Vol. 1. *Selected essays* (pp. 149–171). Chicago: The University of Chicago Press.

Knight, F. H. (1940/1999). "What is truth" in economics? In F. H. Knight & R. B. Emmett (Eds.), Vol. 1. *Selected essays* (pp. 372–399). Chicago: The University of Chicago Press.

Knight, F. H. (1944). Realism and relevance in the theory of demand. *Journal of Political Economy, 52*(4), 289–318.

Knight, F. H. (1956). The role of principles in economics and politics. In F. H. Knight, W. L. Letwin, & A. J. Morin (Eds.), *On the history and method of economics. Selected essays* (pp. 251–281). Chicago: The University of Chicago Press.

Knight, F. H. (1972). Social science. *Ethics, 83*(1), 1–12.

Koopmans, T. C. (1947). Measurement without theory. *The Review of Economics and Statistics, 29*(3), 161–172.

Kuorikoski, J., & Lehtinen, A. (2018). Model selection in macroeconomics. DSGE and ad hocness. *Journal of Economic Methodology, 25*(3), 252–264.

Kydland, F. E., & Prescott, E. C. (1982). Time to build and aggregate fluctuations. *Econometrica, 50*(6), 1345–1370.

Kydland, F. E., & Prescott, E. C. (1996). The computational experiment. An econometric tool. *Journal of Economic Perspectives, 10*(1), 69–85.

Ladyman, J. (1998). What is structural realism? *Studies in History and Philosophy of Science Part A, 29*(3), 409–424.

Laudan, L. (1981). A confutation of convergent realism. *Philosophy of Science, 48*(1), 19–49.

Long, J. B., & Plosser, C. I. (1983). Real business cycles. *Journal of Political Economy, 91*(1), 39–69.

Lucas, R. E. (1972). Expectations and the neutrality of money. *Journal of Economic Theory, 2*, 103–124.

Lucas, R. E. (1973). Some international evidence on output-inflation tradeoffs. *The American Economic Review, 63*(3), 326–334.

Lucas, R. E. (1975). An equilibrium model of the business cycle. *Journal of Political Economy, 83*(6), 1113–1144.

Lucas, R. E. (1976/1981). Econometric testing of the natural rate hypothesis. In R. E. Lucas (Ed.), *Studies in business-cycle theory* (pp. 90–103). Oxford: Basil Blackwell.

Lucas, R. E. (1976/1981). Econometric policy evaluation. A critique. In R. E. Lucas (Ed.), *Studies in business cycle theory* (pp. 104–130). Oxford: Basil Blackwell.

Lucas, R. E. (1977). Understanding business cycles. In K. Brunner & A. H. Meltzer (Eds.), *Stabilization of the domestic and international economy* (pp. 7–29). Amsterdam: North-Holland.

Lucas, R. E. (1980). Methods and problems in business cycle theory. *Journal of Money, Credit and Banking, 12*(4), 696–715.

Lucas, R. E. (1981). *Studies in business-cycle theory*. Oxford: Basil Blackwell.

Lucas, R. E. (1986). Adaptive behavior and economic theory. *Journal of Business, 59*(4), S401–S426.

Lucas, R. E. (1987). *Models of business cycles*. Oxford: Basil Blackwell.

Lucas, R. E. (1994). Review of Milton Friedman and Anna J. Schwartz's 'A monetary history of the United States, 1867-1960'. *Journal of Monetary Economics, 34*(1), 5–16.

Lucas, R. E., & Prescott, E. C. (1974). Equilibrium search and unemployment. *Journal of Economic Theory, 7*(2), 188–209.

Lucas, R. E., & Rapping, L. A. (1969). Real wages, employment, and inflation. *Journal of Political Economy, 77*(5), 721–754.

Lucas, R. E., & Rapping, L. A. (1972). Unemployment in the great depression. Is there a full explanation? *Journal of Political Economy, 80*(1), 186–191.

Lucas, R. E., & Sargent, T. J. (1979). After Keynesian macroeconomics. *Federal Reserve Bank of Minneapolis Quarterly Review, 3*(2), 1–16.

Mäki, U. (2009a). Unrealistic assumptions and unnecessary confusions. Rereading and rewriting F53 as a realist statement. In U. Mäki (Ed.), *The methodology of positive economics. Reflections on the Milton Friedman legacy* (pp. 90–116). Cambridge: Cambridge University Press.

Mäki, U. (2009b). Realistic realism about unrealistic models. In U. Mäki (Ed.), *The Oxford handbook of philosophy of economics* (pp. 68–98). Oxford: Oxford University Press.

Mäki, U. (2018). Rights and wrongs of economic modelling. Refining Rodrik. *Journal of Economic Methodology, 25*(3), 218–236.

Manicas, P. T. (2006). *A realist philosophy of social science. Explanation and understanding.* Cambridge: Cambridge University Press.

Mantzavinos, C. (2014). Text interpretation as a scientific activity. *Journal for General Philosophy of Science, 45*(S1), 45–58.

Mariyani-Squire, E. (2017). Critical reflections on a realist interpretation of Friedman's 'Methodology of positive economics'. *Journal of Economic Methodology, 24*(1), 69–89.

Marshall, A. (1920/2013). *Principles of economics* (8th ed.). New York: Palgrave Macmillan.

McCall, J. J. (1970). Economics of information and job search. *The Quarterly Journal of Economics, 84*(1), 113–126.

Medema, S. G. (2011). Chicago price theory and Chicago law and economics. A tale of two transitions. In R. Van Horn, P. Mirowski, & T. A. Stapleford (Eds.), *Building Chicago economics* (pp. 154–179). Cambridge: Cambridge University Press.

Nagel, E. (1963). Assumptions in economic theory. *The American Economic Review, 53*(2), 211–219.

Newton, I. (1713/1999). *The principia: Mathematical principles of natural philosophy* [I. B. Cohen, & A. Whitman, Trans.]. Berkeley, CA: University of California Press.

Noppeney, C. (1997). Frank Knight and the historical school. In P. Koslowski (Ed.), *Methodology of the social sciences, ethics, and economics in the newer historical school* (pp. 319–339). Heidelberg: Springer.

Nounou, A. M. (2012). Kinds of objects and varieties of properties. In E. M. Landry & D. P. Rickles (Eds.), *Structural realism. Structure, object, and causality* (pp. 117–133). New York: Springer.

Papineau, D. (2010). Realism, Ramsey sentences and the pessimistic meta-induction. *Studies in History and Philosophy of Science Part A, 41*(4), 375–385.

Phelps, E. S. (1967a). Phillips curves, expectations of inflation and optimal unemployment over time. *Economica, 34*(135), 254–281.

Phelps, E. S. (1967b). Money-wage dynamics and labor-market equilibrium. *Journal of Political Economy, 76*(4), 678–711.

Phelps, E. S. (1995). The origins and further development of the natural rate of unemployment. In R. Cross (Ed.), *The natural rate of unemployment. Reflections on 25 years of the hypothesis* (pp. 15–31). Cambridge: Cambridge University Press.

Phelps, E. S. (2006). *Biography of Edmund S. Phelps*. Retrieved April 20, 2018, from Nobelprize.org. https://www.nobelprize.org/prizes/economic-sciences/2006/phelps/biographical/.

Plosser, C. I. (1989). Understanding real business cycles. *Journal of Economic Perspectives, 3*(3), 51–77.

Popper, K. (1962). *Conjectures and refutations*. New York: Basic Books.

Prescott, E. C. (2006). The transformation of macroeconomic policy and research. Nobel lecture. *Journal of Political Economy, 114*(2), 203–235.

Psillos, S. (1995). Is structural realism the best of both worlds? *Dialectica, 49*(1), 15–46.

Psillos, S. (1999). *Scientific realism. How science tracks truth*. London: Routledge.

Psillos, S. (2006). The structure, the whole structure, and nothing but the structure? *Philosophy of Science, 73*(5), 560–570.

Reder, M. W. (1982). Chicago economics. Permanence and change. *Journal of Economic Literature, 20*(1), 1–38.

Reiss, J. (2010). Review of "The methodology of positive economics. Reflections on the Milton Friedman legacy, ed. Uskali Mäki". *Erasmus Journal for Philosophy and Economics, 3*(2), 103–110.

Ringer, F. (1997). *Max Weber's methodology*. Cambridge, MA: Harvard University Press.

Samuelson, P. A. (1963). Problems of methodology. Discussion. *The American Economic Review, 53*(2), 227–236.

Samuelson, P. A., & Solow, R. M. (1960). Analytical aspects of anti-inflation policy. *The American Economic Review, 50*(2), 177–194.

Sargent, T. J., & Wallace, N. (1975). "Rational" expectations, the optimal monetary instrument, and the optimal money supply rule. *Journal of Political Economy, 83*(2), 241–254.

Scaff, L. A. (2011). *Max Weber in America*. Princeton, NJ: Princeton University Press.

Scaff, L. A. (2014). Max Weber in the United States. *Società Mutamento Politica, 5*(9), 271–291.

Schliesser, E. (2011). "Every system of scientific theory involves philosophical assumptions" (Talcott Parsons). The surprising Weberian roots to Milton Friedman's methodology. In D. Dieks, W. J. Gonzalez, S. Hartmann, T. Uebel, & M. Weber (Eds.), *Explanation, prediction, and confirmation* (pp. 533–543). Dordrecht: Springer.

Schmidt, M. (2010). Causation and structural realism. *Organon F, 17*(4), 508–521.

Schwarzer, J. A. (2013). Samuelson and Solow on the Phillips curve and the "menu of choice". A retrospective. *Oeconomia, 3*(3), 359–388.

Shaw, G. K. (1984). *Rational expectations*. Brighton: Harvester Press.

Shiller, R. J. (1984). Rational expectations and econometric practice by Robert E. Lucas, and Thomas J. Sargent. A review. *Journal of Money, Credit and Banking, 16*(1), 118–123.

Shils, E. (1981). Some academics, mainly in Chicago. *The American Scholar, 50*(2), 179–196.

Simon, H. A. (1953). Causal ordering and identifiability. In W. C. Hood & T. C. Koopmans (Eds.), *Studies in econometric method* (pp. 49–74). New York: John Wiley & Sons.

Simon, H. A. (1969/1996). *The sciences of the artificial*. Cambridge, MA: The MIT Press.

Sims, C. A. (1982). Policy analysis with econometric models. *Brookings Papers on Economic Activity, 13*(1), 107–164.

Slutzky, E. (1937). The summation of random causes as the source of cyclic processes. *Econometrica, 5*(2), 105–146.

Smith, V. L., Suchanek, G. L., & Williams, A. W. (1988). Bubbles, crashes, and endogenous expectations in experimental spot asset markets. *Econometrica, 56*(5), 1119–1151.

Snowdon, B., & Vane, H. R. (2005). *Modern macroeconomics. Its origins, development and current state*. Cheltenham: Edward Elgar.

Solow, R. M. (1988). Growth theory and after. *The American Economic Review, 78*(3), 307–317.

Stigler, G. J. (1985). *Frank Hyneman Knight*. Center for the Study of the Economy and the State working paper no. 37. Chicago: The University of Chicago.

Taylor, J. B. (2007). An interview with Milton Friedman (Stanford University, May 2, 2000). In P. A. Samuelson & W. A. Barnett (Eds.), *Inside the economist's mind* (pp. 110–142). Oxford: Blackwell.

Vercelli, A. (1991). *Methodological foundations of macroeconomics. Keynes and Lucas.* Cambridge: Cambridge University Press.

Weber, M. (1904/1949). "Objectivity" in social sciences. In M. Weber, E. A. Shils, & H. A. Finch (Eds.), *The methodology of the social sciences.* E.A. Shils, & H.A. Finch, Trans. (pp. 50–112). Glencoe: The Free Press.

Weber, M. (1906/1949). Objective possibility and adequate causation in historical explanation. In M. Weber, E. A. Shils, & H. A. Finch (Eds.), *The methodology of the social sciences.* E.A. Shils & H.A. Finch, Trans. (pp. 164–188). Glencoe: The Free Press.

Weber, M. (1917/1949). The meaning of "ethical neutrality" in sociology and economics. In M. Weber, E. A. Shils, & H. A. Finch (Eds.), *The methodology of social sciences* (pp. 1–47). Glencoe: The Free Press.

Weber, M. (1927). *General economic history* [F.H. Knight, Trans.]. London: Allen and Unwin.

Weber, M. (1930). *The protestant ethic and the spirit of capitalism* [T. Parsons, Trans.]. New York: Charles Scribner's Sons.

Weber, M. (1968/1978). In G. Roth & C. Wittich (Eds.), *Economy and society. An outline of interpretive sociology.* Berkeley, CA: University of California Press.

Weeks, J. (1989). *A critique of neoclassical macroeconomics.* New York: Palgrave Macmillan.

Whewell, W. (1840). *The philosophy of the inductive sciences, founded upon their history. Vol. 2.* London: John W. Parker.

Whimster, S. (2007). *Understanding Weber.* Abingdon: Routledge.

Wilber, C. K., & Wisman, J. D. (1975). The Chicago school. Positivism or ideal type. *Journal of Economic Issues, 9*(4), 665–679.

Wong, S. (1973). The "F-twist" and the methodology of Paul Samuelson. *The American Economic Review, 63*(3), 312–325.

Worrall, J. (1989). Structural realism. The best of both world. *Dialectica, 43*(1–2), 99–124.

Archival sources

Lucas R.E., Unpublished papers, 1960–2004 and undated. Archival material stored at the David M. Rubenstein Library, Duke University.

5

The end of economics?

Do old fallacies ever die?
Milton Friedman

The theory of hermeneutics draws attention to a twofold prerequisite for careful textual interpretations. The one component is a textual basis as broad as possible. As the meaning of a text stems from the meanings of its parts, such as individual sentences and paragraphs, and, similarly, the meaning of a set of texts, such as the lifework of an author, stems from the meanings of the individual texts, the more component parts we can properly interpret, the higher the probability of a correct overall reading is. Meaning is a complex phenomenon. As individual textual parts contribute to the overall meaning, any decrease in the number of considered parts is likely to distort the resulting interpretation. The other is an appropriate interpretive framework conceived as a constituent part of the pre-given personal knowledge. Its importance is clearly signified by the just mentioned part-whole problem known as the hermeneutic circle in the theory of literature. If the meaning of a whole is dependent upon the meaning of its parts, whilst the meaning of a part is dependent upon the meaning of the whole, it is necessary for the interpreter to find an appropriate point to start from. As interpretive acts are of cyclical and iterative character, this tension between part and whole can be resolved by starting the procedure with proper pre-given knowledge ready to apply.

This concluding chapter aimed at self-reflection sets the analysis performed in the preceding parts into the focus. Besides the establishment of an extended textual basis, the other innovation was the consistent application of semirealism as an interpretive framework that problematizes how entities are causally structured and thus has facilitated a realist interpretation of Lucas's microfoundations project. On this showing Lucas's descriptively unrealistic models have emerged as some sharpened tools of sound causal analysis. Lucas built his microfoundations upon the relevant properties of real-world economic agents. With an explicit requirement of the consistency with micro-evidence and micro-theory, that is, placing the analysis of social actions upon a choice-theoretic fundament, Lucas and his followers have taken a huge step towards the end of economics.

5.1 Hermeneutics in the history and methodology of economics

Human statements are rarely unambiguous. Most of the time we do not take the trouble to put forward the exact intended meanings of our utterances carefully and explicitly. As a consequence, such statements need interpretation (Skinner, 1988, p. 262). Scientific texts are no exception. In the history of economic thought there exist two standards for textual interpretation. Following Blaug (1985, pp. 1–3) they are referred to as absolutist and relativist histories.

Considering these methods or approaches is also useful for the methodology of economics. There are some points in favour of conceiving the history of economic thought as closely tied to or even inseparable from the history of methodology. As we have seen, theoretical improvements sometimes emerge as methodological advancements. In general, our knowledge is directly dependent upon the underlying methodology: what we know stems from the way we acquire this knowledge. The ultimate purpose of social and natural sciences is scrutinizing reality, and the methodology we choose intimately establishes our way of inquiry and hence the inferences we draw. At the bottom-line, studies in the history and methodology of economics have their basic units in common: published and unpublished texts written in economics. For this reason, even if one may have serious reservations about regarding these two sub-disciplines as close-knit, both the methods of historiography and their limitations directly apply to methodology. The problem of textual interpretation is a concern for methodology as well.

As Blaug argues, an absolutist historian of economics pays attention to the development of a theory whilst disregarding the authors' intellectual development, precursors, scholarly connections, and the personality of the carriers and articulators of theories—plainly put, the personal, historical, and intellectual background of economic ideas, referred to as the 'context'. It is only the evolution of ideas living their own lives that matters. A critique of the past follows from this: a critique that rests upon the current state of knowledge (Emmett, 1997, p. 227). As all past theories are judged by present lights, current theoretical knowledge is inevitably assumed to be superior to all past achievements. Even though dead ends and breaks in the progress might have occurred, what we know now is set as the ultimate standard. The motivation for evaluation with hindsight is particularly strong in cases where the history of economic ideas is done in order to avoid past mistakes (see Section 2.1.2 for the place of the history of economic thought in the Chicago tradition). In such a case, any assessment and judgement of economic theories on the basis of their own embedding intellectual and social contexts, a hallmark of the relativist stance, seems to be a mistaken endeavour.

Given Blaug's rather sceptical attitude towards modern economics, the idea of economics making considerable progress is best conceived as reflecting a desired state of affairs or a standard economics fails to meet. The assumption of an overall development of economics is probably the most vulnerable aspect of absolutist histories. Many regard the theoretical evolution after Keynes as a degeneration of economics. In this context Lars Pålsson Syll's (2016) recent passive, destructive, and pessimistic criticism is worth mentioning. On this ground Blaug's idea of an unbroken (albeit possibly erratic) progress from falsity towards 'truth' seems unacceptable. Looking back from present upon the history of ideas, one may find the theoretical evolution linear, though it hardly seemed so for the economists accomplishing the progress. During an evolutionary process a number of bifurcations emerge (Leijonhufvud, 1994). As a consequence, a realized development cannot be regarded as necessary and predetermined. At any bifurcation, economics might have turned to directions that as some unsuccessful initiations could later have marginalized or even come to extinction. A part of the story to tell is why economics as such (Samuels, 1972) has taken the path it has. The history of science is a history of recognitions and discoveries. With hindsight, the evolution of a discipline can really be described as a sequence of milestones, though such determinant events never emerge as necessary and unavoidable turning points. For instance, Lucas's neo-Walrasian 'misstep' was by no means an inevitable consequence of the preceding developments, especially given Chicago's strong Marshallian traditions. Bifurcations signify debates in each of which only an idealized scenario sees a victorious approach emerging. If we disregard these debates, we cannot but miss some key aspects of the history of ideas. It is not an overstatement to say that along absolutist lines even the narrowly conceived task can only be completed at the price of serious distortions.

The purpose of relativist historical reconstructions is to understand what a text or a set of text meant for the contemporaries or for other interpreting communities (Emmett, 2003, p. 533; Skinner, 1988, p. 276), so any text is placed in the relevant context. For this contextualistic attitude, where 'context' does not simply mean textual context, the critique of the past with hindsight is not necessarily a goal. Blaug tries to overrate his own absolutist approach by portraying a frequent mistake of relativism as a necessity. Assessing a theory in its own intellectual environment, or finding some theoretical similarities between texts of different eras, however, do not compel one to regard early classics as forerunners of modern economics or as providers of prescient ideas.

By contrast, absolutist narratives seek the 'genuine' forms of theories to fit them into a sequence. If the primary interest is in identifying an evolution conceived as a chain the links of which are 'theories properly understood', an absolutist is in hot water when it comes to circumscribing the textual basis to be taken into account. What principled grounds can she find to underlie her decision? Where is the border line between texts to study and texts to neglect? If, for instance, the starting point is the fact that Lucas's island models constituted a milestone of modern macroeconomics (a statement even his antagonists would accept), how would an absolutist select the texts for analysis? An obvious answer is his texts from the 1972–78 period, ranging from the neutrality of money (Lucas, 1972) to the implications of the Lucas critique (Lucas & Sargent, 1979). A relativist fly in the absolutist ointment, however, is the question whether Lucas's theoretical and methodological stance can properly be reconstructed on the basis of a half a dozen of texts. Although an absolutist historian would not pose this question in this way and rather play down Lucas's name to facilitate a discussion about micro-founded macroeconomics of the 1970s, both the essence of the problem and the practical question remain the same.

The attitude of contextualist–relativist historians is an answer to this question. As relativists argue, every past theory was somehow a response to the affairs of its own era, which is a point difficult to refute.[1] According to Blaug's critique, from this it takes only one step to get to the alleged and erroneous relativist stance that it is the social and historian circumstances that somehow *cause* the theories to emerge and develop (Mantzavinos, 2016). Blaug regards it as a general relativist mistake, but even if it is, it is not an implication of the relativist historical stance (relativism in general only takes attributing properties to things not in themselves but relative to given frameworks); thus, it is not an inevitable error. This fact in itself discredits Blaug's defence that it is only absolutism that can help to avoid this mistake. The same is true of the other thread in Blaug's critique through which he places the blame upon relativism for not checking the inner consistency of theories. Not even on the basis of relativism is it impossible to study the logical consistency of a theory under scrutiny. What is more, as Emmett (2003, p. 523) points out, such a critical analysis of texts also constitutes an integral part of contextualist interpretations. Contextualists are free to distinguish false, a bit better, and finally good theories against some solid standards, such as semirealism has aided us in the present analysis.

So apart from the absolutist and relativist stances Blaug distinguishes, there is at least one further option: contextualism. As Blaug argues, their relativist attitude deprives relativists of the possibility of absolutist assessment carried out on the basis of current superior state of knowledge. This shortcoming of relativism, however, does not imply the neglect of the context. Likewise, adherents of the contextualist approach do not have to be averse to judging theories by present lights. One thinking that context is highly important can thus take a contextualist stance without becoming a full-fledged relativist as paying attention to the context may easily be conciliated with absolutist assessments. What is more, one would go

---

[1] The most efficient way of refutation would be to prove in a strict sense that any economic theory is independent of its social and intellectual environment.

so far to say that absolutist histories can best be done in a contextualist fashion. Accordingly, gauged against the way how related parts are structured sets limitations to causal understanding in the microfoundations project Lucas's and Friedman's methodologies were clearly judged as successful and unsuccessful attempts (with some caveats regarding their oeuvres, mentioned below), even though paying attention to the context (taken as Chicago economics, the debates, or even the personalities of the leading characters in the story) has been an aspect of crucial importance throughout. These stances on the proper ways of writing histories of economic thought are thus difficult to tell apart. The more so as a lot of work has been done to place absolutist histories into context, so today nothing but contextualist histories, be they histories of science or ideas, can be regarded as the 'best' histories (Pickering, 1997, p. 6). At the same time, contextualism has started to fade into relativism (Price, 2008, pp. xi–xvi), so today absolutist histories of economics can hardly go without treating theories as integral parts of some broader settings. There are fewer and fewer effective arguments for playing down the importance of contexts.

Blaug's objections to relativism are easy to block, whilst the approach he suggests raises some problems to which contextualism has simple answers. As both authors when writing and readers when reading always rely upon their cultural backgrounds, focusing on a narrow set of texts can hardly result in correct or even acceptable interpretations. Moreover, when Blaug (1985, p. 3) admits that no economic thought can claim absolute and eternal validity (as social laws change in space and time), he cannot but implicitly refuse the absolutist stance on the negligibility of the social and intellectual environment. Providing a sketchy overview of the history of economic thought from Adam Smith through Marshall and Walras to Pareto, he himself also tells a relativist history but without making this fact explicit. Establishing his narrative, he takes for granted the well-known interpretation of the invisible hand as a starting point of later developments. However, it is not Smith's only plausible and tenable reading (Mantzavinos, 2014).

It is the absolutist historian's own limited point of view due to which she gets into trouble when selecting the textual basis for analysis. History of economic thought is an interpretive discipline as its very purpose, plainly put, is to unravel the proper[2] meanings of texts. As relativists and contextualists argue, this mission is doomed to failure unless the influences that the author's social and intellectual environment exerts are also taken into account. Even though such circumstances are not necessarily to be regarded as causes of a text in the strict sense of the word, through the author they still leave marks on it as the author reacts to these circumstances with his works. However, one does not have to be a relativist

---

[2] A proper interpretation is not a reading of eternal validity.

to realize: if the purpose is interpretation aimed at suggesting a proper, careful, and comprehensive narrative, then the textual basis is to be as inclusive as possible to cover even the author's unpublished works such as notes, teaching materials, and correspondence (Weintraub, Meardon, Gayer, & Banzhaf, 1998). It is not only standing upon relativist grounds that widening the set of relevant texts makes sense.

An assessment of the relationship between published and unpublished works of an author always requires caution, especially in cases where the unpublished part of the oeuvre significantly changes the evaluation previously formed on the basis of (a subset of) the published writings. Needless to say, such a modification is highly probable. If these textual sources did not alter the way we think of an author, with hindsight they would simply be regarded as insignificant. However, deciding in advance to disregard the unpublished works cannot but lead to presupposed superficiality. It is only after studying a text that it can turn out to be irrelevant to an interpretation. According to the usual argument these texts have remained unpublished as they do not reflect the author's true opinion.[3] The personal and inherently unpublished character of letters invalidates this argument: they are not meant to be published, though in many respects they can shed light on the role the author's intellectual or personal background plays in his professional achievements. Works, however, may remain unpublished for other reasons as well: being pressed for time, losing interest in the topic, the related ideas show up in published writings, disbelief in the appeal of the subject, or even the lack of confidence (Weintraub, Meardon, Gayer, & Banzhaf, 1998, p. 1498). However, if we have good reasons for taking these texts into account, then they inevitably bring along the effects of the social and intellectual environment into the analysis. Such a reason is the case where a subtle relationship between the published and unpublished texts occurs just like the relationship between rehearsals and subsequent actions (Geertz, 1973, p. 7). Notes and other manuscripts are easy to regard as preliminary collections of thoughts to be sharpened. It is no problem if published works only constitute the tip of the iceberg. Such a case, however, is a strong point in favour of paying particular attention to unpublished materials.

The smaller the sample of texts, the higher the probability of the emergence of some rival interpretations. This issue is likely to occur in cases where the competing interpretations focus upon different parts of the corpus. The same problem regards, on the one hand, the relationship between paragraphs of a text and the whole body of the text and, on the other

---

[3] If the additional texts modify the currently accepted interpretation, this argument is difficult to defend. The purpose of broadening the textual basis is to find an interpretation as careful as possible (Mantzavinos, 2005, p. 134) and not to preserve the current reading. To the latter, any incompatible or 'outlying' text ought to be excluded.

hand, the relationship between separate texts and the author's oeuvre. One of the simplest ways of choosing from the rival readings is to increase the number of involved texts. What trivially emerges when interpreting a single text (one ought not to understand a text on the basis of a single paragraph) also applies to the reconstruction of the meaning of an oeuvre. The more texts involved, the more careful the interpretation. Stigler (1965) argues for this suggestion with the case of statistical sampling and confidence. Even if a reader makes do with an interpretation she puts forward in a superficial and brief statement, she inevitably faces the fact that her reading is based upon textual parts that are scattered over the lifework (Emmett, 2003, p. 527). The idea of a consistent interpretation free of conflicting parts is always a presumption in the strict sense. Some conscious efforts to avoid an unnaturally consistent account are thus necessary (highlighting some inconsistencies in Max Weber's methodological works was an aspect of the discussion in Section 4.1.1). For instance, Mantzavinos (2005, pp. 137–145) delineates some alternative readings of Adam Smith's invisible hand metaphor that stem from different textual bases and can equally be regarded as valid. Whether there is an overall consistency or not, converging the sample towards the whole population of texts is the only way of minimizing the interpretive distortions, and the only way of revealing an inconsistency instead of putting forward an array of seemingly competing readings. A careful interpretation seldom leads to a consistent account, which may seem disturbing. Even if such an inconsistency is a theorizing failure, it is not something to eliminate but to highlight. An author having had a change of heart does not necessarily refuse her prior self (a pure case of inconsistency), only refines her stance. We can find such a sharp change in opinion in Lucas's works as well (Lucas, 1990a) when, for instance, he drops the idea of the taxation of capital income.

Weird as it is, an absence of consistency with regard to an author's oeuvre does not inevitably result in inconsistency. This is also true of the Lucas interpretation suggested in Chapters 2–4. In spite of the efforts to pinpoint those texts where Lucas applied a realist language and to suggest a general framework to aid in understanding how he could (and should) be regarded as a realist, there is still a plethora of texts which are rather neutral in the realist-antirealist context. These textual items are neither inconsistent with a possible realist position, nor do they support this reading. This raises the issue of whether it is really necessary for an author to articulate his 'general position' time and again. The emphasis upon empirical performance had grown into a minimum requirement and a widely held norm by the 1960–70s, so it would have made no sense for Lucas to keep pushing it. By contrast, it is rather infringing this common rule that would have required recurrent emphases and a thorough defence strategy. Predictive success, however, is easy to reconcile with the semirealist version of structural realism which, as a framework applied with hindsight, is not a label Lucas could have applied to himself. However, this is only a chronological question. The analysis above was not aimed at creating a position unacceptable for Lucas, but rather applying a recently emerged conceptual background to reconstruct the intended meaning of his texts in the way Skinner (1969) suggested. Efforts were made to identify what Lucas would say today, having the terminology of modern structuralist philosophy in his bag (Emmett, 1997, pp. 227–228). Lucas's realism combined with the ideas of its forerunners (Stigler and Becker; see Section 2.1.1 for more on the imperialism of economics and the realist interpretation of the involved choice-theoretic framework) is an ambition detectable at the textual level. Semirealism has only acted as the framework to aid us in organizing Lucas's analysed texts into a meaningful and plausible system.

A careful conclusion thus emerges according to which having satisfactory empirical performance and connecting to the socio-economic universe via thoroughly built and causally adequate microfoundations were equally important aspects for Lucas. The relationship between micro and macro, and the way entity properties contribute to the formation of causal connections are easy to understand in a structural realist framework. As the vast majority of the analysed texts come from the 1970s, on these grounds, however, no general position characterizing Lucas's oeuvre comes up. In these terms we have some dubious speculations at best. For instance, Vercelli (1991, p. 127) calls attention to the fact that after the 1980s Lucas flew in the face of some of his prior ideas or even demolished them. In the same period his interest became more diverse, but writings from these years were mainly neglected above.

In the 1980s, to be more specific, inflationary considerations started playing a minor role and the usual island framework occasionally got out of sight. Just to name a few scattered examples, Lucas and Stokey (1983) dynamize the Ramsey theory of optimal taxation in a version where there is one commodity and one representative consumer who faces the government levying taxes and buying that one product. Lucas's (1988) concern is the problem of economic development conceived as the growth of per capita income, paying close attention to experienced patterns of economic growth. Theory is still conceived as a dynamic system to put on a computer and run. Such an artificial economy is populated by abstract-idealized agents or robots, as Lucas calls them, in order to reproduce some real-world-like patterns in the outcomes of their interactions. Here Lucas applies a closed-economy framework including a set of competitive markets that are populated by identical rational agents who produce with a constant-returns technology. Lucas's (1990a) question regards how taxation can contribute to the maximal utility of consumers. He applies a variant of the usual representative agent framework built upon a single household as a representation of many. The decision problem is also familiar: the utility of the household is dependent upon consumption and leisure. Lucas (1990b) looks into the problem of capital flows between countries with unequal capital endowments. Even though he performs the calculations in per capita terms all along the paper, he does not use his well-known representative agent framework. Atkeson and Lucas (1992) problematize the allocation of a single product among a large number of agents who face unpredictable shocks to taste affecting their marginal utility of consumption and hence leading to distribution effects. Lucas (1992) places infinitely lived households into a single-product economy to study the distribution effects of shocks to preferences that induce the households to adjust their consumption. Lucas (1993) considers the growth effects of human capital accumulation by suggesting a framework in which the world economy is made up of single economies, each characterized with a production function in which, quite realistically, labour force is regarded as immobile and capital as mobile. In a multi-agent model, Atkeson and Lucas (1995) assuming that agents face employment risk construed as the possibility of being unemployed in each period study the problem of optimal allocation of work and consumption. As workers with opportunity to work may also choose not to take jobs, a moral hazard emerges which is a hindrance to the perfect pooling of job risks.

Besides avoiding the trap of overgeneralization, our conclusion also leaves open the question of the relationship between Lucas and economics after Lucas, especially the issue of the problematic assumptions in DSGE models (see Sections 1.2.3 and 5.4 below for more on this). Paying attention to the changes emerging between Lucasian business cycle models and the degenerative section of the research programme (Lakatos, 1978), if the latter really emerged at all, is far beyond the scope of this volume.

Lucas is highly likely to have acquired the requirement of predictive success prior to the notion of realistic microfoundations as the former had already been a hallmark of the Chicago school in his graduate years (Friedman, 1953/2009). When carrying out the choice-theoretic analysis of the Great Depression of 1929–33 (Lucas & Rapping, 1969) the idea of a reduction to individual decisions was also at hand; thus it is only the general equilibrium framework and the rational expectations hypothesis that were missing. Both had become parts of his analytical toolkit by 1972. However, it is also an important detail that, as we have seen, in 1969 Lucas was already aware of the rational expectations hypothesis. All these theoretical and methodological advancements took place in a couple of years, and these developments effectively underline that Lucas's theoretical and methodological stance in the 1970s is the result of a rapid progress influenced by multiple factors. We can take a snapshot of the theory and the methodology he subscribed to in these years; however, its caption ought not to be something like 'Lucas's overall theoretical and methodological position', which would be a possibly oversimplifying reconstruction to be taken with a pinch of salt. The stronger the efforts to establish coherence in a reconstruction, the higher the risk of distortion. On the basis of the accomplishments above our best bet is to talk of a more or less coherent subset of Lucas's theory, following the suggestions Anthony Waterman (1988, p. 206) made in general. To decide the extent to which this coherence can be extended over his oeuvre, again, is far beyond the scope of this volume. Likewise, the econometric aspects of Lucas's methodology were also hardly touched upon.

As we have seen, by increasing the sample one can enhance the probability of forming a proper understanding of an author's theoretical and methodological position, which, it is to be emphasized again, does not imply either the consistency or the stability of this stance. It is not incidental that in the context of the problem of choosing texts for analysis it makes sense to talk of sample and sample size. As Mantzavinos (2014) argues, textual interpretation due to its implicit and unconsciously applied cognitive background closely obeys the hypothetico-deductive method of the sciences. From this Mantzavinos infers that textual interpretation meets the requirements of modern science, so it is possible to have rational debates over alternative readings and it is meaningful to seek 'true' interpretations. For Mantzavinos a textual interpretation is aimed at reconstructing the accurate nexus of meaning of a text or a set of texts.

In this approach the practice of textual interpretation rests upon two pillars: hypothesis formation and statistical tests, both (especially the latter) conceived very broadly. The phase of hypothesis formation is necessitated by the complexity of interpretation. This is the reason why Mantzavinos treading in Dilthey's footsteps talks of not simple 'meaning' but the 'nexus of meaning' in the case of every single textual expression. Compared to simple meaning the nexus of meaning is a highly complex notion. Its use is explained by the fact that a text is a product of interactions between author and readers as interrelated texts constitute systems. When formulizing an utterance an author relies upon her own intentions, knowledge, and convictions, and takes even the expected reactions of her readers into account (Nehamas, 1981, p. 145). As a consequence, it is contentious whether the intended meaning or the nexus of meaning of a text deprived of its context can properly be revealed. Identifying the correct meaning is oftentimes uncertain even within the context, though. As texts are human actions emerging in a special form (Austin, 1962), what Weber (1968/1978, p. 4) said about the understanding of human actions also applies to textual interpretation. The sharp distinction between subjectively intended and objectively valid meanings holds with regard to speech or linguistic acts and of course texts as well. This gives slightly more room for interpretive work as compared to Skinner's (1969, p. 28) suggestions since the actual meaning may differ from the intended meaning. The accordance of meanings can be an initial hypothesis at best which is to be rejected if some falsifying facts emerge (Skinner, 1972, pp. 404–405; 1988, pp. 269–278). As an obvious example emerges the case when an author erroneously sizes up the ways leading to an end and, as a consequence, the text she puts forward fails to achieve the expected purposes. This is a simple error of the expected effects of a speech act, and it is the interpreter who must underline the differences and emphasize what the author actually does (Manicas, 2006, p. 7). This also means that Mäki's (2009a) efforts to suggest a realist interpretation were not bizarre in spite of Friedman's explicit disapproval (see Section 4.1 for more on the history of the interpretive debate over F53). The meaning that emerges as the result of interpretation is dependent not upon the author's agreement but upon the strength of evidences provided by the contextual matrix. Further instances are some unintended implications in a text—implications having remained hidden even for the author.

The nexus of meaning of a text or a set of texts never opens up immediately. If so, it would be enough for us to read one paragraph by any author. By contrast, any reader proceeds from word to word, from sentence to sentence, and from paragraph to paragraph. Simultaneously, using her pre-given knowledge she keeps interpreting the text from the very first moment. Such interpretations, however, are only interpretive hypotheses in the strict sense as any tentative interpretation may turn out to be wrong the moment we start reading the next paragraph. To keep things short and sweet, the reader assumes the absence of inconsistency both in the individual sentences and at the textual level.[4] However, this assumption is also a hypothesis that experience (i.e. reading) may controvert (Bevir, 1997). Interpretive hypotheses oftentimes regard unobservable 'entities' conceived in the strict sense of the word: such a case is when we discuss the realism of Lucas or novelist Jonathan Franzen. Realism as such is

---

[4] The theory of cognitive dissonance (Festinger, 1957) underlines that human beings in their everyday practices strive towards consistency with regard to their beliefs and actions in order to avoid a related psychological discomfort. Beliefs embrace all kinds of knowledge and opinions, including scientific ideas. We can avoid inconsistency or dissonance or, generally speaking, non-fitting relations among cognitions by reconciling our ideas or by retaining the inconsistency of beliefs, but in a rationalized form. Such a rationalization is when a theoretical inconsistency is made explicit by saying that the current belief is the correct one and the author has changed her mind. In such a case, any change in belief or conviction appears to be a result of a foreshadowing theoretical progress or a step towards the 'right' theory. This is the reason why theoretical consistency is always a good assumption ('no one loves entertaining troublesome contradictions'). However, we must give credit to textual evidence if inconsistency is undeniable. If the author was aware of the contradictions (always a problem for further scrutiny), her rationalizing efforts may be found somewhere. Skinner's (1969, p. 20) strategy is another way of rationalization to mention. He justifies the feeling of discomfort raised by cognitive dissonance by placing emphasis upon the inevitability of inconsistencies.

directly unobservable; thus in order for this hypothesis to be empirically tested, some implications directly comparable to experience are needed. A subtle theoretical stance implies textually observable statements, so after an initial interpretive hypothesis has been formed it is tested via its consequences or implications expected to show up at the textual level.

Having done so, we have at least one hypothesis, and deduction was also applied to bridge the gap between hypotheses and their testable implications. During empirical tests we check the validity of an initial hypothesis on the textual basis. A test may rest upon anything that is judged to be relevant as for the interpretive problem at hand; thus the interpreter is required to go far beyond a hard core of published texts of an author. When conducting tests, interpretive hypotheses may be revised if needed. In case of unaffirmative observations such hypotheses are fine-tuned or rejected once and for all. Simultaneously, if some alternative hypotheses come into play, they are also weighed and compared.

This is the same theorizing pattern as studied in Chapter 2 in the context of the Marshall–Walras divide. Understanding in the natural and social sciences and interpreting activities follow a very similar scheme (Mantzavinos, 2009, pp. 299–300). As we have seen, one of the most intriguing aspects of the debate over the Marshallian and Walrasian approaches regarded the use of pre-given theories. Theorists on the Marshallian side disapproved of pre-given ideas by saying that theorizing practice can be relieved of them by letting the data speak. That is, theories were expected to emerge from observations, and observation-based theorizing was supposed to be the very first stage where any theory ought to step into the process. Now, dwelling upon the interpretive use of the hypothetico-deductive method underlines how untenable an epistemic stance it is. Even if one lets the data speak (and she ought to: interpretive hypotheses are to be modified under the burden of textual evidence), in order to interpret a text she actively applies her background knowledge from the very first sentence as details of the text are to be organized in a theoretical framework. A stimulus can turn into information only if the reader's pre-given or background knowledge is in action. As in Chapter 2, theorizing is conceived as a cyclical interaction of induction and deduction in which the interpreter moves there and back again between theory (i.e. interpretation) and data (words and sentences in a text). Theorizing is successful and, what is more, possible only if a copious amount of pre-given knowledge is applied. It is the act of reading that activates this background knowledge as any reader during interpretation tries to place a text in pre-given schemas. As Gadamer (1960/2004, p. 269) says, a reader always turns to texts with particular expectations. Even if the reader starts reading a text with no pre-given hypotheses, and forms her first ideas on it when reading, she will inevitably think something the moment her eyes meet the first sentence, which would be impossible should she have no pre-given knowledge (but for pre-given knowledge she would even be unable to read the text). This thought will serve as an interpretive hypothesis as she proceeds, so reading and interpretation is a dynamic act. The reader continuously changes and refines her beliefs on a text. Interpretive hypotheses are unstable: the validity of such a hypothesis is checked via comparing its implications to observations, i.e. on textual grounds.

This cyclicality is thus not a circulus vitiosus impossible to leave behind. As a matter of fact, leaving is unnecessary as cyclicality is an inherent component of theorizing and textual interpretation. The course of textual interpretation is commonly described with the 'hermeneutic circle' which refers to an allegedly problematic tension between part and whole. The meaning of a text stems from the meanings of its parts, whilst the meaning of each part is determined by the ideas formed on the whole. The same part-whole relation applies to the relationship between a text and a set of texts (Taylor, 1985, p. 18). If, however, we admit the existence of the hermeneutic circle instead of making efforts to break out of it, the approval of our entering the circle on the basis of appropriate pre-given knowledge can be a possible solution to the related problems (Ricoeur, 1981, p. 18).

As Stigler (1976) suggests, it is the scientific community that endows us with 'proper' pre-given knowledge. As a consequence, it must be noted, the scientific community becomes a hermeneutic authority (Fish, 1980) that infuses the changes in opinions on scientific ideas with a considerable extent of rigidity (Kuhn, 1962). By admitting the contribution of pre-given knowledge Stigler regards the problem of the hermeneutic circle as settled. However, it also follows from his suggestions that a prerequisite of joining the profession is the acceptance of some ready-made interpretations in the history of economic thought. This by no means guarantees correct interpretations, so Stigler only takes notice of how science actually works. Mantzavinos insisting on the terminology modifies the problem setting by completely dissolving the hermeneutic circle in the usual practice of scientific theorizing (for him there exists no problematic hermeneutic circle, only a natural, dynamic, and iterative theorizing cyclicality). At the same time, like Stigler, he institutionalizes the scientific community as a provider of the inevitable pre-given knowledge and as the authority deciding upon the validity of interpretations. This certainly solves one of the two problems: the mystery of the hermeneutic circle is demolished, though objectivity cannot but remain a promise and a hope. As a positive feature, scientific understanding and textual interpretation are placed on a common basis.[5] If Mantzavinos's approach is correct, all the natural, social, and human sciences rest on the same epistemological footing.

---

[5] Without this, historians of modern economics would face problems as economics extensively applies the hypothetico-deductive method in social scientific theorizing. It would be weird at a minimum if the same method proved to be inapplicable in the history of economic thought and economic methodology the purpose of which is the understanding of social actions emerging as texts.

As Mantzavinos (2009, pp. 305–308) argues, the hermeneutic cycle is only an empirical problem that the human mind unconsciously and automatically solves during cognition. Initial interpretive hypotheses show up from the background as literates spontaneously recognize the words and their meanings. In the act of reading the meaning of a text automatically reveals itself from the meanings of single words (more specifically, pre-given knowledge helps the meaning to reveal itself from the text) and from the activated items of pre-given knowledge to form a complex network to be more or less modified and refined by reading the further parts of the texts. Understanding or interpretation is thus not a mystery but rather an everyday skill. The application of pre-given knowledge does not give rise to suspicion. On the contrary, placing an emphasis upon it is necessitated by its inevitability and its role underlying human knowledge (Simon, 1983, pp. 25–27). There is no contradiction in the fact that cognition rests upon previous experience and pre-given knowledge. It is a fact of life.

Conscious interpretive efforts are only needed when one faces confusing texts difficult to understand. In such cases, when interpretation and understanding cannot go spontaneously, some 'focal awareness' is aimed at generating interpretive hypotheses (Polanyi, 1958/2005). Forming hypotheses, however, still rests upon pre-given knowledge including theoretical and scientific knowledge, and scientific interests. Interpretation thus remains the same for the most part. Pre-given knowledge is necessary in all cases. The only question regards how much consciousness or focal awareness its proper application requires. There is no impassable hermeneutic circle even in complicated cases. Pre-given knowledge would be excludable from the game only if a reader could turn to a text with an empty mind. If not, for at a minimum she speaks the language in which the text is written, she cannot but read the text on the basis of her pre-given knowledge underlying the interpretive process.

As scientific texts are oftentimes inconsistent or confusing for various reasons and in various ways and to various extents, the fact that everyday interpretive acts run smoothly does not imply the simplicity of the interpretations of theoretical works. It only follows that interpreting such a text is a meaningful effort and an achievable purpose the cognitive bases of which have been understood by now in due measure. But the inference still holds: increasing the textual basis for an interpretation enhances the probability of finding a correct or at least a widely applicable reading and contributes to the screening out of incorrect interpretive hypotheses, even if the meaning of a text or a set of texts is not ultimate and is not independent of either the author's or the reader's cultural backgrounds. When Zwe talk of a contextualist interpretation this activates the context on both the author's and the interpreter's sides. It is only in such a contextualist way that Fish (1980, p. vii) admits texts having obvious and inescapable meanings. Mantzavinos (2005, p. 138) puts forward a more radical idea.

As he argues, there can be true meanings or interpretations. This is the intended meaning the author had in mind (Hirsch, 1967, p. 8). This, at the same time, underlines that the meaning of a text and its author's intention are impossible to part in certain cases.[6] Like in realist natural sciences, however, sometimes this real meaning, unfortunately, is impossible to find because of the well-known problem of the underdetermination of theory by data: texts may support various readings. For this reason, interpretations are put forward in conditionals in a strict sense. Every reader has their own reading, though among or beyond these interpretations there exists a true interpretive hypothesis grabbing the true meaning of a text. However, finding it may be too ambitious a purpose. As Skinner (1972, p. 393; 1988, p. 280) argues, instead of a state of certain knowledge only plausible and corroborated interpretive hypotheses are achievable.

5.2 Interpreting Lucas on a broad textual basis

This raises the question of how the widening of the textual basis changes our understanding of Lucas's methodology. The simplest way of putting the answer is to study the portray that the published works and unpublished materials of the archives paint together and how this picture differs from the commonly accepted account of his methodology.

As we have seen, all the standard assessments of his methodology highlight the low level of descriptive performance as a hallmark. Accordingly, Lucas's models are regarded as of imaginary nature. Discussing the methodological norms, De Vroey (2016, pp. 176–177) mentions microfoundations and the general equilibrium framework. By contrast, the analyses we have just struggled through (especially in Chapters 3 and 4) focused on descriptive performance and its relationship with Lucas's further methodological tenets, whilst paying particular attention to the microfoundations conceived as the key to the establishment of both causal adequacy and the connections with reality. More specifically, the main question concerned what principles Lucas had established in in his methodology as for connecting his models with reality.

---

[6] If one asks the interpretive question in the form 'What has the author expressed with this text?', the distinction disappears, and interpretation reveals the author's intention (Skinner, 1972, p. 397). Distinguishing intention and motive leads to another problem. For Skinner (1969, p. 49), 'the essential aim [...] must be to recover [the] complex intention on the part of the author.' Nexus of meaning as a key concept requires the interpreter to identify the author's motive in cases where it is identifiable and contributes to an adequate reconstruction (Mantzavinos, 2016). Discovery of the author's intention is a legitimate objective of interpretation, but not the only one. This purpose is of course contentious as both intentional analyses and textual interpretations rest upon texts and contexts. For some different concepts of intention and meaning, see Skinner (1972) and Brown (2003).

In his methodological analysis, De Vroey (2016) places a huge emphasis upon analogue systems which he characterizes as Lucas's key term. An analogue system or analogy is a construct whose behaviour sufficiently mimics the target. This resemblance seems to be wholly of outer nature. If in similar situations a system behaves similarly to the modelled thing, analogy holds (Boumans, 2005, pp. 93–95). From this, De Vroey (2016, p. 179) infers that by manipulating analogue systems, that is, by launching real-world-like macro-shocks to artificial economies, 'we can learn about the functioning of real economies' on the basis of the similarity in behaviour. However, by emphasizing that for Lucas 'a theoretical proposition is a statement about a fictitious economy rather than about an actual economy', De Vroey (2016, p. 180) tries to completely separate model and reality (De Vroey & Pensieroso, 2016, p. 4). Apart from the similarity in behaviour there seems to be no connection in between. De Vroey conceives the only dimension of analogy as the imperative that the outer behaviour of a mathematical model should be in consonance with the behaviour of the target. This is a subtle way of putting the instrumentalism of F53. Vercelli (1991, p. 130 and p. 141) characterizes Lucas in the same way, putting the main conclusion of F53 into his mouth ('Lucas defends himself by asking to be judged not on the realism of hypotheses but on the usefulness of his assumptions'). This sharp demarcation between model and reality and Lucas's admittedly unrealistic terminology is a sufficient basis for De Vroey (2016, p. 71) to introduce Friedman as a realist economist as compared to Lucas. This is quite weird, however, as Friedman (1953/2009) regarded the realism of assumptions as of marginal importance.

However, this interpretation is severely flawed as it conceives realism as a unidimensional concept. To see why, suffice it to recall the sequence of Mäki's (1989, 1994a, 1996, 2000, 2002, 2009a, 2009b, 2011) papers where scrutinizing the way how economics is able to impart sound causal knowledge via theories that seriously distort reality he discusses the problem of the realisticness of unrealistic models. For Mäki this knowledge does not rest upon superficial similarity emerging at the outer behavioural level. He argues that, plainly put, unrealistic concepts and models are capable of substantively grabbing some selected relevant properties of reality.

Identifying the realism of mathematical economics with descriptive realism doomed to failure the critique against the then mainstream theory as early as in the 1970s. Kornai's 'Anti-equilibrium' is an illustrative example (Kornai, 1971). Here Kornai judging by the absence of descriptive realism calls into question modern mathematical economics as a 'real' science: a science that could and does deal with reality (Csaba, 2017, pp. 38–40). The main thread of his argument is simple. He supposed theoretical or social irrelevance to be a direct and inevitable implication of poor descriptive performance. What is more, Kornai argued that, as another consequence of poor descriptive performance, theoretical relevance conceived as efforts towards causal understanding was not even a purpose of theorizing. This perspective, however, was rather weird and off the mark even in those days. In his response to Kornai, Hahn (1973) highlighted both the multi-dimensional character of scientific realism of which descriptive performance is only one and the fact that representing laws and objects in mathematical style by no means renders them propositions of mathematical character. The content that mathematical formalism conveys remains non-mathematical (Manicas, 2006, pp. 26–27), he argued. As far as the causal understanding of complex reality was considered, Hahn also regarded highly abstract models with poor descriptive capabilities as relevant. As Hahn underlined, the absence of descriptive realism does not necessarily ruin causal adequacy.

In his methodological analysis, De Vroey turns to modern macroeconomics via this rather obsolete approach Hahn already rejected. De Vroey also takes it for granted that models with poor descriptive performance cannot achieve theoretical-causal adequacy. On this showing the history of modern macroeconomics where descriptive accuracy has not been a standard thus immediately turns into the history of Friedmanian instrumentalism gaining territory. The fact that De Vroey does not even problematize causal understanding is a clear sign of this mindset. For De Vroey, the only dimension and measure of realism is descriptive accuracy (Galbács, 2016). All this amounts to his intention of providing a methodological analysis on Lucas whilst completely disregarding not only the results of modern economic methodology but also the effective answers his subject, modern macroeconomics, has given to the related criticisms. The result can be nothing but a picture modern macroeconomics has not only rejected but effectively refuted. Even though in the reference section of his 'History', De Vroey (2016, pp. 389–417) mentions Mäki's 'The methodology of positive economics—Reflections on the Milton Friedman legacy' as the only source that contains some relevant papers on the methodological assessment of modern macroeconomics, the same reference section also highlights the fact that no papers of the volume were factually used. By so doing, De Vroey perhaps thinking that a correct interpretation requires no pre-given knowledge tried to reduce his interpretive theoretical basis underlying the methodological analysis to zero. As we have seen, however, due to the cognitive characteristics of interpretive work this is a hindrance to forming an appropriate reading. Authors when doing methodology move far beyond the territory of economic theories narrowly conceived. In order to provide proper renditions, proper interpretive frameworks are needed, but building and applying them are highly unlikely to be spontaneous acts. Without such an explicit, reliable, and fruitful engine, all that De Vroey has is a reformulation of Lucas's methodology and theory in plain English, which inevitably leads to enigmatic statements like his labelling Friedman as a realist economist as compared to Lucas. If descriptive realism is the sole dimension, what about the further aspects? By contrast, even though Boumans (2005, pp. 92–96) relies upon a massive econometric theoretical background, he settles the problem of 'Robert Lucas's artificial economies' on the basis of his 'Econometric policy evaluation—A critique' (Lucas, 1976/1981); 'Understanding business cycles' (Lucas, 1977); 'Methods and problems in business cycle theory' (Lucas, 1980); the introduction to his 'Studies in business-cycle theory' (Lucas, 1981, pp. 1–18); and 'Adaptive behavior and economic theory' (Lucas, 1986).

It is structural realism taken from the general philosophy of science that was applied as a framework for the methodological analysis of Chapter 4. In modern philosophy of science there is a commonly accepted idea that a general theory intended to give account of reality at the most fundamental level must be a form of structuralism. Structural realism proved to be an adequate framework as its central problem regards the relationship between parts and whole, which is also a concern for micro-founded macroeconomics. It is even more appealing as it can aid in extending current realist philosophy of economics to the microfoundations project. The main purpose of the programme is to trace macro-level economic phenomena back to micro-level units (and to other irreducible macro-entities), and it is exactly this relationship, i.e. to interconnect the levels, that stands in the focus of the debates over structural realism. The key question of the controversy taking place in both the philosophy of physics and the general philosophy of science regards what knowledge about the micro-level units is needed in order that macro-level phenomena could be explained and understood.

According to the ontic version of structural realism, entities are unnecessary for analysing phenomena over the entity level. In this framework, entities are only nodes of the structures, so entities are structurally dissolved and reconceptualized in structural terms. Reality is conceived to consist of structures only. However, this framework proved inappropriate for our present purposes. Even the most ardent adherents of ontic structural realism are oftentimes ready to admit that in the visible world, where the units of structures are entities having experienceable properties, the ontic version is too radical and an unnecessarily restricted interpretation of reality. A social scientific consequence of ontic structural realism would be the possibility of analysing macro-social phenomena whilst neglecting the individuals. A radical way of putting it is an imperative that both the existence and the properties of individual entities should be disregarded. Even if there exist entity properties, they all stem from the structures.

Semirealism as a more tenable version reverses this relation by deriving all supra-entity phenomena from the properties of entities, be they of micro- or macroeconomic nature. By so doing, semirealism renders entities and their properties ontologically prior to structures. Thanks to their characteristics, entities can interconnect and form structures, and it is also their properties that determine the roles entities play in causal connections and the way such connections work. The close relationship between causal structures and entity properties explains why causally adequate structure representations cannot do without realist representations of the key entity properties. According to the beautiful philosophy of semirealism, to explain the various levels of reality we do not need various ontologies; thus the tenets on the causal properties of entities as such can easily be extended to cover the agents conceived as the dominant units of economics. It is more than saying that a causally adequate representation of a macroeconomic structure, which does definitely not mean descriptive realism, requires realist representation of entity properties. A more powerful albeit equivalent paraphrase of this statement suggests that theorists should derive all macroeconomic phenomena from the properties of agents and further, irreducible entities. Everything beyond the individuals has the individuals as its ultimate ontological basis. This is an exceptionally strong point in favour of micro-founded macroeconomics. The purpose of abstraction and idealization is to endow the simplified forms of entities with some existent properties that are relevant in terms of the causal mechanisms under scrutiny. This suggestion does not touch upon the problem that a mathematical representation of a structure may lead to inconsistencies. As semirealism argues, this is a problem of mathematical formulization but not of ontology.

At the same time this argument also invalidates the way Hoover (2009) interprets F53. As he argues, Friedman could be a causal realist by setting no requirements as for entity-level assumptions over and above macro-level empirical performance. This paper of Hoover is particularly interesting as it is one of the most striking examples of the misapplication of the contextualist approach (Boland, 2010). Judging by Friedman's persistent admiration for Marshall and Marshallian economics (according to Hoover's simple syllogism, Friedman was a Marshallian, Marshall was a causal realist, Friedman thus could be nothing but a realist), Hoover reads F53 as a causal realist manifesto. His interpretation is thus wholly dominated by the context and Hoover misses suggesting the possibility of an inner inconsistency. As semirealism argues, however, theoretical entities alien to our everyday world can only carry inexistent causal structures. And as Friedman did not insist on realism as a purpose, empirical performance in his case refers to nothing beyond itself. Entity-level assumptions cooked up with a view to predictive success cannot but lead to good macro-level predictions only, and this is exactly what Friedman emphasized in his methodology.

If we do not discredit the idea of a realist Lucas prejudicially, his considerations on the decision problems of agents will show a radically different picture of his theory and methodology. The point of departure from the widely accepted account is the recognition of the simple fact that empirical success does not necessarily imply F53-like instrumentalism. For realists it is also important to have good predictions as realists conceive satisfying empirical performance as a sign of a grip on reality. Friedman's instrumentalism is a simple case as he approved of this account as the correct summary of his methodological stance and the vast majority of the F53-interpretations also subscribe to this reading. Our key question was whether Lucas put forward some purposes similar to the instrumentalist claims embedded in F53. As semirealism argues that macro-level phenomena should be traced back to micro-level properties, the key to the alleged realism of the Lucasian microfoundations project lies in the way he represented agents. Likewise, if Lucas had really built his models in the 1970s in an instrumentalist fashion, instrumentalism could also be identified at this level. An emphasis upon empirical performance at the macro-social level is indifferent in these terms.

His texts do not support an instrumentalist reading of Lucas—if they do, it is only at a superficial level at best. His main objection to Keynesian models regarded the assumed constancy of the underlying parameters. As he argued, these models prove useless in cases where economic policies change. As a change in the policy rule drives agents to change the behavioural rules they previously followed, the purpose of economic theory is to understand the individual's decision problem, or more specifically, to understand how a regime change influences individual behaviour. We can thus find the extremely individualist methodological stance according to which all macro-social phenomena should stem from the agents. As a consequence, the most important question of the analysis above regarded Lucas's ideas on the representation of entity properties.

It is important to realize that when Lucas suggested a reduction to individual decisions (to the extent it was feasible), the thing he had in mind was a far cry from a mere heuristic device. It is more than the fact that the choice-theoretic framework he applied led to predictions well mimicking real outcomes that justified its use. Lucas regarded choice theory as causally adequate and realist since macroeconomic phenomena really emanate from individual decisions, and it also explains the predictive success of models. Lucas suggested no ad hoc or pragmatist assumptions but understanding and modelling the decision problem of real economic agents. Understanding business cycles amounts to the understanding of how changes in the money stock, conceived as evident shocks, can lead to large-scale real economic fluctuations with the transmission of individual decisions. Lucas established the consistency with the available evidence and data as a requirement at two distinct levels. Beyond good empirical performance at the macro level the consonance with micro-economics and micro-level data is also an explicit requisite. In his models analysed above he designed the prototypical individual by exploiting the available theoretical and empirical results about the decision problem of real economic agents. For Lucas individual decision is so obvious a basis that the choice-theoretical framework loses its hypothetical character.

In the background of macro-data there lie individual decisions. The stability of the rules decision makers follow ensures the stability of the relationships between macroeconomic variables. It is possible to superficially mimic macro-level dynamics; however, even the practical benefits, let alone the theoretical merits, of such an endeavour are highly limited. If we fail to understand decisions and, instead, we apply an atheoretical framework (in the style of Sims and his VARs) or some ad hoc theories (Friedman and his Phillips curves), we cannot go farther than some macro-level tendencies and trends, and the way such patterns of actions follow from individual behaviour remains hidden. As a major weakness, these frameworks cannot say anything intelligible about either the changes in behaviour or their consequences or the underlying reasons. They can only refer to some superficial results of behaviour without looking into the way agents act.

Laying down his microfoundations, however, Lucas wanted to dig down to as deep as the level of decisions. This case qualitatively differs from mimicking the consequences of human behaviour. The difference is clearly visible when decision rules change. As Lucas argued, to understand the effects of events that imply changes in decision rules one ought to regard effects as the joint results of changing conditions and stable preferences (see Fig. 5.1). Changes in behavioural rules stem from agents' adaptation. An improper theoretical and methodological basis allows one only to consider some superficial consequences of individual behaviour. In such a case, economists thus are left behind the data. It is only a simple fact of life that models may no longer work in cases where modellers miss some underlying behavioural changes. By contrast, Lucas's purpose was to explain macro-social phenomena with individual decisions that means looking into the real causal mechanism. The causal role of money was well known even before Lucas's time. However, pre-Lucasian theories failed to clarify the mechanism that related the changes in money stock to the emergence of large-scale fluctuations. Lucas suggested a cause-and-effect connection by building his theory of the real causal mechanism upon the most fundamental level that economics can reach.

FIG. 5.1   The Lucasian idea of how economic policy changes lead to behavioural changes.

5.3 How Friedman and Lucas fit into Mäki's framework: An assessment

Mäki's notion of realism is not the same as the concept general philosophy of science has formed on realism as the most tenably construed. In order to understand the dissimilarity it is insufficient to refer to how the naïve and the refined forms differ. As we have seen, even though scientific realism cannot convincingly attest to the truth of theories and the existence of presumed entities, not even the approximate truth of our best theories, realism still entertains the belief that we have theories worth realist commitments. When it comes to assessing the truth of certain theories, realists have definite answers.

By contrast, Mäki argues that not only truth and existence claims, but even the beliefs in existence and truth constitute too strong a requirement against scientific realism. His reasoning rests upon the usual anti-realist footing. Ideas on what to regard as true change from time to time, so our theories currently supposed to be true may fail later falsifying tests: realists thus have no more than the chance of existence and truth. Our theories might be true and the entities realists postulate might exist. This is the most we have, as Mäki (2008) argues. All in all, the overall picture of economics Mäki suggests is a rather liberal one which is capable of covering the vast majority of our theoretical developments. Over and above surrogate systems, realist economics embraces a plethora of substitute systems that may later turn out to be true or used only for developing frameworks to underlie later genuinely realist attempts. Even though substitute systems, statically viewed, do not fit into realist science as they have no targets and provide no support for surrogative reasoning, with time they may turn into or may be utilized in surrogate systems. On this showing, where scientific realism is the defining principle of economics, anti-realism seems only to be a stop along the road towards realism. This is a very instructive and all-embracing concept of scientific realism where even the various manifestations of anti-realism can be reconciled with or subordinated to realism. Along these lines, Mäki has suggested a conception of realism that can apply to more disciplines as compared to the alterative concepts: it can cover immature disciplines or ones having predictive performance weaker than usual (Mäki, 2012, pp. 5–6). This loose notion having a further advantage can help us to conciliate quite a large slice of economics with scientific realism (Mäki, 2009b, p. 73). In any case, this part is larger than the definition built upon theories believed or intended to be true would cover.

When defining realism on the basis of the possibility of being true, Mäki is right to be cautious; the inferences he draws, however, are rather exaggerated and unjustified. Defining scientific realism in terms of beliefs has led to a rather moderate concept, and it is contentious whether further mitigation is needed. Apart from the problems realists face when it comes to demonstrating the truth of theories, the history of science also suggests good reasons for some scepticism. At the same time, it seems gratuitous to call into question the convergence of science towards truth. What is more, even the pessimistic induction may be nothing but an ungrounded and hasty overgeneralization. The selective strategies of scientific realism are all aimed at identifying the zones of reality where the withdrawal of our realist commitments is irrational. Realists conceive everyday scientific practice as of dynamic character: at times, theories we currently believe to be true turn out to be false, and in such cases we must give up our faith in truth. Realists' beliefs may change, some of their convictions may be overwritten, whilst they still refrain from drawing overarching conclusions in order to avoid giving way to the pessimistic induction. However, the primary goal of science is still the same: realists strive towards true theories and existence claims rational to form, even though beliefs are alterable. Realists by no means commit themselves to theories the truth of which is irrational or implausible to assume.

To see why Mäki's possibility-based notion is problematic, it is worthwhile to place his realist ideas in context. Mäki's weakened approach is not without precedents in the literature (Chakravartty, 2017a, Sect. 1.1), where realist commitments taken as believing in the truth of something are also left out of the picture. Some authors try to define scientific realism on the basis of aims, purposes, and ambitions, in contrast with the usual focus on achievements. Van Fraassen (1980, pp. 8–9) provides the paradigmatic example, though he is careful enough not to sidestep the problem of acceptance and belief. On his account, science is an endeavour set to find true theories of reality, and acceptance stems from the belief a theory is true. For van Fraassen placing an emphasis upon aims does not lead to neglecting the truth and belief component of realism. Lyons (2005, 2017), by contrast, goes farther by claiming that the aim of seeking true theories is unrelated to the belief in our (best) theories being (approximately) true, and to give account of how realist science works, he argues, suffice it to focus on aims only. At first sight, this seems to be a promising way as the idea of realist science seems to be defensible on the sole basis of its aims even if some theories are rejected when judged by truth. However, this is the trap itself. Lyons has tried to block some anti-realist arguments by providing a notion of realist science that may be acceptable even to non-realists and, by so doing, he could not but throw out the baby with bath water. As Chakravartty (2017b, pp. 3387–3388) argues, if truth or, in broad terms, the achievements and the success of science, the questions of reference and ontology, and the related beliefs are bracketed in theory assessment, this is no longer realism one is talking about. Setting science the task of seeking truth whilst neglecting whether it ever succeeds is compatible with the idea of never achieving truth, and even an ardent anti-realist would be satisfied with the idea of science only aiming at truth. Conflating realism and anti-realism or reducing realism into anti-realism can hardly be an effective defence for realism or taken as a fruitful approach to realism.

Mäki's step, however, leads to some inconsistency as it is definitely causal understanding that he discusses in the context of realism and he interprets models as providing us with truthful information about the real world. Realism is not realism with no rational belief in the reality of something (Chakravartty & van Fraassen, 2018, p. 23; Kitcher, 1993, pp. 150–151), though, as epistemic structural realists do, one can hide some things behind the veil of agnosticism whilst claiming to be a realist. For Mäki, however, the knowledge of reality dawns on the horizon all the time, it is thus not the epistemological limits of human cognition on account of which he rushes to a weakened concept of realism. As Mäki argues, truth of an assumed causal mechanism or entity property, at least in terms of plausibility, can be judged (Mäki, 1994b). In this vein, Mäki (1992, pp. 342–344) conjoins scientific realism with truth as reality has its structure as an objective feature and thanks to isolation economists can form true messages about this structure hence reality. A further point in favour of the close-knit unity of realism and truth is Mäki's (2002) emphasis upon the commonsensible notions of economics. The vast majority of our abstract-idealized concepts are in harmony with our ideas about ourselves and the world: with ideas we believe to be true (Mäki, 1992, p. 334). And the resemblance relations between model and target also turn into truth when the modeller performs surrogative reasoning (Mäki, 2013). Surprising as it is, whilst Mäki delineates one by one what realists probably know about the way the world works, and whilst all these elements could have been forged into a rigorous concept of realism, in the end he refrains from setting these elements as requisites or constituents of realist science. For Mäki, even though we have rational grounds for believing we know a thing or two about reality, we can be realists with no beliefs in truth or even with no knowledge at all.

Bearing in mind the age-old theorizing habits of economics, Mäki highlights that truth when taken as partial truth is not corrupted by descriptive falsity, so in spite of the unrealisticness of models economics is easy to reconcile with a sufficiently careful idea of truth. This statement amounts to putting forward the tenable idea that descriptive falsity is an insufficient ground for assessing the truth value of any theory (as it is also argued throughout this volume) as a descriptively false theory may still be true in the sense of conveying some true messages about its target. Mäki, however, takes a further step when inferring that scientific realism can live on the simple possibility of being (partially or approximately) true. As a claim it is rather shallow as almost any theory has the possibility of being true, even those that are not intended to be so or those the truth value of which is uncertain at the moment. Judged by this standard, Friedman on the basis of his F53 also seems to be a realist as in his positivist methodology he simply disregards the truth of theories. Friedman does not insist that theories ought to be untrue. For Friedman as an instrumentalist, theories might admittedly be true, but if not, it is not a concern as long as theories provide us with useful predictions (Caldwell, 1992), and for Mäki this admittance constitutes a sufficient ground for labelling Friedman as a realist.

Friedman also showed indeterminacy about truth. It is easy to find some claims under his pen where he, whilst insisting on the importance of empirics, seems to stand on the same platform of realist science as Mäki does:

> The heart of the *General Theory* is an extremely simple hypothesis—that a highly unstable marginal efficiency schedule of investment and a liquidity preference function that is highly elastic at low rates of interest and unstable at higher rates of interest are the key to short-run economic movements. That is what gives investment its central role, what makes the consumption function and the multiplier the key concepts, what enables Keynes to develop his theory [...] without having to introduce the quantity of money.
>
> [...]
>
> I believe that Keynes's theory is the right kind of theory in its simplicity, its concentration on a few key magnitudes, its potential fruitfulness I have been led to reject it [...] because I believe that it has been contradicted by evidence: its predictions have not been confirmed by experience. This failure suggests that it has not isolated what are "really" the key factors in short-run economic change. (Friedman, 1972, p. 908)

No surprise, Mäki (1994a, p. 249) interprets these rows as a clear manifestation of his realist economics. As Mäki argues, here Friedman placed the blame on Keynes for failing to recognize money as a key element or essential factor in triggering large-scale fluctuations. As we have seen, Lucas also took for granted the causal role money played in capitalist economies. Even though Mäki does not use the causalist terminology, the context clearly shows it is the causal relationships between money and the real economy and, in broad terms, causalist economics that he has in mind. This impression is further strengthened by the fact that Hoover (2009) also underlined Friedman's causalist achievements. However, in his F53 Friedman neglected the truth of theories and the related ontological and referential problems, and Mäki also rejected to set truth or even the belief in truth as a prerequisite for realism. As it was argued in Chapters 3 and 4, on the basis of his F53 Friedman could not have been a causal realist, even if he had realist aspirations in the broader context of his oeuvre, which in itself is a good point in favour of why aims in themselves make up an insufficient ground for realism. Friedman's methodological stance is so blurred, to say the least, that to label him as a dedicated realist one needs a rather permissive and occasionally inconsistent concept of scientific realism.

If the truth of theories in causal terms is not a concern, as Mäki insists, Friedman was undoubtedly a realist, even in his F53 (Mäki, 2009a), and all the differences between his and Lucas's methodological principles, ambitions, and achievements inevitably fade away. However, there is more to realism in economics, as Mäki also argues. Even though we can never have more than rational beliefs and the conviction that in certain cases to withhold our realist commitments is irrational or even bizarre, this rationality encourages us to rely upon our knowledge as it is rational for us to use what we believe we know. Lucas has subscribed to a more rigorous concept of realism where truth, plausibility, ontology, and reference have all played a high-ranked aspect, but his relist achievements can be highlighted only if we use a standard capable of telling the difference in the ways models attach to reality. Realism defined in terms of the possibility of truth is not such a standard. By contrast, if realism is meant to imply realist commitments to truthlike constituents of reality, cases of Lucas's causal-structural realism and Friedmanian instrumentalism clearly disengage. Mere statistical correlations are no longer on a par with realist models intended and believed to be true and to provide sound causal explanations. One is free to define scientific realism to her liking, though it is not guaranteed that her definition proves useful in revealing some key dissimilarities a more stringent concept would effectively underline. As we have seen, everything else is similar to everything else if we paint with a wide brush; it is thus no surprise if the differences between strikingly dissimilar methodologies are blurred when we refuse to apply a framework sensitive enough for discerning the peculiarities. Mäki is ready to admit that we have grounds for setting higher standards for economics in terms of rational beliefs and the zones of reality where plausibility and rationality are good guides for us to form commitments; he thus unnecessarily abandons the positions scientific realism tenably has.

5.4 Epilogue

The future of micro-founded macroeconomics is blurred. As we have seen, thanks to Stigler and Becker, the extensive social scientific use of choice theory had already arisen in Chicago years before Lucas's time. Stigler and Becker conceived individual decisions as a basis to which they could reduce a lot of individual and social actions. As a consequence, the scope of economics as a formal science has considerably broadened and it has become possible to explain much by little (Samuelson, 1947, p. 23). As in other disciplines, in economics this 'little' is supposed to mean as few logically independent law-like sentences as possible and the use of the same argument patterns over and over again in order to achieve a form of theorizing efficiency (Kitcher, 1981, p. 514; Mäki, 2001, p. 488).

Social phenomena previously studied by a variety of social scientific disciplines turned out to be analysable in the field of mathematical economics. The understanding of diverse phenomena no longer required a vast array of different theories and theoretical diversity.

This development triggered economics to improve into a unified science. In this new science, however, individual decisions constituting the ultimate basis are not the postulates of a Friedmanian as-if framework, but rather conceived as the real sources of individual and social actions. Lucas's theoretical and methodological achievements were assessed above along these lines. Lucas insisted on the consistent application of the realist choice theory, kept building the unified social science and broadening its scope. His purpose was to provide a choice-theoretic fundament for the study of money-induced large-scale fluctuations which, as it is argued above, he also regarded as a realist basis. Lucas also underlined how powerful an assumption the rationality postulate was if it is not omniscience or infallibility that was meant by rationality. On the contrary, Lucasian rationality properly construed refers to agents' efforts to act rationally, though their attempts are fraught with errors most of the time.

Striving towards unification is an explicit desire of this new economics:

> at any given time there will be phenomena that are well-understood from the point of view of the economic theory we have, and other phenomena that are not. We will be tempted [...] to relieve the discomfort induced by discrepancies between theory and facts by saying that the ill-understood facts are the province of some other, different kind of economic theory. Keynesian 'macroeconomics' was, I think, a surrender (under great duress) to this temptation. It led to the abandonment, for a class of problems of great importance, of the use of the only 'engine for the discovery of truth' that we have in economics. Now we are once again putting this engine of Marshall's to work on the problems of aggregate dynamics. There is much to be done, but there is an exciting sense of real progress in the enterprise, and I am full of hope. (Lucas, 1987, p. 108)

As it is argued in Section 4.3.3 above, real business cycle theory emerged as the next step in this unification process. This stage of the theoretical evolution tried to trace more and more macroeconomic phenomena and causal mechanisms back to the single and well-known choice-theoretic framework (Plosser, 1989). The explicit purpose was to explain as many micro- and macro-level problems as possible in a single, highly flexible, and comprehensive theory, and hence to max out the analytical possibilities of neoclassical choice theory and hence unification. And if the cutting edge of economics really succeeds, the history of economic thought shall inevitably come to an end in a sense Fukuyama (1992) suggests.

Unification, however, is a subtle term with multiple interrelated meanings. It has two versions at least, logical and ontological unification, which oftentimes go hand in hand. Logical unification refers to the technical relation between axioms and theorems. This form labels a process in which more and more statements can be derived from a given set of axioms, or in which a given set of statements can logically be reduced to fewer and fewer axioms, but all this in logical terms only, so there is no ontological ground in the game. In a unified science there exists a general model type as a template that can be customized and used to explain more and more diverse phenomena (Mäki, 2009b, p. 87; Teller, 2004, p. 441). In many cases logical unification also means the consistent and recurrent application of a common mathematical structure[7] (Mäki, 1990, p. 331). Ontological unification, by contrast, has a more profound meaning. This notion claims that equations in models represent real causal relations. Logical unification is thus possible as there exists an ontological basis that facilitates our sorting more and more diverse phenomena under a single theory. Distinct phenomena are understood as manifestations of the interplay of the same entities and their relations, so at the end of the day there exists only one mechanism with various occurrences (Aronson, 1984, pp. 213–216). Using this terminology, we can say that Stigler and Becker endowed the previously recognized logical unification with an ontological basis and Lucas standing upon this ontological fundament could start moving macroeconomics under the choice-theoretic framework.

There are thus two cases: mere logical unification without an ontological basis, and logical unification implied by ontological unity, if the additional case of a presupposed ontological unity going without a successful logical unification is disregarded. When logical unification rests upon ontological unity, logical unification and the use of a shared mathematical structure are facilitated by the fact that the phenomena under scrutiny are really the consequences of a theoretically postulated common mechanism; theorists at least believe in it. Accordingly, the idea of micro-founded macroeconomics is underpinned by the firm belief that macro-social phenomena are the results of individual decisions. There exists a schematic mechanism, the ultimate choice-theoretic framework, in which a representative economic agent placed into a macroeconomic setting faces various shocks and tries to optimize, which leads to certain unintended macroeconomic outcomes as some implications of the invisible hand.

Even though it is dubious whether beyond individual decisions further individual, social, or environmental factors also affect macroeconomic outcomes or not (Mäki & Marchionni, 2009, p. 192), as we have seen, there is a strong conviction that all social processes stem from human decisions at the end of the day (Section 2.1.1). Were these external forces

---

[7] In their case study, Mäki and Marchionni (2009, pp. 186–189) mention mathematical structure as an intriguing limitation to logical unification. Certain tractability assumptions may hinder the theory successfully representing the realistically conceived causal structure. In other words, sometimes theorists want to be realists; however, their mathematics does not allow them to be.

not regarded as some omitted variables exerting influence through the individual, a simple theoretical inconsistency would inevitably follow. The preference system relates individual utility to the consumption of some goods broadly conceived. As a consequence of simplification and omission implied by isolation, there exist factors that in reality do influence the modelled decisions. Such a case, for instance, is the relation of nominal income and demand in the primitive form of the Marshallian cross, or in Lucas's island models the social institutions, or the nominally rigid contracts that the Keynesians suggest. Even though it may make sense to model the restrictive effects of such institutions and contracts, in order to preserve theoretical consistency their effects must always emerge via decisions. What is more, the mere existence of these social facts is to be derived from decisions, exactly within a choice-theoretic model. Social institutions and contracts never force people to call them into being. Likewise, their coercive power never emerges via compelling agents with a shotgun to obedience, where the absence of conformity would result in being killed. When it comes to discussing the coercive effects of external factors in a choice-theoretic model, the discussion only regards the number of variables in the preference system. Doing otherwise we would not take our own assumptions seriously.

But what does unification mean in the case of such an overwhelming idea as the reduction of social connections to individual decisions? Does it inevitably drive model pluralism (Aydinonat, 2018; Grüne-Yanoff & Marchionni, 2018; Mäki, 2018; Rodrik, 2015) to extinction? I do not think so. Model pluralism and hence the complementarity of models follows from social complexity: from the recognition that the underlying causal structure is far more complex than the capacities of a single theory. As we have seen, there is no trade-off between unification and pluralism. Tracing diverse phenomena back to a single theoretical fundament does not eliminate causal complexity. In the case of the microfoundations project the efforts towards unification only amount to the belief that it is the individual with her preference system who stands at the end of every causal chain. The causal structure still needs simplification, isolation, and omission for the sake of analytical success; model pluralism thus remains a part of the big picture. So whilst we have the DSGE framework as 'The' unifying model, this is not one unique core model directly applied for various circumstances, but rather a family of models in which each piece is a customized or modified, context-dependent variant emerging as a result of horizontal development (Kuorikoski & Lehtinen, 2018; Ylikoski & Aydinonat, 2014). Thus we do not need to choose between 'The' model and 'a' model as they are all the same. Even though the DSGE framework is intended to be an all-purpose general framework, all the distinct problems admittedly require its distinguishable and individually customized versions.

It would be a mistake, however, to infer the identity of economics as such with the DSGE framework. Economics refuses to be boiled down to DSGE modelling and hopefully it will always do. Isolation inevitably implies partiality, so models even in the unified framework cannot provide comprehensive causal explanations for social phenomena. The representational role of our tractability and negligibility assumptions is always to be problematized, and these questions cannot adequately be addressed in the DSGE framework. There we can have partial answers at best. Models can aid in analysing concrete events occurring in concrete spatiotemporal settings only if the set of models is regarded as a menu bringing certain causal factors and mechanisms to the fore. The road to whole truth leads through the sum of our partial results. Even though the emergence of the choice-theoretic framework as a unified theory seems to have brought economics to the end of its own history, there is still much to be done. The ongoing debates over the unified framework signify that the development of economics, quite paradoxically, has entered a post-history stage. Only time will tell whether this stage will really turn out to be the end of economics or only a stage of a relatively settled Kuhnian normal science to be replaced once in the future.

Suggested readings

Hermeneutics has a vast and still expanding literature. Zimmermann (2015) provides a brief and useful introduction to hermeneutics. The reader edited by Jefferson and Robey (1987) helps to place hermeneutics in the context of various approaches to textual analysis and interpretation. The compilation by Düppe and Weintraub (2019) is a must-read if one seeks a comprehensive overview of the methodological problems of modern historiography of economics. Blaug (1991) and his authors discuss what role the history of economic thought can play in modern economics. Backhouse and Fontaine (2014) treat the history of economics as a case of disciplinary histories in the social sciences ranging from the history of historiography to the history of sociology or political science.

References

Aronson, J. L. (1984). *A realist philosophy of science*. London: Macmillan.

Atkeson, A., & Lucas, R. E. (1992). On efficient distribution with private information. *The Review of Economic Studies, 59*(3), 427–453.

Atkeson, A., & Lucas, R. E. (1995). Efficiency and equality in a simple model of efficient unemployment insurance. *Journal of Economic Theory, 66*(1), 64–88.

Austin, J. L. (1962). *How to do things with words*. Oxford: Oxford University Press.

Aydinonat, N. E. (2018). The diversity of models as a means to better explanations in economics. *Journal of Economic Methodology, 25*(3), 237–251.

Backhouse, R. E., & Fontaine, P. (Eds.) (2014). *A historiography of the modern social sciences*. Cambridge: Cambridge University Press.

Bevir, M. (1997). Mind and method in the history of ideas. *History and Theory, 36*(2), 167–189.

Blaug, M. (1985). *Economic theory in retrospect*. Cambridge: Cambridge University Press.

Blaug, M. (Ed.), (1991). *The historiography of economics*. Cheltenham: Edward Elgar.

Boland, L. A. (2010). Review of "The methodology of positive economics. Reflections on the Milton Friedman legacy, ed. Uskali Mäki". *Economics and Philosophy, 26*(3), 376–382.

Boumans, M. (2005). *How economists model the world into numbers*. Abingdon: Routledge.

Brown, V. (2003). Textuality and the history of economics. Intention and meaning. In W. J. Samuels, J. E. Biddle, & J. B. Davis (Eds.), *A companion to the history of economic thought* (pp. 538–552). Oxford: Blackwell.

Caldwell, B. J. (1992). Friedman's predictivist instrumentalism. A modification. *Research in the History of Economic Thought and Methodology, 10*(1), 119–128.

Chakravartty, A. (2017a). In E. N. Zalta (Ed.), *Scientific realism*. Retrieved from Stanford Encyclopedia of Philosophy: https://plato.stanford.edu/archives/sum2017/entries/scientific-realism/. (Accessed 26 July 2019).

Chakravartty, A. (2017b). Reflections on new thinking about scientific realism. *Synthese, 194*(9), 3379–3392.

Chakravartty, A., & van Fraassen, B. C. (2018). What is scientific realism? *Spontaneous Generations, 9*(1), 12–25.

Csaba, L. (2017). Comparative economics and the mainstream. *Economics and Business Review, 3*(3), 32–51.

De Vroey, M. (2016). *A history of macroeconomics from Keynes to Lucas and beyond*. Cambridge: Cambridge University Press.

De Vroey, M., & Pensieroso, L. (2016). *The rise of a mainstream in economics. Discussion paper no. 2016-26*. Louvain: Institut de Recherches Économiques et Sociales de l'Université Catholique de Louvain.

Düppe, T. & Weintraub, E. R. (Eds.), (2019). *A contemporary historiography of economics*. Abingdon: Routledge.

Emmett, R. B. (1997). Reflections on "Breaking away". Economics as science and the history of economics as history of science. *Research in the History of Economic Thought and Methodology, 15*(1), 221–236.

Emmett, R. B. (2003). Exegesis, hermeneutics, and interpretation. In W. J. Samuels, J. E. Biddle, & J. B. Davis (Eds.), *A companion to the history of economic thought* (pp. 523–537). Oxford: Blackwell.

Festinger, L. (1957). *A theory of cognitive dissonance*. Stanford: Stanford University Press.

Fish, S. (1980). *Is there a text in this class? The authority of interpretive communities*. Cambridge, MA: Harvard University Press.

Friedman, M. (1953/2009). The methodology of positive economics. In U. Mäki (Ed.), *The methodology of positive economics. Reflections on the Milton Friedman legacy* (pp. 3–43). Cambridge: Cambridge University Press.

Friedman, M. (1972). Comments on the critics. *Journal of Political Economy, 80*(5), 906–950.

Fukuyama, F. (1992). *End of history and the last man*. New York: The Free Press.

Gadamer, H. G. (1960/2004). *Truth and method*. London: Continuum.

Galbács, P. (2016). Review paper. Very deep is the well of the past. *Society and Economy, 38*(3), 413–426.

Geertz, C. (1973). *The interpretation of cultures. Selected essays*. New York: Basic Books.

Grüne-Yanoff, T., & Marchionni, C. (2018). Modeling model selection in model pluralism. *Journal of Economic Methodology, 25*(3), 265–275.

Hahn, F. H. (1973). The winter of our discontent. *Economica, 40*(3), 322–330.

Hirsch, E. D. (1967). *Validity in interpretation*. New Haven: Yale University Press.

Hoover, K. D. (2009). Milton Friedman's stance. The methodology of causal realism. In U. Mäki (Ed.), *The methodology of positive economics. Reflections on the MIlton Friedman legacy* (pp. 303–320). Cambridge: Cambridge University Press.

Jefferson, A., & Robey, D. (Eds.), (1987). *Modern literary theory. A comparative introduction.* London: B.T. Batsford.

Kitcher, P. (1981). Explanatory unification. *Philosophy of Science, 48*(4), 507–531.

Kitcher, P. (1993). *The advancement of science. Science without legend, objectivity without illusions.* Oxford: Oxford University Press.

Kornai, J. (1971). *Anti-equilibrium. On economic systems theory and the tasks of research.* Amsterdam: North-Holland.

Kuhn, T. S. (1962). *The structure of scientific revolutions* (3rd ed.). Chicago: The University of Chicago Press.

Kuorikoski, J., & Lehtinen, A. (2018). Model selection in macroeconomics. DSGE and ad hocness. *Journal of Economic Methodology, 25*(3), 252–264.

Lakatos, I. (1978). In J. Worrall & G. Currie (Eds.), *The methodology of scientific research programmes.* Cambridge: Cambridge University Press.

Leijonhufvud, A. (1994). Hicks, Keynes and Marshall. In H. Hagemann & O. F. Hamouda (Eds.), *The legacy of Hicks. His contributions to economic analysis* (pp. 143–158). London: Routledge.

Lucas, R. E. (1972). Expectations and the neutrality of money. *Journal of Economic Theory,* (2), 103–124.

Lucas, R. E. (1976/1981). Econometric policy evaluation. A critique. In R. E. Lucas (Ed.), *Studies in business cycle theory* (pp. 104–130). Oxford: Basil Blackwell.

Lucas, R. E. (1977). Understanding business cycles. In K. Brunner & A. H. Meltzer (Eds.), *Stabilization of the domestic and international economy* (pp. 7–29). Amsterdam: North-Holland.

Lucas, R. E. (1980). Methods and problems in business cycle theory. *Journal of Money, Credit and Banking, 12*(4), 696–715.

Lucas, R. E. (1981). *Studies in business-cycle theory.* Oxford: Basil Blackwell.

Lucas, R. E. (1986). Adaptive behavior and economic theory. *Journal of Business, 59*(4), S401–S426.

Lucas, R. E. (1987). *Models of business cycles.* Oxford: Basil Blackwell.

Lucas, R. E. (1988). On the mechanics of economic development. *Journal of Monetary Economics, 22*(1), 3–42.

Lucas, R. E. (1990a). Supply-side economics. An analytical review. *Oxford Economic Papers, 42*(2), 293–316.

Lucas, R. E. (1990b). Why doesn't capital flow from rich to poor countries? *The American Economic Review, 80*(2), 92–96.

Lucas, R. E. (1992). On efficiency and distribution. *The Economic Journal, 102*(411), 233–247.

Lucas, R. E. (1993). Making a miracle. *Econometrica, 61*(2), 251–272.

Lucas, R. E., & Rapping, L. A. (1969). Real wages, employment, and inflation. *Journal of Political Economy, 69*(5), 721–754.

Lucas, R. E., & Sargent, T. J. (1979). After Keynesian macroeconomics. *Federal Reserve Bank of Minneapolis Quarterly Review, 3*(2), 1–16.

Lucas, R. E., & Stokey, N. L. (1983). Optimal fiscal and monetary policy in an economy without capital. *Journal of Monetary Economics, 12*(1), 55–93.

Lyons, T. D. (2005). Toward a purely axiological scientific realism. *Erkenntnis, 63*(2), 167–204.

Lyons, T. D. (2017). Epistemic selectivity, historical threats, and the non-epistemic tenets of scientific realism. *Synthese, 194*(9), 3203–3219.

Mäki, U. (1989). On the problem of realism in economics. *Ricerche Economiche, 43*(1–2), 176–198.

Mäki, U. (1990). Scientific realism and Austrian explanation. *Review of Political Economy, 2*(3), 310–344.

Mäki, U. (1992). On the method of isolation in economics. In C. Dilworth (Ed.), *Intelligibility and science* (pp. 317–351). Amsterdam: Rodopi.

Mäki, U. (1994a). Reorienting the assumptions issue. In R. E. Backhouse (Ed.), *New directions in economic methodology* (pp. 237–256). London: Routledge.

Mäki, U. (1994b). Isolation, idealization and truth in economics. In B. Hamminga & N. B. De Marchi (Eds.), *Idealization in economics* (pp. 147–168). Amsterdam: Rodopi.

Mäki, U. (1996). Scientific realism and some peculiarities of economics. In R. S. Cohen, R. Hilpinen, & Q. Renzong (Eds.), *Realism and anti-realism in the philosophy of science* (pp. 427–448). Dordrecht: Springer.

Mäki, U. (2000). Reclaiming relevant realism. *Journal of Economic Methodology, 7*(1), 109–125.

Mäki, U. (2001). Explanatory unification. Double and doubtful. *Philosophy of the Social Sciences, 31*(4), 488–506.

Mäki, U. (2002). Some nonreasons for nonrealism about economics. In U. Mäki (Ed.), *Fact and fiction in economics. Models, realism, and social construction* (pp. 90–104). Cambridge: Cambridge University Press.

Mäki, U. (2008). Scientific realism and ontology. In S. N. Durlauf & L. E. Blume (Eds.), *The new Palgrave dictionary of economics* (pp. 5752–5759). London: Palgrave Macmillan.

Mäki, U. (2009a). Unrealistic assumptions and unnecessary confusions. Rereading and rewriting F53 as a realist statement. In U. Mäki (Ed.), *The methodology of positive economics. Reflections on the Milton Friedman legacy* (pp. 90–116). Cambridge: Cambridge University Press.

Mäki, U. (2009b). Realistic realism about unrealistic models. In H. Kincaid & D. Ross (Eds.), *The Oxford handbook of philosophy of economics* (pp. 68–98). Oxford: Oxford University Press.

Mäki, U. (2011). Scientific realism as a challenge to economics (and vice versa). *Journal of Economic Methodology, 18*(1), 1–12.

Mäki, U. (2012). Realism and antirealism about economics. In U. Mäki (Ed.), *Philosophy of economics* (pp. 3–24). Amsterdam: North Holland.

Mäki, U. (2013). On a paradox of truth, or how not to obscure the issue of whether explanatory models can be true. *Journal of Economic Methodology, 20*(3), 268–279.

Mäki, U. (2018). Rights and wrongs of economic modelling. Refining Rodrik. *Journal of Economic Methodology, 25*(3), 218–236.

Mäki, U., & Marchionni, C. (2009). On the structure of explanatory unification. The case of geographical economics. *Studies in History and Philosophy of Science Part A, 40*(2), 185–195.

Manicas, P. T. (2006). *A realist philosophy of social science. Explanation and understanding.* Cambridge: Cambridge University Press.

Mantzavinos, C. (2005). *Naturalistic hermeneutics.* Cambridge: Cambridge University Press.

Mantzavinos, C. (2009). *Philosophy of the social sciences. Philosophical theory and scientific practice.* Cambridge: Cambridge University Press.

Mantzavinos, C. (2014). Text interpretation as a scientific activity. *Journal for General Philosophy of Science, 45*(S1), 45–58.

Mantzavinos, C. (2016). In E. N. Zalta (Ed.), *Hermeneutics.* Retrieved from The Stanford Encyclopedia of Philosophy: https://plato.stanford.edu/archives/win2016/entries/hermeneutics/. (Accessed 18 December 2018).

Nehamas, A. (1981). The postulated author. Critical monism as a regulative ideal. *Critical Inquiry, 8*(1), 133–149.

Pickering, A. (1997). The history of economics and the history of agency. In J. P. Henderson (Ed.), *The state of the history of economics* (pp. 6–18). London: Routledge.

Plosser, C. I. (1989). Understanding real business cycles. *Journal of Economic Perspectives, 3*(3), 51–77.

Polanyi, M. (1958/2005). *Personal knowledge. Towards a post-critical philosophy.* London: Routledge.

Price, A. W. (2008). *Contextuality in practical reason.* Oxford: Clarendon Press.

Ricoeur, P. (1981). *Hermeneutics and the human sciences* (J. B. Thompson, Ed., & J. B. Thompson, Trans.). Cambridge: Cambridge University Press.

Rodrik, D. (2015). *Economics rules. Why economics works, when it fails, and how to tell the difference.* Oxford: Oxford University Press.

Samuels, W. J. (1972). The scope of economics historically considered. *Land Economics, 48*(3), 248–268.

Samuelson, P. A. (1947). *Foundations of economic analysis.* Cambridge, MA: Harvard University Press.

Simon, H. A. (1983). *Reason in human affairs.* Stanford: Stanford University Press.

Skinner, Q. (1969). Meaning and understanding in the history of ideas. *History and Theory, 8*(1), 3–53.

Skinner, Q. (1972). Motives, intentions and the interpretation of texts. *New Literary History, 3*(2), 393–408.

Skinner, Q. (1988). A reply to my critics. In J. Tully (Ed.), *Meaning and context. Quentin Skinner and his critics* (pp. 231–288). Princeton: Princeton University Press.

Stigler, G. J. (1965). Textual exegesis as a scientific problem. *Economica, 32*(4/128), 447–450.

Stigler, G. J. (1976). The scientific uses of scientific biography, with special reference to J. S. Mill. In J. M. Robson & M. Laine (Eds.), *James and John Stuart Mill. Papers of the centenary conference* (pp. 55–66). Toronto: University of Toronto Press.

Syll, L. P. (2016). *On the use and misuse of theories and models in mainstream economics.* London: College Publications.

Taylor, C. (1985). *Philosophy and the human sciences.* Cambridge: Cambridge University Press.

Teller, P. (2004). How we dapple the world. *Philosophy of Science, 71*(4), 425–447.

van Fraassen, B. C. (1980). *The scientific image.* New York: Oxford University Press.

Vercelli, A. (1991). *Methodological foundations of macroeconomics. Keynes and Lucas.* Cambridge: Cambridge University Press.

Waterman, A. M. (1988). Malthus on long swings. A reply. *The Canadian Journal of Economics/ Revue canadienne d'Economique, 21*(1), 206–207.

Weber, M. (1968/1978). In G. Roth & C. Wittich (Eds.), *Economy and society. An outline of interpretive sociology.* Berkeley: University of California Press.

Weintraub, E. R., Meardon, S. J., Gayer, T., & Banzhaf, H. S. (1998). Archiving the history of economics. *Journal of Economic Literature, 36*(3), 1496–1501.

Ylikoski, P., & Aydinonat, N. E. (2014). Understanding with theoretical models. *Journal of Economic Methodology, 21*(1), 19–36.

Zimmermann, J. (2015). *Hermeneutics. A very short introduction.* Oxford: Oxford University Press.

Index

Note: Page numbers followed by *f* indicate figures.

Printed in the United States
By Bookmasters